Edward A. Wild and the
African Brigade in the Civil War

ALSO BY FRANCES H. CASSTEVENS

Clingman's Brigade in the Confederacy, 1862–1865
(McFarland, 2002)

The Civil War and Yadkin County, North Carolina
(McFarland, 1997)

Edward A. Wild and the African Brigade in the Civil War

by FRANCES H. CASSTEVENS

McFarland & Company, Inc., Publishers
Jefferson, North Carolina, and London

The present work is a reprint of the illustrated case bound edition of Edward A. Wild and the African Brigade in the Civil War, *first published in 2003 by McFarland.*

LIBRARY OF CONGRESS CATALOGUING-IN-PUBLICATION DATA

Casstevens, Frances Harding.
Edward A. Wild and the African brigade in
the Civil War / Frances H. Casstevens.
p. cm.
Includes bibliographical references and index.

ISBN-13: 978-0-7864-2443-6
softcover : 50# alkaline paper ∞

1. Wild, Edward Augustus, 1825–1891.
2. United States. Army—Biography.
3. United States. Army. African Brigade (1863–1865)
4. Generals—United States—Biography.
5. United States—History—Civil War, 1861–1865—Participation, African American.
6. United States—History—Civil War, 1861–1865—Campaigns.
I. Title.
E467.1.W68C37   2005   973.7'415'092–dc21   2003004183

British Library cataloguing data are available

©2003 Frances H. Casstevens. All rights reserved

No part of this book may be reproduced or transmitted in any form or by any means, electronic or mechanical, including photocopying or recording, or by any information storage and retrieval system, without permission in writing from the publisher.

On the cover: Captain Edward A. Wild *(U.S. Army Military History Institute).*
Background photograph: "Contraband of War" *(Library of Congress).*

Manufactured in the United States of America

McFarland & Company, Inc., Publishers
Box 611, Jefferson, North Carolina 28640
www.mcfarlandpub.com

To my six grandchildren,
Simon, Jacob, Amber and Wesley Casstevens,
and Kayla and Corey Campbell, all of whom love history
as much as I do. It must be a genetic trait.
They will be the future guardians of the past.

And to Victor Seiders, my best Yankee friend,
for all his help and encouragement.

Abbreviations

A.A.G.	Assistant Adjutant General
EGSL	Earl Gregg Swem Library, Williamsburg, Virginia
LC	Library of Congress, Washington, D.C.
MHI	Military History Institute, Carlisle, Pennsylvania
NA	National Archives, Washington, D.C.
NCCV	North Carolina Colored Volunteers
NYSL	New York State Library
O.R.	*Official Record of the War of the Rebellion*
UNC-CH	University of North Carolina at Chapel Hill
USCT	United States Colored Troops

Acknowledgments

My thanks to Galen Harrison of Kernersville, North Carolina, who provided the germ of an idea for a book about Edward A. Wild. Mrs. Helen Stevens Whitlock, a descendant of General Wild's sister Laura, shared material collected by her grandfather, Horace N. Stevens, and permitted me to use some of "The True Man of Action," the typescript written by her grandfather and Gershom Bradford.

Anne Clark of the Brookline Public Library, Brookline, Mass., was most helpful, as was the Massachusetts Historical Society in furnishing copies of documents and other information. the New England Historic Genealogical Society found a copy of General Wild's will. Gerri Andrews, Librarian, Corolla Branch Library, Currituck County, N.C., shared information. Dale Beasley of Knott's Island furnished information about Miss Nancy White and her family.

Researcher Carolyn Lackey made several trips to the Military History Institute, Carlisle, Pa., to locate needed information. Bruce Baker transcribed information at Duke University that could not be photocopied.

Melinda Sells, Librarian, and the staff of the Yadkin County Public Library—Mattie Adams, Bonnie Fletcher, Reba Hollingsworth, Betty Kennedy, and Nancy Williams—helped obtain rare books and obscure articles through interlibrary loan.

My thanks to the University of North Carolina at Chapel Hill, Duke University, Harvard University Archives, Boston University, New York State Library and the National Archives in Washington, D.C. for copies of original documents; the Earl Gregg Swem Library, William and Mary College, for the Tyler family information; and the Library of Congress for copies of contemporary photographs taken from 1861 to 1865.

Danny Casstevens created the pen and ink sketches to help illustrate this book.

—Frances H. Casstevens
February 2003

Table of Contents

Acknowledgments   vii
Abbreviations   viii
Introduction   1

I.	Family History and Early Life of Edward Augustus Wild	5
II.	Captain Wild, United States Army, 1861	19
III.	Colonel Wild, 35th Regiment, United States Army, 1862	34
IV.	Brigadier General Wild, United States Volunteers (Colored)	55
V.	Charleston, South Carolina, 1863	73
VI.	Wild's Raid on Northeastern North Carolina and Its Results	93
VII.	Retaliation and Repercussion	117
VIII.	Miss Nancy White and the Wead-Draper Dispute	127
IX.	The Clopton Whipping and Other Civilian Incidents	146
X.	January to June 1864: Fort Powhatan, Wilson's Wharf–Fort Pocahontas, and Other Battles in Virginia	161
XI.	Court-Martial of General Wild	183
XII.	The Final Months of the War, July 1864 to May 1865	194
XIII.	The Freedmen's Bureau in Georgia and the Chennault Affair	211
XIV.	Post-War Years: The Search for Silver	245

Epilogue	264
Appendix: Tables for Chapter VI	267
Notes	271
Bibliography	311
Index	319

Introduction

I first heard of Edward A. Wild at a meeting of the Sons of Confederate Veterans. While presenting a program on letters to and from prisoners, Galen Harrison of Kernersville, North Carolina, mentioned that he owned a letter from Miss Nancy White, one of the women taken hostage by Wild's troops when they invaded northeastern North Carolina in 1863.

The story fascinated me, and I wrote Wild's name down on a scrap of paper to remind myself to find out more about this incident. I began doing research and "surfing" the Internet for information about the infamous "wild General." The more I learned, the more I wanted to know what motivated this unique man to do the outrageous things attributed to him. Were all the bizarre stories and articles about him true? As I continued to search, each document I found added a piece to the puzzle and helped complete the picture of the man. Letters written by the General himself give us his viewpoint about incidents in his life, and allow a glimpse of the real man in the blue uniform.

Wild lived an unusual life. He was a doctor by profession, an adventurer by choice, and a military officer by a sense of duty. Although he was known nationally during his lifetime, Wild is seldom mentioned in books on the American Civil War. Many Civil War historians do not mention him, much less give him credit for his role in turning former slaves and freedmen into first-rate soldiers in the Union Army. Very few books on African-Americans in the military history of the United States mention Brigadier General Wild and his African Brigade. One exception to the lack of information is John G. Barrett's *The Civil War in North Carolina*, which deals with Wild's raid into the state.[1] A recent book by Webb Garrison, *Civil War Hostages: Hostage Taking in the Civil War*, has a chapter about two of the hostages taken by Wild in North Carolina.[2] Thus, there was definitely a need for a book about Brigadier General Edward A. Wild.

Wild was as controversial as the war in which he fought between 1861 and 1865. We are yet unable to agree on a name for this war. Northerners call it the *Civil*

War, Southerners insist it should be called either the *War Between the States* or the *War of Northern Aggression*. There was nothing *civil* about it. It was a bloody, brutal, and cruel war, in which both soldiers and civilians suffered, and communities, villages, towns, cities, and states were devastated both physically and economically.

Opinions are also divided about Brigadier General Edward Augustus Wild. Perhaps, if Wild had died on some battlefield, he would have become a martyr and a champion of black civil rights. If Wild, instead of Colonel Robert Shaw of the 54th Massachusetts, had died at Battery Wagner on Morris Island in Charleston Harbor that 18th day of July in 1863, perhaps his memory would be honored today by both blacks and whites. As fate (or luck) would have it, Wild and his black troops arrived in Charleston Harbor three weeks after the disastrous assault.

Wild survived it all—the carnage of the battlefields in Virginia and Maryland, the loss of an arm from a bullet wound, the hell of Morris Island in the summer of 1863, the heat and cold, arrest and court martial, disease, despair, and demotion—only to be buried so deep in obscurity that few Civil War enthusiasts, history buffs, scholars or students even know of his existence. Even fewer know anything about Wild's work as a doctor during the Crimean War or his work with the Freedmen's Bureau in Georgia.

His peers and contemporaries ignored him. Historians have overlooked and diminished the contributions of Edward A. Wild, the courageous captain of Company A, 1st Massachusetts Regiment. This same Captain Wild cared enough about his men to complain to higher authorities about the inadequacy of the regimental commander, Colonel Robert Cowdin. Cowdin got his revenge for that criticism when he wrote his regimental history, *First Regiment of Infantry, Massachusetts Volunteer Militia*, and entirely omitted Wild's name from the roster and the regimental history.[3]

Dissatisfied with the 1st Massachusetts, Wild continued to provide heroic and courageous leadership as Colonel of the 35th Massachusetts Regiment, until he was badly wounded at South Mountain. The suffering he endured the rest of his life because of the amputation of his left arm was not appreciated and his blood was shed for naught, according to the annals of history.

Wild was an abolitionist violently opposed to slavery. He freed hundreds, perhaps thousands, of slaves, and settled them safely on Roanoke Island. He then not only recruited the freed slaves, but trained them and gave them the opportunity to prove their value as soldiers in the Union army. In spite of all his accomplishments, Brigadier General Edward Wild has been forgotten and given a "back seat" in the saga of American history.

The military career of Brigadier General Edward Augustus Wild is a prime example of the difficulties encountered by white officers who led black troops during the conflict which divided the country. Granted, despite his high ideals and pure motives, Wild did some outrageous and inexplicable things. Were his actions typical of the ways in which war was conducted during the 19th century, or did he act outside the norm and overstep the bounds of civilized warfare? No one has ever hinted that Wild acted to enhance his own glory or for personal gain, but most agree that he was a non-conformist and a staunch abolitionist who hated Southern "Rebels," especially guerrillas, whom he equated to "land pirates." Wild was condemned by both the Union and the Confederacy, and was arrested on several occasions. He was tried in a military court martial. Were those charges valid, or due to personality conflicts with superior officers? Did he deserve to be tried, convicted, and sentenced for his actions, or was he the victim of discrimination?

Perhaps Wild was made the scapegoat. Perhaps the truth about the man might have proved an embarrassment to those who outwardly professed a belief in the abolition of slavery, the equality of all men, and the abilities of blacks to perform as obedient, brave, and outstanding soldiers, as they did under General Wild at Wilson's Wharf. Certainly, the South had no monopoly on discrimination and Southerners were not alone in their hatred and fear of black soldiers. Confederate hatred for black soldiers and their white commanders was publicly proclaimed by the Confederate Congress. Hatred from Northern sources, and within the military establishment, was expressed in more subtle ways, by covert rather than overt acts.

Was he villain or hero, devil or saint? Did he truly hate all Confederate soldiers and Southern civilians so much that he treated them in a very high-handed and cruel manner? What motivated him to defy orders from his superiors and risk a court martial? Was he really as "wild" as he had been described, unmindful of authority, military rules and regulations, bent on doing what he thought was right no matter what anyone said? Was he as monstrous as the South believed him to be, or was he truly a great leader and abolitionist who freed slaves and cared for their families? After his raid on northeastern North Carolina, Brigadier General Wild was called a "cousin to Beelzebub,"[4] another name for Satan derived used in the New Testament to describe the Prince of Devils. Did his actions reflect a strong sense of duty, based on ingrained beliefs about the evils of slavery and the need to abolish it, or did he want revenge after he lost his left arm?

Was he really a cruel, heartless Yankee general who tortured helpless civilians, or was he correct to punish slave owners, Confederate sympathizers, Confederate soldiers, guerrillas and "rebels" regardless of age or sex?

Why has Wild been forgotten? Was he hated because he trained his black troops so that they performed as well as or even better than their white counterparts? One author believed that Wild was "harassed, vilified, court martialed, demoted, and relieved of his last important command position" because many persons, both in the North and in the South, were incensed at his willingness to promote the interests of his black soldiers above those of white Southerners.[5] Southerners openly opposed him and his actions, but the discrimination he met in the North from among his own peers, his subordinate officers, and his superior officers was more subtle, but more devastating to the man, his reputation, his military career and, subsequently, his place in history.

Paradoxically, Edward Augustus Wild was one of the most loved and hated characters of the 19th century. Sadly, the man and his actions were neither understood nor appreciated by military or civilian, black or white, Northerner or Southerner. Some saw Edward Wild as "paranoid, indiscreet, hate-driven, generally obnoxious," while others saw him as "the personification of devotion to principle,—a man of faith," and one who would "have died a martyr for any cause he believed in."[6] His friends and admirers viewed "Ned" Wild as an "original character; true to his convictions on all occasions." His classmates and friends adored him, and his relatives loved him. He had a "genial disposition and made friends wherever he went."[7]

Perhaps it was his nature. As one relative described Wild: "He was not a moderate man and over-reacted to certain situations."[8] Edward Wild was definitely an enigma, an inexplicable man who evoked strong emotions from those who knew him. Wild could be kind to his friends and harsh on "those who denied an emancipated slave his rights."[9] Mrs. Helen Stevens Whitlock, a relative, believed that "He liked a challenge and the greater it was, the better. And part of that challenge was acting on behalf of the oppressed, the Afro-Americans."[10]

Wild expressed his philosophy about his military career in a letter to his wife on October 18, 1861: "I did not come here to be elevated, but simply from a sense of duty, and with the single-hearted objective to serve my country to my utmost ability, feeling within myself that I was the proper man to come." The next month, he wrote, "What courage I have comes from force of reason and of faith and of self discipline and determination. I pray heaven that when I see the need of sacrificing myself, no weakness of mine shall deter me."[11]

Through all the controversy, Wild was steadfast, unmoved by the humiliation of being arrested and the disgrace of court martials. He was ostracized, demoted, and stripped of his command. Yet, he did not let anything deter him from doing what he believed was right—neither public nor private opinion, military or civil authority, the loss of his arm.

Perhaps it is time to look at the impact of Edward Augustus Wild, not only as a military commander in battle, but also his part in a number of bizarre incidents. We may discover that he was the most amazing, audacious, contentious, controversial, outrageous, opinionated, unconventional Union officer who ever lived. In spite of all, he deserves to be remembered as the most courageous man of the 19th century. It is my hope that through this book, a better understanding of this man can be obtained and he will take his rightful place in history. It has been my privilege to explore the life and times of Edward Augustus Wild, and to come to know him as a man, a doctor, a general, and an adventurer. I hope my efforts will help separate fact from fiction to reveal the truth about Brigadier General Edward Augustus Wild. In the process, I hope I have offended no one.

I

Family History and Early Life of Edward Augustus Wild

At birth our death is sealed, and our end is consequent upon our beginning.
—Marcus Manilius, *Astronomica*

Edward August Wild was a complex man. A medical colleague, Dr. J. T. Talbot, described Edward Wild as "one of the most remarkable men" who had ever been a member of the American Institute of Homeopathy. Another medical colleague remembered Wild in an 1892 memorial service by saying that "there was little chance that we should ever have another like him."[1] Wild was "a genius ... a born leader." He associated with those of the "highest literary ability."[2] He was highly intelligent,[3] well educated, and could converse on many subjects. He was an "original character, true to his convictions on all occasions, and the personification of devotion to principle."[4] He was also a "Yankee abolitionist only slightly less zealous ... than old John Brown."[5]

Our opinions of Edward Wild are based on whatever sources are available in the 21st century. Although Wild is seldom mentioned in the biographies and autobiographies of his contemporaries, such as Ulysses S. Grant or Benjamin F. Butler, and he is entirely omitted from many major military works on the period, many documents exist which help paint a picture of this unique man and help to explain some of his more bizarre actions.

In his prime, Edward Augustus Wild was physically fit, tall and handsome. He was meticulous in his personal habits, and he abstained from the use of tobacco and intoxicating beverages.[6] He was said to be "peculiar in many ways," a trait he inherited from his father, who had been "before him, full of all sorts of curious notions, and these were increased in the next generation." Although Edward admitted that he was "always a miserable correspondent," he loved "to read letters," with the qualification that they be "free from flattery."[7] His writing in college was "clear, logical and terse, sparing of rhetoric;" he was definitely a man of few words.[8]

He never sought to be the center of attention, and disdained flattery of any kind, even from his friends.[9] He disdained fame and glory, and declared, "As for me, when I am shot down, let no one put on mourning for me."[10] Yet, when heroic action was needed, Wild was the first to take the lead, such as the time he led the rescue of three men from a capsized boat.[11]

He was seen by some as a "man of faith—who would have died a martyr for any cause he believed in and espoused." Because of his devotion to whatever cause, he inspired devotion in others, and he gathered about him those who shared his devotion to freedom and country.[12] He was not ambitious but saw his military service as a duty gladly performed. He wrote his wife in 1861, "I did not come here to be elevated, but simply from a sense of duty, and with the single-hearted object to serve my country to my utmost ability, feeling within myself that I was the proper man to come."[13] He loved military drill, and was an active member of the Independent Corps of Cadets in Boston before the war. Typically, Edward never missed a single drill.[14]

Wild's most complimentary biographers, his great-nephews Horace Stevens and Gershom Bradford, began their biography by stating that Edward was "adored by his classmates and friends, beloved by his relatives. His genial disposition made him friends wherever he went."[15]

Edward enjoyed music and art, and with little instruction or practice, he could "improvise with ability" and play almost any musical instrument.[16] Those who knew him personally remarked on his "merry" laughter and keen sense of humor, which "shed its sunlight on his pathway through life."[17] Before the war, he played a trumpet in an amateur brass band called The Hypnophonians, but he was limited to playing drums and cymbal afterwards.[18]

The only church in Brookline in the early 1800s was a Unitarian church called the "First Church," which the Wild family attended. Music was sometimes furnished by the members who played a variety of instruments. John H. Pierce, Dr. Charles Wild, and Charles Lyon played the flute; William H. Brown, the bassoon; George Murdock, the bass viola; Job Grush, the clarinet; and Artemus Newell played the "bombadoo [sic]."[19] "Ned" Wild played a "double bass or flute."[20] Edward Wheelwright, a Harvard classmate, remembered that Wild had a taste for music and had "skill as a performer." Wheelwright remembered seeing Wild play the bass viola and the trombone "in the choir of Dr. Pierce's church in Brookline."[21]

Edward Wild enjoyed a challenge. He enjoyed being the champion of those less fortunate, especially the former slaves and their families. He suffered much pain in his life, emotionally because of his activities with the black troops and the Freedman's Bureau, and physically because of the wounds he received on the battlefield. After his arm was amputated, he was never free of pain.[22]

Bradford Kingman noted that "He had the greatest disregard of self, and was of a vivacious turn, enlivening all company into which he entered, which rendered him socially peculiarly welcome to both sexes." His face reflected "kindness," and "benevolence warmed his heart." He was "ever kind, courteous and affable." As a doctor, his "highest motive" was to "relieve the suffering" through the use of his skills, and he worked "with delicacy, as well as with tenderness." He had simple tastes, and was "averse to all hollow pretensions and ceremonial observances."[23]

Yet, with all these fine characteristics, there was a darker side to Edward Wild, a side that prevented him from showing mercy on those who supported slavery and opposed freedom for the blacks or their usefulness as soldiers to the Union Army. He especially hated those Southerners who fought as guerrillas outside of the regular army of the Confederacy. He was not above using force in retaliation for wrongs done to his men, or taking hostages to ensure the safety of his men who had been captured by the enemy. As a brigadier general, Wild could be "harsh and reproachful to those who denied an emancipated slave his rights."[24] As a result of his treatment of Southern civilians and Confederate soldiers, many believed he was a cruel, heartless Yankee.

Family Background

How did Edward Wild reach the point where he was hated by people on both sides of the Mason-Dixon line? To understand the man, we need to look into his family background and education. We need to understand the times in which he lived, and events surrounding him.

The character of an individual is the result of both genetics and environment. The Wild family was of English ancestry. Edward Wild's most famous ancestor was the Reverend Roger Williams (1602–1683), of Providence, Rhode Island. Edward's mother, Mary Joanna Rhodes, was the great-great-great-granddaughter of Roger Williams, who was known as one of the earliest advocates of religious freedom.[25] Williams questioned "the religious purity" of the Massachusetts colony, and he preached the doctrine of separation of church and state. For his actions, in 1636 he was exiled from the Massachusetts Bay Colony. He then settled in Providence, the first "permanent white settlement in what would become Rhode Island."[26]

Edward's Father, Dr. Charles Wild

Dr. Charles Wild, Edward's father, was born in Boston, Massachusetts, on January 15, 1795, the son of Abraham and Susanna Pitman Wild.[27] After graduation from Harvard Medical School in 1818, Dr. Wild moved to Brookline, Massachusetts, where set up his medical practice. For over 40 years, Dr. Wild remained one of Brookline's highly esteemed citizens and a favorite doctor.[28]

A tall man, Charles Wild had a "firm tread and a deep voice," and his eyes had an "unusual piercing look" as he viewed his patients through spectacles. He was devoted in his care of his patients, and often stayed with them for an entire day and night. Charles Wild was known for having a "great good common sense."[29]

On December 29, 1819, Charles Wild married Mary Joanna Rhodes of North Providence, Rhode Island. Edward Augustus Wild was born on Friday, November 25, 1825, the third of nine children born to Charles and Joanna. Out of the nine children, only six lived to reach adulthood.

Edward Wild's Childhood

Edward grew up in "Beautiful Brookline," a typical little country town southwest of Boston. The town was surrounded by dense woodlands, and wildflowers grew everywhere. Small ponds, fed by gentle brooks, were shaded by great oak trees.[30]

Life was simple in Brookline. The inhabitants were mostly farmers, and a few were merchants.[31] Edward's father built a house on Washington Street on two acres of land given him by Mrs. Croft.[32] The Wilds, like every other family, probably kept a cow and a pig.[33]

Edward's early training was influenced by a "Christian home and careful training," and he was tutored in the "habits of industry." His childhood was typical of others who lived in small New England towns. He played ball in the summer, swam in the ponds, hunted in the woods, and went "sliding" down snow-covered hills in the winter months. He probably started to school when he was six or seven years old, and would have continued until about age 14.[34] He suffered usual childhood illnesses and injuries. He injured the metatarsal bones in his foot, the bones between the ankle and the toes.[35]

In the spring there were "May parties" in Perry's Woods. The young men had fun playing kick the "football."[36] "Sociable" gatherings were held at Seaman's Grocery Store, and usually music was provided. Dancing parties were held in the old Lyceum Hall, and food was served from long tables set up in the big room above the hall.[37] Together with older couples as chaperones, young people enjoyed picnics and outings. Occasionally, boys "sailed" down to the harbor at Boston, and went on annual fishing trips.[38]

Everyone in town turned out when a distinguished person passed through Brookline, such as John James Audubon. When General Lafayette, the French marquis who helped the colonists during the American Revolution, rode through the town, the streets were lined with people throwing flowers in his honor.[39]

Two of Edward's closest boyhood friends were Edward Atkinson and Edward S. Philbrick. The three Edwards called each other "Ned," and were very close friends until Edward Wild went to Harvard and Edward Philbrick went to college to become a civil engineer. The friendship of Atkinson and Wild continued throughout their lifetimes, and Edward Wild often poured out his troubles to Atkinson, who offered advice.[40] Wild fondly recalled the days when "we were free from care and therefore happy," when he and Edward Atkinson "used to play together, down at the old house in Cypress Street."[41]

The young people were a tough lot. They preferred to stay outdoors most of the time. Many, like Edward Atkinson, never wore an "overcoat except on Sunday, nor did we wear rubber shoes or boots." The boys wore cowhide boots and kept them well greased to make them waterproof.[42] Winter was the time for building fires along the banks of a local pond, and after the surface had frozen solid it provided the opportunity for ice skating at night. "Ned" Wild and his friends "Ned" Philbrick, "Ned" Atkinson, Frank Howe, Daniel Gilchrist, Charles Heath, and others came together to glide over the ice for evenings of fun to dispel the long, cold winter nights.[43]

The Wild family was involved in many social gatherings, along with a circle of friends from among the Goddards, Heaths, Howes, Pennimans, Sumners, Searls, and other local families. Evenings were spent at the various homes enjoying "music, dancing and friendly conversation." The Heaths were especially musical, and their young sons Charles and Frederick often invited young men to sing in quartets or as single voices to provide excellent entertainment.[44]

The first floor of Pierce Hall (the town hall) served as a public school during the summer months. Various kinds of meetings were held there, and educational "Lyceum lectures." There was also the Classical School modeled after a Greek temple, with Doric columns.[45] Edward began his education under the tutelage of Gideon Thayer at his private school.[46]

Edward's beliefs and values were influenced by his family, his church and his environment. He was an avid reader. He undoubtedly read his father's set of Sir Walter Scott's novels, available by subscription in the United States from 1820 to 1828. Edward chose this set of books as part of his share of his father's estate.[47]

The Anti-Slavery Movement

In the 1830s, the antislavery movement gained followers in Massachusetts and elsewhere. William Lloyd Garrison began publishing *The Liberator* in Boston in 1831.[48] Through his newspaper, "one of the most influential" in the United States, Garrison began crusading against slavery. He denounced slavery "as a sin and slave owners as sinners."[49]

At first, slavery had existed in all the colonies, but it was not profitable in the North. The opposite was true in the South, especially after Eli Whitney invented the cotton gin in 1793, and the demand for cotton greatly increased. The South could supply that demand only with the use of cheap slave labor. By 1860, cotton exports totaled $191,000,000, or 57 percent of the total value of all American exports. Thus, the South saw slavery as essential to their continued welfare and prosperity.[50] The abolitionists presented no solutions to the financial loss to slave owners if slavery were to be prohibited and abolished.[51]

The South resisted the anti-slavery movement. They counted slaves as "property" that was vital to their economic system. If this system of slavery were abolished, it would certainly bring about the "collapse of the whole Southern economy."[52]

Southerners saw their very way of life threatened by the abolitionists, and to preserve the *status quo*, they were willing to exert their constitutional rights to withdraw from the Union. Thus, with the lines drawn, tempers flared and reason flew. It became a case of "sectionalism" versus "nationalism." The men of the North felt compelled to reject slavery and secession both for moral and political reasons.[53] The South defended the institution of slavery as a means of preserving their economy and their lifestyle, and believed that the Constitution gave them the right to protect their interests.

Such was the atmosphere in the state of Massachusetts as Edward Wild became a young man. It was an era of changing views toward slavery and other social mores and customs. Samuel Philbrick, one of Brookline's most influential citizens and the father of Wild's friend Edward Philbrick, was an ardent abolitionist. The elder Philbrick undoubtedly had a great influence on his son and his son's friends. After being visited by Sarah and Angelina Grimke, the abolitionist sisters, Samuel Philbrick became a pioneer in the movement to abolish slavery. Philbrick broke with custom and showed his dedication to the abolition movement when he took a small Negro boy under his protection, and brought him to church to sit in his own pew.[54]

As Edward Wild grew to manhood, the anti-slavery movement also grew. He learned to hate the institution of slavery, and everyone who protected and prolonged that institution. Perhaps this was one of the reasons he fought so bravely for the Union, and dared to defy authority to do whatever he could to free slaves.

Edward Wild Becomes a Doctor

After attending the local schools of Brookline, Massachusetts, and the "classical" school there, Edward was given private instruction under Dr. Samuel Rogers of Roxbury. This additional preparation enabled him to enter Harvard College in 1840 and graduate in 1844.[55]

At the end of his sophomore year, Wild was awarded a "Detur," a book given as a prize for "merit in studies." A bookplate inside bore the inscription, "Detur Digniori," which means "To the more worthy let it be given."[56]

Edward Wild was a member of the Phi Beta Kappa honor society. He achieved "high distinction" in mathematics, Greek and Latin, and achieved the "required rank" in philosophy. At the Commencement exercise, he was assigned "An English Oration, 'The True Man of Action.'"[57] This subject proved to be prophetic, because for all of his life, Edward Augustus Wild, was, in every respect, "A True Man of Action."

After graduating from Harvard with an A.M. degree, Edward continued to study medicine in the office of Dr. Benjamin Eddy Cotting of Roxbury, and with his father, Charles Wild.[58] Dr. Charles Wild had become interested in homeopathy in 1839.[59] The second meeting of the Massachusetts homeopathic fraternity was held in the home of Dr. Charles Wild on February 16, 1841.

Homeopathy, a system of therapy used to treat both chronic and acute illnesses, is based on the theory that large doses of a drug given to a healthy person will produce certain conditions which, when occurring spontaneously as symptoms of a disease, are relieved by the same drug in small doses.[60] By the end of the 19th century, approximately 15 percent of physicians in the United States practiced homeopathy. It declined in popularity, but since the 1980s, interest has been renewed.[61]

Dr. Charles Wild used homeopathic methods in treating patients. He carried books with him as he visited patients, which he studied at their bedside trying to determine from the best authorities the best method of treatment.[62] Edward, aware of this treatment method since childhood, wanted to follow in his father's footsteps in the practice of homeopathy and entered Jefferson Medical College in Philadelphia. He graduated in 1846, "upon a brilliant examination and a full year in advance of the regular course."[63]

Edward Wild began his own medical practice in Brookline in 1847. He became a member of the Massachusetts Medical Society in 1850.[64] When he joined the Massachusetts Society of Homeopathy in 1853, he was appointed to some important committees.[65]

In the 1850s, physicians had few diagnostic tools—the ophthalmoscope, laryngoscope, endoscope, cystoscope, or X-ray did not exist. The hypodermic needle had not been invented, and main treatment forms were bloodletting and the use of purgatives.[66] There were no antibiotics, and sanitary practices were unheard of. As a practicing physician, Edward would have sworn to the Hippocratic oath to do the patient no harm, and to uphold patient confidentiality.[67]

After graduating from Jefferson Medical College, the young doctor Wild spent a year in the practice of medicine with his father. However, during the summer of 1848, Edward's health became "somewhat impaired," and his father advised him to take a break and go to France to visit the hospitals and attend medical lectures.[68]

Travels Abroad

Edward traveled by rail to New York to board an Ocean Steam Navigation Company steamer, which embarked on October 1, 1848. He arrived at the port of LeHavre on October 20.[69] Wild planned to travel to Paris to visit the hospitals and to observe their treatment methods.[70]

While in Europe, Wild kept in touch with his fiancée, Mary Howe. She told his friend Edward Atkinson about one letter she had received from Wild, except the portions that "were written in Latin," which she didn't share. Edward told his fiancée that he had not been seasick, and had arrived in France feeling so "much better," he felt "like a new man."[71]

While on board, Wild made the acquaintance of some of the ship passengers. He met Mrs. Murat, whose husband was the son of the Marshal of France. He also became friends with a Mr. Otis, an architect from Buffalo, New York. Wild and Otis decided to tour Normandy before going on to Paris. Because they wished to travel economically, they started walking on November 1 with their knapsacks on their backs. Otis wanted to examine the architecture of the many ancient churches in Normandy. Edward, a talented artist, made sketches of various buildings, and gained a "considerable knowledge of architecture." The two men had visited Caen, Rouen, and many other places, and Wild acted as Otis' interpreter, the latter being ignorant in the French language.[72]

Edward became involved in a dangerous situation during this tour, a pattern he would follow throughout his life. He and his friend decided to take a shortcut along a beach in Normandy that was only passable at low water. It was a very dangerous place when the tide was incoming. The beach was bordered by a cliff of blue clay. When the two started walking, they were told that the tide was going out. However, when they were only halfway across, the tide had turned and was incoming. A hailstorm came up quickly, and it grew dark. They trudged onward, having to work around masses of clay which had fallen from the cliffs. Luckily, they saw a gap in the cliff cut by a small stream and they climbed upward to a small village. Here, they stopped at the single tavern to dry their clothes by the chimney.[73] Luckily, they suffered no harm from the episode, although they very well could have been crushed against the rocky cliffs or pulled out to sea by the tide.

November 1848 to January 1849—Paris, France

On November 18, Wild traveled to Paris, where he roomed in the same building as did the Murats. The Murat family was very fond of Edward and permitted their secretary to give him lessons in French. Edward enjoyed his days in Paris, and wrote his parents in a "humorous vein" that he was having a grand time: "The atmosphere was filled with mustaches," Edward casually remarked, and added that his own mustache "was flourishing," because the floors were so slippery, and it was "very dangerous to use a razor."[74]

For two months, Wild increased his medical knowledge by visiting hospitals in Paris and attending lectures, although his comprehension was somewhat limited by his knowledge of French. Soon, however, he began to get restless, and decided to travel to Switzerland and Italy.[75] In the 19th century, a young man's education was not considered complete until he had taken the "Grand Tour" to Paris, Rome, Athens, and other ancient cities.

1849—Italy

Wild and a Harvard classmate, George Silsbee Hale, starting out on a walking tour.[76] The two young men planned to "pedestrinize through Italy and Switzerland." This was not the best of times to visit Italy, but very "troublous times." During 1848, revolutions had erupted in many European countries. Italy was involved in a threefold war—Rome was fighting with Naples, the French had invaded Rome, and the northern part of Italy was engaged in combat with Austria.[77]

Wild, always curious and even drawn to danger, did not hesitate to visit a country in the midst of war.[78] Horace N. Stevens believed that the Murats would have known of the danger, and would have warned Edward against visiting Italy at this time. However, like all young men, he "made light of all danger and was looking for adventure so was not to be deterred."[79]

The distance from Paris to Geneva, Switzerland, was approximately 225 miles, as the crow flies. If the Edward and George traveled south through Genoa to Milan, that would have been 150 additional miles. If they left Paris in late January, they should have arrived in Milan in the late spring.[80] The army of King Charles Albert of the Piedmont was positioned just west of Milan. It was attacked on March 23, 1848, by the Austrian forces of Marshal Rudetsky and completely wiped out.[81] Edward and his friend may have witnessed this battle.

At this time, Giuseppe Garibaldi was the leader of the Italian freedom movement, called *Risorgimento* ("revival"). He had organized a corps of 3,000 volunteers to serve Charles Albert, king of Sardinia.[82] The soldiers guarding the border between the territories controlled by Rome and Naples arrested Edward and George as spies. Edward recorded that they "were searched by the troops on both sides of the line, each taking us for spies of the other side."[83]

At Terracina, 25 miles south of Rome,[84] Edward and George were taken before Garibaldi, who quickly determined that they were not spies and released them.[85] The encounter with Garibaldi may have been in May or June of 1849. However, before the pair could get out of Italy, they were arrested again.[86] At Forli, the young Americans were again arrested as Austrian spies, "mobbed and roughly maltreated." They were lucky to escape with their lives. Once released, they traveled northward up the River Po where they were detained again as deserters from the Austrian army. Wild managed to prove who he was, and they were released. Shortly thereafter, on Lake Garda, in northern Italy, he and George were arrested at midnight as suspected robbers, and were thrown into prison. They were successful in getting released.[87]

The revolutions begun in 1848 were based on the growing popularity of nationalism. Most of them were failures. However, serfdom was abolished in the Austrian empire, Sardinia managed to keep its liberal constitution, and the German States got parliaments, even though they were "not of the democratic variety."[88] But peace in the Baltic States is never permanent, and in less than 10 years, the Crimean War would erupt between Russia and Turkey, a war in which Wild would take part.

Wild learned much from his experiences in Italy. He learned what it was like to be incarcerated in Italian prisons. Although he certainly was not pleased at being arrested, his sojourn in Europe "pleased his love of adventure,"[89] but many of his adventures were "neither safe nor agreeable."[90] He observed firsthand the horrors of war and its devastating effect upon the people and the land.[91] These experiences made a lasting impression on Edward.

1850 to 1855—Brookline, Massachusetts

By January 1, 1850, Edward Wild had returned to Brookline and resumed his practice as a physician of homeopathic medicine.[92] He did not marry Mary Howe. Ned Atkinson wrote to Ned Philbrick to report that Wild's engagement to Mary Howe had been broken. Edward Wild was hurt, but "to forget his disappointment," he buried himself in his medical work and in helping his father.[93]

In the nation, tempers flared over the expansion of slavery. Congress tried to avoid conflict through compromise. On September 9, 1850, Congress passed the Compromise of 1850, which included the Fugitive Slave Act. This bill allowed California to be admitted as a non-slave state. As a concession to the South, fugitive slaves found in the North would be returned to their Southern owners.[94]

The people of Massachusetts hated the Fugitive Slave Law and worked to get around it. Brookline, Massachusetts, became part of the "underground railroad" which helped slaves escape from the South to freedom in the North. One of the "stations" along the route to freedom was at the home of Samuel Philbrick in Brookline.

In 1854, an incident involving the arrest of a runaway slave, Anthony Burns, almost caused a riot in Boston. To prevent any trouble when Burns was taken from jail to be returned South, the mayor of Boston hired a bodyguard of 127 "roughs," and called out the entire Boston police force. The state sent 22 companies of the Massachusetts Volunteer Militia, and the United States government sent 1,140 armed soldiers to prevent any possible riot.[95]

Wild joined the Boston Independent Corps of Cadets after his return from Italy. He reportedly never missed a drill. Undoubtedly the Anthony Burns case made an impression upon him. That event, coupled with his knowledge that many in his hometown consistently helped slaves gain their freedom, "laid the foundation for his devotion to the cause of the colored people"[96] for many years and in many different situations.

That same year, Wild began courting Miss Frances Ellen Sullivan. He proposed, and they were married in Boston by the Reverend A. L. Stone on June 12, 1855, in what was described as a "notable social event." The 26-year-old bride was the daughter of a prominent Boston couple, John Whiting and Marian (Dix) Sullivan. The groom was 29 years old.[97]

The bride's mother, Marian Dix Sullivan, composed "The Blue Juanita," a popular song during the 1850s. Marian was the sister of General John Adams Dix.[98] A War of 1812 veteran, Dix studied law and rose in politics in New York state to be come a United States Senator from 1845 to 1850.[99] In 1861, Dix was Secretary of the Treasury, and was appointed by President Lincoln as a Major General of the United States volunteers on May 16, 1861, and commander of the Department of Annapolis.[100] He was later Governor of New York, and Minister to France.[101]

1855 to 1856—The Crimean War

The Crimean War[102] was the first war to have on-the-spot news coverage printed in newspapers such as *The Times* of London. *The Times* reported the casualties of the war from battle injuries, and even more deaths from disease. A British news reporter noted in December of 1854 that there were as many as "3,000 invalids in the hospital at Balaklava, 4,000 at Scutari, and a considerable number in the hospital marquees at the camp." The "new Turkish reinforcements were dying by wholesale ... from mere famine and misery...."[103]

Undoubtedly, Edward knew of the conflict when he embarked on his honeymoon. Two weeks after his wedding, Dr. Edward A. Wild took his young bride, Ellen,[104] and sailed for Constantinople on their honeymoon cruise.[105] In the area centered around the Black Sea, the Crimean War had been raging since October 1853. It involved Turkey and Russia and eventually France, Britain, Sardinia,[106] and a number of independent American volunteers.

By the time Edward Wild arrived in Turkey, the two most important events of the Crimean War had already occurred. The first was the development of modern nursing techniques by Florence Nightingale. Since diseases and starvation killed more troops than the enemy, Nightingale's reforms in the way military hospitals were maintained and patients cared for were invaluable and probably saved many lives.[107]

The second memorable event was the "Charge of the Light Brigade," immortalized in a poem of that same name by Alfred, Lord Tennyson. This "suicidal" charge was made on October 25, 1854, by a British light cavalry brigade. Because of either a misunderstood order or an order that was poorly planned, the brigade charged in the wrong direction across an open plain to die from Russian heavy artillery. Two-thirds of the 650 men who made the charge were killed.[108]

The Crimean War began over access to the key to the main door of the Church of the Holy Sepulcher in Bethlehem—in a dispute between the Greek Orthodox Church and the Roman Catholic Church. A fight over the key erupted and several Greek Orthodox monks were killed. This gave the Russian Tsar Nicholas, who was also the head of the Greek Orthodox Church, the excuse he needed to intervene in the affairs of the Ottoman Empire. Nicholas saw this as the perfect excuse to make trouble for the Church of the Holy Sepulcher, which had been controlled by the monks of the Roman Catholic Church, under the protection of France since the time of the Crusades.

When the newlywed couple arrived in Constantinople, Edward, the adventurous young American, left his bride and offered his services as a doctor to the Turkish Sultan,[109] Abdul Mejid. Turkey, that part of the Ottoman Empire known as "the sick man of Europe," was in the midst of a bitter conflict with Russia. Known as the Crimean War for the Crimean Peninsula which juts into the Black Sea, the conflict had begun in 1853.

Why did Edward Wild become involved? Was he moved to offer his services to gain experience, or because he craved adventure? The large military salary offered was incentive enough for some.[110] But did that interest Wild?

Perhaps Wild saw this as an opportunity to further his medical education and experience. Since Florence Nightingale had already organized the British and French field hospitals, perhaps Wild may have wanted to try the same service for the Turkish forces in the summer of 1855.[111] Certainly, his services were badly needed. In January 1855, a letter to the editor of *The Times* pointed out that of 130 deaths during the month, those from "dysentery or diarrhea was more than 100." Only a few deaths resulted from fever or wounds.[112]

Upon arriving in Constantinople, Edward probably offered his services to the Turks through the American ambassador. Wild was welcomed by the Sultan Abdul Mejid, and was given a commission as Surgeon of Artillery with the rank and pay of a Lieutenant Colonel. He was given the name *Kholoussy Bey,* meaning "sincere commander."[113] He was assigned to the staff of Omar Pasha, the commander of the Turkish forces in the field. Omar Pasha, a Hungarian who had fled to Turkey from his own country, had worked his way up through the ranks to become Commander-In-Chief. He was described as "a cold and stern man but a great general."[114]

Shortly before Wild arrived in Turkey, Omar Pasha had made a reconnaissance, and the good news was that the Russian force was now believed to be much smaller than had previously been perceived. In addition, the Allied forces had succeeded in gaining a more advantageous position from which to fire upon the Russian fortifications at Sebastopol.[115] The town withstood the siege for 11 months, until the Russians finally surrendered in September of 1855.[116]

Wild was not the only American doctor to volunteer for service in the Crimean War. More than thirty young doctors served with the Russians. Ten died in the war, and one disappeared. Those who did survive returned home to use their skills in the many hospitals in United States filled to overflowing with casualties from the American Civil War.[117]

Whether serving the Tsar's Russian army or the forces of the Turkish Sultan, American doctors did so at grave risk to themselves. All suffered from the cold and illnesses such as typhus fever, cholera, and smallpox.[118] To add to the deadly diseases, the winter of 1855–1856 was one of "constant snows, rains, fog, and mud...."[119]

Dr. Wild's duties as Surgeon of Artillery took him to several points around the Black Sea. He visited the ports of "Sinoub (Sinope), Trebizond, Tatoum, Redout Kalek (Kemhal), Sokhoum Kaleh." From Kemhal, Wild and Omar Pasha's forces moved to Mingrelia and Georgia, where they encountered enemy forces near Kutais. They advanced near to Tifliss and spent the winter near Sokhoum Kaleh in the foothills of the Caucasus Mountains.[120] In his memoir of the Crimean War, Wild noted that he had also made two trips into Abkhasia and Chirkesslik (Circassia).[121] There, during the winter of 1855–1856, near the Caucasus Mountains, Wild used some captured Russian hospitals for his medical facilities. Even after the peace had been declared in February of 1856, Dr. Wild continued in charge of "extensive military hospitals in Trebizond," which were filled with a large number of sick and disabled former soldiers. After about nine months, Edward returned to Constantinople, and arrived there about the first of May 1856.[122]

Before leaving Turkey, Dr. Edward Wild was given two medals and two diplomas by the Sultan Abdul Mejid in recognition of his services. With one of the medals, War Medal (Sefer-nishaui), he also received the Decoration of the Mejidieh with its accompanying *beral* (diploma) and an autographed letter from Omar Pasha "recommending me for that high honor."[123]

The other medal, the *Nichan-berati,* was enclosed in a silver case which bore the Sultan's coat of arms. A diploma with the Nichan medal stated that "the Nichan" had been struck to commemorate the courage and zeal shown by the commanders, officers and soldiers in the performance of their respective duties.[124] Wild's medal and diploma were for distinguished service and were "bestowed upon him as a testimonial of my Imperial satisfaction with his conduct."[125] The Sultan honored Dr. Wild by giving him the " imperial decoration of the fifth grade and the present *beral* or diploma" in testimony of his actions.[126] Dr. Wild, the "appointed physician in the imperial corps d'Armee at Batourn [who] has shown good service in his position" was one among many employees who received medals for the performance of good service to the Ottoman Empire during the Crimean War.[127]

Wild was in Turkey for 15 months, and 9 of those months were spent in actual service to the Sultan.[128] When the war ended, Edward and his wife resumed their honeymoon. He wrote that he "visited with my wife all the banks of the Bosporus."[129] They stayed in Constantinople until the fall of 1856, and visited Trebizond, the Bosporus, the gulf of Nikiomedia, the islands of the Marmora (Prinkipo), and the Troad. Continuing their leisurely journey, they visited Greece and some of the islands of the Archipelago. The couple remained long enough on the island of Malta for Edward to become initiated into the order of Freemasonry, and to obtain three degrees in Saint John's Lodge.[130] From Malta, Edward and Ellen visited Sicily, and they spent most of 1857 in Italy.[131]

It was late in the fall of 1857 before Edward thought about returning to the United States. Perhaps he procrastinated because he still wanted to return to Turkey to work in the hospitals there. To that effect, he wrote to inquire if a position was available. The reply to his letter from Lord Napia, dated October 18, 1857, was not favorable. Wild was informed that there were no vacancies in the medical department and that several persons had been denied employment "in whom he [Lord Napia] was deeply interested."[132]

That ended the matter, and the Wilds crossed the Atlantic for home. They arrived in Brookline, Massachusetts, after having been gone for two and a half years.[133]

Results of the Crimean War

The Crimean War temporarily halted the advance of Russia into the Balkan states.[134] At the end of the war, the Treaty of Paris of 1856 was very favorable to the Ottoman Empire, and provided for the neutralization of the Black Sea. The Crimean War left in its wake much hatred and unresolved nationalistic sentiments. Austria, which had remained neutral, was no longer deemed a Russian ally.[135]

This war, like other wars fought in the Balkan states, never completely resolved anything. Only a quarter of a century later, the Russo-Turkish War of 1877–1878 was settled by the Treaty of San Stefano in 1878, in which the independence of Serbia and Rumania was recognized. Austria was allowed to occupy and control Herzegovinia and Bosnia, where dissatisfaction erupted in Sarajevo, Bosnia, in on June 28, 1914 (sixty years after the start of the Crimean War) with the assassination of the ArchDuke Francis Ferdinand, heir to the throne of Austria.[136] In 1917, the Pact of Corfu proclaimed that all Yugoslavs would unite after World War I to form a kingdom under the Serbian Royal House. After being freed from German Occupation during World War II, a monarchy was abolished and Yugoslavia came under the control of Marshal Tito and the Federal People's Republic of Yugoslavia. When Tito died in 1980, the three ethnic groups—Serbs, Croats, Muslims—began fighting among themselves.[137]

On June 25, 1991, Croatia and Slovenia proclaimed their independence from Yugoslavia. The world watched through the media of television the brutal fighting and atrocities committed against civilians in Bosnia, Serbia, and Croatia brought about by the resurgence of nationalism and the intolerance of religious differences intensified by the breakup of Yugoslavia. A peace treaty was finally signed in Paris on December 14, 1995. NATO forces have kept a close watch since that time.[138]

Sadly, perhaps the only enduring elements of the Crimean War of 1854–1856 were Florence Nightingale's advances in nursing care and Tennyson's epic poem immortalizing the unnecessary deaths of the brave horsemen of the Light Brigade.

After returning to America from the Mediterranean, Dr. Edward Wild opened his medical practice in Brookline and became popular as a physician. He became a member of the American Institute of Homeopathy in 1859. The following year, he gave the annual oration to the Massachusetts Homeopathic Medical Society, and he spoke on "mind over matter."[139]

1861—War in America

Events in Charleston, South Carolina, would soon drastically change America forever. Confederates fired on Fort Sumter on April 12, 1861, and thus began the American Civil War (known in the South as the War Between the States). Edward Wild had no idea when he joined the 1st Massachusetts Volunteers in 1861 that his life would be so drastically altered. Not only would his medical career be ended, but soon his physical capabilities would be greatly impaired.

II

Captain Wild, United States Army, 1861

Accurst be he that first invented war.
—Christopher Marlowe,
Tamburlaine the Great

War between the states erupted with the attack on Fort Sumter on April 12, 1861. This one act, "more than any other act committed in the interest of secession," divided the country.

War was inevitable after Confederates fired on Fort Sumter and forced the surrender of Major Robert Anderson and his Union troops within the fort. On April 15, 1861, President Lincoln proclaimed the seven southern states that had already left the Union (South Carolina, Mississippi, Florida, Alabama, Georgia, Louisiana, Texas) as being in a state of insurrection, and he called for 75,000 volunteers to put down the rebellion. The reaction to Lincoln's call for troops was the deciding factor in sending the four southern states still in the union (North Carolina, Virginia, Arkansas, and Tennessee) over to the other side to join the Confederacy.[1]

Wild was destined to play a major role in this war, and in bringing about changes in the United States Army. Before he could assume his role as a "recruiter" for black troops, he would have to undergo a baptism of fire, and sustain wounds that would render him unfit to practice his pre-war profession as a doctor. For his willingness to promote blacks as soldiers and to help them and their families, and for his treatment of slave-owners, Confederate guerrilla forces, and civilians who were Confederate sympathizers, Wild would be discriminated against, court martialed, arrested, vilified, demoted, and damned by both Union and Confederate governments, by military personnel and civilians on both sides of the conflict, and on both sides of the Mason-Dixon line.

Background and Events Leading to War

For decades, politicians had attempted to legislate a peaceful solution to the slavery question and other differences between the northern and southern states. The Wilmot Proviso, enacted in 1846, carried an amendment which stipulated that none of the territory acquired by the Mexican War would be open to slavery. This bill created more bitterness over the extension of slavery.

After Lincoln was elected president in 1860, events moved quickly. South Carolina seceded from the union on December 20, 1860, and six of her sister states soon closed ranks to form the Confederate States of America. After South Carolina seceded, Christopher Gustavus Memminger, later Secretary of the Treasury of the Confederate States, wrote the "Declaration of Causes of Seceding States." He listed the reasons why South Carolina left the union.

At the Convention of April 26, 1852, South Carolina had protested the "encroachments upon the reserved rights of the States," but in "deference to the opinions and wishes of other slave-holding States," South Carolina did not take action at that time. However, since then the situation had worsened, and encroachments on the rights of states had continued. South Carolina and the other original states were granted from Great Britain the right to be "free, sovereign, and independent states," and won two basic rights through the American Revolution: (1) "the right of a State to govern itself;" and (2) "the right of a people to abolish a Government when it became destructive of the ends for which it was instituted."

One of Memminger's arguments hinged on the "doctrine of *States' Rights*," which was written into the Constitution of the United States, and guaranteed in the Tenth Amendment to the Constitution, which clearly states that all "powers not delegated to the United States by the Constitution, nor prohibited by it to the States, are reserved to the States, respectively, or to the people." Other concerns expressed by Memminger concerned the fugitive slave laws. He ended with a declaration that:

> The State of South Carolina has resumed her position among the nations of the world, as a separate and independent State; with full power to levy war, conclude peace, contract alliances, establish commerce, and to do all other acts and things which independent States may of right do.[2]

In his first inaugural address, President Abraham Lincoln mentioned the legal and constitutional sanctions of slavery, and addressed the issue that the Union of the states was "perpetual." This concept, he said, "is implied, if not expressed, in the fundamental law of all national governments."

Overriding the slavery question, Lincoln believed that no state could "lawfully get out of the union...." He saw acts of violence within any State or States against the authority of the United States as "insurrectionary or revolutionary."[3]

Governor John A. Andrew

John Albion Andrew, Governor of Massachusetts from 1861 to 1866, was a powerful ally and friend to Edward Wild. Throughout the war, he and Wild corresponded frequently to exchange ideas. Governor Andrew wanted more regiments and he wanted good men to lead them. Andrew, a staunch abolitionist, had once helped raise money for the defense of John Brown. Born in Maine, Andrew became a lawyer and, to further his anti-slavery ideals, entered politics and helped organize the Free-Soil Party. He later became a Republican and was elected as a member of the Massachusetts House of Representatives in 1858.[4]

As governor, Andrew was the Commander in Chief of all the Massachusetts troops. It was due to Andrew's efforts that the Massachusetts state militia was prepared for war, and the 6th Massachusetts was the first armed force to enter Washington after Lincoln's call for volunteers.[5]

John A. Andrew (1818–1867) of Massachusetts, one of Wild's staunchest friends and supporters. (Property of Frances H. Casstevens.)

April 1861—Preparing for War

Only a few days after Fort Sumter surrendered on April 14, 1861, Governor Andrew wrote Simon Cameron, Secretary of War, and offered to protect Boston Harbor and to prepare men "by exact drill and discipline for active service." Andrew wanted 1,000 to 2,000 called up for active service as militia.[6] Governor Andrew promised to send "4,000 more troops from Massachusetts within a very short time after the receipt of a requisition for them." Andrew sought permission from the Secretary of War to enlist into the United States army the "Irish, Germans, and other tough men, to be drilled and prepared here for such service." Andrew was confident that "We have men enough of such description, eager to be employed, sufficient to make three regiments."[7]

Sentiments were running high in Brookline, Massachusetts, in the spring of 1861. All the young men were eager whip the Rebels. They soon saw action in Maryland. The 6th Massachusetts Regiment was attacked in Baltimore by a mob on the 19th of April. Three soldiers of the 6th were killed and 10 wounded.[8]

Edward Wild undoubtedly would have been influenced to some degree by such avid abolitionists as Harriet Beecher Stowe, whose book *Uncle Tom's Cabin* began appearing in serial form in 1851. He had been brought up to believe that slavery was wrong, that injustice could only be overcome by armed resistance, and acting on that belief, he was quick to join the 1st Massachusetts Volunteers (1st Mass.) and offer his services to the Union after the outbreak of war. He began to raise a company of volunteers in Brookline and Jamaica Plain.[9]

The citizens of Brookline "were wealthy and public-spirited," and they spared neither their lives nor their fortunes in lending support to the government.[10] When news came of the attack on the 6th Mass., town meetings were held and practically every man in Brookline attended. The first meeting was held in the town hall on April 20, 1861; the second was held on April 22. The crowd heard speeches by a number of men, and the "selectmen were asked to furnish a drill ground for the drilling of the companies." A military committee was formed, which included Edward A. Wild and other prominent Brookline men.[11] Wild had to decide whether he would serve as a surgeon in the hospitals in Massachusetts or become a battlefield doctor. He had gained much experience in treating battle wounds during his months with the Sultan's forces in the Crimean War. Horace Stevens and Gershaom Bradford believed that what he desired most was to preserve the Union and free the slaves. His travels abroad had shown him what a wonderful country America was, and he knew it "must be kept intact to grow and become a great nation which it could never be if divided." He was an ardent abolitionist, and he sympathized with the plight of those fugitive slaves he had seen at the home of Samuel Philbrick. Edward had the highest moral standards and a "strong sympathy for oppressed people." He saw the war as his chance to do something to help them. Although those sympathies would get him in trouble on many occasions, once Wild made up his mind, he would not be deterred from his course. He feared "neither God, man or the devil."[12]

The first Brookline resident to enlist was William D. Goddard. Another was the young lawyer Wilder Dwight, who was inducted as a major in the 2nd Regiment of Infantry, Massachusetts Volunteers.[13] Dwight would later die at Antietam.[14] (See Chapter III.)

Others soon followed. Edward A. Wild and his friends William L. Candler and Charles P. Chandler volunteered to raise a company. A hall was rented on the corner of Boylston and Washington streets in which to recruit and drill those who signed on. Soon a company of 30 to 40 men was formed, and they were drilled by Edward Wild and his two lieutenants, Candler and Chandler.[15] First Lieutenant Chandler was adamant about getting the men in good shape to march. Once, he marched the company "double-quick from the Town Hall to Corey Hill," then on to Jamaica Plain before returning them to the Town Hall.[16]

Over the next year and a half, Wild would see action in several major battles (Bull Run, Williamsburg, Fair Oaks, South Mountain), and he would gain a reputation "as a courageous and capable officer."[17] The 1st Mass. was always in the forefront, and even after Wild was no longer a part of it, this regiment saw action at Second Bull Run, Chantilly, Fredericksburg, Chancellorsville, Gettysburg, the Wilderness, and Spotsylvania.[18]

May 1861— Call for Volunteers

On May 3, President Lincoln issued a call for volunteers to serve a period of three years or the duration of the war. Governor Andrew had to wait to learn how many regiments were needed to meet the state's "quota." Wild grew impatient and anxious to begin equipping and training his men. Characteristically, he cut right through the "red tape" and wrote directly to the Governor of Massachusetts for the needed equipment. His answer came promptly from Binney Sargent, aide-de-camp to the Governor, who wrote on May 11, 1861, that he was sorry that the "arms which you desire are not to be obtained by us at present."[19]

Lt. William L. Candler (left), Capt. Edward A. Wild (center), Lt. Charles P. Chandler, Officers of Company A, 1st Massachusetts Infantry, 1861. (Courtesy of Massachusetts Commandery, Military Order of the Loyal Legion, and U.S. Army Military History Institute, Carlisle Barracks, Carlisle, Pa.)

A thousand volunteers were waiting for arms and equipment. On May 22, Secretary of War Cameron notified Governor Andrew that six regiments of infantry were to be raised from Massachusetts and ordered that "that number must not be exceeded." Cameron stated that each regiment was "to have the regular army organization of ten companies of ninety-eight men each and the regulation number of officers."[20]

Wild spent the months of April and May of 1861 recruiting men in his hometown of Brookline and in nearby Jamaica Plains for a company of volunteers.[21] He resigned from the Brookline Military Committee, and with his company of Brookline Rifles, persuaded enough men to join to fill a company of 78 men. As soon as the company was organized, Wild traveled to the Adjutant General's office in Boston

Captain Edward Augustus Wild, of Company A, 1st Massachusetts Volunteers. (Courtesy of Massachusetts Commandery, Military Order of the Loyal Legion, and U.S. Army Military History Institute, Carlisle Barracks, Carlisle, Pa.)

and offered his company to Governor Andrew. His was one of the "first complete companies to be accepted," and was designated Company A, First Regiment of Massachusetts Volunteers." [22]

On May 22, 1861, Captain Edward Wild, age 35, of Company A, 1st Massachusetts Volunteers, came under the command of Colonel Robert Cowdin.[23] He was "mustered" into the service as of May 23, 1861.[24] Captain Edward Wild was described as a tall, slender man, with a "reddish beard."[25]

His company was mustered into service at the old Franklin School House in Boston, by Colonel Harrington of Brookline. The company was recruited and "equipped entirely by the town of Brookline." The Military Committee presented each of the three commissioned officers with a "camp-chest" and $125. Privates received $5.00 to be used to buy equipment. The ladies of the town obtained the necessary shirts, stockings, and other clothing.[26]

June 1861—Marching to War

When the 1st Mass. left the barracks in Faneuil Hall, they moved to Cambridge, from whence they marched to war.[27] On June 1, 1861, the 1st Mass. went into camp at Fresh Pond, near Cambridge. The regiment was then transferred to Camp Cameron, at North Cambridge, on June 13, then marched to Boston on June 15. Here, the City of Boston presented the regiment with a flag, and the regiment embarked on the railroad cars after tearful good-byes from relatives and friends.[28]

The 1st Mass. left the state with Colonel Robert Cowdin in command, and field officers Lieutenant Colonel George D. Wells and Major Charles P. Chandler. Chandler was killed in one of the battles between the Chickahominy and the James rivers, and his body was never recovered.[29]

From Camp Cameron near Philadelphia, the 1st Mass. took railroad cars on June 15 to Baltimore, Maryland. They proceeded cautiously, remembering that the 6th Massachusetts Militia had been attacked in Baltimore on April 19. Ten rounds of cartridges were given to each man as a precaution against attack, and the men loaded their muskets. They marched toward the Washington depot by way of Baltimore Street. The people who crowded the along the sides of the streets watched silently as the regiment marched by. Women watched from the windows of the houses along the way. Once the soldiers reached the depot without incident, they boarded railroad cars which were to take them to Washington, D.C.[30]

It did not take Captain Wild very long to see that the military organization needed much improvement. On June 17, 1861, he wrote his friend Governor John A. Andrew to report a lack of discipline and "want of system" which was so great "as to vitally impair its efficiency as a military corp. on active service...." While the situation had been bad when the men were camped at Cambridge, Wild reported that conditions had worsened on their removal to Philadelphia, "causing great and unnecessary delays, especially in embarking and disembarking, causing discomfort, suffering, sickness, and even danger, to the troops." Wild had hoped that conditions would improve, but they had grown worse since the entire regiment had been "brought together in camp." Wild believed Colonel Cowdin was totally unsuited as commander, and was "wanting in system, and in the comprehension of details—wanting in tact, especially in military matters—wanting in presence of mind, when disturbed by the confusion about him—and completely wanting in military foresight and calculation." Wild begged the Governor to use his influence to have Colonel Cowdin removed from command of the regiment.[31] Wild knew that by going over the head of his superior officer he was guilty of insubordination. This first act of insubordination would not be his last.

Governor Andrew took no action on Wild's request, and Colonel Cowdin continued to command the regiment. However, Colonel Cowdin did not forget Wild's criticism.

On June 19, Wild and his regiment camped on the banks of the Upper Potomac River near the "Chain Bridge."[32] Once the regiment reached Washington, they "formed in a column by company, and marched up Pennsylvania Avenue to Seventh Street." The men were soon settled. A few men were placed in an "unoccupied building on Seventh Street." Another two companies were assigned a building on Sixth Street. In Washington, no rations were available, and since they had not eaten since leaving Philadelphia, the officers had to give the men money to purchase food.[33] On June 21, the regiment was formed in a column and marched in front of the White House, where they were reviewed by President Abraham Lincoln. They then proceeded past Georgetown College, set up tents and camped in an open field on the Potomac River. They called this "Camp Banks," in honor of Major General Nathaniel P. Banks, an ex-governor of Massachusetts.[34]

The men of the regiment celebrated the 4th of July by participating in a parade in full dress, and the regimental band played the national anthem. Afterwards, an

American flag was presented to them by Senator McGougal on behalf of "Boston citizens resident in California."[35] A beautiful silk banner was presented to Colonel Cowdin by Colonel Ellis of the First California regiment on behalf of the San Francisco City Guards, because their commander, Captain Moore, had formerly served under Colonel Cowdin. Speeches were made by various senators and representatives.[36]

The regiment remained at Camp Banks until July 8, when they were ordered on an 8-hour, 18-mile march to Great Falls on the Potomac. Any marching was hard on the men because of the extreme heat during the month of July, their heavy woolen uniforms, and the necessary guns and equipment for survival each man carried. Until July 16, the regiment was engaged in daily skirmishes with enemy pickets, but did not sustain any casualties.[37]

At the beginning of the war, the Federal forces of the Army of the Potomac were commanded by Brigadier General Irvin McDowell, a West Point graduate who had served in the Mexican War.[38] McDowell gathered five divisions of troops to Washington, the first commanded by Brigadier General Daniel Tyler, which consisted of four brigades. The fourth brigade was commanded by Colonel Israel Bush Richardson,[39] nicknamed "Fighting Dick," a veteran of the Seminole War and the Mexican War.[40]

The 1st Mass. was ordered to return to Camp Banks, and on July 17, 1861, they were placed in Richardson's brigade.[41] Richardson reported that his brigade consisted of "the Second and Third Michigan Regiments, the First Massachusetts Regiment, and Twelfth New York." It also included a battalion of light infantry, made up of 40 men from each regiment for a total of 160.[42]

As part of Richardson's Brigade, the men of Company A, 1st Mass., marched bravely across the Chain Bridge into Virginia to meet the Army of Virginia. The regiment reached Centreville by night and made camp.[43] It was a hot and dusty march, and the men were not acclimatized to a sweltering Virginia summer.

July 18, 1861—Blackburn's Ford, Virginia

After the fall of Fort Sumter, the war moved to Virginia. The first major encounter took place around the strategic railroad intersection Manassas Junction, 25 miles southwest of Washington. The Manassas Gap Railroad ran west through Manassas Gap and into the Shenandoah Valley, giving access across the Appalachian Mountains into Kentucky. The Federal advance into Virginia relied on General Irvin McDowell's move against Manassas Junction, while at the same time, a smaller force under General Robert Patterson would cross the Potomac, take Harper's Ferry, then move south through the Shenandoah and keep forces of Confederate Joseph E. Johnston engaged and away from the Manassas Gap Railroad.[44]

Union General McDowell marched proudly out to meet the opposition forces under Confederate General P.G.T. Beauregard on the afternoon of July 18. McDowell ordered Brigadier General Daniel Tyler and his division to proceed to Centreville to scout out the roads from Bull Run to Warrenton, Virginia. Tyler was not to "bring on an engagement, but keep up the impression that we are moving on Manassas."[45] By mistake, Richardson's Brigade turned left in Centreville, and marched to Blackburn's Ford.[46]

The road ran along a ridge, then went down an incline into woods near a creek called Bull Run. The Federals advanced unchallenged to a point about a mile from Centreville, where they halted at a spring to get water for the men on that hot July day. Richardson and Tyler, with a squadron of cavalry and two companies of infantry, moved ahead to make a reconnaissance. They arrived about a mile from Blackburn's Ford and saw that the enemy had a battery there in position to "enfilade the road." Richardson ordered the battalion of light infantry to open fire. After several rounds had been fired, the enemy answered with their own gunfire. The skirmishers moved forward to the edge of some woods, and Richardson ordered the 1st Mass. to move up in support of the skirmishers. He ordered two 12-pound howitzers moved up. The enemy began to fire upon the road. The 12th New York was moved to the left of the Federal battery, formed into a battle line, and ordered to charge the enemy's position. He positioned the 1st Mass. and the 2nd and 3rd Michigan Regiments on the right of the battery. This was barely accomplished when the enemy forces sent heavy musket and artillery fire along their whole line. The 12th New York fell back "in disorder" under the intense fire. The howitzers and cavalry had also withdrawn, leaving the left flank exposed. The three remaining regiments on the right "remained firm and determined."[47] The Massachusetts regiment, which included Captain Edward Wild and Company A, stood firm.

Federal skirmishers moved close enough to the enemy breastworks to kill Confederate officers behind the works. "One Union man was shot through the shoulder" by a Confederate with a revolver, and a cannoneer was bayoneted while he loaded his cannon.[48]

At one point, the Confederates came out of the woods and headed for the 1st Mass. The men of the 1st Massachusetts stood firm, but the enemy fire was so heavy they were ordered to lie down. They remained on the ground for about 30 minutes.[49]

The Confederates formed a line of battle on the edge of the wood but retreated under fire from a Union artillery battery. Colonel Richardson asked General Tyler for permission to charge and drive the enemy back. Tyler refused, as he had been ordered to do only "reconnaissance" to establish the enemy's strength. So, the men withdrew. Three regiments fell back in an orderly fashion, but they had to leave their dead and wounded.[50]

Captain Wild noted about the Battle of Blackburn's Ford: "Our regiment in advance made the first attack" and suffered considerably. "Reconnaissance being made, we retired in perfect order. Bivouacked on the field until July 21st."[51]

At Blackburn's Ford, Colonel Cowdin provided an excellent target for Confederate sharpshooters as he stood "conspicuously in white shirt sleeves." When told to sit down, he replied, "The bullet is not cast that will kill me today." He was right and lived to see a number of major battles. He served until his commission as Brigadier General expired in March of 1863.[52]

Tyler's reconnaissance at Blackburn's Ford against the men of James Longstreet's force was repulsed with 83 casualties. The Confederates lost 68.[53] Casualties among the men of the 1st Mass. Infantry were one officer killed, and 9 enlisted men killed and 22 injured.[54] (A list later compiled by Lt. Col. William F. Fox showed 14 killed, including those who died later from injuries received at Blackburn's Ford, who were members of the 1st Mass. Regiment.[55])

The heaviest skirmishing was done by the men of the 1st Mass., and Companies G, H, and F, which suffered the most casualties.[56] Wild and his company had one casualty.[57]

The fighting at Blackburn's Ford was unplanned. No orders had been issued to General Tyler to engage the enemy at this point. In fact, McDowell had ordered Tyler to only "Observe well the roads to Bull Run and to Warrenton."[58] Tyler did not get along well with General McDowell, and he managed to turn a simple "reconnaissance at Blackburn's Ford into a substantial engagement" that alerted the Confederates to the movement of Federal troops.[59] Unfortunately, the affair seems to have been "badly managed." Horace Stevens believed that with a "little more skill and a little more support for the 1st Mass., the enemy should have been driven back into his lines and kept there instead of the whole days fighting going by default and nothing coming of it."

"Except for the short time the 12th New York was under fire," it was the men of the 1st Mass. who bore the brunt of the fighting, and were exposed to enemy fire for about two hours, with the "support of any other infantry." Under the circumstances, the men and the officers behaved courageously.[60]

What action was taken by Captain Edward Wild in this encounter is unknown. He did not mention his role in any surviving accounts, but Stevens and Bradford believed that Wild and his men were "fearless under fire and that his calmness and courage was transmitted to his men," so that Company A acquitted itself well. Wild's men had passed their first test with merit to their company.[61]

On the night of July 18, the 1st Mass. fell back to Centreville and remained there during the night. On July 19–20, the regiment was engaged in skirmishing and advanced on a new position which they held.[62] Colonel Cowden reported that on July 19, the men moved forward again, to halt in some woods near the main road about a mile from the site of the previous day's battle. Companies I and K took possession of a farmhouse, and Cowden's pickets exchanged gunfire with Confederate pickets. The rest of the regiment remained in the woods until the afternoon of July 21, when they moved forward to become engaged in battle. They were attacked by a "small brigade, and a sharp skirmish" resulted.[63]

First Battle at Bull Run (First Manassas), Virginia, July 21, 1861

A major battle took place near Manassas, Virginia, on July 21, 1861. The fighting began early at about half past 7 o'clock in the morning and continued throughout the day. The result was a rout of the Union forces. The 1st Mass. retreated and camped the night of July 21 at Centreville. On July 22, the 1st Mass. acted as the rear guard for the retreating Union army. It was a grueling task, and the regiment was forced to march 22 miles "through a severe rain storm without any rations for twenty-four hours." Upon reaching the Chain Bridge, the regiment "was kept standing for four hours" while awaiting "permission to enter its camp" on the opposite side of the Potomac River.[64]

Of his first major battle, Wild wrote:

> I was sent in command of two companies to hold a small wood in advance of our front of the 18th inst., and protect the artillery that opened the fight. The chief battle took place some distance on our right. But the enemy also attacked to the left of us smartly. Stampede occurred in the afternoon from 4 to 5. But we could see nothing of it, only judge by hearing, that our men were driven back. Was not relieved; and received no orders, although I went for them. Finding ourselves abandoned and apparently surrounded, I started, after six o'clock, marched back in good order through woods to Centreville heights and found our Brigade drawn up in hollow squares. Retained that position and formation until after eleven at night. Then commenced retreat. We brought up the rear for several miles. Were afterwards relieved by the German Regiments.[65]

The first major battle of the war ended with the Federal forces fleeing back to Washington. Both sides learned from this encounter that it would not be a short war. The Union had lost the battle but not the war. One soldier of the 1st Mass. was killed at Bull Run on July 21. The 5th Mass. lost 9 killed, 2 wounded, and 22 taken prisoner.[66]

The 1st Mass. crossed the Potomac the next day, and moved into quarters at Camp Scott, where they remained for a few days before going to Fort Albany. In camp, the men drilled frequently as "artillerists," cut timber, and performed guard duty around the fort.[67] The regiment was ordered on July 24, 1861, to Arlington Heights, Virginia, to take possession of Fort Albany. They remained there until August 7. Attached to General Joseph Hooker's Brigade, they marched to Camp Union at Bladensburg, Maryland, and remained until September 10, 1861. Daily drills were occasionally viewed by President Lincoln and General George B. McClellan.[68]

July 28, 1861—Wild's First Arrest

On July 28, 1861, Special Order No. 23 was issued for the arrest of Captain Edward Wild at Fort Albany. Wild demanded that Colonel Robert Cowdin immediately inform him of "the reasons of said arrest."⁶⁹ On August 5, 1861, Wild received an order from Acting Brigadier General Richardson, of the 4th Brigade, 1st Division, to release him. Wild pointed out that "Article 79 of the Articles of War, would, 4 hours hence, have released me from a *lawful* and *regular* arrest." He again demanded to know the "reasons of my *arrest*."⁷⁰ General Order No. 73 had been issued by Richardson and forwarded to Colonel Cowdin with a note to release "Capt. Wild from arrest; no charges having been made against him."⁷¹

No charges were ever filed and this arrest came to naught, but it probably did not improve relations between Wild and Cowdin. In fact, his arrest might have been precipitated by Wild's letter of complaint to Governor Andrew about how Cowdin ran the regiment. Wild makes no mention of his arrest in account of his "Military Life." However, he does state that on August 9, he (and his regiment) transferred from Richardson's Brigade to the original Brigade of General Joseph Hooker. The unit then removed to Bladensburg, Maryland.⁷²

September 1861

Wild and his regiment spent September in Maryland in search of Confederate arms and military stores. In doing so, the men marched 272 miles. The object of the foray into Maryland was to maintain peace during the upcoming elections, and to discover the truth of rumors about recruitment in Maryland for the Confederate army. One of the highlights for the men was the capture of a Confederate flag which hung from the courthouse in Calvert County. It was not an easy time for the men, because they had to sleep on the ground without tents.⁷³

On September 11, 1861, Governor Andrew asked President Lincoln and his Secretary of War to authorize his state to "raise whatever regiments you wish additional." Andrew assured Lincoln that he would "fulfill" his commitment to send Brigadier General Thomas W. Sherman the troops ordered by the Secretary of War, and to send others as fast as possible. He also agreed to assist General Benjamin F. Butler as much as possible.⁷⁴ When Butler's militia was committed to the Federal government in the spring of 1861, Butler became one of the Union's "earliest, and least likely, heroes." He quickly moved to safeguard the city of Washington, D.C., and within the next month, had occupied Baltimore, Maryland, which helped keep Maryland in the Union. This gained him the rank of Major General in the Union army.⁷⁵

Benjamin F. Butler had moved to Massachusetts with his widowed mother before the war. He graduated from Waterville (later Colby) College, and taught school for a while. He studied law and was admitted to the bar. Butler also developed military ambitions. He advanced quickly through the ranks of the Massachusetts militia, and was promoted first to colonel, then to brigadier general. In 1860, he was a delegate to the Democratic National Convention, where he nominated

Jefferson Davis for president.[76] Before the Civil War, Butler's name was almost a household word in New England. After 1861 everybody who had ever heard of Abraham Lincoln had also heard of Benjamin F. Butler, and both of them were discussed all over the world. Butler was one of the best-loved and worst hated men of the nineteenth century. His friends who spoke most kindly of him were mostly common people, for he was truly a democrat and always a fighter on the side of the poor and lowly. His enemies, both during his lifetime and after his death, were wealthy businessmen and their political retainers.[77]

October 1861

The 1st Mass. Regiment "marched and countermarched" over 200 miles during a month's time. On October 7, 1861, they returned to their camp at Bladensburg, where they remained for two weeks. General Hooker was given the command of the division, which included his old brigades and Sickles' and the New Jersey Brigade. Colonel Cowdin assumed command of the brigade, with Lieutenant Colonel George D. Wells in command of the regiment.[78]

On October 12, 1861, Wild's regiment marched 50 miles down the Potomac River to Budd's Ferry and set up their winter quarters. The camp was on Chicamoxen Creek, just opposite the Confederate batteries at Shipping Point, Occognan Creek, situated so that the Federal troops could hear the constant fire from the Confederate batteries on the south side of the river. A part of the regiment was engaged in a skirmish at Shipping Point and captured some arms and military stores.[79]

On October 25, Hooker's division marched along the shores of the Potomac River to the Posey Plantation, opposite the Confederate fortifications at Dumfries and Shipping Point. They halted at Camp Hooker in Charles County, Maryland. There were daily drills. A picket line was established, and a party was sent out at night to the outpost at Stump Neck on Chickamoxen Creek. The men felled trees and built log houses which provided comfortable winter quarters.[80]

November 1861

From Camp Hooker, William Candler, Wild's friend and fellow officer, wrote to his brother to report the news that he (Candler) had been released from command of Company C, 1st Mass., and told to report for duty to Captain Wild since the Company's former commander had returned to duty. Candler had mixed feelings about being in command, because he was "not strong enough to take charge of a company like that and give it the attention and labor" which it needed. He described the men of the entire regiment as being composed of "rough, hardy set of men, who have been neglected and abused shamefully."[81]

When Wild and his men were stationed at Camp Hooker, they received items of clothing from the Brookline War Committee, for which Wild wrote a thank-you letter. Although 100 shirts and 100 "drawers" had arrived, still missing was a promised box of stockings. Wild reported that his men were being kept busy building log houses for winter quarters, an activity that occupied "our men's thoughts, and [kept] them from grumbling and brooding over the long continued inaction." Always quick to take advantage of opportunity, Wild reported to the War Committee that the boxes in which the clothing arrived would be used to "floor & fit up the quarters of the officers of Co. A." He mentioned the "strong brown wrapping-paper" would be enough to "paper all the walls and roof" of the log quarters, and they were considering using tar to make a "tight roof." Wild was certain that their log houses would remain standing when he and his troops moved on, to shelter other troops, or to be used after the war for the "slaves (if there be any??) for probably four generations." The troops were camped for miles along the river, and the weather was "more stormy than that of Boston." He believed the storms were "more frequent and more violent." One windstorm had blown down "half the camp of the 26th Pennsylvania," but they had lost only about 8 or 10 tents. The winter camp was made as comfortable as possible with the addition of chimneys to the log cabins and constantly burning fires to warm the tents.[82]

Although military activity was usually curtailed during the winter months, Wild and his Company A and a few men of Company E were involved in the rescue of a schooner, *Delaware*, which was shelled by Confederates as it attempted to move up the Potomac River on November 14, 1861. The schooner, loaded with pinewood, had stalled under Confederate batteries. After the crew abandoned the ship, and Confederates, commanded by Brigadier General Louis T. Wigfall, boarded the beached ship and set it on fire.[83]

When the action began, Wild was presiding over a "Regimental Courtmartial." Although only a captain, Wild was Officer of the Day in the absence of the regimental Colonel Cowdin. Wild was notified that the Confederates had started out in boats toward the schooner.[84] He immediately dismissed the court and ordered Company A under Lieutenant Chandler to the landing. Wild took 30 men in a "seine boat" and rowed 3½ miles.[85] Under heavy Confederate fire, Wild's men got close enough to force the Confederates to abandon the ship. Wild and his men boarded the disabled boat, although the fire had burst through the hatchway and had engulfed the rigging, and "burned off half the mainsail." Wild's men were able to extinguish the fire, although the ship sustained significant damage. This was accomplished while the Confederates fired "eighty-three shots" at Wild and his men. Wild barely missed being wounded when a shell burst within three feet of his head. The men of Company A "behaved admirably," according to Wild. The schooner was eventually towed to safety by a steam tug.[86]

Captain Wild reported minimal casualties, and although they had been "struck several times by shot and shell ... no man [was] hurt." One Confederate was killed and several wounded.[87]

December 24–26, 1861

Captain Wild took a 3-day leave over the Christmas holidays, and traveled to Philadelphia on December 24. He probably stayed with his sister, Susanna, and her husband, George A. Wood, who lived in Philadelphia.[88] Wild returned to his command on December 26, 1861.[89]

Wild's Treatment of Southern Ladies

Wild's men were devoted to him, and knew he had "powers of fascination." On one occasion, he was ordered to take his company and search a house for hidden rebel stores. When he arrived at the house, he was confronted by two young ladies who denied him entrance to their home unless it was "over their dead bodies." Wild did not argue, but quietly withdrew his troops some distance away. Then he ordered that all the outbuildings searched. In short order, Lieutenants Candler and Chandler started to return to the house to report that they had found what they searched for hidden beneath some hay. From inside the house, they heard singing. They looked in a window and saw Captain Wild and one of the ladies "singing darkey melodies, while the other accompanied them on the piano."[90]

After Wild lost his arm, his gallant behavior was not extended to the Southern ladies in North Carolina or Georgia (see chapters VI and VII).

III

Colonel Wild, 35th Regiment, United States Army, 1862

War spares not the brave, but the cowardly.
—Anacreon, *The Palatine Anthology*, VII, 160

On January 13, Captain Wild went to Washington on regimental business, and remained for three days.[1]

Otherwise, along the Potomac River, there was little action—only sporadic gunfire from the two opposing forces of the Union and the Confederacy during January 1862. Confederates held Shipping Point, on the south side of the river, almost directly across from Camp Hooker on the north bank, in Charles County, Maryland, where Wild was stationed. On January 12, Federal pickets from Camp Hooker were fired upon by Confederates in a boat which approached from Shipping Point.[2] There were no injuries.[3]

In January another schooner attempting to run the blockade up the Potomac ran ashore and was fired upon by Confederate batteries. Confederates tried to board the ship, but were thwarted when the 1st Massachusetts arrived. Company A, 1st Massachusetts, reached the schooner by boat, and Company B arrived by land. There was an exchange of fire, but with little or no effect.[4]

Wild was mainly occupied with non-combat activities. He served on a court martial from January 17 to March 6, 1862, which convened at the "old Posey's House, at Budd's Ferry." Presiding over the court was Colonel Joseph W. Revere of the 5th New Jersey Volunteers, later a brigadier general. Judge advocate was Wild's friend Major Charles P. Chandler of the 1st Massachusetts Volunteers (who was later killed at the battle at Glendale near Richmond on June 30, 1862). The court tried 55 cases. Wild remained in command of his company during this time.[5]

Wild noted that the "Rebels evacuated their batteries across the Potomac" on

March 9. On March 10, the 1st Massachusetts and a New Jersey brigade marched to Rum Point, and then were transported by barges to Shipping Point. At the site they found abandoned food, ammunition, and furniture. They removed all usable siege guns, ammunition and stores, and destroyed the rest, which had been fired upon by Federal gunboats in a bombardment that ignited an explosion seen and heard for miles.[6]

March to July 1862—Peninsular Campaign in Virginia

Major General George B. McClellan succeeded the aging General Winfield Scott as Commandeer in Chief of the Union army. McClellan, a West Point graduate, was a "brilliant military organizer, administrator, and trainer," but, despite a year in Europe observing foreign military methods, lacked the ability to command and move large forces in battle.[7] McClellan came up with a plan to capture Richmond, Virginia, the Confederate capital, and in the middle of March 1862, McClellan's army moved down the Potomac River. He then positioned 12 divisions at Fort Monroe at the mouth of the James River for the planned assault.[8]

The men of the 1st Massachusetts complained frequently about being left idle while the rest of the Union army "distinguished itself."[9] Their wishes were soon granted, as the Federal forces advanced up the peninsula on April 4, 1862.[10]

April 1862

On April 5, 1862, Hooker's Division, which included the 1st Massachusetts, and Captain Edward Wild of Company A were loaded on the steamer *Kennebec* and transported to Fort Monroe. They arrived on the morning of April 10, and expected to disembark. Wild noted that "being caught in a storm at the mouth of the Potomac, we did not land until April 11 at Ship Point."[11] Their destination was changed, and they moved up river to Poquosen Creek, an inlet in the Chesapeake Bay. They camped on shore in the woods near the landing. The next day, they marched seven miles and camped on the opposite side of the creek. On April 16, the division moved to Yorktown, Virginia.[12]

Wild's Second Arrest

On April 14, Brigadier General Henry Morris Naglee issued Special Order No. 59, which required commissioned officers to appear in uniform "prescribed by Regulations at all parades." Line officers were not permitted to "appear with their pantaloons inside their boots."[13] At Camp Winfield Scott, three days later, Naglee sent a reminder to Colonel Robert Cowdin about appearances while on parade. This memo threatened: "If Captain Wild appears again in the gray overcoat which he has worn of late, you [Colonel Cowdin] will be held responsible."[14] Subsequently, Colonel Cowdin issued Special Order No. 64, which charged Captain Wild with disobeying orders by appearing "in uniform contrary to the regulations," and he was placed under arrest. Wild was to remain "in his quarters until further orders releasing him." Additionally, his sword was confiscated by Lieutenant Joseph Hibbert.[15]

On the bottom of Colonel Cowdin's order, Wild wrote: "In view of all these circumstances, I remonstrate against the extreme harshness of the treatment I have received from Col. Cowdin, which seems to me unnecessary, partial, and unjust."[16]

Wild penned a lengthy protest to Lieutenant Joseph Hibbert, Adjutant, 1st Massachusetts Regiment. Wild stated that he understood the order regarding "prescribed uniform" to refer to "occasions of parade, not being applicable to fatigue duty, marches, etc." He made it clear that he had no "intention to disobey such orders," yet circumstances necessitated that he wear a gray overcoat the previous night while he was on guard duty.[17]

Wild explained that he had not had the time to change because early that morning the entire regiment was ordered to move their encampment. He was charged with the task of supervising and assisting in the removal of his tent and kitchen. Those who might have helped him were on fatigue duty. Wild regarded the gray overcoat as his "working dress." He and his regiment had been ordered to move from their previous post rather hastily, and all extra baggage left in storage. Since he had no other overcoat with him, and he did not have the time to send for one or the money to pay for it, he had worn the gray one.[18]

Under the circumstances, Cowdin may have overreacted, but he may have believed he was carrying out Brigadier General Naglee's orders. In June, 1st Lieutenant William Latham Candler wrote his brother that "old *Cowdin* is growing more and more of a lunatic." Candler wanted to get out of this regiment, because of Cowdin and a group of new line officers, none of whom he liked very much.[19] Did Colonel Cowdin dislike Wild and other officers as well?

April 5 to May 4, 1862—Yorktown, Virginia

McClellan's Peninsular Campaign began on April 5 with fighting at Yorktown and continued through May 4, 1862. The Peninsula was defended by Confederates in Magruder's Army, commanded by Major General John Bankhead "Prince John" Magruder, an experienced soldier of the Seminole War, and in Mexico. His nickname came from his "courtly manner" as well and his "reputation for lavish entertainment" while stationed at Norfolk, Virginia. He resigned from the Union Army, became a Colonel in the Confederate Army, and won recognition for his victory at Big Bethel on June 10, 1861. (At the end of the war, Magruder refused a parole, and went to Mexico to serve as a Major General under Maximilian.)[20]

At Yorktown, Captain Wild was ordered to take a position in a *redoubt*, a fortified enclosure usually placed in front of a permanent fortification.[21] The Federal assault was carried out by Heintzelman's Corps, and Hooker's Division was the center of that line. The 1st Massachusetts Regiment did routine "picket and fatigue duty," and stood "to arms" before and after daylight for 1½ to 2 hours each morning.[22]

Wild's brigade commander, Brigadier General Naglee, was replaced by Brigadier General Cuvier Grover on April 24.[23] Grover previously had served in the Union artillery, infantry and cavalry. He would be breveted for his service at Williamsburg, Fair Oaks, other campaigns.[24]

On April 26, Companies A, H, and I of the 1st Massachusetts were "detailed under Lieutenant Colonel George D. Wells for special duty." Artillery and rifle fire from the Confederate redoubt were a danger to Wild's regiment, and they were ordered to capture it. The men started out at 3 A.M. in a drizzling rain, reached their picket line about daylight, and succeeded at their task.[25] Undoubtedly, Captain Edward Wild was involved and probably led this expedition. He noted that at Yorktown, he and his men "shared in all the work and fighting of the siege."[26]

Wild described the part his regiment played in the capture of Yorktown:

> April 26. At day light captured a Lunette by storm; with three companies under Lt. Col. Wells, 1st Mass under the supervision of General Grover. Then while we pursued the enemy, and made a reconnaissance, two companies of the 11th Mass. Vol. with shovels and picks leveled the Lunette. This being one of the enemy's chain of fortifications, we were subjected to a severe fire from the others. We captured a number of prisoners and lost as many in killed and wounded.[27]

As usual, nothing went according to plan. Several major problems upset McClellan's grand design. Without McDowell's Corps on hand, the planned encirclement of Yorktown could not be accomplished. The maps were incorrect — the Warwick River was an unforeseen impediment. Confederate batteries at Yorktown and Gloucester prevented a Federal amphibious landing. McClellan finally decided he could not undertake "a formal siege," and he put Fitz John Porter in charge with assistance from Brigadier General William Farquhar Barry, Chief Engineer of the Army of the Potomac, and Brigadier General John Gross Barnard, Chief of Artillery. About 100 heavy Parrott guns, howitzers and mortars were positioned, and firing on Yorktown began May 1. The town, defended by Confederates under Major General John Magruder, held out until the night of May 3, when they withdrew. The Federals then entered the abandoned works where they encountered land mines. There was a brief encounter between Federals and Confederate rear guard forces at Williamsburg the next day.[28]

The 1st Massachusetts and Hooker's Division remained at Camp Winfield Scott before Yorktown, on duty in the trenches through the night of May 3.[29] Out of three companies of the 1st Massachusetts, four were killed and 14 wounded during the siege of Yorktown.[30]

May 4–5, 1862—Williamsburg, Virginia

Magruder's retreat was covered by the cavalry of Brigadier General J.E.B. Stuart, and they were pursued by the George Stoneman's Federal cavalry. On May 5, the Federal troops were bogged down by deep mud, but they closed ranks and attacked the Confederate line. Hooker's forces launched an attack against the center at Fort Magruder, "the strongest part of the line." Hooker tried to repulse a counterattack, but his reinforcements were late in coming because of the road conditions. Confederates under General D. H. Hill reinforced General James Longstreet's left flank. The Federal troops of W. F. Smith's division attacked the Confederate fort around noon. General Winfield Scott Hancock's division surrounded the Confederate left, captured several unoccupied redoubts, and held them against Confederate counterattacks. During the night, the Confederate forces withdrew further up the peninsula.[31]

At Williamsburg, Wild's sword was hit by a bullet, and his head was injured by splinters from a tree.[32] He described the Battle of Williamsburg:

> We fought long and hard, all day, under Hooker. First struck the enemy's skirmishers on abattis about 6 A.M. Cleared the abattis. Attacked Ft. Magruder. The enemy after a while were reinforced, turned upon us, and after repeated flankings and reflankings, we were driven slowly back by overwhelming numbers through the abattis, losing about an eighth of a mile. We received reinforcements about 4 P.M. after constant fighting for ten hours in a continuous rain storm. The enemy were then rapidly driven and the whole field was gained by dusk.[33]

Table I Casualties from the Williamsburg Battle, May 4–5, 1862[34]

Numbers engaged	Killed	Wounded/Missing	Total
Federals 40,768	456	1410/373	2,239
Confederate 31,823	?	?/(133 missing)	1,603

On May 5, twelve men of the 1st Massachusetts Regiment were killed.[35] The division lost 2,017, the majority of the total Federal losses (see table above). Wild was "hit four times but not hurt." After the fighting ended, the Federals remained camped about Williamsburg, "burying the dead and performing provost duty in the city &c."[36]

On May 15, Wild and his men marched to Baltimore Crossroads. Ten days later, they marched to Poplar Hill, where they remained guarding the White Oak Swamp bridge until June 4, when they moved to Fair Oaks. At Fair Oaks, the men did picket duty, and skirmished "without cessation until June 25."[37]

June 25, 1862—Fair Oaks (Oak Grove), Virginia

The battle at Fair Oaks (also called Oak Grove, Henrico, King's School House, or The Orchards) was the first of the "Seven Days' Battles," and part of the Penin-

Fair Oaks–Seven Pines Battlefield with 32-pound howitzer in foreground. (Courtesy of Library of Congress, Washington, D.C.)

sular Campaign. McClellan had moved Federal corps south of the Chickahominy River, and was ready to march against Richmond. Heintzelman's III Corps, located at Fair Oaks–Seven Pines, was ordered to attack the outpost of Confederate Major General Benjamin Huger's division. Hooker's Division moved forward early in the morning, led by Sickles' brigade, along the Williamsburg Road. Hooker met superior forces, and D. B. Birney's brigade was ordered up to support him. McClellan's chief of staff viewed the situation and ordered Hooker to withdraw. At 1 P.M., McClellan ordered the attack to resume. Palmer's brigade was ordered up as reinforcements. DeRussy's battery moved forward and drove the Confederate pickets back with their canister. Federal infantry occupied the positions vacated by the

Confederates, but the advance was halted by nightfall. The next day, the Confederate forces took the initiative at Mechanicsville, [38] the second of the Seven Days' Battles, which resulted in heavy Confederate losses.

Federal casualties at Fair Oaks/Oak Grove were 626, Confederate casualties, 441.[39] The 1st Massachusetts had 14 killed and several wounded on June 25.[40]

Wild described the events on June 25 at the Battle near Fair Oaks:

> Our position (the left) of McClellan's lines attacked the enemy along our front; drove them through the Swamp across an open plain, carried their line of entrenchments and held them all day. We met with heavy loss. I was struck twice."[41]

Wild was one of those casualties on June 25. He was wounded on the knee by a minnie ball, and through his right hand by a "small rifle ball."[42] He was treated by Dr. Richard Henry Salter, but he lost the use of two fingers on his right hand. After the war, to assist Wild with obtaining an increase in his invalid pension, Dr. Salter wrote: "Although the wound was serious, the chances for saving the hand would be enhanced under treatment away from the camp. Accordingly, only simple water dressings were used, and the said Captain Wild was sent to the General Hospital...."[43]

The next day, Wild left the battlefield and traveled to Philadelphia. He stayed at the home of his sister, Mrs. Susanna S. Wood, and her husband George Augustus Wood, from June 27 through July 23.[44] The wounded captain was joined by his wife, Frances, who had not seen him since he enlisted the year before.[45]

Wild stated when he applied for an increase in his invalid pension that the bullet had entered his hand "between first and second knuckle joints," and then made its "exit in the palm injuring the thumb and metacarpal bones of the 1st & 2nd fingers." The injury left him with "no power of grip" in his right hand.[46] Wild noted that his knee joint came within a "hair breadth" from being injured.[47] While Wild stayed with his sister, he was treated by George Wood's family physician and surgeon, Dr. George W. Norris, "without cost to the government."[48]

William Candler, one of Wild's friends, was also in the battle at Fair Oaks. Candler reported the 1st Massachusetts Regiment lost "11 officers in two days fighting, and many more are *hors du combat* from sickness and exhaustion." He noted that several officers, including Captain Smith of Company B, have "resigned and gone home." Candler stated his "love and respect" for General Joseph Hooker, but also he knew that Hooker's health had failed, and the General had "taken a permanent leave of absence." Candler had lost everything "except the clothes on my back," and since the paymaster was behind, he had had to spend $150 to reoutfit himself. Candler complained: "The Army is getting to be rather an expensive place to live in...."[49]

July 1862—A New Regiment

Candler referred to Edward Wild as "Ned" in letters to his family. Three weeks after Wild was wounded, Candler wrote his brother that he had been told "Ned"

Wild was to be promoted to Major, and that he would not return to the 1st Regiment. Candler was also dissatisfied with the 1st Regiment, and had lost confidence in its officers, especially General Cowdin, who had acted like "a perfect child" on the battlefield. Others soldiers in the regiment had become as dissatisfied with General Cowdin as Wild had been early in 1861. In July, Captain Smith, of Company B, and Captain Adams of Company F, of the 1st Massachusetts, resigned.[50]

On July 19, 1862, Captain Edward Wild returned to Boston.[51] Five days later, on July 24, 1862, he was officially promoted to Major in the 32nd Massachusetts Volunteers, and placed in command of recruits at Camp Stanton, at Lynnfield, Massachusetts.[52] His duties were to recruit and train men for the new regiment, which would become the 35th Regiment of Massachusetts Infantry. On July 28, 1862, Wild received orders to "drill and discipline" men who had been accepted into the regiment after only a cursory physical examination. It was not an easy task. The camp was crude. They lived in tents and slept on straw with no blankets at first. The regimental quartermaster eventually furnished the men with uniforms and other necessary articles, including woolen blankets. Yet, even under less than optimal conditions, Major Wild quickly turned raw recruits into a disciplined, well-trained fighting force.[53]

While recovering from his injury, Wild went home to Brookline. The citizens there were eager to hear the war news. A resolution was passed on August 19 requesting Wild to attend a meeting of the Town. A 5-man delegation called upon him to ask him to attend the meeting, and in a short time, they returned accompanied by Wild. The people welcomed him with great enthusiasm, and exhibited the love and admiration which they felt for him. Wild thanked the citizens for "their warm sympathies and interest" on behalf of his men, and promised to "bear the remembrance of this hour with gratitude when far away." The meeting adjourned with "three rousing cheers" for the Union.[54]

August 1862—Formation of the 35th Massachusetts Regiment

The 35th Massachusetts was mustered into the service of the United States on August 21, 1862.[55] When Wild first joined the 35th Massachusetts, his right arm was still in a sling from the injuries he had received at Fair Oaks.[56] He wrote the "story of the 35th" Massachusetts Regiment and "its doings" for the year 1861, which was published in William Schouler's *Massachusetts in the War*.[57] At the request of Governor John Andrew, Colonel Wild also wrote an account of the 35th Massachusetts from August 1861 to January 1863.[58] The 35th continued to be a viable military unit until the men and officers were mustered out of service on June 9, 1865.[59]

Because Governor Andrew wanted only the best leadership for his state troops, he asked the Secretary of War Edwin Stanton for experienced field officers. Stanton replied that "such officers were scarce and the military situation was critical."⁶⁰ However, when Governor Andrew asked Stanton for Edward Wild to train his new recruits, Secretary of War complied. On August 12, 1862, Stanton wrote Governor Andrew that the Adjutant-General had been directed to "muster out Major Wild ... as requested." He also told the Governor that his request for experienced field officers would not be answered immediately because "the demand for them is so great for the new enlistments, and the exigencies in the field so critical, that it is sometimes impossible to comply with the requests...."⁶¹ This correspondence took place after the battle at Cedar Mountain, Virginia, on August 9, 1862, in which Major General Nathaniel P. Banks was actually "out generaled" and defeated by Confederate forces of Thomas "Stonewall" Jackson.⁶²

Wild had been assigned briefly to the 32nd Massachusetts, although historical accounts conflict on whether he actually served.

Wild wrote that on July 24, 1862, he was "promoted to Major of the 32nd Regt. Mass. Vols. and was placed in command of Camp of Recruits at Camp Stanton, Lynnfield, Mass." On August 7, 1862, he was promoted to "Lieut. Colonel of the 32nd Mass. Vols. and continued in charge of Camp of Recruits, [which were] rapidly increasing up to 3500 men."⁶³ The next notation was August 20, when he was promoted to "Colonel of the 35th Regt. Mass. Vols."⁶⁴ Few accounts mention the brief time Wild reportedly served in the 32nd Regiment. *The National Cyclopedia of American Biography*⁶⁵ does list his promotion to "major of the 32nd regiment." Report No. 3627 of the 57th Congress of the House of Representatives, in regard to House of Representatives Bill # 806 which granted a pension to the General's widow, makes no mention of service in the 32nd, but does mention that he served in the 1st Massachusetts, the 35th Massachusetts, and that he was appointed as brigadier general of volunteers.⁶⁶ *Massachusetts Soldiers, Sailors and Marines in the Great Civil War* gives August 11, 1862, as the date Wild was commissioned a Colonel in

Colonel Edward A. Wild, 35th Massachusetts. (Courtesy of Massachusetts Commandery, Military Order of the Loyal Legion, and U.S. Army Military History Institute, Carlisle Barracks, Carlisle, Pa.)

the 35th Massachusetts, with a muster-in date of August 21, 1862, but does not indicate that Wild was ever in the 32nd Regiment.[67]

Modern sources such as Warner's *Generals in Blue: Lives of the Union Commanders*[68] and Sifakis' *Who Was Who in the Civil War* omit any reference to Wild's service in the 32nd Massachusetts.[69] When his widow applied for a pension and indicated that her husband had served in the "32nd," a form referred to the Chief of the Record and Pension Office of the War Department was returned with the notation that "the name Edward A. Wild has not been found on the rolls of F and S 32 Regt. Mass. Inf." Although he never fought with the 32nd Regiment, Wild served as a recruitment and training officer until the 35th Regiment was completed. This service has been almost entirely overlooked in most biographical articles about him — another case of credit not being given where it was due.

In fact, Wild was promoted within the ranks of the *32nd* until the recruitment and mustering in of *35th* was actually complete on August 21, 1862. Wild was subsequently mustered out of service on August 21, 1862,[70] a formality that allowed him to be "mustered into" another branch or regiment of the Army. This date was the same day that the 35th Regiment was mustered into service, so in actuality, Wild was being transferred from the 32nd Regiment to the 35th Regiment.

Special Order No. 557, by William Schenler, Adjutant General of the Commonwealth of Massachusetts, issued at the command of Massachusetts Governor John A. Andrew and dated July 24, 1862, directed:

> Major Wild of the 32d Regiment, Mass. Vols. will take command of the companies for the 32nd Regt now at Camp Stanton, Lynnfield, and of all other recruits at that Camp, except those of the 33d Regiment. Maj. Wild will report to Col. Maggi of the Post, from whom he will receive orders.[71]

In a later widow's pension claim, his widow, Frances E. Wild, altered her story:

> The records of the Adjutant General's Office of the Commonwealth of Mass. show that my husband was *mustered* as *Major* of the *32d Mass.* Volunteer Infantry *July 24, 1862*, and *Lieut. Col.* same Regiment *August 6, 1862*, but that is [unreadable word] an error as he never joined for duty in the 32d being disabled by wounds received at Fair Oaks, Va. Till he joined for duty with the *35th Mass* about Sept. 1, 1862.[72]

Special Order No. 562 described Major Wild's authority and duties with the 32nd Mass. Volunteers. He was to take command of a camp for recruits at Lynnfield for all corps of Massachusetts Volunteers in actual service and needing recruits (as well as recruits for his own regiment). He was to drill, discipline and instruct them while in camp, and to deliver them to the proper regimental recruiting officers to be forwarded to their regiments. He was authorized to make requisitions "for all articles needed, for the encampment, clothing, transportation and subsistance of recruits raised...."[73]

Wild did not care whether he was promoted or not. He wrote his wife from Camp Union, Bladensburg, Maryland, on October 18, 1862:

> As for promotion you must recollect that I did not come out here to be elevated, but simply from a sense of duty, and with the single-hearted object to serve my country to my utmost ability, feeling within myself that I was the proper man to come. Should I be broken or cashiered, I would immediately enlist as a private, for the same reason, and do my utmost in that capacity. If I should be promoted by those who are competent to judge and who think that I could serve my country better by filling a larger sphere, I should obey orders, and consent to the promotion though it must be strong inducement that could draw me away from my present company and my present regiment, for I am proud of both. If ... I should not be promoted ... I should not be disappointed, but shall continue to work on, as I only intended to serve during the war and then retire to obscurity. You must remember that I spoke in the same tone when I left Brookline.[74]

Wild's rise through the ranks had been almost meteoric. Over the course of a few weeks, he was promoted from Major to Lieutenant Colonel to Colonel. This put him in the position of a field and staff officer. On August 21, 1862, Wild received Special Order No. 651 from the Governor of Massachusetts, which ordered him and his new regiment to Washington, D.C., to report to Major General Silas Casey. Troops were needed to work on a new line of entrenchments connecting the fortifications of Arlington Heights.[75]

After the last companies of the 35th Regiment were mustered in, they left Camp Stanton, Lynnfield, Massachusetts, on August 22, 1862, "poorly armed and equipped."[76] Of the 960 Enfield rifles issued, many were defective, and a large portion of them were returned.[77] That the men were poorly armed was not Wild's fault. He had requested the necessary arms for his 35th Regiment and had been assured by Lieutenant Colonel A. G. Browne his request had been forwarded through proper channels, and that he [Browne] had urged those in charge to "spare no effort to complete the preparation" of Wild's regiment for duty in the field.[78]

Governor Andrew proudly notified Secretary of War Stanton that he had sent "no better material to the war" than the 35th Regiment, just raised by Wild, "full to maximum."[79]

At full strength, a Federal regiment contained a maximum of 1,025 men; the minimum number was 845. Regimental strength varied over the course of the war, but a large staff was necessary to maintain a regiment. Commissioned regimental officers were: colonel, lieutenant colonel, major, adjutant, quartermaster, surgeon, two assistant surgeons and a chaplain. Non-commissioned officers included a sergeant major, quartermaster sergeant, commissary sergeant, hospital steward, and two principal musicians. Regiments usually consisted of 10 companies, numbered alphabetically from A to K, with the letter J always omitted. A full company consisted of 101 officers and men. Company officers were: captain, 1st lieutenant, 2nd lieutenant, 1st sergeant, 4 additional sergeants, 8 corporals, 2 musicians, and 1 wagoner.[80]

On August 22, the men and officers of 35th Massachusetts arrived in Boston, and marched through city streets lined with people who cheered as the troops went from Blackstone Street to the State House. They cheered Colonel Wild, who was "handsomely mounted with his arm still in a sling." In a flag-presentation ceremony at the State House, the men were given their colors and a state flag.[81] Governor Andrew was away from the State House when the regiment arrived. He later apologized to Colonel Wild for having missed seeing them. "The handsome, soldierly appearance of the command was universally noticed and spoken of with enthusiasm," the Governor noted with pride. He expressed "the utmost confidence in the honor and welfare of the regiment," and the "zeal, capacity, and manly virtue" of its commander. Andrew knew that the men of the new regiment would "perform the duties of a soldier" with "excellence and competence to win its laurels."[82] He commented on the "patriotism and intelligence, instructed and refined by the culture of our schools, and the best influences of Massachusetts homes." He saw the departing troops as "some of our best, as well as some of our bravest," equal "in every arm and in every rank of the Service."[83]

The 35th Regiment traveled to Fall River and boarded a steamer. They arrived on August 23 at Jersey City, and then moved on to Philadelphia.[84]

The Philadelphia Incident

In Philadelphia, an incident showed just how unpredictable and unconventional Wild could be. A firm believer in total abstinence of alcoholic beverages, Wild knew the "demoralizing effect" that liquor could have on the troops, "especially when en route to a military destination." Wild described the incident:

> In the immediate neighborhood of the Union Volunteer Refreshment Saloon, where we were supplied with a meal by the hospitality of the citizens, there are a large number of drinking shops, which have been a pest to every regiment passing through. I personally ordered the proprietor of each establishment to sell no liquor to my men, warning him of consequences; at the same time setting a guard at his door. Soon after, detecting them enticing men in at back doors, to drink and fill canteens, I ordered the stock to be cleaned out at two places, a hotel and a saloon. This order was summarily and thoroughly carried out by my men. No serious personal violence was committed, although we had occasion to overawe a large party of Zouaves and other bullies.[85]

As a result of Wild's actions, the city authorities followed him with "two writs of arrest," but he refused to accept them. He threatened the policemen that "if they caused us any delay," he would "be obliged to take aldermen and all with me to Washington." He reasoned, "In time of armed rebellion, the exigencies of the military service must take precedence of all else."[86] Wild dared defy authority on any level, and he bluffed his way out of being arrested in Philadelphia. Although he was followed to Washington, there were no further repercussions from the Philadelphia incident.

However, he would not be so fortunate as to escape the consequences in the future when he attempted to act both as judge and jury of those he believed were wrongdoers. Over the next few years, this type of incident would become a common occurrence with Wild, as he used his rank and the power of the military to right wrongs, according to his own personal beliefs and his puritanical upbringing.

Wild recorded the arrival of the 35th Regiment in Washington, D.C., on August 24, and they were placed under Major General Silas Casey's command. They were ordered across the Potomac, and Wild and his men camped beyond Arlington Heights.[87] Casey, a veteran of the Indian wars and the Mexican War, was famous for his 1861 book, *System of Infantry Tactics*, adopted by the United States Army. A later a book was entitled *Infantry Tactics for Colored Troops*.[88]

On August 27, the 35th was transferred to the command of Brigadier General Amiel Weeks Whipple and put to work on the entrenchments connecting the fortifications of Arlington Heights, Virginia.[89] From August through November 1862, Whipple commanded a division charged with the protection of the Military District of Washington. (He was mortally wounded at Chancellorsville and died on May 6, 1863.)[90] South of the Potomac, Brigadier General Whipple commanded a division of 21 regiments, including that of Colonel Edward A. Wild's 35th Massachusetts Regiment.[91]

The 35th Massachusetts was then assigned to the brigade of acting Brigadier General Van Volkenburg, and they continued "to dig till Sept 6." The regiment was then transferred to General Ambrose E. Burnside, and ordered to follow "in light marching order." They marched through Washington and into Maryland. Burnside assigned them to the brigade of Brigadier General Edward Ferrero, along with the 21st Massachusetts. The men continued short marches and bivouacs until September 14.[92] Three weeks later, Wild and his men would find themselves engaged in a fierce struggle with enemy forces at the Battle of South Mountain.[93]

South Mountain, Maryland, September 14, 1862

After invading Maryland in September of 1862, the Confederate forces of General Robert E. Lee marched toward Harper's Ferry. They were pursued by Union Major General George B. McClellan to Frederick, Maryland, and then on to South Mountain, part of the Appalachian Mountains that ran north and south across western Maryland. There, heavy fighting occurred over control of the passes through South Maintain at Crampton's, Turner's, and Fox's gaps.

It was imperative that the Confederates prevent the Federal troops from crossing South Mountain and moving on to Boonsboro, where Lee's supply trains were camped. Lee had not intended to fight either at South Mountain or Sharpsburg.[94]

The Lost Dispatch

Neither the battle at South Mountain nor that event of three days later at Sharpsburg (Antietam) should ever have happened. From Frederick, Maryland, Confederate General Robert E. Lee had sent a plan of his movements to General

III. Colonel Wild, 35th Regiment United States Army, 1862

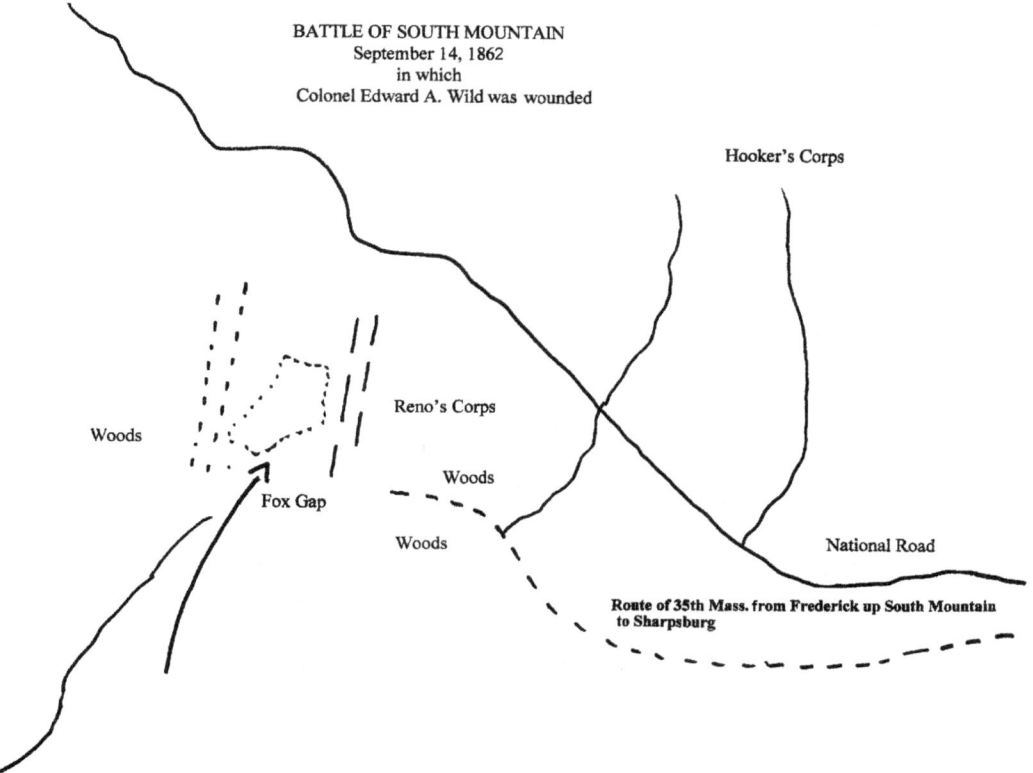

Arrow indicates cleared area defended by General Reno's IX Corps. As darkness approached, the Confederates attacked. Reno was killed; Colonel Wild and others wounded. (Danny Casstevens, artist)

D. H. Hill, in which he directed General "Stonewall" Jackson to capture Harper's Ferry, and ordered generals Longstreet and D. H. Hill to move to Boonsboro, on the west side of South Mountain.[95] A copy of General Lee's Special Order 191[96] (known also as the "Lost Dispatch") was found lying on the grass wrapped around three cigars. It was given to General McClellan, who learned from the "Lost Dispatch" that Lee planned to split his forces in order to capture Harper's Ferry and then concentrate on the town of Sharpsburg, Maryland. McClellan, who had always hesitated to attack Lee because he believed, erroneously, that Confederate forces opposing him were much larger than they actually were, now found the confidence he needed to "defeat Lee."[97] Within an hour after receiving Lee's lost orders, McClellan had his whole army on the move and by the next day, he had caught up with Confederate forces at South Mountain.

Lieutenant General D. H. Hill described the battle at South Mountain as "one of extraordinary illusions and delusions." The Federals believed they faced a formidable Confederate army. Although actually few in number, Confederates, by moving about, were able to make the Federals believe that this was so.[98]

Over the course of the day, fighting would erupt three different times at Fox's Gap alone, in addition to fighting at the other gaps through South Mountain. The action began when a Federal cavalry unit located Confederate General D. H. Hill's division, which was guarding Turner's Gap, and the main road across South Mountain. By 9 o'clock that morning, Union General J. D. Cox and some of the IX Corps under Union General Jesse Lee Reno arrived and began an attack through Fox's Gap. Hooker's I Corps arrived and launched another attack about a mile to the north at Turner's Gap. General Burnside coordinated the operation and commanded the right wing of McClellan's forces, which consisted of the I and IX Corps.[99]

Wild and his 35th Massachusetts Regiment were a part of the Second Division, 2nd Brigade of the IX Corps of the Army of the Potomac, directly under the command of Brigadier General Ferrero.[100] Before the war, Ferrero, of Italian descent, operated a dancing school established by his father in New York City and taught cadets at West Point. He was also active in the state militia and had obtained the rank of Lieutenant Colonel by 1861.[101]

In his report of the fighting at South Mountain on September 14, 1862, Ferrero described how his brigade arrived at South Mountain on Sunday, September 14, and engaged the enemy in battle. At 3 P.M., they moved up the Hagerstown Road, to the summit of the mountain, and there formed a line of battle in support of other units already engaged in combat. At 3:30 P.M., Ferrero moved to the top of the mount and encountered enemy fire from the direction of some woods. This produced "temporary confusion" in one of Ferrero's new regiments. Yet, they quickly regrouped and advanced from their position to occupy the field. They managed to hold their position throughout the night by having the whole force on guard. There was no further action from the Confederates, who had withdrawn the main body of their troops. Ferrero's men captured 100 prisoners, and he proudly reported they had "behaved with the greatest bravery."[102]

At Fox's Gap, the 35th Regiment had advanced into the woods on the east side of the cleared area, where they formed a battle line in a cornfield on the eastern side of the mountain. Company A led the charge, and reached cleared land. The regiment prepared to charge across an open space to a sunken area in which many dead and dying Confederates lay. When they reached the woods, they located the road that led downward in to a valley to the southwest. At the point where the road entered the wood, Colonel Wild stood "shouting loudly and waving his men" onward in pursuit of the enemy. The Confederates had retreated, leaving behind a pile of knapsacks and some dead and wounded soldiers. One of the wounded Confederates fired, and the Yankees immediately began rushing forward with bayonets fixed. However, Wild stopped them and shouted, "We do not hit the wounded."[103]

As evening approached, the men rejoined their units and were ordered to form two lines, with the 51st New York and the 51st Pennsylvania in front and the 21st Massachusetts in the rear. The 35th Massachusetts formed behind the 21st, near the woods to the east of the open area. As darkness fell, Colonel Wild was busy getting his men in line when a burst of musket fire came out of the woods to the west, thick with Confederates who had just returned. The Federals returned their fire, but there was much confusion. The Union troops were ordered back to the woods for more protection, but the enemy kept up a steady fire. "The front file of the brigade kept up a steady fire as did the enemy while the rear file of the 35th lay on the ground listening to the bullets whizzing through the trees."[104]

The actions of the 35th Regiment were described in detail by Wild up until the time he was wounded:

> My regiment entered the fight about 4 P.M. Drove the enemy through the forest, over rough, rocky, mountainous ground—and then rejoined the brigade. [We] Were forming line to pass the night, just about dusk, when the enemy attacked us suddenly from a dark wood; they were repulsed. I was wounded, my left arm being shattered by an explosive bullet.[105]

Wild was severely wounded in the first round of enemy fire, but he managed to make his way to the rear and down the mountain. He walked over two miles to a crude building that was being used to shelter the wounded.[106] Wild's friend and fellow officer Lieutenant Colonel Candler learned that Wild had been wounded. Even though Candler had not slept for 24 hours, he set out to find the wounded Colonel Wild. It was a dark and rainy night, but Candler would not be deterred. He searched for four hours until he finally located his wounded friend. Reunited, the two men "broke down, swamped in the emotions," in the midst of wounded and dying on a rainy night in Maryland.[107]

Ferrero reported that Colonel E. A. Wild, of the 35th Massachusetts Volunteers, "was wounded severely in the arm while forming his regiment under the enemy's fire." Casualties in Ferrero's brigade (51st N. Y. Volunteers, 51st Pennsylvania Volunteers, 21st Massachusetts Volunteers, and 35th Massachusetts Volunteers), totaled 116 men—10 killed, 83 wounded, and 23 missing.[108] Union General Jesse Lee Reno was killed. Confederate Brigadier General Samuel Garland, Jr. was also killed.[109] Two future presidents were wounded at South Mountain. Lieutenant Colonel Rutherford B. Hayes, later the 19th President of the United States, was serving with the 23rd Ohio when he was severely wounded in the arm.[110] William McKinley, a commissary sergeant in Hayes' regiment who had bravely carried food and coffee to the regiment during the fighting, was not severely wounded. Although McKinley escaped death at Stone Mountain, as the 25th President, he would die from an assassin's bullet exactly 39 years later on September 14, 1901.[111]

Wild believed that the men of his regiment had performed well at South Mountain in their first combat:

> In this battle, the first ordeal of the 35th, their behavior was excellent, and considering their total inexperience, their very brief period of mutual acquaintance want of confidence in weapons & especially their utter want of drill, the nature of the ground, it was very remarkable that they should have held together so well as they did. The lack of drill was severely felt; as we had had no opportunity at all for battalion drill; and that by companies had been quite limited. They were ready to do anything they were ordered, if they only knew how to do it.[112]

Although the Confederate forces failed to stop the advance of McClellan's army at South Mountain, they did manage to save Lee's trains and artillery, and to "reunite his scattered forces." They took pride in the fact that, for a number of hours, a force of about 9,000 Confederates held off a Federal force almost three times that number.[113]

While the Battle of South Mountain was only a preliminary action to the major battle that would occur at Antietam, it was a Union victory.

Table II Battle of South Mountain, near Sharpsburg, Maryland, September 14, 1862

Numbers Engaged	Killed	Wounded	Missing	Total
Union—28,480[114]	325	1,403	85	1,813
Confederates—17,852	325	1,560	800	2,685
Total: 46,332	**650**	**2,963**	**885**	**4,498**

Confederate figures were estimated by Livermore, based on official reports, supplemented by "experience factors." He did, however, state that "losses were probably higher."[115]

In Wild's 35th Regiment of Massachusetts Volunteers, 5 men were killed. Other regimental losses from the state of Massachusetts at South Mountain were minimal.[116]

Wild's injury was caused by round shot. Two days later, on September 16, his left arm was amputated by Dr. Rogers.[117] As a surgeon in the Crimean War, Wild had seen such injuries many times, and knew what the results could be. He demanded that his arm be amputated.[118] "Take it off at the shoulder and don't let me wake and find it here," Wild ordered. Dr. Rogers tried to save part of the arm in the first operation, but "the result was not satisfactory." Wild's plea to remove his arm at the shoulder was based on experience. When limbs were shattered by bullets they quickly developed gangrene and death was painfully inevitable.[119] Although the amputation of a limb was a painful, permanent disability, the loss of his arm did save Edward Wild's life, and after a short time, he was back on his feet. His wound did remain quite sore and an "abscess would form," testified Dr. William Hunt, who cared for Wild's injury for many years. When his shoulder finally healed, Wild had to wear "a false shoulder to support his clothing. Yet, all his life, Wild remained a "very uncomplaining man, not speaking of any of his complaints to anybody."[120]

September 17, 1862—Battle of Antietam (Sharpsburg, Maryland)

The battle at South Mountain was and still is overshadowed by the battle at Antietam (Sharpsburg, Maryland), the bloodiest day of the war. Confederates refer to battles by naming them after the nearest town; Federal authorities named battles after the nearest creek or stream. Thus, the Confederates' battle of *Sharpsburg* is called *Antietam* by the Federal forces.

Because of his injuries, Colonel Wild was not able to remain with his troops. While he was recovering, his 35th Regiment fought bravely at Antietam on September 17, 1862, only three days after the battle at South Mountain.

For three hours, 550 men from three Georgia regiments of Brigadier General Robert Toombs held off the advance of Major General Ambrose Burnside and 11,000 Federal troops across the bridge (thereafter known as the "Burnside" Bridge). By midday, Toombs knew that his men could not hold off another Union assault on the bridge. From their position above Antietam Creek, on a 100-foot-high bluff on the west side, the Confederate infantry and sharpshooters had a great advantage and could fire down on any Federal soldiers who attempted to cross the bridge. Eventually, the Confederates ran low on ammunition, and Toombs ordered his Georgians to move half a mile to the rear. The third assault on the bridge was headed by the 51st New York and the 51st Pennsylvania under the command of Colonel Edward Ferrero. The fire from the Confederates broke up their formation as they approached the bridge, and the Federals were forced to take shelter. Just before 1 P.M., the Federal troops suddenly rushed across the bridge and reached the other side. Although now across Antietam Creek, the Federals had suffered heavy casualties.[121]

Brigadier General Ferrero reported casualties on September 17 for his 2nd Brigade, Second Division, IX Army Corps at Antietam as 95 killed, 271 wounded, and 6 missing, a total of 372. When the 116 casualties from South Mountain were added (10 killed, 83 wounded 23 missing), the total was 488.[122]

Wild's history of the 35th Massachusetts, based on information obtained from others of his regiment, noted that the 35th "bore a conspicuous part" in the fighting at Antietam and in taking the Burnside bridge, as well,

> under Lt. Col. Sumner Carruth, who was soon shot through the neck and obliged to retire. The Major being about on special duty, the command devolved upon Capt. Wm. S. King of Co. K who nobly sustained his party to a place of safety; for by that time the whole color guard were disabled. At the decisive moment of this great battle, it became necessary to take hold the Bridge over the Antietam Creek and its approaches—Our Regt. supported the 51st New York made a charge over the bridge, drove the enemy from the top of the first rising ground and likewise from the second, never stopping till themselves occupied the crest of the second hill; which position they held sometime, though subjected to slaughtering crossfires, with a steadiness that veterans might be proud of, until ordered to retire a little to a more sheltered spot. Their behavior was admirable throughout, & considering the drawbacks above mentioned, it was magnificent.[123]

Wild reported heavy casualties suffered by the 35th Massachusetts in Maryland in the two battles—South Mountain and Antietam: "We had 2 captains killed & 4 wounded. Of Lieutenants, 1 killed, 10 wounded. Of enlisted men about (250)." Of those present, "we had ⅔ of the officers, and nearly ⅓ of the men disabled."[124] At Antietam alone, Wild's 35th Regiment lost 48 killed, 160 wounded, and 6 missing, for a total of 214 casualties.[125]

Antietam still holds the record for the most casualties in a single day's battle. At Antietam, Federal losses were 2,108 killed, 9,549 wounded, 753 captured for a

Confederate dead after Battle at Antietam/Sharpsburg, September 1862. (Courtesy of Library of Congress, Washington, D.C.)

total of 12,410.¹²⁶ Confederate losses at Antietam were 1,512 killed, 7,816 wounded, 1,844 missing, for a total of 11,172.¹²⁷ If the casualties at Harper's Ferry, Crampton's Gap, South Mountain, and Sheperdstown are added to those at Antietam, Confederate losses totaled 12,601.¹²⁸

Although not physically wounded, Major General George McClellan was a "casualty" of Antietam. For his failure to follow up on the Union victory at Antietam, Lincoln replaced him with Major General Ambrose E. Burnside as commander of the Army of the Potomac.¹²⁹

October to November 1862

Colonel Wild recuperated at Middletown, Maryland, for two weeks, September 16–30. His wife joined him there. On October 1, he was well enough to be moved to his sister's home in Philadelphia, where he remained for two more months.¹³⁰

Dr. Oliver Wendell Holmes traveled to Sharpsburg, Maryland, in search of his son, a soldier wounded at the battle there. His travel log, entitled, "My Hunt After 'The Captain,'" was published in the *Atlantic Monthly*.¹³¹ Holmes' account of his journey from Massachusetts to Maryland mentioned a lady whom he met on the train from New York, as both were traveling "down to Maryland."[132] Having learned of her husband's injury, the lady intended to join him at Middletown. Although Holmes mentioned no names, he described her as "the light of our party while we were together on our pilgrimage, a fair, gracious woman, gentle, but courageous." Years later, Wild told his friend, Dr. Francis H. Brown, "You can recognize me and my wife from the description."[133]

When Dr. Holmes arrived several days after the battle was over, the carnage remained. There were hundreds of wounded and dying men, both Yankee and Confederate. Holmes described the death and destruction vividly, and the horror of it all, from seeing a soldier dying with lockjaw to the stench of dead horses still lying beside the roads. He was horrified at the numerous mounds that served as mass graves for the thousands who were killed at Antietam.[134]

December 1, 1862

Two and one-half months after his surgery, Edward Wild had recovered sufficiently to go home, and he left for Boston on December 1, 1862.[135] In constant pain, almost completely helpless, and unable to command his regiment, Wild was suffering a low point in his life. He received reports of the "splendid performance" of his regiment at Antietam and in other engagements.[136]

Wild had trained his men well and, even after the heavy losses they suffered at Antietam, his regiment continued to fight with distinction at Jackson, Mississippi; Knoxville, Tennessee; and in most of the major battles in Virginia—the Wilderness, Spotsylvania Court House, Cold Harbor, Petersburg, and the Weldon Railroad.[137]

Summary of Wild's Military Activity 1861–1862

From July 18, 1861, through September 14, 1862, Wild stated that he had actually been engaged in fighting for "less than six days." He had taken part in battles at Blackburn's Ford, First Bull Run (First Manassas), Yorktown, Williamsburg, Fair Oaks–Seven Pines, and South Mountain. In addition, he had been involved in several skirmishes and in siege operations at Yorktown.[138] During the first two years of the war, Wild suffered devastating and permanent injuries to the his fingers of his right hand and his left arm. Disabled, maimed, in constant pain, and unable to function as a commander, Wild's future looked dim. However, there were those who believed in Edward Wild and his unique abilities.

Wild would be promoted to brigadier general, and work toward recruiting an army of black soldiers. In the process, he would create enough havoc to make both the North and the South notice the "wild" General. As commander of the "African

Brigade," he would provide grist for the mills of rumor and scandal, and become an embarrassment to government officials. He would become a savior to many of the slave families he freed from bondage, and become a leader of the colored soldiers he recruited and trained to fight under his command. As a brigade commander, Wild would also engage in acts that no "Southern gentleman would dream of," and thus evoke the wrath of the Confederate Government, and the people of the South, especially the states of North Carolina, South Carolina, Virginia, and Georgia.

Edward Wild looked forward to 1863 with hope, especially when his 20 of his Harvard classmates, to show their love and appreciation, sent him a New Year's Eve present. That present was an "elegant sword of the regulation pattern, very elaborately chased, heavily gilded, with gold cord and tassels and a shark-skin sheath."[139]

Edward Wild could not foresee that in recruiting blacks as Union soldiers into his "African Brigade," he would meet with hatred, discrimination, arrest, and court martial. He would have to deal with situations that would test his abilities to the limit.

IV

Brigadier General Wild, United States Volunteers (Colored)

He is one of the bravest men and one of the best, most accomplished and experienced officers....

—Governor John Andrew to Major General
John G. Foster, May 14, 1863

In the spring of 1863, Wild could not have foreseen the amount of opposition to enlisting black soldiers that he would encounter, nor the widespread distribution of that discrimination toward those new black soldiers and toward himself. Opposition to Wild and his black soldiers came not only from Southerners, but also from Northerners—his military subordinates and superiors, the Federal government, and the public at large.

There was an almost "impenetrable wall of prejudice" against the use of "colored men in military service." It was widely believed that "they could not be made soldiers; that they could not fight; that to employ them would prolong the war; that white soldiers would not serve in the same army with them; and that they would prove a source of demoralization to our armies in the field." It was feared that the use of blacks as soldiers would result in "civil discord" in the states loyal to the Union, and would prove "ruinous to the Union cause."[1]

Evolution of Black Troops and Opinions Regarding Them

The evolution of an all white army into one that was integrated was a slow process, but once the key elements were in place, the ranks of the Union Army were swelled by black men from many states, both North and South, all eager to fight for freedom for their brothers and sisters still being held in bondage.

President Abraham Lincoln had long toyed with the idea of freeing the slaves, but had held off until the proper time because he was afraid "half the officers would fling down their arms and three more states would rise [in rebellion]." Secretary of State William Seward suggested the President wait to issue the Emancipation Proclamation until there was a clear Union victory on the battlefield. Otherwise, Seward reasoned, it would look like "a cry of help" to blacks.[2] The proper moment came after the Battle of Antietam (Sharpsburg), a bloody battle, but a Union victory. The preliminary Emancipation Proclamation was adopted on September 22, 1862, to take effect on January 1, 1863. It not only freed the slaves in the states currently in "rebellion against the United States," but it guaranteed that "such persons of suitable condition will be received into the armed service of the United States to garrison forts, positions, stations, and other places, and to man vessels of all sorts in said service."[3] This was the key to allowing blacks to serve in the United States armed forces.

Lincoln's Emancipation Proclamation freed only the slaves in the states currently in rebellion against the United States—the Confederate States of America.[4] Although a great political move, the proclamation actually gave very few slaves their freedom because it did not apply to those slaves in the border states or areas under Federal control. The states "in rebellion" totally ignored it.

Freeing the slaves had not been Lincoln's original purpose, but as the war continued, he saw it as a means to gather needed support, both at home and abroad. Lincoln explained to newspaper editor Horace Greely that his primary objective was "to save the Union, and is not either to save or to destroy slavery. If I could save the Union without freeing any slave, I would do it; and if I could save it by freeing all the slaves, I would do it; and if I could do it by freeing some and leaving others along, I would also do that."[5]

This one act totally changed how the world viewed the American Civil War from a contest over states' rights to a crusade to end slavery. Massachusetts Governor John Andrew believed the proclamation was "wrong in its delay until January, but grand and sublime after all."[6] Shortly after the Proclamation took effect, an order was issued to raise volunteer companies for duty, and those volunteers could be "persons of African descent, organized into special corps."

As the war continued, casualties mounted, and the terms of service of many soldiers who had volunteered in 1861 would soon be up. More men would be needed to replace them. Stanton tried to postpone a draft, but the Enrollment Act of March 3, 1863, resulted in bloody riots in several states.[7] When state governors were ordered to impose a draft, riots erupted in Wisconsin and Indiana, and there were threats of riots elsewhere. Anti-draft riots took place after the battles at Gettysburg, Pennsylvania, July 1–3, 1863, which left thousands of soldiers dead or wounded, and decimated the ranks of both armies. A "draft law" was not welcomed at this time.

Hatred of blacks erupted in violence during the New York City anti-draft riots July 13–July 16, 1863. A Negro church and an orphanage for 250 Negro children were burned. Military troops were ordered to help the city police force, but over 1,000 people were killed or wounded.[8]

The mob's fury also targeted military officers who attempted to quell the riot. Colonel H. F. O'Brien, of the 11th New York, ordered his men to fire howitzers and rifles into a crowd, and several rioters were killed, including four women. After the police force moved on to another area, O'Brien dismounted and walked to a drug store. A crowd gathered in front of the store and threatened him. Bravely, he drew his sword and revolver and walked out onto the sidewalk. He was hit on the head, savagely beaten, mutilated, then dragged through the streets until he died.[9]

Draft riots occurred in Vermont, New Hampshire, and Ohio. In Boston, a mob stoned Federal troops and dispersed only after the troops had killed several rioters. The draft was wisely postponed until August 19.[10]

To ease the need for a draft, it was imperative that the ranks of the Union army be replenished with black volunteers. The recruitment of blacks was one of the most difficult jobs of the white officers assigned to the black regiments because every kind of obstacle imaginable was placed in their path, and there was little in the way of "assistance or incentive" to help with the job of recruiting blacks.[11]

If captured by the Confederate Army, a black Union soldier or his white commander could face execution. This was sanctioned by the Confederate government, which had met in secret session on Friday, May 1, 1863, and passed a resolution condemning the "Government of the United States, its authorities, commanders, and forces" who would free slaves in the Confederate states, abduct slaves, incite them to insurrection, or use them in the "war against the Confederate States...." This resolution specifically targeted "every white person being a commissioned officer ... who ... shall command Negroes or mulattos in arms against the Confederate States...." It also specified that any who attempted to "arm, train, organize, or prepare Negroes or mulattos in any military enterprise ... shall, if captured, be put to death or be otherwise punished, at the discretion of the court."[12] Negroes or mulattos caught fighting against the Confederacy were to be "delivered to the authorities of the State or States in which they shall be captured to be dealt with according to the present or future laws of such State or States."[13] The resolutions passed by the Confederate government were widely publicized in newspapers, such as the Wilmington *Journal*. The editor of this Southern paper wrote: "The Yankee officers who would put themselves at the head of a Negro brigade ... should fight with halters around their necks."[14]

The action of the Confederate government was mirrored in July of 1863 by President Lincoln's policy of retaliation for any Federal prisoners of war executed by Confederates.[15] Lincoln promised protection to all citizens, "whatever class, color, or condition," especially "soldiers in the public service," and "for every soldier of the United States killed in violation of the laws of war, a rebel soldier shall be executed; and for every one enslaved by the enemy or sold into slavery, a rebel soldier shall be placed at hard labor on the public works...."[16] Retaliation was carried out on both sides of the conflict. When Brigadier General Wild executed Confederate deserter and guerrilla, Daniel Bright, Confederates retaliated and hanged one of Wild's black soldiers.

Major General Benjamin F. "Beast" Butler

Major General Benjamin F. Butler. (Courtesy of Library of Congress, Washington, D.C.)

Even before the Emancipation Proclamation was issued, the controversial Major General Benjamin Butler had used blacks as soldiers. This rotund politician was the first major general appointed by President Abraham Lincoln, and was the first to coin the term *contraband of war* to apply to the freed slaves who fled to safety behind Union lines.[17] In 1861, when three slaves had sought refuge at Fort Monroe, Butler refused to return them to their owner; since Virginia was no longer in the union, the owner had no rights under the Fugitive Slave Act. Butler deemed the slaves and anything else taken from the Confederate states as "contraband of war."[18] This term was shortened to *contraband*, and referred to the thousands of slaves who fled to the Union lines or were liberated when Federal troops took control of a formerly Confederate area.

Butler and all who advocated freeing slaves and using them as soldiers in the Union Army were hated by Southerners and slave owners. The officers and soldiers under Major General Butler were specifically targeted in General Order No. 111, a proclamation issued on December 24, 1862, by President Jefferson Davis. This order declared Butler's commissioned officers "robbers and criminals deserving death," and if captured "reserved for execution." However, Butler's private soldiers and non-commissioned officers, if captured, were to be treated with kindness and humanity and sent home on parole with the promise that they would not aid or serve the United States in any capacity during the continuation of this war unless duly exchanged.[19]

Sent to New Orleans in May of 1862, shortly after the city surrendered, Butler had used three regiments of freed slaves of Louisiana Native Guards to help him hold the city. On September 27, 1862, the 1st Regiment Louisiana Native Guards became the first African-American regiment, in which all the platoon and company commanders were black.[20]

Although a capable military governor, Butler's actions in New Orleans so enraged the citizens of that city that he was removed in December of 1862 and transferred. Vilified in the South and declared an outlaw by President Jefferson Davis, Butler was even accused of stealing the silverware from the New Orleans house in which he made his headquarters.[21] This accusation resulted in the nickname "Spoons," which "clung to him ever after."[22]

"Contraband" of war, a term coined by Major General Benjamin F. Butler. (Courtesy of Library of Congress, Washington, D.C.)

Butler's General Order No. 28 decreed that any female of New Orleans who should "by word, gesture, or movement, insult or show contempt for any officer or soldier of the United States" would be "regarded and held liable to be treated as a woman of the town plying her avocation." [23] If the ladies of New Orleans didn't respect Union soldiers, they would be treated as prostitutes. Butler soon became known as the "Beast of New Orleans" for his treatment of the people of that city.

Another controversial act was the hanging of a New Orleans gambler, William B. Mumford.[24] In defiance to Union rule, Mumford had pulled down the United States flag that flew at the New Orleans Mint. Arrested and tried, Mumford was found guilty and sentenced to hang "at or near the Mint" where he had committed his crime. Everyone expected Butler to pardon Mumford, but he did not. He was not even moved by pleas from the condemned man's wife and children. However, after the war, when Mumford's widow found herself in dire financial straights, she approached Butler for help. The General secured a clerical job for her in the Internal Revenue Department of the United States government. During the Hayes administration, a number of job cuts again left Mrs. Mumford without a job. She called on the general a second time for help, and he made the rounds of government agencies until he found her a job in the United States postal department.[25]

The idea of having black soldiers, whether in blue or the gray, was abhorrent to many people. Southerners harbored an ingrained fear that their slaves would rise up and massacre them in their sleep. Their need for ample slave labor was overshadowed by their fear of slave revolts. This was especially true in states which had a high ratio of blacks to whites.[26]

Slave insurrections have occurred throughout the history of slavery in America and increased in proportion to the number of slaves.[27] The first major revolt occurred in New York City in 1712. The Negro Plot of 1741 in New York caused mass hysteria over rumors of a slave conspiracy, which resulted in a trial. Eleven Negroes were burned to death, and 50 deported to the West Indies.[28] In Charleston, South Carolina, the "Stono Revolt" of 1739 resulted in 50 slaves being hanged. Laws to prevent future revolts were passed. These limited the number of hours slaves could work to not more than 14 or 15 daily, and forbade working on Sunday. Slave gatherings were forbidden, as was teaching a slave to read and write.[29] The Citadel, the military college in Charleston, was established in 1824 as a direct response to the danger of slave uprisings.[30]

The most famous slave uprising was the Nat Turner Rebellion on August 21–22, 1831, in Southampton County, Virginia. It resulted in the massacre of 55 white people by a mob of runaway slaves, estimated at 450 (probably only about 60) who came out of the Dismal Swamp. All, including their leader Nat Turner, were executed.[31] While in jail awaiting his execution, Turner was questioned, and his answers were published as *The Confessions of Nat Turner (1800–1831)*.[32] This rebellion had a great impact on the psyche of the nation, which has been perpetuated by William Styron's The *Confession of Nat Turner,* winner of the 1968 Pulitzer Prize for fiction.[33] The memory of this rebellion was still fresh at the outbreak war in 1861.

In the summer of 1861, when Lincoln first presented his Cabinet with the idea of freeing the slaves in the Confederate States, it was not without consideration for the repercussions that might occur. It was only after many battles had been fought and countless lives of both Union and Confederate soldiers had been lost that Lincoln used the Emancipation Proclamation as his "ace in the hole" and, like any good poker player, he held his trump card to play at the most advantageous time.

As the war progressed, the need for more soldiers led both sides to consider using blacks in the military. Samuel G. Howe, Commissioner of the American Freedman's Inquiry Commission, submitted a report to Secretary of War Stanton on various aspects of the freed Negroes, including their ability to function as soldiers. The Commission believed that military training was the best, quickest, and most efficient means of helping the colored race cultivate self-respect and self-reliance, if under judicious officers, who would treat them firmly and kindly. Thus, if the Negro was employed as a soldier, the war would become a blessing, and one "cheaply bought at any price."[34]

The Commission saw no difficulty in getting black men to enlist, "provided those now in the field shall be regularly paid, and provided the determination of the Government to protect them in all rights of the white soldiers shall be clearly made known to them," especially if this was sanctioned by President Lincoln.[35]

Black Troops Become a Reality

Southerners long resisted the idea of the Confederacy arming slaves to fight alongside whites, but when the North actually did so, the new black regiments were not welcomed on either side of the Mason-Dixon line. After the Burnside expedition of 1862, hundreds of "contraband" had fled into the territory in eastern North Carolina now under the jurisdiction of Brigadier General John G. Foster. However, Foster hesitated to raise any black units under his command.[36]

Once the policy of recruiting colored troops was approved, it was quickly implemented on a large scale in the North. The Adjutant General began to work with recruiting and organizing blacks in the Mississippi Valley, and Nathaniel P. Banks organized a corps of colored troops he named "Corps d'Afrique." Recruitment was begun on the East coast, with the hope that the enrollment of blacks would ease the hated "conscription" law enacted in 1863.[37]

General Order No. 143, dated May 22, 1863, established a Bureau for Colored Troops.[38] Charles W. Foster was appointed chief of the bureau as Assistant Adjutant General. With the establishment of a central bureau in Washington, black regiments would be organized on a "uniform national basis," regardless of the states in which they were recruited.[39]

Lincoln's goal was to recruit 200,000 Negro troops by the end of 1863. On June 30, 1863, the American Freedman Inquiry Commission of the Freedman's Bureau reported that "Docility, earnestness, the instinct of obedience" were qualities that made a good soldier, and that these were qualities, "as a general rule, of the colored refugees who enter our lines."[40] However, the Commissioner of the Freedman's Bureau wisely surmised that the efficiency of the black troops hinged upon having white officers who were "in sympathy with them, have gained their confidence, and can arouse their devotion."[41]

54th Massachusetts Volunteers (Colored)

The 54th Massachusetts, an all black regiment, was largely the idea of Governor John A. Andrew of Massachusetts. Governor Andrew was a "tireless abolitionist" who had strong support from Frederick Douglass, Harriet Beecher Stowe, and other abolitionists. He was able to convince the War Department to allow him to raise a regiment of free blacks from Massachusetts. Andrew began searching among the brightest young Massachusetts white men to command it.[42] He envisioned the 54th as "a model for all future Colored Regiments."[43]

The young and handsome Robert Gould Shaw was one of the first to accept command of a new black regiment. Shaw had been serving since May of 1861, first with the 7th New York National Guard, then in the 2nd Massachusetts Infantry. He had fought in several major battles, including Antietam.[44] Governor Andrew, always an advocate of black soldiers, wrote Francis George Shaw, a wealthy merchant and abolitionist, for help.[45] Andrew asked Shaw to speak to his son, Captain Robert Gould Shaw, about accepting the command of a black regiment.[46] At first the younger Shaw refused Andrew's offer, but after soliciting opinions from several friends, and after hearing encouragement from his parents, he accepted.[47] Philosopher William James praised Shaw for having the courage to join in "this new Negro-soldier venture [where] loneliness was certain, ridicule inevitable, failure possible, and Shaw was only twenty-five."[48] Shaw knew the risk to "officers of coloured [sic] regiments" and that he would be "in rather a ticklish situation, if caught by the Rebels...."[49]

Another officer of the 54th was Lieutenant Garth Wilkinson James, the younger brother of two famous American authors—Henry James and William James. The ranks were joined by Lewis and Charles Douglass, sons of the famous black abolitionist Frederick Douglass. The regiment spent the spring of 1863 training and by May the 54th Massachusetts Regiment was ready for action.[50]

Colonel Shaw was very pleased with his regiment and, although some had been skeptical at first, once they saw Shaw's 54th Regiment, they had "no more doubts of Negroes making good soldiers."[51]

Darien, Georgia, Destroyed

Once Shaw's regiment had received basic training, it was ordered to Darien, Georgia, on the Altamaha River, under the command of Colonel James Montgomery. Although Montgomery was energetic and devoted to the cause, Shaw deplored his "terrorist methods." Montgomery was a "bush-whacker—in his fighting, and a perfect fanatic in other respects." Although Montgomery neither "drinks, smokes or swears," he considered "praying, shooting, burning and hanging" the "true means to put down the Rebellion."[52] Montgomery took eight companies of Shaw's 54th Massachusetts Regiment on a raid with the 2nd Regiment South Carolina Infantry and burned the town of Darien, Georgia, on June 12.[53] "One rebel was killed by a shell, and the only persons we saw were one old colored woman and two whites, who requested to be left behind." By sundown the whole town was enveloped in flames, which could be seen "burning from 3 o'clock in the afternoon till daylight the next morning." One soldier told the *New Bedford Mercury:* "The town of Darien is now no more."[54]

The burning of Darien did not endear the 54th Massachusetts to the people of Georgia or South Carolina, and revenge against the 54th was not long in coming. On July 18, 1863, in front of a little palmetto and sand fortification called Battery

(Fort) Wagner, at the tip of Morris Island in Charleston Harbor, the 54th Regiment Massachusetts were catapulted into history. Shaw and many of his men were killed in the assault.[55] Shaw, two other officers and 31 men were killed; 11 officers and 135 men were wounded, and 92 were missing—272 out of the 650 Union men engaged.[56]

Wild Promoted to Brigadier General

Wild's promotion to the rank of brigadier general resulted from the need for more Federal troops, and this need was to be met by the use of black soldiers.

Wild had been seriously wounded at South Mountain. He had spent several months recuperating, but his friend, Governor John A. Andrew, did not allow Wild to remain idle very long. The Governor soon had Wild working, often late into the night, to help organize an all black regiment, the 54th Massachusetts Volunteers. Andrew wanted to tap the vast pool of adult black males, both free men in the North and freed slaves in the South, who could be used to augment the ranks of the Union Army. Wild totally agreed with Andrew, and supported his ideas.[57] Wild spent the months of February, March and April assisting Governor Andrew in "raising and organizing colored troops."[58] This was a cause Wild believed in and it was something he could do, even though severely handicapped by his injuries.

On April 1, Andrew wrote Secretary of War Stanton and urged him to find some "able, brave, tried and *believing* man" who could organize colored troops in North Carolina into a brigade. Andrew firmly believed that 2,500 to 5,000 men could be raised, but in order to be successful, "it needs a *man* always for the soul of any movement.... And the right man is the main point." Stanton subsequently forwarded Andrew's letter to General Foster in North Carolina. However, Foster did not believe that "not more than one Regiment ... could be raised in this Department." Foster was concerned that any troops raised from among the contraband or freedmen would be "antagonistic ... to the feelings of the white troops."[59]

Governor Andrew wanted to raise another black regiment (the 55th) in addition to the 54th. He wanted Wild to take charge of the new regiment, and he wrote Secretary of War Stanton on April 6, 1863, that he would see Colonel Wild the next day. Although Wild had not yet accepted the offer to raise a regiment, Andrew believed that Wild would "need little time here to select [a] portion of officers" if he accepted.[60]

Thinking ahead, Governor Andrew looked past the regimental level to the formation of an entirely new brigade, and he recommended that Wild be promoted to the rank of brigadier general, to "facilitate the work of forming a brigade." However, Stanton disagreed and insisted Wild's commission be "withheld until he had already raised a brigade." This strained the good relationship Stanton and Andrew had enjoyed since the beginning of the war.[61]

Governor Andrew wanted a brigade commander who could provide the quality of leadership equal to that of Colonel Robert Shaw of the 54th Massachusetts.

Brigadier General Edward A. Wild after he lost his left arm at South Mountain, September 14, 1862. (Courtesy of Massachusetts Commandery, Military Order of the Loyal Legion, and U.S. Army Military History Institute, Carlisle Barracks, Carlisle, Pa.)

Wild was one of those considered for the post to command a brigade of black troops, but he had not been Governor Andrew's first choice. He had originally wanted Brigadier General Francis "Frank" Channing Barlow of New York to command the new black regiments, but Barlow was still recuperating from wounds received at Antietam in September of 1862.[62] Andrew believed Barlow was "next to" Wild in his ability to take charge of colored soldiers.[63]

Colonel Robert Shaw, before his death at Battery Wagoner, had also favored Barlow as a brigade commander, and declared: "He is just the man for it, and I should like to be under him." [64] Barlow had tutored Robert Shaw at Shaw's Long Island home in 1856 to enable the younger man to pass the Harvard entrance examination. Barlow practiced law in New York, and also wrote for the New York *Tribune*. He enlisted as a private in the 12th Regiment New York Infantry on April 19, 1861. Subsequently, he was promoted within the ranks to Lieutenant Colonel and Colonel, and saw service at the siege of Yorktown, and at Fair Oaks. After the battle at Antietam, Barlow was promoted to Brigadier General.[65]

The Governor believed there were great numbers of colored men in North Carolina who might be enlisted as soldiers, and he suggested Wild's name to Stanton as a brigadier general who could organize those men. He knew of no one else to whom "the duty could be safely and well be committed." Again, Governor Andrew wrote to the Secretary of War extolling Wild's abilities, his experience, and his "zeal for work." Wild was preparing to return to his 35th Massachusetts Regiment when he was sidetracked by an offer to "become a brigadier general and raise a brigade...." Wild was unconcerned about rank and pay, and was too "interested in the work to make a point of either." Wild was more interested in getting the job done and was "willing to forget himself in it."[66]

In April, Shaw learned that Edward Wild would probably be given the command of the brigade, that he had wanted Barlow "very much" to have.[67] Although Shaw described Wild as an "excellent man," he wondered if Wild, due to the extent of his wounds, would be able to remain active in the military service. He knew that Wild was "determined to try it."[68] Later, on July 7, 1863, only a few weeks before his death on Morris Island, Shaw wrote to Walter Wild, Edward's brother, to tell him how pleased he was with Wild's success in recruiting troops in North Carolina.[69]

On April 29, 1863, the Paymaster General issued Special Order No. 194 concerning Colonel Edward A. Wild, who, because of his wounds, had tendered his resignation, and was given an honorable discharge, to take effect on April 14, 1863, because he had been appointed a Brigadier General of Volunteers. Wild also received $1,591.52, less income tax, being his full pay from August 20, 1862 to April 24, 1863.[70]

In spite of his disabilities, Wild was the man for the job Governor Andrew had in mind. The Governor had confidence in Wild, and that confidence was not unwarranted. Wild had experience. He had been in six major engagements, and had acted with daring and courage on the field of battle.[71]

Handicapped by battlefield injuries, Wild still accepted the challenge, although at first he doubted his ability to do the job. "I am not the man I was a year ago," he told a friend. Yet, he wanted to help in any way he could. He had some experience in recruitment, and had helped recruit for the 35th Massachusetts after being wounded at Seven Pines. He wanted to "work" for his country as "long as I can, and ... do what is set before me."[72] In addition to his willingness to serve his country in any capacity, Wild's belief in the "value of black soldiers," his hatred of the Confederacy, and his determination to overcome all obstacles made him perfect for the job.[73]

Wild was asked to help select white officers for the black regiments. His job was to "receive applicants for commissions," and to judge their commendations. He was to examine candidates, and to advise with Colonel Robert Shaw and Lt. Colonel N. P. Hallowell, of the 54th and 55th regiments, respectively, in selecting officers.[74] This enabled Wild to familiarize himself with a number of men, some of whom he would later appoint to his own regiments. His success also justified Governor Andrew's faith that Wild had the "ability to raise and lead black troops."[75]

All obstacles were finally overcome, and the paperwork completed. On April 13, Secretary of War Edwin Stanton authorized Wild to "raise a brigade (of four regiments) of North Carolina volunteer infantry" to serve for three years or the duration of the war. The organization of the brigade was to follow regulations set out in General Order No. 126 of 1862. Recruitment was to be done in "accordance with the rules of the service and the orders of the Secretary of War."[76]

Officially still a member of the 35th Massachusetts Volunteers, Colonel Edward Wild was sent by Governor Andrew to Washington on April 21, 1863. On April 24, he was appointed "Brigadier General of Volunteers." Wild accepted and began finalizing his plans. He received his instructions, and the officers of his first regiment were appointed.[77] He set about building his brigade from scratch. One regiment had to be completed before the second could be begun.[78]

Wild was delighted with his job of recruiting free blacks and former slaves as Union soldiers. Once he had recruited enough men to fill its ranks, he would have his own brigade. That task was not without peril, and Wild would be assailed from all sides when he attempted to free, recruit, and train black men for his "African Brigade."

Many of the men who commanded black regiments were not as well qualified as Wild, or as sympathetic to the problems of the blacks. Wild knew many of the Northern abolitionists, and he had proven himself a "courageous and capable" military leader.[79] It could never be said that Wild's appointment had been politically motivated. Governor Andrew described Wild as "one of the bravest men and one of the best, most accomplished and experienced officers in the Mass. Volunteer Service." He was not just a thinker but a doer. His other good qualities, according to Governor Andrew, were his "exemplary patience and quiet though not unenthusiastic perseverance."[80] Wild was described by Foster in General Order No. 79 as a "gallant and accomplished soldier and gentleman."[81]

Moreover, Wild understood the psyche of his men. They "are not veterans ... they must be led, you cannot order them forward and expect them to go alone, you cannot station them in a heavy fire and expect them to stay without flinching ... though they be the bravest men on earth; example is everything." Wild knew that to lead his men, he must set the example for them. "They are not afraid to do what they think you are not afraid to lead them in yourself, but let them suspect you of flinching, they think something is impossible or going wrong, they are like sheep without a shepherd; one firm man can support a whole corps."[82]

Wild tried his best to live up to that principle. His motto was, "If you want a thing well done, do it yourself."[83] This was evident in everything he did, from handling details to writing reports himself, even though he had to compensate for two injured fingers. On horseback, he held his sword in his right hand and the reins in his teeth.[84]

Although Wild was well qualified to raise and train troops, he also had several negative aspects to his personality. The wounds he received in the war had left him embittered toward the entire slave-holding population. That deep hatred was evident in some of the harsher actions he took against slave owners, Rebels, and guerrillas, and may very well have stemmed from the loss of his arm and his constant pain.[85]

Phantom limb pain was first described by S. Weir Mitchell in the *Atlantic Monthly* in the case of George Dedlow. Dedlow awoke in a hospital complaining of pain in his leg, only to be informed that both his legs had been amputated. Since that time, the phenomenon of phantom limbs has become well known, and the "terrible pain in these invisible appendages" is very real.[86] Brigadier General Edward Wild suffered from this malady the rest of his life.

55th Regiment Massachusetts Volunteers (Colored)

After the 54th Massachusetts Volunteers was complete, Wild, George L. Stearns, and others began to develop a network of black recruiting officers through the northern states, and eventually had enough volunteers to form the 55th Regiment.[87] By June 22, all the companies had been recruited and the regiment was mustered into service. When presenting a flag to the 55th Regiment, Governor Andrew noted in his presentation speech: "I know not when, in all human history, to any given one thousand men in arms has been committed a work so proud, so precious, so full of hope and glory, as the work committed to you." [88]

The officers of the new all-black regiment were: Colonel Norwood P. Hallowell, Lieutenant Colonel Alfred S. Hartwell, Major Charles B. Fox, Surgeon William S. Brown, Assistant Surgeon Burt G. Wilder, and Chaplain William Jackson.[89]

A month later, the 55th Massachusetts was ordered to Boston to board ships that were to carry them into the heart of the war being waged in Charleston Harbor, and there they would become part of Brigadier General Edward Wild's African Brigade.[90]

As a brigadier general in charge of an entire brigade, Wild had a large number of men at his command. A brigade consisted of two or more regiments. Federal brigades usually averaged 4.7 regiments, or about 2,000 men. Confederate brigades were somewhat smaller, made up of 4.5 regiments, which included about 1,850 men. Northern brigades were officially designated by a number within their division. "3, 1, IV" was the designation for the 3rd Brigade of the First Division of the IV Corps. Confederate brigades were named after their commanders, such as "Clingman's Brigade." Wild's African Brigade, in the spring of 1864, was actually the 1st Brigade, 3rd Division of Colored Troops, XVIII Army Corps, Department of Virginia and North Carolina[91] (1, 3, XVIII). By May 5, 1864, Wild's brigade of four regiments had become part of the Army of the Potomac.[92]

Raising Troops in North Carolina

The decision to raise colored troops in North Carolina was the result of several factors. By 1863, Federal troops occupied a number of counties on the coast of the state, and thus a large number of freed male slaves were available for induction into the Union army. When the Confederates attempted to retake the town of "Little" Washington, North Carolina, defended by an insufficient number of Federal troops, the Federals had organized all the "able-bodied males" in the town, armed them, and put them into the battle line. William Derby described this "first experience with armed Negroes," and he noted how the white soldiers fought alongside the blacks without protest. The willingness of the freedman to fight to prevent the

Confederate takeover of Little Washington convinced many that they would make good soldiers.[93]

With high hopes for success, Governor Andrew of Massachusetts wrote to Major General John Foster to advise him of Brigadier General Edward Wild's departure for Foster's district headquarters in New Bern, North Carolina, in May of 1863. The Governor described Wild as "one of the bravest men and one of the best, most accomplished and experienced officers" in the Massachusetts Volunteers. He was knew Wild was "peculiarly adapted—by reason of his cosmopolitan experiences as a Surgeon, a soldier and a traveler and as a man of ideas and not simply of routine."[94]

Staffing the 1st North Carolina Colored Volunteers

After finishing the task of screening applicants for commissions, Wild began putting together his "prototype" regiment as the 1st North Carolina Colored Volunteers (NCCV). He staffed his regiments with men who were both "committed to abolition and temperance." Although not in the majority, there were some African-American officers in Wild's brigade. Wild had problems finding enough white, non-commissioned officers with military experience to serve as officers because he could not take them from the Army of the Potomac, and he was forced to chose them from units stationed elsewhere or from the ranks of disabled soldiers. Thus, Wild turned first to Massachusetts and other New England states. However, to balance out this disadvantage, Wild was authorized to select men he believed were qualified and to "establish their relative seniority" within his regimental hierarchy. Therefore, he was able to staff his 1st NCCV regiment quickly and efficiently. Within three days after accepting his appointment as brigadier general, Wild had placed the majority of officers in the required positions in his regiment. On April 28, 1863, 26 officers were appointed. The colonel and lieutenant colonel were appointed on June 1.[95]

It was not easy getting good men to lead the black troops. Colonel Charles E. Griswold of the 2nd Massachusetts Regiment declined an offer of the "colonelcy of the 1st North Carolina Regiment of black troops," because he was not allowed "to nominate any of my officers, especially those of my personal staff."[96] Wild had also wanted Dr. Francis M. Lincoln, previously with the 35th Massachusetts, for the Surgeon for the 1st NCCV. Lincoln declined because he had not recovered from "diarrhea" and to accept an appointment under Colonel Griswold.[97]

Wild was successful in getting his own brother, Walter H. Wild, a First Lieutenant with Shaw's 54th Massachusetts, transferred to his brigade. Considering Wild's disabilities, it was probably very comforting to have his brother close at hand to perform needed personal services, and for moral support during times of stress and tension.[98]

The majority of the officers selected by Wild for the 1st NCCV had previously served in Massachusetts regiments. The first was James Chaplin Beecher, who had been a lieutenant colonel in the 141st New York Regiment. Another was Lieutenant Colonel William N. Reed, a New Yorker who had graduated from a military school in Germany, where he had reached a rank of *etat* major in the Imperial Army. Reed may have been a mulatto, and if so, he was the highest-ranking man of African descent in the Union army.[99] John V. De Grasse, a black doctor, was appointed assistant surgeon and given the rank of major. De Grasse had received a medical degree in 1849. He was the first black man to become a member of a medical organization when he was accepted by the Massachusetts Medical Society in 1854.[100] De Grasse was later court martialed supposedly for "intoxication," but more than likely because he was black.[101]

Wild also commissioned the Reverend John N. Mars chaplain of the regiment. Mars was black. At age 58, Mars resigned his commission in 1864 because of the harshness of army life and its effects on his "chronic rheumatism."[102]

After the regiment was no longer under Wild's wing, both Dr. De Grasse and the Reverend Mars were replaced with white officers.[103] Thus, a brigade that began as an integrated entity eventually succumbed to the ravages of war and widespread white hostility. While it was highly improbable that another black doctor could have been found to replace De Grasse, the chaplain's position could possibly have been filled by another man of color, if those in authority had so desired.

In order to attract blacks as recruits into the Union forces, placards were posted in New Bern, North Carolina, calling for 4,000 men for "Wild's colored Brigade."[104] It had already been determined that there were enough ex-slaves to fill the four new regiments which were to become Wild's African Brigade. In March of 1863, a census compiled by Private Henry A. Clapp indicated the number of freed blacks in the counties of coastal North Carolina under Federal control totaled at least 8,500 black refugees in New Bern and nearby camps.[105] With an adequate supply of manpower, Wild needed and received help with recruiting from a valuable ally, a black Massachusetts recruiter named George N. Williams. Williams reported the plan to recruit blacks troops to the Philadelphia *Christian Recorder*. His comments were published on May 19, 1863, regarding the "ten thousand" freedman of African descent in the area. He said they were "generally intelligent, and are greatly elated at the idea of being made soldiers." Problems arose almost immediately when a young black man assigned to watch the baggage of some white officers was kicked by a white quartermaster from a Rhode Island regiment. For this act, General Wild personally arrested the quartermaster and had him punished.[106]

With only part of his officers appointed, Wild gathered the men and sailed from New York to New Bern, North Carolina, on May 15. Three days later, Wild was ready to begin recruiting blacks for his brigade. He worked out a system whereby he personally visited "every part of the Department."[107] After enlisting the adult males, Wild was concerned for the families they would leave behind. He gave "much time and labor to the care and provision of Negro families."[108]

Wild took a personal interest in those around who served him, either black or white. Shortly before going into North Carolina, Wild requested "a favor" from his friend Edward Wilkinson Kinsley.[109] Abraham H. Galloway, a mulatto and former spy who was Wild's "special and confidential recruiting agent," had gotten his slave mother sent from Wilmington to New Bern. Abraham wanted her sent north to safety with a Mr. Stevenson of No. 12 Arch Street, in Boston. Wild asked his friend Kinsley: "Will you get her started? Perhaps bring her with you hither, and forward her from here?" Wild was most anxious to help his agent, "who has served his country well, since the commencement of the war." Wild closed his letter by giving the woman's location in the house of "Edward Hughes, barber, at the corner of Middle and Broad Streets in New Berne."[110]

The colored women of New Bern were grateful to Wild and proud of the black regiment. They ordered a flag to be presented to the 1st NCCV. The flag was made of "blue silk, with a yellow silk fringe around the border," on which the Goddess of Liberty rested her foot on a copperhead snake. The flag carried the word *Liberty* in large letters over the sun. The flag was made in Boston, and "consecrated" by Massachusetts Governor Andrew.[111]

On July 25, 1863, the 55th Massachusetts joined Wild in North Carolina, and Capt. John Wilder's Company A, 2nd U.S. Colored Troops (USCT), was sent to him from Fort Monroe near Norfolk.[112]

By June of 1863, the recruitment process was in high gear. Former slaves in eastern North Carolina were urged to enlist in the 1st NCCV. Wild's regiments became part of the Department of North Carolina, under the jurisdiction of Major General J. G. Foster, who commanded a Federal force of approximately 9,000 men. With the main district under Foster at New Bern, troops were also stationed in the Districts of Beaufort, Albemarle, and Pamlico.[113]

Captain Josiah C. White, of the 1st NCCV, was the recruiting officer at Beaufort, North Carolina. Wild learned that there was to be a 2-day camp meeting, and he offered to send Captain White a party of "well drilled men" to march to the meeting place, where White could "hold them in attendance as long as you think proper; keeping them always together in a soldierly manner." Wild hoped to exhibit his troops, and "prove to the colored people of that vicinity that we are in earnest," and that this would encourage the blacks to enlist. Wild warned White that he must maintain order at the meeting, but "should any *violence* be attempted by hostile parties," he authorized White to "put it down at once with ball cartridges." If White was fired upon from within a dwelling, Wild gave him permission to "burn it to the ground *with all* its contents." Once the meeting was over, Wild wanted his troops sent back to New Bern. Wild also cautioned Captain White to warn his soldiers to "avoid plundering," but any fugitives who fled to the Union lines were allowed to "bring *all that they can*, especially food." If the fleeing blacks brought their families with them, they were soon to be settled in a "colony of contrabands" on Roanoke Island.[114]

In late July, Wild wrote his friend Kinsley to report that he had "much more on my hands now, than I can do well, between the military general business, the military recruiting business, the colonization scheme, and the endless appeals of the oppressed for protection." He felt the weight of responsibility: "All seem to look to me—At times when I see the weak, or the false and rotten course pursued by different provost marshals, it exasperates me so."[115]

Wild was not without a sense of humor. He jokingly wrote his friend Kinsley that he was going to try to outdo Dr. Winship: "He with both hands, can lift a dozen men—I want to show that I can with three fingers raise a whole brigade of men...."[116] He did proceed to raise a brigade, and very quickly at that.

Wild's long absences from home probably had a bearing on his relationship with his wife. As is true of all soldiers, serving one's country diminishes the time available to spend with family. His wife did seem to love him very much, and she tried to understand his lack of personal attention and his failure to write her. In the fall of 1863, after he had been accepted the task of recruiting Negro volunteers for the United States Army, Mrs. Wild wrote to her husband's friend Edward Kinsley: "I know now how hard the poor soul has been working and can excuse his long silence, for it is better for him to spend his time in working for his country than in writing to me, though I can not always persuade myself to think so."[117]

Funds for recruiting were not always forthcoming. When Major George L. Stearns accepted the position of recruiting black volunteers, he got the "run around" and was shuttled from Major General Foster at Fortress Monroe to Brigadier General Naglee at Norfolk when he attempted to get help with the recruiting. Foster was willing to help, and promised to even "subsist, arm, and clothe the recruits," but said he had no money to pay the recruiting expenses. Captain Wilder, superintendent of contrabands, reported that an order had gone out a few weeks earlier to "impress all able-bodied colored men for service in the Quartermaster's Department at Washington, and that all who could be secured had been sent forward; that many had escaped and in fright had taken to the woods, where they remained...." Wilder also said that the number of recruits could be greatly increased "by the payment of the recruiting fee." Naglee refused to give him any information "without a positive order." Wilder learned that "General Wild had used his own funds in recruiting his brigade."[118]

Roanoke Island Freedmen's Colony

After General A. E. Burnside's victories on the coast of North Carolina, many of the area slaves escaped to freedom behind Union lines. A number of them fled to the safety of Roanoke Island. After New Bern was captured in March of 1862, Vincent Colyer of New York was appointed Superintendent of the Poor in the Department of North Carolina. He was replaced by first Sergeant Thompson and then in May of 1863 by the Reverend Horace James, who was appointed to the position of Superintendent of the Blacks in North Carolina. James was ordered to establish a "colony of fugitive slaves on Roanoke Island." James planned to settle families there, educate them, and train them to be able to sustain a "free and independent community."[119] James returned to the North in June of 1863, and while he was gone, Brigadier General Wild received orders from General Foster to "take possession of, and assign to the Negroes, the unoccupied and unimproved lands of the island, laying them out in suitable lots for families." Wild complied and sent Serg. George O. Sanderson, of the 43rd Massachusetts Regiment, to make a preliminary survey and open "the first broad avenue of the new African town."[120]

The citizens of Brookline, Massachusetts, were concerned about the freed slaves on Roanoke Island. By early 1864, those freed people on Roanoke Island were in sad shape, having suffered the "ravages of the small-pox." Edward W. Kinsley, a Boston merchant and philanthropist, visited them and saw their lack of clothing, bed linen, food and shelter. Kinsley reported this information to a Brookline committee and a wagon went from house to house to collect contributions. This was repeated daily for as long as people of Brookline continued to make contributions. Items collected were then to be taken to Boston and shipped to the freed people's colony on Roanoke Island. The New England Educational Commission for Freedmen hoped to give "courage and cheer to the brave and absent husbands and friends of these distressed ones," to "remove a heavy burden from the heart of General Wild," and to "render immediate aid to his suffering Colony."[121]

This work transporting the families of freedmen to Roanoke Island was interrupted when Wild was assigned to Folly Island in Charleston Harbor, a position with which he was not happy.

V

Charleston, South Carolina, 1863

The bravest are surely those who have the clearest vision of what is before them, glory and danger, alike, and yet not withstanding go out to meet it.
—Thucydides, *Funeral Oration of Pericles*

Only recently has the struggle that raged on Morris Island in Charleston Harbor been brought to the attention of the nation. The award-winning movie *Glory* focused on the assault of the 54th Massachusetts on Battery Wagner on July 18, 1863. It depicted how the 54th Massachusetts Regiment, "despised by the South" and "distrusted by the North," overcame insurmountable odds "to join the war for freedom." The 54th met every challenge, from "racism within the ranks" to the horror of death in front of Battery Wagner.[1] The movie could not tell the full story of the fight to capture Morris Island, or describe the role of other units and other events in the struggle to capture Charleston, the "cradle of secession."

Charleston, South Carolina

One of the oldest towns in the United States, *Charles Town* was established in 1670 under the Lord Proprietors and named for the English king, Charles II. During the American Revolution, it became *Charlestown*, and was incorporated in 1783 as *Charleston*.[2] A city with a long and illustrious past, Charleston was the queen of the culture of "moonlight and magnolia," a culture perpetuated by slave labor, and all the dark aspects that went with it.

The war began in Charleston on April 12, 1861, when South Carolina troops fired upon the Federal-held Fort Sumter and forced Major Robert Anderson, the fort Commander, to surrender. In the North, the city was held responsible for all the heartache, pain and suffering that the war created. *Charleston had to be punished for starting the war—Charleston had to be captured and destroyed!*

The battles that raged in Charleston harbor during the summer of 1863 were overshadowed by the fall of Vicksburg and Lee's defeat at Gettysburg, events which occurred during the first week of July in the same year. Those events did not make the fighting on Morris Island any less fierce or the deaths any less heroic, but it is sad that those who fought and died there are seldom remembered.

The importance of Charleston to the life of the Confederacy was understood by both sides. The Confederacy could not manufacture enough materials to supply the demands of the war, and relied on the import of foreign-manufactured items. The Federal fleet attempted to prevent foreign imports by blockading Southern ports. By 1863, Charleston was one of only a few harbors still open through which the South could obtain needed supplies. New Orleans had already fallen into Union hands in the spring of 1862, and a Federal fleet attempted to blockade Confederate trade entering through the ports of Wilmington, North Carolina, and Savannah, Georgia. Yet, a number of "successful blockade runners" slipped through the Federal blockade.[3] The Federal navy was never able to completely stop the flow of cargo in and out of Charleston, and every ship that slipped past the blockade helped prolong the war.[4]

Confederate Brigadier General P. G. T. Beauregard[5] (commander of the defenses of the Carolina and Georgia coast) and city officials decided that Charleston would not fall into Yankee hands as had New Orleans. He vowed to let Charleston "be laid in ashes sooner than surrender it."[6] Although Beauregard did not believe such an event would occur in the immediate future, the capture of Charleston by the Union forces would be a severe blow to the Southern cause. Anticipating a siege, Beauregard built up the defenses around Charleston. The harbor was surrounded by a number of heavily armed forts. Fort Sumter was the primary defensive element.

The Key to Charleston

After numerous Federal attempts to capture Charleston failed, a new plan was begun in the spring of 1863. Intense military activity was directed at Charleston both from land and sea by the Federal forces. The first step was to capture Morris Island, a little three-mile strip of sand only about 2,500 yards from Fort Sumter, on the south side of Charleston Harbor. Here were two well-armed fortifications at Battery Wagner[7] (called "Fort" Wagner by Union sources), and at Battery Gregg, on the tip of the island. If Battery Wagner fell, the Federals would be able to bombard and force Fort Sumter to surrender, and Charleston could not be defended.[8]

The Federal plan was to begin with the landing of troops on Folly Island, south of Morris Island. The two batteries on Morris Island could be fired upon by heavy guns installed on Folly Island. On April 6–7, 1863, Colonel Joshua B. Howell's XVII

V. *Charleston, South Carolina, 1863*

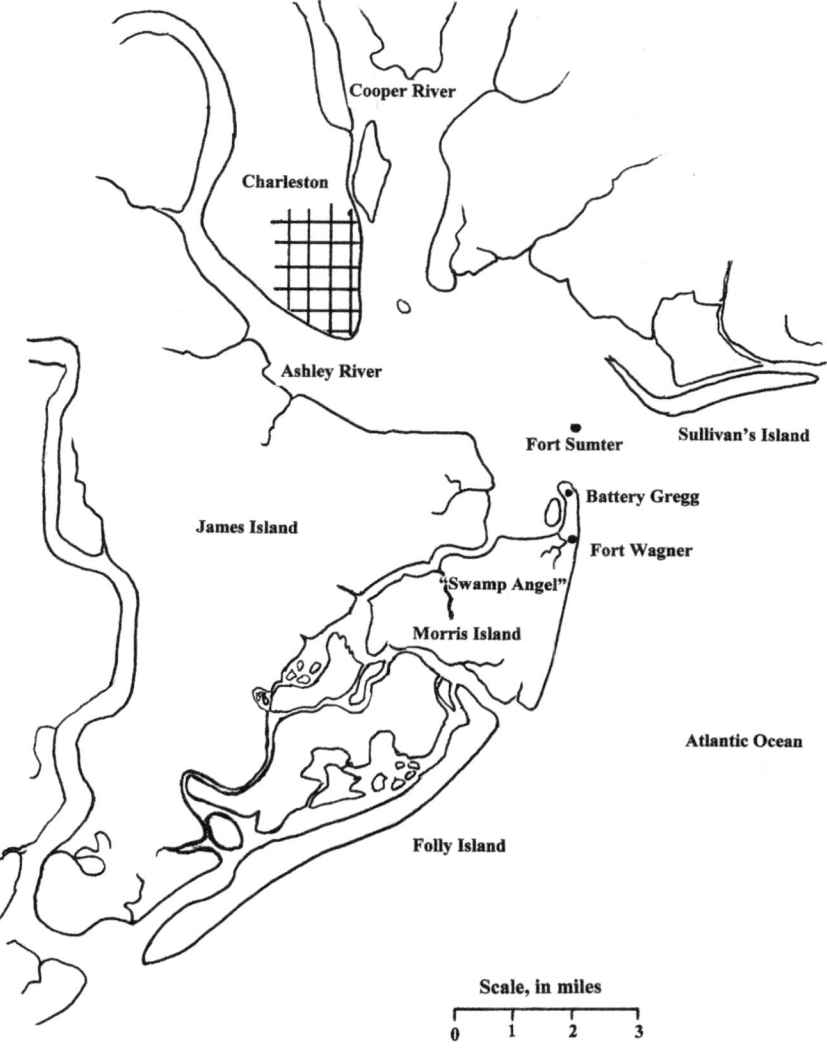

CHARLESTON & CHARLESTON HARBOR

Danny Casstevens, artist

Army Corps and part of General Alfred Terry's X Army Corps of 10,000 soldiers landed on Folly Island, and the campaign began.[9]

The Federal assault on April 7 failed against the outer defenses of Charleston by way of Folly Island and Morris Island. Major General David Hunter was replaced by Brigadier General Quincy A. Gillmore. Rear Admiral Du Pont was replaced by Rear Admiral J. A. Dahlgren.[10] Brigadier General Israel Vogdes remained on Folly Island with a brigade, and was told to stay hidden.[11]

Brigadier General Gillmore spent the first three months secretly preparing for an attack on Morris Island to be launched on July 10. Gilmore had managed, undetected, to install heavy guns and mortars on the northern end of Folly Island within ⅜ of a mile of the Confederate rifle pits on the south end of Morris Island.[12] Beauregard was taken totally unaware. He did not believe the Federal attack would come by way of Folly Island, and withdrew the Negro laborers from Morris Island to strengthen the fortifications elsewhere. Later, when it was discovered that General Vogdes was doing some work on Folly Island, Confederates built among the sandhills of the "south end of Morris island nine independent I-gun batteries" to face the 47 guns in the hidden Federal batteries on Folly Island.[13]

After Cole's Island was abandoned by Confederates in 1862, the Federals were able to occupy it and Battery Island. From there, the Federals easily occupied densely wooded Folly Island, where their operations could easily be concealed. The Federals slowly advanced to the north end of Folly Island, then to Light House Inlet, and hidden by trees and shrubbery, built formidable batteries. The attack was then launched on the southern end of Morris Island.[14]

July 18, 1863 — Federal Assault on Battery Wagner by the 54th Massachusetts

As the Federal offensive to capture Charleston continued, more troops were needed. From New Bern, Major General John G. Foster ordered Wild and his "African Brigade" to move from New Bern, North Carolina, to Charleston, South Carolina. Foster believed the colored troops would "do well and fight well under their fighting general."[15]

Wild and his men had not arrived in Charleston when one of the major Federal assaults was made against Battery Wagner. The fighting on July 18 was fierce, as the Federal troops attempted to overrun Battery Wagner, defended by the Confederate forces of the Charleston Battalion, and the 31st, 51st, and 61st Regiments of Brigadier General Thomas L. Clingman's Brigade from North Carolina.[16]

The dry portion of Morris Island was narrow, so the 54th split into two wings of two ranks, with one right behind the other. The 6th Connecticut and the 48th New York followed. A third section was made from regiments of Strong's Brigade, and following them was a brigade commanded by Colonel Haldimand S. Putnam, and behind Putnam was the brigade of Brigadier General Thomas G. Stevenson. Putnam did not think that Battery Wagner would be taken easily. He told another officer: "We are going into Wagner like a flock of sheep."[17]

The men of the 54th were told to lie down and wait. A long stretch of sandy beach lay between the advance lines of Gillmore's guns and the parapets of Battery Wagner. General Strong rode up and asked the men of the 54th if they would follow him into Fort Wagner, and every man replied "yes." It was a straightforward charge. The men had their bayonets fixed to their rifles. The charge began about 7:45 P.M., when Shaw moved to the front of the 54th and addressed his men: "Move in quick time until within a hundred yards of the fort, then double quick and charge." Then he ordered the charge with "Forward." They advanced ¾ of a mile along the sand, led by Shaw with sword in hand. The Confederate guns on Sumter, Sullivan's Island and James Island began firing on the advancing Federals. Colonel Shaw actually reached the top of a parapet and before he was shot, he yelled, "Come on, men! Follow me!"[18]

The Federals lost 246 killed and 880 wounded, and another 389 were captured or missing.[19] The 54th received the deadly fire from the Confederate defenders inside Battery Wagner. About half of the 650 men of the 54th were injured in the assault.[20] Colonel Robert G. Shaw, commander of the 54th, was killed and two field and staff officers were wounded.[21]

A Confederate gunner reported "both white and black were killed on top of our breastworks as well as inside." Colonel Shaw was buried in a trench with "45 of his men."[22] (See the video *Glory* for a vivid reenactment of these events.)

The death of Colonel Shaw undoubtedly affected Brigadier General Wild. Both of these young men had been chosen to recruit and command the first black regiments from Massachusetts. They shared similar backgrounds and worked toward common goals.

One soldier of Wild's 55th Regiment thought that they, too, should have a "chance to distinguish ourselves as well as the 54th," although the efforts of the 54th resulted in a fearful loss of life.[23]

Wild's African Brigade

General Wild was supposed to remain in North Carolina until he had raised a full brigade, but his stay was cut short by the need for more troops to take Battery Wagner in Charleston Harbor. Captain Charles Bowditch hoped that after the capture or evacuation of Charleston, the brigade would be allowed to return to North Carolina.[24]

Before leaving New Bern, Wild had a few days to drill his new brigade. Shortly after the arrival from Boston of the 55th Mass. on Sunday morning, July 26, the men set up wall tents for the officers and shelters for the men. Wild ordered a brigade drill for Sunday afternoon.[25] Additional drills were ordered on July 28 and 29 in brigade movement, and in "firing blank cartridges by file, company, wing, rank, and alternate battalions," both while advancing and retreating. The evening drills, however, seemed to affect the health of the men, and there was much sickness. By July 28, the camp had been made neat and orderly, and the men had recovered somewhat from their voyage.[26]

Wild ordered the regiment to leave New Bern in "light marching order." The men wore their "blouses" and carried their blankets. Knapsacks, stores, tents, officers' baggage, and even horses were left behind along with men too sick for duty. These were left under the care of Lt. J. T. Nichols and Commissary Sergeant Becker, under the supervision of the quartermaster. The positions left vacant by the sick were filled with new recruits destined to become members of the 2nd North Carolina Colored Volunteers (NCCV).[27] Wild left New Bern on July 30, 1863, with a brigade of 2,154 men—the 1st NCCV, a detachment of the 2nd NCCV, and the 55th Mass.[28] In addition, he had under his command one company of the 3rd NCCV.[29]

55th Massachusetts Volunteers (Colored)

The 55th, the second colored regiment raised in Massachusetts, was filled with free African Americans recruited from many states. The 55th mustered in on May 12, 1863, and when the 54th Mass. left for South Carolina, the new regiment moved into the vacated barracks at Readville. Here, they received basic trained by Colonel N. P. Hallowell and Lt. Col. A. S. Hartwell. As part of their training, the men did guard duty, patrolled the grounds, inspected barracks, went on fatigue details, and drilled in "squads, companies, and battalions." Marches over 4 to 6 miles were ordered frequently.

> No regiment left Massachusetts with a better outfit than the fifty-fifth. Few, if any, in better drill and discipline for the length of time they had under instruction; none with more faithful, intelligent, and efficient corps of officers, or men more thoroughly devoted to the cause which they had undertaken.[30]

On July 21, 1863, the 55th sailed from Boston on the steamer *Cahawba* to Morehead City, North Carolina. They had originally been ordered to march to New York, but the draft riots there made that inadvisable.[31] The *Cahawba* arrived at Morehead City on July 25. After disembarking, the regiment marched along the railroad tracks to a line of "earthworks erected for the defense of the place, where arms were stacked and ranks broken to await the train from New Bern." The men were loaded on open train cars, and arrived on the south bank of the Trent River, near New Bern, between 7 and 8 P.M. They were formed into a column by company to meet Brigadier General Wild and his staff. A campground was assigned the men on the bank of the river below Fort Spinola, and they camped near the men of the 1st NCCV, who shared hot coffee and welcomed the new arrivals.[32]

Captain Charles Bowditch, of the 55th, described the camp near New Bern in a letter to his father. Setting up the camp had been hard work "especially for the officers." He and other officers had to put up the "shelter tents" for the men "almost with our own hands, besides our own tents." There were two wall tents to each company, which gave him one for himself. "We have pitched them in rather a novel but very luxurious style." Two tents were set to face each other, and "a fly" was stretched "over the interval," which provided a covered space of about 26 feet.[33] The 55th was now part of Brigadier General Edward Wild's African Brigade.[34]

1st North Carolina Colored Volunteers
(35th Regiment, United States Colored Troops)

The 1st Regiment, North Carolina Colored Volunteers, later designated the 35th Regiment, United States Colored Troops, was a regiment of infantry made up entirely of men of African descent. It was organized at New Bern, North Carolina, and Portsmouth, Virginia, on June 30, 1863.[35] In August of 1863, this regiment was combined with the 55th to form Wild's African Brigade. Unlike the men of the 55th, many of the men of the 1st NCCV were former slaves who had deserted their plantation homes and sought protection with the Union army only a few months before. Brigadier General Wild set up a camp for the freed slaves and their families on Roanoke Island. Colonel James C. Beecher trained the regiment. He also established a school for the former slaves.[36] Colonel Beecher was the son of Lyman Beecher, the Congregationalist preacher, and the brother of Henry Ward Beecher; he was a half brother to Harriet Beecher Stowe, author of *Uncle Tom's Cabin.*[37]

Lacking a chaplain, Colonel Beecher also "took over the spiritual care" of the men of his regiment. He wrote many letters to friends and family about the 1st NCCV. Early in July, Beecher noted that his "regiment is a buster," improves every day, and "such a line of battle as we form. It would make your eyes shine to see these six weeks soldiers go through dress parade."[38] The 1st NCCV carried a "beautiful banner of the Republic which had been presented [to them] by the colored ladies of New Bern...."[39]

2nd NCCV (36th Regiment, United States Colored Troops)

The 2nd NCCV was organized at Portsmouth, Virginia, in 1863. Its numeric designation was changed to the 36th United States Colored Troops on February 8, 1864.[40] This regiment was commanded by Colonel Alonzo Draper. (For more on Draper, see Chapter VIII.)

3rd NCCV (37th Regiment, United States Colored Troops)

A company of the 3rd NCCV, commanded by Captain John Wilder, joined Wild on Folly Island in August of 1863. However, this regiment was not complete until January 30, 1864. It was designated the 37th Regiment, USCT, on February 8, 1864.[41]

August 3 to October 20, 1863—Folly Island, South Carolina

Part of the 55th Massachusetts (400 men) sailed on the schooner *Recruit*. Wild and his staff boarded the steamer *George Peabody*, and both ships departed simultaneously. Six hundred men of the 55th were aboard the steamer *Maple Leaf*, which arrived on August 3 at Pawnee Landing on Folly Island. About 60 men on the *Maple Leaf* were transferred to the schooner *William A. Crocker*.[42]

Once on Folly Island, the 55th proceeded along the beach to the northern end of the island, and they set up camp on the sand. "So urgent was the call for men that heavy details for fatigue were made at once," and it was five days later before the troops of Wild's African Brigade were assigned a campsite. That camp had been vacated by the 47th New York. It was situated about 400 yards south of Light House Inlet, "in a small grove of palmetto."[43] A map of the camp of the 55th Mass. was drawn by Major Charles Fox on November 14, 1863. The original is archived by the Massachusetts Historical Society, but is reproduced in *Whom We Would Never More See*.[44]

The 1st NCCV landed on Folly Island on August 3 and set up camp directly north of the 55th. [45]

From the southern end of Folly Island, the men of the 55th Mass. marched to the north end of the island and bivouacked on the shore. The next day they received orders to establish a camp there. However, the rising tide on the night of the August 3 threatened "to float us out." The next morning, the entire battalion were ordered to do "fatigue-duty at Morris Island." On August 5, they moved to a camp in the woods near the shore.[46] Fatigue duty was work, in addition to drill, such as camp maintenance and policing.

By August 6, some of the ships carrying Wild's men had still not arrived, so General Wild and Colonel Hallowell went out on the steamer *Mary Benton* to search for the missing transport ships. They located one ship and found the men suffering from a shortage of water. On August 8, Lieutenants Gannett and Harman and their 50 men arrived. Finally, on the afternoon of August 9, Major Fox and 800 men of the 55th arrived on Folly Island.[47]

The last of Wild's men, on the schooner *Recruit*, arrived six days after the first men of the brigade had reached Folly Island.[48] The *Recruit* had been "beset by calms and light air for ten days," which delayed its arrival until August 9.[49] Wild made several trips out to sea on a tug to locate his missing men before they ran out of water.[50]

By August 9, all of Wild's African Brigade had arrived in South Carolina and were assigned to Folly Island.[51] They set up camp on the north end of Folly Island, the part closest to Morris Island. Wild and his troops were placed under the command of Brigadier General Israel Vogdes, an artillery veteran from Pennsylvania who had taught mathematics at West Point. Vogdes served in the Seminole Wars and on the western frontier. As a Major of 1st United States Artillery, he had been captured on October 9, 1861, at Santa Rosa Island off the Florida coast, and imprisoned until August of 1862. Vogdes commanded forces on Folly Island from July 19 to December 16, 1863.[52]

Wild in Trouble for Leaving Island

Almost immediately after Wild arrived on Folly Island, he and General Vogdes clashed. Wild did not report to General Vogdes as soon as he arrived, but had reported to General Gillmore instead. Vogdes felt slighted, and Captain Bowditch believed Vogdes put Wild on his "hit list." Vogdes threatened to charge Wild with being absent without leave, and further vented his rage by harassing the Brigade Adjutant with orders about reports and other trivial matters.[53]

Although all of Wild's men had not yet arrived, Vogdes assigned Wild to be the "General Officer of the Day" on August 6, and ordered Wild to report to headquarters at 9 o'clock.[54] Wild could not be found because he was on a ship trying to locate some of his men. When Wild did not report at 9 A.M., his absence was noticed by General Vogdes, and at 10:20 A.M., a request was sent to Wild that the General Commanding wanted an explanation as to why he had left the island without permission.[55] A 1:10 P.M., Vogdes demanded to know why Wild was "absent from this Island."[56] Wild was in danger of being counted "absent without leave." The next day, Wild was ordered not to leave the island "without permission from proper authority."[57]

When he returned from his quest, Wild angrily replied to Captain S. L. McHenry, Assistant Adjutant General, to explain his absence. He had been ordered by Major General Foster, Commander of the Department of North Carolina and Virginia, to bring all his men, "properly armed and equipped," to Charleston Harbor "for *temporary* service" to this Department; and that after numerous delays and accidents, caused by insufficient transportation, he had arrived "with a portion" of his command. However, the majority of his troops were still at sea, "with provisions plenty, but *a very limited supply of water*." Because of their long voyage due to headwinds, he had become very "anxious to relieve them." Wild did not believe he was obligated to report for duty until he obeyed earlier orders and had his troops landed and encamped. Fearing that he should needlessly be hindered by "existing and by new regulations," which might involve a "fatal waste of time," he purposely "abstained" from reporting for duty until he had seen his men safely on shore.[58]

Wild explained that on the day he was to have been "General Officer of the Day" he had been on a boat in the Atlantic Ocean, trying to locate the rest of his troops. When additional messages had been sent to him, he was again out at sea. Wild was aggravated because he had previously "explained the whole matter to yourself verbally," and the reason for his actions.[59]

A notation on the margin of the order in Wild's handwriting stated, "When this came I was at sea. Detail was changed."[60]

Wild was not about to be intimidated by Vogdes or anyone else, and he stated his case. He claimed he had never received any orders "to report myself in person to Gen. Vogdes," and that he was still under his "original sailing orders" from Major General Foster. He said that his absences were of the "dictates of common humanity, and of military exigency," referring to the needs of his troops on their unexpectedly long voyage. Wild did not consider that he was absent from his command, since he had left a minority of them "encamped," and under the charge of "competent commanding officers." He had done this solely to "go to the relief of a majority thereof, afloat, separated in 3 detachments, and *not* in condition to take care of themselves." As to the charge of "absent from the Island without permission," Wild declared that, since he had not reported for duty, he was not obliged to obtain special permission from General Vogdes for his movements, "so long as I was able to get the assistance of the Quartermasters for a landable object." Typically, Wild ended his letter with the statement that under "similar circumstances, I should feel it my duty, to follow the course I have done."[61]

Wild's explanation did not satisfy General Vogdes, who ordered Captain McHenry to have Wild answer several more questions. Vogdes wanted to know, in writing, if Wild had been ordered by General Gillmore to report to him on Folly Island, and he wanted the name of the quartermaster who furnished the transportation used by Wild to search for his troops, and "by whose authority was such transportation assigned for such duty under your orders."[62]

Wild did not hesitate to answer the additional questions. To Captain McHenry, he stated that the only orders he had received were "Special Orders No. 459," which made no mention of any men except "Those upon the Steamer Maple Leaf and ignored myself entirely notwithstanding that I telegraphed before landing that I was present in command." Wild was annoyed that he had to "make the statement twice before being believed." Wild mentioned that he had talked personally with General Gillmore and had learned that Gillmore "desired me to remain in the Dept. of the South for the present and directed me to act under the orders of General. I. Vogdes," and to remain in command of the "detachment" from his brigade "until further orders."[63]

Wild expressed his gratitude to Quartermaster Captain Dunston, and Captain Moore for the use of the steamers. Captain Williams, the Post Quartermaster at the north end of Folly Island, had supplied "Boats both large and small." Wild closed his letter with: "I have the honor therefore to report for duty to the Gen. Comdg U.S. Forces, Folly Island."[64]

Life on Folly Island, Summer and Fall 1863

Wild's African Brigade was dispatched with such haste that the men arrived on Folly Island with only the arms needed for field service. They had left their knapsacks, camp equipage, and baggage behind.[65] Wild tried continuously to get himself and his troops moved back to North Carolina. When Colonel Hallowell requested that he be allowed to return to get the items left behind in New Bern, General Wild at first refused because he hoped to use the excuse that his men on Folly Island were "without fit equipage" as a means to get them returned North again. However, this did not work, and upon a second request, Colonel Alfred Stedman Hartwell was authorized to return, contingent upon General Gillmore's consent.[66]

Finally, a month after the Brigade's arrival, General Gillmore sent Lieutenant Colonel Alfred S. Hartwell and another officer from the brigade to return to New

Bern, and ordered Major General Peck, commanding at New Bern, to give them a steamer to bring the baggage and other abandoned items to Charleston.[67] One wonders how the men managed during the interim. What little was left of their equipment did not arrive until September, most of it having been destroyed or stolen.

Wild criticized Lieutenant Colonel Hartwell, of the 55th Mass., who had been sent to New Bern to supervise the removal of the baggage left by Wild's men. Hartwell replied to a note from Brigadier General Wild, which censured him for neglect of duty, and said that he had personally seen that the items were collected and loaded upon railroad cars and the boat at Morehead City. He had ordered a detail of 50 men and the quartermaster to pick up whatever they could of the effects left by the men of his regiment and others in Wild's Brigade. He had tried to safeguard the property by posting three guards and a corporal from his regiment had been placed in charge of the property left at Pawnee Landing. However, Hartwell reported that although the "guard is still there, some few of our things [are] still remaining."[68]

Wild asked Hartwell to look for a "box placed on board by Capt. Drayton" for him. He described the box as being 1 foot, 7½ inches long, and 1 foot 3 inches wide, 30 inches high, and said it had contained 24 cans of "preserved meats," each weighing 2 pounds and each clearly marked with his name on a card, which might have fallen off, and the cans would only have the mark of the maker, *Underwood Co., Boston*. Wild urged him to search immediately for the missing cans of meat within his regiment and to begin his search in the officers' quarters.[69] The contents of the missing cans probably disappeared in the stomachs of the men and officers.

Disease, Illness, and Death

Without any of the comforts of home, the rigors of life on an island in Charleston Harbor took its toll on the men of Wild's African Brigade. The 55th, mostly from northern states, suffered from the heat, and disease decimated their ranks. Twelve men died during the first 7 weeks, and by the end of December, 23 had died.[70]

Captain Walter H. Wild (brother of Brigadier General Wild) described conditions on Folly Island during the summer of 1863 to his sister, Laura W. Phipps. From Wild's headquarters, Walter reported the "weather full as warm as a year ago at this time, but my duties a little easier to perform.... I have just escaped a fit of sickness, the result of exposure, fatigue, both bodily and mentally." He noted that Brigadier General Wild had not escaped the sickness, and would probably "be sicker before he gets better." The General's arm "troubles him often and his head swims constantly." Walter reported that the General insisted on treating himself "with homo [homeopathic medicine] and refused to be considered sick enough to be waited on and I hope he will weather it through, but it is a hard test for the best constitutions...." Typhoid and dysentery had taken a toll on the men. One lieutenant had just been buried and three more were "dangerously ill." Quite a few more men and officers were "unfit for duty."[71]

Walter Wild described the daytime heat as almost unbearable, and the only respite came at night with the breeze from the ocean. The camp on Folly Island necessitated "lying on the *sand*, breathing *sand*, eating and drinking *sand* and actually turning into *sand*, some of us." High winds had almost "buried our tents out of sight in the sand."[72]

Over a period of several months, the 55th Mass. lost 54 men to combat, 4 to accidents, and 112 to disease. Of the 112 who died of disease, 63 of those died in the first weeks the regiment was on Folly Island from various illnesses. Typhoid fever took the most lives, but the heavy workload, the heat, and the poor diet were contributing factors. There were few drugs or medicines available to treat the sick. Opium and alcohol were the only pain relievers. Hygiene was unknown.[73] Lieutenant Frank Heimer, an officer from the 144th New York Volunteers, whose camp was next to one of the Massachusetts regiments, reported that while on Folly Island, "very near every man in the Regiment got sick; the cause being ... that everlasting marching in Virginia in the hot summer and then being transplanted to a sandy island in South Carolina, with bad and unhealthy water to drink. Well, for about three days I was the only officer for duty, the other reporting sick...." After some of the other officers had recovered, Heimer himself was stricken and lay sick for two weeks before he recovered enough to eat.[74]

Brigadier General Vogdes, the division commander, had no love for the black soldiers. At one point, he believed that the number of men out because of sickness was too large, and insinuated that some of the men were faking illness. Dr. Burt Wilder was "indignant" at Vogdes' remarks because the doctor knew Vogdes had ordered 400 and 500 men to do duty for 4 and 5 nights in succession.[75] Exhaustion had made the men more susceptible to illness.

Those of Wild's brigade who died were buried in the brigade cemetery adjacent to the regimental campsite, which was uncovered in 1987 when the land was being cleared for new construction. Extensive excavations of the campsites and graves on Folly Island have revealed much about how the men of the 55th Mass. lived and died.[76] Since the excavation, developers have been pushing to turn the site into a housing development, and to annex the area to the city of Folly Beach.[77]

Mosquitoes were a great pest, and there was no escaping them. In addition, the men were bothered by sand fleas, ticks, and flies. Other dangers came from the sea. A Lt. Thurber brought a "Portuguese Man-of-War" on a stick into camp. When Assistant Surgeon Burt Wilder tried to examine the creature, it stung him on the hand. Immediately, there was pain up his arm and into his chest, so that he could barely breath. The excruciating pain lasted about an hour before subsiding.[78] Sharks lurked beneath the waters of the Atlantic Ocean that lapped at the beach on Folly Island. Some of the soldiers caught a crocodile that weighted 1,100 pounds, and it had already had its leg "bit off by a shark."[79]

To make matters worse, the water was "brackish and unhealthy." The water was obtained by "digging below tide-mark and curbing with barrels." The best well was made by "cutting into a sand dune and making a winding passage to the water, thus placing the water continually in the shade and protecting it from dust and dirt...."[80] (One such barrel, still in excellent condition, has been found during the excavations in recent years on Folly Island.[81])

Obtaining food was a daily problem. Generally, the soldiers subsisted on a diet of "spoiled canned meats, moldy hardtack, and coffee." Occasionally, they were given oranges and fresh vegetables, and sometimes they received food from home, such as sweet potatoes, dried apples, honey, jelly, and lemon syrup. Fish were caught from the beach, and supplemented with crabs and oysters. Later archaeological excavations have uncovered the bones of cows, pigs, turkeys and sheep that had been butchered, cooked, and eaten on the island.[82]

Daily Duties

In spite of the adverse conditions, Wild's men had duties to perform. From August 10, 1863, until the opening fire upon Fort Sumter on Sept. 5, 1863, "heavy details for both night and day fatigue were made from the regiment, amounting on the average to at least three hundred and fifty men each twenty-four hours." The work involved cutting timber, making gabions, building wharves, loading and unloading stores and ammunition, hauling heavy guns to the front, and working in the trenches on Morris Island. Most of the work was under fire.[83]

Fatigue duty, involving cleaning up the camp, repairing roads, and other routine maintenance, was ordered every day. Daily, there was work in the trenches on Morris Island, in addition to the heavy manual labor the men were ordered to perform. The regimental returns for the 55th reported "continuous fatigue duty on Morris Island," involving over 400 men each day. They were also sent to the surrounding areas of Long Island and Botany Bay Island.[84]

Colonel James C. Beecher, of the 1st NCCV, was angry when his men were ordered to "clean up the camps occupied by white troops." Beecher voiced his resentment about the treatment of his black troops as servants and their being given menial tasks:

> I have never before known such duty imposed upon any Regiment.... They have been slaves and are just learning to be men. It is a drawback that they are regarded as, and called, "d—-d niggers" by so-called "gentlemen" in the uniform of U.S. Officers, but when they are set to menial work doing for white regiments what those Regiments are entitled to do for themselves, it simply throws them back where they were before and reduces them to the position of slaves again.[85]

Captain Bowditch, of the 55th Mass., complained that his men had been ordered to "lay out camps, pitch tents, dig wells, etc. for white regiments, who have lain idle until the work was finished for them." When General Wild learned of this, he made objections to Colonel Hallowell and asked him to tell the officers in charge of the details "to disregard such orders in the future," on his authority. Bowditch agreed that this was the right thing to do, and in order to maintain the "self-respect and discipline" of black soldiers, they should not be asked to perform the "work of menials for men who are as able to do the work themselves as the blacks." The officers in charge of black troops were looked down upon. Even after Morris Island was captured, discrimination against the black troops continued. Captain Pratt, in charge of building a new fort between Battery Wagner and Battery Gregg, was treated shamefully by the engineers under him. "They obey, but at the same time do it sullenly, not liking to be placed under the command of a captain of a Negro regiment."[86]

Several days later, Wild issued an order which forbade Negro troops from digging wells and doing other menial tasks for white troops. This order was supported by General Gillmore, but Bowditch believed that it was too late, somewhat like "shutting the barn door after the horse is stolen."[87]

Daily, the Union forces slowly but surely dug their way to the very walls of the little sand and palmetto battery called Battery Wagner. Black soldiers were employed in digging a series of trenches which enabled the Federals to move closer. When the call went out, "Cover, Wagner," meaning enemy fire was coming at those in the trenches from the Confederate battery, Federal soldiers "particularly Negroes, [were seen to] fall flat on their faces, under the delusion that they were obtaining cover from mortar shells exploding over them, when ... their chances of being hit were much increased by this posture."[88]

One of the parallel trenches on the approach to Battery Wagner, about 350 yards from the fort, was opened from the beach to the marsh. Here, the black troops of the 3rd USCT dug a trench to place a "flying sap," consisting of gabions.[89] A gabion was a cylindrical basket with open ends, made of brush or metal ribbon woven on pickets used in field works.[90]

On August 30, the 3rd USCT, on "fatigue duty in the advanced trenches since the 20th instant," were finally relieved by the 54th Mass., "it being desirable to have older troops for the important and hazardous duty required in the advance of this period." The infantry officers in charge of fatigue details believed that it took "more effort to make the men work than fight under the same fire."[91]

Even though Wild's African Brigade was not actually involved in combat and the siege of Battery Wagner, they were frequently under enemy fire. Once, from Sullivan's Island, Confederates fired into the Federal camp on Folly Island and killed two men.[92]

In the heat of the Charleston summer, the men could not work "more than one-fourth of the time." A greater amount work increased the sick list. Eight hours out of 32 hours, or 8 hours on duty and 24 off, was the most effective schedule. Neither engineers nor the blacks assigned to dig on work duty "carried their arms into the trenches," but the white infantry "usually did."[93]

Brigadier General Vogdes disregarded the recommendations and worked Wild's African Brigade hard, and assigned them to details that often lasted 36 to 48 hours.

One detail was required to work for 60 hours without rations, until finally Assistant Surgeon Burt Wilder complained. The work was hard and dangerous, and frequently men were injured.[94] Dr. Wilder treated many injuries that resulted from work involving lifting heavy objects. One man nearly had his toe crushed off, another had a finger crushed. One man dislocated his arm, and another accidentally was shot in the hand.[95]

The men of the 55th were involved in heavy manual labor, hauling cannon, building gun emplacements, as well as standing guard.[96] In addition to the heavy workload, they were required to do guard duty and picket duty. The daily routine of the 55th Regiment, and other regiments of Wild's Brigade was to:

> be under arms at four A.M. and to remain until daybreak.... It was considered very unhealthy for the men to stand still or lie down in the open air before sunrise, and the regiment was frequently drilled upon the beach, by company or battalion, during this morning hour.[97]

Beecher's 1st NCCV were put to work "digging in the trenches," which permitted "no chance to drill or learn the use of their guns; it was dig, dig, and they were kept at it with no respite till December." The men needed to march and drill. When they occasionally found time to drill, it was usually at night on the beach. One news account described this scene:

> The hard white beach, the ocean waves tumbling in, dashing, moaning, continually splashing along the reach of sand; and that long line of black soldiers, their guns shining in the moonlight, the low words or command, the prompt, soldierly obedience—a regiment of slaves, but lately come out of captivity, drilling there at midnight in sight of the great land of slavery.[98]

As a result of their nocturnal drilling near the salt water of the ocean, their "second-hand guns" rusted.[99]

The officers sometimes used the night hours to teach illiterate black soldiers to read. By the time the regiment was sent to Florida in February of 1864, 300 had learned to read and write.

Dangers were not always apparent. On August 25, the Federals discovered buried wooden torpedoes loaded with explosives in front of Battery Wagner. One torpedo exploded and threw a corporal from the 3rd USCT "25 yards, and depositing him, entirely naked, with his arm resting on the plunger of another torpedo...." His body, discovered next morning, gave rise to the "absurd story that the enemy had tied him to the torpedo as a decoy."[100] Torpedoes often were easily disabled by boring a small hole through the wood, and pouring in enough water to "destroy the explosive power of the powder." Sometimes they used "sharpshooters" to explode the torpedoes by "firing at their plungers."[101] The Federal forces found more than 60 torpedoes "planted in the ground" in front of Battery Wagner, probably placed there after the heavy assault of the 54th Mass. on July 18.

The hardships of Folly Island were only slightly less than those of Morris Island. One New York trooper wrote that Folly Island "was probably the worst place in the army. If there is a worse place than these islands I don't want to see it."[102] Within the bombproof shelter of Battery Wagner on Morris Island, conditions were so bad that the Confederates were forced to rotate the defenders every five days.[103]

Under such adverse conditions, morale deteriorated. The men expressed their dissatisfaction with General Vogdes, whom they described as "the meanest man alive." Vogdes was also the "greatest coward in the Army" who kept a "whole company" guarding his headquarters, and was "afraid to go out at night."[104] Did he fear his own men? Captain Bowditch of the 55th believed Vogdes wanted revenge on Wild and his men, and that he assigned some of the 55th to do "Night work (which keeps them out from one evening till the next morning) three nights running, thus depriving them of sleep...." Bowditch thought it a rather "mean way to vent one's spite upon a man, by taking his revenge on those whom he commands."[105]

Fortunately, as the weeks passed and the weather turned cooler, the morale of the troops improved. Another improvement was a move to establish winter camp at the back of Folly Island.[106]

Occasionally, Brigadier General Wild took his turn as "General Officer of the Day." In that capacity, one hot day in August, he toured the island accompanied by his brother Walter, who served as Wild's aide-de-camp. Walter Wild wrote to his sister that late one evening, he and his brother were walking near the end of Folly Island at Stono Landing when they heard a "band of Germans playing their evening pieces before Colonel Fairchild's tent. There was only a dozen of them, but they played so artistically some old opera airs that carried me right back into the corridors of old Music Hall in Boston and into one or two salons, that they started tears once more."[107] Both Wild and his brother Walter loved music, but Walter remarked that while on Folly Island, our "constant music is the booming roar of cannon of the largest caliber and bursting shell, with now and then the variation of a dull *whang* from a tremendous mortar which makes the sand tremble beneath our feet."[108]

Brigadier General Wild was also called upon for court martial duty. On August 26, he presided over the trial of a sutler. On the court with him was Brigadier General Richard S. Foster, and Colonel Alford.[109]

Discrimination Against Black Troops

Although the black troops of the 55th Mass. and the 1st NCCV worked hard and wanted to be good soldiers, they met prejudice at every turn. They were given the "worst equipment, the worst supplies, and the worst guns in the army because many high ranking Union officers thought so little of these soldiers."[110]

They were also discriminated against in pay. By July 16, Beecher believed that his regiment "could make a fair fight" if need be, but he complained that his men only received $7 per month in pay, while the white troops received $13.[111] Black soldiers received $10 per month, less $3.00 for clothing, while white soldiers received

$13, plus an additional $3.50 for clothing.[112] When Massachusetts Governor Andrew offered to make up the difference, the men of the 55th Mass., as a matter of principle, refused his offer. Some of the men of the 55th Mass. even wrote to President Lincoln. They complained that after having been in the field for 13 months, they had received no pay and had only been offered $7 per month. The Paymaster told them that was all he was authorized to pay "Colored Troops." The men of the 55th responded (original spelling retained) that this was "not according to our enlistment," and that, consequently, "We Refused the Money ... we came to fight For Liberty justice & Equality. These are gifts we Prise more Highly than Gold For these We left our Homes our Fameleys Friends & Relatives most Dear to take as it ware our Lives in our Hands To Do Battle for God & Liberty...." They demanded their pay from the date of enlistment, or they wanted to be immediately discharged, "Having Been enlisted under False & Pretence as the Past History of the Company will Prove."[113]

Eventually, Congress did authorize equal pay for black and white soldiers to date from January 1, 1864. Retroactive to April 19, 1861, back pay was finally distributed in October of 1864.[114]

Early in the war, the abilities of black troops to perform their duties on the battlefield were still questionable, although blacks were eager, able, and willing to prove themselves in battle. Because of prejudice, discrimination, and ignorance about the capabilities of the new black regiments and the thoroughness of their military training, black troops were usually relegated to menial tasks and duties. Some of these tasks were necessary, since a lot of hard, manual labor was involved in conducting a siege operation. A detailed report from the Engineer's Office on the siege of Morris Island listed having the availability of "colored troops for work" as one of the 19 "most important items of engineer material expended on the siege works."[115] Thus, the men of Wild's African Brigade stationed on Folly Island were mainly involved in non-combat work. This was fine with the white privates, as one put it: "I did not come to war to work, but to fight."[116]

During the summer and early fall of 1863, black troops were assigned to perform various duties. How they performed those tasks was closely scrutinized. On September 10, 1863, after Battery Wagner had been taken, Major T. B. Brooks issued a circular asking for opinions about how to use colored troops for work, and how they compared with white troops. Brooks stressed the importance of the survey. He asked that the questions be answered carefully and that only honest, unbiased opinions about the performance of colored troops be given. He asked about:

1. Courage, as indicated by their behavior under fire.
2. Skill and appreciation of their duties, referring to the quality of the work performed.
3. Industry and perseverance, with reference to the quality of the work performed.
4. If a certain work were to be accomplished in the least possible time, when

enthusiasm and direct personal interest are necessary to attain the end, would whites or blacks serve best?

5. What is the difference, considering the above points, between colored troops recruited from the free States and those from the slave States?[117]

Six officers replied to Brooks' questionnaire. The conclusions were that blacks:

1. were "more docile and obedient, hence more completely under the control of his commander," and were influenced by example;
2. were less skillful, but were skilled enough for most work involved in a siege;
3. could do more work than whites, because they worked more constantly;
4. could not be hurried in their work, no matter what the emergency; and
5. those recruited from free states were superior to those recruited from slave states.[118]

Blacks had been sick less than whites (13.9 percent vs. 20.1 percent), and blacks had performed more fatigue duty than whites (56 hours vs. 41 hours). However, he also noted that white soldiers had done more grand-guard duty, which he considered "more wearing than fatigue" duty.[119] Lieutenant Talcott reported on how the work on a road to Battery Meade was done: "My infantry detail for this work were blacks. I found that they did at least one-fourth more than the whites who were with me on the preceding night."[120]

Wild's brigade got a favorable report from C. W. Foster, Assistant Adjutant General of Volunteers, in a report to Secretary of War Stanton on October 31, 1863. Foster reported that two colored regiments had been raised in Massachusetts, and that in North Carolina, one regiment "had been recruited by Brig. Gen. E. A. Wild, U.S. Volunteers." Wild's 2,000 "colored troops have already established for themselves a commendable reputation. Their conduct in camp, on the march, in siege, and in battle attests their discipline, their endurance, and their valor."[121]

A commission, headed by Robert Dale Owen, James McKay and Samuel G. Howe, was set up to review the condition of black troops. The Commission praised the black soldiers for being neat in their "care of their persons, uniforms, arms, and equipments, and in the police of their encampments." They were skilled as "cooks and providers and exhibit much resource in taking care of themselves in camp." The Commissioners reported: "These qualities will be apparent to any one who inspects the Negro regiments under Brigadier-General Wild in North Carolina...."[122]

Wild's Staff

Although a staff had been authorized by the War Department on July 28, by September 1, Wild's staff was still incomplete. He had "*no* Staff officers, commissioned as such." So, on the authority of General Gillmore, Wild detailed a number of line officers for that purpose: Captain James S. Draper, 1st NCCV, Acting Brigade Quartermaster; Captain Walter H. Wild, 2nd NCCV, aide-de-camp; and Captain Thorndike D. Hodges, 1st NCCV, Acting Assistant Inspector General. Two other officers Wild wanted for his staff were "on duty at New Bern, N.C., with the portion of the Brigade remaining there." The situation, explained Wild, existed because his brigade was "still in [the] process of formation; that our proper field is North Carolina."[123]

Looking toward the future and assignment away from Charleston and back to North Carolina, Wild continued to work to secure good officers for his African Brigade. He wrote to Sergeant George H. Willis, of Company G, 40th Mass. Volunteers, on October 1, 1863, to tell Willis of his appointment as 2nd Lieutenant in the 3rd Regiment of Wild's Brigade. The General ordered Willis to proceed to New Bern, North Carolina, where he would receive his commission. Wild advised Willis that he would not need to "procure a full dress uniform, but only a plain working suit, with shoulder straps, sword and belt, and black felt hat." A sash would not be required. Wild suggested a "suit of thin blue flannel" for warmth was recommended, and "low shoes, with cloth garters for marching." Willis was told to bring as "little baggage as possible," because "no enlisted man will be allowed to act as officer's servant." His brigade, Wild announced, would be "organized and conducted on the principle of strict temperance," and if Willis accepted the commission that acceptance was an automatic agreement to the temperance rule.[124]

October 20, 1863—Wild Is Released from Duty on Folly Island

Although Brigadier General Wild had been placed in charge of colonizing Roanoke Island with refugee Negroes, because of his extended absence from North Carolina, this job was given to another. On September 10, 1863, Major General Peck, commanding the Department of Virginia and North Carolina, placed Chaplain Horace James, who was already superintendent of blacks for the District of North Carolina, "in charge of the colonization of Roanoke Island with Negroes." Using his own discretion, James was authorized to "take possession of all unoccupied lands on the island, and lay them out and assign them ... to the families of colored soldiers, to invalids, and other blacks in the employ of the Government, giving them full possession of the same until annulled by the Government or by due process of United States law."[125]

Perhaps Wild learned of this change, because on September 22, he wrote Major General J. G. Foster to report his dissatisfaction with his position on Folly Island. Wild stated that his troops had "done good service," considering the "enormous amount of fatigue duty imposed upon them." He also said that his men had been "somewhat abused" and noted the amount of sickness and deaths that had occurred. Wild worried that his "recruiting service will be utterly spoiled by my long absence," and he pointed out that his work in the Department of North Carolina "has been going backward since my departure." Wild told Foster that he had "tried to get away, without avail." In addition, Gillmore now declared that he had no authority to send Wild to North Carolina. Wild pleaded with Foster to use his influence to have him returned to North Carolina under Foster's command. Wild seemed almost desperate when he described the Department of the South as "a trap, where nothing that enters in, can ever get out." Wild's letter was forwarded to higher authority, and on October 4, Chief of Staff Henry W. Halleck referred the matter back to General Gillmore, giving Gillmore the authority to send Wild back to North Carolina "whenever his services can be spared."[126]

Wild's Final Days on Folly Island

Wild's brigade spent the time from September 17 to October 28 on Folly Island, engaged in guard, picket and fatigue duty. The work in the hot, humid summer, the constant fatigue and guard duty, the ever-present fear of bombardment from enemy guns, and the stress of survival on Folly Island took its toll on men and officers alike. Colonel N. P. Hallowell, who still suffered from a wound he received at Antietam, was honorably discharged. He was replaced as commander of the 55th by Alfred S. Hartwell.[127]

Yet, as long as Battery Wagner was in Confederate hands, a constant vigil had to be maintained. Even after Confederates abandoned Wagner, Wild ordered Colonel Samuel M. Alford to have the troops under his command always ready to move at a moment's notice.[128]

The addition of black troops to the siege of Battery Wagner had had a positive impact on the Federal situation in the Charleston area. Within two weeks after the arrival of Wild and his troops, Brigadier General Q. A. Gillmore demanded that the Confederate commander, General P. G. T. Beauregard, evacuate both Morris Island and Fort Sumter. Gillmore's Federal troops had advanced close enough to Battery Wager that he could now threaten to "open fire on the city of Charleston" if Beauregard did not comply with his ultimatum "within four hours."[129] Ignoring Gillmore's demand, the Confederates held out on Morris Island until the night of September 6, when, under cover of darkness, the Confederates abandoned Battery Wagner.

After Battery Wagner fell, the fighting around Charleston continued. Wild and his African Brigade remained on Folly Island for some time before they returned to Norfolk, Virginia. On October 10, 1863, Wild was relieved from his duties in the Department of the South and ordered to New Bern to continue his recruitment duties and to complete the organization of the 3rd NCCV.[130] He embarked on October 21, leaving his brigade behind.[131] He reached Hilton Head Island on October 22, and was back in New Bern, North Carolina, by October 24.[132]

VI

Wild's Raid on Northeastern North Carolina and Its Results

A Wild General.
— *The New York Globe,*
March 4, 1864

Back in New Bern by the last week in October, 1863, Wild began reorganizing to continue recruitment of blacks. This was cut short when he was ordered to report at Fortress Monroe, and he arrived there on November 1.[1]

Major General J. G. Foster, commander of the Department of Virginia and North Carolina, ordered Wild to report to Brigadier General James Barnes, commander of the Norfolk and Portsmouth District from October 1863 to January 1864.[2] Wild was to assume command "of colored troops," and other units as General Barnes should designate.[3] Wild assumed command of the 1st USCT, 2nd NCCV, 10th USCT, and detachments of the 1st NCCV, 3rd NCCV and 55th Mass. Colored Volunteers.[4]

By the end of October 1863, there were 58 regiments of colored troops in the Federal army, with a total strength of 37,480.[5] With a larger number of black units, the risks associated with their command increased proportionately. Wild saw the enormity of the job he had been assigned, and knew the risks involved; but always one to welcome a challenge, Wild did not hesitate. In addition to his recruitment duties, he was responsible for the "contraband camps," to which the freed slaves flocked daily.[6] These escaped slaves sought protection from the Union forces and worked as cooks, teamsters, or body servants.[7]

On November 10,[8] Major General Butler replaced Major General Foster as commander of the Department of Virginia and North Carolina. On November 17, the 5th USCT was added to Wild's brigade, and he began a series of recruiting raids into neighboring counties to bring in contraband families. Wild sent Colonel Alonzo

Draper and 100 men of the 2nd NCCV on a raid which resulted in the capture of several guerrillas, including Major Burroughs.[9]

Wild in North Carolina

During the summer and fall of 1863, military activity in eastern North Carolina had been minimal. There had been a few raids by armed bands of Negroes and Union bushwhackers, called "Buffaloes," but these were insignificant when compared to the raid of the Federal troops led by Brigadier General Edward Wild.[10] Wild had a threefold purpose in going to North Carolina: (1) to free slaves, and send them north or settle them in the colony for freedmen on Roanoke Island; (2) to enlist those freedmen as soldiers in his brigade; and (3) to clear the area of guerrilla forces and partisan rangers. In addition, he was to administer the Oath of Allegiance to as many citizens who wanted to take advantage of the protection that the oath afforded.[11]

Wild announced boldly to the slave owners in the five northeast counties of Currituck, Pasquotank, Perquimans, Gates, and Chowan that: "All slaves are now at liberty to go where they please, or to stay. By assisting them on their way with food and transportation, you can save yourselves the necessity of visitations from the colored troops."[12]

Federal View of Confederate Guerrillas and Partisan Rangers

The North took a dim view of partisan rangers and guerrilla forces. In 1862, Columbia University professor Francis Lieber was asked to state his views on guerrilla warfare. In an essay entitled, "Guerrilla Parties Considered with Reference to the Laws and Usages of War," Lieber distinguished between guerrillas and partisan rangers. *Guerrillas* were "bands of armed men engaged in conducting irregular warfare because of their irregular origin." *Partisan rangers*, on the other hand, were organized "to injure the enemy by action separate from that of their own main army." The latter were part of a genuine army and entitled to the privileges afforded them by the laws of warfare.[13] On December 17, 1862, Lieber and three major generals were appointed to a board to propose changes in the "Rules and Articles of War," and regulations for conduct of armies in the field, as set out by the laws of war.[14]

Land Pirates

Wild was not as lenient in his views of guerrillas and partisan rangers. In the fall of 1863, there was resistance from Confederate militia and home guard forces in the counties of northeastern North Carolina. One of the goals of Wild's North

Carolina foray was to find and destroy the guerrilla camps hidden deep within the swamps, and to kill or capture those Confederates he saw operating as guerrillas.

Wild hated guerrilla warfare—war conducted by irregular troops in short, sharp engagements, sudden raids on supplies and communications, and other small-scale actions designed to harass the enemy. Wild saw the "North Carolina Defenders"—as guerrillas and partisan rangers were called—as "improper" organizations that "ought not to be recognized," although Governor Vance had authorized their officers to raise companies for State defense.[15]

Wild did not hesitate to make his views on guerrillas and partisan rangers known to the people of the coastal counties:

> All guerrillas are on a par with pirates, and are to be treated as such. The fact of their being paid by the State, and being called "Partisan Rangers," does not help the matter. Neither the Governor of the State nor Jefferson Davis can legalize such a style of warfare.[16]

He told the people of North Carolina that it would be in their best interest not to harbor guerrillas or partisan rangers, and to refuse to give them food or shelter and to report their location to the military authorities.[17]

Confederate View of Partisan Rangers and Guerrillas

Even in the southern states, there was much controversy over guerrilla warfare, such as that carried out by William Quantrell in Missouri and Kansas. The Confederate Congress, in an act passed on April 21, 1862, legalized the partisan ranger units "to [have] the same pay, rations, and quarters during their term of service, and be subject to the same regulations as other soldiers."[18] Partisan ranger units operated in Alabama, Georgia, Florida, Louisiana, Mississippi, North Carolina, South Carolina, and Virginia. North Carolina had nine known partisan ranger units.[19]

In August of 1863, the 66th Regiment of North Carolina Troops was organized at Kinston, North Carolina, from the 8th Battalion of Partisan Rangers and other ranger companies. Soldiers of the 66th were from the counties of Carteret, Duplin, Franklin, Lenoir, New Hanover, Onslow, Orange, Nash, and Wayne.[20] The 68th North Carolina was made up of 10 companies of men from the counties of Pasquotank, Camden, Hertford, Bertie, Chowan, and Gates.[21] The 68th was raised during the summer of 1863, but it was never turned over to the Confederacy, although it operated under orders of Confederate generals. James W. Hinton, of Pasquotank, Colonel of the 68th, had previously been a Lieutenant Colonel of the 8th Regiment, North Carolina Troops. The second in command, Lieutenant Colonel Edward C. Yellowly, had also served as a Major in the 8th Regiment.[22]

Wild learned firsthand about guerrillas and partisan rangers while he was in North Carolina, but that knowledge did not change his opinion of them.

Each captain is his own mustering officer; musters men into the service of North Carolina, and the men are paid, or expect pay, from the State only. Governor Vance supplied them with excellent arms (new Enfields) and ammunition. There appears to be some person acting as commissary near each company, to keep a small stock of provisions in camp; but the bands do not scruple to live on the inhabitants, individually and collectively. The captain is allowed to encamp where he pleases, and to operate when and where he sees fit, his proceedings being as independent, arbitrary, and irresponsible as those of any chief of bandits. The men have never been obliged to report to anybody except the captain. The captain only must go at stated intervals to Murfreesborough or to Raleigh, probably to vouch for the pay.[23]

Background Precipitating Wild's Raid

As a prelude to Wild's raid in 1863, Colonel Charles C. Dodge, of the 1st New York Mounted Rifles, on a foray into eastern North Carolina in May of 1862, found the people at Hertford "very bitter in opposition" to the Confederate Government. At Edenton, Dodge was "kindly received by the people," who fed his men and entertained the officers. He found strong Union sentiment in the area. In the Dismal Swamp area, sentiments were "much divided," but the people feared persecution and retribution from the Confederate government, and did not express Union support. A large number of local men had left to join the Confederate Army. Dodge learned from an escaped slave that his former master was "mustering in recruits" to be sent to the Confederate Army. Acting on this information, Dodge marched to Sunbury and surrounded the house of the Confederate recruiter. He "roused him from his bed" and forced him to mount his horse and accompany the Union soldiers. Dodge learned from him the names of the officers in his regiment. With 20 handpicked men, and guided by his Confederate prisoner, Dodge surprised the Confederate officers in their beds. He captured a colonel, a captain, and four lieutenants, and he took them to Union headquarters in Norfolk.[24]

The Great Dismal Swamp—Hiding Place for Guerrilla Forces and Others

The Great Dismal Swamp of northeastern North Carolina and southeastern Virginia extends nearly 30 miles from north to south across the state line. The swamp may have covered as much as 2,200 square miles, but has been reduced by drainage to 750 square miles. The area is a mixture of waterways, swamps and marshes, inhabited by the black bear, white-tailed deer, opossum, and raccoons, and cottonmouth water moccasins. Even alligators roamed the murky waters in times past.[25]

In addition to serving as a wildlife refuge, the Dismal Swamp was a hideout for anyone running from the law. The swamp often echoed with the sound of bloodhounds and shotgun blasts as outlaws, runaway slaves, and deserters were tracked by slave owners, soldiers, or bounty hunters. Harriet Beecher Stowe's *Dred, a Tale of the Great Dismal Swamp,* is based on stories of runaway slaves who hid out in the swamp. Confederate soldiers sought deserters from their ranks there, and Wild and other Union troops hunted down Confederate guerrillas.

Stories abounded of the dangers in the swamp, both real and imaginary, from ghosts to savages. Parents warned their children of the natural dangers from poisonous plants, deadly snakes, hungry alligators, or quicksand.[26]

In 1728, while surveying the boundary line between North Carolina and Virginia, William Byrd II described the Dismal Swamp as a "vast wasteland" and believed it should be drained and used for agriculture.[27] It was:

> a mere quagmire, trembling under the feet of those that walk upon it ... towards the heart of this horrible desert, no beast or bird approaches, nor so much as an insect or reptile.... Nor indeed do any birds fly over it ... for fear of the noisome exhalations that rise from this vast body of dirt and nastiness.... With all these disadvantages the Dismal is in many places pleasant to the eye, though disagreeable to the other senses, because of the perpetual verdure, which makes every season look like spring, and every month like May.[28]

David Hunter Strother, under the pseudonym "Porte Crayon," described the swamp in *Harper's Magazine* in 1856—how "Lofty trees threw their arching limbs over the canal, clothed to their tops with gauze-like drapery of vines, walls of matted reeds closed up the view on either side, while thickets of myrtle, green briar, bay and juniper hung over the black narrow canal until the boat could scarcely find a passage between...." He wrote of the dense undergrowth, which could be seen surrounding "pools of black, slimy water, from which rose the broad-based cypress, and grouped around, those strange, contorted roots, called knees, knarled and knotted like stalagmites in a cave."[29]

Federals Act to Protect the Dismal Swamp Canal

Beginning in 1793, slaves toiled 12 years to complete the Dismal Swamp Canal, a 22-mile waterway. By 1805, flat-bottom boats using the canal were charged a toll to help defray the continued cost of construction and maintenance.[30] The canal ran south 16 miles from Norfolk on the east bank of the Elizabeth River, and ended at South Mills on the Pasquotank River in North Carolina.[31] The canal allowed passage of "steamers and light-draught vessels" from Norfolk to Elizabeth City and into the Albemarle Sound.[32] A second canal, started in 1855 by the Albemarle and Chesapeake Canal Company, was completed in 1858–1859, just before the war.[33]

In March of 1862, Confederates erected batteries and dug entrenchments to protect the end of Dismal Swamp Canal near South Mills in Camden County. General Burnside learned that the Confederates were building ironclads and intended

Butler Takes Command

In the fall of 1863, Union General J. G. Foster, in charge of the Federal forces in Eastern North Carolina, was replaced by General Benjamin F. Butler. That change was not favored by some. General Robert Schenck commented that Butler could do "the most atrocious things—steal or murder—and be let alone."[35]

When Wild returned from Charleston, he was sent to serve under Major General Butler. Butler found Wild to be a man "with spirit and ideals much like his own." Butler had gained an unsavory reputation for his harsh treatment of civilians while in command of New Orleans, but Wild, a devout abolitionist with a number of personal eccentricities, would soon make Butler appear mild in comparison.[36]

Wild Moves to Eradicate Guerrillas

As part of the Federal plan to eradicate the guerrilla forces, Wild sent Colonel Alonzo G. Draper, along with the 6th USCT, in late November of 1863 on a raid through Princess Anne County, Virginia. Wild gave Draper the authority to capture and disperse bands of guerrillas, and told him that if "fired upon you will at once hang the man who fired." If the shots came from a house, "burn the house immediately. In case of a hanging, you will label the body according to the nature of the case, as 'Assassin's' 'Guerrillas' &c."[37]

Wild decreed that guerrillas were "not to be taken alive." He told Draper if he should find firearms "in any house," he was to "bring the owner in as prisoner."[38] This raid was very successful, according to an article that appeared in the New York *Times,* and its success encouraged Butler to authorize a similar raid into North Carolina, to be headed by Brigadier General Wild himself. Draper did succeed in enlisting of a large number of recruits. He freed from bondage hundreds of slaves, and captured a guerrilla chief. The results encouraged General Wild, "with the approbation of Maj.-Gen. Butler, to plan a raid of a similar character, but on a much more extensive scale, beyond our lines into North Carolina."[39]

The captured guerrilla chief was subsequently tried, and Colonel Draper was required to be in attendance during the trial. Thus, he was late in joining Wild in North Carolina[40] on what is known as "Wild's Raid."

Wild's Raid into Northeastern North Carolina

Once commander of the Department of North Carolina, Butler wasted no time in sending Brigadier General Wild and his brigade of Negro troops to northeastern

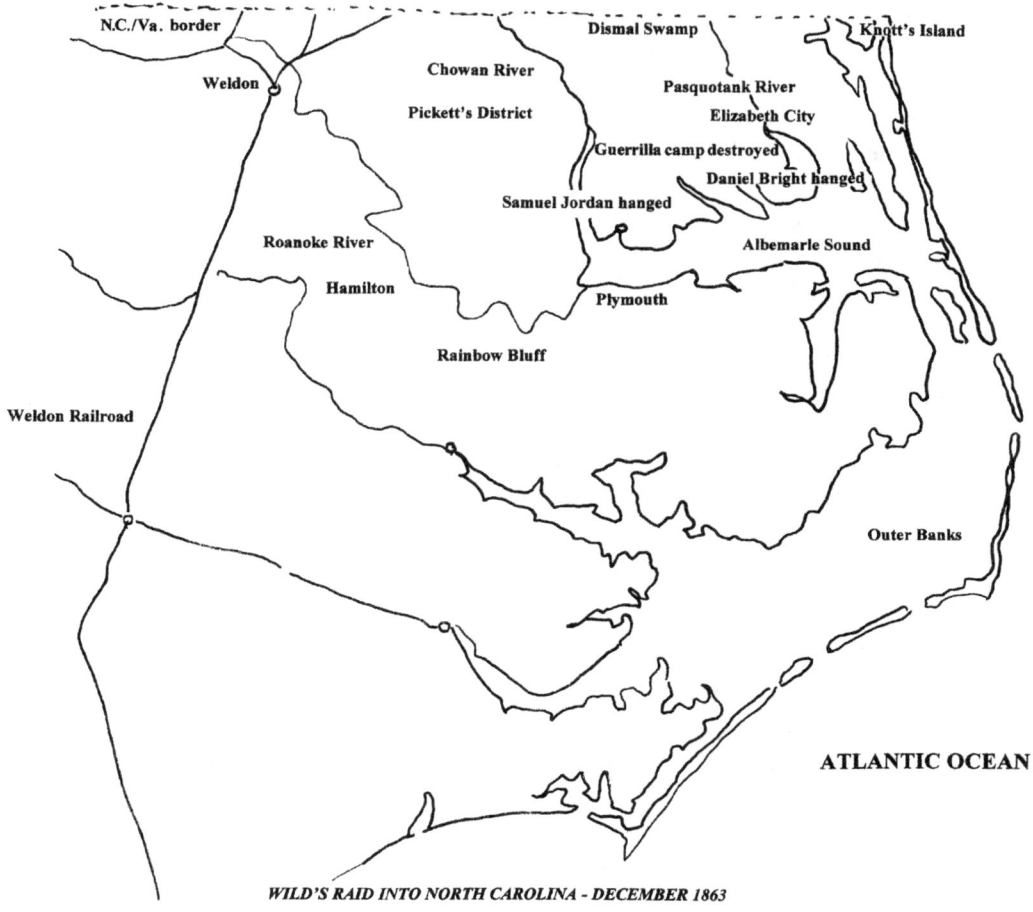

WILD'S RAID INTO NORTH CAROLINA - DECEMBER 1863

Danny Casstevens, artist

North Carolina. Butler had become an embarrassment to the government by his actions in New Orleans the previous year. He had been "stored away" at Fortress Monroe, and "troops and supplies" were withheld from him to make sure that he stayed "shelved." When Butler requested more troops, the War Department sent him more brigadier generals. Butler was not to be outdone, so he attempted to solve his manpower problem by recruiting and training black troops, "for whose capabilities and potentials" he had great respect. Thus, Wild was the means Butler used to free slaves and enlist them into the Union Army.

Because navigation on the Dismal Swamp canal had been interrupted, and Union sympathizers in the area were being plundered and harassed by guerrillas forces, Butler felt justified in sending Brigadier General Wild to North Carolina with a force large enough to remedy the matter.[41] Wild's orders were to clear out bands of Confederate guerrillas operating in the Dismal Swamp area, free any slaves he found there, and recruit able-bodied black males for his regiments from among those freed slaves. With that sort of "license," Wild was free to give the people of the northeastern corner of the state a taste of what Georgia would experience in 1864 under General William Tecumseh Sherman.[42] As a "Yankee abolitionist," Wild was "only slightly less zealous in this respect than old John Brown." Wild hated slave owners and was bitter over the loss of his arm at South Mountain.[43]

Wild's force consisted of about 2,000 men—700 men from the 1st Regiment USCT, commanded by Colonel John H. Holman; 400 men from the 2nd NCCV, commanded by Colonel Alonzo G. Draper; and 530 men from the 5th Regiment USCT, commanded by Colonel James W. Conine. There were also another 100 men from "detached units" of the 1st NCCV, and a detachment from the 55th Regiment Massachusetts Infantry.[44] (Some sources do not mention any involvement of the 55th Massachusetts in Wild's Raid into North Carolina during December of 1863.[45])

Just before starting on the raid into North Carolina, Brigadier General Wild and his brother, Captain Walter H. Wild, requested permission for a short leave of absence. Together, they traveled to Philadelphia on November 24 to visit their sister Susan.[46]

December 5, 1863—Wild's North Carolina Raid Begins

When Wild's black troops first arrived in Virginia, they were assigned to Fort Monroe, Yorktown, Norfolk and Portsmouth.[47] From these points, Brigadier General Wild began his trek to free slaves, and to inflict "damage upon the enemy" along the coast of North Carolina[48] (see Appendix, Table I). Wild's troops began their march at daylight on December 5, and they left so secretly that only one representative of the press was aware of their movement. The expedition was reported eventually in Northern newspapers by a reporter, "Tewksbury," who accompanied the expedition. A detailed account of Wild's Raid appeared in the New York *Times*.[49]

Wild's destination was Elizabeth City, North Carolina, 50 miles from his headquarters in Norfolk, Virginia. He and his men traveled southward along the road which ran beside the Dismal Swamp Canal.[50] Elizabeth City had been occupied in 1862 by Federal forces, when according to tradition, the "sheriff and many citizens set fire to their own houses at the approach of the Federal fleet, and the brick courthouse also was burned."[51]

Because roads were few, it was difficult to go from Virginia to eastern North Carolina without using the Dismal Swamp Canal or the toll road beside it. A stagecoach traveled along this road between Norfolk and Elizabeth City.[52]

Wild's men moved in two columns. Wild, leading the first column of about 400 men of the 1st USCT and 400 from the 2nd NCCV, left Portsmouth by way of Deep Creek and the Dismal Swamp Canal. They camped the first night at Deep Creek, nine miles south of Portsmouth. Then they followed the towpath along the Dismal Swamp Canal, which began at the mouth of Deep Creek, and marched 18 miles the next day. The men camped that night on the Ferebee Farm, and remained there until the middle of the following day while they awaited the boats which were to bring rations and forage. However, the boats did not arrive, but General Wild was still "determined to advance, trusting to Providence and the country for the subsistence of his men."[53] He sent word back to have the supply boats meet him in Elizabeth City.[54] The supply boats had taken a wrong turn, so the troops were forced to begin immediately "living off the country." The troops devoured everything in sight, like the Biblical "cloud of locusts."[55]

The second column left from a camp northeast of Norfolk and moved by way of Kempsville, Great Bridge, and Northwest Landing to South Mills. This column consisted of 530 men from the 5th USCT, 100 from the 1st NCCV, and a detachment from the 55th Massachusetts.[56]

Resistance Within the Ranks

On this raid, Wild met resistance from some unexpected quarters. When the plan to free slaves to get new recruits became known, it was almost sabotaged by Union cavalry outriders of Colonel John Ward's 8th Connecticut Regiment. The cavalry was sent in advance of Wild's black soldiers to warn the population that the "nigger-stealers were coming to plunder them of everything."[57] Historian Richard Reid describes this action against Wild: "It was not the first time, nor would it be the last, that the General's attempts to raise and lead black troops were hamstrung by racist white soldiers prejudiced against blacks in general, and against any white officer who would consider leading them."[58]

The success of any raid depended upon "the secrecy with which it is undertaken and the rapidity with which it is executed—a dash into the enemy's country, rest nowhere, and a hasty return."[59] However, someone learned about this raid and had enough authority to attempt to negate one of Wild's main objectives.

Brigadier General George Washington Getty commanded forces at Norfolk and Portsmouth, Virginia, from July 1863 until January 1864.[60] Wild knew that he would be freeing slave families, so before he left Norfolk he relayed to Brigadier General Getty the orders issued by Butler that "all colored men, women, and children coming into our lines from the enemy's country are to be welcomed by our forces wherever met, and are to be assisted on their way as much as possible." Wild knew there would be many slave families coming in, and he promised to punish severely any who attempted to "obstruct" them in any way.[61]

Brigadier General Getty had the authority to command Colonel John Ward's 8th Connecticut Cavalry regiment. On December 4, when Wild complained to Major R. S. Davis, Assistant Adjutant General of the XVIII Army Corps, about Ward's interference, Davis forwarded to headquarters both Wild's letter to Brigadier General Getty and Getty's reply. The Commanding General "considered the tone" of Wild's letter "very improper."[62]

On December 12, 1863, from Elizabeth City, Wild wrote to General Barnes that when he returned he had some "serious complaints to make against Colonel Ward, of Brigadier General G. W. Getty's Command, for his attempting to defeat the objects of our expedition." Wild charged that Colonel Ward had tried to thwart his expedition by sending out a force of U.S. Cavalry to give advance warning to the inhabitants of coastal North Carolina.[63] Getty replied to Wild's complaint, but stated that he had "no knowledge of the expedition referred to in your communication."[64] Was Getty lying to cover his own involvement, or the involvement of his subordinate, Colonel John Ward, or was he carrying out the wishes of a superior officer, someone other than Major General Butler?

Butler did everything he possibly could to prevent trouble involving the black troops. On the day Wild began his march into North Carolina, Butler issued General Order No. 46, which specified how colored troops were to be treated. Butler declared: "The recruitment of colored troops has become the settled purpose of the Government." Butler proclaimed it was the "duty of every officer and soldier to aid in carrying out that purpose ... irrespective of personal predilection." Assistance was necessary, Butler told the men, because of the new rights acquired by the colored soldiers, and the "new obligations imposed upon them, the duty of the Government to them, the great stake they have in the war, and the claims their ignorance and the helplessness of their women and children make upon each of us who hold a higher grade in social and political life...."[65]

Butler reminded his white soldiers that the colored soldiers did not have access to "'State aid' for the support of their families while fighting our battles ... nor the generous bounties given by the State and National Governments in the loyal States," but an even greater reward awaited them—"freedom for himself and his race forever!"[66] Butler listed 16 items which defined the rights and benefits of black soldiers in the United States army. Paragraph XV noted the judicial process for offenses committed by black soldiers or against black soldiers by others:

> Court-martial and courts of inquiry in relation to all offenses committed by or against any of the colored troops, or any person in the service of the United States connected with the care, or serving with the colored troops, shall have a majority of its members composed of officers in command of colored troops, when such can be detailed without manifest injury to the service.

All offenses by citizens against the Negroes, or by the Negroes against citizens—except of a high and aggravated nature—shall be heard and tried before the provost court.[67]

Brigadier General Wild was to have occasion to use Paragraph XV when he was brought up before a court martial. He would use the first part in his own defense, and he used the second part when he tried Confederate soldier-guerilla Daniel Bright in a "drum-head court martial," found him guilty, and then hanged him.

December 11, 1863—Wild Occupies Elizabeth City

When Wild approached Elizabeth City, he found that the bridge over the Pasquotank River had been burned by guerrilla forces. Although he saw "nothing of it remaining visible but the charred tops of the piles," that did not stop him. When he learned a nearby house and barn belonged to a member of a guerrilla band, Wild took matters in hand and "killed two birds with one stone." He adopted a novel means by which to restore the bridge and punish the guerrilla at the same time. "A thousand men were put to work in demolishing the house and barn. Suitable portions of the timber were selected ... and in six hours the whole force had moved across the new bridge and on to Elizabeth City."[68]

Wild and his men had encountered trouble from the start of the expedition. Initially, he met with little military resistance, and he captured Elizabeth City with only two of his men wounded. One of his men was captured by guerrillas.[69] (The captured soldier may have been Private Samuel Jordan, later hanged by Confederates.)

The gunboat transporting their "forage" developed engine trouble, and the cylinder exploded. Those supplies finally did arrive on another steamer. In anticipation of further trouble, Wild sent a request to General Graham to send a replacement boat.[70]

Wild then learned that his naval support would not arrive. The steamer *Frazier* brought the news that the gunboat *North State*, "which had been sent from Old Point with orders to report to Gen. Wild, had burst her steam-pipe and was lying disabled in Currituck Sound." The failure of the gunboat to arrive could seriously hamper the "success of the expedition, which contemplated cooperation by water." There was also a chance that a "formidable rebel force might be sent hither from the Blackwater [in Virginia]," and it would be impossible for Wild "to retreat or to hold the city for any length of time without the aid of a gunboat." Since it would take over a week to get another gunboat from Fort Monroe, General Wild sent for help from Captain Flusser, who commanded the naval force at Plymouth.[71]

Wild set up headquarters in Elizabeth City. The people of the town believed that "Beelzebub himself had taken up residence."[72] The sight of armed blacks frightened the citizens more than anything they had ever seen. Ironically, historians believe the town of Elizabeth City and the county of Pasquotank suffered "more spoliation from roving bands of buffaloes and guerrillas than from the Yankees." Many of the homes that existed in the 1860s can be seen today, such as the Judge Small house, built in 1800, the Fearing home, the Charles home, and the Beveridge house.[73]

Wild worked from his headquarters and sent details out into the surrounding countryside. He was "besieged from daylight until dark by persons desiring passes to and from the country, to reclaim horses and carts taken for the removal of the effects of the slaves, to have guards stationed at their houses, to take the oath of allegiance." Instead of delegating work to his staff, the General did "nearly all the writing himself." No detail, however trivial, escaped his notice, and he personally superintended everything.[74]

Wild sent his men through Currituck and Camden counties to engage in a number of minor skirmishes with "land pirates," as Wild termed Confederate partisan rangers, and guerrilla forces.[75] He did not differentiate between the two groups, nor did he confine his activities to military targets or military personnel, but brought war to the civilian population. Wild saw those units as "virtually bandits, armed and hired by Governor Vance," and believed all they could do was "harass us by stealing, murdering, and burning; by stopping Negroes from reaching us, and by driving them over the lines, and harass their own State by plundering, terrifying, and even murdering Union citizens." Wild knew there had been attempts to combine the various units of infantry operating between "Hertford and the Atlantic" and that there was also quite a large mounted force around Gatesville. A new unit, the 66th Regiment, North Carolina State Troops, had a force of about 300 to 450, and one field piece. They were camped about 3½ miles out of Hertford.[76]

Wild planned to destroy the Confederate camp near the village of Hertford, but had to change his plans because of a lack of transportation "over the various waterways encountered."[77] Eventually, he did succeed in destroying several of the guerrilla camps in the swamp.

December 12, 1863 — Foray to Hertford, Perquimans County

On December 12, Colonel Holman and his men were sent on a foray to Hertford, about 15 miles southwest of Elizabeth City. The troops had difficulty reaching their destination because Confederate guerrillas burned the bridges across the Little and Perquimans rivers. Holman tried to find the camp of Captain John T. Elliott, of Company A, of the 68th North Carolina Volunteers.[78] Holman followed the "Sandy Cross" Road for six miles toward Hertford, then sent his men into the swamp. There, they burned a Confederate camp, which consisted of two large buildings that housed forage and provisions. In the same neighborhood, they burned several houses and barns and returned to Elizabeth City with one "guerrilla as prisoner."[79]

December 11 (or 12), 1863 — Mrs. Wright's Dairy, Camden County

Camden County, between Currituck and Pasquotank counties, was the scene of much discord and fighting between the Home Guard and the "Buffaloes," who were the Union sympathizers. Friends and neighbors fought against each other and became "bitter enemies." There were skirmishes, raids, ambushes, as well as outright murder and other forms of violence in the county.[80]

Mrs. Catherine Edmondston recorded in her diary the details of the "outrages committed about the 11th of the month" (or December 12?) in Camden County by Wild's men:

> they went to the house of a Mrs. Wright & entering her dairy against her will drank all her milk. That night two of the wretches [Wild's soldiers] were taken violently ill & died, when they returned to the house & accusing Mrs. W. of having poisoned the milk seized, *tied* & threw her in a cart & sent her to Norfolk for trial. In vain she protested that she was innocent, that the Negroes (for the band was composed of them under white officers) had been eating fish, oysters, & every thing else that the country afforded & then drinking quantities of milk it produced its usual effect in inducing cholera morbus. They would listen to no reason, but sent her as she was to Butler's tender mercies.[81]

Was this "Mrs. Wright" an unaccounted-for prisoner taken by Wild's men? If so, what happened to her? She is probably the wife of William T. Wright, mentioned in the "Tewksbury" report, whose house Holman reportedly burned on December 12. Was her arrest only rumor or Confederate propaganda?

Mrs. Munden Taken Hostage

The first documented female hostage taken by Wild's men was Phoebe Munden, about 35 years old, wife of Lieutenant William J. Munden, an officer in Company 1, 68th North Carolina Regiment.[82] Lieutenant Munden later testified that he was at his home about five miles from Elizabeth City on the day his wife, Phoebe, was arrested and taken to Elizabeth City.[83] Munden swore that Wild and his troops had burned his house and its contents, "stables, crop, and nearly everything on the premises." Munden testified that Wild's men also burned the house of William T. Wright, a commissary to Company E. "They also burnt a barn of corn, wheat, and other things belonging to Ed. Jennings, a citizen not connected with any military organization." He stated that he had heard that an additional six or seven houses in Camden County were burned.[84]

On December 12, Mrs. Munden was taken from her home and forced to leave her three children, the oldest only ten, without parental supervision. She was taken to Elizabeth City, where she was placed in a room "without fire, bed, or bedding, with several male prisoners, and tied by the feet and hands." What was even worse in the minds of Southerners was that "a Negro guard was placed in charge" of Mrs. Munden and the other prisoners.[85] Her imprisonment was described in several accounts, and verified by the Special Committee of the Confederate Congress, in several depositions, when the Committee collected evidence about the hostages and their treatment.

Confederate "Guerrilla" Captured and Mrs. Weeks Taken Hostage

On Sunday, December 13, Colonel John Holman took another female hostage, Mrs. Elizabeth Weeks, and captured Daniel Bright, believed to be a Confederate guerrilla.[86]

Mrs. Weeks, the wife of Private Pender Weeks, was confined in a room with Mrs. Munden at Elizabeth City. Mrs. Munden's home had been burned, and she had no clothing except what she wore. The ladies were confined in a room until Thursday, December 17, before they began the trip to Norfolk, Virginia. Mrs. Munden's husband was told that her wrists were bleeding from "the stricture of the cords with which she was bound."[87] The ladies were held as hostages, under constant guard, to assure the safety and good treatment of the colored soldier being held by Captain Elliott. Wild vowed that he would treat the ladies the same way his Negro soldier held captive by Confederates was treated, "even to hanging."

Mrs. Catherine Edmondston was especially upset by the taking of female hostages.

> A detachment of men under Lieut. Munden having taken some of the Negroes prisoner, they went to his house &, without warning of any sort seized Mrs. Munden, tied her, & took her to the Elizabeth City jail where she was confined in a cell with two black sentinels constantly in her room for some days, they sending him word that whatever was done to the Negro prisoners would instantly be visited in like manner on her. My God, is it not horrible! Can such things be?[88]

Confederate Colonel Joel R. Griffin also reported that Mrs. Munden had been arrested, "tied, and placed in jail at Elizabeth City." A few days later, both she and Mrs. Weeks were taken in irons to Norfolk with their "feet tied."[89] Both ladies were "compelled to sleep on the naked floor without bed or bedclothes or other covering, and without fire." Dr. W. G. Pool finally convinced the Federal guards to let the ladies have some blankets.[90] Since it was mid–December, blankets and heat were needed for comfort.

The citizens of Camden County saw Wild's actions as "extreme measures," because of his holding hostage the wives of suspected home guardsmen.[91] Wild claimed that these hostages were taken to guarantee the safety of his captured soldier, Private Samuel Jordan.[92]

December 17, 1863 — Court Martial of Prisoners

On Thursday, December 17, Wild assembled a "drum-head court" to try his captives. Wild's soldiers had captured 20 men suspected of being guerrillas. They were placed in irons and put on trial before Wild left Elizabeth City. Nine were found innocent; eight were convicted and sent to Norfolk.[93] One of them, Daniel Bright, who Wild believed was a "guerrilla," was convicted and sentenced to death by hanging.[94] Wild then sent a note to Confederate Captain Elliott to assure good treatment of the colored soldier being held by Elliott. He urged Elliott to "renounce" his present course as the leader of guerrilla forces, "or join the regular Confederate Army."[95]

December 18, 1863—Hanging of Confederate Guerrilla/Soldier Daniel Bright

On a very cold morning with drenching rain, Wild and his 1,300 men marched toward South Mills and stopped at "Hinton's Crossroads" to hang his condemned prisoner, Daniel Bright. The hanging was attended by Wild's officers and a crowd of colored soldiers. The other prisoners, including the two ladies, were forced to watch Bright's execution. Spiritual guidance was offered the condemned man by Lieutenant Colonel Giles W. Shurtleff,[96] a graduate of the seminary at Oberlin College. The hastily made gallows malfunctioned, and when Wild kicked the barrel out from under Bright, his neck was not broken and he did not die instantly. Instead, Bright hung there and strangled for nearly "twenty minutes" before he died. Wild ordered a placard attached to the body.[97] A New York newspaper reported the gruesome details:

> About noon, the sun coming out, a halt was ordered. The General and his staff rode toward to a small unfinished building designed for a post-office, standing upon a knoll at a crossroads. Sufficient boards and laths were knocked off to afford an unobstructed view of the proceedings from two sides, when one of the officers, producing a cord, tied a hangman's knot at one end of it and, standing upon the head of an empty cider-barrel, made the other fast to one of the joists overhead. After considerable experimenting, the barrel was made to serve for both the scaffold and the drop, being ingeniously balanced upon one of the floor-timbers, and held in place by a wedge which could be instantly removed. From this to one of the windows a board was laid, and thence another to the ground outside, forming an inclined plane. Meanwhile most of the officers had ridden forward and tied their horses to the fence of an adjacent farm-house, whose inmates had closed all the window-blinds, and a crowd of colored soldiers encircled the building, watching in silence these ominous proceedings. Lieut. -Col. Shurtleff, of the Fifth United States, was appointed spiritual adviser to the criminal, and went back with a guard to bring him to the place of execution. When informed that he had but a few minutes to die, and was counseled to improve this time in making his peace with God, he dropped to his knees in the road and prayed: "O, merciful Father, look down upon me! O, merciful Father, look down upon me!" These words alone he repeated a hundred times, until the acting Chaplain stopped him. He then rose to his feet, walked up the inclined board with a firm step, at the point of the bayonets the colored guard, advanced quickly to the head of the cider barrel, and stood under the noose. This being placed around his neck, Col. Shurtleff involved the throne of grace in behalf of the guilty wretch. As the word "Amen" dropped from his lips, the General, who

had taken charge of the drop, pulled the wedge—the barrel tipped, the guerrilla dropped. He was a man of about thirty, a rough stout fellow, was dressed in butternut homespun, and looked the very ideal of a guerrilla. He died of strangulation, his heart not ceasing to beat for twenty minutes. Then a slip of paper was pinned to his back, on which the General had previously written, "This guerrilla hanged by order of Brig.-Gen. Wild, Daniel Bright, of Pasquotank County." And the body was left hanging there, a warning to all passing bushwhackers.[98]

The Confederate Congress appointed a special committee to inquire into matter. The Special Committee reported that a large force, under Brigadier General Wild, had invaded Pasquotank County, and arrested a citizen of the county at his own residence, and hanged him on the side of the public road. The Committee also noted the wording on the placard placed on the body, which was left hanging.[99]

The committee reported that Daniel Bright, the man hanged by Wild, was a member of the 62nd Georgia Regiment, commanded by Colonel J. R. Griffin, and that Bright had authority from the Governor of North Carolina "to raise a company in that county for local defense." Bright, however, failed in his efforts, and he "retired to his farm, and was there seized, carried off, and executed."[100]

December 18, 1863—Skirmish at Indiantown/Sandy Swamp

A 200-man detachment of Wild's men, from the 5th Regiment USCT commanded by Captain George B. Cock, was involved in a skirmish on December 18 at Sandy Swamp near Indiantown. About 11 A.M., while the men were marching, Lieutenant Bennet reported that he thought the enemy was nearby. The detachment was halted, and the vanguard moved forward to reconnoiter. From about 400 yards away, a volley was fired at the Federal troops from a dense pine thicket. Two men were killed instantly, one mortally wounded, and another severely wounded. Cock ordered his men to "lie down and fire on the enemy from behind the fence," which they did, and thus they escaped being injured by a second volley of shot. After a few more minutes, both sides were rapidly firing. The Captain sent out two companies, one to the right and one to the left, to flank the enemy. The remaining men were to launch a frontal attack. Cock and his men moved by the road to a point in front of the thicket from where the firing had come. He gave the order to "fix bayonets," and then moved by the right flank into the piney woods. The enemy had already fled, so Cock and his men returned to their original position, and picked up their dead and wounded. In Company G, 5th Regiment USCT, Privates Richard H. Fox and Jeremiah Franklin were killed; Jordon Dorton was mortally wounded by a shot in neck and died the next morning. David Quan was shot through the right lung.[101]

After the Indiantown skirmish, the nearby home of Dr. McIntosh was overrun by troops and "contraband" alike. The scene was like a nightmare. Garden fences were demolished, and fence rails were burned. Horses were hitched to every available tree or post. The ground was covered with carts loaded with contraband, and all the outbuildings were broken into and used for a variety of purposes. The doctor's office housed a lieutenant colonel and a captain, their weapons, saddles and bridles mingling with medicine bottles used by the doctor. The wounded were tended by three surgeons while they lay on beds of cornhusks. Civilians and soldiers alike were engaged in a wide variety of activities, from pumping water to plucking chickens.[102]

December 19, 1863

The day after the skirmish at the Indiantown Bridge, the combined forces led by Wild went back to attempt to find the guerrillas. Wild reported that he "drove them a long chase into their swamp, and after much trouble struck their trail," which was over a series of "single felled trunks leading into their citadel." In order to reach their camp, Wild and his men had to walk "single file" over those tree trunks.[103]

Major Gregory, an elderly man, was taken hostage.[104] *Major* was his given name, not his rank. Colonel Draper found Gregory's name on a roster when they raided the camp of the 68th North Carolina Militia in Camden County. Because of this, Mr. Gregory's home was burned.[105] The original "Muster Roll, N. C. Defenders" is preserved in the Edward Wild papers at the University of North Carolina at Chapel Hill.

Wild's men went to Gregory's farm and took him prisoner. He was an old man, probably about 70-odd years, and he probably never took part in the war. Wild's men set fire to his dwelling and outhouses, and "stripped him of all his personal estate, and brought him a prisoner to Norfolk." The old man, already in bad health, wept "in sorrow on his sad and melancholy fate," and declared "before God and man he never had raised his hand in aid of this unholy war."[106] Wild sent a note to Willis Sanderlin, Captain of the Guerrillas (Company B, 68th Regiment, North Carolina Troops),[107] regarding Major Gregory and Wild's black soldier held by the guerrillas: "I shall treat him equally as your people treat that soldier. If they hang him, I shall hang Major Gregory. And you know by this time, that I keep my word."[108] Wild implied that Mr. Major Gregory had been taken hostage to safeguard the treatment of one of Wild's men who had been captured near Shiloh. Although Wild had threatened to hang Gregory, on December 22 he offered to exchange him for the soldier held by the guerrillas. That exchange was to have taken place at the village of Deep Creek near the end of the Dismal Swamp Canal.[109] The exchange never took place, because the soldier captured at Shiloh escaped. Wild did release Gregory, but unfortunately, the old man died within a few days, having suffered a stroke while being held prisoner.[110]

December 20, 1863—Pursuit of Guerrilla Forces to Crab Island

One of the Confederate camps sought by Wild's men was located on a 3-acre island known now as Guerrilla Island in Camden County, where the local Confederate soldiers "made their last stand" and escaped from pursuing Federal forces of Colonel Alonzo Draper. In the brief skirmish, a few men on both sides were killed. Resentment against Wild and his men still lingers among some of the descendants of those soldiers. Two of these descendants vow that they would "gladly join the guerrillas under the same circumstances," and after what Wild did in their county, one stated he would have "tried to hunt Wild down and shoot him."[111]

December 21, 1863—Raid Ends, Troops Return to Virginia

About the time the Wild was preparing to return to Virginia, Confederates mobilized and moved into the area. Wild received a warning from Colonel De Forest at Northwest Landing that "the rebels were moving in force, with cavalry and artillery" to cut him off. Wild heeded the warning because, since he had already dispatched much of his force homeward, he had only about 400 men with him. These men were "very much the worse for wear." Wild was also hampered by a train of 73 teams and "many contraband families."[112]

On December 21, 1863, Brigadier General G. W. Getty learned from "fugitives from South Mills" that a Confederate force of cavalry and infantry was positioned between Elizabeth City and South Mills, 8 miles from the Pasquotank Bridge.[113] That same day, Brigadier General Getty advised Major General Butler that if "General Wild is in Currituck County, it would be well to send a steamer to Pungo" to be ready to transfer the 98th New York from there to Coinjock Bridge or Northwest Landing. Getty had already sent a squadron of cavalry to the area around South Mills to watch enemy troop movements. Butler, Getty's superior, had instructed post commanders to "afford all possible assistance to General Wild."[114] Getty then ordered General Graham, in command of a Naval Brigade at Norfolk, to send a gunboat to Pungo, prepared to move the Federal troops from the area quickly, if warranted.[115] The threat to Wild and his men was real, as reported by Major General Getty. A considerable Confederate force advanced from the Blackwater and passed through Gates County to oppose the march of the troops under General Wild, who intended to march from Elizabeth City on Hertford and Edenton, and from there through Gates County to Suffolk, Virginia. Part of the Confederate force advanced as far as the Pasquotank. They destroyed bridges, ferries, etc., and returned. To draw attention from the Confederate force being sent against General Wild, "infantry and artillery were concentrated at each of the points, Franklin and Zuni, for the purpose of making a demonstration in the direction of Suffolk. The force at Franklin advanced as far as Carrsville." The opposition was suspended when Wild withdrew his force to the east side of the Pasquotank.[116]

The next day, Getty heard from Wild that the enemy force which had been at South Mills had retired, some across the Blackwater River and some across the Chowan River. Thus, it was impossible to overtake them by a force "marching via Suffolk."[117]

In a report dated December 21, 1863, from Currituck Court House, Wild described the slow movement of the remainder of his troops homeward. He had already sent ahead the "cavalry, artillery, prisoners, sick, contraband train, and Colonel Holman's regiment." His men moved in three columns—one landing at Powell's Point, another "ferried across at Camden Court-House and marched down through Shiloh, and then up via Indiantown," and a third column from South Mills to Indiantown and upward. Wild gathered all his forces for the return to his base at Norfolk, "including our steamboats" and the gunboat *Flora Temple*. Although eager to return home as quickly as possible, Wild allowed his "sadly worn" men a day of rest before seeing some "contrabands to Roanoke Island."[118]

The *Three Brothers* and a bateau were loaded with the "sick, lame, and wounded, a few prisoners, and a good pile of contrabands, with their baggage," and sent to Norfolk.[119]

On December 23, Wild sent Colonel Alonzo G. Draper and a detachment to Knott's Island. That excursion resulted in the taking of a third female hostage (see Chapter VIII).

December 23–24, 1863—Wild's Brigade Back at Fort Monroe, Virginia

After 20 days of "hard scouting, without overcoats or blankets," Wild's Brigade returned to their home camp in Virginia. They had traveled 25 to 30 miles per day.[120]

On the last leg of the return march to Norfolk, just as Wild and his men reached the Virginia line, an attempt was made by the Confederates to trap them. The commander of the attack, Captain Henry A. Chambers, of Ransom's Brigade, described their efforts in his diary:

> We now begin to double-quick and the nearer town [Suffolk, Virginia] the faster we were required to go. We did not understand the object of this until we were rising over the hill just this side of town when we were met by a little Franco-Louisiana Zouave who had been sent back to urge us on. He was in perfect fever of excitement and, rising in his stirrups, with his sharp stirring voice, he would cry, "Colonel, for God's sake hurry your men on or you will be too late." Turning on the men he would rush along with "Run, boys, run, and we will catch the G—D—niggers yet!" We were nearly exhausted with our long double-quick, but when told that "the hated Negroes had been encountered," we received as it were renewed vigor, and on we pushed.[121]

In hot pursuit of Wild's Brigade, Ransom's Confederates were almost exhausted when they reached Suffolk. The people in the town ran out to offer them water. Most of Wild's column managed to escape, "but several stragglers were surrounded in a house on the far side of town." One of Ransom's men was killed in an attack on the house. The house was set on fire, with the black soldiers still inside.[122]

No sooner had Wild arrived back in Norfolk when a civilian was shot and killed by the sentry in front of Wild's headquarters. The dead man, James Hill, had once "kept a bar" but his most recent occupation was acting as bartender for Mr. David Esby on Market Square in Norfolk. Some who knew the man reported that the deceased had a "habit of drinking." Esby, Hill's employer, reported that he, Charles Green, and Hill were at a saloon called "The Office," eating oysters. Hill had gone outside and was talking to a Mr. John Ford. When Esby approached the two men, he heard someone "open a window and say if he advances another step shoot him." Green said that he had been in "The Office" about 9:30 P.M. with Hill, and he believed that Hill had argued with the sentinel at the door, but could not remember what was said. Green believed that Hill was a "secessionist," because he had seen him carry a sling shot or billy.[123]

No harm came to Wild because of this incident, but Wild and his men had to be alert for assault not only from enemy troops, but from civilians.

Performance of the African Brigade

Confederate sources were critical of Wild's black troops. The Milledgeville, Georgia, *Southern Recorder* reported that "the Negro ran riot during the Yankee stay in the Albemarle country," but when they were fired upon they "fled like wild deer."[124]

A Northern reporter wrote that the "irregular service" of the raid was "especially suited to the nature of colored troops," and that they would prove "far better guerrilla hunters than whites."[125] Wild reported that the black soldiers on his expedition in December of 1863 had "marched wonderfully, never grumbled, were watchful on picket, and always ready for fight. They are most reliable soldiers."[126]

Union cavalry soldiers said that "no soldiers have ever done as hard marching through swamps and marshes as cheerfully" as did the black troops of Wild's Brigade. The cavalry thought if they had to follow Wild's troops for "any length of time it would kill their horses."[127] Some months later, as the soldiers were being transferred from Norfolk to Yorktown, General Isaac J. Wistar wanted Wild's Brigade to "march up from Old Point Comfort, as I should like to have them somewhat familiar with the hardships incident to the march." One can almost visualize the slight twinkle in Wild's eyes, as he replied, "If that is all, let them go on the boat, for they are veterans already in marching."[128]

Results of the Raid

Wild's raid was significant because it was the first on a large scale undertaken by Negro troops, and it settled the question of their efficiency as soldiers. The black soldiers were "thoroughly obedient to their officers, during a march of three hundred miles their conduct on every occasion was truly admirable." These men, new to soldiering, performed their duties just as any of their white counterparts. They scouted, skirmished, did picket and guard duty, and fought well. Colonel Draper reported that the black troops performed well under fire, and that he had every confidence in them.[129] That their actions were not always courteous or kind toward Southern ladies was reported to the Special Committee of the Confederate Congress.[130] The raid definitely had an impact on how blacks as soldiers were viewed by both North and South.

Although not overly happy with Wild, his superiors considered his time in North Carolina as a success because he had quelled Confederate sympathy in the region, and guerrilla and partisan activity had almost ceased.

Confederates and Yankees generally agreed on what had occurred on this raid into northeastern North Carolina (see Appendix, Table II). Confederates believed that Wild had seized more than one hundred thousand dollars' worth of personal property in the adjoining counties, and stripped the farmers of every living thing and carried it away, leaving hundreds of people without a pound of meat or a peck of meal.[131]

The people of the area suffered. The old, the young, male and female—no matter whether connected with the military activities of the Confederate troops and homeguard or not. They suffered losses because they were Southerners who lived in North Carolina, one of the Confederate States of America. North Carolina newspapers reported that Negroes were permitted to curse and abuse defenseless ladies, to strip them of their jewelry and clothing, and offer them indignities which would offend delicacy to repeat.[132]

The citizens of Northeastern North Carolina were terrified by Wild and his men. Rumors spread quickly from plantation to plantation. As Wild expected, the people were "panic-stricken," and many families fled into the swamps. It was reported that the Confederate units and the guerrilla forces operating in the area had also been removed from that part of the state.[133] One newspaper described the raid as "a Reign of Terror." Wild reports only to General Butler. Wild has visited the surrounding country with "fire and sword," and has devastated whole provinces. He threatens that this is "only the beginning of that terrible vengeance" which he will call down upon defenseless women and children.[134]

After Wild's raid, the Confederate authorities described conditions in eastern North Carolina as "deplorable." Property of all kinds had been destroyed or confiscated. Horses and mules, especially, had been the "objects of plunder." Wild's men not only foraged for food items, but they seized valuable household furniture and sent it North. Local citizens believed that regiments of "bummers" had ruined many stately homes and mansions.[135]

The extent of the damage caused by Wild's raid varied according to who was reporting. An account by "Tewksbury," dated January 4, 1864, tallied the results:

> 2000–3000 slaves released from bondage;
> 350 ox, horse, and mule teams were captured;
> 75 saddle horses, some valuable animals;
> 13 guerrillas were killed and wounded;
> 10 dwelling houses were burned; 2 distilleries were burned;
> 4 guerrilla camps were destroyed; 1 guerrilla [Daniel Bright] was hanged;
> 100 rifles taken, plus uniforms and infantry equipment.[136]

Milton M. Holland, a soldier in Wild's Brigade, wrote home to say that "thousands of slaves belonging to rebel masters were liberated."[137]

After reading the newspapers in mid–January, Mrs. Catherine Edmondston expressed her fear of the freed slaves and her disgust at the outrageous acts committed by Wild in Eastern North Carolina:

> Armed Negroes, originally run-aways from their owners to the Yankees, now disgusted with their new rulers, fugitives in turn from the Yankee army, demoralized & lost to all restraint or sense of dependence, their Masters mostly absent, rove through the country & seize from the defenseless inhabitants what they list. God help them & keep us from a like fate. The tender mercies of Abolitionism![138]

The loss of slaves was financially devastating to slave owners. The price paid for nine slaves at an auction in Franklin County in January of 1864 was $29,132, an average of $4,348 each. One 44-year-old female slave sold for $1,375. A 40-year-old male sold for $3,000. A 16-year-old female brought $3,600, and a 14-year-old female brought $3,700. A 28-year-old male brought, $5,457. Two others, both in their 20s, brought $6,000 and $6,450, respectively.[139]

Wild's Wins and Losses

By December 29, 1863, Mrs. Catherine Devereux Edmondston could comment that Wild and his men "did not escape unscathed, however, more than a hundred having been shot by the citizens & Guerrillas in their made progress through the country."[140]

After Wild was safely back in Norfolk, Brigadier General James Barnes cited Wild's losses at "4 men killed, 1 mortally wounded, and 2 taken prisoners; about 12 men wounded."[141]

More accurately, the casualties suffered to the men under General Wild's command were 7 killed and 9 wounded, and two men had been taken prisoner. Wild also reported that one man had died of poison, and 3 had died from illness. A number had fallen ill from "fatigue and exposure," while nine had been sick with smallpox, and many had the mumps. He noted that 3 horses had been "fatally shot," which included one officer's horse. He enumerated the loss of guns, "4 by the swamping of a boat, 4 by the accidental conflagration of a temporary smallpox hospital, and 1 captured"[142] (see Appendix, Table III).

Wild had taken 14 prisoners and 4 hostages, but his main purpose of recruiting black soldiers was only minimally successful. He had enlisted only about 70 to 100 former slaves as soldiers.[143] This number was low because most of the able-bodied slaves had already left their masters and fled the area.[144] Wild seemed satisfied, however, and noted that he had "gained many recruits and rescued great numbers of slaves; killed and captured a number of guerrillas, besides destroying their swamp camps, their arms and other property."[145]

The "wild" General was happy that he had been able to liberate a large number of slaves, believed to be between 2,000 and 2,500, although he was never sure of the exact number. That number varied because people were constantly joining and leaving his column of troops.[146]

Wild determined that a majority of the people of the area were reasonably neutral, although their sympathies lay with the South, and "they were tired of war, or weary of their own distresses and privations; harassed by the frequent alternation of masters, being plundered by both sides." Some were despondent over the "ultimate success of the South;" others were "convinced of the doom of slavery." Some were aware of the "mischief arising from the presence of guerrillas in their midst." Those people who were really neutral, or who sympathized with the North, were afraid to speak their minds for fear of retaliation by guerrillas.[147]

Confederates saw Wild's actions as criminal, uncivilized, and unjustified. They said Wild had "outraged all the laws of civilized war."[148] They saw his actions as "atrocities that make the blood run cold." One newspaper hinted that even General Butler did not "countenance to these acts of inhumanity," and reported having seen a "letter from General Butler directing General Wild to make no arrests without specific charges; the prisoners to be sent immediately to Gen. Getty for investigation; to seize no property unless under military necessity." Confederates believed that Wild had disobeyed Butler's orders; he had not returned confiscated property, nor released the hostages that were still being held in jail.[149]

After the raid, even Wild's fellow officers were unhappy with him. Colonel J. W. Shaffer urged Butler to "get rid of Wild," even if he could not get a replacement. Shaffer begged Butler to tell Secretary of War Stanton that he could have Wild, if Stanton would "give us one good substitute common sense man ... I wish Wild was elsewhere. He has no common sense and does harm!"[150]

Wild's raid did seem to solidify Union sentiment in the counties where he had made his presence known. It also solidified sentiment against the Federal forces, and placed the blame for the "atrocities" in North Carolina on someone.

Wild believed he had done what he was ordered to do. Yet, he received little praise except from Major General Butler. Perhaps only his "sable soldiers" believed that Wild was "the right man in the right place." One of them wrote that, although Wild had lost an arm, "with his revolver in hand, he was at the head of our regiment cheering us on to victory."[151] What greater praise could a commander wish for than the approval of his men? But it is not the opinion of the common foot soldier that matters, for they have no power to make or break brigadier generals. Rather it was Wild's peers and superiors who had the authority to promote or demote, or arrest and court martial him, and they used that power.

Lingering adverse opinions of Wild's activities in North Carolina and his subsequent actions in Virginia would put his career in jeopardy by mid–1864. Controversy over his failure to release the hostages, his hanging of Daniel Bright, and the fight over the "possession" of Miss Nancy White would cast a dark shadow over Wild's career, and result in a court martial.

Because of the actions of Wild and his African Brigade in North Carolina, Brigadier General Wild suffered damage to his reputation and his military career.

VII

Retaliation and Repercussion

Grow like savages, as soldiers will
That nothing do but meditate on blood.
—Shakespeare, *Henry V*

Just before Brigadier General Edward Wild began his raid into North Carolina, a letter to Secretary of State Stanton in the New York *Times* on November 28, 1863, pointed out that death awaited Union officers connected with colored troops captured by the Confederates. None had been captured alive and held in the South as a prisoner of war, nor had any colored Union soldier who had been captured in the South been "accounted for as a prisoner of war." A letter dated at Port Hudson, November 3, 1863, from a captain in the 7th Regiment reported that "First Lieut. George B. Coleman, Jr., of New York City, who was captured about two months ago while out on a raid, was hanged within twenty-four hours afterward, together with some twenty privates (colored) who were taken with him." This letter also pointed out that those connected with the "Corps d'Afrique" when captured were either "murdered, cast into prison, or sold into slavery. They are not recognized in the South as soldiers."[1]

For prisoners, death was always a possibility, especially if the prisoner was a black Union soldier being held by Confederates. Prisoners held by Union forces could suffer the same fate, and did. Brigadier General Wild captured and tried Confederate soldier Daniel Bright, found him guilty, and sentenced him to hang. The sentence was carried out by the general himself. Retaliation for this hanging was not long in coming.

Wild soon learned what kind of retaliation would be forthcoming. Confederate Colonel Joel R. Griffin wrote Wild to chastise him for his actions against prisoners and hostages, and to describe what Confederates had done as a result of Wild's actions.[2]

> Your Negro troops fired on Confederates after they had surrendered and they were only saved by the exertions of the more humane of your white officers. Last, but not least, under pretext that he was a guerrilla, you hanged Daniel Bright, a private of Company L, Sixty-second Georgia regiment [cavalry] forcing the ladies and gentlemen whom you held in arrest to witness the execution. Therefore, I have

obtained an order from the General commanding, for the execution of Samuel Jones, a private from Company B, Fifth Ohio, whom I hang in retaliation. I hold two more of your men—in irons—as hostages for Mrs. Weeks and Mrs. Munden. When these ladies are released, these men will be ... treated as prisoners of war.[3]

These two executions brought Wild to the attention of both the North and the South.

January 12, 1864—Private Samuel Jordan Hanged

Confederate Colonel Joel R. Griffin complained to Confederate Major General George Pickett (famous for "Pickett's Charge" at Gettysburg) about the cruel treatment of the female hostage, Mrs. Phoebe Munden, and the other ladies.[4] Wild had even threatened to execute the ladies. It was this complaint that probably led to the execution of Wild's black soldier, Samuel Jordan.

On December 17, a month before Jordan was hanged, Wild wrote to John T. Elliott, "Captain of Guerrillas," that Mrs. Munden and Mrs. Weeks had been taken as hostages to safeguard the life of one of his colored soldiers who had been taken by the guerrillas. Wild threatened: "As he is treated so shall they be: even to hanging. By this time you know that I am in earnest."[5]

Wild's activities were watched closely by Confederate forces. Colonel Joel R. Griffin of the 62nd Georgia Regiment, operating in North Carolina, reported on December 19, 1863, to Major General George Pickett that the enemy (Wild's men) had 2,900 Negroes and 500 cavalry at Elizabeth City. He also reported the hanging of "Private Daniel Bright of Company L, of my 62nd Georgia Regiment." Griffin reported that Bright had been hanged from a beam in a house, and that his body had "remained suspended forty hours."[6] The 62nd Georgia, of which Griffin was in command, was also known as the 2nd Georgia Calvary, a unit of Partisan Rangers. From September 1863 through May 1864, this unit was assigned to the Department of North Carolina. The 62nd had originally been organized with seven Georgia companies and three North Carolina companies.[7]

First Lieutenant William J. Munden reported that he and a "portion of company E [66th Regiment] had captured and made prisoner a Negro, a private in a regiment called the 'Fifth U.S. Colored.'"[8] This was Private Samuel Jordan. Confederates, enraged because Wild had hanged Daniel Bright, retaliated by hanging their prisoner, Private Samuel Jordan. By the middle of January, the body of Private Jordan, one of Wild's black soldiers, had been found.

The first report of the hanging of the colored Union soldier came in a letter to General Getty, signed by 11 citizens of Pasquotank County, North Carolina. Fearful of retaliation against themselves, the citizens wrote on January 13:

> There was found this morning a dead man and still hanging in our neighborhood, as the enclosed script which was found pinned to his back will show you by whom it was done. We have made a suitable box and buried him near the place he

was found hung. Should his friends wish to get his body they can get it by applying to any of the subscribers. We trust that you will not attach any blame to any of the citizens of this neighborhood, as we were entirely ignorant of any of the circumstances until we found the body, from all we can learn he was brought across the Chowan River to this place and as soon as the men who had him in charge had hung him they went back.[9]

On January 17, 1864, Major General Benjamin F. Butler was erroneously told that "Private Jones, Company B, Fifth Ohio Volunteers" was singled out from among other Union soldiers being held in Richmond, turned over to General George Pickett, and hanged.[10] Butler had been notified by Colonel Samuel P. Spear about the incident and also that, as of January 16, 1864, Speer had "the body" in his possession, and promised to have it properly buried at 2 P.M. on the date the letter was written. Spear enclosed with his letter to Butler the letter from citizens of Pasquotank County, North Carolina. A copy of the placard which was attached to the body was also enclosed, with the following inscription:

"Here hangs Private Samuel Jones of Company B, Fifth Ohio Regiment, by order of Major-General Pickett, in retaliation for Private Daniel Bright, of Company L, Sixty-second Georgia Regiment (Colonel Griffin's), hanged December 18, 1863, by order of Brigadier-General Wild."[11]

This document, referred to by Andy Phrydas, Military Records Archivist for the state of Georgia, has been described in "Autographs and Manuscripts: The American Civil War, Catalogue No. 46," by Kenneth W. Rendell, Inc., which listed "A true copy" of the notice that was attached to the body of Private Samuel Jones [sic] and signed with the original signature of Col. Samuel F. Spear, which noted that the hanging was in "retaliation for Private Daniel Bright, of Co. L, 62nd Georgia Regt. (Col. Griffin's)."[12]

A letter to Colonel Spear from M. B. Smith gave the details of the hanging, which took place on Tuesday, January 12. He also reported that a Mr. Williamson, who lived nearby, made a coffin, cut the body down, and buried him in a nearby field. The soldier had been in handcuffs when executed, and these were transferred to Colonel Spear.[13] As it turned out, the name of the soldier who was hanged in Pasquotank County was not Samuel Jones from the 5th Ohio, but was Private Samuel Jordan, a member of Company D, 5th USCT.[14]

One of the men in Jordan's regiment wrote home that Private Jordan had been found "with a note pinned to his flesh." The soldier vowed that "Before this war ends we will pin their sentences to them [Confederate soldiers] with Uncle Sam's leaden pills."[15]

The Retaliation Policy

Although the Confederates retaliated for the hanging of Daniel Bright (and Wild threatened to retaliate for that hanging by also hanging his female captives), Federal policy, as set out in Section I, No. 28, General Order No. 100, opposed retaliation. Retaliation will "never be resorted to as a measure of mere revenge, but only as a means of protective retribution, and moreover cautiously and unavoidably ... retaliation shall only be resorted to after careful inquiry into the real occurrence and the character of the misdeeds that may demand retribution." The philosophy behind this ruling was that: "Unjust or inconsiderate retaliation removes the belligerents farther and farther from the mitigating rules of regular war, and by rapid steps leads them nearer to the internecine wars of savages."[16]

The life of Samuel Jordan could possibly have been spared if Wild had released Mrs. Munden. A plea for Mrs. Munden's safety was sent shortly after she was taken by the Captain of Company E, 66th North Carolina Troops, to Brigadier General Wild. Although addressed to a "colonel," this letter was undoubtedly intended for Brigadier General Wild. This letter was the result of a note Lieutenant Munden had received from his wife. Although Mrs. Munden understood that she was being held as hostage for the colored prisoner taken "a few days ago," she was in "great distress" and she feared that if Wild's colored soldier "was held or hung she would be treated the same." The Confederate Captain asked that Mrs. Munden be treated with respect, and promised that he would have the Federal prisoner released. To date, the Union prisoner had been treated honorably as "a prisoner of war." Although he had been sent to Raleigh, the Captain promised he would "go immediately after him."[17] The colored prisoner referred to by the Captain was Samuel Jordan.

There is no doubt that Samuel Jordan of the 5th USCT was hanged in retaliation for the hanging of Daniel Bright, as well as for the hostages still held by Brigadier General Wild in Norfolk as of January 15. Colonel James W. Hinton wrote Major General Butler from Murfreesboro, North Carolina, on January 15, 1864, and asked plainly: "I desire further to call your attention to the fact that the ladies whose names are mentioned in General Wild's letter are ... still held in close confinement in the city of Norfolk. I want to know whether it is your purpose to hold these ladies as 'hostages' for a soldier legitimately captured?"[18]

Efforts to Free the Female Hostages

The controversy over the hostages continued to rage. Undoubtedly, everyone took Wild's threat to hang his female hostages seriously, especially after it was known that Confederates had hanged one of Wild's black soldiers. Yet, Pickett disregarded Wild's threats to hang the female hostages, and dared to call Wild's bluff when he hanged Private Jordan.

After a thorough investigation, the Special Committee appointed by the Confederate Congress reported that the ladies were still in custody on January 26, even though General Benjamin F. Butler had "countermanded the order" for the execution of the ladies in retaliation for the hanging of a colored soldier.[19] A North Carolina newspaper reported late in January 1864 that the two ladies "of high character" had been handled roughly by a brutal Negro soldiers, and after having been brought to Norfolk, were kept "confined in a close room."[20] In a report of his operations in

North Carolina, Wild noted that he wanted to keep the hostages in custody, "to be dealt with as they shall deal with the prisoners taken from my party."[21]

As opposition to Wild and fear that he would harm the hostages increased, Major General Butler received orders from President Lincoln. Butler replied: "All executions have been stayed until further orders from you."[22] Butler believed that the execution of Private Jordan in retaliation for the hanging of Daniel Bright would not affect the treatment of the ladies while being held prisoner.[23] However, to be on the safe side, Butler stepped in and forbid Wild to hang the women in retaliation for the hanging of Jordan. He further clarified the hanging of Jordan and Bright, by pointing out that "no difference was made between Jordan and Daniel Bright on account of color, one being hanged in retaliation for the other by the rebel authorities, the case presupposed by General Wild ... that some different treatment would be meted out to his soldiers because of his color not having arisen...."[24]

Yet, Butler defended Wild's action in hanging Daniel Bright and stated emphatically that Bright was a deserter from the 62nd Georgia, and although he "was not engaged in warfare," Bright was engaged "in pillage and murder, as a guerrilla; was duly tried by court-martial, sentenced, and hanged; and the execution of Private Jordan [was] in retaliation for that act...."[25]

Butler further covered for Wild by saying in a letter to Colonel James W. Hinton that Bright "and his company had refused to obey any order emanating from you or the Governor of North Carolina, because you had frequently ordered the squad of which he had pretended to be one across the Chowan River, and they had refused to obey." Butler stated that these facts were brought out in a "court martial" in which Daniel Bright was tried, and that, as Butler understood the definition, Bright was "within the strict meaning of the term 'guerrilla.'" Butler firmly believed that if the Confederate Captain John T. Elliott and his men had refused to obey orders and march where they were supposed to, and had, in fact, remained in "a peaceable county against the will of the inhabitants, plundering and burning," as the Federal authorities had been informed, then they "deserved a like fate as Daniel Bright by every rule of civilized warfare." He assured Hinton that if his regiment did not fall within the definition of "guerrillas," they had nothing to fear "worse than imprisonment." However, if they were actually "guerrillas," Butler advised that it would be best for "them not to get into our hands." Butler emphasized and staunchly defended Wild's actions as being carried out only against "guerrillas."[26]

However, Butler "passed the buck" on the matter of the hanging of Private Samuel Jordan to the authorities in Washington. These actions temporarily cooled matters, but Confederate General George Pickett developed "an enthusiasm for hanging Union soldiers he designated as hostages."[27]

Private and Public Outrage Over Wild's Raid

A letter posted from Norfolk, Virginia, December 28, 1863, about the "atrocities in North Carolina" was originally published in the New York *Daily News* and reprinted in the Raleigh *North Carolina Standard* a month later. It pointed out the differences in the administration of General Naglee, which was "marked by many courtesies and kind acts," compared to the "Reign of Terror" of Brigadier General Wild.[28]

Major General Benjamin F. Butler had high praise for General Wild, and was "much indebted to Wild and his Negro troops for what they have done." Yet, he admitted there were some complaints because of actions authorized by Wild "against the inhabitants and their property." Butler pointed out, however, that "all the committees agree that the negro soldiers made no unauthorized interference with property or person, and conducted themselves with propriety."[29]

Butler knew there was a "considerable degree of prejudice against the colored troops," and that impediments had been thrown "in the way of their recruiting, and they [were] interfered with on their expeditions." Butler promised to look into that matter. He also admitted there were some "incompetent officers in the negro regiments." He firmly believed that the "negro troops, to have a fair chance, ought to have first-class officers" because they were more prone to depend on their officers than white soldiers.[30]

Citizens of North Carolina Hold Meetings

The white citizens of northeastern North Carolina were terrified of the black soldiers, and they did not want them back in their area. General Butler had warned the citizens of Currituck, Pasquotank, Perquimans, Gates, and Chowan counties that he would return the "colored troops" if they did not help drive the "Partisan Rangers" out of the area. Butler was intent on exterminating "all guerrillas east of [the] Chowan River," and would use whatever means necessary. He was not above laying to waste an entire county. Butler warned the citizens that if they wanted to prevent "universal destruction of their property," they should help Federal authorities "in ridding this country of these land pirates." With Wild and his men in the area, the Federals had sufficient force "to accomplish our purpose, and we shall immediately enter upon the work."[31]

Wild warned the people of retaliation if they harbored guerrillas or Confederates. As a result, the residents of several northeastern counties held public meetings, and 523 people signed petitions to have Confederate forces withdrawn from their counties.[32]

In order to prevent the "universal destruction" promised by both Major General Butler and his subordinate Brigadier General Wild, the citizens of each county acted quickly. Petitions were sent to North Carolina Governor Zebulon B. Vance to beg the Governor to "remove or disband" the Rangers. While this was done under duress, it was believed to be necessary to prevent another raid like the one Wild had just made.[33] As a result, "The guerrillas have also been withdrawn from these counties," much to the relief of the inhabitants. Butler rewarded those people with a promise that as long "as they remained quiet, keep out the guerrillas, and stop blockade running" that they would be protected by the Federal troops, and "be allowed to bring their products into Norfolk and receive goods in exchange."[34] Butler was pleased that the citizens of the five eastern North Carolina counties had all passed resolutions asking the Governor of North Carolina to withdraw homeguard units from their neighborhoods.[35]

Efforts Toward Return of Hostages and Property

The raid was officially over, but the controversy had just begun. Not only did Confederate sympathizers suffer, but those supposedly loyal to the Union were treated just as badly. Mr. Morrisetts, of Camden County, N.C., presented his certificate of loyalty when his property was about to be confiscated. "General Wild paused for a moment, took the property, but promised to return it when he reached Norfolk." Even though the old man followed Wild to Norfolk, and pleaded for the return of his property, he was told that the property "belonged to his Negroes, and his loyalty did not protect him." The old gentleman left with tears in his eyes and muttering, "I am a ruined man; my children are beggars."[36]

On December 31, 1863, only a few days after Wild returned to Norfolk, Attorney J. Parker Jordan of North Carolina wrote a long letter to Major General Butler. Jordan voiced a number of complaints against Wild. Outrages had been "perpetrated alike on the loyal and disloyal." The attorney also mentioned that Butler had sent a letter to Wild which "demanded" that whatever arrests Wild made in North Carolina, those persons should be "sent immediately to Gen. Getty for investigation." Wild had been ordered not to seize property "unless under military necessity," nor was he to "require the oath of allegiance of the citizens unless he was able to protect their rights." Contrary to orders, Wild had "seized and destroyed more than one hundred thousand dollars worth of property, belonging to citizens in N.C.," much of which belonged to citizens who were loyal to the Union and who also held a "certificate of protection" from the United States Government. Jordan's letter is one of very few accounts that not only mention the two married ladies that Wild took hostage, but also mentions that a Miss White had been "treated very badly." Parker viewed Wild's actions in North Carolina as "acts of barbarity," and he pleaded for the return of the property that had been seized, and that the female hostages be released.[37]

Wild was soon besieged from all sides and condemned for his actions in North Carolina. Colonel James W. Hinton, commander of the 66th Regiment North Carolina Troops, wrote to Major General Butler and included a copy of Brigadier General Wild's note to Captain John T. Elliott, "Captain of Guerrillas," in which Wild justified his holding Mrs. Munden and Mrs. Weeks.[38]

Confederate officials tried other methods to get the hostages taken by Wild released. North Carolina Governor Zebulon B. Vance wrote to Judge Ould, the

Commissioner of Exchange, at his headquarters in Richmond to complain about conditions along the Chowan River and in eastern North Carolina:

> As you will see by the letters from a Yankee General by the name of Wild, which Col. [James W.] H.[inton] will show you, they refuse to treat them as prisoners of War, although regularly commissioned by law. They have also murdered several soldiers, and have arrested two respectable ladies whom they keep handcuffed as hostages for two Negro soldiers and declare their purpose to hang them in case the Negroes are hung. I must ask you to see if some arrangement cannot be made to include these troops within the cartel of exchange and repress if possible this horrible, cowardly and damnable disposition on the part of enemy to put women in irons as hostages for Negro soldiers![39]

Governor Vance did not hesitate to express his disapproval of General Wild: "Such men as this Wild are a disgrace to the manhood of the age, not being able to capture soldiers' they war upon defenseless women! Great God! What an outrage!"[40]

The Governor of North Carolina made some promises of his own, and declared that if his men were not "treated as prisoners of war," and if these "outrages upon defenseless females continue, I shall retaliate upon Yankee soldiers to the full extent of my ability, and let the consequences rest with the damnable barbarians who begun it."[41]

Confederate military officers applied pressure for the release of the hostages. From his headquarters on the Blackwater, near Franklin, Virginia, Confederate Colonel Joel R. Griffin wrote General Wild to chastise him for his actions against prisoners and hostages, and to describe how the Confederates forces would retaliate:[42]

> Probably no expedition, during the progress of the war, has been attended with more bitter disregard from the long established usages of civilization or the dictates of humanity than your late raid into the country bordering the Albemarle. Your stay, though short, was marked by crimes and enormities. You burned houses over the heads of defenseless women and children, carried off private property of every description, arrested non-combatants, and carried off ladies in irons, whom you confined with Negro men ... I hold two more of your men—in irons—as hostages for Mrs. Weeks and Mrs. Munden. When these ladies are released, these men will be ... treated as prisoners of war.[43]

Shortly after Wild and his men had returned to Norfolk, the *North Carolina Standard* reported on Wild's activities, and that he had taken two ladies and held them as hostages for the safety of one of his Negro soldiers who had been captured. The ladies were "imprisoned in Norfolk jail, badly treated, and guarded by Negroes." The article described Wild, because of his actions against the women, as a "demon in human form." It added, "Is there no retaliation by which such monsters can be compelled to not have some regard for the usages of civilized warfare?"[44]

An affidavit was submitted to the Special Committee of the Confederate Congress from First Lieutenant William J. Munden, Company E, 66th Regiment, North Carolina Troops, the husband of female hostage Phoebe Munden. Mrs. Munden had been confined "in a room over a store with some fifteen or twenty others," all men, except Mrs. Munden and Mrs. Elizabeth Weeks, who were held for three days with their hands and feet tied. When allowed to answer the "calls of nature," they were accompanied by a Negro guard, "who stood over them with muskets, and they were compelled to "do this in a public street."[45] The Confederate Congress had no power to force Wild to release the hostages.

Was the Hanging of Bright Legal?

How could Brigadier General Wild, a Federal officer out in the swamps of eastern North Carolina, make any kind of accurate judgement as to the military status of the prisoner Daniel Bright? How could he determine whether Bright was a Confederate soldier in a regular unit or acting as a guerrilla? What were Wild's motives? Why were the captured prisoners even tried? A trial was usually held by the army that had captured deserters from its own ranks. The prisoners were not deserters from the Union army, but were Confederate soldiers, and as such, should have been treated by the rules of war as military prisoners. Why did Wild think that he had the authority to hang one of the captured soldiers, even after he had been tried and pronounced guilty? He even went so far as to carry out the hanging himself, and to add insult to injury, he ordered a placard placed upon the dead man which told who had done the deed.

Early in March of 1864, an article in the New York *World* condemned Wild for the hanging of the Confederate guerrilla. "If he was a guerrilla, Wild had no right, under the laws of War, to hang him, and under any other government he would have been promptly court-martialed, and either cashiered or shot." At that time, Wild had not "even [been] rebuked ... but he cost a poor Union soldier his life, for the rebels promptly retaliated, as they were justified in doing by the laws of War...." The article criticized the Federal government for not objecting to the hanging of Samuel Jordan, because, as the article alleged, of "Wild's atrocities" in North Carolina. In addition, Wild's raid did motivate the Confederate military to send an army to eastern North Carolina to recover lost territory, and the raid did seem to put an end to the "peace movement in the Old North State."[46]

Just what was Daniel Bright's proper military status? The Georgia Department of Archives and History, in Atlanta, replied to an inquiry that they had been unable to locate the Compiled Service Record of Daniel Bright. Although Bright "is listed as Daniel Bright, Company L, 62nd Regiment, Georgia Volunteer Cavalry, we have found only one (1) record, documenting his service from Georgia.... It appears that the 62nd Regiment was composed of and consolidated with units from Georgia and other states, including North Carolina."[47] Colonel Griffin did acknowledge that Daniel Bright was a private in Company L, of his 62nd Georgia Regiment, and even if operating as a partisan ranger, Bright should have been made a prisoner of war.

The Federal government did issue orders after Wild's raid to all commanders of Union troops that according to Section IV, No. 81, p. 157, General Order No.100,

"Partisans are soldiers armed and wearing the uniform of their army, but belonging to a corps which acts detached from the main body for the purpose of making inroads into the territory occupied by the Enemy. If captured, partisan rangers were entitled to all the privileges of the prisoner of war." Undoubtedly, Wild incorrectly believed that Daniel Bright and others he captured were "war rebels," defined as those "who rise in arms against the occupying or conquering army.... If captured, they may suffer death, whether they rise singly, in small or large bands, and whether called upon to do so by their own, but expelled, government or not. They are not prisoners of war; nor are they if discovered and secured before their conspiracy has matured to an actual rising or to armed violence."

Confederate officials were probably justified in their outrage over the taking of female hostages and their treatment. Whether or not the women were treated cruelly, they should not have been taken. However, once they were taken hostage, they should have been kept separate from the male prisoners, and if their guards had been white officers, there would have been fewer complaints.[48] Confederates were understandably angry over the wanton destruction of property by Wild's men, without regard to whether the property belonged to Confederate or Union sympathizers. Wild's men had foraged for food from the very beginning of the raid because their supply boat had failed to arrive (see Chapter VI).

Wild's treatment of Bright is questionable. Wild had just come from the horrors of Morris Island where the black troops under General Robert G. Shaw had been slaughtered, mutilated, and buried without dignity. Rumors persisted that no black troops captured would be allowed to live. Wild was greatly concerned with the safety of any of his men captured by the guerrilla forces or any regular Confederate force. However, Bright's execution would seem to have forced a similar act by Confederates, rather than prevent it.

Horace Stevens and Gershom Bradford questioned how Daniel Bright had come to be "disassociated" from his Georgia regiment, and why he supposedly was living "peacefully" at his home in Pasquotank County. Stevens and Bradford reasoned that it probably would have been better to have taken Bright as a prisoner of war.[49]

A few years after Wild's death, Edward Wheelright made a notation on an announcement of a meeting of the Colonial Society of Massachusetts. "With regard to the hanging of the bushwhackers by Gen. W. in N. C., Mrs. W[ild] says there was one man hung much to her regret & she thought the case should have been referred to Gen. Butler under whose orders Wild then was & that the responsibility should have been left with him."[50] Perhaps she was correct.

VIII

Miss Nancy White and the Wead-Draper Dispute

For fools rush in where angels fear to tread.
—Alexander Pope,
An Essay on Criticism (1711)

Among the many bizarre events involving Brigadier General Edward Wild, the abduction and detention of three female hostages, including a young, unmarried lady from Knott's Island, had the most far-reaching ramifications. The events surrounding the taking of the two married women have been described in Chapter VI.

A foray to Knott's Island on December 21, 1863, by Colonel Alonzo Draper ended in his taking hostage a 23-year-old lady, Miss Nancy White. There is little in the official reports about this particular hostage, but taking Miss White into custody caused major problems.

Why did Brigadier General Wild send Colonel Draper to Knott's Island at the end of the raid into North Carolina? What were Wild's orders? Did Draper carry out those orders, or did he act independently? Was Draper specifically ordered to take a "hostage," or was Miss White taken on the spur of the moment as the result of threats from her mother, Susan White? Was she abducted in retribution for the *Maple Leaf* escape?

That a single, white female should be taken hostage was an act so vile, so uncivilized, so unchivalrous, that the perpetrator should be punished and condemned by society on both sides of the Mason-Dixon line. Although Wild was not even present at the time of Miss White's abduction, he was condemned and criticized by both Union and Confederate military, individuals, and civilian groups because she was taken by one of his subordinate officers, and supposedly on his orders. Whether or not the hostage was taken on specific orders issued by Brigadier General Edward

Wild is not known. However, he did order one of his officers to go to Knott's Island, and that officer did take a young lady from her home.

The actions committed by Wild, his white officers, and his black soldiers fueled the flames of outrage and indignation, and would eventually cause major problems for Brigadier General Edward A. Wild and others involved.

History of Knott's Island

Knott's Island, a peninsula 5 miles long by 3.5 miles wide, may be the oldest continuous settlement in North Carolina. One of the settlers of Virginia in 1623 was James Knott, and some of his descendants moved south to Knott's Island, hence the name.[1] Settled in the mid–1600s, Knott's Island was claimed by both Virginia and North Carolina for more than 50 years, as both colonies authorized land grants and tried to collect taxes. In 1728, William Byrd II of Virginia was authorized to survey the line between the two states. Byrd's survey placed the greater portion of Knott's Island in North Carolina. The dividing line cut across Dozier's Island, then across an "Arm of the Sound into Knot's Island, and there Split a Plantation belonging to William Harding." Byrd said the soil was good, and the climate was temperate, although in the summer the inhabitants suffered because of "mosquitoes." Byrd noted that a "Mr. White, who keeps open House for all Travelers, that either Debt or Shipwreck happens to cast in his way," was the "Principal Freeholder" on Knott's Island.[2]

Solomon White, the innkeeper mentioned in Byrd's *History of the Dividing Line*, was one of the children of Patrick and Elizabeth White.[3] He was an ancestor of Miss Nancy White, the subject of this chapter. The White family's sojourn on Knott's Island began with Patrick White, who was brought to the Virginia colony as an indentured servant. Patrick obtained 50 acres of land in Lancaster County, Virginia, in 1653. One Patrick White and his brother William obtained land patents on Knott's Island in 1682 and in 1683.[4]

The western part of Knott's Island, called "Mackey's Island," was the estate of Joseph P. Knapp in the early 20th century. In recent years, a wildlife refuge has been provided by the Federal government. Knott's Island is composed of flat farm lands, forests, swamps, and marshes. Isolated from the rest of North Carolina, the people maintain close ties with Virginia.[5] Even today, it is easier to travel 40 miles to Norfolk, Virginia, via Highway 615 than the county seat at Currituck, which can only be reached from Knott's Island by ferryboat.[6]

The Maple Leaf Escape—June 10, 1863

Some people believe that Miss Nancy White was taken hostage from her home on Knott's Island because of an event that happened six months earlier in June of

1863—the escape of a number of Confederate officers from the steamer *Maple Leaf*. An account by W. B. Browne, "Stranger Than Fiction," published half a century after the events, supposedly was based on a personal interview with Miss Nancy White, and the diaries of Lieutenant A. E. Asbury of Higginsville, Missouri, and Colonel J. J. Green of Covington, Tennessee, two of the Confederate officers who escaped from the *Maple Leaf*. Browne tried to prove a connection between the escape of Confederate officers from the *Maple Leaf* and Colonel Alonzo Draper's foray to Knott's Island that resulted in a young lady being taken hostage.[7] There may be a connection, since both events involved members of the White family.

A chain of events began on May 25, 1863, when Union General Henry W. Halleck issued orders that "No Confederate officers will be paroled or exchanged till further orders." The prisoners were to be kept closely confined and guarded. In addition, any officers who had already been paroled were to be confined.[8] About this time, a group of Confederate prisoners were being transported and some of this group escaped from the *Maple Leaf*.[9] The order halting paroles probably provided the incentive needed for these officers to escape.

The Federal steamer *Maple Leaf* left New Orleans in early June with 75 to 80 Confederate officers who were prisoners of war. The ship arrived in Norfolk, Virginia, and 26 additional Confederate officers were taken aboard before the ship headed out to sea on June 10 on its way to Fort Delaware. The Confederates' escape plan was set in motion when prisoners engaged the sentinels on duty in conversation. Other prisoners stood near where the guards had stacked their muskets, and others were ready to overpower the crew once the signal, the ringing of the ship's bell, was given. As the bell tolled, the prisoners sprang into action so quickly and quietly that they soon had control of the steamer. Upon commandeering the ship, the prisoners gave the "Rebel yell," which "rang out over the waters of the Chesapeake Bay." The ship was now commanded by Captain E. C. Fuller, former captain of the Confederate gunboat *Star of the West*.[10]

According to Browne, all the Confederate officers who were able to leave the ship did so. They disembarked to the beach and fled. Among those who had to remain on board because of injuries was the gallant Captain Fuller, who was "promptly placed in irons upon arrival at Fort Monroe."[11] Fuller died shortly on July 25, 1863, in the Federal prison on Johnson's Island.[12]

The freed officers wanted to go to Nassau, but the supply of coal was inadequate for that distance. Instead, they landed about 10 miles south of Virginia Beach, close to Knott's Island. The steamer was returned to her Yankee captain, with his promise to take the sick and wounded prisoners to Fort Delaware.[13] The escape was accomplished without violence or loss of life.

Major General John A. Dix, Union commander of the Department of Virginia from June 17, 1862, to July 15, 1863,[14] reported that the "97 rebel officers" had overpowered the guard and had taken possession of the steamer. Dix, humiliated over the escape, sent Union cavalry after the escapees. To save face, Dix noted in his brief report that some "thirty prisoners refused to join in the plot and had returned on the steamer."[15] Formerly United States Secretary of the Treasury, Dix was famous for his "American Flag Dispatch," in which he decreed that if anyone attempted to "haul down the American flag, shoot him on the spot." This order was issued January 29, 1861, in New Orleans when W. Hemphill Jones, captain of a revenue cutter, *McClelland*, refused to surrender his ship.[16] Dix was also the uncle of Edward Wild's wife.

A detailed report of the escape was filed on July 7, 1863, by William H. Ludlow, Lieutenant Colonel and Agent for Exchange of Prisoners. Ludlow promised that if the Confederate officers who escaped from the *Maple Leaf* were recaptured, unless exchanged, they "would be hung."[17] Union officials were greatly embarrassed by this escape.

The former Confederate prisoners, now free from their Yankee captors, found themselves in Princess Anne County, Virginia, and knew they would be safe if they could reach North Carolina and its swamps. To get there, they had to travel south down Knott's Island, then cross Currituck Sound to the mainland. The officers walked 30 miles at night. Before crossing Currituck Sound, they stopped at the south end of Knott's Island.[18]

On Knott's Island, the Confederate officers were sheltered and fed supper at the home of Confederate sympathizers. W. B. Browne interviewed the daughter of a "Mr. White" (reportedly the Nancy White who was later taken prisoner by Colonel Draper). She told Browne that after the officers had eaten at her home, Mr. White took many of them in his own boat across Currituck Sound to the mainland, where he let them off near the Currituck Courthouse. Soon after the officers left Knott's Island, the Federal cavalry arrived in pursuit of them, and were intent on arresting anyone they could find. A "little maid of less than ten summers" (Miss Nancy White or someone else?) was arrested by the cavalry and brought a prisoner to Norfolk and charged with aiding and abetting the escape of rebel prisoners.[19] According to Ed McHorney in 1899, the girl's father, Henry White, and other family members were arrested, and their homes burned.[20]

Confederate authorities were soon aware of the plight of the escaped Confederate officers. In order to help them, Secretary of War J. A. Seddon wrote General D. H. Hill that the escapees from the *Maple Leaf* were hiding out in Camden County, on the east side of Pasquotank, and that they were in danger of being found by the cavalry sent out by General Dix. Seddon advised Hill to send Confederate cavalry to create a diversion to allow the prisoners to avoid capture.[21]

The Confederate officers also were helped in their flight by Dempsey Knight, a blockade-runner from Currituck County. Knight led the Confederates up the Albemarle Sound and the Chowan River to Confederate lines. Later, on one of his runs, he was captured by the Federals, who discovered who he was. The Federals promised to release him if he would tell where the missing Confederate officers were. Knight refused, and he was "strung up by his thumbs and tortured." When released, he jumped in the water and "drowned himself rather than confess."[22]

The Federal cavalry failed to find the escaped prisoners, because they had been hidden in the swamps by Colonel Green, the "guerrilla captain." Colonel Green subsequently escorted the officers to Richmond, Virginia.[23]

Prisoner exchange agents for both the Confederacy and the Union bickered over the escape of the Confederate officers. Confederate Agent Robert Ould justified their escape by raising questions about parole. He asked: "Can parole and imprisonment go together?" Ould believed the prisoners were justified in escaping, because a parole was a contract "not to bear arms if released," but a contract that a prisoner had the right to reject. Ould stated that up until the officers reached the Fort Monroe, they had been under "little or no guard. Their imprisonment was nominal." The situation changed upon reaching Fort Monroe, and the Confederate officers were put in something like a dungeon, with "eighteen in a room fifteen feet square, with an armed sentinel always at the door."[24] Because Union officials ended the possibility of exchange or parole, the Confederate officers believed it was necessary to escape.

The Confederate officers succeeded in reaching Richmond, Virginia, partly because of the help they received from people on Knott's Island. Accounts differ as to the part the White family played in giving aid to the escaping officers. Stories have persisted that when Federal troops visited Knott's Island to interrogate Mr. White, he was not at home, and the Federal troops "took a young girl to Norfolk" in his stead.[25] The *undocumented* story of the abduction of a 10-year-old girl in July may have gotten "telescoped" with the *documented* abduction of Nancy White, a 23-year-old, in December of 1863 by Colonel Alonzo Draper.

It is documented that six months after the officers escaped from the *Maple Leaf,* Miss Nancy White of Knott's Island was arrested in December of 1863 (although no charges were ever brought against her), taken to Norfolk as a prisoner of the Union forces and placed in the custody of Brigadier General Edward Wild. The question remains: Was Miss Nancy White taken a hostage in retaliation for the escape of the officers from the *Maple Leaf,* or was she taken because her mother spoke with disrespect and threatened Colonel Draper? Was it a coincidence that six months after the escape from the *Maple Leaf* Brigadier General Wild was sent to the area, or was the entire raid planned by General Dix as a means of revenge? We may never know the real reason, but the story gets even more complicated after Miss White's abduction.

Colonel Alonzo Granville Draper

The Union officer who took Miss White hostage was Colonel Alonzo Granville Draper. Draper was almost as unconventional and unpredictable as his superior officer, Brigadier General Wild. Ten years younger than General Wild, Draper was born in 1835 and grew up in Boston.[26] He was intelligent and had a "thirst for knowledge." At age eight, he was pronounced a "lawyer in embryo." He graduated from the Otis School in Boston in 1850, where he received the Franklin medal. Continuing his education, he graduated from the English High School in 1854, and received another Franklin medal and three additional prizes.[27]

Almost as adamantly against alcoholic beverages as Wild, Draper "delivered a temperance lecture" before he was fifteen years of age. He then helped organize a temperance society in Boston, and he drafted its constitution and bylaws.[28]

Draper's life was also marked with involvement in controversial causes. As a young man, Draper was a "man of ability, and conservative as a leader, invariably counseling moderation, and deprecating, at all times, any resort to violence." He was a fluent speaker, and early on in his life, he took up a cause to right the wrongs against conditions which existed among the industrial class.[29] Unable to enter college, Draper studied law. In 1859, he became the editor of *New England Mechanic*, a newspaper dedicated to the interests of journeymen shoemakers. In 1860, he organized the Shoemaker's Strike—the first large movement of its kind.[30]

Colonel Alonzo Granville Draper, 36th United States Colored Troops, Brevet Brigadier General, United States Volunteers. (Courtesy of Massachusetts Commandery, Military Order of the Loyal Legion, and U.S. Army Military History Institute, Carlisle Barracks, Carlisle, Pa.)

Always a maverick, Draper fell in love and married "without his father's consent." The bride was 17-year-old Sarah Elizabeth Andrews of Boston. Alonzo and Sarah eventually were the parents of six children, including a set of twins.[31]

When the war began in 1861, Draper, at age 25, was living in Lynn, Massachusetts, with his growing family. He was one of the first to volunteer for military duty, and raised a company in Lynn. For two months he paid for the services of a drillmaster and supported the men of his company until they were accepted. He was mustered in as Captain, Company C, 1st Massachusetts, Heavy Artillery, on July 5, 1861. He and his troops were drilled both as an infantry and an artillery regiment, and were stationed along the Potomac for the defense of Washington. On August 22, 1862, Draper was assigned as an Instructor in Infantry and Artillery to the 107th New York volunteers. Promoted to Major on January 16, 1863, he was placed in command of Fort Albany. When being considered to command colored troops, Colonel Thomas B. Tannat told Governor John A. Andrew that he thought Draper was "a too severe disciplinarian for that race." However, this proved incorrect, and the black troops soon learned that Draper made no distinction between blacks and whites "under his authority." Draper accepted the promotion to Colonel of the 2nd North Carolina Colored Volunteers on August 1, 1863.[32]

Both Draper and Wild were from Massachusetts, and both men had served as captains of companies in the 1st Massachusetts. It is not known whether they were friends, but certainly they had known each other since 1861. Both had risen in the ranks, and by 1863, Draper's 2nd NCCV was a part of Wild's African Brigade.

December 21, 1863—Draper Sent to Knott's Island

On Monday, December 21, 1863, Brigadier General Wild sent Colonel Alonzo G. Draper and a detachment of 250 men from the 2nd NCCV to Knott's Island. Wild's men were to travel by steamer to Knott's Island and then march to Norfolk.[33] Although Draper wrote a lengthy report on December 24, 1863 (three days after he took Miss White hostage), he only reported on an encounter with enemy forces at Shiloh in Camden County. He also reported an ambush near Sandy Hook as he and his men marched to meet Wild at Indiantown, and described his pursuit of the guerrilla forces and that he had burned their camp on Crab Island. Draper made no mention of his raid on Knott's Island, the burning of several homes there, or the incident that led to his taking Miss White hostage.[34]

After several encounters with guerrilla forces and a search for them in the swamps, Colonel Draper may not have been in the best of moods by the time he reached Knott's Island. According to one story, Draper had asked a North Carolina woman for the location of a guerrilla camp. She gave him directions but, fortunately, he took another route. Had he followed her directions, he and his men would have marched "into a pit which had been prepared in the roadway, and where the guerrillas were lying in ambush on either side."[35]

Wild Tells Draper's Side of the Story

The events on Knott's Island were described second-hand in a report penned later by Brigadier General Wild. Wild defended the actions of Colonel Draper, and reported that Mrs. Susan White stood up to Colonel Draper and threatened him. She warned the Colonel that "if you burn my house, there will be no houses left standing on this Island," which Draper took to mean that her family would burn the houses of Union sympathizers on Knott's Island. Draper then insisted that Mrs. White accompany him. When Mrs. White found herself under arrest, she began to beg off. Colonel Draper remained firm, because the nature of her threat made it imperative she be taken into custody. However, someone pointed out to Draper that Mrs. White was very pregnant, and near her time of confinement. Draper relented, but asked Mrs. White's daughter Nancy if she would surrender in her mother's place.

The young lady hesitated some 5 minutes, so Draper decided for her, and demanded that she go with them. Immediately, Miss White thought of her clothing, and gave a typically female reply that she had "nothing to wear." Colonel Draper allowed her to take her trunk along, and promised to give her time to dress at another house where they were to pass the night.[36]

At the time Nancy White was taken hostage, she was living with her parents, Henry and Susan Ann Fentress White, and several brothers and sisters. The youngest child, Marshall, was born, according to family tradition, the night that Nancy was taken hostage by Colonel Draper and his men. Henry had three brothers—James, age 37, Caleb, age 24, and William, age 22.[37]

After destroying the homes of Caleb White and Henry White, Colonel Draper and his troops left Knott's Island, taking Nancy White[38] in tow as a hostage. He and his men headed back to Virginia by way of the Federal outpost at Pungo Point on the east bank of the North River. Lieutenant Colonel Frederick F. Wead, post commander at Pungo Bridge, and the 98th New York Infantry had their winter quarters there. Draper and company arrived at Wead's headquarters on Tuesday, December 22.[39] Draper told Wead that he had taken the lady as a hostage "in obedience to orders of Gen. Wild," in retaliation for a "man of his command taken by guerrillas." Undoubtedly, Draper thought his actions were acceptable, since General Wild already had two female hostages under guard.

Drapers in America adds a few more details to the incident. After having taken a "Southern lady as hostage," in order to leave Knott's Island by a land route, Draper and his men had to cross a district under the command of a New York colonel. Upon arriving at Frederick F. Wead's headquarters, Draper and his hostage were invited to dine with Wead. That hospitality soon turned sour, and Wead took away Draper's sword "with the intention of releasing the lady." However, Draper ordered his regiment to his rescue.[40]

Wead's Side of the Story

Brigadier General James H. Ledlie and Lieutenant Colonel Wead had been assisting General Wild in his raid in North Carolina. A gunboat had been ordered to go to Pungo in case the 98th New York needed to be transported to Coinjock Bridge, Currituck courthouse, or Northwest Landing, as the situation demanded.[41] Wead was "an energetic, capable and meritorious officer" who had built up his regiment from a badly demoralized one to the best in the Department of Virginia and North Carolina.[42] Wead was a handsome young man with a high, wide forehead and a full beard.[43] He had an open, honest look about him. In contrast, Draper had the fierce, hard look of his "pirate" ancestor, softened only by his light-colored eyes.

Animosity between Draper and Wead existed before the argument over Miss White. After learning that Draper and his men had gone to Knott's Island and fearing a repeat of the outrages in Virginia and North Carolina, Wead sent Draper a

VIII. Mrs. Nancy White and the Wead-Draper Dispute 135

letter by Lieutenant Seyden of the 3rd N.Y. Cavalry. Seyden returned and reported that Draper had "burned the houses" of Caleb and Henry White "who were said to belong to Coffee's Guerrilla Co.," and that Draper had turned Henry White's wife, "who was within a few days of childbirth" out of doors, and Draper had taken White's daughter as hostage.⁴⁴

Draper arrived with his hostage the next day at Wead's headquarters, and asked for help in getting his men across to river so that he could rejoin Brigadier General Wild. At first, Wead offered Draper refreshments and extended to him every courtesy. Then, Draper's men arrived at Wead's headquarters with a carriage, and ushered Miss White into the house. A disagreement arose between Draper and Wead. Wead did not want Draper to take the lady out of the district without first referring the matter to Captain A. H. Davis, Ledlie's Assistant Adjutant General. Wead offered to give Draper "a receipt" for Miss White, but Draper

Lieutenant Colonel Frederick F. Wead, 98th New York Volunteer Infantry. (Courtesy of Division of Military and Naval Affairs, New York State Adjutant General's Office, Albany, New York, and the U.S. Army Military History Institute, Carlisle Barracks, Carlisle, Pa.)

refused and "attempted to force her out of the house and on my failure to remove from the door where I was standing, rushed into another room, seized his sword and thrust at me with it." Wead ordered his men to seize Draper and disarm him. Draper then swore he would call up his men to take Miss White away, and ordered his men into Wead's camp to form a "column of attack." Draper threatened to attack Wead's men, who had formed a line of defense in front of Wead's headquarters. Wead, along with Colonel Cullen of the 96th N.Y. Volunteers and Captain Kruntzer of the 98th N.Y. Volunteers, attempted to reason with Draper and "endeavored in the most temperate and courteous manner to dissuade him from his mad purpose." Draper finally agreed to take the lady to Captain Stevens' headquarters, and Wead reluctantly let her go, because he felt he had deviated from his duty in his desire to prevent bloodshed. Wead truly believed that bringing the lady to his headquarters was wrong because it was an "unwarranted infringement" upon his "territorial jurisdiction," and because it was contrary to the rules of civilized warfare.⁴⁵

Wead told Draper that the treatment of Miss White and her family "was a criminal violation of the law of war." He argued that Draper had "no authority to operate in Brigadier General Ledlie's district," and he wrote immediately to Captain A. H. Davis to complain that Draper did not have the authority to take the lady from his territory.[46] General Wild sided with his colonel, and reported that Wead had "severely abused" Draper and his officers, and had refused to allow Draper to leave with Miss White.[47]

Wild's first reaction was to support his subordinate officer, and he filed a complaint against Wead. In the complaint, Wild said that Colonel Draper had clashed with Lieutenant Colonel Wead over the possession of a hostage, and that Wead had "attempted to take a prisoner from him *vi et armis*" (with force and arms). Wild described the "personal violence inflicted upon Colonel Draper ... and the imminent danger of a pitched battle between the respective armed parties."[48]

One can just imagine the two hot-blooded young men and their supporters arrayed for battle almost at the point of coming to blows over the possession of a beautiful young damsel in distress. The news reporters would have been elated if they had learned of the affair.

Although Wild may not have ordered Draper specifically to take Miss White hostage, he came under fire because of the situation, especially when he did not release her for several weeks. She was still being held hostage on January 10, 1864, when Wild had to make a report to General Barnes regarding her situation. He explained that there were no charges against the young lady, but that she was being held "as hostage, to be offset against any of my colored soldiers taken prisoner by the Guerrillas." Wild stated that Miss White had been "uniformly well treated—and comfortably lodged in company with 2 other women—wives of guerrillas." He noted that she had not complained about her situation, and he dismissed allegations that she had not been allowed to write her mother, or that news of her family had been kept from her. On the contrary, in writing to her mother, Miss White had "praised our kind treatment and consideration," although she did say, "After all, it is not like home."

Wild continued to defend Draper's actions as necessary because of the threats made by Mrs. Susan White to burn the homes of Union sympathizers on Knott's Island. However, he assured Barnes that Miss White was now being held only as a witness in the Draper court martial. After that matter was resolved, she would no longer be needed as a witness, and would be released sometime in mid–January of 1864.[49]

The new year came, but Wild still held his three female hostages in Norfolk, Virginia. As the news spread, more and more people became upset over the action of Wild during his raid into North Carolina. Wild's threat to hang his female hostages was taken seriously. Wild's men believed that they were holding one of the "fair daughters" of the Confederacy for the "good behavior of her husband, who is a guerrilla officer, toward our beloved soldiers."[50]

Wild and his men were bombarded daily with inquiries about the location of the hostages, but their location was kept secret. Wild defended his actions as necessary because of the many "Secessionists" of Norfolk. Wild "snubbed them all," and even turned some out of his office. When approached by Attorney Charles W. Butts as to the whereabouts of the hostages, Wild told the lawyer "it was none of his business."[51] To ignore some of these complaints was a mistake. Attorney Butts either presented a *writ of habeas corpus* and brought charges against Wild, or had enough political clout to have pressure put on Wild to release the girl.

In addition, there was a letter of complaint to Major General Butler about the hostage from Miss White's uncle, James White.[52] Wild believed James White's letter was only a ploy to find out where the hostages were held, with a "view to further mischief."[53] Wild questioned the honesty of James White and Soloman W. Coffee, the authors of the letter. White was the brother of two guerrillas and uncle of the third. The co-signer of the letter, Soloman W. Coffee, was the brother to John T. Coffee, Captain of this same guerrilla company, as well as a brother-in-law to Henry White, the Lieutenant of the company of guerrillas. This same *Soloman W. Coffee* was on the company muster roll which had been used as evidence in the military trial of a captured Confederate, Major Burroughs.[54]

Wild pointed out that White and Coffee avoided any mention of the fact that Miss Nancy White was the daughter of a "Lieutenant of guerrillas." While Wild admitted that Draper and his men burned the houses of Miss White's relatives, he noted that the burning of Mr. White's house and barns or those of his brother, another guerrilla, was not mentioned in James White's letter, "lest it should be asked why they were burned." James White had only said that Miss White's father "was in the Confed. Service." The truth, Wild declared, was that her father, Henry White, was a Lieutenant of Capt. Coffee's Company of guerrillas. Henry White's brother, Caleb, was a Sergeant in the same company, and his son, William Henry White, was also a member of that company. Wild also pointed out to General Barnes that at the time "their houses were burning and Miss White arrested," Mr. White had gone to Camden County to join forces with other bands of guerrillas there to help in "waylaying my colored troops and slaughtering as many as they could with safety to themselves." Wild was certain that it was Mr. White and his guerrillas that "had made repeated attacks" against him and his men, and he also believed that this "very company was guilty of attacking our steamers in the C & A canal, burning one and firing into another."[55]

Wild turned sarcastic in his comments about James White's statement that he was "ignorant of the nature of the offence that Gen. Wild charges her with having committed, or the *offence* that *any other person may have committed*. I have been told on the streets of Norfolk that she is held as a hostage." Wild declared that the taking of Miss Nancy White was a well-known and much-talked-about incident. James White could have learned from her mother or from every inhabitant of Knott's Island. He thought it absurd that James White "should be the only man in all this region ignorant of the piratical deeds of his own family."[56]

Court Martial Charges

After the argument between Colonel Alonzo Draper and Lieutenant Colonel Frederick F. Wead, the two officers almost came to blows and the men under their commands came very close to engaging in a battle to defend their respective officers. Wead was so enraged because Draper would not leave Miss White with him that he brought charges against Colonel Draper, charges that could only be resolved by a military trial.[57]

Draper and his soldiers left Pungo Point, taking Miss White with them. They did not go directly to Norfolk as planned, but joined Wild and his remaining forces at Northwest Landing. Draper reported the incident with Wead to Wild, who, in turn, reported it to General Butler. Wild saw the incident as unlawful interference on the part of Wead. Meanwhile, Wead, not to be outdone, filed an indictment of nine charges against Draper. These charges are reproduced in full as Appendix D of Witt's *Wild in North Carolina*. Briefly summarized, those charges were:

(1) violation of 54th Article of War; (2) disobedience of orders; (3) conduct unbecoming an officer and a gentleman; and (4) conduct prejudicial to good order and military discipline.

The other five parts were listed as "specifications" under the four main charges.[58] Also among the papers of Frederick F. Wead, housed in the New York State Library, are the charges Wead brought against Colonel Draper regarding Draper's burning of houses and the taking of two married women as hostages.[59]

Wead was concerned that his actions might be construed as motivated by hostility to Negro troops, but he discounted that by stating "only their commanding officer was concerned in it." Wead believed that the incident would have taken place had "an officer of white troops acted equally intemperate and regardless of law." He also reminded his superior that it had only been a month since he (Wead) had reported "bad conduct of Col. Draper's regiment on their former march through this county." Wead believed that his actions then as post commander had gained him "ill will" from both Colonel Draper and his "Brigade Commander" (Wild). Wead gave as further evidence a statement made by Colonel Draper's surgeon that "all this was expected. Gen'l Wild told Col. Draper that Col. Wead was a copperhead and if he interfered with his operations to shoot him down." Wead came to the conclusion, perhaps wrongly, that the affair was provoked on purpose by Wild when he sent the detachment from Currituck. Wead also denied that he was a "copperhead," and insisted that he was an abolitionist who did not oppose the government's use of Negro Troops. He swore he was one of the earliest and most constant advocates of that policy. He declared he was a "believer in the necessity of discipline among those troops as well as others," and of the "indispensableness of a decent regard for the usages of war," and the rights of other officers, especially those commanding colored troops.[60]

Upon learning of the Wead-Draper dispute, Major General Butler ordered Wead removed from his regiment.[61] A few days later, Brigadier General James H. Ledlie wrote the Governor of New York that Lieutenant Colonel Wead was coming to New York state to fill up his "depleted ranks," and to obtain commissions for a number of "competent non-commissioned officers." Ledlie believed Wead to be a very capable and meritorious officer, and his regiment one of the best in the Department of Virginia and North Carolina.[62]

Major General Butler agreed to an investigation after he saw the charges Wead brought against Draper, charges that had been approved and endorsed by two generals. Butler, however, had to make an unexpected trip to Washington, and while the final outcome of Butler's investigation is not known, a compromise was reached.[63] The trial was held on January 12, 1864, and Draper was cleared. However, the next day, Butler ordered Lieutenant Colonel Frederick Wead to resume command of his regiment.[64]

Butler's General Order No. 8 of January 16, 1864, detailed the issues and the decisions on those issues. Only Wead's "good character" saved him from being dismissed from the military service, and Draper was found "entirely justified" in the whole transaction. Wead was ordered to make an "ample apology" to Draper for the "personal indignity suffered." Wead was publicly reprimanded for a "grave breach of military discipline and subordination." Always the politician, Butler saw the affair as a "misunderstanding of the rights & powers of officers commanding posts or having a military district assigned to their command." Butler concluded that an "inferior" officer can "never be responsible, either in moral or military law, for the acts of his superior officer, and if either do wrong, both are responsible to the common head." The decision was that any officer who attempted to "interfere with the acts of another officer not under his command, by force, thereby endangering a collission [sic] between bodies of troops, will be held to the strictest responsibility."[65]

Miss White Released

In a postscript to his letter to General Barnes, Wild excused his actions in keeping Miss White because she was needed as a witnesses in the trial between Colonel Draper and Lieutenant Colonel Wead, to take place before Major General Butler. Wild admitted he had been willing to release the girl ten days earlier, but since the trial of Draper had to be postponed until January 12, he had to retain her in custody. He declared: "She must appear at that time. And I do not intend to have her in the meantime tampered with by Lt. Col. Wead and his gang. I therefore keep her as close as ever." He promised to release her immediately after the trial, since she was no longer needed as a witness.[66]

It is not known what Miss White said at the court martial of Colonel Alonzo Draper. She appeared not to have suffered any harm during her imprisonment, except that she was greatly humiliated by her captivity. She was not kept in a public jail, but was housed in the home of Captain James Croft and his wife. Croft was a member of Wild's staff.[67]

The purpose of her letter to Brigadier General Wild is unclear. More than likely, she was asked to write the letter as a sort of "thank-you" note, for being released. Perhaps her letter was intended to stem the tide of criticism against Wild for holding her. Whatever her motivation, Miss White wrote Brigadier General Wild on January 14, 1864:

During the time that I have been a prisoner under you and confined in Capt. Croft's Quarters, I have been treated very kindly, indeed more than I could expect and have had every thing done that could conduce to my comfort and shall ever feel grateful to you for your bounty, and to Capt. Croft and family for the many kindnesses that I have received during my imprisonment.[68]

The envelope in which Miss White sent her letter has been reproduced in Galen Harrison's *Prisoners' Mail from the American Civil War*. Before her release, Miss White was required to pledge "her word and honor as a lady not to give Aid and Comfort to the Rebels," and to "do all in her power to restore the United States Government to its former Supremacy."[69]

Once the trial was over, as promised, Wild released Miss White from custody. He ordered Lieutenant G. H. Willis of the 3rd NCCV to escort her by "Streamer to Pungo Bridge" to be given over to the care of some of the officers of the 98th New York Volunteers.[70] Ironically, upon her release, instead of keeping her away from Wead, Wild sent her to him, with the note: "Wishing to restore her to her family, I now send her to Pungo Bridge, and I take the liberty of consigning her to your care, trusting you will forward her to Knott's Island, and believing also, that it will give you pleasure to do so."[71] Wead complied and reported back on January 16 that he had taken Miss White, the former "Hostage," to the "site of her former home." Wead expressed his gratitude to Wild and admitted that the Brigadier General had been right in believing it "affords me pleasure to return this lady to her friends. It is always pleasant to see a wrong redressed."[72]

One would hope this story had a happy ending, and that after the differences were resolved between Wead and Draper, and between Wead and Wild, that the matter would be forgotten. This was not the case.

Mid–January 1864—Hostages Still Being Held

Major General Butler had no choice but to become embroiled in the hostage controversy. When President Lincoln was informed of the hostage situation, he contacted Major General Butler. Butler replied to the President: "All executions have been stayed until further orders from you."[73] After Butler received orders from Lincoln, he could then alleviate the fears of Lieutenant W. J. Munden and Private Pender Weeks, the husbands of the female hostages. Butler assured the men that nothing had been done to their wives "to annoy, insult, or injure them, except the detention...." He promised the husbands that their women would not be hanged, and Butler overrode Wild's threats and declared that Wild's order to execute the women in retaliation would be revoked.[74]

Butler tried to calm the waters with a "judicial" approach and proposed an exchange of the two married women for their husbands. He still believed he needed someone to hold hostage because Confederates were "still talking about reprisals." On the other hand, Butler wanted to "observe all the rules of civilized warfare" so long as the Confederates did the same.[75] Butler promised that he would return the women to Northwest Landing on the condition that the husbands placed themselves "in his hands in their stead, to be treated as prisoners of war unless some outrage not justified by civilized warfare is perpetrated by the men of your commands, [and] the two women, Mrs. W. J. Munden and Mrs. Pender Weeks, will be delivered to their friends.[76] In this, too, Butler used his rank to overrule Wild's authority.

Butler's letter of January 26 referred to the two married women who were still being held hostage, since Miss White had been released 12 days earlier. That exchange may never have taken place. The two married women were held even after Miss White was released.

Investigation by Confederate Congress

The Confederate government was so concerned about Wild's raid it would not let the matter rest, and the Confederate Congress authorized a full investigation. The Confederate House of Representatives began its inquiry into the events in eastern North Carolina in open session on Friday, January 8, 1864. A resolution by Smith of North Carolina proposed the appointment of a Committee to conduct the investigation. On Monday, January 11, 1864, Swan, from the Committee on Military Affairs, presented the House of Representatives with "A bill for the benefit of citizens and noncombatants seized by the enemy," to be referred to the Judiciary Committee. This was ordered. A motion was passed that authorized the special committee appointed to investigate the outrages of the enemy in North Carolina to send for "persons and papers."[77]

Several months later, a resolution was adopted by the House of Representatives of the Congress of the Confederate States of America:

> Whereas information comes to us through our public journals, and from private sources, which leaves but little doubt our enemies are sending organized bands of raiders through the country, whose mission it is to murder in cold blood noncombatant citizens, unoffending women and children, to violate the persons of our females, and perpetrate other crimes and outrages disgraceful to humanity and practiced only by barbarians: Therefore, *Resolved*, That it be referred to the Committee on the Judiciary to inquire into the truth of these reports, and if true, to report a bill authorizing the infliction of such measures of retaliation as will effectually protect our people from these outrages.[78]

Although protests were made to Major General Benjamin F. Butler about Wild's actions in North Carolina, Butler neither demoted nor reprimanded Wild. Instead, he gave Wild command of all the troops, both black and white, in the Norfolk-Portsmouth area.[79] At the end of January 1864, the structure of Federal troops in the Department of Virginia and North Carolina, under Major General Benjamin F. Butler, listed Brigadier General Edward A. Wild and his African Brigade as being stationed at Norfolk and Portsmouth. Wild's African Brigade, commanded by Colonel John H. Holman, included the 2nd NCCV, with Colonel Alonzo G. Draper in charge; the 3rd NCCV, under Lieutenant Colonel Abial G. Chamberlain; and the 1st USCT, commanded by Major Elias Wright. In addition, Wild had access to the 27th Massachusetts, the 20th New York Cavalry, six companies of the 2nd Massachusetts Heavy Artillery, and the 7th New York Battery.[80]

Wild Is Demoted

On March 5, 1865, a scathing article entitled "A Wild General" appeared in the New York *World,* a paper with nationwide distribution. This criticism did not help Wild's image or that of his colored soldiers. The article pointed out that the "abolition journals were glorifying a certain General Wild for a raid he made in North Carolina while in command of a body of negro troops. Those same negro troops, the article alleged, had committed "all manner of atrocities." The Lincoln administration was denounced for placing "two-penny tyrants," Major General Butler and Brigadier General Wild, "in responsible military positions."[81]

Then, in April of 1863, Wild was relieved of his duties and replaced by General Charles K. Graham. Although Wild was still in the Department of Virginia and North Carolina, commanded by Major General Benjamin F. Butler, he now was in Major General William F. Smith's XVIII Army Corps. Next in the hierarchy of command was the Division of Colored Troops, with Brigadier General Edward W. Hinks in charge. Wild was left in charge of only the 1st Brigade, now composed of the 1st USCT, commanded by Col. John H. Holman; the 10th USCT, commanded by Lt. Col. Edward H. Powell; and the 23rd USCT, commanded by Col. Joseph B. Kiddoo.[82] This was just the beginning of a downward spiral in the military career of Brigadier General Edward A. Wild.

Was Wild Justified in Taking Hostages?

Hostages were frequently held to insure the safety of other captives by the enemy. In June of 1863, in South Carolina, Union General David Hunter ordered Colonel James Montgomery: "Every rebel man you may capture, citizen or soldier, you will send in irons to this place to be kept as hostages for the proper treatment of any of your men who may accidentally fall into the hands of the enemy."[83]

Although rare, the taking of female hostages was not without precedent. The Richmond *Dispatch* reported that in June of 1863, eleven "Yankee ladies were taken from Winchester to Richmond" where they were imprisoned by Confederate authorities in Castle Thunder.[84] However, these "female prisoners" were soon sent to Washington, where they were lodged in the United States Hotel.[85] However, "two wrongs do not make a right," and Wild may have overstepped his authority in taking these women hostage.

VIII. Mrs. Nancy White and the Wead-Draper Dispute

Male hostages were executed by both sides. Six months before Wild's raid into North Carolina, Union officer Lieutenant Colonel Assistant William H. Ludlow informed Confederate Exchange Agent Robert Ould that two Confederate officers, Brigadier General W. Fitzhugh Lee and another, had been selected as hostages for Capt. H. W. Sawyer, 1st New Jersey Cavalry, and Capt. John M. Flinn, 51st Regiment Indiana Volunteers, and had been "chosen by lot for execution." Ludlow vowed that if he learned that those two men were executed or "any other officers or men in the service of the United States not guilty of crimes punishable with death by the laws of war," that the Confederate officers held by the Union forces would "be immediately hung in retaliation, without giving you other or further notice." Ludlow had the authorization to promise that the "United States Government will proceed to retaliate for every similar barbarous violation of the laws of civilized war."[86]

Prisoners and their punishment became a serious issue, and some clarification of the rules of war was needed. On April 24, 1863, the revised rules of conduct of the military in the field, entitled "Instruction for the Government of Armies of the United States in the Field," were issued as General Order No. 100.[87] Lincoln ordered that the report be "published for the information of all concerned." Although General Order No. 100, section I, No.7, defined martial law as extending to "property, and to persons, whether they are subjects of the enemy or aliens to that government," there were many limitations as to what could and could not be done under martial law. Section I, No. 16, stated that "Military necessity does not admit of cruelty—that is, the infliction of suffering for the sake of suffering or for revenge, nor of maiming or wounding except in fight, nor of torture to extort confessions." Section I, No. 22, p. 150, also stated that "the unarmed citizen is to be spared in person, property, and honor as much as the exigencies of war will admit." In Section III, No. 54, p. 154, a hostage was described as "a person accepted as a pledge for the fulfillment of an agreement concluded between belligerents during the war, or in consequence of a war. Hostages are rare in the present age." Private citizens (Sec. I, No. 23, p.150) "are no longer murdered, enslaved, or carried off to distant parts, and the inoffensive individual is as little disturbed in his private relations as the commander of the hostile troops can afford to grant in the overruling demands of a vigorous war." The rule for modern warfare had advanced from suffering being inflicted on private individuals to "protection of the inoffensive citizen of the hostical country is the rule; privation and disturbance of private relations are the exceptions" (Sec. I, No. 25, p. 151).

The regulations described the treatment of prisoners, and that they were not to be subjected to "intentional suffering or indignity." They were to be fed "plain and wholesome food."(Sec. III, nos. 75, 76, p. 156). Certainly, Wild's female prisoners suffered "indignity," if nothing else.

Wild had his own interpretation of General Order No. 100. He found that ordinary measures were of little avail, and so he was forced to use a more rigorous style of warfare; he burned their homes and barns, ate their livestock, and took hostages from their families.[88]

Although Wild may have felt justified in doing so, taking three female hostages did not ensure the life of his own soldier, and Samuel Jordan was executed as Confederates retaliated. The hostage situation, combined with other more bizarre actions by Wild, led eventually to his arrest and court martial, and ended what might have been an outstanding military career.

Epilogue to the Nancy White Story

After Nancy White was released, she returned home to Knott's Island. She eventually married Eugene Ballance, son of Willoughby and Arsenth Ballance, on May 25, 1875. Nancy was born November 27, 1840, and died May 8, 1920. The couple had two children to die in infancy, Nannie Ballance (August 27, 1879–June 4, 1880), and Susan Ballance (October 7, 1882–August 14, 1883).[89] Her only surviving child, Mary Ballance, married a Mr. Dey. Mary Dey died in Norfolk, Virginia, about 1945. A family legend relates that Nancy White kept a diary about her days as a hostage, but that her daughter, Mary Ballance Dey, would never release it.[90] Alyda White (Mrs. Emory Beasley), 74-year-old great-niece of Nancy White, wrote an account stating that Nancy "thought it was a disgrace to stay in jail." Alyda had heard also that Nancy was only 16 at the time of her abduction. She also said that Henry White was not on Knott's Island when Draper and his Federal troops arrived and began burning homes and outbuildings, but that he watched his barn and boats burn from a safe distance. Mrs. Beasley also notes that Marshall White was born the same night Nancy was abducted.[91]

Tombstone of Nancy White Ballance on Knott's Island. (Courtesy of Dale Beasley, Knott's Island, North Carolina.)

Alyda White was the daughter of William Fentress White and Verna Irene Bowden, granddaughter of William Henry White (Nancy White's brother) and Lenora.[92]

Lieutenant Colonel Wead Honored

Within a short time, Lieutenant Colonel Frederick F. Wead was promoted to full Colonel, but three months later he was killed while leading his men at Cold Harbor.[93] General Butler ordered that a redoubt be named in Wead's honor.[94]

Brigadier General Alonzo Draper Killed

Shortly after his court martial, Colonel Alonzo Draper was assigned to command the prisoner of war camp at Point Lookout, Maryland.[95] He was promoted to brigadier general on October 28, 1864. He survived the war but did not live long afterward. Having been ordered to accompany his command to Texas, he was shot by a stray bullet, supposedly from an unknown Federal soldier.[96] The bullet lodged in his spine. When told of the hopelessness of his situation, Draper replied: "Gentlemen, I am not afraid to die." Draper died on September 3, 1865, just short of his 30th birthday.[97]

While both Wead and Draper died while still young men, it seems that Lieutenant Colonel Frederick F. Wead got the better deal out of the court martial, and was promoted. Draper, on the other hand, may have been "punished" by being sent to Point Lookout, undoubtedly not a very coveted position among officers. Yet, Draper served admirably at Point Lookout for several months until recalled to the battlefield.

IX

The Clopton Whipping and Other Civilian Incidents

A lion is in the streets.
—Proverbs 26:13

During the later part of 1863, the whole country, both North and South, was shocked by reports that three women and one old man had been taken hostage by Brigadier General Edward Wild on his raid into North Carolina. Other actions directed toward civilians by that same "wild" general, in 1864 in both Virginia and North Carolina, would prove to be even more shocking. These incidents would add to the already tarnished reputation of General Edward A. Wild. In the upcoming year, it would not be the Confederate Arm that would cause Wild the most trouble; it was the civilians and how Wild dealt with them that would cause Wild major problems.

Miller's Raid and the Ferebee Incident

During the last week of January 1864, Wild sent an expedition commanded by Captain Henry F. H. Miller, of the 2nd NCCV, to northeastern North Carolina. As Miller and his men approached Elizabeth City, his soldiers went to the house of Edwin Ferebee and took from him "ten slaves, one horse, and one mule & two carts." Captain Miller learned from the slaves that Ferebee had been feeding guerrilla bands, and a group of 26 guerrillas had eaten supper at the Ferebee home a only a few nights before.[1]

After Wild read Miller's report, he ordered Edwin Ferebee to come to Norfolk. A note from Dr. R. C. Perkins attested to the "bad health" of Ferebee and said he was "still confined to his bed and could not travel to Norfolk" without endangering his life.[2] Another note from Pastor R. R. Overby, of the Baptist Church, promised that Ferebee would "come to Norfolk whenever required and his health will admit, or before it is demanded." The Pastor also swore that he knew Ferebee to be "a peaceable [sic] and quiet citizen" and that he had not "of choice given any aid to the Guerrillas." Pastor Overby acknowledged the fact that the guerrillas had been to Ferebee's house several times, and "demanded something to eat."[3]

Miller also encountered Mrs. Shaw, the wife of a "rebel" colonel, who acted very "unlady-like." He was exasperated by her and declared if "she had been a man, I should have bound her hands & feet & carried her to Norfolk." She evoked General Butler's order, and refused to let him take her slaves, and said that "they did not want to go, & that they were very afraid of my soldiers," while at the same time, those very same "men, women & children were crying to me for help to save them from the hand of oppression." Mrs. Shaw "raised a cane above the head of Sargent [sic] Davis without any provocation," except that he had said, "Madame, you dare to strike." She asked, "Are you not ashamed to be the leader of a gang of negroes?" The Captain replied, "It seems you were not ashamed to hold these men, women & children in bondage, & why, do tell me, should I be ashamed to lead them on to sweet liberty." She retorted that if her husband were there with his regiment he would soon remove the negro troops. Miller was unmoved, and replied, "That, Madam, would depend entirely upon the sword & the bayonet."[4]

Leaving the Shaw plantation, Miller and his train of freed slaves were followed by guerrilla forces. They continued on a forced march of 33 miles through a dense swamp and did not stop until 11 P.M. Miller complimented his troops and their handling of the problems common to moving trains of contraband. They arrived back in Norfolk on February 2 with a train of "150 contrabands, 35 carts & wagons, 28 mules, 8 stears [steers] & several horse." The greatest accomplishment was, however, that they had given the enemy "a warning that we are not afraid to meet them on their own dear soil."[5]

Seizure of Private Homes for Military Quarters

When a city is under martial law, civil law is suspended and military law takes precedent. General Order 100, of 1863, stated that "property of any Secessionist was liable for seizure." However, if a citizen of a state in the Confederacy agreed to take the Oath of Allegiance to the United States, that oath afforded the amnesty offered by President Lincoln and was supposed to guarantee safety and security.[6]

John Williams House Confiscated

Housing was always in short supply, especially when an army was in residence. Wild's brigade needed housing and there were several houses in Portsmouth that were owned by John Williams, reported to be an "out and out Rebel." When Wild ordered the Provost Marshal to take Williams' property, Williams protested and hired a lawyer, Charles W. Butts. Butts had come from Pennsylvania to practice in Norfolk. He tried to circumvent Wild's order by having Williams appear before Lieutenant Colonel Weldon, the Provost Marshal at Norfolk. Butts hid the fact that Williams was a resident of Portsmouth, and he asked the Provost Marshal to administer the Oath of Allegiance to his client. No sooner had Williams taken the oath than he began bragging that he was still "a Rebel as before and only took the oath to save his property." Of course, Wild learned of this and canceled the oath, then had it erased from the records. Butts, thinking to bypass Wild, wrote to Attorney General Edward Bates in Washington, but did not mention his action which had resulted in Wild's cancellation of his client's oath.[7] Bates wrote the Secretary of War, and made the comment that Wild's order was "extraordinary and seems to me a great stretch of power without and against law." However, Secretary of War Stanton knew that Wild was acting under martial law, and forwarded Bates' letter to General Butler. As a result, Attorney Charles Butts was ordered to leave the District of Norfolk, and a subsequent order decreed that he leave the Department.[8]

Mrs. Newton's Property

Still seeking adequate housing, General Wild noticed a house near his headquarters which belonged to Mrs. Courtney Newton. He ordered the Provost Marshal to seize her property. Mrs. Newton, however, had earlier taken the Oath of Allegiance. When she learned her property was to be taken, she went directly to Major General Butler's headquarters. Butler found that legally she was entitled to keep her property because she had taken the oath, and because of her loyalty. Yet, there remained the question of "military necessity." Butler ruled that while a "commanding general would have no difficulty in taking the homes of persons of known disloyalty for the convenience of his officers and men, nothing but urgent necessity would justify the taking of homes of loyal persons."[9] Butler ruled that if Wild and his staff should be without shelter in "inclement" weather, he would be justified in taking the home of a loyal citizen. However, the owner of the house would have a claim against the Federal government for rent. Butler, therefore, again sided with a civilian against Wild, and set aside Wild's order to confiscate the Newton property. Wild had probably thought the title to the property was in Mrs. Newton's husband's name, and since he had died as a Confederate soldier, the property could be confiscated.[10]

The Reverend Wingfield's Punishment

Wild extended his authority to control to church congregations and those who mounted the pulpits. From his headquarters in Norfolk, Wild issued General Order

No. 2 on February 11, 1864, which appeared in area newspapers, including the Wilmington *Journal*.

> All places of public worship in Norfolk and Portsmouth are hereby placed under the control of the Provost Marshals of Norfolk and Portsmouth respectively, who shall see the pulpits properly filled, by displacing when necessary the present incumbents, and substituting men of known loyalty and the same sectarian denomination, either military or civil, subject to the approval of the Commanding General.
>
> They shall see that the churches are opened freely to all officers and soldiers, white or colored at the usual hour of worship, and at other times, if desired; and they shall see that no insult or indignity be offered to them, either by word, look or gesture, on the part of the congregation.[11]

Apparently, the Reverend S. H. Wingfield, an elderly Episcopal minister of Portsmouth, disregarded and defied Wild's order. His actions were brought to the attention of General Wild, and Wingfield was subsequently disciplined by the general. Wild prescribed punishment on February 25, 1864, in Special Order No. 44. He ordered Wingfield to clean the streets of Norfolk for "secessionist behavior," because, according to Wild, Wingfield had been disrespectful to the President of the United States during prayer at a church service, which served to "annoy and disgust the loyal portions of the congregation."[12]

Wild had branded Wingfield "an avowed Secessionist," one who had taken every opportunity "to disseminate his traitorous dogmas," to the annoyance of his loyal neighbors. Wild believed it necessary to make an example of Wingfield, and he had the Provost Marshal to arrest the Rev. Wingfield and turn him over to Colonel Sawtelle (without a trial) to begin his sentence of cleaning the streets of Norfolk and Portsmouth for three months. This was to atone for Wingfield's "disloyalty and treason."[13]

The New York *World* described the Rev. Wingfield as a "man of high character ... of education and ability." They dismissed the charges against the minister as untrue, "but, true or not, he had no trial," and had been punished only because someone had reported him to General Wild.[14]

The citizens were outraged at the punishment imposed on the elderly minister. Again, because of public outcry, Major General Butler had to step in to overrule Wild's orders and give Wingfield a reprieve.[15]

Confiscation of "Sherwood Forest" Plantation

During the Peninsular campaign, Union forces continued to press on toward Richmond. The plantation of "Sherwood Forest," situated on the north side of the James River near Wilson's Wharf, was overrun by Federal troops. On May 7, 1864, a black troop under the command of Brigadier General Wild, part of the 1st Brigade, Hinks' Division, XVIII Corps, crossed the James River at Kennon's Landing and occupied Sherwood Forest, the home of a former United States president, John Tyler. During the fighting at Wilson's Wharf, while Wild's men were under siege by Confederate Fitzhugh Lee, some of the outbuildings at Sherwood Forest were burned, "by (some believed) retreating Confederate cavalry." Robert Seager II, in *and Tyler too,* described "a reign of terror" that was unleashed against the "defenseless county by the conquerors."[16]

John C. Tyler, nephew of the former president, wrote to the President's widow, Mrs. Julia Tyler: "General Wilde [sic] has landed at Kennon's with coloured troups [sic] and taken everything through the county—I hear they have not left five dollars' worth on Sherwood Farm."[17]

"A Fate Worse Than Death"

Another casualty of the war and the Federal occupation of Charles City County, Virginia, was Maria Tyler, a niece of former President Tyler. When Federal troops arrived at her home, Sherwood Forest, a terrified Maria fled to the safety of the William H. Clopton plantation, "Selwood." In her absence, Sherwood Forest was almost completely dismantled, by Wild's orders, and the house, barns, and outbuildings were taken over by "neighborhood Negroes who wandered aimlessly through the countryside."[18] Unknowingly, poor Maria Tyler had jumped from the frying pan into the fire by going to Selwood.[19]

Although both generals Butler and Wild had given Maria Tyler permission to go North, and assured her friends that she would be "shielded," Maria would not leave Charles City County. Brigadier General Wild answered Mrs. Julia Gardiner Tyler, the ex–President's widow, on June 6, 1864, about Maria's whereabouts. Wild wrote that Miss Maria Tyler had "left the Tyler Mansion about 3 weeks ago, and took up her residence at Mrs. Clopton's, where she has been living up to the present time." Wild contacted Miss Maria to see if she wished to join Mrs. Julia Tyler on Staten Island, but she declined. Wild reported that Maria had decided not to leave Charles City County, because she was "liable to hemorrhage from the lungs." Wild promised that "When Miss Tyler's decision is made, I will notify you further."[20]

In reality, Maria did not want to leave because she had married 20-year-old Union Private Kirk, "a little Dutchman" from Buffalo, New York, who was "entirely without any of the civilities of life about him."[21] Sad to say, neither Maria's friends nor her relatives would welcome Maria's Yankee bridegroom into their homes. Even Julia Tyler refused to visit her, and declined a pass offered by General Butler. She believed Maria was mentally ill, and had been "bordering on insanity" for weeks. She attributed the girl's mental condition to the "terrible scenes" she had recently witnessed.[22] The delicate, orphaned 27-year-old Maria, desperate for security, committed the "unpardonable sin" when she did the "unthinkable" and married a Yankee soldier,[23] a situation considered by true Southern women to be a "fate worse than death." The problem created by this Southern belle having a Yankee husband was soon resolved when Private Kirk was arrested by the military police after it was discovered he already had a wife back in New York state.[24] Maria Tyler's reputation was ruined.

May 6, 1864—Arrest of Englishman James Challiner

Activity along the James River and around Wilson's Wharf was escalating as the move toward Richmond continued. James Challiner was taken prisoner on May 6 when Wild sent a party to surprise the "Rebel Signal Station" at Sandy Point on the banks of the James River, some miles below Wild's position. The Federals had traveled in a gunboat and then landed in small boats, two or three miles above the destined point, in order to block any retreat. As Wild's men approached the embankment, they saw a couple of people watching them. They hurried to arrest the man, James Challiner, to prevent him from spreading information of their arrival. Challiner's companion got away. Although Challiner was questioned, he would give no information. The detail soon learned that the man who had escaped had indeed rushed to the Signal Station to warn the Confederates of their presence in the area. Wild's men followed and were able to apprehend the escaping Rebels. A search of the Challiner premises revealed two muskets concealed, and a lot of "old army clothing and equipment being probably remains of McClellan's Army."[25]

Wild's soldiers attacked the Rebel Signal Station at Sandy Point. The 10 Confederates at the station put up some resistance, and 5 were killed, 3 wounded and 2 caught. The dead were buried on the spot. The wounded were taken to Fort Monroe. Wild reported that of the 10 at the signal station, 8 were soldiers and 2 were citizens. One citizen was killed and one was wounded. The officers in charge of the capture were Captain Eagle and Lieutenant Rice of the 1st Regiment USCT. Wild complimented them for "skillfully carrying out the plan."[26]

The wounded Confederates were taken prisoner. Private W. D. Wise had received a flesh wound in his left hip; Private T. R. Vincent was wounded in his right side; and Grenbow Gordon, a private citizen, received a slight flesh wound in his left shoulder.[27]

The Walker Incident

Other captured civilians—George Walker, A. H. Ferguson, J. L. Egman, and W. S. Graves—were sent by Wild from Wilson's Wharf to the Provost Marshal at Fort Monroe on May 17, 1864. In a transmittal letter, Wild noted that Ferguson was to be treated as a "prisoner of War." George Walker had been proved to have been a guerrilla for a long time. Although he had been "wounded by one of my men after his capture," Wild warned that the prisoner "should be carefully guarded." Wild ordered that Graves and Egman, both citizens, be detained for three weeks to keep them from relaying information to Confederates.[28]

The Walker incident has several versions. George Walker was shot by Wild's black soldiers. Walker claimed he was trying to stop the soldiers from plundering. Walker survived his wound and was sent to prison.[29]

Testimony concerning George Walker's activities obtained from Confederate deserters who were imprisoned by the Federal troops presented a different version of Walker and why he was shot, from that of Brigadier General Wild.

Charles J. Major, one of Walker's neighbors, gave a statement to Wild. He lived four miles from Walker, and had always known him. Walker had been Sheriff and Constable before the war, and that he had always been a "secessionist—was so, many years before the War." During the war, Walker had helped the Confederacy "in every possible way—has provided provisions forage etc." He was known to have "persecuted Union men,—and was constantly haranguing and trying to influence others." Walker's official capacity was not as conscription or "enrolling officer" but he helped in that endeavor voluntarily. Major reported he had heard that as McClellan was retreating from Harrison's Landing, "an officer of his army went home to eat a meal, alone." As he was returning to his post he was "waylaid and killed by this George Walker, who afterwards boasted of it."[30]

According to Joseph Bryant of Charles City County, Virginia, Walker was "active in carrying out the conscript act." When Bryant deserted from the Confederate army, Walker had "hunted" him down. Bryant added to Walker's guilt by stating that he also had heard rumors that Walker often bragged of "killing a Yankee officer during McClellan's retreat from Harrison's Landing." Bryant testified that Walker "habitually led scouting parties" between Charles City County and James City County.[31]

Another acquaintance of George Walker was Charles H. Kruger. Kruger stated to Brigadier General Wild, on May 16, 1864, that he was a deserter from Company D, of the 10th Virginia Cavalry, in which he was a bugler. He stated that he had known George Walker for two years while he had been stationed in the county, and had been on picket duty in the area. Walker, he said, was known to be a "Rebel," and that he "entertained officers and soldiers of the rebel army at his home constantly." A Confederate signal station had been set up at Walker's house for "more than a year." He believed the report that Walker had "fired at Yankees of McClellan's Army," but he could not say he had heard Walker say anything about this personally. However, Kruger did remember Walker telling him: "I can tell any man that won't kill a Yankee, by looking at his eye, and such a man is a yankee himself."[32]

May 8, 1864 — Civilian Prisoners Sent to Fort Monroe

On May 8, Wild compiled a list of prisoners who were to be sent to Fort Monroe from Wilson's Wharf, and how long each was to be imprisoned.

Mrs. Wilson—wife of Dr. Wilson, runaway (confine)
Mr. R. H. Ealey—scout—head hurt—(prisoner of war)
Mr. John H. Freeman—Capt. of Reb steamer conscripted & furloughed (Prisoner of war)

Mr. Josiah Wilson—runaway from his slaves (confine him 6 weeks)
Master George W. Wilson—his son (confine one month)
Master William B. Bunt—brought in from Major's house (confine 1 month)
Mr. George B. Major, brought in by foraging party (confine 1 month)
Mr. William G. Smith—Signal Corps (prisoner of war)
Mr. Dennison Worthington—Signal Corps (prisoner of war)
Mr. John Challiner—Englishman (detain 1 month)
Mr. S. P. Carrington—Prisoner of war
Mr. J. C. Tyler—citizen (detain 1 month)
Mr. James Vaughan—citizen (detain 1 month)

Wounded Prisoners

W. D. Wise, private Signal Corps (slightly) Prisoner of war
[T?] S. R. Vincent, private Signal Corps (slightly) Prisoner of war
Dunbar Gordon, citizen with arms (slightly) Prisoner of war

Contraband

Richard B. Randall, Samuel Randall, James Hall, Tabornto Randall, Charles White, and several others.[33]

Among the plantation owners arrested were John C. Tyler, nephew of the late President Tyler, as were G. B. Major, A. H. Ferguson, R. J. Vaiden, J. C. Wilson, and Thomas Douthat of "Weyanoke." These men were taken to Fort Monroe, under General Benjamin F. Butler's jurisdiction, and kept prisoners. Their wives and children were left defenseless.[34]

James Challiner, captured at the Sandy Point Signal Station, was brought to Wild at Wilson's Wharf and retained, because he could pass along important information to the enemy if released. He was held from May 6 until June 30, when Wild suggested that he was "sufficiently punished for his indirect aid and communication with the enemy," and that the prisoner might now be released, since his information was out of date. He ordered, however, that Challiner not be landed at Wilson's Wharf, but released at some point below there. Other prisoners now being held at Fort Monroe now could safely be released, especially those who were "not charged with special offences and who are not liable to exchange."[35]

May 9, 1864—The Shooting of Lamb Wilcox and Others

Wild earned another black mark when Virginia planter Lamb Wilcox was killed. According to one version of the story, Wilcox was standing unarmed in his doorway when he was shot dead because he refused to salute Wild's African Brigade.[36] Just who fired the shots is unknown, but as their commander, Wild was held responsible for the actions of his soldiers.

William Clopton wrote to Mrs. Tyler on June 8 to tell the news about various incidents involving neighbors and Federal soldiers that would make her "blood curdle" in her veins. He told how Lamb Wilcox had been "shot down in cold blood." Another by the name of Adams had been "shot dead" standing in his own door. Bunt and Gordon had been shot but not killed, and George Walker was "lying at the Hospital, shot without another word said." Other "vile and indecent actions" had taken place at the home of William Majors.[37]

The Holt Affair

According to Wild, Mr. Holt and his family were are all rebels who lived close to Wilson's Wharf, "but across the creek, and a mile from the shore, concealed by dense woods." Holt had two sons who had volunteered for the Confederate Army, and one daughter who was "affianced to a Staff Captain, probably in Fitzhugh Lee's Staff."[38]

Wild became suspicious that Holt was "harboring and aiding scouts to examine our position from these woods," after some movement in the woods was noticed. Federal gunboats fired shells into the area. The next morning Wild went with a party to examine the area, and found traces that a large mounted party probably had been harbored at Holt's house all night and "some had slept in his beds." Wild questioned the Holt family but they would not give him any information as to the "numbers or rank of their guests." The Holts would only say that they had all departed, "being obliged to report to Fitzhugh Lee the same evening." Wild knew that whoever had been in the woods was there to reconnoiter for another attack upon his position. The plan was frustrated doubtless by the movement of Grant's army to the south.[39]

Wild could do nothing at the time, but he remembered, when was relieved from his command at Wilson's Wharf, to warn his successor at the post to be wary of Holt. Wild advised his successor to keep a sharp lookout for the Holts, "and to catch this quiet and peaceable old man." Wild believed that Holt, "like all the slave holders of that region," was "excessively pious, and a man of honor." Wild had put off Holt's punishment because his men had been "too busy just at the time" and he wished to do it thoroughly. Wild did send a small party on his last day with orders to take hastily what "availables" they could find at the Holt house, but they returned to report that the "9th Army Corps had saved them all the trouble."[40]

Confederate Dog

The Federals at Wilson's Wharf were "hounded" by a Confederate spy, in the form of a large, white dog who came from the Holt place, with whom Wild had a long "acquaintance." The dog belonged to some guerrilla and was seen many times prowling about the Federal pickets, at all hours of night and day. Its appearance heralded shots fired at Federal pickets by Confederate sharpshooters.[41]

The Whipping of William H. Clopton

While the imprisonment of a number of wealthy, influential Virginia plantation owners brought censure to Wild, the incident involving the whipping of a member of that class is, undoubtedly, one of the most bizarre happenings from among all the strange and unconventional actions attributed to General Wild.

On May 10, 1864, William H. Clopton, and several other Charles City County, Virginia, planters had been taken prisoner, and sent to Fort Monroe. Wild's reason for taking Clopton and other citizens prisoners was "to prevent their giving information to the enemy; until change of military positions shall render such precautions unnecessary." Along with the prisoners, Wild sent packages belonging to them, and items found on their persons.[42]

William H. Clopton wrote to Mrs. Julia Gardiner Tyler on May 17 that when he approached General Wild to obtain permission to remain with his family, he learned that "some young negro women" had preceded him and had told General Wild that he (Clopton) "was a most cruel master," and, consequently, he was "stripped and whipped most cruelly by negroes."[43]

Wild was told by half a dozen women former slaves among the refugees that Clopton had often whipped them "unmercifully." Wild said that Clopton was notorious as being the most cruel slave owner in the region, but that he put up a front and appeared in his presence to be a "Sniveling Saint." Wild allowed his hatred for slave owners to influence his common sense. Wild decreed that the punishment should fit the crime, as the *Old Testament* decreed, "An eye for an eye." He had Clopton tied to a post and stripped to the waist. Then, Wild gave a whip to the women, and three of them took turns in "settling some old scores on their master's back." A black man finished the administration of poetic justice. Wild remarked without remorse, "I wish that his back had been as deeply scarred as those of the women, but I abstained and left it to them."[44]

Because of this incident, Wild was described as a "fanatical abolitionist." One source said the whipping was begun by one of Wild's soldiers, William Harris, of the 1st U.S. Colored Troops, who had formerly been owned by Clopton. Harris struck 15 to 20 blows, and each so severe "that blood flew at every stroke."[45]

May 11, 1865—More Prisoners

Another group of prisoners, including both civilians and soldiers, was sent by Brigadier General Wild to Capt. John Cassells, Provost Marshal. Charles City

County farmers included William H. Clopton, Samuel Morrison, J. M. Vaiden, Robert Vaiden, Richard M. Graves, Wm. R. Walker, G. W. Colgin, and R. W Bullifant. Golmore Croper, a Surry County farmer, was also sent. Confederate soldiers M. F. Vaiden and Nelson R. New had been captured while on furlough. Last on the list was Charles Marklin, a fisherman and British subject. Wild specifically ordered that Clopton, New, and Vaiden were to be considered "prisoners of war." The others he ordered to be "detained for a month or less, to prevent their giving information to the enemy," or until changes in military position made their retention no longer necessary.[46]

After Clopton was whipped on May 13, he was sent to tell his story to Major R. S. Davis at Bermuda Hundred. Davis was informed that Clopton had stated that "he came into our lines of his own free will to report himself and to obtain such information in relation to his future conduct as would guide him so as not to transgress any of our laws or rules." Several officers at the post had called the attention of the post commander to Clopton, including the Post Adjutant, and other officers of the garrison. He was told that upon General Wild's orders, Clopton had been tied up and "flogged by Negroes and that his back and arms bore the marks of the fearful punishment." Clopton told the Post Commander that he had been punished because "some one reported that he had been a cruel Master." Clopton had requested that he be allowed to "contradict" that report with testimony from his own servants. After seeing Clopton's body, the Post Commander decided to send him to the Major General Commanding (Butler) for a "personal inspection and investigation," because he knew that the Butler would not approve of such punishment.[47] After he was whipped, Clopton was taken to Old Point where some of the officers learned of his whipping and preferred charges against General Wild. Later, Clopton was detained by General Butler, who agreed that Clopton had "been badly treated," and promised to investigate the matter.[48]

Clopton wrote his friend and former neighbor, now a resident of Staten Island—Mrs. Julia Gardiner Tyler—on May 17, to tell her the terrible local news. He reported that John C. Tyler had been taken prisoner the previous week, and that Miss Maria Tyler had fled to his home.[49]

On May 31, William H. Clopton again wrote to Mrs. Julia Tyler to tell her he had visited John C. Tyler and others being held at the Chesapeake Hospital Prison. He conveyed a rumor that "Gardie" (David Gardiner Tyler) was safe with Robert Tyler, but he had had no news of his own son. He advised Mrs. Tyler not to return to Virginia until the war was over. He convened the sad news that all her furniture "but the crib & piano were destroyed." Clopton also expressed his concern over his separation from his wife, who did not know that he had been paroled from prison for a week.[50]

On June 8, Clopton told Mrs. Tyler that he had heard from his wife Luella and Maria Tyler and that both were well. He reported that Colonel John C. Holman, one of Wild's officers, had visited his wife and Miss Maria Tyler at Selwood and had shown them "marked courtesy." He knew that the visit was a result of Mrs. Tyler's letter to General Butler.[51]

While William H. Clopton was out on "parole," he managed to see John C. Tyler and gave him $50 to purchase some "summer clothes." While in prison with the "greasy & dirty of the county," Tyler had caught the "itch," and was bothered by other vermin (lice) common to prisons.[52] From prison in Fort Hamilton near Fort Monroe, John C. Tyler wrote on May 20 to Mrs. Julia Tyler to tell her he had been taken from "Sherwood some 12 days past [May 8, 1864] & was not permitted to take a suit of clothes & have no money." John had been quite ill, but was now feeling better. In the same room with him were several others, including G. B. Major, Ferguson, the two Vaiden men, Wilson, and his little son. John reported that there had been "no trial" and he could not find out what the charges were against him and the others. William H. Clopton had been left at Fort Monroe. John described his own treatment by the officers at Fort Hamilton as "kindly," and that they were well fed, but he had no appetite. He got to exercise some in the yard, but he had to sleep in a room with 16 others, many of whom had been "sick since our arrival here."[53]

Although General Butler did treat the planters with respect, he still did not release them until pressure was brought by Mrs. Julia Gardiner Tyler.[54] Mrs. Tyler's complaints were published in the *Evening Post & Evening Express* in June of 1864. She described her property, Sherwood Forest, a plantation of 1,400 acres on the James River, left to her by her husband, the late President Tyler, which, until the arrival of Federal troops in the spring of 1864, had been in "perfect order & under a high state of cultivation." She said up until the spring of 1864, she had been treated with all courtesy due the widow of an ex-president by both the Northern and Southern armies, but since then, her "beautiful estate" had been wrecked, "the sanctuary of her home invaded, & the operations of her farm prevented by the seizure of all her stock & the imprisonment of her manager, and elderly gentleman engaged in the inoffensive pursuit of conducting the business of her plantation."[55] Her letter was in reply to an article reprinted from the Cincinnati *Commercial*[56] which disclosed information from letters found in the Tyler home. The letters emphasized ex–President Tyler's Southern sentiments. After Mrs. Tyler's letter, the editor of the *Evening Post & Evening Express* criticized her husband, a man who "had sworn to support the constitution of the United States," but who had attended the Peace Convention "called to prevent the issues of civil war, where he professed the most unbounded devotion to the Union, and an utter detestation of the South Carolina secessionists." Yet, the editor pointed out, Tyler had "returned to his own state to engage almost immediately in inflaming the excitement against the Union, and in precipitating Virginia into the vortex of southern madness." Thus, instead of Tyler helping to keep Virginia in the Union, he and the state had chosen the Confederacy, and the result was that the "fields [of the state of Virginia] are ravaged, her women are widows, and her children orphans."[57]

The tongue-lashing Mrs. Julia Tyler gave Colonel Joseph Holt, Judge Advocate General, resulted in charges being brought against Brigadier General Wild before the Judge Advocate General of the Army. Mrs. Tyler, outraged because of Clopton's whipping and the destruction of Sherwood Forest, wanted to see Wild punished.⁵⁸ Wild wrote his wife on June 22 that "Mrs. Ex. Pres. Tyler keeps stirring up the Clopton whipping matter." By this time, the matter had been referred to the Judge Advocate General, and Wild knew that he faced a court martial. He did not let his wife know that he was worried about it, and he quipped lightly that "whatever I might lose in military, I might gain in civil or political life."⁵⁹

Wild's Explanation

What was the reason behind the destruction of Sherwood Forest, the Tyler plantation? Was it destroyed because Tyler had supported the Confederacy? Was it destroyed by Wild's orders or orders from someone higher up? Were the James River plantation owners singled out for harsher treatment than was necessary or warranted? Why were civilians, whose only crimes were that they were Southern plantation and slave owners, detained as "prisoners of war?" Why were civilians killed or whipped?

On May 11, 1864, Wild received a terse letter from the Division Commander, Brigadier General Edward W. Hinks, who demanded an explanation for the "killing of a citizen by an armed party" from Wild's brigade, and for the "whipping of a Citizen Prisoner of war." Hinks also wanted the names of all the officers connected with these two events. Hinks told Wild that he hoped that "these extreme acts were not perpetrated without sufficient cause."⁶⁰

In his defense, Wild detailed his actions, as requested by General Hinks, but he did not reply directly to Hinks. Instead, Wild addressed his explanation and a protest of Hinks' accusations to Major Robert S. Davis, Assistant Adjutant General of the Department.

> Not being in the habit of accepting rebukes for acts not committed, and feeling that I can judge of "the qualities becoming to a man or a soldier" quite as well as I can be informed by Brig. Gen. Edw. W. Hinks, in *such a letter* ... I protest against the whole tone of the above [Hinks'] letter, as unbecoming and unjustly as being full of harsh rebuke, administered before ever making any inquiry; and therefore, as *pre* judging cases against me, and taking for granted that acts perpetrated by me, are necessarily barbarous and cruel, and not admitting the possibility of any justification, nor the probability of any excuse.⁶¹

Wild's Version of the Wilcox Shooting

Wild described the events that led to the Wilcox shooting. A party was sent out before daylight to surprise a "squad of Rebels, who had been playing as *Guerrilla*," and who had attacked Wild's men three times. Wild knew that Confederates would be spending the night at a "certain house," and he sent out his men, hoping they would arrive before daylight. However, the distance was greater than he had been told, and the Federal soldiers did not arrive until daylight. There, they found 11 Rebels commanded by an officer in uniform, reported to be an Adjutant. The advance detail of 5 mounted Union soldiers advanced on the Confederates. One was killed and another wounded. The Confederates escaped into a swamp, and encountered a smaller group of Union soldiers who were awaiting the main body of Wild's men to approach. The Confederates escaped in two boats and crossed the Chickahominy River. The citizen killed was believed to be "Wilcox, owner of the house, and the enrolling officer of the District." Wilcox was buried in the yard at the house, and the house was burned. The officers in charge of this expedition were Major Cook, 22nd USCT, and Henry Harris, of Captain Choat's 2nd USCT Battery. Wild stated emphatically: "I wish it to be distinctly understood by Brig. Gen. Hinks, that I shall continue to kill Guerrillas, and Rebels offering armed resistance; whether they style themselves citizens, or soldiers."[62]

Wild's Version of the Clopton Whipping

Wild reported that William H. Clopton had been brought in by pickets, because "He had been actively disloyal, so that I held him as Prisoner of War, and have sent him as such to Fortress Monroe." He had also learned that Clopton was the "most cruel slave-master in this region." Among the refugees at Fort Monroe, Wild found several women who said that Clopton had whipped them, even totally unclothed and in the "presence of whites and blacks." Wild admitted that he had Clopton's back laid bare, and had placed the whip in the hands of the women. Three of them took a turn in settling some "old scores on the master's back." In addition, William Harris, of the 1st USCT, a black man who had been "abused" by Clopton, "finished this administration of poetical justice." This is contrary to other reports, which said that the black man began the whipping.[63] Wild stated in the order that accompanied a number of prisoners to the care of the Provost Marshal that Clopton, "besides being an active Rebel," had been "a very cruel slave master." He had him tied up and allowed his own slaves to whip him before being sent to Fort Monroe.[64]

Wild could not help commenting that he wished Clopton's back had been as "deeply scarred" as those whom Clopton had whipped, but he did not push the whipping to that extent. He absolutely refused to apologize for the Clopton whipping, and declared that he would do the "same thing again, under similar circumstances." Wild called Clopton a "high minded Virginia Gentleman," and noted that Clopton had lived for many years next door to John Tyler, the late ex–President, and was intimately connected with the Tyler family.[65] This seems to indicate that Wild harbored prejudice or hatred for the late President Tyler as well as his neighbors of the planter class. It was Clopton's connection with the Tyler family that would come back to haunt General Wild.

Hinks replied by saying that he would not proceed with Wild's arrest, but hoped that an "order to that effect" would come from the Department Headquarters, and that Wild would be tried by a military court and that he would "be relieved of his command and examined by a commission to determine and report on his soundness of mind."⁶⁶

Hinks added that Wild had told him personally that "some of his soldiers had killed a citizen and buried him in his own yard. Wild explained that this was because the "citizen attempted to take a musket from a soldier." A notation on the margin beside this paragraph in Wild's hand reads: "*lie!!!*" Beside this word, he placed his initials as well, "E.A.W."⁶⁷

The attitude Wild exhibited in his reply to General Hinks so enraged Hinks that he asked Butler to arrest Wild for insubordination and for "using excessive methods in dealing with rebel sympathizers." Wild had actually been present only at the Clopton whipping, but had not been present when George Walker was killed or when Wilcox was killed. While he was responsible for the acts of his men, these incidents should not have been cause for a court martial.

General Wild was sharply reprimanded and "his rampaging troops finally brought under control." The planters he had arrested and imprisoned at Fort Monroe were treated by Butler with "marked respect," and formal charges were brought against looters. Clopton brought charges against Wild, "but nothing came of them."⁶⁸

For Brigadier General Wild, however, the animosity generated by these and other events resulted in scandalous publicity in national and local newspapers, and fed hatred and discrimination toward black troops and their commanders. All these factors combined to culminate in the arrest and court martial of Brigadier General Wild (see Chapter XI).

"Poetic Justice" vs. "Emphatic Prose"

This whipping of a slave owner by his former slaves was an act for which Wild was criticized by both civil and military authorities. Historian and poet Carl Sandburg, in his biographical work on Abraham Lincoln, said Wild had earned quite a name for himself "by giving former slaves whips with which they lashed the bare back of their former owner." Attorney General Edward Bates wrote that Wild was "the same ruffian that caused a gentleman [Clopton] to be stripped and whipped by his own slaves, and called it *poetic justice!* The wretch ought to be punished in emphatic *prose.*"⁶⁹

Brigadier General Edward Wild would find that he was to be the recipient of some poetic justice in the months ahead.

X

January to June, 1864: Fort Powhatan, Wilson's Wharf–Fort Pocahontas, and Other Battles in Virginia

We will try it.[1]
—Brigadier General
Edward A. Wild,
May 24, 1864

The new year would bring changes—some good, some bad, and some unexpected.

The United States War Department made changes in how the military units were designated. All black units came under Federal jurisdiction, i.e., the 2nd NCCV became the 36th USCT.[2]

January 1864—Troop Movement and Command Changes

After the raid in North Carolina, Wild and his brigade returned to Virginia. Major General Butler, head of the Department of Virginia and North Carolina, ordered Wild to send the 10th USCT from their camp near Craney Island to the eastern shore of Virginia to replace the officers and soldiers then on duty there. Butler advised Wild to instruct the officers in charge of the 10th Regiment to exercise the "strictest diligence and vigilance" so that "no outrages of any sort are committed by his troops, for both he and his officers will be held personally responsible by me if any such are committed." Butler reminded Wild that the civilian inhabitants "fear greatly the quartering of negro troops in their midst." Butler wanted the black troops to be on their best behavior "to correct that misapprehension," but he also warned that "the most summary punishment will be visited upon them for any breach of discipline, especially any that shall affect peaceable men."[3]

Wild's 5th USCT was sent to Yorktown, and detachments of the 1st NCCV and the 55th Massachusetts rejoined their regiments on Folly Island just outside Charleston Harbor.[4]

On January 18, Henry T. Schroeder, Acting Assistant Adjutant-General, directed Brigadier General Edward Wild to take over the command of Brigadier General James Barnes.[5] Barnes, a former teacher at West Point, was commissioned a Colonel in the 18th Massachusetts in 1861. He saw action at Antietam, Fredericksburg, and Chancellorsville. Barnes was in command of the Norfolk and Portsmouth District from October 1, 1863, until January 8, 1864. Wounded at Gettysburg, Barnes continued to command, but he never fully recovered.[6]

In his new post, Wild had command of the 27th Massachusetts Regiment, the 2nd Regiment Massachusetts Heavy Artillery, Regan's 7th New York Battery, and a detachment of the 11th Pennsylvania Cavalry, in addition to his "colored troops."[7]

On January 19, Laurence Bradford, master's mate of the gunboat *Shockokon*, went to Norfolk to see Lieutenant Hayward. Hayward presented him to General Wild, and Wild invited the young man to his house. There, they had lunch at 12 noon, which was improved by some fine Scotch ale. In the afternoon, they rode horseback around the country. Bradford could stay no longer but had to return to his ship by 8 P.M.[8]

Again, on January 21, Bradford ate dinner with Brigadier General Wild at Norfolk, and attended the theater with Captain Walter Wild. Bradford noted that Walter paid for the tickets and would not allow him to pay.[9] (Bradford later married Hattie Phipps, General Wild's niece.)

February 1864

As post commander, Wild had a variety of duties, one of which involved sutlers. In compliance with General Order No. 27, sutlers were required to submit for approval itemized lists of various items they offered for sale to the soldiers with their costs and the sale price. Sutlers sold everything from boots to butter, at a great profit to themselves.[10]

Administrative duties included making recommendations for promotions. Wild submitted a list of names to Major Thomas M. Vincent, A. A. G., of the War Department: 1st Lieutenant Joseph J. Hatlinger to Captain (to replace Peter Winsor, discharged for disability); 1st Lieutenant George B. Proctor to Captain (to replace George W. Ives, dismissed for drunkenness); 2nd Lieutenant Leonard T. Gaskill to 1st Lieutenant; 2nd Lieutenant Parker to 1st Lieutenant; and 2nd Lieutenant Titcomb to 1st Lieutenant.[11]

Wild suggested Richard F. Andrews, Corporal, Company C, 1st Regiment Massachusetts Heavy Artillery, stationed at Fort Tillinghast, Arlington, Virginia, to replace Leonard T. Gaskill, who was being promoted; Private Algernon Draper, Company C, 1st Regiment, Massachusetts Heavy Artillery, currently a hospital steward at Fort De Kalb, to 2nd Lieutenant; and Private Edward C. Gaskill, Company B, 25th Regiment, Massachusetts Volunteers, to 2nd Lieutenant.[12]

As men moved up through the ranks, regiments of troops were shifted to meet the changing needs of the war effort. During February the 1st USCT was sent to New Bern, North Carolina, and the 2nd NCCV (the 36th USCT) was sent to Point Lookout, Maryland.[13]

March 1864—Grant Takes Command

Lieutenant General Ulysses S. Grant was made "General in Chief of the Armies of the United States" on March 12, 1864. With Grant in command, the war took a different turn. Beginning in the spring of 1864, the battles in Virginia would go down in history as some of the bloodiest ever fought. Each encounter allowed the Union forces to move one step closer to victory. The horror of the wounded being burned alive at the Wilderness, the deaths in the "Bloody Angle" at Spotsylvania, the huge number casualties sustained by Grant's men at Cold Harbor, and the siege of Petersburg, punctuated by the explosion of the "Crater" are examples of war at its deadliest.[14]

Grant's plan to take Richmond was presented to President Lincoln and Secretary of War Stanton. It was approved, and Grant was given the authority to move the Army of the Potomac south to concentrate on Richmond. In conjunction, Major General Butler was to move his troops up the James River.[15] The move up the James River was part of General U.S. Grant's "Overland Campaign" of May and June, 1864, to capture Richmond. Once he began his move, Grant did not back down or retreat, but moved steadily toward his goal—Richmond.

On March 13, 1864, Wild's command encompassed the District of Norfolk and Portsmouth, and included a number of large civil duties. He was still under the command of Major General Benjamin F. Butler, who was in charge of the Department of Virginia and North Carolina. Only six weeks later, on April 23, Wild was relieved of command of the District, and ordered to report to Camp Hamilton, near Hampton, Virginia, a camp for colored troops. He was assigned command of the 1st Brigade, Third Division, XVIII Army Corps, under Brigadier General Edward Winslow Hinks, Division Commander. Major General William Farrar "Baldy" Smith was Corps Commander. Wild and Hinks would not have a good relationship.

Federal Troops Move Up the James River

Brigadier General C. A. Heckman made a "cavalry reconnaissance to Pig Point," but found no signs of any enemy troops. The citizens in the area claimed that there had been no Confederates in that "section of the country since their evacuation of Suffolk."[16] With the exception of Plymouth, North Carolina (recaptured in April of 1864 by Confederate forces of Brigadier General Robert F. Hoke), the coastal areas of Virginia and North Carolina remained in Union hands until the end of the war. Heckman reported to Wild on March 5, 1864, that all was quiet in North Carolina in the "District of Currituck" near South Mill,[17] the territory Wild raided in December the previous year.

Heckman reported enemy forces at Suffolk, and that both sides had pickets out "facing each other."[18] Intelligence reports were often erroneous concerning the strength, location, and movement of the enemy. Major General Benjamin Butler wrote Major General John J. Peck that he was preparing to meet Confederate forces at Suffolk. Butler questioned a report that 25,000 Confederate soldiers were in North Carolina, and concluded that if this were true, "the enemy must be not only ubiquitous but more numerous than the sands of the sea." He noted that Brigadier General Hugh J. Kilpatrick had just returned from a cavalry raid, and had sworn that Confederate General George Pickett's division was at "Bottom's Bridge." The reports conflicted: Brigadier General C. A. Heckman insisted that the enemy was "in front of him," while Major General Peck believed just as strongly that the enemy was on his front.[19]

Massacre at Fort Pillow, April 12, 1864

With the exception of the battles at Milliken's Bend, Louisiana (June 1863), and Fort Pillow, Tennessee (April 12, 1864), colored troops had not been engaged in waging defensive battles.[20] This changed at Wilson's Wharf when Wild's black troops repulsed a major attack by Confederate forces, and the success of this battle challenged the widely held belief that black troops could not perform in battle as well as whites. The effort exerted by Wild's troops in the defense of Wilson's Wharf was perhaps motivated by events at Fort Pillow the previous month.

Originally part of a string of Confederate fortifications, Fort Pillow sat on a bluff above the Mississippi River about 50 miles above Memphis. When Confederates abandoned the fort, it was occupied in the spring of 1864 by the 13th Tennessee Cavalry (Union), commanded by Major William B. Bradford. Coincidentally, the Union major and the Confederate general, Nathan Bedford Forrest, were from the same county in Tennessee.[21]

At Fort Pillow on April 12, 1864, the Confederate forces of Major General Nathan Forrest were accused of "murdering most of the garrison after it surrendered, burying Negro soldiers alive, and setting fire to tents containing Federal wounded."[22] An investigation was launched by the United States House of Representatives, and many survivors were interviewed. The conclusions of the Committee were published in Report No. 65, 38th Congress, 1864. Historians tend to agree with the findings; Southerners believe the report was pure Yankee propaganda.

Several of those eyewitness accounts were published in *Official Records of the War of the Rebellion*.[23] Some accounts allege Confederate forces were bent on killing any black soldiers they found. Private George Huston remembered hearing: "A rebel officer rode up to the bank and said that General Forrest ordered every damned nigger to be shot down. So the enemy kept on firing on our defenseless men, and killed a great many of them."[24] Other witnesses testified that Union soldiers waving a white flag to surrender were shot down by Confederates.[25]

Eddy W. Davison and Daniel Foxx disagree. Fort Pillow, they say, was a relatively "minor battle in the sweep of the War Between the States engagements [and] continues to inflame emotions to the present day." This is true partly "because of the immediacy with which rumor and innuendo spread, along with other reports of the battle and its aftermath." Casualties, although heavy, were not outside the range of many battles. Of the 557 Union soldiers and civilians defending Fort Pillow, the number of those who survived have been reported to range from at least 336 to as many as 350. The numbers of those killed range from 180 to 225, a 31–42 percent mortality rate.[26] This can loosely be defined as a *massacre*—the needless or cruel killing of many people, a wholesale, pitiless slaughter. Is this not also the definition of *war*?

Massacre or not, the battle at Fort Pillow had an impact on Wild's troops a month later at both Fort Powhatan and Wilson's Wharf–Fort Pocahontas in Virginia. Here, colored troops in defensive positions faced Fitzhugh Lee's Confederate Cavalry. For black troops, the possibility of being executed if they fell into the hands of Confederates gave them an incentive to fight even more aggressively. White officers of black troops placed their own lives in jeopardy, along with those of their men, when it came down to the question of fight and live or surrender and be killed. All of Wild's men would soon fight desperately to avoid being captured by Confederates.[27]

April 1864

On April 1, General Grant inspected Butler's troops at Fort Monroe, and Wild's Brigade at Norfolk. At this time, Grant still had a favorable opinion of Butler's military capabilities, but to ensure success in the move toward Richmond, he assigned Major General William F. Smith and Major General Quincy Gillmore, two experienced and very capable generals, as corps commanders. Grant ordered Butler to assemble all available troops, even those on garrison duty that could be spared. Gilmore was to bring 10,000 troops up from Charleston, South Carolina, and General Kautz was to move with 3,000 cavalry stationed at Suffolk, Virginia, to the south side of the James River. Butler was then to proceed with his army up the James, to capture City Point, and prepare for battle.[28] Butler began assembling his army between Fort Monroe and Yorktown. It included the two corps of colored soldiers, the X and XVIII Corps.[29]

On April 20, 1864, there were more changes in command. To make the United States cavalry force as efficient as possible, Brigadier General A. V. Kautz, chief of cavalry, was ordered to join Heckman and to take command of all the cavalry in Heckman's department. General Charles K. Graham was ordered "to relieve General Wild and assume command of all the forces in Norfolk and Portsmouth."[30] However, Graham was told not to "interfere with any of Heckman's arrangements."[31] Wild was given command of the 1st Brigade and Colonel Samuel A. Duncan had command of the 2nd Brigade, in a Division of Colored Troops commanded by Brigadier General Edward Hinks.[32] After Wild was relieved of his duties as "Military Commander of Norfolk," he was ordered to report to Camp Hamilton. Wild's 1st Brigade was now part of Hinks' Third Division of the XVIII Army Corps.[33] The 1st Brigade consisted of the 1st USCT, under Colonel John H. Holman; the 10th USCT, under Lieutenant Colonel Edward H. Powell; the 22nd USCT, under Colonel Joseph B. Kiddoo; and the 37th USCT, commanded by Lieutenant Colonel Abial G. Chamberlain.[34]

Wild recommended Lieutenant Colonel Abial G. Chamberlain be appointed Colonel of his regiment, and 2nd Lieutenant Waldo F. Hayward, of the 36th USCT, be appointed 1st Lieutenant of the 37th USCT. However, Hinks blocked Chamberlain's promotion by stating that, although Chamberlain was an "officer & gentleman" whom he would be happy to recommend for a promotion, his regiment was too small. He also advised Wild that Lieutenant Hayward had already been "ordered as desired in his own regiment."[35] Hinks, commander at Point Lookout, Maryland, was replaced by Colonel Alonzo G. Draper.[36] Draper had served with Wild in North Carolina, and had been involved in a dispute with a fellow officer over a hostage (see Chapter VIII).

By the end of April 1864, the Division of United States Colored Troops was under the command of Brigadier General Edward W. Hinks. Brigadier General Wild was in charge of only the 1st Brigade, which included the 1st, 10th, and 22nd USCT.[37]

Brigadier General Edward Hinks, now Wild's superior commanding officer, was born in Bucksport, Maine, in 1830. He became a printer for the *Whig and Courier* in Bangor, Maine, and then moved to Boston in 1849. By 1855, he was elected to the Massachusetts legislature. Hinks was appointed a 2nd Lieutenant of the Regular Army while serving as a lieutenant colonel and colonel of a 90-day regiment of militia. On August 3, 1861, Hinks became a colonel of the 19th Massachusetts Infantry, and saw action in all the major engagements beginning with the disaster at Ball's Bluff in October of 1861. He was badly wounded twice at Sharpsburg (Antietam) in September of 1862. While convalescing, Hinks was promoted to brigadier general on November 29, 1862. He was engaged in court-martial and recruiting duties until March of 1864, when he was placed in command of the prison camp at Point Lookout, Maryland, for a couple of months. Hinks was given command of a division of black soldiers of the 18th Corps involved in the Petersburg offensive until July 1864. From then until the end of the war, Hinks was involved in daft and recruitment until he resigned his commission June 30, 1865.[38]

Hinks and Wild had much in common. Both were from Massachusetts, and both had been in the war almost from the beginning. Both had been injured in battle about the same time, Wild at South Mountain and Hinks at Antietam. Both men had risen to the rank of brigadier general, and both were involved in the recruitment of blacks. Yet, Wild has been described as a man whose "rabid idealism, tinder-dry temper, and thirst for conflict gained him nearly as many enemies in blue as in gray."[39] Wild believed Hinks had subjected him to a great deal of petty tyranny, and Wild suspected Hinks was "copperheadish." Wild even told his wife that Hinks was "a mean spirited fellow." "Bakalum!" exclaimed Wild in reference to Hinks which, in Turkish means, "We shall see."[40] Perhaps they did not get along because Hinks was ill, and Wild was in constant pain,[41] which did not help the disposition of either man.

May 1864—Action at Fort Powhatan and Wilson's Wharf–Fort Pocahontas

On May 1, 1864, from Point Lookout, Maryland, Colonel Alonzo G. Draper reported that a large force of rebel cavalry, "supposed to be Fitzhugh Lee's," had crossed the Rappahannock River at Port Royal on April 30, and Confederate officers had "crossed into Maryland in citizens' dress." Draper sent some cavalry to conduct a search.[42] He warned Butler that a force of thousands, "principally cavalry," was intended "as a flank movement against General Grant."[43] This information was conveyed to Grant.

The control of the James River was crucial to the Federal cause. If Confederates gained the bluffs around Wilson's Wharf, they could command the river for several miles in each direction, and prevent the passage of Federal ships carrying supplies to the army in the field and in front of Petersburg.[44]

Richmond, the Confederate capital, was the goal of the movement that began on May 5. The XVIII Corp and the X Corp were moved up the James River from Fort Monroe to City Point and Bermuda Hundred. Along the way, detachments were placed at strategic points, and some of Wild's Brigade were stationed at Wilson's Wharf (Fort Pocahontas) on the north bank of the James River. The rest were put ashore at Fort Powhatan on the south bank, 6 or 7 miles above Wilson's Wharf.[45]

In preparation for the move up the James River, Hinks issued instructions to each brigade and regiment in his Division as to what they could take with them to Wilson's Wharf and Fort Powhatan. Each regiment was to have one wagon and four horses, and one wall tent. Brigade headquarters were to take 2 wall tents and 3 fly tents. Regiments were to take only camp kettles and mess pans. The regiments were allowed to take 60 rounds of ammunition per person, and to carry 40 rounds in boxes on the boats in which the men were to be transported. One wagon and one ambulance were allotted to two batteries. Only 5 horses were allowed for each regiment's Field and Staff officers. Hospital stores were to be transported on the boats with the men. Each brigade was allotted one ambulance, two hospital tents, and one medicine chest.[46]

In May 1864, Wild commanded the 1st Brigade of United States Colored Troops (USCT), part of the Third Division, under the command of Brigadier General Edward W. Hinks. Wild's brigade consisted of the 1st, 10th, 22nd, and 37th regiments of USCT. A second brigade of colored troops was under the command of Colonel Samuel A. Duncan, which included the 4th, 5th and 6th U.S. Colored regiments.[47]

Wild was promoted to "field command" in the Army of the James, under the command of Major General Butler. This Army was divided into two corps. Wild's unit numbered 2,000 men, "half of an all-black division in the XVIII Corps" of Brigadier General Edward W. Hinks.[48]

Sherwood Forest

From 1842 until his death in 1862, ex–President John Tyler's home was "Sherwood Forest," a plantation near Wilson's Wharf. Tyler was the 10th president of the United States. The plantation was part of a land grant made in 1616 known as Smith's Hundred. President William Henry Harrison inherited the property in the late 1700s. The plantation had several owners before Tyler bought the house and 1,600 acres in 1842 from his cousin, Collie Minge. Tyler named it Sherwood Forest to reflect his reputation as a political outlaw. The house was built circa 1730 is the classic Virginia Tidewater design. It is the "longest frame house in America." Tyler expanded its length when he added a 68-foot ballroom, where the "Virginia Reel" was often danced. Members of the Tyler family still reside on the plantation. (The house was restored in the 20th Century. Only the grounds are open for tours from 9:00 A.M. to 5:00 P.M. daily.)[49]

Brigadier General Wild confiscated several items from Sherwood Forest. He took "two canes and a secession flag" and sent them to his commanding officer, Major General Butler. Wild suggested that the items be sent to Philadelphia for the Sanitary Commission Fair. Wild believed that the sale of the items could raise "a very large sum of money, for the benefit of our soldiers," and "for the public good." One of the canes was a sword cane and the blade had been inscribed. Wild also suggested the items be sent to his brother-in-law, George Wood, at his home (237 South 18th Street, Philadelphia). He knew Wood would see that the items reached the fair.[50]

Fort Pocahontas at Wilson's Wharf

Fort Pocahontas served as a Federal supply depot. It was built and manned by Wild's colored troops. One soldier described the works as "one of the best arranged breast works I have seen...."[51] The fortifications were designed by Major General Godfrey Weitzel, who had taught engineering at West Point before the war. Weitzel commanded the 2nd Division, XVIII Corps, and was Chief Engineer for the Army of the James. Promoted to Major General in August of 1864, he assumed command of the XVIII Corps after General Ord was wounded in action.[52]

Fort Pocahontas is situated on a high bluff overlooking the James River. One of the best-preserved sites in Virginia, Fort Pocahontas is on the National Register of Historic Places. During the war, out of 2,000 acres, 500 acres were planted in corn by Mr. Wilson, the owner, but advancing troops prevented the cornfield from being plowed and it grew up in weeds.[53]

Two pencil sketches, one of Camp Wilson's Landing (Wilson's Wharf–Fort Pocahontas) and another of an ironclad in the river in front of Fort Powhatan, were drawn by Edward Lamson Henry (1841–1919) in the fall of 1864. Henry was a captain's clerk on a Union supply transport which moved on the James River. The sketch of Fort Pocahontas shows a number of tents on the bluff above the river.[54] The soldiers who stayed in the fort also lived in structures made of earth, wood and brick.[55]

As part of Grant's plan to take Richmond, a massive troop movement was begun. On the morning of May 5, 1864, "the whole transport fleet was assembled at Newport News," and these ships, led by ironclads, moved up the river, under the direction of Acting Rear-Admiral S. P. Lee. Along the way, Wilson's Wharf was seized and occupied by Federal forces. Major General Benjamin F. Butler seldom mentioned Brigadier General Edward A. Wild, but he did comment that Wilson's Wharf was "seized and occupied by two regiments of colored troops," as was Fort Powhatan, which lay seven miles above Wilson's Wharf. These sites had been occupied by regiments of black troops, "all under the immediate command of Brig.-Gen. E. A. Wilde [sic], who had remained in the service although he lost an arm...."[56]

May 6, 1864

The Federal signal corps kept communications open between the gunboats and the land forces, and took an active part in the events at Wilson's Wharf. The signal officer at Wilson's Wharf went with a detachment of the 1st USCT to capture a rebel signal station and equipment at Sandy Point on the James River. The Confederate "signalists" resisted and the sergeant and three of his men were killed (see Chapter IX). On May 7, a temporary "intermediate" signal station was set up at Turkey Bend to assist in communications between the flag ship *Malvern* moving on the James River to Curl's Neck. The Navy Department was informed of the loss of the gunboats *Shawsheen* and *Commodore Jones*; the first was destroyed by a Confederate battery, and the second by a torpedo.[57]

On May 16, 1864, the 22nd USCT, under Colonel J. B. Kiddoo, was ordered to proceed with his regiment to Fort Powhatan, where he was to relieve Colonel Stafford, commander of the 10th USCT and commander of the station. Stafford and his regiment were ordered to report to Brigadier General Wild at Wilson's Wharf.[58]

From the headquarters of the Third Division at City Point, Captain Solon A. Carter warned Wild an attack was expected on Fort Powhatan. If an attack occurred, Carter authorized Wild to send "one of your regiment to the relief of the garrison immediately."[59]

Confederate officers were aware of the Federal presence along the James River. Major J. F. Milligan, a Confederate signal officer for General Beauregard, advised General Braxton Bragg that five ocean steamers carrying about 2,500 men had been sent by Butler. The Confederates noted that the force at Fort Powhatan was commanded by General Wild and was "composed of negroes, numbering about 2000." They knew that the Federals had a small force at Berkeley on the north shore of the James River, and that the "Yankees" had "repaired all the wharves from Berkeley down to Grove's Wharf" along the river's north side.[60]

After the failure to take Drewry's Bluff from Confederates May 12–16, 1862, Butler had withdrawn his X and XVIII Corps to Bermuda Hundred, a peninsula surrounded by water, in which he was contained.[61] After this fiasco, Benjamin F. Butler was known as "Bottled-Up Butler."

In anticipation of a battle soon to involve his men, Wild, at his headquarters at Wilson's Wharf, issued instructions "to be read by my company commander to his men, with whatever comments may be necessary to make *every one* understand *fully*."

> You should kill all *armed* rebels, whether soldiers or citizens, who are offering resistance.
> You should kill all *armed* rebels who are running away.
> You should kill all prisoners who are attempting to escape, either by *running* or *fighting*.
> You should *not* kill *un*armed rebels, who surrender themselves, nor those who are *not taken in arms*. After they once become prisoners, and do not attempt to escape, they should be regarded as helpless, like women and children.
> You should not kill guerrillas, *until* it is *proved* that they have been guerrillas. *If found in arms*, it *is* proved at once by *the very arms* themselves, and you should kill them at once. If not found in arms, you should *wait* until it be proved that they *have* carried arms—that is, until they have been *tried* by *court-martial* and condemned- for fear that you may kill some innocent person.[62]

A notation on the side of Wild's order explained that "a recent occurrence has made the issue of these instructions necessary."[63] This probably refers to the massacre at Fort Pillow.

May 21, 1864—Action at Fort Powhatan

Fort Powhatan, 7 miles west of Wilson's Wharf, was the headquarters of the 22nd USCT. Colonel Joseph Barr Kiddoo, post commander, had seen action in many of battles—Yorktown, Williamsburg, and Fair Oaks. At Malvern Hills, he was commissioned a Lieutenant Colonel of the 137th Pennsylvania. Kiddoo was promoted to a Colonel in March of 1863. He fought at South Mountain, Antietam, Fredericksburg, and Chancellorsville. Promoted to Major on October 5, 1863, he became commander of the 6th USCT, and then as a Colonel he commanded the 22nd USCT. (Kiddoo was severely wounded at Petersburg. Promoted to brigadier general of United States Volunteers, he eventually rose to the rank of Major General.)[64]

On May 21, Fort Powhatan was attacked by Confederate cavalry. Colonel Kiddoo signaled General Wild at Wilson's Wharf that "the enemy had appeared on my picket-line in a small force, but had withdrawn." Wild answered that if Kiddoo needed help to send word. When the enemy reappeared, Kiddoo requested a regiment of infantry from General Wild. A section of "Captain Howell's battery" was moving on Federal gunboats dispatched from City Point to Wilson's Wharf. Kiddoo signaled the boat, and had it move ashore to help in the defense. Kiddoo had been assured by General Wild that he would give whatever assistance was needed. However, before Wild could arrive at Fort Powhatan with the men of the 1st USCT, the enemy reappeared at the fort. Once Wild arrived, he and Kiddoo rode along the line of defense. They concluded that the approaching enemy was only a "reconnoitering party," and so Wild left with his 1st USCT and the section of Howell's battery. The pickets helped hold the fort. While one man was holding his post, he fired round after round from his rifle, and eventually fenced with a "rebel officer till he disabled the officer." During this confrontation, the Union soldier received a saber cut across his face. Kiddoo also needed a detachment of cavalry to scout the area to inform him more timely of the approach of any enemy forces. He requested that Captain Howell's battery remain, and said more troops were needed to effectively perform both fatigue duty and picket duty, because he did not have enough men for both tasks.[65]

On Wild's orders, 1st Lieutenant H. W. Allen reported that Fort Powhatan had been attacked and that General Wild had gone there with one regiment. Allen requested assistance from General Hinks. Hinks arrived at Fort Powhatan with the 5th Regiment, but found all was quiet. The enemy's cavalry had only made a demonstration and then left after a few shots were fired from within the fort. Hinks noted that Colonel Kiddoo had not requested any assistance, and was "well prepared for any attack at that point."[66] Hinks did not believe it necessary to send a squadron of cavalry to Fort Powhatan, because Kiddoo was "well prepared for any attack of the enemy, and equal to any emergency that is likely to occur at that point."[67] Hinks reported to Butler and "belittled the affair" at Fort Powhatan. He appeared to be irritated by Wild's request for assistance, however prudent it may have been.[68] This did not help Wild's relations with Hinks. Wild was pleased, however, and noted that the reconnaissance of the Confederate cavalry and the attack Fort Powhatan was repulsed with little difficulty.[69]

May 24, 1864 — Wilson's Wharf–Fort Pocahontas

Wild inspected and improved upon the defensive fortification at Wilson's Wharf, which consisted mainly of abatis pointed at the field around it. A small stream ran in front of the semicircular fort, and served the function of a medieval

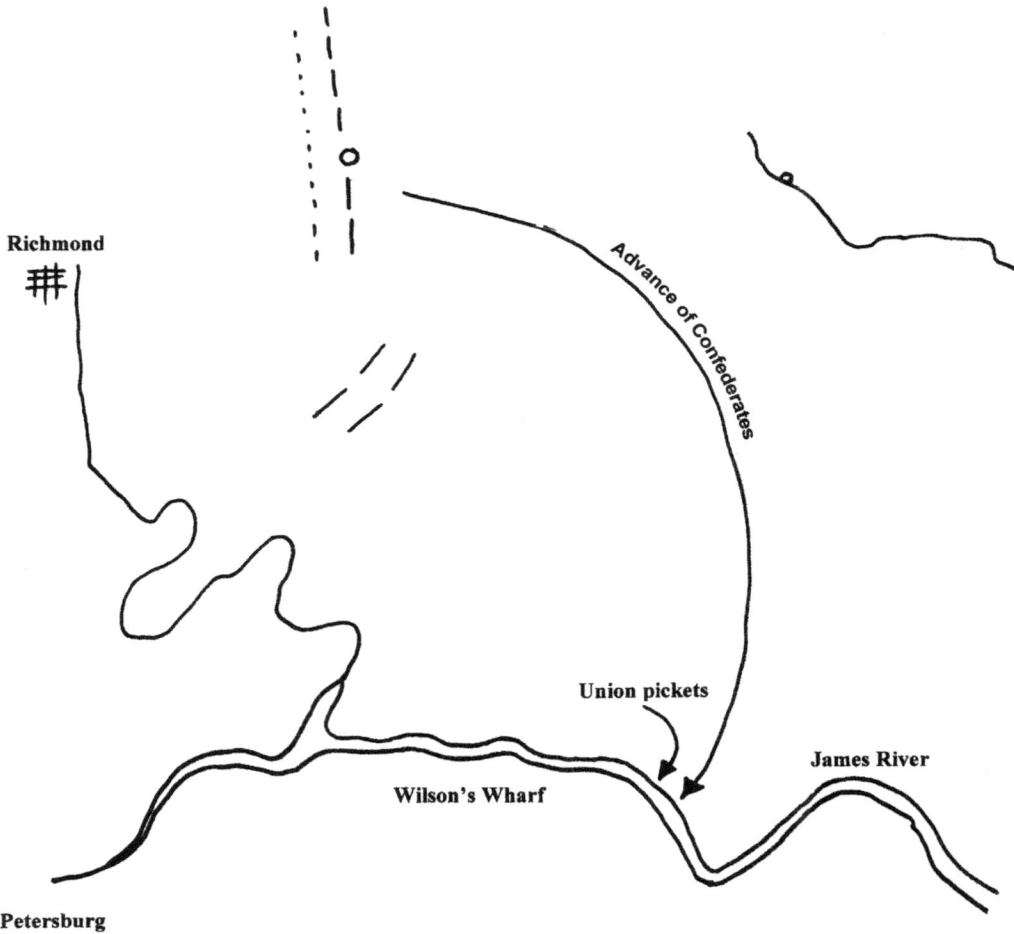

**BATTLE OF WILSON'S WHARF
(FORT POCAHONTAS)
Defended by Brigadier General Wild and the 1st and 10th USCT**
Danny Casstevens, artist

moat. The troops cleared trees and underbrush from the bluff, and positioned batteries to defend the fort from attack.[70]

Wild and his troops had little protection from enemy fire except from within rifle pits and the abatis. His force consisted of colored troops—the 10th USCT, and half of the 1st USCT—with "one section of light battery (Battery B, USC Artillery). He had only two 6-pound cannons.[71]

Fitzhugh Lee Attacks

The assault on Wilson's Wharf was launched by the Confederate cavalry of Major General Fitzhugh Lee, nephew of General Robert E. Lee. Fitzhugh had served on the staffs of Ewell and Johnston during the Peninsular Campaign, and had ridden with J.E.B. Stuart. Promoted to brigadier general in July of 1862, Fitzhugh commanded a cavalry brigade at South Mountain and Antietam. In August 1863, after the battles at Chancellorsville and Gettysburg, he was promoted to Major General. Fitzhugh Lee was a seasoned and fearless fighter, but he was not accustomed to fighting black soldiers,[72] especially black soldiers and white officers who were afraid if they were captured they would be massacred like the defenders of Fort Pillow.

After riding all night from Richmond, Fitzhugh Lee and his cavalry arrived at Wilson's Wharf on the James River early on the morning of May 24. His force included the 5th North Carolina Cavalry[73] and the 2nd Virginia Cavalry. Lee surveyed the situation, and determined that the black Federal soldiers at Wilson's Wharf posed a double threat: "not only were they well entrenched," but "they were black, and defeat at their hands would be humiliating." Undaunted, Lee was confident that his men could capture Fort Pocahontas and Wild's black troops. His decision may have been influenced by the reports published in the Richmond *Daily Examiner* that these black soldiers had committed "the most atrocious outrage on the people," and he was determined to avenge the citizens of Charles City County.[74]

Lee advanced his mounted soldiers quietly through the woods, and ordered them to dismount. The Confederates believed their numbers were superior to those in the fort, and that if they gave their famous "Rebel yell," the black troops within the fort would surrender. At 12:30 P.M., the Confederates gave their blood-curdling cry and launched their attack. They were met by black Federal soldiers led by Captains Stephen A. Boyden and Giles H. Rich of the 1st USCT. After several skirmishes, the Federals fell back behind their earthworks. The Confederates occupied the front of the fort and the woods on the north bank of the river, hoping to cut communications with any Federal gunboats that might attempt a rescue. Fitzhugh Lee ordered his men to charge across an open field, to climb a ravine, and capture the fort,[75] not an easy task.

Inside the fortification, Wild ordered his men to hold their fire until the Confederates were in close range. They waited impatiently as the Confederates advanced quickly toward the fort, but they slowed when they became tangled in the abatis. Then, Wild gave the order to open fire on the enemy. After 90 minutes of fighting, the Confederates fell back and raised a white flag of truce. Wild ordered his men to stop firing. Then, Fitzhugh Lee tried another tactic: he ordered the commander of the fort to surrender.[76] Lee made a major error in judgment, because the commander of the fort was Brigadier General Edward Augustus Wild, and his troops were black.

Fitzhugh Lee sent a note to Wild to demand his surrender, and promised Wild that if he and his men surrendered, "they will be turned over to authorities at Richmond and treated as prisoners of war. Should they refuse," Lee could not be responsible for the consequences.[77]

Lee's reference to the "consequences" was a reminder of the atrocities committed at Fort Pillow six weeks earlier.[78] It was an offer made by Fitzhugh Lee to assure the black Federal soldiers that they would be treated the same as white prisoners of war if they surrendered.

The rumors of the massacre at Fort Pillow had put fear into the hearts of many, especially black Union soldiers. Considering the nationwide publicity in newspapers and magazines such as *Harper's Weekly* of the events at Fort Pillow, it is no wonder that Wild refused to surrender, and that his men fought as hard as they could to hold Wilson's Wharf. Wild was not cowed by the Confederate demand, and he was determined that his men would not meet the fate of those at Fort Pillow. He gave a curt reply on an "old envelope taken from his pocket" to Fitzhugh Lee without wasting any words: "We will try it." Wild meant what he said. He and his colored troops then proceeded to repel the Confederate cavalry and save an important position for the Federal army on the James River.[79]

After Wild had sent his reply to Fitzhugh Lee, fighting resumed about 2:30 P.M. Lee was determined to conquer the post and Wild was determined to hold it. The Confederates kept up a steady fire all along the front and left flank in an attempt to dislodge the black troops. Lee's 5th North Carolina Cavalry advanced in a charge on the fort, moving "as fast as the obstructions would permit." When they reached the breastworks, Wild's black soldiers held their positions and rained a heavy crossfire on the advancing cavalry. General Wild, with his pistol in his right hand, "urged his men to victory." The fighting was hard and bloody. The earth reverberated when the heavy artillery guns fired and the air was thick with smoke. A Union officer wrote that Confederates came "with a yell, but our boys gave a louder yell, and poured so much lead among them, that they broke and ran like sheep."[80]

The Confederate attack stalled only 30 feet from the parapets, and Lee wisely ordered a retreat. A member of the 5th North Carolina cavalry described the retreat: "We retired under that awful fire from the most useless and unwise attack, and the most singular failure we were ever engaged in."[81]

Confederates launched three separate attacks at Fort Pocahontas. As night approached, Lee ordered his men off the field, and by 6 P.M. the battle was over. After dark, Wild sent pickets to find Lee's campsite. The next morning, Wild ordered his brigade to advance on the Confederates. However, the men of Fitzhugh's Cavalry had slipped away in the night.[82]

Official Reports of the Battle of Wilson's Wharf

Major General Benjamin F. Butler, commander of the Department of Virginia and North Carolina, reported that General Fitzhugh Lee had "abandoned his attack on our post at Wilson's Wharf during the night, having completely failed." Butler reported 20 Confederates were killed, including Confederate Major Breckinridge of the 2nd Virginia Cavalry. The Federals captured 19 prisoners, while they lost only "1 man killed, 20 wounded, and 1 missing." Butler credited the success of the battle to Brigadier General Wild, who commanded, "in person," a defensive force of 1,800 men, "all of whom were negroes."[83]

Brigadier General Edward W. Hinks, commander of the Third Division, XVIII Army Corps, reported from City Point: "All is now quiet at Wilson's Wharf, the enemy having abandoned the attack during the night."[84] He made no mention of the actions of Wild and did not compliment the black troops for their bravery. Hinks would later lock horns with General Wild in a court martial.

Second Lieutenant Julius M. Swaim, Chief Signal Officer, was in a position only 10 yards from the Federal rifle pits on the bank of the river at Wilson's Wharf. He counted Confederate cavalry to be over 3,000. As the fighting continued, Swaim sent two men to the gunboat to direct the gunfire and communicate with Fort Powhatan. Although Swaim was hidden from view by the riverbank, a detachment of Confederates approached within about 70 yards from where he was stationed. They opened fire on Swaim, and he had to abandon his post and seek protection behind the earth works. He was able to open a signal station on board a transport ship near the wharf, and to direct the fire from the gunboat to "successfully stop the enemy's movements on our right." About 7 o'clock that evening, the enemy retired, but left dead and wounded on the field. Swaim commended Wild, and expressed his thanks to Private Mott for flagging messages while under enemy fire.[85] Swaim filed a report of his actions in the Signal Corps during May.[86]

The Chief Signal Officer of the Department of Virginia and North Carolina commended 2nd Lieutenant J. M. Swaim for his actions in directing by signal the fire of the gunboats toward the Confederate force attacking Wild's brigade at Wilson's Wharf.[87]

Brigadier General Wild's report was the longest, and probably the most accurate:

> This post was attacked yesterday at noon by a considerable force of the enemy, supposed to be cavalry, having three guns, probably horse artillery. The attack was evidently made in earnest, with a design of rushing in upon us suddenly, but they received so decided a check from our pickets, that a large portion of the force dismounted and made their approach more cautiously. They encompassed our front, and filling the woods on the river bluff to the north, tried to stop all communication with steamers coming to our aid, and harassed our landing place. They also made it uncomfortable for the gunners to serve their pieces on our gunboats.[88]

After fighting for and hour and a half, the Confederates sent a man with a flag of truce, and a note with "a summons to surrender in the name of Maj. Gen. Fitz. Lee." Wild forwarded the note to department headquarters.[89]

In regard to the demand to surrender, Wild reported simply, "I declined." They then "went at it again." Lee's troops were massed on the extreme right, concealed by wooded ravines. They made a charge, while keeping up a steady attack all along Wild's front and left flank. They approached the parapet, but "failed under our severe crossfires. They fled back into the ravines, and after another hour gradually drew off out of sight." Wild sent out three parties who found the enemy still "drawn up in skirmishing array beyond the woods." The picket was left to watch them, and his men brought in a few wounded and prisoners. The enemy built campfires and spent part of the night, but had disappeared when, at sunrise, Wild's men advanced toward them.[90]

An officer of the 1st USCT described the battle: "We had a fight with Fitzhugh Lee, and whipped him completely. He had 2,000 men.... We had about 1,100 men. He came down with cavalry and charged on our pickets, expecting to cut them off, and then surprised the camp. But he "reckoned without his host.""[91]

Wild did not rest on his laurels, but after the Confederates left the area, he enlisted the help of passing steamers. He called "ashore all troops aboard them, took them into our service, arming some with the guns of our wounded men and other spare guns, and working others in various ways." He expressed his thanks for those volunteers, especially the artillery men of the 1st Connecticut Heavy Artillery, for relieving several of his men who "had dropped with the heat...." Wild was also appreciative of the cooperation he received from the gunboat *Dawn* that had helped repulse the attack by shelling the enemy on "both flanks." He commended the actions of Captain Quackenbush's ensign (William F. Chase) who took the wheel of the tug *Mayflower* when both the captain and the pilot had been shot. Most of all, Wild was appreciative of the men of his command who "behaved steadily and well." He was especially grateful for the fine "conduct of the pickets and skirmishers under Capt. Giles H. Rich," of the 1st USCT.[92]

Results and Statistics—The Battle of Wilson's Wharf–Fort Pocahontas[93]

Wild's two black regiments had about 1,800 men; Fitzhugh Lee's cavalry division, about 3,000 men. Casualties were estimated at 165 total. It was a Union victory.

Sergeant George W. Hatton, 1st USCT, believed that the heroism of his regiment at Wilson's Wharf had secured for them "unfading laurels" to be engraved on the pages of history. Chaplain Henry M. Turner, who was also at Wilson's Wharf that day in May, remembered the encounter as a "terrific battle," but also he remembered "the coolness and cheerfulness of the men, the precision with which they shot, and the vast numbers of rebels they mercifully slaughtered, [which] won for them the highest regard of both the General and his staff, and every white soldier that was on the field.... The rebels were handsomely whipped." Rufus Wright, of the 1st USCT, said simply: "We whipp the rebs out."[94]

The New York *Times* described the battle at Wilson's Wharf: "The chivalry of Fitzhugh Lee and his cavalry division was badly worsted in the contest last Tuesday with negro troops, composing the garrison at Wilson's Landing." Southerners saw only the outrages and atrocities committed by the black soldiers on the "defenseless inhabitants" of Charles City County.[95]

Although little has been published about the battle at Wilson's Wharf–Fort

Pocahontas, it was a Union victory, and one of few defensive battles won by black troops alone. With only part of two black regiments, Wild's forces repulsed an attack by a much larger force of the Confederate cavalry of Major General Fitzhugh Lee. Wild's losses were minimal. However, among the wounded was his brother, Captain Walter H. Wild, who was acting assistant inspector general.[96] Walter was hit in the head by a spent bullet, and a plate of silver the size of a "half dollar" was inserted into his skull and remained throughout his life.[97]

Wild estimated Confederate losses at about a dozen killed, "including a captain and a major." He had also captured and brought in 6 wounded Confederates and 4 prisoners, from an enemy force he estimated as double or triple that of his own. Prisoners stated that "they had detachments from three cavalry brigades, comprising all their available men." Wild also learned from a memorandum book taken from the pocket of the dead Major Cary Breckenridge, of the 6th (2nd) Virginia Cavalry, the names of the units involved, but not their numbers.[98]

A notation made by Wild at the end of his own account in his "Military Career" outline from information he had seen in *Medical and Surgical History of the Rebellion* gives 2 Union soldiers killed, 24 wounded, 0 missing; Confederates had 20 killed, plus 100 wounded, and 19 missing.[99] Brigadier General Edward Hinks reported to Major General Butler that Federal casualties at Wilson's Wharf were 1 killed, 20 wounded and 2 missing.[100]

The final count of casualties of Union troops under Major General Butler's command for the period May 5 through May 31, 1864 (including the battle at Fort Powhatan and Wilson's Wharf), was 21 in the Third Division, Brigadier Edward W. Hinks commanding, 1st Brigade, commanded by Brigadier General Edward A. Wild. Among them were 2 soldiers killed, 2 officers wounded, 10 men wounded, 1 man missing from the 1st, 10th, 22nd, and 27th USCT.[101]

Performance of Black Troops

Wild was pleased with the performance of his men. Under fire, they had proved wrong those who doubted the value of blacks as soldiers. Not only did black soldiers fight just as well as whites, but at Wilson's Wharf they "had fought even better." "Within my own command, all behaved steadily and well," and they "stood up to their work like veterans [against a force] at least double my own, and probably triple."[102] Wild believed that if his men had not been "short of artillery ammunition," they could have killed twice as many of the enemy. Ammunition had been in short supply because of a recent change of batteries at the post. Thus, they had been careful not to use all their ammunition at once, in case the siege was a lengthy one.[103]

Butler commented that "the Negroes held firmly ... and Lee retired beaten in disgrace, leaving his dead on the field." Fitzhugh Lee even admitted that his men had found "a foe worthy of their steel."[104]

Acting Rear Admiral S. P. Lee visited Fort Powhatan and Wilson's Wharf on

May 28, and reported to Secretary of the Navy Gideon Wells that the *Pequot, Atlanta, Dawn,* and *Young America* would be able to "effectually help the troops." He noted that there was one colored regiment at each place, "to hold against great odds these important positions, which the army is fortifying." He noted also that General Wild had only 900 colored troops at Wilson's Wharf and two 90-pound Parrott guns when Wilson's Wharf was attacked by at least 2,000 of Confederate cavalry. Wild thanked Lee for the help of the gunboats in repelling the attack.[105]

For saving this vital link in the Federal lines of communication, Wild was widely praised. Newspapers acclaimed Wild as a fighter and as an "enthusiast on the subject of colored troops.... He has the most implicit confidence in his troops, and so have they in him." Even General Hinks praised Wild for his defense of Wilson's Wharf and Fort Pocahontas.[106]

Aftermath

Wilson's Wharf was the heart of tidewater Virginia. The land was divided into large plantations of 1,000 to 20,000 acres, graced by fine plantation homes filled with valuable furnishings.[107] In the aftermath of the battle at Wilson's Wharf, looting of those homes did occur, but it may have not been done by any of Wild's black troops. The white troops who replaced the black troops at Fort Pocahontas apparently were not as well behaved, but spent a lot of time "appropriating resources" from nearby homes. A. R. Arter, of Company C, 143rd Regiment Ohio Infantry, attested to the damage at Sherwood Forest. The house was ransacked again by Union troops:

> A lot of the boys went out yesterday [June 22, 1864] and broke into President Tyler's house and took and destroyed lots of stuff. They say he has the nicest kind of a mansion the house furnished in the best of style. They brought in some very nice furniture such as sofas looking glasses stands carpeting &c of the very costliest kind and destroyed the pyana [piano] & large looking glasses & such other stuff they could into Bring in. There was also a foraging Party went out from this post yesterday on a steamer and came back last evening with a full load & they Brot [brought] in 80 head of sheep some 20 or 30 head of cattle lots of mules & Horses & among the rest eighty negroes they were mostly women & children good many of them young women one old nig 105 years old so he says.

Arter remarked that "our men shows the rebs, in this section no mercy [but] take everything."[108]

Black Soldiers Executed

Hinks forwarded a report to Butler about the execution of two men of the 22nd USCT the day before the attack on Fort Powhatan. The black soldiers had been "shot to death" in Petersburg at a place called the "Gallows" where condemned criminals were executed. The fate of five other prisoners who had also been captured from his division was unknown. Hinks asked Butler to ascertain if the report was correct, and to find out what had happened to the other five prisoners. If the reports were true, Hinks wanted to retaliate by executing Private Heaton of the 24th Virginia Regiment captured on May 18, and all the other "prisoners captured from General Fitzhugh Lee during the attack" to retaliate for the murder of two soldiers of the 22nd Regiment, and any other soldiers of his division who have "met with a like fate."[109]

On June 11, Wild received his full commission as a Brigadier General, United States Volunteers, dated June 1864, to rank from his original appointment by the Secretary of War on April 24, 1864.[110]

Cold Harbor, Virginia—May 31 to June 12, 1864

Part of Wild's Brigade fought at Cold Harbor in the 1st Brigade, of Hinks' Division (Third Division), of William F. "Baldy" Smith's XVIII Corps.[111] Later, Wild's Brigade rejoined the X Army Corps.[112]

Wild's men marched 25 miles from White House on the Pamunkey River to Cold Harbor on June 1. They found that a battle had already begun, and the enemy were "strongly posted in thick woods behind well-constructed breast-works, with slashed timber in front." In order to reach the entrenched Confederates, the Union forces had to cross "an open plowed field, fully 1,250 yards wide," and came under heavy fire from both muskets and artillery. However, the troops, upon reaching the edge of the field, moved quickly and drove the enemy from the woods to their second line of works. Once behind the second line, the Confederate defenders began to bring heavy fire upon the right flank of Wild's brigade, but they held their position throughout the night, and captured 400 prisoners. When they were ordered to charge, "they neither faltered nor wavered," and although the men were "greatly fatigued by heavy marches and night labor, they went as directed to and over the enemy's works as if there had been no obstacle in their path, and with a dash of enthusiasm that could hardly have been anticipated."[113]

Trouble with Hinks

Either there was a mix-up in orders for troop movements, or Brigadier General Hinks purposefully made trouble for Wild. On June 2, Hinks asked General Butler if he had ordered General Wild to send men to him. Wild had dispatched Colonel Holman with 1,000 "with the intention of going to Petersburg," reportedly on orders from General Hinks. However, Hinks denied issuing any orders, and feared "it is a ruse to weaken Powhatan." Hinks wanted to know if he should send the men back "immediately," because he had made no preparations for them.[114] Butler answered Hinks: "You will allow the troops from Wild's brigade to disembark at

Spring Hill, refresh and rest themselves. The same boat may bring over a portion of one of the regiments of Colonel Duncan's brigade so as to reunite his regiments."[115] Captain Dodge told General Hinks that he had no boat, because he had sent General Wild all of his small boats. "Will make a change with you as soon as they return," Dodge wrote to Hinks.[116]

Wild found time to write to United States Senator Henry Wilson to recommend a promotion for Captain George H. Johnston. Wild helped those persons he liked in any way he could. Wild had known Johnston since the days when they were both in the 1st Regiment of Massachusetts Volunteers and, since that time, Johnston had been training as "Adjutant of Regiment, Brigade, Division, Corps, and Post." Wild had high praise for his friend, who "As Post-Adjutant of Norfolk, recently under my command, he has shown himself thoroughly competent, both for his military duties, and for the functions of civil government; which, in a place like Norfolk, is a consideration of the first importance." Wild also mentioned that Johnston was "better fitted for such work by reason of his deeply-rooted antislavery principles." Wild believed this qualification should be "considered indispensable in all present and future officials set over the South."[117]

Petersburg, June 15, 1864

The 1st Regiment of the 1st Brigade, Third Division, commanded by Brigadier General Wild, was the only regiment of this brigade to participate in the fighting before Petersburg on June 15, 1864. On June 16, brigade headquarters was moved from Wilson's Wharf to Point of Rocks, and on June 21, moved again to a field near Petersburg. The brigade was involved in picket duty along the Appomattox River through the end of June.[118]

Butler ordered two regiments of Ohio Volunteers to Wilson's Wharf on June 16. They were to hold that point and relieve General Wild, who was to report with his command at City Point, by taking the same steamers that brought the Ohio Troops. Reinforcements were also sent to Fort Powhatan to relieve the regiments there. He ordered Colonel Stafford to bring his colored troops and report to General Hinks "before Petersburg or wherever he may be."[119]

Wild's troops were replaced at Wilson's Wharf by white troops from Ohio, New Hampshire, New Jersey, and New York, who remained until the site was abandoned in June 1865.[120] Major R. Davis ordered the 153rd and 163rd Regiments, Ohio Volunteers, to Wilson's Wharf so Wild could report to City Point. Wild received this order on June 16 at 5 P.M. The Ohio troops arrived June 17.[121] This did not give Wild much advance notice.

Wild Leaves Wilson's Wharf

Wild was relieved from duty at his post at Wilson's Wharf by new three-months' troops, and he proceeded to join his command to the battlefront. He reported at City Point, and he and his men were ordered to go to Bermuda Hundred and set up camp. On June 21, the whole Third Division marched from Bermuda Hundred to a position in front of the town of Petersburg, which was now under siege.[122]

When Wild left Wilson's Wharf for City Point, he was confident that he had left Wilson's Wharf so strongly fortified that the Confederates would not be able to take it without a full corps or a siege. From there he was sent to the Point of Rocks, where he and his men camped "a mile inland," then moved again. Wild wrote his wife on June 22 that he and his men "have encamped in six different places since leaving Wilson's Wharf." [123]

On June 19, the 1st, 10th, 22nd, and 37th USCT, and the 1st U.S. Colored Cavalry (USCC) (dismounted) were assigned to the 1st Brigade, under the command of Brigadier General Edward A. Wild. A second Brigade was to be composed of the 4th, 5th, 6th USCT, the 2nd USCC (dismounted), and the 5th Massachusetts Colored Cavalry (dismounted).[124]

June 22, 1864 — Petersburg, Virginia

When Wild wrote to his wife on June 22, she was staying at the "Mansion House, Mt. Carbon, Pottsville, Pennsylvania." From there, she forwarded her husband's letter to his friend, Edward W. Kinsley. Wild reported: "We are here in front of Petersburg—considerable cannonading going on, but not any of us hurt at present." They were almost immediately put to work, and "were taken out twice to be put into the trenches—kept waiting some time, & countermanded...."[125]

General Wild told his wife that his brother Walter was able to rejoin him at Petersburg. Walter had arrived "last night late—looks pretty well."[126] No doubt, the General was happy to see his brother, who had been wounded in the head at Wilson's Wharf.

Eventually, Wild's colored troops received recognition for their defense of Wilson's Wharf. They were also commended for fortifying City Point, Fort Powhatan, and Wilson's Wharf, and for securing communications there. They had, according to Edward W. Smith, A.A.G., "practically moved Fort Monroe as a base within fifteen miles of the rebel capital—there to remain till that travels." For their actions in defeating Fitzhugh Lee's Confederate cavalry, the 1st and 10th Regiments of the Third Division earned the right to have inscribed on their colors the name *Wilson's Wharf*. The 1st, 4th, 5th, 6th, and 22nd USCT earned the right to have *Petersburg* inscribed on their banners, and the quartermaster was directed to furnish new flags so inscribed. A number of the colored soldiers were also awarded the Congressional Medal of Honor for their actions in battle.[127]

Casualties suffered from June 15 to 30 included 184 losses in Wild's 1st Brigade. Wild had been under arrest during part of this period and his brigade was part of the Third Division commanded by Brigadier General Edward W. Hinks. This division also included the 5th Massachusetts Colored Cavalry (dismounted), the 1st

U.S. Colored Cavalry (dismounted), and the 1st and the 10th USCT. These units suffered 21 men killed, 13 officers wounded, 125 men wounded, and 25 men reported missing during this period.[128]

For Brigadier General Edward Wild, the fight on the battlefield was over for a while, but the battle before a military tribunal had just begun (see Chapter XI).

XI

Court-Martial of General Wild

A tawny lion, pawing to get free.
—John Milton,
Paradise Lost, VII

Wild, the adventurer-physician-humanitarian, was accustomed to making decisions independently. Therefore, he sometimes purposefully and willfully disobeyed orders. He "flouted discipline" in many ways, and he might even have been "cashiered" out of the army for such conduct, had it not been for his heroic action on the battlefield at Seven Pines.[1]

Wild's unconventional actions resulted in his arrest on several occasions (See Chapter II). Early in the war, *Captain* Wild wore "elements of civilian attire on the parade ground," and was subsequently arrested by his brigade commander. The true reasons behind some of those arrests were not always apparent in the charges listed in the indictment. Some were the result of personal conflicts with superior officers. Other arrests were perhaps due to prejudice because he was a commander of black troops. Wild and other officers who commanded black troops were not appreciated as they should have been, but were treated as villains and traitors by many, including some of their fellow officers, and superior officers. Eventually, Wild's actions resulted in formal charges and court martial proceedings. From December of 1863 to June of 1864, Wild did many things which shocked and humiliated people (see Chapters VI, VII, VIII, IX). Wild's propensity to disregard authority and obey only those orders he thought "lawful" caused him problems throughout the war. Wild's methods, which had always been unorthodox, became even more bizarre during the spring of 1864.

The year 1864 did not begin well for Wild. His father, Dr. Charles Wild, died in North Providence, Rhode Island, on February 3, 1864, at age 69.[2]

In the spring of 1864, Brigadier General Edward W. Hinks was Wild's superior officer. Although both were from the state of Massachusetts and both, supposedly, were in favor of using black soldiers, Wild and Hinks could not get along.

Hinks, enraged over Wild's whipping of William H. Clopton, and the killing of a citizen (see Chapter IX), demanded an explanation.

Hinks wrote to Wild on May 11 and demanded a full report of the "killing of a citizen" and the "whipping of a citizen Prisoner of war, within your camp." Hinks expressed his doubts that there could be any "justification" for those two "extreme" acts, and he sincerely hoped that they were not committed "without sufficient cause." Hinks further stated in no uncertain terms that he would not "countenance, sanction or permit any conduct on the part of my command not in accordance with the principles recognized for the Government of belligerents in modern warfare between civilized nations, and for any departure from these rules all officers concerned will be held individually accountable." He ended his caustic letter with: "Barbarism and cruelty to persons in our power are not among the qualities that are becoming to a man or a Soldier."[3]

Wild was not cowed by his superior officer, and not afraid to speak out when he disagreed, but Wild absolutely refused to admit to any wrongdoing in these matters. Instead, he answered Hinks arrogantly: "I shall continue to kill guerrillas and rebels offering armed resistance, whether they style themselves citizens, or soldiers.... I shall do the same thing again, under similar circumstances."[4]

Wild's reply only added fuel to the fire, and he and Hinks continued to be at odds. When Hinks asked Wild for an explanation about the incidents involving Clopton and the citizen killed, Wild answered in a letter addressed to Major Robert S. Davis, and took exception to the accusations made by Hinks. Wild went into great detail to explain the situation at the Rebel Signal Station, in which a civilian was killed, and to defend the actions of his troops.[5]

> I would respectfully inquire for my own information and guidance whether it has been definitely arranged that black troops shall exchange courtesies with Rebel soldiers? And if so, on which side such courtesies are expected to commence? And whether any guarantees have been offered on the part of the Rebels calculated to prove satisfactory and reassuring to the African mind.[6]

The animosity between Wild and Hinks continued to build and eventually resulted in Wild being brought before a court martial.

Two days later, on May 13, 1864, Hinks listed his complaints against Brigadier General Wild, and sent them to Department Headquarters. Hinks requested that action be taken, and stated what Wild had told him about the killing of the citizen:

> Gen. Wild ... said to me that some of his soldiers had killed a citizen and buried him in his own yard. I inquired what the occasion was. He replied the citizen attempted to take a musket from a soldier. This affair Gen. Wild now sees proper to describe with other language.[7]

Even Wild's own officers were appalled at the Clopton whipping. Colonel Holman, 1st USCT, one of Wild's regimental commanders, was the one who reported that General Wild had caused Clopton, a "prisoner of war to be tied up by his hands to a tree in front of his—Gen. Wild's—hd. qrs. Stripped, and whipped by command in his camp..." Hinks promised that "Proper charges against Gen. Wild will be forwarded as soon as prepared." [8]

Hinks stated that he had not yet placed Wild under arrest, "but requested that an order to that effect" come from Department Headquarters. He desired that Wild "be tried by a military commission, or that he be relieved of his command and examined by a commission to determine and report upon his soundness of mind."[9]

>COMPLAINT: THE CLOPTON WHIPPING AND DEATH OF CIVILIAN
>Initial Charges Filed: May 12, 1864
>Charge No. 1: Conduct Unbecoming An Officer and a Gentleman
>Charge No. 2: Conduct to the Prejudice of Good Order and Military Discipline
>Charge No. 3: Disobedience of Orders
>Plaintiff: Brigadier General Edward W. Hinks.[10]

June 23, 1864

Wild was arrested for a third time on June 23 and charged with "disobedience" of orders from Brigadier General Hinks.[11] Major General "Baldy" Smith was left without a "proper officer to command a division," whose value depended upon its leadership. In an urgent letter to General John A. Rawlings, Chief of Staff of the Armies of the United States, Smith complained that Brigadier General Hinks, who commanded the "colored division," had to give up his duties because of ill health. Smith pointed out that General Wild, the second in command, "is entirely unfitted for the command, and besides is in arrest at present for insubordination." This left no commander for Hinks' division of about 5,000 men, of which about 2,200 were as "yet undrilled in loading their muskets...." Hinks thought them "unfitted by reason of ignorance of drills for service in the field." Smith recommended that the four untrained regiments, three of which were dismounted cavalry, be "sent back so to some point where they can be instructed and aided in holding entrenched lines or positions which will have to be held wherever the main army be." Smith believed the subject of his letter warranted immediate attention.[12]

>COMPLAINT: REFUSAL TO REMOVE QUARTERMASTER
>Arrested: June 23, 1864
>Charges: Two charges of Disobedience of Orders, Conduct to the Prejudice of Good Order and Military Discipline (Chronic Insubordination Special Order # 52, Paragraph III).
>Failure to Obey Orders to Dismiss his Quartermaster
>Plaintiff: Gen. Edward W. Hinks.[13]

When ordered to remove Lieutenant Birdsall as quartermaster of the 1st Brigade and replace him with a "competent officer," Wild had the audacity to refuse. He replied that he was perfectly satisfied with Birdsall and had no reason to remove him. Wild stated emphatically that he "must respectfully decline to comply with the said orders; against which I protest as an *unlawful order*."[14]

Hinks could take no more from Wild, and he asked Butler to arrest Wild for insubordination and for "using excessive methods in dealing with rebel sympathizers."[15] Subsequently, one of Hinks' staff officers was sent to General Wild with a second request of the order, but Wild told the staff officer to tell General Hinks, "I know my rights and will maintain them."[16] This open defiance of a direct order gave General Hinks a reason to order Wild's arrest. That arrest led to a court martial.

Brigadier General Edward W. Hinks issued Special Order No. 52 on June 23, 1864, for the arrest of Brigadier General E. A. Wild "for disobedience of orders." Wild was to be brought under arrest to the Headquarters of the XVIII Army Corps at Petersburg. That same order turned over the command of the 1st USCT, 1st Brigade, Third Division, XVIII Army Corps to Colonel John H. Holman.[17]

The court martial of Brigadier General Edward A. Wild was based on several charges—the Clopton whipping episode, Wild's refusal to obey orders to remove Lieutenant Birdsall, and Wild's use of disrespectful language and protest against "an unlawful order."[18]

Brigadier General Edward W. Hinks first brought charges against Wild on May 12, 1864. At that time, Wild was at Wilson's Wharf and soon was engaged in a major battle defending his position against an attack by Confederate cavalry under Fitzhugh Lee.

On the first charge, "Conduct unbecoming an officer and a gentlemen," Hinks alleged that Wild had caused a prisoner of war, William H. Clopton, to be "stripped of his clothing, tied up and whipped by contrabands" in front of General Wild's headquarters at Wilson's Wharf on or about May 10, 1864. Hinks also charged that Wild, when asked for a written report of the whipping, had replied in "words to the effect that he had so whipped a prisoner of war and that he wished it to be distinctly understood that he should do the same thing again."[19]

The second charge, "Conduct prejudicial to good order and military discipline," was the result of a statement to the contrary when Hinks commanded Wild not to allow whipping of prisoners by officers of Wild's command.[20]

The third charge, "Disobedience of orders," came about when Hinks ordered Wild to report the circumstances pertaining to the killing of a citizen by an armed party, and the whipping of a prisoner of war, Wild "did fail, neglect, and refuse to make such report as required."[21] Wild protested that he was not in the "habit of accepting rebukes for acts not committed ... and feeling that I can judge the 'qualities becoming to a man or a soldier' quite as well as I can be informed by Brig. Gen. Edw. W. Hinks in *such* a letter.... I protest against the whole tone of the above letter."[22]

In his own defense, Wild explained the circumstances in detail to Major Robert S. Davis. Concerning the death of a citizen, Wild said that he had sent a detachment on Friday, May 6 "to surprise a Rebel Signal Station at Sandy Point." The signal station was in a house and when his men approached, those at the station ran into the swamp. Those attempting to escape ran into another of Wild's detachments. The Confederates offered "considerable resistance" but the Federal soldiers prevailed. Five "rebels were killed, three wounded and two caught. The dead were properly buried on the spot—the wounded and prisoners were brought into camp," and later sent to Fort Monroe. Wild continued his activities in the area of Wilson's Wharf against Confederate soldiers, civilian Confederate sympathizers, and guerrillas. On May 9, he sent a detachment to arrest a group of guerrillas who were spending the night at the home of a citizen. His men found 11 rebels who offered substantial resistance under a Confederate officer. Five of Wild's mounted soldiers charged, killed one, and wounded another, and the rest escaped into the swamp and across the Chickahominy. The citizen killed was "Wilcox, the owner of the house," who was also a Confederate "enrolling officer of the district." He was "properly buried in the yard, his house was burned." Wild repeated his threat to continue to "kill guerrillas and rebels offering armed resistance whether they style themselves citizens or soldiers."[23]

As to his reasons for having William H. Clopton whipped, Wild declared that he had testimony from "half a dozen women among our refugees, whom he [Clopton] had often whipped unmercifully," sometimes entirely naked. Wild believed the women's testimony and he admitted that he allowed three women and one man to whip Clopton. His only regret was that Clopton had not been as badly scarred as the former slave women.[24] Wild continued to be unrepentant for his actions and promised that he would do the same thing again "under similar circumstances."[25]

In addition to the specifications in Charge 2, Hinks filed a supplement on June 4. In this charge, Hinks referred to Wild's letter to Major R. S. Davis, Assistant Adjutant General, in which Wild questioned how his black troops were to respond to the rules regarding how "black troops shall exchange courtesies with rebel soldiers, and if so, on which side such courtesies are expected to commence...."[26] In other words, were his black troops to bow down before the Rebels, or defend themselves?

Hinks complained that in Wild's letter to Davis, Wild had used "unbecoming and defiant and disrespectful language" to express his "contempt and disrespect towards his commanding officer," and had willfully disobeyed "lawful commands" from his commanding officer.[27] Hinks now had just cause to proceed with a court martial.

The first specification of a charge of "disobedience of orders" regarding the Quartermaster resulted from Wild's refusal to "select from his command a competent officer as Acting Quarter Master of his Brigade, and relieve Lt. Birdsall as Acting Quartermaster of the 1st Brigade and return him to duty with his Regiment." This took place in camp before Petersburg, on June 23, 1864. The second specification alleged that Wild, when ordered by "his commanding officer Brig. Gen. E. W. Hinks through Capt. Thos. L. Livermore, A.A.D.C., to comply with the requirement of

Part II, Special Orders No. 52," and to "report his compliance within one hour," he "did neglect to do."[28]

On June 24, Wild wrote to Captain Solon A. Carter, A.A.G., defending his position regarding the quartermaster: "To every General Officer is reserved the right of appointing his own Staff, I appointed Lieut. Birdsall (Senior Regtl. Q.M.) to act as Brigade Quarter-Master." Wild further stated that he was "perfectly satisfied of his competency, and his good conduct." Since Wild could see no reason for Birdsall's removal, he refused to "comply with said order; against which I hereby protest as an unlawful order."[29]

Just about the time Brigadier General Wild was being arrested, his wife was writing to Edward Kinsley to relay news from her husband, and to express her concerns. She disliked General Hinks, and told Kinsley, "I never heard any good of him, but I have had a dislike of him for a long time." She believed Hinks was "mean and spiteful." Mrs. Wild wished that her husband could be under a "really good commander," if he had to be under anyone less than a Major General. She also believed that her husband should not be "sacrificed to the spite of a *Copperhead*," referring to Hinks' political tendencies. She was concerned, as always, with her husband's welfare, and she feared that because of General Hinks' dislike of Wild, that he might be placed in "some needlessly exposed position, where if he does not lose his life, he would receive some terrible wound that would make him utterly helpless for life." Wild must have mentioned to his wife some of the problems he was having with Hinks, because in her letter, Mrs. Wild reminded Mr. Kinsley that it took "a great deal of abuse to make the Gen. speak ill of any one (not secesh), particularly of his superior in rank." The lady stated that her husband had "been under tyrants before," and that the Lord "has delivered him from their persecution." She was optimistic and hoped that he would be saved again. Yet, to be on the safe side, she asked Kinsley to put in a good word for her husband.[30]

Wild wrote Major Russell, Assistant Adjutant General of the XVIII Army Corps, to protest his arrest. The arrest was "unjust." Wild believed that General Hinks had issued an unlawful order when he commanded him to dismiss one of his staff—his quartermaster. Wild took exception to the order, and "declined to obey it," and thus he was arrested.

Wild also saw the order as "*oppressive;* and *intentionally* so," a method used by General Hinks perceived by Wild to "entrap" him. Furthermore, Wild contended that the timing was bad for the service. In addition, Wild believed that his being arrested while he was "Corps officer of the day" was aimed less at him than at the Major General Commanding.[31] If he is referring to the commanding officer of the XVIII Army Corps, that was Major General William F. "Baldy" Smith. The commanding General of the Army of the James during this period was Major General Benjamin F. Butler.[32]

Hinks would not let the matter rest, but he continued to find instances of insubordination with which to charge Wild. From City Point on June 27, he filed "Supplemental Specification to Charge 2nd of Charges and Specifications preferred against Brig. Gen. Edward A. Wild."[33]

June 29, 1864—Court Martial of Brigadier General Edward Wild

Major General Smith knew of Wild's refusal to obey Hinks' orders, and he stated that Wild was a "chronic insubordinate ... entirely unfitted for command." Thus, Smith proceeded to call a court martial jury and Wild was found guilty of "flagrant insubordination."[34]

Wild had only a few days between his arrest on June 23 and the time his court martial was scheduled to begin. General Order No. 74, dated June 28, 1864, set the trial date and listed those who would hear the case: Brigadier generals T. H. Hill, J. W. Turner, A. Ames, and H. Burnham; Colonels G. A. Steadman, N. M. Curtis, Wm. L. Schley, and Gibson; and Lieutenant Colonels J. B. Rawlston, and J. Coughlin. Captain Gilchrist, Provost Marshal of the 23 Division, was to be the Judge Advocate. The court was to convene at the headquarters of the XVIII Army Corps at 10 A.M. on the 29th of June 1864.[35]

Wild appealed to Major General Butler "for protection, not only against my Corps commander, but against the Court Martial appointed by him." Wild urged Butler

> either to suspend proceedings until he can investigate the circumstances, or to annul the order convening the court (as the members have not yet been sworn) and then further direct matters as he shall think proper. I had also intended to enter a formal complaint and protest against the whole course of treatment which I have endured at the hands of Brig. Gen. Hinks, for 2 months past, as being oppressive and insulting and *designed* to be intolerable. But if, as I hear it stated, he is to be relieved from command of this Division, such complaint seems now superfluous.[36]

In his military career history, Wild records the following:

> June 29—I appeared before a General Court Martial, a detail of 11 officers, of which Brig. Gen. Thomas H. Neill was President and Capt. Gilchrist was Judge Advocate, convened in Front of Petersburg by Maj. Gen. W. F. Smith, by G. O. No. 74. HQ 18th A.C., dated June 28, 1864, for the purpose of trying me on 2 setts [*sic*] of charges and specifications preferred by Brig. Gen. E. W. Hinks, as follows:
>
> 1st Sett—Charge 1. Disobedience of orders + 2 specifications.
> 2nd Sett—Charge 1. Conduct unbecoming an officer and a gentlemen + 2 Spec.
>   Charge 2. Conduct to the prejudice of good order and military
>   discipline + 2 spec.
>   Charge 3. Disobedience of Orders + 2 spec.[37]

Because of the short amount of time between notification and the trial,[38] Wild did not have adequate time to prepare a defense. On the first day of the trial, Wild voiced an objection because "with one exception, all members of the Court were his junior." In addition, none of those on the court had ever or were presently commanders of "black troops." The authority for this objection came directly from Major General Benjamin F. Butler's General Order No. 46, which required a "majority of such officers" making up a court "trying [the] commander of black soldiers" should also be commanders of black troops. This court, however, chose to ignore Butler's order. Therefore, the next day in court, Wild objected to the members as "being prejudiced against my past course and present position, raising and commanding negro troops."[39]

Wild had petitioned General Smith, the Corps commander, on June 25, for release from arrest. After 2 days, when he had not received a reply, Wild sent another copy to Smith's headquarters. His only reply was a "summons to appear before General Court Martial today." Wild stated that he had received a copy of the charges on "June 26th at 11 P.M." Another set of charges was "first received June 27th at 8 P.M." He stated that his "first notice of impending court martial was about 10 P.M. of June 28th summoning me to appear at 10 A.M. June 29th (12 hours after) by Gen. Orders No. 74." To further complicate matters, Wild declared that he had never received a copy of General Order No. 74, "nor did I ever see it until entering the Court room." Thus, he was "wholly in ignorance of the list of members of the court, until it convened; and of course, unprepared to challenge them, and unprepared with witnesses, defense &c."[40]

During the trial, Wild objected to all the members of the court except Brigadier General Neill as being his "juniors." His objection was overruled. One of the key points of his defense was the disregard for Butler's General Order No. 46. Wild considered this to be of "very great importance in the trial on the charges growing out of the Clopton case, this being *essentially* an affair of negros." This objection was also overruled. Wild then tried another tactic, and objected to one member as being "an officer of the Regular Army, sitting in judgment on me, a volunteer." This objection was overruled on the grounds that the member of the Regular Army had been detailed for the Court as a brigadier general of volunteers. Wild then asked for time "to consider challenges against some members of the Court, on the score of prejudice." The court allowed this request, and adjourned until the next day, June 30, at 10 A.M.[41]

That same day (June 29, 1864) Wild wrote his appeal and addressed it to Major Robert S. Davis, A. A. G., to ask for "protection against the oppression and injustice of my superior officers." He explained the situation in detail how he had been arrested for not replacing his quartermaster.[42]

Although Wild did not get any help from Major General William F. Smith, Smith did endorse the back of Wild's appeal, and indicated that the appeal would be "forwarded without comment and that Gen. Wild will only be tried on charges brought against him since his service here. Should the Major Gen. Commanding receive any explanation they will be given on any points. The general spirit of the letter is altogether unworthy [of] a soldier who is not afraid to have his peers look into his conduct."[43]

The trial continued on June 30, but the all of the charges and specifications in the 2nd set were withdrawn. Wild raised his objection to the members of the court martial on the grounds of "individual bias and prejudice against myself, my reputation and my previous course in relation to both negros and Rebels." This objection was "overruled."[44]

Wild protested the proceedings, and the ruling of the Court. He believed that the "only conceivable grounds on which my first two objections could be overruled, must be that no other than those named could be detailed without manifest injury to the Service."

Wild cited section XV of Butler's General Orders, No. 46, dated December 5, 1863, in his defense during the court martial of July 1864:

> Court-martial and courts of inquiry in relation to all offenses committed by or against any of the colored troops, or any person in the service of the United States connected with the care, or serving with the colored troops, shall have a majority of its members composed of officers in command of colored troops, when such can be detailed without manifest injury to the service.
> All offenses by citizens against the negroes, or by the negroes against citizens—except of a high and aggravated nature—shall be heard and tried before the provost court.[45]

Wild believed that, if proper time were allowed, after the press of the campaign was over, and the question be referred to a higher authority, a proper and competent court could be appointed to try a brigadier general. He believed that was nothing in the "nature of the charges requiring such urgent dispatch in the proceedings," but that it could wait until a proper time for settlement. In the meantime, he thought the United States army should "be profiting" from his services. He believed that the "proceedings are marked by an indecent haste, which is in itself unfair, and which is convincing evidence of unfair intent in all parties concerned." He complained that he was being tried "as no brigadier general was ever tried before. Would not a corporal have a right to complain of such treatment?"

Results of Court Martial

On July 1, Wild put his defense into writing, and the case was closed. The finding of the court was "guilty."[46] The first two charges pertaining to the Clopton whipping were dropped because that incident had been referred to the Judge Advocate of the Army. That left only one charge, "disobedience of an order," which referred to the removal of Birdsall, for Wild to defend himself against. Wild argued that the order "was an unlawful one" that he should have not been compelled to obey. His authority was based on the right enjoyed by general officers "to select their staff, and they could not be ordered removed unless some clear reason was given." However, he failed to convince the court, and was found guilty of that charge. The court sentenced Wild to be suspended both from "rank and pay for six (6) months, and to be reprimanded in General Orders by the General commanding the 18th Army Corps," General William F. "Baldy" Smith.[47]

Wild Appeals Verdict, Decision Overruled

Wild refused to comply with the verdict, and appealed to Butler. He stated that the court had failed to meet "a standard imposed by the army leader himself."[48]

Wild could only conclude from the verdict of the court that the charges had grown "out of the odium on the part of most of our Army officers, which I had incurred in consequence of my being early, active, and somewhat prominent in raising and leading Colored Troops—being in fact a pioneer therein."[49] He did not believe it had anything to do with the Clopton beating, but stemmed from prejudice against him for his leadership of black troops. He managed to convince Major General Butler to help him. Late in July, Butler got Wild acquitted and freed him from arrest. Perhaps Butler had been moved by Wild's plea: "I was one of the very earliest to start the raising of negro troops ... [and to be] identified with their cause. On this account I have had nothing but prejudice, jealousy, misrepresentation, persecution and treachery to contend against" from Smith and Hinks, his immediate superiors.[50]

Butler overruled the action of the court martial, mainly because of the court's failure to recognize the importance of his General Order No. 46. Butler had written that order specifically to assure that the prejudice ingrained in some of the white officers would not affect their judgment and negate an impartial trial of an officer who commanded black troops. Butler also stated that there "were other grave objections to the course of this trial." He believed, as well, that Wild had been "sufficiently punished for an erroneous and impudent assertion of his rights." Subsequently, the Judge Advocate General's office approved and confirmed Butler's reversal of Wild's trial.[51]

On July 30, 1864, Butler issued General Order No. 86.

> Par II. The proceedings, findings and sentence in the foregoing case, having been approved by Major General W. F. Smith, the officer convening the Court, and having been forwarded from the action of the Major General Commanding the Department, the following are his orders thereon:
> *Proceedings disapproved.* General Orders No. 46, of the series of 1863, is still in force in this Department and was duly pleaded by Brigadier General Wild. No notice of the plea seems to have been taken by the Court. With the reason for that order, the Court had nothing to do. It was an imperative order; and the Court was bound to obey it,—especially a court assembled to try an officer for insubordination. There are other and more grave objections to the course of this trial as disclosed by the record, but until his orders are obeyed, a sense of propriety will not permit the Commanding General to explain or discuss the proceedings of the Court. For this reason only, therefore, so far as the record will show, the proceedings are set aside, and Brigadier General Wild is released from arrest and returned to duty.[52]

Clearly, General Order No. 46 had not been obeyed in Wild's court martial, because the members of the court were not officers who commanded colored troops. Butler went on to note that he had found "prejudice among some officers—now happily dying out—so strong so inveterate and deep rooted" that "such officers would not form an impartial tribunal for the trial of an officer in command of colored troops." Butler wisely made it clear that he was not insinuating that any of the "very respectable officers composing" the court for the court martial of Wild were prejudiced, but it was sufficient that when Wild had pointed out a lack of officers commanding black troops on the court, this information had been disregarded, when it should have been taken into consideration. Butler concluded that "Brigadier General Wild has been sufficiently punished for an erroneous and impudent assertion of a right on his part, which resulted in no detriment to the public service, in being deprived of his sword for more than thirty days, during a campaign in which he might have earned for himself honorable distinction."[53]

Subsequently, Butler's ruling was reviewed by the Judge Advocate General in Washington, and was "approved and confirmed." Wild was saved for the time being.

Wild Resumes Recruiting After the Court Martial

Since the recruiting rendezvous was to be established at Fort Monroe and New Bern, Butler thought it more practical that Brigadier General Wild, rather than Colonel Draper, be assigned there, because Wild was "admirably fitted." Butler asked Grant if he would apply for the change to Wild instead of Draper.[54] Grant replied that he had a "telegram objecting to the recruiting rendezvous at either place." Grant, himself, was not in favor of the change, and stated: "I don't want States to get the benefit of recruits obtained in that way; besides, the men so obtained are worth more in keeping present organizations filled."[55]

Grant must also have changed his mind. Since both Grant's and Butler's orders were dated July 24, it is hard to determine which came first, probably Grant's. Major General Benjamin F. Butler ordered Wild to be released "from arrest and to report to Fortress Monroe to await orders there." Wild was permitted to take his personal staff.[56] Butler also telegraphed Major General Ord that Wild was to be released.[57]

The order to release Wild was probably issued after a note from Grant asking Major General Halleck to change the order to place Colonel A. G. Draper, of the 36th U.S. Colored Troops, in command of recruiting at Fort Monroe, Virginia. Grant insisted that Draper was needed at City Point, and urged that the order be changed so that Brigadier General Wild would take Draper's place as recruiting commander.[58] That this request was even made was probably because of pressure applied by Butler for Wild's release from arrest and his reinstatement as a recruiting officer. Wild was kept under arrest until July 24 when a telegram arrived from Major General Butler instructing Wild to proceed to Fort Monroe and await further orders.[59]

Although Wild was convicted by a court martial, that conviction was overturned by Major General Butler. Thus, although found guilty, Wild was freed on a technicality.[60]

XII

The Final Months of the War: July 1864 to May 1865

Only those who have neither fired a shot nor heard the shrieks and groans of the wounded who cry aloud for blood, more vengeance, more desolation. War is hell.

—William Tecumseh Sherman,
Graduation Address,
Michigan Military Academy,
June 19, 1879

Brigadier General Wild spent most of the month of July under arrest while Major General Butler worked on his behalf to put him again in charge of a center for the recruitment of blacks. Wild's job was in jeopardy because Lieutenant General U.S. Grant was not in favor of maintaining recruitment centers. Grant wrote Major General H. W. Halleck to express his view that having a recruiting center at Fort Monroe was not only expensive, but it would require two officers "who cannot be spared from the field, and will not add a man to the service." The practical Grant saw no need for such centers since "Every negro that comes in is now taken into the service, the best specimens physically being enlisted in companies already organized," while those not physically able were used as "laborers in some of the departments or sent north." Expeditions were also being sent out to "bring back all the negroes they can find."[1]

However, late in July, Wild was officially detailed as "chief mustering and disbursing officer for the rendezvous" at Fort Monroe. Colonel Alonzo G. Draper was assigned elsewhere.[2] Subsequently, all recruiting officers were ordered to report to Brigadier General Wild at the fort.[3]

Ever mindful of the problems of Negroes, Wild wrote Captain C. E. Wallbridge that he tried to help "a dozen or more black teamsters who had been employed by Capt. Bradley," the quartermaster at New Bern, North Carolina. They had been sent to Fort Monroe, but rather than being released, they had to serve another month as teamsters. After working a second month, "against their will," the distressed teamsters complained that their families had been left in New Bern "without habitation or shelter." Wild obtained passes for two men to talk to the division Commander, but they were met by Wagon-Master Styles. He refused to look at their passes, and had the Provost Marshal return them to their wagon train. Wild took exception to the high-handed treatment of the teamsters, and asked that their "right" and claims be investigated.[4]

Another incident involved some of his soldiers and their families. The soldiers asked Wild to help get their families to safety from Smithfield. The men obtained sailboats, and Wild sent Captain Whiteman and 15 men from a dismounted cavalry unit with them, with strict orders to "abstain from plundering," and to injure no one, but to get the women and children and return promptly. The rescuers encountered a

Bust of Brigadier General Edward A. Wild. (Courtesy of Massachusetts Commandery, Military Order of the Loyal Legion, and U.S. Army Military History Institute, Carlisle Barracks, Carlisle, Pa.)

head tide and calm wind, so their slow progress down Smithfield Creek was noticed. The group in boats was attacked by an enemy force of about 100 men with horses and dogs, armed with shotguns and rifles from behind some breastworks, and one man and one woman were killed. The "contrabands" rowed to the opposite bank and all scattered in the marshes. When the last boats with the Union soldiers approached, the captain landed to attack the enemy force, but found that they were outnumbered. They returned to their boats and made their way "past the danger, by wading his men behind the boats," with baggage and bedding piled up on the boats to shield them from enemy fire. Wild praised the "coolness and ingenuity of Captain Whiteman," and credited the escape to his efforts. Wild learned later that there were signal stations in the neighborhood and, in retaliation, he ordered "the burning of a dozen or twenty houses," in accordance with General Order No. 23.[5]

On August 4, the whole post was moved to Newport News, where Wild acted as superintendent of all recruitment of Negroes in Virginia.[6] Newport News was a healthy place, with plenty of water and wood. The 1st Regiment of Colored Cavalry did guard duty for the camp and kept the new recruits inside. They would soon be assigned to a regiment.[7]

The August organization report in the Department of Virginia and North Carolina, under the command of Major General Benjamin F. Butler, listed Wild stationed at Newport News commanding only the 1st U.S. Colored Cavalry (three companies, dismounted). He was part of the District of Eastern Virginia, under Brigadier General George F. Shepley.[8]

September, 1864—On the Battlefields in Virginia

Wild's 1st Brigade participated in the battle at Chaffin's Farm (also called Fort Harrison, Fort Gilmer, New Market Heights and Laurel Hill) on September 29–30, 1864, under the command of Colonel John H. Holman. The 1st Brigade sustained 119 casualties; the 2nd Brigade, under Col. Alonzo G. Draper, had 455 casualties, and the 3rd Brigade, under Colonel Samuel A. Duncan and then Colonel John W. Ames, had 387 casualties. All of the regiments in these brigades were colored troops.[9]

On October 28, 1864, Secretary of War Stanton ordered Butler to relieve General Wild "from recruiting service," because the recruiting posts in Newport News and at New Bern were being discontinued.[10] The War Department telegraphed Wild to move to the battlefront.[11]

November 1864—Wild Put "On the Shelf"

Relieved of his recruiting duties, Wild was at Butler's disposal. Eager for news from Newport News, while stationed near Chaffin's Bluff, Wild wrote to his brother Walter on November 18. Brigadier General Wild was bored. He had been "absolutely idle" waiting for General Butler to return and "assign me a position." He had spent his time reading, and "a daily ride on horseback" had been his "sole occupation."[12]

December 1864

The war was coming to a close. After Union General William T. Sherman had completed his infamous "march to the sea" from Atlanta eastward across Georgia, and Savannah had been captured, attention turned to the North Carolina coast, and Fort Fisher, below Wilmington.

Wild had been reduced in rank and relegated to performing the duties of a courier or "errand boy." Butler trusted Wild to carry confidential dispatches to Brigadier General I. N. Palmer,[13] Commander of the District of North Carolina, and Rear Admiral David Porter, commander of the Union fleet of the coast.[14] In conjunction with Butler's planned attack on Fort Fisher, he sent a diversionary expedition up the Roanoke River to capture the Confederate works at Rainbow Bluffs (Rainbow Banks). Wild carried dispatches to Admiral Porter which asked his assistance and cooperation in the endeavor.[15] Rainbow Bluffs was a steep embankment along the Roanoke River, near the town of Hamilton.[16]

In preparation for the expedition, Butler ordered Colonel Webster, Chief Quartermaster at Fort Monroe, to help Wild in every way "in your power." Captain Homer A. Cooke endorsed the order and noted that "transportation will be individually afforded and all possible facilities placed at the disposal of Gen. Wild." The orders were forwarded to Brigadier General Wild at the front before Richmond.[17] Palmer was to "Rendezvous a sufficient land force at Plymouth, N.C.," and cooperate with the fleet in an advance to Rainbow Bluff and a joint attack upon Fort Branch. Once the mission was carried out successfully, the land forces were to move on to Tarboro and destroy the railroad bridge. The utmost secrecy was to be maintained.[18]

December 1864—The Rainbow Bluff Expedition

Wild left at sunrise on December 1 to meet Admiral Porter at Hampton Roads. He explained his mission and obtained Porter's cooperation in Butler's venture before sending dispatches to Commodore Macomb, commander of the naval forces in the Albemarle Sound.[19]

The next day, Wild reached Roanoke Island, where he delivered the naval dispatches and then proceeded to New Bern.[20] Butler issued an order on December 2 for Wild to report "in person to Major General Weitzel," who still commanded the XXV Corps, but Wild did not receive this order until December 24, because he was "absent—at Wilmington, N.C."[21]

Butler and about 6,500 men set out from Bermuda Hundred on December 7. Two days later, from Fort Monroe, Butler wired Admiral Porter that the army portion of the "conjoint expedition against Wilmington" was ready to begin. Porter, however, had his doubts about the outcome of the expedition, and did not believe that Butler knew what he was doing by depending on an "explosion to do all the work."[22] Porter was proven correct in the fiasco on December 24.

December 9, 1864—Rainbow Bluffs

The Rainbow Bluff expedition involved the 27th Massachusetts, 9th New Jersey, 16th Connecticut, 85th New York, and 176th Pennsylvania regiments. There was also Battery A of the 3rd New York Artillery, and the 12th New York Cavalry. The force was commanded by Colonel Savage of the 12th New York Cavalry.[23] Wild noted that General Palmer sent "all the detachments of troops that could be spared, to concentrate at Plymouth under Col. Frankle," and the 2nd Massachusetts Heavy

Artillery. Wild accompanied the troops on the expedition in an advisory capacity. They traveled on a naval gunboat, which had trouble landing. On December 9, the Federal troops moved further up the Roanoke River, where they were engaged in skirmishes all along the way with rebel outposts.[24]

On the morning of December 10, Confederate troops were posted on a bluff high above a creek, and with artillery and cavalry support, they attempted to destroy Gardner's Bridge. The Federals drove the Confederates back away from the bridge, and skirmishing continued to Foster's Mill. Bringing up artillery, the 2nd and 27th Massachusetts and the 9th New Jersey engaged the enemy for half an hour while the bridge was being repaired to allow troops to cross.[25]

After several hours, the Federal force advanced and drove the enemy beyond Williamston. Union troops camped at Williamston the night of the 10th to await the naval gunboats. The 85th New York was left at Williamston to await the arrival of the boats and to forward supplies when they arrived, while the main body of troops moved out at midnight to Spring Green Church, a mile from Butler's Bridge, where Confederates were entrenched. Colonel Frankle divided his forces and sent the 27th Massachusetts and the 9th New Jersey to the right to come up behind the enemy. A joint attack was planned from front and rear upon the enemy's position.[26]

The Federal forces passed the town of Hamilton, and arrived at Rainbow Bluffs before sunrise on December 12. Here, they found that the Confederates had received reinforcements. This made the planned surprise attack impossible, "frustrating the main object of the expedition." During the night, the Federal soldiers managed to capture a number of Confederate soldiers, and "several commissioned officers, including a colonel."[27]

Fort Branch

It was a bitterly cold December night as the soldiers made their way across field and stream. They encountered the road connecting Hamilton to Fort Branch. The Federal troops followed the road and with the Confederates in their rear, were not free to survey the enemy's strength and position at Fort Branch.[28]

The Federals saw Colonel Hinton, commander of Fort Branch, at a house near the intersection of the roads. He saw the Federals advancing but, in the dark, he believed them to be his reinforcements. He mounted his horse and rode up to Captain Russell of the 3rd New York Artillery and said, "Good morning, Captain! Never so glad to see anyone in my life." The Yankees pretended they were Confederates and answered him. Hinton extended his hand to Colonel Bartholomew, and remarked, "Good morning, Colonel! Just in time! There's fun ahead!" Then, Bartholomew walked over to admire Hinton's horse, a gray. He shook Hinton's hand while at the same time grasping the bit in the horse's mouth, and said, "I'm awful glad to see you!" Then he ordered the Confederate Colonel: "You may get off that horse! You won't need it any longer, as you are my prisoner!" Hinton was naturally surprised, and replied, "The devil you are! I thought you were the Weldon Junior Reserves."[29]

With the Confederate colonel captured, the Federals soon tricked the guard at the log barracks and enticed them to come outside. The Junior Reserves were seen approaching from the rear, and when the Federal artillery was engaged, the Junior Reserves scattered. The 27th Massachusetts and the 9th New Jersey rushed down the road and charged the enemy behind their entrenchments, and captured a large number.[30] Colonel Hinton and 40 others were captured by Colonel Frankle.[31]

Colonel Frankle moved his men forward to occupy the forks of the road while artillery was being brought up across Butler's Bridge. However, the plan to attack the entrenched Confederates from both front and rear had fallen through.[32]

Instead, the 27th Mass. and the 9th New Jersey made a reconnoiter toward Fort Branch, where they found the Junior Reserves positioned before the fort. The two Federal regiments wanted to assault the fort, but had only 4 rounds of ammunition left. After consulting with Brigadier General Wild, Colonel Frankle ordered the troops to pull back toward Williamston. The attack could not be carried out because of the failure of the navy to cooperate. The extra ammunition was on board the ships, and because of the great degree of secrecy, the land forces had no idea where the boats were.[33]

Brigadier General Wild described the expedition: "The whole affair and all the details were planned with judgment and carried out with coolness and steadiness."[34] From New Bern, Brigadier General I. N. Palmer, commander of the District of North Carolina, reported that General Wild left New Bern on December 16 to see General Butler to "explain matters to him."[35]

Because of the cold temperature, some of the troops were "badly frost bitten," so they returned the way they had come. The naval gunboats had attempted to follow them, but were hindered by obstructions in the Roanoke River. Two of the gunboats were sunk by Confederate torpedoes. Thus, the cooperative effort came to naught, and Wild and the troops returned to Plymouth, where the various units dispersed to their previous posts.[36]

Intelligence received from Union Commander Macomb on December 21 advised that the enemy was concentrated on the bluffs at Poplar Point. Help was needed to dislodge their sharpshooters. However, by that time, the men of the expeditionary force were out of supplies, and the men "so chafed and footsore that fully one-half the force had been placed upon the sick list by the surgeons." Commander Macomb was so informed, and the force returned to Plymouth.[37]

In December of 1864, changes were being made in the organization of the Army of the James. The X and XVIII Army Corps were done away with and the white infantry troops in those units were to be consolidated into a new corps to be called the XXIV Corps, and become a part of the Department of Virginia and North Carolina. The colored troops in the Department of Virginia and North Carolina were organized into the new XXV Corps, to be commanded by Major General George Weitzel.[38] This change also placed Brigadier General Wild in the XXV Corps.

Anticipating Wild's return to General Butler's headquarters, Palmer asked Captain A. J. Fitch to inform General Butler "immediately upon the arrival of General Wild at this place the force was dispatched to Plymouth." An attempt to regain Plymouth was being readied, as well as to threaten Kinston from New Bern. Palmer also described several naval expeditions, and said they had encountered obstacles in the Neuse River, as well as damage by torpedoes in the Roanoke River near Plymouth.[39]

On December 20, 1864, Wild returned to Norfolk, Virginia, where he reported to Lieutenant Colonel Smith that he and his men had "failed to surprise the enemy on Rainbow Bluff." Confederates had been reinforced and "the navy could not help us on account of the multitude of torpedoes." He informed Smith that the Federal navy was still in the process of "making their way up the river."[40] Wild telegraphed Butler at the headquarters of the Army of the James for orders, but Butler was with his troops on the first, and subsequently disastrous, expedition against Fort Fisher.[41]

Butler's Fiasco at Fort Fisher— December 20–27, 1864

Fort Fisher was the key to maintaining the defenses of the Cape Fear River area. Butler, with the land forces, and Admiral Porter, with the naval forces, launched a joint assault on December 20. However, bad weather prevented any action until December 23. Butler planned a massive explosion at the base of the fort. A boat was loaded with 215 tons of powder and moved to within 200 yards of the fort. However, when the "powder" boat exploded about 1:45 A.M., the results were not what Butler expected. Colonel William Lamb, the fort commander, assumed that a blockade runner had run aground and exploded. It did little damage. Federal troops moved into position on the morning of December 24 and began bombarding the fort. On December 25, the Federals advanced to within 75 yards of the Confederates in the fort, but did not attack. General Butler unwisely decided that the "defenses were impregnable," and called off the attack. He had his men loaded onto ships from the Union fleet, and they left the Fort Fisher area.[42]

Although General Robert F. Hoke and a large Confederate force were at Sugar Loaf, only a few miles from the fort, General Braxton Bragg, sent by President Davis to take charge of the action, failed to order Hoke to assist at Fort Fisher. As a result, the fort capitulated under the renewed Federal attack which began January 12, directed by General Alfred H. Terry (who had replaced Butler). After bitter hand-to-hand fighting, both Colonel Lamb and General Whiting were wounded, and Fort Fisher surrendered on January 15, 1865.[43]

Wild received his much-delayed orders to report for duty to Major General Weitzel, commander of the newly formed XXV Army Corps, on December 24. This corps was composed entirely of colored troops.[44] Since both Smith and Hinks had left the army, Wild was appointed a division commander of the XXV Corps, "the first and only American army corps composed entirely of black units."⁴⁵ Weitzel had just returned from the failed assault on Fort Fisher when Wild reported on December 30. He assigned Wild to command the First (previously Third) Division, XXV Army Corps. He and his men were stationed on the lines in front of Richmond, at Chaffin's Farm, on the north side of the James River. He was to remain there for the next three months.⁴⁶

The "wild" General was soon embroiled in another controversy, this time with one of his former regimental commanders, Alonzo G. Draper, now Brevet Brigadier General.

January 1865

Because of the fiasco at Fort Fisher, Major General Butler was relieved of command. Some saw Fort Fisher as "the occasion, rather than the cause of Gen'l Butler's removal," which was universally approved by both the army and the country. Although Butler had great administrative abilities, and was skilled in diplomacy and statecraft, he was inadequate as a military commander. William P. Derby believed that Butler was "at his best as the military governor of New Orleans,"⁴⁷ although there are many who would disagree with that statement.

Butler was replaced by Major General Edward O. C. Ord. With Butler gone, Wild was deprived of the support of the only man who had always stood by him in his actions and helped him avoid trouble. Butler had bailed Wild out of more than one prickly situation.

Stationed at Fort Brady, on the James River, Wild watched for enemy troop movement on land and on water. On January 24, 1865, Wild reported a large body of enemy troops on the opposite side of the James River moving toward Bermuda Hundred.⁴⁸ Five enemy boats went up the river, but only one of them was hit on its iron sides by gunfire from Fort Brady. Wild noticed the boats traveled slowly, and did not return the fire from Fort Brady, and that the only sign of life was "the setting of a lantern on the bows of the third boat after she was struck the third time." Federal pickets soon shot out the lantern.⁴⁹

Brigadier General Wild wrote a protest to Brigadier General Turner, Chief of Staff of the XXV Army Corps, about a rebel steamer which had come down to Cox's Ferry in daylight. Wild believed the enemy would be able to "examine everything—the position of our pickets on both sides of the river, the exact bearing of the guns at Fort Brady, the disposition of our forces." He feared that if allowed river passage, the Confederates would learn that they had "no troops in the neighborhood of Cox's Ferry, and no new batteries; nothing but Fort Brady itself." Most importantly, Wild did not want the enemy to learn that the Federal forces had not placed obstructions in the river to "prevent a repetition of their naval descent." He saw that the chief objective of the request was to "spy out precisely this information."⁵⁰ Undoubtedly Turner took Wild's advice and ordered that "parties from such boats will not be allowed to land," and ordered General Wild "to put pickets, not to exceed twenty-five, in the field in front of his position to look out for such landing above the wharf."[51]

General Wild sent pickets to several points to prevent "boat parties of the enemy landing in the neighborhood of the graveyard." The idea was "not to attract the attention of the enemy," which might draw fire from the batteries on the opposite shore and inflict injury upon the men in the trenches, but to show the enemy that they are "forbidden to come onto this ground," while not arousing their suspicion that "we are about to engage in any enterprise."[52]

On February 6, 1865, Major General Ord wrote General Heckman, commander of the XXV Corps, to have General Wild send out scouts to determine if Confederate rams were moving down the river.[53]

February 15, 1865 — Draper Files Charges, Wild Arrested Again

Charges: Conduct prejudicial to good order and military discipline
Plaintiff: Brevet Brigadier General Alonzo G. Draper

Wild's former regimental commander, Alonzo Draper, now a Brigadier General in his own right, preferred charges against Wild on February 15, 1865. Draper accused Wild of exhibiting conduct "prejudicial to good order and military discipline."[54]

Specifically, Draper alleged that Brigadier General Edward A. Wild, while in command of the First Division, XXV Army Corps, had talked with others about Draper. Wild was reported to have told Colonel Robert M. Hall, 38th USCT, an officer under Draper's command: "You must not be too much influenced by General Draper, he has strong prejudices...." Draper alleged that on another occasion, Wild told Colonel Hall, "I can scarcely think that General Draper is actuated by malice, but it sometimes looks like it. I go home and begin to think I am mistaken, when some other evidence of the interest he takes in this case, makes me think it must be so," or words to that effect.[55]

Was Wild becoming paranoid? Did he believe that everyone was prejudiced against him and his black troops? Wild's explanation does not support this.

Wild's Reply to Draper's Charges

Four days after Draper filed charges, Wild wrote Lieutenant Colonel Edward A. Smith, A.A.G., Department of Virginia. He explained that "In the first place, this was not mere gratuitous scandal or gossip, intended to injure Gen. Draper, as it might appear to one cursory reading the specifications. I was giving some advice to Col. Hall, while engaged in making certain official inquiries."[56]

Wild claimed that his "advise was limited to a single point or topic,—whereas the language ascribed to me in the first specification, appears to be general and unlimited in its affliction." Wild said that he was only advising Colonel Hall to "make up his own estimate of the character qualifications and relative value of the officers of his command (with a view to expurgation) and to rely upon his own opinions, unbiased by retorts from within or without and to take a reasonable time in doing so."[57]

Wild warned Hall not to be "too much influenced in this matter by Gen. Draper, as he is a man of strong prejudices, and if you were to act solely on his representations (incomplete, of course), you might perhaps be led into individual injustice, or injustice towards some individual."[58]

Wild repeated his warning for emphasis: "You must form your own judgment about your own officers. I say this because it would be very natural for you, a stranger, coming into a strange regiment to go directly to your Brigade Commander, not only for advice, but to accept his opinions exclusively in a matter like this."[59]

Wild explained that his words were "meant to apply explicitly to this one matter solely of estimating personal character and could not be made to apply to any other situation without good cause, as my language was very explicit." It was not meant to "disturb the influence of Gen. Draper over Col. Hall, or any other inferior officer in any other fields of good order, or channel of military discipline but this one," and was only intended as advise to Colonel Hall "to avail himself of his proper prerogative as a regimental commander, who is always presumed to be the best judge of his regimental officers."[60]

Wild then addressed the "case of one of his officers, whom Gen. Draper had born down upon constantly and sharply, and sometimes unnecessarily." Wild told Colonel Hall that he should look himself for some "virtue" in the officer. In this case, Wild said his language and his advice to Colonel Hall was only to "acquaint" him with that officer.[61]

The circumstances that led to his talk with Colonel Hall had arisen because a group of documents had been received concerning different officers in the 38th USCT. One of the documents was sent to Wild by General Heckman, the Corps commander, requesting Wild's opinion. Soon thereafter, another document was received, and several additional ones involving "similar inquiries." To answer the inquires, Wild had to talk with a number of enlisted men. Thus, he went to the quarters of Colonel Hall, and during that investigation, "I was led into giving the above advice to Col. Hall. But the advice was given privately and reached no ears but his." In his defense, Wild claimed that while his visit to Hall "might give color to the suspicion that I went out of my way to gossip and slander Gen. Draper for the purpose of prejudicing Col. Hall against him," the truth was that he "was obliged to go there in following out the directions of Gen. Heckman and was perfectly innocent of anything but the most honest intentions." Wild believed that some other officer had probably persuaded General Draper to "make the complaint of me," and to bring charges. Wild claimed that Draper was aware of his visit to Colonel Hall and the reason for it, because he had first gone to Draper's quarters and informed him of his errand, and talked with him "on the same subject and partly to the same effect."

Major General Weitzel sent Draper's charges to Lieutenant Colonel E. W. Smith, Assistant Adjutant General, Army of the James, at the XXV Army Corps headquarters. Both Colonel Hall and Brevet Brigadier General Draper had contacted Weitzel to file a complaint, but Weitzel had reservations. First, he did not want General Wild "to be tried" on the charges, but he wanted the Commanding General to see that this "grave Military offence on the part of Gen. Wild" corroborated the observations of General Heckman and others on his staff that General Wild's views of military discipline and command were peculiar, and entirely different from his. In the best "interests of the Corps, and the welfare of the army," Weitzel suggested that Brigadier General Wild be relieved "from duty with this Corps, and assigned to some other duty."[62]

On February 14, 1865, Wild requested a leave of absence of six days[63] because he had to have some dental work done. This was the day before Draper filed the charges. On February 17, 1863, Wild's request was granted for leave to go to Philadelphia. He left on February 20, and returned on the 25, having been absent from duty "5 days and 10 hours."[64] He returned to headquarters of the First Division, XXV Army Corps on February 25, "some thirteen hours" ahead of the time he was required to return.[65] Typical of Wild, he made no mention of any charges brought by Draper in his outline of his "Military Career."

On February 24, Major General Ord contacted Brigadier General John Aaron Rawlins and asked for "a good brigadier-general in place of Wild, who has charges against him and does not satisfy Gen. Weitzel." Ord asked if General Curtis could be used to head the division.[66]

March 1865

The Union tightened its net around Lee's army, and the war neared an end. Wild's military career was also coming to an end. An order from Major General Weitzel directed Brevet Major General Augustus V. Kautz to relieve Brigadier General Wild of command of the First Division of the XXV Army Corps. General Kautz was now Wild's commanding officer.[67] He assigned Wild to command the 2nd Brigade of the First Division of the XXV Army Corps.[68]

Wild was bitter at being demoted to a brigade commander. He was highly critical of Ord, who commanded most of the army in front of Petersburg, and left the less favored units, including Wild's Brigade, at Bermuda Hundred. Wild was sure that Ord had taken a dislike to him and was determined to deprive the black troops of the honor and glory due them.[69]

Fall of Richmond, April 3, 1865

On the Osborne Pike picking up rebel stragglers, Captain George A. Bruce, 13th New Hampshire Infantry, reported that on April 2 or 3, he was overtaken by

General Wild and staff, and a company of colored soldiers "marching by the flank, who passed the supports to our skirmishers, who were also marching by the flank." Bruce ordered his reserves "to move past the colored troops," and for the "skirmishers to advance more rapidly." Bruce did not want enter the city behind the colored troops of General Wild.[70]

By April 3, Richmond was being evacuated. President Davis and his cabinet had already fled, along with the funds from the Confederate treasury and the banks of Richmond. Wild's brigade of black soldiers (part of Kautz's Division, Weitzel's XXV Corps) was one of the first groups of Federal soldiers to enter the city.[71] Former slaves, recruited into the Union Army by Wild, were among the first infantry enter the "sacred precincts" of Richmond, Virginia.[72] Because of Ord's troop placement, on April 3, 1865, Wild was able to enter Richmond at the head of his black troops.[73] This gave Wild "great satisfaction," but Ord soon put a damper on Wild's happiness. As soon as General Robert E. Lee surrendered, Ord approached Wild and ordered: "You must get these damned niggers of yours out of Richmond as fast as you can!" He ordered Wild and his men to the Petersburg area to the camps newly vacated by white troops.[74]

Wild and his troops were in Richmond before sunrise well in advance of all the infantry forces. Wild reported that the city was "occupied and guarded by provost guards and patriots of our cavalry," all of whom were kept busy trying to put out the fires that had been set by "Rebel soldiers, and even by the Rebel *owners themselves*." Wild and his brigade occupied the forts and lines about the city until April 12.[75]

General Weitzel entered Richmond just behind a cavalry vanguard of about 40 men and the XXIV and XXV Corps. He found the city on fire, and the citizens crowded onto the grounds of the capitol to escape the fires. Weitzel's first order was to put General Ripley's brigade to work to put out the fires. Upon learning that General Robert E. Lee's wife was at her home on Franklin Street, Weitzel sent men to guard her residence. He also placed a guard at the Masonic Temple, "the oldest in the country." He then rode to City Hall and officially took possession of the city, and telegraphed Grant: "We took Richmond at quarter past eight this morning...."[76]

Union forces suffered considerable losses during the "Appomattox Campaign," during the last days of the war from March 29 through the surrender on April 9, 1865. The combined forces of the Army of the Potomac, the Army of the James, and Sheridan's cavalry lost 197 officers killed and 579 wounded; 1,269 men killed and 7,180 wounded. A total of 96 officers were captured or missing and 1,658 men were either captured or missing, for a grand total of 10,979. Luckily, Wild's 2nd Brigade did not suffer any losses, which indicates they were not engaged in any battle or skirmish.[77]

On April 13, Major General Ord relieved Brigadier General Wild of his duties in the XXV Army Corps, and directed Wild to report to Lieutenant General U.S. Grant. Wild received those orders on April 16 and complied.[78]

When Weitzel asked President Lincoln what should be done first to help the people of Richmond, Lincoln replied, "If I were in your position, General, I think I would let them up easy, let them up easy." Weitzel was kind to the people of Richmond, and he offered the stores of the Army of the James to them, and dispensed food, blankets, clothing and medicine. He saw that the streets were patrolled to prevent looting. Unfortunately, the kind treatment handed out by General Weitzel ended after President Lincoln was assassinated.[79]

April 14, 1865 — President Lincoln Assassinated

The assassination of President Abraham Lincoln at Ford's Theater changed the course of history. For the next decade, the "Reconstruction" policy instigated after Lincoln's death had a tremendous impact on the defeated Southern states. John Wilkes Booth, the gunman, shot Lincoln and then jumped from the presidential box onto the stage. With both arms in the air, he shouted, "Sic semper tyrannis."[80] Booth, a Confederate sympathizer and well-known actor, unknowingly did the South a great injustice, and left the Confederate states to the mercy of the Radical Republicans and those who wanted to see the South punished for the war. As the remnants of the Confederate government fled south, the nation prepared to mourn President Lincoln.

April 19, 1865 — Washington, D.C.

According to Walter Wild, Brigadier General Edward Wild took his staff with him to Washington for President Lincoln's funeral.[81] The funeral service began at noon on Wednesday, April 19, in the East Room of the White House. It was conducted by the Reverend Thomas Hall, pastor of Epiphany Episcopal Church of Washington. Simultaneously, services were taking part all across the country. After the service, the coffin was placed on a hearse and, guarded by soldiers of the Veterans Reserve Corps walking on each side, the procession marched slowly to the Capitol building, where the body would lie in state. The next morning, the doors were opened and thousands of people entered to view the catafalque and pay their last respects to Lincoln. Then, the casket was loaded on a special train that would travel 1,600 miles over 14 days to Springfield, Illinois, for burial. At each city the train passed, thousands of people lined the tracks and waited hours for the train to go by.[82]

On April 20, 1865, at the request of Major General E. O. C. Ord, Lieutenant General U.S. Grant issued Special Order No. 78, which relieved Wild of his duties and ordered him to report to headquarters in Washington, D.C. Wild was then ordered to proceed to his home, and to contact by "letter" the Adjutant General of the Army in Washington, D.C., for orders.[83]

April 23, 1865

On April 23, all the colored troops in Richmond were ordered to march to

Petersburg. They marched through the streets of Petersburg in "triumphal procession," and then passed through to camp on the south side where they had camped when the city was under siege.[84]

By April 23, Wild was back home in Brookline, Massachusetts, awaiting further orders.[85] He was not idle, nor did he remain there long.

Wild Discovers Who Had Him Demoted

While in Washington, Wild discovered why he had been demoted. General Weitzel had written a letter to Massachusetts Senator Henry Wilson, Chairman of the Committee on Military Affairs, to complain that Wild was "incompetent to handle a division." After Wild was acquitted in the Draper case for lack of hard evidence, Weitzel would not let the matter rest until he had ousted Wild. Wild was surprised, because he thought Weitzel was more amicable toward him. Wild suddenly found himself without a command, and that he was also "stigmatized as incompetent," and expected to be "dropped." While he had not envisioned a long military career, Wild was concerned that the freedmen would lose "their truest friend," and at a time "when they will have the greatest need of friends to elevate them to their new political status...."[86]

Wild believed that he was being penalized because, as one of the first to champion black soldiers and to "raise black troops," he was "identified with their cause." Wild bitterly complained that he had had "nothing but prejudice, jealousy, misrepresentation, persecution and treachery to contend against ... from every quarter—even from General Butler himself, who aimed to be considered the most prominent friend of the Negro in the whole country."[87]

Wild's removal came after Major General Weitzel recommended that he be permanently transferred because Wild's views were opposed to his own.[88] Subsequently, Major General Edward O. C. Ord, who had replaced Major General Butler, agreed with Weitzel's sentiments, but failed to take any action.[89] Wild was humiliated, and only a public statement by Weitzel could clear his name and allow him to continue in command. General Weitzel did say that his letter to Senator Wilson had only been intended to show his preference for General Theodore Read, and that he still considered Wild to be an "honest, sincere, patriotic, and brave man." In Weitzel's favor is the fact that his letter to Senator Wilson had been written just after Weitzel joined the Corps, and Weitzel admitted that he had "received unfavorable reports" about Wild from several sources, which he subsequently learned were greatly "exaggerated." Weitzel also claimed that Wild's removal from command had been "without his knowledge."[90] In fact, Wild had been removed by the order of Major General Ord. Ord was an "arch-rival" of Butler's, and after Ord took command of the Army of the James, he began looking for a replacement for Wild, "who has charges against him." Ord stated that his was also the view of General Weitzel. Ord pretended to be a friend of the blacks, but was really not. Wild believed that

Ord disliked him personally because he believed that Wild was Butler's pet. Wild also contended that this view was fostered by the "Nigger-haters" on Ord's staff. This is substantiated by the limited use of black soldiers and by Ord's order to remove black troops from the city when Richmond was captured.[91]

May 10, 1865 — Wild Accuses Ord

Wild continued his feuding with Ord, and on May 10, 1865, he sent a "one of the most scathing indictments of a superior officer ever penned by an American soldier" to the Senate Military Committee, headed by Senator Henry Wilson of Massachusetts. Wild described Ord as "a man of the smallest calibre … vacillating, uncertain … arbitrary, hasty…. He can be influenced by any one who can get a good chance to talk to him … and can be swung round to a point diametrically opposite to his opinion of an hour before." Ord had acted "hastily, rashly, and one-sidedly." He said Ord was prone to reprimand subordinates "in the most insulting way possible," while praising and showing favoritism to others. Wild declared Ord was a bigot and was dishonest, and while he appeared to believe in the freedom of blacks, Ord had "done the meanest things to, and for, the negroes." He concluded that Ord had "gained the utter contempt of all."[92]

Wild's protest did little to repair the damage to his reputation or to restore his position.

Undoubtedly a major shakeup in command was being undertaken in regard to the commanders of the colored troops.[93] All three division commanders—Charles J. Paine, William Birney, and Edward Wild—were removed shortly after Ord took over the Army of the James. These men had similar backgrounds—all had been civilians before the war; two were lawyers, and one (Wild) was a doctor. All of them had led white units at the beginning of the war, and all had volunteered in 1863 to recruit and lead black soldiers. They had been successful in recruiting black troops, and all three had been removed or transferred from Virginia within two months after Ord assumed command.[94]

Wild was not alone in his opinion of General Ord. Major General Birney believed that he had been removed because "of his support for black soldiers," and he had expressed that opinion to Butler. In addition, Birney believed his removal was because "to be a 'Butler man' was to be doomed."[95] Birney told Butler that he had been ordered to command a "separate division" which included City Point, Fort Powhatan, and Wilson's Landing. This was an insult because General Ord had no control over City Point, and the forces at the other two sites were under the command of General Carr, who was Birney's superior in command. In actuality, Birney had no command at all. Birney attributed his removal to the "same cause that led to the removal of Foster, Heckman, Shepley, Harris & Wild…." Birney thought Ord was so "flighty and eccentric" that he should not be permitted to occupy a position of much influence. Birney stated that Ord's "discrimination against the colored troops" had been so noticeable that it has attracted "general attention." In the recent campaign, Ord, according to Birney, had treated the colored troops badly. He threw them "behind hand, threw them out of the flank, gave them hard work to do, encamped them where there was no water, separated them unnecessarily from their supply train, and kept them back upon the front whenever he could." Birney said Ord was "chagrined" because Birney and his troops got into Petersburg first," and he had censured him.[96]

May 23–24, 1865—Review of the Grand Army of the Republic

Wild's last act as part of the Grand Army of the Republic was to march in the grand review in Washington May 23–24. Approximately 150,000 men paraded before President Andrew Johnson and other government officials and commanding generals. After the review, the volunteer army was disbanded.[97]

Then Edward headed home with his two colored servants. They were back in Brookline by May 26. He wrote to George Griggs for rooms for his servants in the "old Whyte house."[98]

Review of Grand Army of the republic in Victory Parade in Washington, D.C. (Library of Congress, Washington, D.C.)

Thus ended the military career of Brigadier General Edward Wild. Unable to practice medicine, he sought another form of employment. Wild had made some bitter enemies during his years in the army, but he also still had some friends. Governor John Andrew saw that Wild was offered a job with the Bureau of Refugees, Freedmen, and Abandoned Lands (the Freedmen's Bureau). Wild would soon find himself in Georgia embroiled in controversy again. Because Wild could not let injustice go unpunished, and he soon found himself entangled in events that would lead to an attempt on his life, and his removal from the Freedmen's Bureau would end his career in the service of the United States government.

XIII

The Freedmen's Bureau in Georgia and the Chennault Affair

The wicked flee when no man pursueth; but the righteous are bold as a lion.
—Proverbs 28:1

The course of events in the South might have taken a different path if Lincoln had not been assassinated. Lincoln had favored a lenient policy toward the devastated South, one not based on revenge. His death changed everything, and President Andrew Johnson issued his own policy. Johnson's "proclamation of amnesty" required an oath of loyalty by all who wanted their rights and property (with the exception of slaves) restored. High ranking Confederate officers and governmental officials, and those who owned property worth more than $20,000, were still excepted. Johnson required those classes to appeal directly to him.[1]

The Bureau of Refugees, Freedmen and Abandoned Lands (Freedmen's Bureau) had been set up in the spring of 1865 to help the 4 million freed slaves until they could provide and care for themselves.[2] The Bureau had been established by Lincoln to help the thousands of freed negroes who had been left jobless and homeless. After Lincoln's death, the Radical Republicans in Congress increased the power of the Bureau to guarantee that Negroes had certain rights, and "equal justice before the law."[3]

The Freedmen's Bureau was given the power to feed, house, and clothe the refugees and freed slaves. Abandoned lands in Confederate states could be used for the refugees and freedmen, and the Bureau could assign 40 acres of land to freedmen for three years, "at an annual rent" not to exceed 6 percent of the value of the land as of the 1860 tax appraisal.[4] It operated under the authority of the War Department, and Bureau offices were set up in the former Confederate states. The Democrats in Congress opposed the Bureau on the grounds that it was "unconditional and unnecessary." In the South, the Bureau was criticized for fostering hatred between the races, and of "advancing" the rights of the Negroes over those of the whites. Originally only meant to be a temporary solution, Congress continued to pass various acts that extended the life of the Bureau to June 30, 1872.[5]

This newly created bureau had vast powers, and it needed administrators and agents, men who believed in fair treatment and civil rights for the Negro, men who were willing to go into a defeated but not subdued South and risk their lives to see that the system of slavery and slave labor was ended. The Freedman's Bureau needed men like Edward A. Wild.

At the end of the war, General U.S. Grant had ordered Wild home, but Wild did not remain idle. Governor John Andrew believed that there could be no better defender of the rights of the Negroes than Edward A. Wild, and the Governor went to Washington to get Wild a job with the Freedmen's Bureau in Georgia.[6] Wild was given new chance to serve his country, but even in Georgia, he could not leave his troubles behind. Wherever he went, he seemed destined to become embroiled in controversy, to generate hatred, and to incur the wrath of civilians and those in authority. In Georgia, Wild would soon find himself in the midst of one of the great mysteries of the war: the lost treasure of the Confederacy and the stolen Virginia bank funds.

There was much work to be done in Georgia, and Edward Wild was eager to take up the challenge. He was told to report to Major General Rufus Saxton, Assistant Commissioner of the Bureau of Refugees, Freedmen, and Abandoned Lands.[7] Saxton, a 41-year-old native of Greenfield, Massachusetts,[8] was a veteran of the Seminole War[9] who once taught at West Point. After Saxton accepted an appointment with the Bureau, he continued the wartime policy of settling freed people on any available property, and he encouraged his subordinates to do likewise. Saxton believed that when the freed slave became a landowner he was on his way to becoming an independent citizen.[10]

Saxton believed that agents for the Freedmen's Bureau should be men who were in sympathy with the "agency's charge." He wanted to staff the Bureau with "Yankees whom he could trust and who shared his own views about Reconstruction." Local citizens or even most army officers would not make good agents. Saxton preferred to enlist the help of men with whom he was familiar and had worked with before.[11] John Emory Bryant was one of Saxton's appointees, and he was given the post of "general superintendent of the freedmen" in the Augusta, Georgia, area. Saxton soon needed more help.[12]

On June 5, 1865, Wild wrote Major General Rufus Saxton about his own appointment. Wild had many questions concerning his new position. Would he be allowed staff personnel, and would they be "detailed or assigned?" Did the Bureau have clerks and other personnel? Would there be "civil employees," and if so, how would they be paid?[13]

Saxton had not worked with Wild before, but he knew of Wild's reputation, and his background and personal courage. Wild's record of recruiting black troops was admirable, but the Brigadier General also was known for his "rashness and insubordination." He had a reputation of "harsh and violent treatment of rebels," perhaps because of constant pain from the loss of his arm.[14]

Saxton replied that Wild's position would be Acting Assistant Commissioner, with his headquarters in Macon. Wild was to establish agencies at Columbus and Atlanta as soon as possible, and at other points as needed to enforce the government's policy towards the refugees and freedmen. His authority would extend across Georgia west of the Altamacha, Ocmulgee and Yellow rivers, and north of Sheffield and Laurence to Cumming. Saxton enclosed "all the orders and circulars from the Freedmen's Bureau yet published relating to your duties," including Circular No. 1 and General Order No. 1.[15]

The situation in Georgia was volatile. The white population still had not come to grips with the new status of the freedmen. Until the end of the war, the Emancipation Proclamation had no effect except in limited areas. In the spring of 1865, much of Georgia remained untouched by war and held on tightly to its system of slavery. This changed with the arrival of agents of the Freedmen's Bureau and the occupation by the United States military.

Even the freedmen were unsure of their status. They had no homes, no jobs, and no food. It was up to the Freedman's Bureau to protect the rights of the former slaves and to get the economy moving again.[16] Wild's job was to help the freedmen understand their new status, and to secure their newly acquired rights. Former slave owners were to be made aware that slavery was not recognized by the Federal Government. Saxton gave Wild leave to settle freedmen and refugees upon abandoned lands in his district. In addition, Saxton expected Wild to look after the "Educational, Industrial and all the other interests of those under your charge" and to protect their rights. In cases of extreme need, Wild could issue army rations to prevent starvation.[17] In the early months after the close of the war, when the "freedmen could not or would not earn their living, supplies from the Bureau kept many of them from starving. Between June and September, 1865, 847,699 rations were furnished" in the state of Georgia alone.[18]

The only restrictions were that Wild should follow the general principles set out in documents sent by Saxton, who promised to send further instructions from time to time. He requested that Wild make full reports to his headquarters about all matters.[19] Wild was given a monumental task, responsibilities far too large for one man, and great power and authority, but no staff to do the work.

Society in the South was topsy-turvey. Former plantation owners were destitute, impoverished, and their way of life destroyed. The blacks who had once been their slaves were now free, but their economic condition was worse. Some stayed on their plantations and continued to work, but many former slaves tested their new freedom by leaving the only homes they had ever known.[20] Many freed slaves left the plantation and went to the cities, where they stood on street corners or huddled in crude huts; some had no shelter at all. A Georgia newspaper insisted there was a need to turn to "the military authorities for protection against vagrants," and even went so far as to suggest that "the commander of the posts require all negroes coming into the city to register, allow them reasonable time to secure work, and then send all those still idle to plantations on the coast or hire them to work on the railroads." The freedmen survived by stealing. Plantations suffered both from loss of a labor force and theft of their crops and other property. Some left reluctantly. One former Georgia slave recalled:

> The master had three boys to go to war, but there wasn't one come home ... he lost all his money, and the house soon begun dropping away to nothing. Us niggers one by one left the old place, and the last time I seed the home plantation I was standing on a hill. I looked back on it for the last time through a patch of scrub pine, and it looked so lonely ... [The master] was a-setting in a wicker chair in the yard looking out over a small field of cotton and corn. There was four crosses in the graveyard on the side lawn where he was setting. The fourth one was his wife.[21]

June 19, 1865 — Wild Begins New Job with Freedmen's Bureau

Wild arrived in Beaufort, South Carolina, on June 19, 1865, and reported to Major General Saxton. He was sent at once to begin work as a supervisor of the Bureau of Refugees, Freedmen and Abandoned Lands.[22]

Wild's arrival on the *Fulton* was announced in the *New South*. The paper noted that he would set up headquarters at Macon, Georgia, gave a brief outline of his military career, and mentioned the injuries he received at Fair Oaks and South Mountain. He was credited with organizing the "54th and 55th Regiments of Colored Troops, which have done such signal service in this Department."[23]

Wild, with his impetuous and impatient nature, was thrust into an already unstable situation. His sympathy for the blacks and his hatred for those who oppressed them led him to act in ways that were contrary to keeping the peace in Georgia. Wild went to Georgia with an "attitude." He did not believe that Southerners had surrendered, and he expressed his opinion when he wrote Senator Henry Wilson of Massachusetts: "I am sure that the submission of the Rebels is as hollow and treacherous as all their previous course—that they will continue to nurse schemes of future treasonable resistance...."[24] Wild harbored a grudge against former Confederates, and believed they were planning further resistance. He favored a "lengthy, firmly supervised Reconstruction," otherwise "peace will be only temporary and precarious." Wild saw his job with the Bureau as part of an effort to firmly secure the "fruits of victory."[25]

Wild moved to Augusta on June 30 to start his duties. He decided not to go to Macon, but to wait until General Saxton could inform him of the outcome of a conference with Major General Oliver Otis Howard, head of the Freedman's Bureau. Howard, known as the "Christian General," was a native of Maine and former commander of the Army of the Tennessee.[26] Howard lost his right arm at the Battle of Fair Oaks.[27] Wild expected this conference to clarify the agency's authority. Wild had already learned of a "jurisdictional dispute" between John Emory Bryant and the post military commander. Wild believed the jurisdiction issue should be settled before he went any farther into the country.[28]

Wild wrote to Massachusetts Governor John Andrew on July 3, 1865, to report his progress in the new job, and to thank the Governor for his efforts on his behalf which resulted in his new position.

> The work will be laborious, and perplexing, and for some time to come, dangerous. The worst opposition which we have to meet is that of the military, big and little. The natives yield doggedly, sullenly, but with the evident conviction that open resistance will be useless; so that the danger is from secret attacks. [29]

Wild began work as an agent of the Freedmen's Bureau without any specific instructions. He had to use his own judgment to deal with the many problems, and he was more radical than John Emory Bryant, the Bureau agent in Augusta.[30]

Wild soon discovered that "slavery exists everywhere except under the immediate shadow of our flag." He knew that it would take months before those persons living in the rural districts would "turn over a new leaf." He also knew that it would take much longer to correct all abuses, and safeguard the civil rights of the negroes. Wild was appalled at the conditions he found in the state. He reported to Governor Andrew that, although he thought he had "learned something of the abominations of Slavery," he was "staggered by the daily reports of awful outrages that come into this city."[31] Cases of rape, murder, and assault, and other crimes were committed almost daily against the former slaves. There were also, of course, crimes committed by blacks against whites.

Wild believed it was utterly useless to hope for any improvement in the condition of the freed Negroes until there was a return to prosperity, which would convince the white population of the benefits of free labor. Wild was optimistic, however, that eventually "Blacks will compete with the Whites in point of *property*, and will surpass the great mass of the Whites in point of *education*."[32] Wild did not see negro suffrage coming about for a number of years "as a voluntary measure." Ahead of his times, he believed that Negro suffrage could be obtained through a "*uniform Suffrage law*, to be forced universally in *all* the States."[33]

Early on, it was apparent to Wild that there was conflict between the Freedmen's Bureau and the military establishment. To Governor Andrew, Wild described the many obstacles placed in his way by the military commanders, who "have it in their power to trammel all our proceedings by withholding aid, either of men or supplies." In order to avoid punishment or criticism, the military commanders did not "directly" refuse to help the Freedmen's Bureau, but through devious and subtle methods of "delays & detentions of all sorts" managed to thwart the efforts of the Bureau. Another method was for the military personnel to say that "they have not what we ask for just then...."[34]

Wild also was hampered in his work by a lack of staff. He said, "I cannot do much until my staff arrive, but shall have to work hard." He had encountered opposition and "mean tricks" from the military ever since his arrival in Georgia. John Emory Bryant, the Augusta agent, also was "overwhelmed almost with such cases & with other work," involving outrages committed by both planters and negroes.[35]

The only good news was the upcoming 4th of July celebration. Wild hoped it could be held without violence. He closed his letter to the Governor on an encouraging note: "The work before me is vast, and often discouraging—but *grand* and I repeat my thanks to you for my being here," and declared, "For they really need such men as I am."[36]

The 4th of July celebration in Augusta proceeded without incident. After a speech by a black preacher there was a "procession" through the streets. The white folk watched from their windows and doors. Wild was glad when the day was over, because if there had been trouble, the small military force there might have had difficulty putting down a disturbance or a riot.[37]

Wild told his wife that conditions in Georgia were not safe: "This will be no place for you for a long time yet. The rebels are beaten but not subdued. There is danger enough here from secret attacks & I am to go in to Macon & other places in the interior where it is still worse."[38] On July 15, Wild wrote his wife that he had traveled by rail to hold public meetings and give "addresses to the Blacks & Whites in separate meetings." Assisting him was Dr. Mansfield French, a Chaplain and Methodist minister, who did most of the talking. They did not confine their activities to Georgia, but one trip took them into South Carolina, to one "of the hardest districts."[39] French, a native of Vermont,[40] had been working with the freedmen on the Port Royal experiment on the Sea Islands since 1862. French wisely prophesied that the "real elevation" of the former slaves would "be slow work."[41] The blacks loved Dr. French, and called him their "white Jesus." He preached to them, taught them, and married them for a fee.[42]

At each meeting, Dr. French was introduced by Brigadier General Wild. French then told the freedmen to "remain with their late owners, or within their present employers, at any rate of compensation, even if it is a bare subsistence, rather than become idlers or vagrants." French then addressed the whites in a separate meeting.[43] The negroes who attended French's meeting in Washington, Georgia, on July 21 dressed in their "holiday attire." Miss Eliza Andrews recorded in her diary that the sermon was interrupted by a thunderstorm, and "the poor darkeys" got "their Sunday clothes spoilt." She hoped that "The Frenchman," as she called Dr. French, would "catch a cough that will stop that pestiferous windpipe of his." She noted that the blacks believed French had "done more for them than Jesus Christ ever did." She believed that he was making the former slaves "insolent and disconnected, and after a while ... they will succeed in making them thoroughly unmanageable, but come what will, I don't think I can ever cherish any very hard feelings towards the poor ignorant blacks."[44]

At least three big meetings were held during the summer of 1865 by the

the Reverend French and General Wild. The first was at the 4th of July celebration in Augusta, where there was a parade through the streets "led by a colored regiment," and then a crowd "ten thousand strong" heard an oration. Two days later, French and Wild held a meeting at Edgefield, South Carolina, near the grave of Preston S. Brooks. The third meeting was held in a grove near the Robert Toombs mansion in Wilkes County, Georgia. The freedmen sang, "Blow ye the trumpet blow; the year of jubilee is come," while Toombs, a hunted fugitive, hid in the swamps not twenty miles away.[45]

Robert Toombs—lawyer, orator, and statesman—not only served in the Georgia legislature, but in both houses of the United States Congress. He had been one of the wealthiest planters in the state. He was the first Secretary of State of the Confederacy, but resigned to become a brigadier general in the Army of Northern Virginia. Wounded at Antietam (Sharpsburg) in 1862, he resigned and was named Division Adjutant in the Georgia militia. After the war, Toombs fled to Cuba and then England. He eventually returned to Georgia, but never asked for a pardon under the laws of Reconstruction. Although he rebuilt his fortune through a large law practice, he suffered a series of personal disasters. His wife died insane and he became blind.[46]

Steedman Sent to Georgia

Major General James Blair Steedman, commander of the Department of Georgia, during the early days of the Bureau, was one of several officers sent south by President Andrew Johnson to investigate Commissioner Howard's agency.[47] Steedman came down to Georgia with instructions from the President himself to reestablish civil jurisdiction. Wild described Steedman as "clear headed, firm," and hoped that he and Steedman could work well together.[48]

By mid–July, the scope of Wild's authority and that of other Freedmen's Bureau agents had been defined by Major General Steedman. Wild felt secure enough in his position to outline his duties and limitations in a letter to Captain A. P. Ketchum in Savannah, who was to be a Sub-Commissioner. With Major General Saxton absent, Wild, as Assistant Commissioner, believed, "it devolves upon me to give you directions." Based on the Bureau's Circular No. 5, Wild knew agents had the power to adjudicate in certain cases. Wild may have received additional informational from Major General Steedman as well. As Steedman interpreted the Bureau's authority, Wild and other agents could make decisions in disputes concerning wages and labor contracts, and award damages for broken contracts. They had no authority in cases of claims for damages from acts of violence or accidents, or in criminal cases, such as rape. The agents could not rule on the permanent title to property, but they could dispose of property after it had been handed over to the Bureau by right of military seizure.[49]

Steedman ordered that the civil courts be reestablished as soon as possible, and in anticipation of that occurrence, he closed the Provost Court in Augusta. That left the District without any court, but Wild obtained the use of the courtroom and began a Freedman's Court of Claims. Wild advised Ketchum that he was to "follow every case wherein a negro is concerned, into Court," and counsel the negro. When the Provost Court in Savannah was abolished, he advised Ketchum to open a Freedman's Court of Claims there, similar to that established by John Emory Bryant.[50]

Bureau agents could issue summonses to the involved parties to appear in court, and levy fines for contempt of court or for failure to appear, but they could not force defendants to come into court. That came under the province of the military. Any fines levied in the claims court would go to the Freedmen's Bureau to be used for the benefit of refugees and freedmen. Wild ordered a strict accounting of all monies collected and expended.[51]

Wild specifically requested that in records from the claims court, the word *colored* be omitted, and especially when giving information to newspapers which published court proceedings. He hoped that this would help eliminate "discrimination between whites & blacks." He did make an exception in some official documents when it was necessary to specify "colored" to "show cause why the case is brought into your court."[52]

Abandoned lands included not only plantations but city lots as well. If seized as abandoned "rebel" property, everything was taken—house(s), all fixtures upon the land, and anything which could be used for refugees or freedmen, which was not actually used for military purposes. The Bureau's Circular 3 stated that "no military authority can give it back to Rebels, nor even listen to their claims." To strengthen the Bureau's authority, War Department General Order No. 110 decreed that "all property that has once been set apart for the use of Freedmen, must now be turned over to the Bureau." As a safety measure, anyone attempting to reclaim property from the Bureau was to be dealt with by the military. Nothing short of a military emergency could cause a commander to remove, invade or disturb any of the Freedmen's Bureau property. Wild advised Ketchum that this policy would "hold good until countermanded" by Major General Saxton. Any appeals from Ketchum's decisions were to go through Wild, rather than the military.[53]

July 1865—Wilkes County, Georgia

In mid-July, Wild went to Washington, Wilkes County, to investigate charges that slave owners were still treating the freed people as slaves. He seized several public buildings in Washington, including the courthouse, and used them for "the educational advancement of the freed people." He planned to confiscate all state property and the railway system in Georgia, "because it had been used to aid and abet the rebellion."[54]

Wilkes County is situated in the northeastern section of Georgia, bounded on the east by Lincoln County and the Savannah River. Across the Savannah River lies the state of South Carolina. Washington, the county seat, is sometimes called "Washington-Wilkes" to distinguish it from the national capital of Washington, D.C. A number of exceptional Confederate generals were from Wilkes County or had relatives there.

Edward Porter Alexander was probably the best known Confederate officer from Wilkes County. He began as an engineer and signal officer under General P. G. T. Beauregard. Promoted to Chief of Ordnance of the Army of Northern Virginia, he soon commanded a battalion of Artillery in Longstreet's Corps, and fought in most of the major battles. Promoted to Brigadier General and Chief of Artillery, Alexander and his battalion were part of Lee's Army at the surrender at Appomattox Court House.[55] Porter Alexander was a friend of President Cleveland, and the two of them spent many days hunting ducks on Alexander's land, which is known today as Yawkee Wildlife Preserve.[56]

Confederate Major General Jeremy Francis Gilmer, originally from Guilford County, North Carolina, married Louisa Fredericka Alexander, sister of Brigadier General Edward Porter Alexander. A West Point graduate in 1839, Gilmer was deemed the most outstanding military engineer in the service of the Confederate Army.[57]

Another Confederate general from Wilkes County was Paul Jones Semmes, who died from wounds received at Gettysburg. Semmes faced Wild in battle from the Peninsula Campaign to South Mountain.[58]

The Confederate Treasure and the Private Bank Funds

Funds comprised of gold and silver, Confederate paper money, and bonds which belonged to the Confederate government were stored in Richmond, Virginia, until near the end of the war. A number of banks in Richmond and other Virginia cities also held money belonging to private citizens.[59] The treasure train was the last train to leave Richmond before it was evacuated by Confederate troops.[60] On April 3, 1863, the "midnight train" from Richmond, Virginia, carried two separate treasures—the Confederate treasure and the private bank funds. The Virginia bank funds were supervised by Judge W. W. Crump and junior clerks from six banks. Each container was stamped with the name of the bank from which it came. These were not opened on the journey south.[61] The train carried at least $200,000 from the banks of Richmond.[62]

The Confederate treasure, in "double-eagle gold pieces, silver bricks, gold ingots, and silver coin," was packed in bags and boxes was guarded by Captain William Harwar Parker, 60 midshipmen and Treasury Department teller Walter Philbrook, and loaded on the train headed south to Danville.[63]

The treasure train had scarcely left Richmond when rumors began circulating, and with each telling the size of the treasure grew. Today there are a number of theories about what happened to the money, the amount and value, and the location of buried portions that remain undiscovered.[64]

April 10–12, 1865 — Davis Meets Johnston in North Carolina

On Monday, April 10, Jefferson Davis and his government left Danville and moved to Greensboro, North Carolina, to meet General Joseph Johnston. Only hours after the train that carried Davis and his cabinet crossed over the Dan River into North Carolina, Union cavalry of George Stoneman burned the railroad bridge.[65] When the treasure train left Danville, Virginia, it reportedly carried silver coin and gold bullion valued at $327,022.90. In Greensboro, North Carolina, approximately $29,000 in silver of the Confederate treasure was left behind to pay the soldiers of General Johnston's army.[66] Davis met with Beauregard in Greensboro on April 12, and Major General John C. Breckinridge informed them that the Army of Northern Virginia "had capitulated."[67] The treasure train continued on to Salisbury, just ahead of Stoneman's troops.[68]

April 1865 — Transport of the Treasure

By April 17, the train had reached Abbeville, South Carolina, where the money was taken off the train and loaded onto wagons headed for Washington, Georgia. The wagons arrived in Washington on April 19. In Washington, the boxes were again loaded on a train bound for Augusta, Georgia, where they were stored in local vaults. On April 26, Parker and the cadets returned the treasure to Washington. Parker included documents and records in the gold and silver leaving in a wagon train for Judge Garnett Andrews' home to be stored. On April 29, Parker and the remaining cadets marched back to Abbeville as guards for the treasure. Parker was accompanied by General John F. Wheless of Tennessee, Confederate Navy paymaster, and Judge Crump of Richmond, assistant treasurer and caretaker of the Virginia bank funds.[69]

Parker learned that President Davis was expected to arrive shortly, so he again loaded the treasure on railroad cars "with a locomotive ready under full steam." When the President and his party arrived on May 2, Parker was ordered to turn over the funds to Acting Secretary of the Confederate Treasury M. H. Clarke, who placed General Basil Duke in charge. Relieved of his duty, Captain Parker "disbanded" his young "midshipmen" who had served so gallantly as guards of the monies.[70] A Georgia native, Medora Perkerson, recounted the story of the Confederate treasure in her book, *White Columns in Georgia*. She added that Parker decided to take the treasure to Augusta by railroad cars when he learned that Macon had been captured, but when he learned of Lee's surrender, he retreated with the treasure back to Washington. Here, the gold and silver was again loaded on wagons to go back to Abbeville. In Abbeville, the treasure was "unloaded and placed in a warehouse." (For years, people have searched in the tunnels under the town of Abbeville, South Carolina, looking for the lost Confederate gold.)[71]

In Abbeville, the responsibility of guarding the money was given to General Basil Duke and his cavalry. General Wheless was given $1,500 to pay Parker and his men, who had been dismissed. Lieutenant Bradford of the Confederate marines was to be given $300. Wheless went to the train, got the money in gold, and then rode to Washington to give Bradford his money.[72] When M. H. Clarke assumed the office of Acting Secretary of the Treasury, the Confederate funds were stored along with the monies from the Virginia banks.[73] In 1882, Clarke made a full accounting of how the Confederate treasury funds had been disbursed along the way.[74]

When Davis' presidential party stopped at Abbeville, where the train tracks ended, five brigade commanders—S. W. Ferguson, George G. Dibrell, J. C. Vaughn, Basil W. Duke, and W. C. P. Breckinridge—met with General Braxton Bragg and President Davis. Davis asked their opinions as to how to proceed with the war. The generals pointed out that recent events had removed all "hope that a prolongation of the contest was possible." Davis finally agreed and declared that "all was indeed lost," and the march to Washington, Georgia, was resumed.[75]

General Breckinridge ordered Duke to get wagons to transport the treasure, and it was loaded from the open boxcars onto six wagons. A detail was made up of men from all five brigades.[76] The treasure was loaded onto wagons at Chester, South Carolina, and then hauled to Newberry, then Abbeville, South Carolina, and then 40 miles to Washington, Georgia.[77]

The men of Duke's, Dibrell's and Vaughn's brigades had not been paid for some months. On May 3, while the wagons were camped on the Chennault property on their way south to Washington, General Breckinridge learned of a plot afoot to seize the gold. He made a brief speech to the men, and exhorted them "to remain faithful Southern soldiers and gentlemen." He also arranged for the Quartermaster General Alexander Robert Lawton to give the soldiers their back pay, "and thus quell any threat of revolt." Breckinridge also gave Mrs. J. D. Moss of the Chennault household "a chest laden with silver and jewels." (On May 22, some weeks later, this chest was seized by Federal troops along with all the other Chennault family silver and jewelry.)

The wagons were reloaded and arrived in Washington on May 4. There, Lawton authorized $108,322.90 to Breckinridge to pay the cavalry and other guards. Each man received $26 to $32. A sum of $10,000 of what had been given to Breckinridge was given to General Robert Toombs who, in turn, gave it to R. H. Vickers to distribute to returning Confederate soldiers at the rate of $2.50 per man. Orders were also issued that all "unattached officers and men should receive a month's pay."[78] The above distributions all came out of the *Confederate treasury funds*.

May 2, 1865 — President Davis in Washington, Georgia

Again, the funds were directed toward Washington, still free from Federal troops, but with a cavalry escort this time. Washington had escaped the wrath of William T. Sherman and the town was peaceful and quiet when Davis and his party arrived after 12 hours in the saddle.[79] Davis went to the home of General Robert Toombs and remained there about 36 hours. With Davis now were his wife Varina and their four children, and her sister, Miss Howell, and brother, Midshipman Howell, as well as other Confederate officials.[80]

On May 4, Clarke returned to Washington with two wagons of "coin and bullion." He transferred $40,000 in silver to Major Raphael J. Moses to be used by the Commissary Department to help paroled soldiers in Washington and Augusta. An additional $86,000 in gold was to be smuggled out of the country for the "continuance of the Confederate Treasury in absentia." This was accomplished by putting the gold in a carriage with a false bottom, and sent to Charleston or Savannah to be taken on board a ship.[81]

May 4, 1865 — Death of the Confederate States of America

The Confederacy officially died in Washington, Wilkes County, Georgia, on Thursday, May 4, 1865. The last official meeting of the Confederate government was held in the bank in Washington, a branch of the Bank of Georgia, the place being provided by Dr. J.J. Robertson, the bank cashier.[82] On Friday, May 5, the Confederate officials separated, and only Reagan accompanied the President westward.[83] That same day, Federal troops entered the town of Washington and occupied it.[84]

Private Bank Funds

The officers of the Richmond banks accompanied their money from Richmond, and swore "it was never mixed with the Confederate treasury funds, but kept apart and distinct. Dr. Robertson, the cashier of the Georgia bank, refused to permit any part of the Confederate treasure to be placed in the bank, fearing to jeopardize this Virginia money. The bank officials remained in Washington with the money until it was considered safe to remove it.[85] Some accounts fail to keep the two separate, resulting in misinformation about the fate of both funds.[86]

When the Federal troops arrived in Washington, they took possession of all the Confederate provisions stored there, as well as the Virginia bank funds in the

Washington bank vault. Judge Crump left on May 8 for Norfolk, Virginia, to make arrangements for the gold to be returned to the banks in Richmond. On May 14, two bank officials arrived in Washington to discuss the situation with Judge Andrews, and they planned to send the bank funds secretly back to Richmond with the aid of Federal guards.[87]

The bank cashier, Dr. Robertson, had gone to southwest Georgia to look after his plantation, and during his absence the bank officers decided to return with their treasure to Richmond by wagon. They foresaw no trouble so they used no precautions. They came openly to the bank in the early morning, loaded their wagons with boxes of specie, and departed about 10 A.M. They camped the first night near Danburg, a little town about twelve miles from Washington.[88]

Thus, after remaining safely in a bank in Washington, Georgia, for three weeks, the private funds from the Virginia banks were loaded on wagons. These were guarded by only a few Federal soldiers. Word soon spread about the movement of the money, and they were eyed by many who were "determined not to allow the treasure to remain in the hands of Federal authorities."[89] In fact, not long after the wagons left Washington, they were relieved of their burden of gold and silver. This happened when the wagons stopped to camp for the night at the Chennault plantation in Lincoln County near the Savannah River on May 24, 1865.

Bank Gold Disappears on Chennault Plantation

No one is sure what happened, but the funds from the Virginia banks disappeared from the campsite at the Chennault plantation. An article appeared in *The New York World* on August 21, 1865, which described how a half a million in gold and jewelry, not part of the alleged Confederate treasure but from private deposits in a Richmond bank, had been stolen from officials attempting to return it to Richmond. The *World* story was written by Miss Eliza Frances "Fanny" Andrews,[90] daughter of Judge Garrett Andrews, whose diary of the last year of the war and the early days of Reconstruction was published as *The War-Time Journal of a Georgia Girl*. She told the editor that she had written her article as if she "were a Yankee sojourning at the South, in order to make some of the hard things it was necessary to say in the telling the truth, as little unpalatable as possible to a Northern public."[91]

What became of the Virginia bank money? Was it buried on the Chennault plantation? The Chennault plantation became known as "golden farm," and for years people have searched there for the missing treasure, and gold coins have been found in the area. Or is it buried at the junction of the Apalachee and Oconee rivers, or was it divided among the local residents?[92]

Most of the Confederate government treasure had already been disbursed to Confederate soldiers and various officials by the time it reached Washington, Georgia. [93] The rest, the money belonging to the banks, was believed stolen from the

Chennault Plantation, near the Savannah River, in Lincoln County, Georgia. Only part of this money was ever recovered.

Mr. Taylor and Mr. Weissiger, in charge of the bank money, removed it from the Washington bank on May 24, 1865. With an insufficient number of guards, they started toward Richmond in wagons by way of Abbeville, South Carolina, instead of a somewhat safer route by way of Augusta and Savannah. A soldier in Washington saw the wagons being loaded, and gave that information to two men, who were both named "Maston and [to] other stray cavalry from East Tennessee." These former Confederate cavalry soldiers thought the money was Confederate "government money," and was therefore considered "lawful plunder," especially since these soldiers had not been paid for some time.[94]

The wagons carrying the bank money camped the night of May 24 near the Savannah River on the Chennault (Chenault) plantation. The officers in charge of the wagon train had received permission from the Reverend A. Dionysius Chennault to camp on his property. Five wagons were parked in an enclosed horse lot. The guard reportedly fell asleep, and the robbers attacked and carried off the money. During the night the wagons were ransacked, and gold and silver were scattered everywhere as the thieves loaded themselves and their saddlebags with as much loot as they could carry. The bank officers were "bound and the escort scattered." The next morning, the bank officials were able to recover about $40,000 which had been dropped by the robbers. Taylor and Weissiger posted a reward of $5,000 plus 10 percent of any money recovered. Many were eager to help, once it was learned that the money did not belong to the Confederate government, but belonged to the widows and orphans of many Confederate soldiers. Eventually, with the help of some Danburg residents, approximately $15,000 to $17,000 was recovered, and several robbers were arrested. A number of thieves were involved, and one of the Chennault men was sent by the robbers to negotiate for them. Once they learned the money was private property, the thieves agreed to give it up, and they agreed to encourage their associates to bring in the rest, if the bank officials would not have them arrested. They then proceeded to gather a total of $70,000 from various hiding places, and eventually about $110,000 was returned to the bank in Washington, Georgia.[95]

A former member of Vaughn's Brigade, Lewis Shepherd, reported that some of Vaughn's Brigade were responsible for the theft of the Virginia bank funds. Some of the officers and men of Vaughn's Brigade learned that a train of specie was being carried north under Federal escort and wrongly concluded that it was the property of the Confederate government. They believed that their four years of hard service for the Confederacy entitled them to a share of this gold and silver, provided they could succeed in securing it from the Federal guard.[96]

Shepherd said these former Confederate soldiers had followed the train and waited for a suitable moment to attack. They "charged the train, captured and disarmed the guards, and proceeded at once to knock the heads out of the kegs and the lids off the boxes containing the coin and to fill their forage sacks with ten- and twenty-dollar gold pieces." Several of the men escaped with as much as $60,000, others with lesser amounts. One of the robbers only got about $4,000 in silver, and when his companions refused to share their gold with him, he told what he knew. Several of the robbers were caught and forced to give up their booty. Shepherd recalled that several men got away. Two went to Kansas City, Missouri, with over $120,000, where they started a business. Two more wound up in California with $100,000, and invested that money in a business. Shepherd said one of the richest men in Texas "got his start with money secured from these kegs, and still another made good as a stockman, being now a cattle king."[97]

May 26, 1865—Some Stolen Gold Recovered

After $60,000 of the money had been recovered, former Confederate Brigadier General Edward Porter Alexander, one of the most highly respected Confederate officers, and a group of "paroled" Confederate soldiers went out to capture the culprits who had stolen the Confederate treasure. Alexander and some of the old Irvin Artillery men caught some suspects, but while they were looking for others, the people of Danburg "armed themselves and made a rescue."[98] Camped near Danburg for the night, several men offered to guard the prisoners. However, instead of guarding them, the men of Danburg released the prisoners. They reasoned that the "arrest of the highwaymen" was a breach of the agreement Weissiger had made, and that they were "honor bound to release then." Much of the money reportedly found its way into the hands of negroes, who watched the robbers hiding and visiting their treasure. A group of highwaymen banded together and scoured the countryside, beating and whipping negroes, "and hanging them up by their thumbs to extort treasure from them." Eventually, a servant of Mrs. Morse came into town and "demanded" protection from the federal authorities. As luck would have it, the authority in Washington, Georgia, was none other than Brigadier General Edward Augustus Wild. [99]

By June 6, the five men who had been caught and accused of the robbery had managed to escape. Georgia residents were not too upset by this, because they had rather Southerners and ex–Confederates have the money than see it fall into the hands of Yankees. Miss Andrews wrote that the Northern press seemed to made a "great ado" about the robbery of the money of the Virginia banks by Confederates, but they failed to mention the $300,000 taken by the Yankees from the bank at Greenville, South Carolina, and thousands of dollars of property that had been stolen from private homes.[100]

Some of the stolen treasure was found in sacks in a nearby stream, some in the woods, and some in wells. All that was recovered was taken back to Washington and stored in the bank.[101] Eventually, the part of the Virginia bank money that was removed to Atlanta was seized by authorities, sent to Washington, D.C., and turned over to the Federal government.[102]

This was the situation on July 21, 1865, when Brigadier General Wild and Rev.

French went to Wilkes County to investigate the murder of an old Negro woman. The residents of Washington, Georgia, feared the murder "would bring their vengeance upon the town." Judge Garrett Andrews was counsel for the defense. One of the killers reportedly shot the woman, while the other "broke her ribs and beat her on the head with a stone" until she was dead. They then left her "unburied in a lonely place, and the body was not discovered" until ten days later. General Wild, "despite the stench," examined the body of the woman with "ghoulish curiosity," and he even went so far as to pull out the broken ribs to look more closely at them. Since Wild was a doctor, he "didn't seem to mind the most sickening details." The attorney for the defendant, Garrett Andrews, said he had "rather have the sharpest lawyer in Georgia as his opposing counsel than these shrewd, painstaking Yankees." They were meticulous, and one of the Federal officers even found the stone with which the woman had been killed. On the testimony of other former slaves, two men were arrested, one was a married man with children, the other a young man of only about 20 years.[103] Eventually, Andrews was able to take advantage of a mistake in the conduct of the trial, and saved his client. Even though Andrews was a "strong Union man," his daughter believed that he detested "the brute" General Wild.[104]

Dr. French and General Wild socialized with the black population, and made a habit of dining "two or three times a week" with some of the Negroes at "Old Uncle Spencer's." Captain Cooley, a Union soldier who had been in Washington for some time, said that Wild and French had "given him more trouble than all the rebels he ever had to deal with," and was often heard to "'damn' them soundly." Although Cooley was a Yankee, he was respected by the town residents, and was even invited to a barbecue held by some of the young men of the town.[105]

Wild Becomes Involved in Treasure Hunt

The missing gold was the focus of attention in Wilkes and Lincoln counties. The Federals combed the county looking for the missing money. A small portion had been recovered, and Wild turned his attention from murder to the stolen Virginia bank funds.[106]

In mid-July, nearly two months after the bank money was stolen, Brigadier General Edward Wild was approached by Angelina, a servant of the Chennault family. She told Wild a story of gold and jewelry in possession of the Chennault family, and promised to aid Wild in his search. In hopes of locating some of the missing money, Wild and his men went to the Chennault plantation.[107]

The Chennaults were a respected Lincoln County family. The Reverend Dionysius ("Nish") Chennault and his wife had served as hosts for Mrs. Jefferson Davis and her party as she traveled from Abbeville. Chennault was widely known because he held camp meetings in order to spread the Gospel.[108] As Wild and his men rode up to the Chennault house, the family dog, "Jeff Davis," began barking.

Sketch of Chennault home, Lincoln County, Georgia. (Danny Casstevens, artist.)

Wild's soldiers shot the dog, and then pierced him with their bayonets, while they laughed and shouted, "Kill Jeff Davis! Kill Jeff Davis!"[109]

Wild sent some soldiers out to arrest various persons whom he believed guilty, or "guilty of being suspected." Several members of the Chennault family—two brothers, their wives, the son and two daughters of the older brother were arrested. Wild's suspicions were valid, because the treasure-carrying wagons had camped on the Chennault land.[110]

Torture of the Chennaults

Wild ordered the two Chennault men strung up by their thumbs, with their hands behind them. This quite painful ancient form of torture can cause permanent damage to the hands and arms if continued for a long period of time.[111] From stories he heard handed down in his family, author Robert M. Willingham, Jr., believed that Wild was personally in charge of the torture of the Reverend Dionysus Chennault, his brother John N. Chennault, and John's son, Frank Chennault. The prisoners were taken into some nearby woods and interrogated all day and into the night. Tom, the son of Angelina who had informed on the Chennaults, was also tortured, but he denied knowing anything about the gold.[112]

The Rev. Nish Chennault reportedly weighed over 300 pounds. His brother, John N. Chennault, was ill with "consumption."[113] John had been discharged from military duty with the 180th District Militia in March of 1864.[114] General Robert Toombs had fled to John Chennault's home at the end of the war.[115] The three Chennaults were strung up so they could "hear each other's groans and shrieks," which added mental anguish to the torture.[116] An account written two years later said Wild was escorted by 12 negro soldiers, commanded by Lieutenant Seaton of the 156th Regiment of New York Volunteers. John was tortured twice, and cut down only after he fainted. The Rev. Chennault was also "hung up twice by his thumbs," and was finally released after he had given many cries of pain and agony. The younger man, Frank Chennault, was hung up only once, and when it looked as if he would faint, he was cut down. According to this account, General Wild and "his subaltern" were both present and directed the whole process. Finally, all except John Chennault, who was "unable to be moved," were sent from their home in Lincoln County under guard to be jailed in Washington, Wilkes County, Georgia.[117] The arrest and torture of the Chennault family did not sit well with the local residents, or with Federal officials when they learned of the matter.

Hanging by the thumbs was called "trysting up," and was a common practice, most often used as a punishment for sailor, according to testimony given at an inquiry about treatment of prisoners at Castle Thunder in Richmond.[118] Captain Cooley had hung two men by their thumbs for robbing the orchard of Judge Andrews. The punishment had no effect and since food was so scarce, the theft of peaches and pears from the Andrews' orchard continued.[119]

While Wild interrogated and tortured the Chennault men, another group of Wild's soldiers entered the Chennault home and threatened the women and children. The youngest two children were spirited away by a family servant. Six-month-old John Chennault, Jr., was taken to the cabin of his nurse, Mandy. A maid, Mary, carried another child on her back for three miles to the home of Captain James Willis. Other children were cared for at James Barksdale's home.[120]

The Chennault ladies were confined in a room of their home, and then were stripped to their undergarments. Although they protested, one of Wild's lieutenants would not be satisfied until they had been reduced to a state of nudity. After this, the house was searched, and $15 in gold was found. A watch was taken from Miss Chennault. The ladies were detained in the woods for the day before being brought into the town of Washington. There, they were confined several more days and sustained on a diet of bread and water. Their condition evoked sympathy from even their Yankee guard, who smuggled in fruits and melons to the lady prisoners.[121] A search of the premises had failed to turn up little more than a "small cache of gold" and "watches taken from the women."[122]

Mary Ann Chennault, the 17-year-old daughter of John N. Chennault, reportedly was stripped and searched in the presence of a lieutenant, who was charged with the execution of the order. Her garments were taken from her one by one, and because of her modesty, "she threw herself upon a bed and sought to conceal her person with its covering [and] she was ordered to stand out upon the floor until stripped to perfect nakedness."[123] Another account stated that the Chennault women were "subjected to search and other indignities by Angelina,"[124] the colored maid who had turned traitor.

The Chennaults were arrested on the charge that they had "shared in the plunder of a box of jewels that the women of the South had contributed for building a confederate gunboat...." That box of jewelry had been among the Confederate treasury that had been stolen near the Chennault home.[125] Probably, the jewelry Wild's men took from the Chennault women were their own personal items.

Mrs. Dionysius Chennault and Mrs. John N. Chennault were formally charged by Wild on July 28, 1865, with a number of instances of cruelty and beating of blacks within their households. Beside the 13 charges against Mrs. Dionysius Chennault were the names of witnesses, i.e., Mrs. Dionysius Chennault was accused of having "brutally whipped Keziah," and Keziah was listed as the witness. She was alleged to have beaten Aunt Fanny (age 50) with a "piece of grape vine having a large knot on the end—about 25 blows." This incident was witnessed by Aunt Fanny, Lula Snelson, Mary, and Matilda. Mrs. John Chennault was charged with whipping several of the freed women with a "clap board."[126] All of the incidents that the Chennault women were charged with were minor, but could result in charges of assault being brought against them.

The Chennault women had been having trouble getting their former slaves to obey them. On July 6, Mrs. Dionysius Chennault had threatened her "hands" that she would "shoot their brains out" if they bothered her. She then began loading her pistol, but had to get Reuben Snelson to finish loading it. Four persons testified about that incident.[127]

One of the most damning statements was attributed to Mrs. Dionysius Chennault, reported to have said on July 17 that "if Yankees came into her yard to talk about freedom, she would fire at them if she got killed for it."[128] These offenses probably did not warrant the women being strip-searched and incarcerated for several days. Nothing was mentioned in the formal charges against the women about the stolen Confederate gold.

Miss Andrews condemned General Wild, Dr. French and all those "precious missionaries of the gospel of abolitionism [who] have come out from philanthropic Boston to enlighten us benighted Southerners on our duty to the negroes, while they take a sterling old Wilkes county planter and treat him worse than we would do a runaway negro!" She compared Wild's "diabolical" treatment of the Chennaults to that under King James I of England and his "thumbscrews."[129]

Mrs. John N. Chennault was held for a few days and given only bread and water in one of the jury rooms at the courthouse. She had been forced to leave her 9-month-old (some accounts say 6 months old) "nursing infant." Local citizens Francis G. Wingfield, Richard T. Walton, and John G. Weems tried to persuade General Wild to allow Mrs. Chennault to be moved to a private home. Each of the men was willing to give bond in any amount General Wild would set to see the lady removed to better quarters. Wild declined their offers, but did allow her friends to see that she had "suitable food at the place of her confinement."[130] Samuel Barnett and Judge Andrews were hired as attorneys for the Chennaults, and after a conference with Federal authorities in Augusta, secured the release of the family. After they were released, the money and jewelry that had been confiscated from them was returned, but the horrors of their interrogation and confinement remained forever in their minds.[131]

Wild's torture and mistreatment of the Chennault family did not result in the recovery of the stolen bank money or knowledge of who had taken it. He failed to find any evidence whatever of the complicity of the Chennaults in the robbery.[132] Wild defended his actions to Major General James B. Steedman in trying to recover the treasure stolen from wagon trains in this region, because he believed that it was Confederate States Government money, and was "*now* due to the U.S.,—and should be collected by me, as abandoned property,—because, when the C. S. Govt. collapsed, all their public property became abandoned, for want of a proper owner."[133]

Wild was skeptical when agents of banks in Richmond claimed that the money was being returned to Richmond when it was stolen. The only "evidence which they show here, consists in passes and recommendations [since procured] from military officers in Richmond." Wild finally decided to "take the whole, (including *$110,000* already collected by them) report it to Gen. Oliver O. Howard, and send it to him if called for; and let these Bank Agents recover it from those who are competent to decide their claim, viz;—the U.S. Govt at Washington." Wild ended his report by asking advice as to what steps he should take.[134]

Major General Howard was breveted for the battle at Ezra Church and the Atlanta campaign, and was one of 15 to receive the "Thanks of Congress" for Gettysburg. He was awarded the Medal of Honor for Fair Oaks. Named a commissioner on the Freedmen's Bureau on May 12, 1865, he did much to help the freedmen. However, he lacked the "executive abilities to keep the bureau from becoming corrupt." After many charges of dishonesty, he asked for and was exonerated by a court of inquiry in 1874. Although he wrote extensively, Howard "never published anything on the Civil War."[135]

July 18, 1865—Mrs. Toombs Ordered to Evacuate Premises

On July 28, 1865, Wild declared the Robert Toombs home "abandoned by its proper owner." Wild seized the premises on behalf of the United States and in the name of the Bureau of Refuges, Freedmen, and Abandoned Lands. The property could then be occupied for the "purposes of said Bureau, and be divided for the benefit of Freedmen," as authorized by Congress in the act which established the Freedmen's Bureau on March 5, 1865. Although Mrs. Toombs was in residence, the property could be seized because it was owned by Robert Toombs, a former

Confederate official and officer who was now a fugitive from the United States authorities and had been declared an outlaw. Wild gave Mrs. Toombs and the occupants of the house 24 hours to leave.[136] The stately Toombs mansion can be seem in Perkerson's *White Columns in Georgia*.[137]

On July 30, Wild went to the Toombs house and ordered the family out. Mrs. Toombs was allowed to take her clothes and a few personal items. Wild had her trunks searched for any contraband after they were packed. The General even cut open a small pincushion to see if it held any jewels. After this incident, Miss Eliza Frances Andrews began to refer to Brigadier General Edward Wild as "the Duke of Alva," a nickname which recalled the cruel treatment of the Duke of Alva to the people of Holland. The use of the nickname also prevented servants who might be eavesdropping from relaying any uncomplimentary comments about Wild.[138]

Wild occupied the Toombs house and established his headquarters there, but not for very long. General Steedman countermanded Wild's order, and the next day, on July 31, 1865, Wild found himself under arrest. The Savannah *Herald* reported that Mrs. Robert Toombs, "the wife of the great rebel remains."[139]

July 31, 1865—Wild Arrested

Wild's arrest negated his plan to open a school for negro children in the basement of the Toombs house. Dr. Mansfield French was eager to begin the school.[140] Before he left Wilkes County, however, Wild contacted W. P. Russell of the American Missionary Association and suggested that he establish a school in the buildings he had confiscated in Washington. By August 3, the missionary-teacher had freed people cleaning up a confiscated building for a school. Wild's aggressive solution to the school building shortage was not used by those who followed.[141]

The Chennaults were still being held, but the women had been removed from the courthouse to "an upper room on the square, where they were confined on a diet of army rations." Two men suspected of trying to signal the women were arrested as they stood in the street looking up at the female prisoners standing at the window. According to Miss Andrews, General Wild was "cold and hard" and he seemed to "glory in making himself hated." She rejoiced when Wild was arrested.[142] However, her father wisely counseled that he feared their happiness over Wild's arrest was in vain. Judge Andrews believed that "such a wily rascal would hardly commit himself as he has done, without good authority." Andrews thought that perhaps Wild had orders from a higher power than General Steedman, and that he would not remain under arrest very long. The Judge feared that if Wild were released and returned to Washington, his "desire for vengeance would make him worse than ever, and then, woe to the Toombses and Chennaults, whose complaints to Gen. Steedman caused his arrest." Some Washington residents could not contain their joy at Wild's arrest, and the young men fired off an old cannon.[143]

Wild's negro bodyguard left the county the next day, August 1. Some of the white Yankee officers, such as Colonel Drayton, condemned Wild's conduct. Miss Andrews also thought that Wild's negro troops had been "exceedingly insolent," and they almost caused a riot at the depot when leaving. She recalled how "They cursed the white citizens who happened to be there, threatened to shoot them, and were with difficulty restrained by the Yankee officers themselves from making good their threat."[144]

Wild and Dr. French left Washington on August 2, 1865. Miss Andrews noted in her diary that the "Reign of Terror" in her town was over. She only hoped that Wild's superiors would "cashier" him, then she might have more respect for Federal officers. To her, Wild was "the most atrocious villain extant."[145]

Schurz Sent to Georgia

German-born Major General Carl Schurz was one of several agents sent by President Andrew Johnson to report on the condition in the southern states. He crusaded for reforms in the civil service.[146] Schurz arrived early in July to survey the situation and the temperament of the people there. He quickly assessed conditions and found that most people were "submissive but not loyal."[147] Contrary to the findings of others, including General Grant, Schurz found that there was *"an utter absence of national feeling ... and a desire to preserve slavery ... as much and as long as possible."*[148] Although there had been "no organized guerrilla warfare," there were many confrontations between blacks and whites, and much bloodshed. The planters had no understanding of the idea of "free labor," and, although the Freedmen's Bureau was as yet quite imperfect, whatever labor agreements had been reached between the planters and freedmen was due to the Bureau's efforts.[149]

Schurz believed that Wild was "entirely unfitted for the discharge of the duties incumbent upon him. He displays much vigor where it is not wanted, and shows but little judgment where it is wanted." The Bureau, Schurz discovered, was so understaffed, it was necessary to temporarily send provost marshals across the state, "one to every four counties." Schurz also determined that settlement of "difficulties between whites and blacks" could not be left to the civil courts, and that the only solution was to adjudicate cases in a military court, "until the people of the State have a more accurate idea of the rights of the freedmen." He believed it would be a long time before power was back in the hands of the people of Georgia, and that military intervention would be necessary until the "sentiments of the people of Georgia have undergone a very great change."[150]

Although Schurz defended the work of the Freedmen's Bureau, he reported to President Johnson that "some of the officers" were men of "more enthusiasm than discretion, and in many cases went beyond their authority." He was undoubtedly referring to General Wild in this instance. However, he knew that greater "confusion and disorder" would have resulted if not for the presence of the Bureau. The agency had prevented Southern society from falling into chaos.[151]

Wild's Side of the Story

After Wild left Washington, Georgia, he wrote a lengthy letter to Major General Steedman to explain his actions there. Steedman and Wild had conspired, but when events did not go as planned, Steedman blamed Wild. Wild stated that he had "only intended to carry out successfully the *private plans* which we formed in Augusta at starting." That plan was to go to Wilkes County and capture General Robert Toombs, and "ferret out the Rebel gold, and it was expressly for these objects that you [General Steedman] furnished me so large an escort."[152]

Wild admitted that he failed to capture Toombs (but he did confiscate his home and evict his family). As to the Confederate gold, Wild understood that if it was found, it would be used to benefit the Bureau. Wild believed that Steedman had expected him "in both these schemes ... to carry out the details in the best way I knew how." Unexpectedly, in Wilkes and Lincoln counties, Wild encountered a number of "very hard characters ... the whole neighborhood was bad—and full of outlaws...." He found it necessary to treat them somewhat "roughly." Wild held a low opinion of the whites he encountered in Wilkes County, "not only on account of their connections—and their antecedents but because of their open defiance of the U.S. Regulations concerning slavery—and their barbarous abuse of the Freedmen—in particular Dionysius Chenault...." Wild claimed that Chennault, although counted a minister, was "only a preacher of recent generation." In addition, he kept "a public house," and was a noted "nigger breaker." Chennault at present was charged with "shooting at negros in 4 instances (8 bullets) *within the last month.*" Wild does not mention the Chennault women in this letter, but he had brought charges against both wives for mistreating their former slaves. Wild did explain to General Steedman that he "treated the men what they really were,—aides & harborers of guerrillas." He continued: "I do not mean that I proceeded to arrest and punish them *as such*, but merely that, in ferreting out treasure, I used means such as I would use with such characters—and *only for the special end in view (treasure).*"[153]

Wild declared he had received "no definite instructions on many points," and after General Steedman arrived in Augusta with instructions, he had accepted Steedman's interpretation, which was "much more recent, more definite and explicit than anything that had reached me."[154] However, since the events in Wilkes and Lincoln counties, Wild had received instructions which were much "altered & restricted" from Colonel Joseph S. Fullerton. He found that he "had no business with the treasure in either case." He admits he made an error in this respect, but it "was an innocent one." He blamed Steedman: "I may plead that I was misled by your self.—And *this error* made my method of recovering the treasure a worse error—which, under other circumstances, might have been no error at all, but the right way to treat such characters, and the *only* efficacious way." Wild tendered his apology to Major General Steedman, and asked that Steedman consider all the circumstances in the case before making a decision. Wild ended with a denial of any intent to disobey orders.[155]

Wild did deny he had mistreated the Chennaults. This mistreatment was verified by John B. Weems, who claimed that the facts in his letter to Henry Clay Dean could also be substantiated by many citizens of Wilkes and Lincoln counties and the town of Washington, Georgia, including "John M. Dyson, Gabriel Toombs, Green P. Cozart, Hon. Garnett Andrew, Dr. J. J. Robertson, Dr. James H. Lane, Dr. J. B. Ficklin, Richard T. Walton, Dr. John Haynes Walton, and David G. Cotting," the present editor of the Augusta, Georgia, *Republican*.[156]

Major General Saxton still had faith in Wild, although his actions had been somewhat overzealous. He displayed that faith by increasing Wild's jurisdiction to all mainland Georgia, except the district of Savannah.[157] Yet, Wild's methods did not help Saxton as he tried to expand the Bureau in Georgia. By early August, there was no organization beyond Augusta and Savannah to safeguard the newly freed slaves. Wild had failed to establish a Bureau in Atlanta, and this caused embarrassment for Saxton. Complaints about the affairs in Georgia were forwarded to Commissioner O. O. Howard.[158]

On August 17, 1865, only a few days before a lengthy article appeared in *The World*, a New York paper, about the robbery, Wild's immediate superior, Major General Saxton, wrote to Wild: "I fully approve of your action and wish to express my entire satisfaction with the energy and discretion you have displayed in the discharge of your varied duties."[159]

Both Saxton and Wild came to believe that if the Bureau was to be successful, suitable personnel would have to come in the form of an "occupying army." This would require a good relationship between the Bureau and the commander of the military, Major General James B. Steedman. At first, Steedman seemed to be sympathetic to the freed people, and willing to assist the Bureau. In mid-July, Wild had been confident that Steedman was willing to help the Bureau, but by August when Steedman returned from leave, he proved unreceptive to Wild's requests for officers "to serve on detached service with the Bureau or to act as Bureau officials" at the same time they performed their "military duties." This was because Steedman held the Georgia Freedmen's Bureau in low esteem.[160]

The staff problem continued to plague Wild throughout his term with the Freedmen's Bureau. Since no funds were allocated for civilians, the military establishment gained control. In late August, Wild set out the difficulties he had had finding agents. The only "competent military officers" he could find were just about to be mustered out of service, and he hesitated to ask them to remain. Wild had only praise for the efforts of Dr. French "in gradually opening the heart of the people to see some good in the Freedmen's Bureau." French had urged the people it would be better to help the Bureau, "rather than obstructing it." Wild reported he had appeared with French as often as possible.[161]

Dr. French assisted Wild with some of the duties of the bureau, because Wild had no staff. Wild's efforts to obtain staff had been thwarted by General Gillmore, who had "refused my application for staff." However, he had spent much time in trying to find agents and put them to work. Yet, he saw his chances of accomplishing anything for the Bureau as being "sent into Georgia to make bricks without straw."[162]

Wild would like to have employed civilians. He knew a number of people back in Massachusetts who would gladly serve. He even had a long conversation with Major General Carl Schurz, but Schurz insisted that Wild must employ military men, and not civilians. Schurz was sympathetic to the problem of securing agents, and had advised officials in Washington.[163]

Wild could not get competent army officers to stay in Georgia and help the Bureau. Many were "less than enthusiastic about being detailed to the agency," finding the assignment to be detrimental to their military careers, too taxing a job, or simply a disagreeable duty. It did not help matters that Steedman considered Wild a man "lacking in judgment and unfit for duty." Problems arose among Steedman and Wild and Bryant. Steedman thought both men had overstepped their authority. Steedman believed the Bureau's jurisdiction should be confined to matters concerning jobs for the freedmen. In other matters, Steedman believed that the Bureau should handle matters only if military tribunals or civilian courts were not available or if the local courts "failed to give the freed people justice." Steedman expressed his views to Wild that the Bureau should not become involved in matters of "abandoned or confiscated property other than as the executor of military or judicial decisions." Wild ignored Steedman's advice, and challenged the legality of returning property within the Sherman Reservation to white owners. Tension increased between the Bureau and the military when Steedman closed Bryant's court of claims because he thought the agent had overstepped the "prescribed limits of Bureau authority by adjudicating criminal matters." Bryant warned Saxton that the "military authorities will swallow up the Bureau if possible."[164]

Steedman believed Wild had exceeded the Bureau's authority. Wild had appointed army officers to supervise the Bureau in Columbus and Albany, Georgia, without military approval. Steedman believed that Wild was trying to "do the department commander's job," and complained that "Wild was playing hell in Georgia." Even Lieutenant Colonel Joseph S. Fullerton, Commissioner Howard's adjutant general, became skeptical of Wild's abilities to stay within the limits of the Bureau's authority and to carry out his duties. Fullerton warned Commissioner Howard, "there is no telling what he may do," because he believed that Wild was "a little crazy." Only a few weeks later, Commissioner Howard realized that Wild had done "more harm than good," and ordered his removal from the Bureau.[165]

Repercussions from Confiscation of the Toombs House

As to the confiscation of the Robert Toombs house, Wild reported that Colonel Fullerton, who was passing through the state, had "directed me verbally but officially to drop the case, as Gen. Howard had decided that an estate was not abandoned if the owner left any of his family in it." Wild had to abide by this decision, but he argued that "Circular No. 13 seems to contradict it again—so that I am still in doubt."[166] Circular No. 13 had been issued by Commissioner O. O. Howard, without waiting for Presidential approval. This circular authorized that instead of merely taking abandoned lands under the agency's jurisdiction so that the agency could use the income from the lands for temporary relief, the confiscated lands could be given to the freedmen in 40-acre plots. Howard cited the Act of March 3, 1865, for authority.[167] Issued on July 28, 1865, Howard's Circular No. 13 decreed that assistant agents of the Freedmen's Bureau, including Wild, should:

> select and set apart such confiscated and abandoned lands and property as may be deemed necessary for the immediate use of Refugees and Freedmen, the specific division of which into lots, and rental or sale thereof according to the law establishing the Bureau, will be completed as soon as practicable and reported to the Commissioner.[168]

Until September, when this order was rescinded, a policy was enforced of a "region-wide redistribution" of abandoned and confiscated lands in the South. This policy was "understood (if not put into practice) by army officers in the South." The impracticality of the policy was soon apparent. There was no way that every slave family could receive land.[169] After drafting Circular No. 13, Howard left on vacation. Perhaps this was his way of avoiding responsibility for the policy and forcing President Johnson to either approve or disavow it.[170] Circular No. 13 was marked "not promulgated" in the records, and was officially rescinded. It was supplanted by Howard's Circular 15, which defined confiscated land as only those "few lands sold during the war under court decree" and ordered the Bureau to restore all other lands whose prior owners had been pardoned. On September 27, Colonel J. S. Fullerton assured President Johnson that all of the assistant commissioners in the field had been wired that the new Circular 15 was to be "strictly observed."[171]

Wild knew there would be repercussions from his confiscation of the Toombs home and his treatment of the Chennaults. He began playing a cat and mouse game with his superiors. On August 10, Major John Emory Bryant, of the Freedman's Bureau stationed in Augusta, Georgia, wrote to the Commander of Military Forces in Macon, Georgia, to inquire about Wild's whereabouts. Bryant wanted to get a message to Wild that General Saxton, Wild's superior officer, had returned to Beaufort, South Carolina. A return reply from Macon informed Bryant that Wild was indeed in Macon.[172]

Wild's confiscation of individual and government property in Wilkes County frightened white property owners. They thought that the Bureau would turn them out of their homes and give them to the freed people. Although Saxton had used the threat to confiscate property to force planters to make work contracts with the freed laborers, this "unenforceable" threat was only that. During these early months of Reconstruction, the agency's main purpose was to educate the whites to the wisdom of the new economy, and to persuade them of the logic of free labor.[173]

On August 18, Brevet Major General R. Saxton telegraphed Bryant to ask if General Wild was in Augusta, and to order that all communications be forwarded.

Bryant replied on August 21 that Wild was not in Augusta, and promised that he would "communicate with him as soon as possible." Bryant had already telegraphed him at Macon, but had received no reply. Bryant then proceeded on August 25, 1865, to inquire of Brigadier General F. Crofton, commander of U.S. Forces at Macon, Georgia, about Wild's location. Crofton replied that Wild was in Macon, Georgia, on August 25. Bryant then telegraphed Wild in care of Brigadier General Crofton, to find out when Wild would be in Augusta. He told Wild that he had "very important orders" for him and a large number of letters. Bryant asked if he should keep the documents in Augusta. He noted that Major General Saxton wanted to know where Wild was. Finally, on August 26, 1865, from Macon, Wild telegraphed Bryant that he was in Macon and would be in Augusta the next Wednesday, and for Bryant to keep his letters.[174]

Wild makes no mention of the Chennault affair or other activities connected with his stay in Georgia in his "Report of the Military Services of Edward A. Wild, Brig. Gen. U.S. Vols."[175]

Wild seemed to be adjusting. He had been assigned the territory around Augusta. He had found another agent, 2nd Lieut. John G. Barney, of the 187th Ohio Volunteers, and was working to finalize paperwork for additional agents. He wrote:

> All the reports for this part of the country would amount to nothing as yet—but now that Augusta is added to me [per General Order No. 7], I must see Capt. Bryant and take in his statistics. Although considerable time has been spent in traveling, it has not been lost; for beside the incalculable good disservice created by the addresses—and the visiting & working at each Post—and the establishing of 3 good agents—beside these I have learned a great deal about the practical working of the Bureau, or what it should be—much more than I even could have learned by establishing a Headqrts & sitting down there at first—I have learned that the state of the county & crops,—learned the needs of the peoples—learned about the making of contracts for labor and what they ought to be—learned the actual new relation between Blacks & whites and the practical bearings thereof—I have learned the real temper of the people on both sides.[176]

By the first of September, offices of Freedmen's Bureau had been established in Albany, Macon, and Augusta. Wild listed himself, and a staff of two—J. W. Lawton, Surgeon, and J. V. (?) De Hanne, Assistant Surgeon—that were stationed at headquarters.[177]

Wild's actions in Wilkes County were not forgotten. On September 1, Saxton telegraphed John Emory Bryant to notify General Wild that he must "see him on business of importance."[178]

Assassination Attempt on Wild

Agents of the Freedmen's Bureau risked their lives because of their advocacy of rights for the former slaves. Their policies provoked violence, and angered Georgia's white planters.[179] Early in September there was an attempt to assassinate Wild. Which of Wild's actions precipitated this attack is not known. It may well have stemmed from his treatment of the Chennaults, or simply because he was with the Bureau. The attempt on Wild's life failed but Captain Healy was killed.[180] Healy, one of John Emory Bryant's assistants in Augusta, was returning to his quarters from his office when he was attacked by three Confederate veterans, "who fired equally deadly balls into his body" and finished the work with knives.[181] The attack occurred on August 2. Bryant had also received an anonymous threat. General Saxton stated that "most of the returned rebel soldiers endeavor to embarrass in every way the operations of the bureau for freedmen."[182] Conditions in Georgia were in a "terrible state of affairs." After the death of Healy, the attempt on Wild, and the threats to Bryant, Lieutenant Firmer, another officer of the 33rd Colored Troops, was reported killed at Beaufort. Saxton noted that the "first families of Augusta cherish an antipathy to the 33rd U.S. Colored troops in particular, if not to colored troops in general."[183]

By September 16, Wild had learned that he was to be relieved of duty. He wrote his longtime friend Edward Atkinson of his plans to resign from the Freedmen's Bureau. The Bureau, he said, was "sadly mismanaged," and was falling "entirely into the hands of the military, to be run as a Provost Marshal's machine—very pretty as a machine—but death to the negro." Wild said the Department of Georgia was entirely under General Steedman, and that his hands were "completely tied by the military." Wild believed that Steedman had had him removed. Also, Steedman had stopped all of Wild's agents by "disapproving their detail, after they had made excellent beginnings." The only agent that remained was John Emory Bryant at Augusta, a civilian, who was being paid by General Saxton. Wild stated that he had no money with which to pay civilians. He seemed disappointed, to say the least, that all his hard work had been "nullified; leaving nothing to show for my ministry."[184]

Wild was sorry he could not continue to serve with the Freedmen's Bureau, under the present policy of the government "for it was ruinous," but he was certain that the "North would find out, after it is too late to stop the slaughter." He correctly foresaw "awful times ahead." Since there was no fighting at present, "either within or without," Wild could see nothing in the Army "worth staying for." His only recourse was to resign. He had come to the end of the line and had decided that he had "been kicked round long enough." He was still willing to "bear the kicking" as long as his country needed him. If there were to be another war with England, he would gladly stay in the Army and fight against the English "with a relish." He did not believe that there would be war with Mexico, which proved correct, as the French withdrew their support of Maximillian, and eventually he was deposed and executed.[185]

Wild concluded that he had done "all that patriotism" required of him, so he would not be kicked around any longer. Apparently Atkinson had suggested that there might be another avenue of employment open to the handicapped general, and Wild wanted to know if Atkinson had any definite ideas. Wild did not want to resume his medical practice because of his "crippled condition." Also, he was four years behind in medical practice and would have much to learn in order to resume. He did not think a return to his practice was economically feasible, since he would have to hire assistants to help him in his practice and in traveling to visit patients. He gave his permission for Ned Atkinson to relay the news that Wild was thinking of resigning, but advised him to keep the rest of the letter to himself, "unless you can swing around the whole administration to change its entire policy with the South. For there lies the root of the difficulty."[186]

By mid–September, Wild was still in Augusta, Georgia. He continued to try to get men for positions with the Bureau, and his choices were military men under Steedman's command. He was thwarted at every turn, and complained to General Saxton that Major General Steedman, while "willing to detail officers," could not spare "more than *eight* commissioned officers in the whole State of Georgia for this purpose." Steedman was of the opinion that men could not report to two department heads at the same time, "that they cannot perform these double duties." Wild was offered some non-commissioned officers and some privates, but Wild was not satisfied. He reminded Saxton that "all the capable men are already detailed for various military duties."[187]

Grant Orders Wild Removed from the Bureau

Wild managed to generate hatred and animosity among the residents of Wilkes and Lincoln counties, and they complained to Federal officials. Reports of Wild's activities were brought to the attention of Lieutenant General Ulysses S. Grant, who sent a telegram to Edwin Stanton, Secretary of War, demanding Wild's removal from his post on the Bureau.

To Stanton, Grant wrote: "Men should be appointed who can act from facts, and not always guided by prejudice in favor of color." He also thought it advisable that General Comstock make an inspection tour of Georgia, Alabama, and Mississippi, and to report "on the situation and management of the freedmen in those States." From Comstock's report, Grant believed that General O. O. Howard could "correct abuses, if there are any."[188] The Secretary of War then referred Grant's orders to Major General Howard, "with directions to relieve Gen. Wild, as recommended by the Lieutenant General." Howard then notified Major General Rufus Saxton to "relieve Gen. Wild as soon as you can," and order him to report to the "Commander of the Army for orders."[189]

Saxton did not agree that Wild should be removed and wrote to assure Wild that he had had nothing to do with this action. Saxton regretted Wild's removal, and was "at a loss to understand this order."[190] Saxton soon learned that there was a "new conciliatory policy," and Wild had been removed from the Freedman's Bureau because "he persisted in pursuing hostile measures, when conciliatory ones were necessary."[191]

Wild was asked to remain in Augusta for several days until General Saxton could arrive to talk with him.[192] Wild complied, and reported to Saxton before going home to Brookline, Massachusetts. There, he awaited further orders.[193] On September 15, Wild received Saxton's Special Order No. 16, which relieved him of his duties in the Freedmen's Bureau in Georgia.[194]

Colonel Drayton, of Major General Steedman's staff, was sent to Washington, Georgia, to examine witnesses and determine the facts. He forwarded his findings to Steedman. Subsequently, Wild was arrested, and "charges were preferred against him, but the public is not advised that even as much as a reprimand was ever administered to him."[195] However, his subsequent departure brought "rejoicing of both rebels and Yankees," according to a newspaper account, which also declared: "The arrest of General Wild gave unbounded satisfaction to the southerners, as showing that there is protection for them yet under the shadow of the old flag."[196]

The northern papers picked up the story. Mr. Truman, "the reliable southern correspondent" of the New York *Times*, quoted General Steedman as to why Wild had been removed from the Freedman's Bureau:

> He (Wild) was, no doubt, an honest and conscientious man. But there was no practicability in him. He proposed to redress the multiplicity of slumbering wrongs which had been spent for a century upon the unfortunate blacks—he was inclined to instantaneously square up for the innumerable and incalculable cruelties inflicted upon this oppressed people for an age—in fact he fallaciously and mischievously went to work to educate and elevate the black man with an utter disregard of the feelings and rights of the white race, who at least, had claims, if only as equals. He mounted a body of black men, who rode at large over the country and committed excesses of the most infamous character. The people generally suffered at the expense of every man who had a black face. A perfect reign of terror was rife; everything became unsettled; and an implacable hatred between the two races was the natural offspring. He not only did not co-operate with the commanding general, but he zealously worked to clog his efforts in all particulars.[197]

General Steedman made particular note of Wild's treatment of the Chennault family but, naturally, mentioned nothing about the plan he and Wild had developed to find the missing Confederate gold. Undoubtedly, Steedman thought Wild had exceeded the limits of humane and civilized treatment of civilians. His comments in the article continued:

> Two outrageous acts of Gen. Wild are brought to my notice. For some alleged reason or other, he caused an old gentleman weighing over two hundred pounds to be tied up by the thumbs until the entire flesh was torn from the bones [Dionysius Chennault]. Only a few days before Gen. Wild was released he arrested two of the first ladies of the county, and had them stripped naked and examined by two colored women, an indignity I have never heard of before during the war.[198]

A newspaper article dated September 17, 1865, that focused on the opposition to the Freedmen's Bureau noted that General Wild, one of General Saxton's best officers, had just been relieved by orders from General Grant. Wild was rather "flat-footed" on the subject of the freedmen, and General Saxton had been "well-pleased with this course since he [Wild] was assigned to duty under him." Saxton liked Wild because of his "energy, for his earnestness in the cause, and for his fearlessness in his dealings with the former masters." The news correspondent believed that Wild would have been "less offensive if the prejudice was in favor of the whites."[199]

From the War Department, Special Order No. 501, issued September 19, 1865, directed Major General O. O. Howard to make a "tour of inspection through the Southern States" to gather information to correct the "abuses in the agencies connected with" the Freedmen's Bureau.[200] That same day, Wild wrote his friend, Colonel Frank E. Howe, in New York that he would be there soon. He asked Howe to hold his mail until he could come and pick it up.[201]

Eventually the struggle for power among the Freedman's Bureau and the abolitionists and the military might came to a head. Military might won out. Wild had struggled to function in the midst of a power struggle since he first arrived in Georgia. His actions in Lincoln and Wilkes counties and his treatment of the Chennault family worked against him in the game of control.

Circular 13 vs. Circular 15

Initially, under Circular Order 13 of July 28, 1865, procedures had been set up for the distribution of confiscated land to former slaves. However, that was replaced by Circular Order 15, directed by President Andrew Johnson, which ordered agents to "return confiscated land to pardoned rebels." Those men to whom Andrew Johnson objected were removed from office. In addition to Wild, another man, C. B. Wilder, was court martialled on suspicious "charges and acquitted," but the trial led to his dismissal.[202] While this change in policy was advantageous to white Southerners and former Confederates, Wild's removal and the removal of other white officials who worked with the freedmen to protect their rights seriously weakened the Bureau.[203]

This policy also revealed the inherent prejudice directed against those who worked for racial equality. Wild's reputation suffered greatly, and he was described as "negligent, corrupt, unconcerned with the condition facing the freedmen, and brutal to the point that he personally generated great bitterness among white Georgians which took a long time to allay." Richard Reid, in his article "General Edward A. Wild and Civil War Discrimination," believed that these charges could be traced back to Assistant Adjutant General J. S. Fullerton and were highly suspect, especially when compared to Saxton's praise of Wild's work.[204]

The end result was that in a span of only two years, from the summer of 1863 to the fall of 1865, Edward A. Wild went from being a wounded war hero and respected and admired military leader to become the arch villain who was subjected to arrest, court martial, and removal from office with the Freedmen's Bureau. He was demoted and relieved of his command. While Wild undoubtedly caused some of the problems, some historians, such as Richard Reid, believe that most of his problems "were the result of persons hostile to his cooperation with blacks and his willingness to place their interests ahead of the interests of the white Southerners."[205] In his wake, Edward Wild left a trail of hatred and bitterness.

By mid-October Wild was in New York City. He sought advice from his old friend, Governor John Andrew, to whom he wrote that he was going to resign, unless Governor Andrew advised him otherwise. Wild stated his appreciation to Andrew for the Governor's intervention and personal efforts on Wild's behalf. Wild felt obligated to the Governor to let him know what he had planned. Wild asked the Governor: "If you see any point to be gained, either for yourself, or for the Negro, or for the Country, by my remaining in the Service,—I will wait." Wild was of the opinion, however, that he should "resign now." He saw himself as a piece in the "game of reconstruction" that was being played by President Andrew Johnson, his "Regular Army officers and his Provisional governors."[206]

Wild was bitter about his situation with the Bureau. Because he was not given any funds, he had to rely on an uncooperative military. "They were profuse in professions and promises, but never in performance. I could get nothing done, that was not afterwards undone. And they managed to block and defeat every move of mine. I could not get a single agent detailed."[207]

In answer to an inquiry from John W. Sullivan, Wild's father-in-law, General Howard's secretary replied that Wild's removal was not "because he had, or appeared to have, any bad intentions; it was simply because he persisted in pursing hostile measures, when conciliatory ones were necessary; or at least adequate." Howard explained that the government's policy had changed, and that they wanted to "procure peace on all sides, and the right of person and property to the freedmen, with as little delay as possible." Howard explained that the life of the Freedmen's Bureau would be of "short duration" and that its "work will probably soon be over;" and now conciliatory measures were needed to make friends of the former slave owners. The measures instigated by Wild did not fit this pattern, and measures of a "more friendly nature" were needed.[208]

Wild took Grant's telegram almost as a "compliment," because he believed that Grant was being used "in ways which he does not perceive." Wild had come to the conclusion that Andrew Johnson had no use for the Freedman's Bureau. The Bureau had made progress, but in the "new districts it cannot make headway against both the Military and the Rebels." Without funds, the Bureau had had to rely "solely on military details, or else leave everything to the Rebels. In his particular case, he was "absolutely at the mercy of the Military; where I found *no mercy*."[209]

Wild wondered what would become of the Negroes, and he foresaw the great mass of the Negro population "worse off than ever before." He dreaded to think what would become of them during the winter months, and knew that "Many thousands must perish by violence, starvation and exposure."[210]

Wild felt helpless. Even if he were in Georgia instead of New York, he could think of nothing he could do, either as a civilian or as a military man, to stop the "deliberate design of the Reg. Army officers" to "annihilate the Bureau." So, he simply gave up the fight. There was nothing left for him to do but resign. Yet, he still held out hope that if Governor Andrew could see "any daylight ahead, worth waiting for," he would be willing to remain. He urged the Governor to let him know within eight days. If he received no reply by that time, he would send in his resignation.[211]

Brigadier General Edward A. Wild was "honorably mustered out of the U.S. Service" on January 15, 1866, along with 120 general officers, as stated in War Department General Order No. 168, dated December 18, 1865.[212]

Brevet Major General Rufus Saxton's action to remove Wild from the Bureau of Refugees, Freedmen and Abandoned Lands was supported and confirmed by Special Order No. 652, issued by E. D. Townsend, Assistant Adjutant General, of the War Department, on December 22, 1865.[213]

After Wild's dismissal from the Freedmen's Bureau, repercussions continued. John W. Weems of Macon, Georgia, wrote to Henry Clay Dean of Mount Pleasant, Iowa, and described the incident involving the Chennaults. This letter was published in 1868 in *Crimes of the Civil War*, a book written by Dean, a self-proclaimed "lover of the Government and the Union of the States," because he believed that the Congress of the United States had failed in its duty to investigate war crimes. A congressional resolution had been adopted on July 10, 1867, which authorized a congressional committee to investigate the treatment of prisoners of war and Union citizens held by the Confederates, and the victims of "arbitrary power and military usurpation by the authority of the Federal Administration." In short, the book hoped to show that the Civil War of 1861–1865 conducted by the Federal Government was not based on "modern civilization and the precepts of Christianity." This same letter was reprinted in the first volume of the Southern Historical Society Papers.[214] Neither of these publications improved Wild's reputation, but served to permanently blacken it.

Mr. John N. Chennault apparently suffered no permanent damage from the treatment he received from Wild and his men. He died at his home near Danburg at age 63 on July 30, 1889.[215]

The Richmond banks did not emerge unscathed. After having spent huge sums of money to recover the stolen specie, the bankers decided to concentrate their efforts in a lawsuit. After nearly 30 years, the case of William G. Taylor and William Isaacs and Company was finally settled on June 22, 1893, in the United States Court of Claims. A settlement was reached and the Virginia banks were awarded the sum of $16,987.88, which supposedly ended the case of the stolen bank gold.[216]

Perhaps Wild found solace when the 13th Amendment was ratified on December 6, 1865. Section 1 decreed that "Neither slavery nor involuntary servitude, except as a punishment for crime whereof the party shall have been duly convicted, shall exist with the United States, or any place subject to their jurisdiction." Section 2 gave Congress the authority to enforce the amendment by "appropriate legislation."[217]

Although Wild's career with the Freedman's Bureau was ended, "Reconstruction" had just begun in the South. Wilkes County, Georgia, suffered under Reconstruction, and Federal soldiers remained in Washington, Georgia, "off and on" for nearly seven years after the war.[218]

Southern whites still view the Reconstruction years from as a dark and dreary time, best forgotten, neither remembered nor reported. A New South grew out of the ashes of war and Reconstruction. For black Southerners, once the protection of the Freedmen's Bureau was no longer available to them, Southern states began adopting "Black Codes" that allowed the former slaves some rights, but denied or restricted their civil rights in other areas.[219]

Wild was not defeated. He was resilient, if nothing else. He put the Freedmen's Bureau behind him and looked forward to a new life of action and adventure in the gold fields of California and the silver mines of Arizona and Canada.

XIV

Post-War Years: The Search for Silver

He was very heroic, he would not give up, he had a very strong will and proved it all his life.
—Mrs. Frances E. Wild, June 17, 1897,
Pension Claim

The final service rendered by Brigadier General Edward A. Wild as a soldier in the service of the United States and the State of Massachusetts was to take part in a parade and flag surrendering ceremony. The ceremony took place in Boston on Friday, December 22, 1865, the 254th anniversary of the landing of the pilgrims at Plymouth.[1]

The procession began with military punctuality at 11 o'clock. First came the escort of Independent Cadets with two howitzers. They were accompanied by the Brigade Band. Next came the commanding general and his staff, headed by Chief of Staff Brigadier General Edward W. Hinks and his aides, the Surgeon, and then the aides to chief of staff. They were followed by a brigade of cavalry, headed by Brigadier General E. A. Wild.[2] Wild's brigade was composed of the 3rd Cavalry, Colonel D. P. Muzzey, 20 officers, and 100 men; the 5th Cavalry, Major C. F. Adams, Jr., and 50 men; and the Frontier Cavalry, with 40 men.[3]

It was a cold but pleasant day. A light dusting of snow covered the ground. The streets were filled with spectators. Once the procession returned to the State House, General Couch addressed the Governor, who accepted custody of the returned flags on behalf of the people of Massachusetts. He promised that the flags would be "preserved and cherished ... as mementos of brave men and noble actions."[4] After the parade, the colors were delivered to Governor John Andrew by Major General Couch and Colonel Francis N. Clark.[5]

Wild's Post-War Health Problems

Because of his injuries, Wild's daily activities were severely hampered, especially by the loss of his arm. Amputees often suffer "phantom" pain after the loss of a limb, and Wild suffered constant and "intolerable pain" in his wounded shoulder. Some believed that his "roving life" was an attempt to forget the pain he suffered.[6] In 1868, Wild met Dr. J. Heber Smith of Boston. He visited the doctor's house with a former staff officer, James Spencer Drayton. Wild continued to consult Dr. Smith in "person and through Major Drayton," for "neuralgia in the terminal nerves of the stump of his amputated arm." The cause of the pain, according to Dr. Smith, was pressure from scar tissue "upon bulbous nerves." Wild told the doctor that he had been loosing sleep, and that his health in general was affected by "almost constant suffering," which had begun shortly after the initial amputation in 1862.[7]

Shortly after his discharge from the military, Wild applied for an Invalid Pension and was awarded $30 per month, beginning January 15, 1866, through the Assistant Clerk, Police Court, City of Boston. Wild gave a Brookline address.[8] A pension was granted because of his "total permanent" disability from the loss of his left arm. His pension certificate was number 65,294.[9]

Yet, despite his pain, Wild remained cheerful. If he was in Boston at Commencement time, he attended Class Meetings. He made light of his "mutilated condition," and was later close-mouthed about the business of his mines or the lawsuit he instigated, and referred to the latter only as "fighting the enemy."[10]

Wild began to suffer from chronic diarrhea while in Austin, Nevada, during the summer and fall of 1866. His wife knew that he suffered, and encouraged him to "diet himself." Since he was a homeopathic physician, Wild treated himself. He did not explain to his wife "how he controlled the disease," and she "never asked him." He prescribed medicines for himself, but occasionally he was treated by Dr. Thayer in Boston. Mrs. Wild stated in her pension application that her husband had "attacks of diarrhea in winter and summer," and the he was subject to attacks at anytime after he returned from the military service.[11]

Wild was laid low by an attack of malaria about 1875. Mrs. Anthony Jones recalled that he had been at Green Lake, New Jersey, and she believed she heard Wild say that it was malaria.[12] His brother Walter wrote that Edward got it in New Jersey. He then returned to Boston and was treated by Dr. David Thayer.[13] During many of his visits to the Anthony Jones family, the General had trouble with his bowels.[14] Often Wild was sick for a week or two at a time.[15] In the fall of 1875, Wild went to the home of Anna F. Sullivan in Central City, Colorado, where he remained for more than four months. While there, Mrs. Sullivan testified that he suffered from "chronic diarrhea more or less all the time." At times, he had to go to bed.[16]

Late in 1875, Wild applied for an "artificial limb, or commutation for the same." He elected to receive the commutation in the form of money.[17] On January 26, 1878, Wild's friend and former army comrade, William L. Candler, submitted an "Officer's Certificate of Disability," attesting to the facts of Wild's disability.[18] Then, Wild applied for an increase in his invalid pension on January 28, 1878, and attached Candler's affidavit.[19] He was given an increase in his pension to $50 per month, to begin March 6, 1878. This claim was based on additional information about the injury to his right hand at Fair Oaks on June 15, 1862. The address given on this form indicated that Edward and Mrs. Wild were living at 131 Devonshire Street, Boston.[20]

In November of 1878, Hannibal Williams and J. H. Thompson, of San Francisco, California, signed an affidavit attesting to Wild's physical condition. They swore that during the past 12 years, Edward Wild had "performed no manual labor, nor has he been able to perform any owing to the crippled condition of his only hand." His friends stated that he had been "debarred" from practicing medicine because of his disability. Although he was not completely helpless, they believed that Wild "needs some assistance from others every day, such as cutting his food, certain parts of his dress, &c."[21]

On June 9, 1879, from San Francisco, California, Wild applied to J. A. Bentley, Commissioner of Pensions, for the arrears in pension payments due him. An Act granting payment of Arrears of Pensions had been approved on January 25, 1879. Wild was granted an increase of $20 per month, to take effect on March 6, 1878. He also claimed the arrears to extend back to January 15, 1866, the date of his discharge, up to March 6, 1878.[22] By the time of his death, Wild was receiving $80 per month.[23] However, the pension was never enough to support Wild and his wife, so he sought other sources of income.

Wild Heads West to the Silver Mines

As soon as Wild was discharged from the Union Army, his friends urged him to resume his medial practice. He replied: "What can a doctor do without hands and arms." He wrote to his friend and financial advisor, Edward Atkinson, on September 16, 1865, concerning his return to the practice of medicine. "Firstly: I can not do justice to myself and my profession by reason of my crippled condition. Secondly: I am much more than four years behind the times in

In 1882, Edward A. Wild appeared far older than his 57 years. (Courtesy of Massachusetts Commandery, Military Order of the Loyal Legion, and U.S. Army Military History Institute, Carlisle Barracks, Carlisle, Pa.)

medical matters." A third consideration was economics. If he did return to medicine, he would have to hire extra help—one to manipulate his medicines, and another person to drive. He would consider a return to his medical profession, only as a last resort and "if nothing else offers I must go to work again in the old track."[24]

Since his military service had left him unfitted to return to the medical profession, he became interested in mining in Nevada Territory, "and with varying fortunes, spent many years of his life, replete with adventure and hardship, in the wildest regions of the west."[25]

Edward had been thinking about the mining industry for some time. In 1864, at Chaffin's Bluff, Edward wrote his brother Walter about a silver mine: "I have reflected quietly and patiently on the mining company, N.C.C.G. & S. and I have become convinced of its certain success, promising vast profits. All the New York Stock has been sold and there only remains a small quantity in the hands of Mr. Sullivan (of Brookline)." Wild had written Sullivan to save him some stock, which he would "pay for as I can save it from my pay."[26]

Although Wild was not addicted to alcoholic beverages, he did have "silver fever." Soon after he left Georgia and the Freedmen's Bureau, he traveled to the mining districts of the western states.[27] A few of his friends pooled a moderate amount of money which they invested in a mine in which he was superintendent. Although fortunes were sometimes made, more often the reverse was true. Wild kept at this occupation, and sometimes "disappeared from sight for some years," and only his closest friends ever heard from him. However, when the mining ventures did pay off, he immediately offered to buy the shares of stock from his friends in a failed venture, to be paid for from the money he made in the new and successful enterprise.[28] He reportedly accumulated a fortune, lost it, and made another fortune, only to lose it also.[29]

The lure of silver was strong, especially when some of the silver mines were known to have produced fabulous wealth. Although silver was worth $1/10$ the value of gold, an "exceptional vein of silver-bearing ore might fetch $7,000 a ton—considerably more than their average gold-bearing ore." One of the most famous silver strikes was the Comstock Lode, which produced over $105 million in silver in a twenty-year period.[30] The Comstock Lode was discovered by accident in 1859, while prospectors were looking for gold. An assayer valued a sack full of discarded blue-black sand at $3,000 in silver and $876 in gold per ton.[31]

Silver is harder than gold but softer than copper, and it is the best conductor of heat and electricity. Pure silver is now mined in Mexico; Peru; British Columbia; and Ontario, Canada. Ontario is the third largest producer of silver among the 50 United States and the provinces of Canada.[32]

Wild Begins a New Career in Mining

Although Wild's friend Edward A. Atkinson was opposed to investing in mining ventures, on February 8, 1866, he authorized General Edward A. Wild as "Trustee for my children" to "subscribe for twenty shares of one hundred dollars each in the Diana Silver Mine."[33] The Diana Mine was near Austin, Nevada.

June 1866 to June 1869—Austin, Nevada

Today, Austin is one of Nevada's most interesting "ghost towns," 165 miles east of Virginia City. After gold was found in Pony Canyon by one of the Pony Express riders in May of 1862, prospectors streamed into the area and a mining district was organized. The second mining camp established was named *Austin*. Austin grew quickly, and was chosen as the county seat. The town soon boasted 366 houses, and a road led up through the canyon to Austin. On a single day, as many as "19 passenger wagons, 3 pack trains, and 274 freight teams" brought people to Austin. On a single day, 69 men arrived on horseback, and 31 came walking into the town. The population of the town doubled and tripled, and continued to increase from week to week.[34]

Samuel Bowles wrote in 1869 that Austin, Nevada, was "the most representative mining town we had yet seen." The population, once 6,000 to 8,000 in 1863, decreased in 1865 to about 4,000, and by 1869 was "probably no more than three thousand." Houses were built everywhere, then streets cut to get to them. Houses were built to conform to the lay of the land, and might have four stories on one side, and only one or two on the other side. The town boasted bathhouses, barbers, and a "first-class French restaurant," as well as a daily newspaper. The Mammoth Lager Beer Saloon, in the basement of a building at the corner of Main and Virginia streets, advertised "choice liquors, wines, lager beer and cigars, served by pretty girls, who understand their business and attend to it...."[35]

The town of Austin prospered through the 1860s and into the 1870s, even with the price of Austin's silver somewhat less than that at Virginia City. However, the location of the town of Austin posed problems and it was more costly to transport the ore, and as the high-grade deposits were depleted, it soon became "uneconomical to work there." The town desperately needed access to a railroad. In 1875, the town of Austin got financial backing from the county to build a spur line to the closest depot of the railroad at Battle Mountain. The county put up $200,000, but allowed Austin only five years to finish the rail line. Efforts stalled for the want of someone to construct the line. Finally on August 30, 1879, an "eastern mining syndicate agreed to do the work." Work was begun, and as the deadline approached, the railroad was still "two miles from Austin on noon of February 9, 1880." The town had only 12 hours left or the money would be forfeited. It had snowed heavily, and the train which carried the rail to the construction site was stalled. However, a grand effort put the rail within half a mile of Austin. As the county grant had specified that the rails must reach the town of Austin by the deadline, the city council met and extended the town limits to reach the end of the tracks. At 10 minutes until midnight, the train rolled over the tracks and into the extended town of Austin.[36]

The lure of silver was described by Fred Hart, a "roving prospector and part-time" writer, and editor of the Virginia City *Enterprise*. In Austin in 1868, about the same time that Wild was there, Hart wrote of seeing a sample of silver. "It was not necessary that a person should be an expert to determine that the rock was rich. A man who had never in his life seen a silver mine, or never before handled a piece of silver ore, could tell at a glance that it was metal."[37]

The Diana Mine

Wild invested in the Diana Mine near Austin, Nevada territory. He arrived there in November of 1865. The local paper, *Reese River Reveille*, noted: "This morning General E. A. Wild arrived from San Francisco and will remain for a time. We believe that General Wild is the agent of the New York and Austin Mining Company to which the Florida and other mines belong."[38] Wild become Superintendent of the Diana Mine. In addition to the regular duties of a superintendent, he also "practiced his original profession of medicine."[39]

The Diana mine had a vein of silver that was not so rich on the surface but at a depth of 50 feet, it improved, and at 130 feet, it produced the finest ore in the Reese River valley. Near the bottom of the mine, the vein of silver was nearly three feet thick—"This is the best one of the veins in the District,"[40] one account reported. The Diana Mine was discovered on January 20, 1863, the first of the mines on "Reservoir Hill." The mine was explored by digging a vertical shaft for 110 feet to cut through the vein, "which slopes east from the croppings." Since the time the shaft was dug and the "incline completed," the mine had netted $200 per ton, on the average, above all mining expenses.[41] After only one year of operation, the Diana Mine had produced 1,200 ounces of silver out of less than two tons of ore.[42] It was one of 27 mines owned by the Reece River Consolidated Company of Austin, Lander County, Nevada.[43]

By 1865, The Diana Mine was described as "one of the best mines in the district. It had a vein that "was not rich at the surface ... but at the depth of fifty feet became rich, and continued to increase in richness so far as it has been followed," to the present depth of 130 feet vertically. Near the bottom of the point at which the vein was being worked, it was nearly "three feet thick."[44]

Edward Atkinson tried to advise Wild against risky ventures. However, on occasion Wild did urge Atkinson to purchase stock in the Diana mine, and others. But Wild warned that it would not be wise to buy anything "without examination." Wild wanted to invest in other ventures, but he did not have the money, because he "had been obliged to use all my money to run Diana." The financial return on the Diana mine improved under Wild's management.[45] Although Atkinson had initially purchased 20 shares in the Diana Mine for his children early in 1866, he subsequently rejected Wild's suggestion that he invest $2,000 and became opposed to Wild's involvement in the mine. By the end of that year, Atkinson did not "want any interest in such property under any circumstances...." Atkinson told Wild that the "very name is hated in Boston, so many people have been cheated."[46]

Because more stock was issued "than the mine could produce a profit for," there were no dividends. If the daily profit was $200 per ton per day, the return to ten investors would be $20 per day. However, if there were 100 investors, the return would only be $2.[47]

By the fall of 1866, Wild was still trying to make the Diana Mine a profitable venture, but received no encouragement from his friends. He ran the mine more frugally than anyone else in the area. By 1867, Mrs. Wild urged her husband to abandon the mine and come home. Her wishes were conveyed by Edward Atkinson, who promised that if Wild returned, he would help him fine "desirable employment."[48] Atkinson suggested to Mrs. Wild that if Edward were to come home, he was sure that he would be able to find "steady regular and profitable employment." Some possibilities were state or federal jobs. Atkinson had often begged Wild to return home, and had assured him that he would help get him a job "where he will make money."[49] Atkinson told Wild, in no uncertain terms, that he should "put your pride in your pocket and come home." He assumed Wild was not succeeding in his mining venture in Nevada, and the financial situation was bad even in Boston.[50]

Wild wanted to buy a claim from a gentleman from New York. To close the deal, Wild needed to $2,000 in gold, and he wanted Atkinson to either loan it to him, or to join the venture with him.[51] However, Atkinson would not go along with the scheme, and told Wild that he must not count on him for $2000, "or any other sum for investment in mines for me or yourself. I never authorized any such draft." Atkinson was afraid that Wild would lose all his money investing in mining ventures. If Wild needed $2000 "for personal expenses, and then you can have it, but I cannot change from my often avowed distrust of mines and mining and I cannot advance money for such purposes."[52]

Although Wild and Atkinson had their differences over investing in mining property, Atkinson continued to act as Wild's agent and financial adviser. In November he sent an itemized list of things he had done for Wild. Atkinson had paid Annie Urann $150 as Wild had asked. He had collected $228.85 of Wild's pension and "credited" it to the "Indian Mills books." Atkinson told Wild there had been no increase in the amount of pension to officers, "only to privates, in certain cases." He reported that he had not heard from Major Drayton nor had he found him. He had received Wild's "oil certificates," and he reported that work on the Colorado mines had all but ceased. He advised Wild to pay nothing on the "North Clear Creek" mine. Atkinson reminded Wild that he had written letters and sent telegrams telling him to "make no mining investment" on his account nor to draw any money for that purpose. Atkinson sent Wild a tax bill, which he had refused to pay because Wild had "ceased to be a citizen of Brookline before May 1."[53]

Mrs. Wild kept Edward Atkinson informed as to her husband's financial wishes. One proposed plan was thwarted, as Atkinson informed him, because "you may not have quite money enough to make it sure." Atkinson continually advised against Wild putting more money into questionable mining schemes. "I have never given much support in your mining enterprises because I could not take the chance." He urged Wild to "settle down to some more prosaic occupation...."[54] However, Wild kept insisting Atkinson invest in mining property. He received a terse letter from his friend, dated December 3, 1866, in which Atkinson declared:

> The very name [Diana] is so hateful in Boston, so many people have been cheated. I do not think the proposition to buy and hold for sale to be a good one— for the reason that there is an immense amount of mining property in California, Colorado, New Mexico, etc.—more accessible and I suppose ere long we shall have all northern Mexico and lower California. Also ere long the Southern branch of the Central Pacific R. R. Will be about to Santa Fe and then into the Pacific.[55]

Atkinson advised: "Beware of the history of the Frenchmen, always finding richer mines but always poorer." Atkinson still hoped that the Diana Mine would pay off, but believed that Wild would do better in the "insurance business" than in the mining business.[56]

June 1869 to September 1869—Boston, Massachusetts

The Wilds remained in Nevada until June of 1869, when they returned to Boston. This three-year period was the longest continual period that they lived together during their 36 years of marriage.[57]

In addition to learning much about the mining industry, Wild's time in Nevada gained him a reputation for honesty and integrity.[58] During his years in Nevada, Wild acquired a considerable amount of property by "pre-empting" land. He later sold the land for a large profit. However, whatever profits he gained from the sale of land, he lost through the "fraudulent failure of bankers in San Francisco." He instigated a lawsuit which dragged on for years, but Wild finally recovered his losses. However, the cost of the litigation outweighed any gain derived.[59]

Mrs. Wild termed this a "barren victory" because of the cost of the lawsuit.[60]

October 1869 to April 1870—San Francisco, California, and Austin, Nevada

In September of 1869, Wild moved to California, and lived at several places. By 1870 Wild was working at the Mohawk Lode. This mine soon played out. However, Wild continued in the mining industry at various sites, sometimes making enough profit to send small amounts to Atkinson to put in a trust fund.[61] That trust fund was for his wife. She wrote Atkinson on in 1881: "I never forget that I owe all I have to you. If you had not interposed in my behalf, all would have been safely planted in some promising mine."[62]

Mrs. Wild reported Wild was "coming and going" between Boston and the western states, and then he began commuting between Canada, New York and Boston.[63] Edward Wild continued to be interested in mining, and he traveled several times to California. He returned to Nevada, and also went to Colorado, Minnesota, and Canada. In between mining ventures, he visited his wife in New York and his brothers and sisters in New Jersey and New York.[64] Brother Walter stated that Edward traveled "all over the country engaged in mining." His family, therefore, saw little of him.[65] Walter declared that although there was "no divorce between him" and Mrs. Wild, they "did not live but very little together." Mrs. Wild would not go with him on "his mining trips or live with him when he got squatted down, but when he would come East he would live with her." Edward provided for her, and she had an income of $10,000 that he "settled" on her, and she lived off the interest. Walter described his brother's wife as "an excellent woman, but never made a good home for him."[66]

Walter Wild had bought stock in the mining property in Austin, Nevada. On April 22, 1875, at Edward's request, Walter transferred "all claim to any mining property I ever had in Austin, Nevada either for myself or for him, to the firm of Brower & Colgate of New York, Trustees."[67]

August 1879 to 1880 — Ontario, Canada

Over the last century, mines in Ontario Province of Canada have produced over 158 million ounces of gold; over 1 billion ounces of silver; nearly 9.5 million tons of nickel; over 13 million tons of copper; and over 9 million tons of zinc.[68]

By the summer of 1879, Wild was in Canada following the lure of silver. Wild liked Canada, and spent much time on Thunder Bay of Lake Superior. He became involved in the Rabbit Mountain Silver Mine.[69] Wild did not actually own the mine, but may have had shares in it. He did, however, own claims on "each side of the Rabbit Mountain property."[70]

His brother, Walter, spent one winter with Edward about 1880 or 1881. Edward seemed to enjoy the climate in Canada.[71] About 1874 in New York City, Wild made the acquaintance of Anthony Jones, an engineer. They soon become friends and were involved in various social and business activities. During the winter of 1875–1876, the former general and his wife Frances spent nearly the entire winter with Anthony Jones and his wife, at Green Lake, New Jersey. Wild also visited the Joneses in Middletown, New York, and Mont Clair, New Jersey. He would stay with Jones and his wife for "months at the time." Emily J. Jones, wife of Anthony, recalled that General Wild and his wife had stayed with the Jones family for two weeks in 1883 at their house at Mont Clair, and she and Frances Wild stayed at Monmouth Beach for two weeks.[72]

After the Joneses moved to Brooklyn, Wild often came to their house and "remained all winter. Anthony Jones often visited Wild in Canada.[73] Wild employed him to go to Canada in the fall of 1883 with three assistants to make a survey. This may have been a survey of the property lines. Wild wrote his brother about Jones' work and that Daunsis and McFhee, his New York investors, thought Wild's plans "absurd; and I have found their impractical hence a deadlock. He got mad. So I shut down."[74]

Letting his partners in the Rabbit Mountain Mine cool their heels for a while, Edward took time off and went to Providence, Rhode Island. There, he undertook to settle his mother's estate, a house and large farm near North Providence which she had inherited from her Jencks ancestors.[75]

Wild was back in Canada by the summer of 1884. While staying at the Queen Hotel in Canada on June 21, 1884, a fire at the hotel destroyed all his baggage. In his baggage was a pension check which had been issued May 81, 1881. Wild filed a claim to have the burned check replaced.[76] Except for frequent business trips to New York, Boston, and Brookline, as well as visits with friends, he remained at Thunder Bay until 1891.[77]

Near the Rabbit Mountain mine at Thunder Bay, Wild built a one-room log cabin "around a large tree" in the woods. The sleeping bunk had only a mattress, no springs. A block of wood, "recessed to receive a head," served as a headrest, similar to the headrests of the Japanese. Perhaps this manner of sleeping kept Wild immobile, so that he did not turn in his sleep and cause more pain to his shoulder.[78] He led a very Spartan existence, isolated and lonely at times, but exciting at others. His wife did not stay at the cabin because it was not a "fit place to take a lady."[79] She seldom accompanied him on his mining ventures, but remained in the East. Whenever Wild came East, he "came wherever" she was staying.[80]

Wild had an "Aladdin stove," invented and given to him by Edward Atkinson. He tried the stove out in a boarding house in before taking it to his cabin. He cooked sturgeon and some chunks of "tough beef" and both came out very tender.[81]

Wild found a good friend in Thomas A. Gorham, a barrister, the English equivalent of lawyer. Gorham had a quarrel with Wild, but soon discovered that the General was right. He apologized for his error, and the two became fast friends. Gorham came to learn that Wild had a vast knowledge of many subjects, and they spent hours together in discussion. Gorham gave an apt description of Wild:

> His power of observation was great and keen. He was such an extremely modest man that no one would realize the greatness of his character and the vastness of his knowledge, much of it gained by experience, until one had become thoroughly intimate with him, spending months and even years in his society. Take him all and all he stood above the standard man, he quite reached that man fitly termed the noblest work of God....[82]

Gorham found that words were in adequate to describe Edward Wild. Mere words could not convey the "tone of voice, the expression of the eye, a gesture...."[83]

When activities at the Rabbit Mountain mine began to slow down, Wild spent more time in Brookline. He also visited Plymouth, Marion, and Marblehead, often for weeks at a time.[84]

After Wild left Canada, his friend Gorham wrote: "There are many people in the woods of Canada, on the northern shore of Lake Superior, that will miss him, and possibly none more than myself." [85] Gorham would never see Wild again.

Death in Colombia, South America

All the illnesses and injuries Edward Wild suffered eventually took their toll on his health. It was a gray-haired, frail-looking man who embarked on the new adventure to South America, an adventure from which he would not return. Undoubtedly, his continued "hardship and exposure brought on premature age, which was graced by dignity and nobility ... but quenched not the fire and daring of his early life."[86]

In July 1891, Anthony Jones invited Wild to travel to South America with him. Jones had a contract to "lay a railroad line in Colombia, South America. Wild accepted the invitation. The former general was always eager for a new adventure.[87] Although his health was feeble at that time, and he was very emaciated, his wife did not try to dissuade Edward from going to South America, because it "would have been of no use." She said that he had the "spirit of adventuring about him." After being in Canada for some years, Wild had wanted a change of scenery.[88] Rebecca P. Hunt, wife of Dr. William Hunt of Philadelphia, who had treated Wild on many occasions, recalled that General Wild "always appeared to be a frail delicate man, but she never heard him speak of any disability other than his arm...." She described wild as looking "like a sick man always after he came out of the army."[89]

The former general was not one to complain. Hiram W. Allen had served on Wild's staff as Acting Assistant Adjutant while on Folly Island in September of 1863, and he continued on Wild's staff until April 23, 1865. He knew Wild from their days together in Company A, 1st Massachusetts Infantry. Allen believed that Wild had never recovered from the loss of his arm, but "he had a wonderful mind and will and never made any complaint; he was not that kind." However, Allen could tell by watching Wild's face to "see it twitch with pain" and he would know that he was in agony, but the General never said a "word of complaint."[90]

The last days of General Wild's life were as unique as had been his whole life. In July 1891, he and a party of civil engineers, under the leadership of Anthony Jones, traveled to Colombia, to survey the route for a new railroad. Although having been habitually bothered by diarrhea, Wild set off on the voyage in "apparently good health, and high spirits," with his longtime friend, the Englishman Anthony Jones. Jones thought that Wild "seemed to enjoy the trip very much, from the time of leaving New York until our arrival at Puetro Berrio."[91]

The group left from New York City on July 9, 1891, aboard the *Philadelphia*, a ship of the Red D Line. They arrived on the island of Curaçao and stayed there several days, then sailed for Savanilla.[92]

After landing on the Colombian coast, the party traveled up the Magdalena River in heat and high humidity. The next leg of the journey involved travel by mule for four days to Medellín, the capital city of Antioquia, a province of Colombia.[93] Anthony Jones later related to the widow that for the first three days, Wild seemed to fare "better than many of us; but on the fourth day it seemed to tire him very much." The last 29 miles were traversed in a carriage.[94] Medellín is high in the Andes Mountains, northwest of the capital of Bogotá. Enrique Naranjo, the Colombian consul, described the city of Medellín as "very clean and pretty," and remarked that it was the "second most important city in the country, with a very mild climate, and famous for the hospitality of its very laborious inhabitants."[95]

The whole group of engineers were "greatly fatigued," but the journey greatly affected the 66-year-old Wild. He collapsed before reaching the city. However, after a few days' rest, he seemed well again, and went about "sight-seeing" with the other members of his party.[96] Wild seemed to have enjoyed it very much. Then, about three weeks before his death, the General complained "of not being very well, felt an oppression in his bowels," which he attributed to the effects from a fall he had taken at Port Arthur, "coupled with the shaking of the mule ride." To obtain relief, he loosened the clothing around his waist, and began wearing suspenders. He reported that he felt a "change immediately." It was then that the diarrhea began.[97] The "fall" had occurred in Port Arthur about 1889. Wild tripped over a "wire which had been placed across the side walk on All Hallow Eve." Because he could not soften his fall because of his missing arm, he injured his ribs and was "laid up some time."[98]

Thinking that the General was improved, Anthony Jones left for a few days. The next room in the hotel was occupied by a fellow passenger, Mr. Frasquieri, who spoke both English and Spanish. When Jones returned on Wednesday, August 19, the General was "sick in bed with a severe diarrhea and quite weak." Jones advised that a doctor be called, but Wild would not allow it. He was weak and "could not take much nourishment, but basically scalded milk with a beaten egg," with a "little brandy or rum added," which he drank three times a day. This was supplemented with "beef-tea, milk toast, toast and water, rice, milk, etc." Then Wild decided that he did not need to take so much "stimulant," and changed the alcoholic beverage to champagne, a good amount of which was available to him. He seemed to improve, but then he again was very weak and the diarrhea increased.[99]

Jones became concerned and called Dr. Zuleta, a young doctor who had graduated in New York, and was well respected in Medellín. As soon as the doctor saw the General, he knew that his condition was serious, and so he called in doctors Perez and Arango, "two of the best physicians in the city." All concluded that the General might die "before morning." The doctors gave Wild a "rubbing off all over with alcohol, hypodermic injections of caffeine, etc., and a little champagne every fifteen minutes," until he went to sleep. Dr. Zuleta remained in the hotel all night, and Mr. Frasquieri and Jones watched over Wild together. A last spoonful of champagne was given him about 11 o'clock on Thursday night, and he slept peacefully until about ten minutes past one o'clock, when his breathing stopped, and he died "without a struggle."[100]

Edward Augustus Wild died early on the morning of Friday, August 28, 1891, in Medellín, Department of Antioquia, Colombia, South America. He had been attended to during his illness by member of the group, and by the resident American, English, and French families. He had refused medical help at first, insisting on treating himself homeopathically. However, when he at last allowed an "allopathic practitioner" to treat him, it was too late.[101] Jones did not believe that Wild realized the seriousness of his condition, but once he allowed Jones to call the physicians, he "submitted so quietly to them," and Jones was convinced he realized his danger.[102] Possibly, had there been a homeopathic physician in the town, Wild "would probably have consented to call in advice sooner."

The cause of Wild's death was chronic diarrhea, which had lasted for some time and apparently "wore him out."[103] His family believed he may have contracted malaria, and according to a letter dated August 2, he had had an attack of vomiting in addition to the diarrhea, so that he had "to lie down by the roadside and wait until the carriage could be sent for...."[104]

Because of Colombian customs, a funeral had to be held within 12 or 15 hours. This was held at 3 o'clock on the same day of his death. The Governor placed the Commandant at the disposal of Jones and Wild's companions. Jones thought that the General would have liked a "quiet and private" funeral, but a military escort was obtained. There were not many soldiers in the city, but they all attended. The Governor, Secretary of State, and Treasurer all called and offered their services. American Vice-Consul Senior Luciano Santa Maria helped by preparing and sending out invitations to the funeral by special messenger to all who could be reached in time to attend. The funeral procession was escorted to the cemetery and attended by the Governor and all the officers of the government, all of whom remained during the service, which was conducted by a Protestant minister, Mr. Touseau. The bells of the cathedral across the street began to toll as the funeral started, and two beautiful wreaths of flowers were sent, one by the Protestant ministers and the other by Mr. and Mrs. Pike, an English couple.[105] Wild was buried with full military and Masonic honors, and a military escort. The "funeral rites were performed amid a large concourse of friends, including the Governor and officers of the State," who gave him the honor due a man of his station.[106]

To wind up the sad affair, the American Vice Consul agreed to notify the Secretary of State in Washington about the death of Brigadier General Wild. All expenses were paid by Anthony Jones, including the cost of the plot in that part of the Catholic church cemetery which had been set aside for non–Catholics. Jones was to have the grave marked.[107]

Mrs. Wild received a telegram at Swamp Scott, where she was spending the summer, on Tuesday, September 1, informing her of the General's illness.[108] The news of his death was not relayed quite so quickly, but came by dispatch from one of those on the mining expedition with Wild in Colombia.[109] The letter, dated September 3, 1891, describing Wild's last days and his death was sent to Mrs. Wild by his companion on the trip, Anthony Jones. Jones was still in South America, and the letter probably took several weeks to reach its destination in Boston.[110] According to the Secretary of the Harvard Class of 1844, Edward Wheelwright, Mrs. Wild had only gotten the news of her husband's death the previous week, which would have been about October 6 or 7.[111]

Jones sent Mrs. Wild her husband's pocket book and contents, and later sent his gold watch. He also included a "small piece of the General's hair, also of his beard taken after death." He asked Mrs. Wild what her preferences were on the disposal of the remaining effects of the late General Wild.[112]

The General's widow held up bravely, but was distraught at times, for she "really loved him, and she was always writing to him, and looking out for anything which would interest him." She had had a premonition that she would "never see him again" when he left for South America. "How strange," she said, "it is to think of him at rest."[113]

Grave of Brigadier General Wild, Colombia, South America. (Courtesy of Harvard University Archives, Cambridge, Massachusetts.)

In October of 1891, an obituary listing briefly some of the highlights of Wild's unusual life appeared in *JAMA* (the *Journal of the American Medical Association*).[114]

Nine years after Wild's death, Charles Patrick Decker, an Englishman traveling in Colombia, chanced upon the General's grave. Decker wrote the Massachusetts Department of Grand Army of the Republic (G.A.R). that General Wild's remains lay in a "neglected grave marked by a decayed wooden cross." Decker was appalled that the brave General's last resting place was so neglected. He wrote: "Here he lies, unhonored, unsung and unwept. I placed a bouquet of roses on the cross, and as long as I live here I shall place a bouquet on each Decoration day and a small flag if I can get them." Decker thought that Wild's remains should be "reinterred" in his hometown of Brookline, Massachusetts.[115]

However, Wild's widow had other ideas, and was not in favor of the removal. As an alternative, one veteran suggested that the G.A.R. should place a bronze tablet on a "bolder in the Brookline cemetery." Mrs. Wild had no objections to that suggestion. Another suggestion was for the War Department to have the General's remains brought home in a "metallic coffin and give them reinterment with full military honors." Again, the widow objected, and pointed out that her husband had "always avoided notoriety." She indicated that this was the reason that he had never joined the G.A.R.[116] A letter that he wrote in 1861 to his wife sums up Wild's feelings about his death:

> As for me, when I am shot down let no one put on mourning for me. Rather hang out the stars and stripes and be proud. Say what you will, I am not a rash person, neither am I so brave as a hundred thousand others; I mean naturally and constitutionally brave. What courage I have comes from force of reason and of faith and of self-discipline and determination. I pray heaven that when I see the need of sacrificing myself, no weakness of mine shall deter me.[117]

Wild's Legacy

After ten years of living and working in the Thunder Bay area of Canada, Wild's assets, according to Colonel Samuel M. Ray, banker of the firm of Ray and Street, included the deed to 1,500 acres of land, "valued at $3,000; cash $5,000; a note for $1,000; and a railroad bond $6,000." The total of $15,000 was a substantial sum in 1891.[118] Of the original 2,000 acres of Canadian land owned by Edward Wild, only a small portion was left to his brothers and sisters. The land was practically worthless but annual taxes had to be paid. Eventually, the heirs lost interest in it except for Elsie Wild Munroe. She paid the taxes for years through Wild's agent, Colonel Ray. About 1920, Horace N. Stevens joined with Elsie to help share the cost of the taxes. By then, the amount of acreage had dwindled to about 400 acres. Some of the land had been lost for failure to pay the taxes on some of the acreage. Eventually, Elsie and Horace divided the land into lots. The location of the land was isolated, "entirely wild and covered with timber."[119] It was accessible only by water. The property acquired by Stevens was inherited by his children, Mary Vic Griswold, Helen S. Whitlock, and Horace N. Stevens, Jr. They sold it to a group that planned to develop the area into a public park.[120]

When all is said and done, perhaps we may come to a better understanding of the many facets of the personality of Edward Augustus Wild—doctor, soldier, revolutionary, humanitarian, liberator of slaves, champion of the rights of black soldiers, friend and protector of the families of his black soldiers, non-conformist, heartless abductor and jailer of helpless women, executioner of Confederate soldiers, and sadistic torturer of helpless prisoners, but most of all, a man who was cool under fire and unmoved by military or political pressure, and one who dared to take action based on his values, beliefs and ideals.

Edward Augustus Wild was outrageous, courageous, and cantankerous. He was also a very exceptional person, and his contributions deserve to be remembered. He sometimes disregarded authority and military rules and regulations, which resulted in his being arrested several times and tried in a military court martial. Yet, he risked his life to improve the situation of slaves and freedmen.

No one ever accused Edward Augustus Wild of being cowardly, dull or boring. He overcame physical disabilities, and prejudice from both friend and foe. He was unafraid of what others thought, and he did not seek fame and glory. Wild lived his life as a "true man of action."[121]

Wild was a man who not only held strong beliefs in individual freedom but his actions were based on those beliefs. No matter what challenge he faced, he refused to compromise, regardless of the consequences. A staunch abolitionist, he was an outspoken advocate of the rights and fair treatment of blacks. He hated anything and everyone who was connected to slavery, and at times, that hatred caused him to overreact in his treatment of slave owners and Southerners in general.

His faith in the abilities of blacks as soldiers, and his careful training of them, changed the image of black soldiers forever. Major General Benjamin F. Butler valued black troops for their "fidelity as guards." The valiant stand Wild's men made at Wilson's Wharf helped to erase the humiliation of Fort Pillow. They were praised for fortifying City Point, Fort Powhatan and Wilson's Wharf. Even when not under Wild's direct command, his regiments were praised for their conduct at Deep Bottom, New Market, and Fort Harrison. A number of Wild's men were singled out for special commendation and many received the Medal of Honor.[122]

His career was like a meteor, blazing bright with religious fanaticism fueled by military power. But that light soon dimmed, as Wild became embroiled in one incident after another that shocked and outraged both the citizens of the North and the South, as well as his own army peers, superiors and subordinates. Honorable, brave, and loyal, he was a freethinker who refused to be bullied into obeying orders he believed to be unfair or discriminatory. He knew his rights under the articles of war, and when he was unjustly arrested, he was quick to express those rights. However, as oftentimes is the case, the prejudicial views of others were not easy to overcome, even with civil and military law on his side.

While he seemed "temperamentally unsuited to a career" in the military, he had always possessed an interest in soldiering and had been a member of the Boston Cadet Corps while in school at Harvard.[123] His firsthand observations of the Bourbon dictatorship being opposed by Garibaldi's "Redshirts," and later his observations while serving as a surgeon with the Sultan's forces in the Crimean War, forged a determination to act on his belief in a true democracy, and when the war came to America, he took the opportunity to enlist and fight "slavocracy."[124]

He was not one to wallow in self-pity, but managed to overcome two devastating wounds and resume his career as an effective military officer. After his death, many of his army comrades recalled that he insisted on leading his men when they charged in battle, even after he had to have his left arm amputated in 1862. To overcome this disability, Wild wrapped his horse's reins around his neck, so that he would have his right arm free to wield his sword or pistol.[125]

After his death, he was remembered during the week of June 13–17, 1892, at the 48th anniversary of the American Institute of Homeopathy, in Washington, D.C. Wild was among those honored in the usual Memorial Service for deceased members.[126]

Also in 1892, some of Wild's Harvard classmates from the Class of 1844 placed a plaque of stone and bronze on the wall of the Walker Memorial Porch on the west end of Memorial Hall.[127] Beside the shield of the plaque are emblazoned the insignia of his military rank, the badges of several army corps to which he belonged, and a

A plaque erected by Harvard Classmates, Class of 1844, lists battles in which Wild served, and carries a Latin phrase which means "To act and suffer bravely." (Courtesy of Harvard University Archives, Cambridge, Massachusetts.)

notation of wounds he received at Williamsburg, Fair Oaks and South Mountain.[128] The Latin inscription seems to embody the life of Edward Wild, who did suffer from his wounds: *Et facere et pati fortiter.*[129] Translated, the inscription reads: *To act and to suffer bravely.* And that, he did.

Portrait Presented to Town of Brookline

In 1893, a life-sized portrait of General Wild, painted by J. Harvey Young, was presented to the town of Brookline, Massachusetts, and placed in the public library. At the ceremony, Martin P. Kennard spoke on behalf of those who had contributed funds toward the painting. Other Harvard classmates made remarks.[130] The portrait committee presented the portrait to the town in honor of Edward Augustus Wild, Brookline's most "distinguished son" as a "gift of the citizens and as a memorial to the heroes who died in the Civil War." The committee included friends, neighbors, and former fellow officers Edward Atkinson, W. I. Bowditch, John W. Candler, W. L. Candler, Latin Professor Dr. Tappan E. Francis, Charles Capen, W. Y. Gross, M. P. Kennard, A. L. Lincoln, J. P. Stearns, and Fergus B. Turner.[131] The painting was accepted on behalf of the town of Brookline by Horace James, chairman of the Board of Selectmen.[132]

An inscription placed below the portrait noted that Wild was "the most distinguished son of Brookline." A plaque summarized Wild's life, his education and his military experience during the War of the Rebellion.[133]

The portrait, along with various personal articles of Brigadier General Edward A. Wild, including his uniform and spurs and the sword he carried during the war, are preserved in the Brookline Public Library.[134] The articles Wild brought back from Turkey were displayed in 1897 at the Brookline Public Library. The exhibit focused on the Turkish decorations and medals presented to General Wild by Sultan Abdul Nejid during the Crimean War, which had been presented to the library by his widow, Mrs. Frances Ellen Sullivan Wild.[135]

In 1926, an article in *The Chronicle* recalled the 1897 event, and noted that Wild had served as an example of "unselfish service and unquenchable spirit." Among the collection are his uniform, his commission as a brigadier general signed by President Abraham Lincoln, his "Personal Narrative of an Incident in the War of the Rebellion," and a book of testimonials "of appreciation" signed by members of the 35th Regiment, Massachusetts Volunteers. The Turkish "Fez" worn by Wild when he was in Turkey and his Turkish coffee cup are in the collection.[136]

Martin Kennard remarked at the portrait unveiling ceremony that General Wild's "biggest problem in the army may have stemmed from his honest belief that blacks were the equals of whites as soldiers and citizens—an idea inimical to most officers of the day."[137]

Friend, neighbor, and fellow officer John W. Candler described Wild, as "a marked and original character, true to his convictions on all occasions, the personification of devotion to principle—a man of faith, he would have died a martyr for any cause he believed in and espoused." Candler admired Wild and knew him as "a leader of men" who gathered "about him kindred spirits in his devotion to freedom and his country."[138]

The true legacy left by Edward Wild was the way in which he lived his life, not ever cowed by anything or anyone. He was described in only glowing terms by friend Bradford Kingman:

> Fear did not enter his mind to prevent him from carrying out his purposes; indeed it has been often said of him he did not know the definition of the term. His mind was ever on the duty to be performed, and stopped not to weigh the risk attending the same. He had the greatest disregard of self, and was of a vivacious turn, enlivening all company into which he entered, which rendered his society peculiarly welcome to both sexes. Kindness beamed in his countenance, and benevolence warmed his heart. He was ever kind, courteous and affable, and in his profession the highest motive of his mind was to relieve the suffering of humanity by his skill, and every duty was performed with delicacy, as well as with tenderness. His friendship was firm and confiding. In his tastes simple, and averse to all hollow pretensions and ceremonial observances.[139]

Not only was Wild a "brave soldier," but he set an example to his men that was one of clean living and devotion to duty. Yet, he never sought glory for himself. While harsh in his interpretation of his authority as a brigadier general and quick to punish those who had supported slavery, Wild could be humorous, kind, and caring, and at the same time "full of patriotism and intense enthusiasm," a man who put all his efforts into performing the tasks assigned him. As he fearlessly replied to General Fitzhugh Lee at Wilson's Wharf: "We will try it," and he did. What more can anyone do?

Epilogue

Edward Wild led an exciting life. He traveled many places, and was engaged in several occupations as doctor, soldier, Freedman's Bureau agent, and mining superintendent. However, he was not overly ambitions, and making and keeping money was not one of his strong points. He was more idealistic than materialistic.

Through the provisions of his will, dated March 4, 1888, Wild did set up a trust fund for the "use and benefit of his wife, Frances Ellen." He stipulated that if the "annual income should exceed $1500.00 in any one year," then any "excess" should either be "reserved" or caused to "accumulate," or be distributed to any of his brothers or sisters who his trustee-executor deemed needful. Since Wild and his wife had no children, after his death, he wanted all his property distributed equally among his siblings, or their offspring.[1]

He named a number of executors: his brother, Captain Walter A. Wild, Springfield, Massachusetts; Hannibal Williams, of San Francisco, California; Samuel W. Ray, of Port Arthur, Ontario, Canada; Anthony Jones, of Brooklyn, New York; and Edward Atkinson, John Gibbs, and William T. Bowditch, all of Brookline, Massachusetts.[2]

Mrs. Wild contested this will, and it was in Probate Court of Norfolk County, Massachusetts, as late as 1895. She was opposed by the other heirs, represented by Arthur Cushing. The question of where the former general resided after the war was an "issue in the case," and if it could be "proved by the heirs that his domicile or residence was at any time, during that period, outside of Massachusetts," Cushing believed his clients could win their suit.[3]

The relatives of Edward Wild had little to do with his wife. A nephew, Horace N. Stevens, wrote in 1947, that Mrs. Wild, "while socially his equal," was "far from being his mental equal and was probably partly the cause of his becoming such a wanderer."[4]

The Federal Government passed its first pension act for the benefit of Union soldiers on March 3, 1865. That act was amended on January 29, 1887. On June 27,

1890, further pension laws were enacted that applied to invalid veterans and their widows. A widow could claim a pension if her husband had served in the United States Armed Services for at least 90 days during the war of 1861–1865. She had to furnish proof of death, but that death did not have to have been caused by his military service. Another stipulation was that the widow had to be "without other means of support than her daily labor." The widows must not have remarried.[5] Further acts and amendments were passed up to the last one on June 9, 1930, which increased the amount of pension received for pensioners at various ages.[6]

Beginning in April of 1892, Mrs. Wild began the process of applying for an "accrued pension for widows."[7] On June 9, 1893, Frances Wild, age 64, filed a "Declaration for Widow's Pension." She listed her residence as 10 Fremont Street, Boston, Massachusetts.[8]

Mrs. Wild continued her efforts for number of years to get a pension for her husband's military service. She obtained affidavits and depositions from a number of his friends and former military associates, relatives, and doctors who had treated the general. Her pension application on the grounds that Wild's death was due to chronic diarrhea acquired during his military service was rejected April 2, 1898.[9]

It took an act of Congress to settle the matter. On March 3, 1903, through Private Bill No. 931, both the Senate and House of Representatives of the Congress of the United States authorized that she be placed on the pension rolls, and was to receive a pension of $30 per month. This pension was granted for Wild's service in the United States Armed Forces as a Major in the 32nd Massachusetts Infantry, a Captain in Company A of the 1st Massachusetts Infantry, and Colonel of the 35th Massachusetts Infantry, as well as his service as a Brigadier General who was "honorably mustered out of service" on January 15, 1866.[10]

However, by an act of May 1, 1920, a widow could draw $30 per month regardless of her financial condition.[11] Mrs. Wild continued to draw the $30-per-month pension until her death on October 3, 1923. At the time of her death, the 95-year-old widow was living at 67 Toxteth Street, Brookline, Massachusetts.[12] Funeral services were held at her home on October 5, at 2 P.M.[13] The cause of death was cited as "hypertrophy of heart." A contributing factor was "old age." She was buried in the Walnut Street Cemetery, in Brookline, Massachusetts.[14]

Frances E. Wild wrote her will on March 13, 1917, six years before her death. She appointed Frederick C. Bowditch of Brookline the executor. She willed Amelia B. Shaal $1,000, and $100 to Miss Harriet B. Pasco of Wellesley, Massachusetts, both to be free of all "legacy and succession taxes, both State and National." The remainder of her estate, both real and personal, was to be divided between her cousins, Florence Dix, Evelyn Dix, Roger Sherman Dix, and Lucy Dix Bolles, or their survivors. She had written a letter stating how she wanted certain articles of personal wear or ornament disposed of.[15]

Mrs. Wild was buried in Brookline and her husband, Edward Wild, in Colombia, South America. Sadly, they were separated in death, as they had been so often during their married life.

Appendix: Tables for Chapter VI

Table I—Timeline of Events during Wild's Raid in North Carolina,[1] December 5–24, 1863

Sat.	12/5/63	Wild and troops departed Norfolk & Portsmouth, Va. in 2 column at dawn, marched 9 miles to Deep Creek.
Sun.	12/6	From Deep Creek, marched 18 miles to Ferebee's farm, camped overnight.
Mon.	12/7	Wild stayed at Ferebee's farm till noon waiting for supply boats, which never came.
Tues.	12/8	Wild's troops moved from South Mills to Camden Court House; reinforcements from 5th USCT, 11th PA, and 7th NY (cavalry & artillery).
Wed.	12/9	Wild arrived to find Pasquotank Bridge destroyed. Rebuilt bridge. Fired upon by enemy, 2 men wounded, 1 captured by guerrillas
Fri.	12/11	Wild's troops occupy Elizabeth City for 6 days. His headquarters at Dr. Pool's house; Wild begins ferrying freed slaves to Roanoke Island.
Sat.	12/12	Wild sent 4 detachments to forage for food and firewood, find guerrillas, and free slaves near Hertford; Col. John Holman and 1st USCT capture Daniel Bright and take Mrs. Phoebe Munden hostage; Camden County, Wild's men drank all the milk in Mrs. Wright's dairy, 2 sickened and died. Mrs. Wright arrested and taken to Norfolk for trial (11th, 12th, or 13th?).[2] Wild writes to Gen. Barnes to complain about advance warning given area slave owners by Union cavalry.[3]

Sun.	12/13/63	William T. Wright (husband of Mrs. Wright?) house burned by Holman; Mrs. Elizabeth Weeks also taken hostage; Wild sent Dr. Ray to Capt. Flusser of the *Miami* for assistance, after he learned that gunboat *North State* had burst steam pipe.
Tues.	12/15	Brig. Gen. Wessel arrived from Plymouth to confer with Wild.
Thurs.	12/17	Draper's men attacked Shiloh Church; Draper and 400 men go from Elizabeth City to Indiantown; Wild wrote Capt. Elliott, offered to exchange hostages. Trial held for 20 prisoners, Bright sentenced to hang.
Fri.	12/18	Elizabeth City evacuated. Wild and 1,300 men leave in cold rain going north to South Mills. Daniel Bright hanged by Wild at Hinton's Cross Roads 2 miles S.W. of South Mills.[4]
Fri.	12/18	Draper ambushed twice. Draper plus 400 men of 1st & 5th go to Camden Court House. Skirmish near fork of Indiantown & Dog Corner Roads—3 dead, 8 wounded, 13 Confederates killed; Capt. Charles H. Frye & 250 men leave by steamer for Powell's Point, then to march to Coinjack. Wild sent cavalry, artillery, plus Holman & 1st & 5th USCT to Norfolk.
Fri.	12/18	Wild and 500 men marched 15 miles to Indiantown to rejoin Draper. Draper & Wild meet at Indiantown; Draper's men attacked at Indiantown Bridge, 1 killed.
Sat.	12/19	Draper and Wild pursued guerrillas in Camden County, and find roster of Co. B, 68th N.C. Militia (Sanderlin's company). Major Gregory's name on roster, he taken, home burned. All Federal forces gathered at Currituck Court House, including contraband, steamboat, and gunboat *Flora Temple*.
Sun.	12/20	Draper and 120–170 men attacked Capt. Cyrus W. Grandy's camp on Crab Island in swamp, 4 miles from Sligo; contraband sent to Roanoke Island.
Mon.	12/21	Wild's raid ended, troops started toward Virginia. Confederate force at South Mills. Col. Draper takes detachment to Knotts's Island via steamer. Miss Nancy White taken hostage. Her home and other homes burned; Wild is at Currituck Court House.
Tues.	12/22	Wead-Draper dispute erupts over Miss White. Wild offered to exchange Major Gregory; wrote Capt. Sanderlin.
Wed.	12/23	On way back to Fort Monroe, Wild's men attacked by Confederates near Suffolk.[5]
Thurs.	12/24	Wild's Brigade back at Fort Monroe, Virginia.

Table II—Results of Wild's Raid into North Carolina[6]

Event	Total Numbers
Freed slaves	2,500 (approximately)
New black recruits	70–100
Guerrilla camps burned	4
Guns captured	50
Other equipment—drum	1
Ammunition, etc.	Not stated
Houses burned	12+
Distilleries burned	2
Prisoners taken (6 who were paroled, 1 hanged; 2 women, 1 old man taken to Norfolk, Virginia)	10
Captured boats	4 large
Horses captured	many

Results of Colonel Alonzo Draper's Detail, December 17–20, 1863[7]

Confederates killed and wounded at Sandy Hook	13
Draper's Union soldiers killed	1
Guerrilla Camps destroyed (Capt. Grandy's on Crab Island)	1

Table III—Wild's Losses During Raid into North Carolina[8]

Outcome	Total numbers
Soldiers killed	7
Soldiers wounded	9
Soldiers taken prisoner	2
Soldiers died of poison	1
Soldiers who died from sickness, fatigue, exposure	3
Soldiers with smallpox	9
Soldiers with mumps	many
Horses shot and killed	3
Guns lost by swamping of boat	4
Guns lost by fire in temporary smallpox hospital	4
Guns captured	1
Total Union Soldiers Killed/Died	11

Notes

Introduction

1. John G. Barrett, *The Civil War in North Carolina* (Chapel Hill: The University of North Carolina Press, 1963), pp. 177–181.
2. Webb Garrison, *Civil War Hostages: Hostage Taking in the Civil War* (Shippensburg, Pa.: White Mane Books, 2000), pp. 69–78.
3. Cowdin, Robert, compl. *First Regiment of Infantry, Massachusetts Volunteer Militia* (Boston: Wright and Potter Printing Co., 1903), p. 18.
4. Creecy, "Old Times in Betsy," *Elizabeth City Economist,* August 24, 1900. Cited in Witt, *Wild in North Carolina*, p. 55.
5. Richard Reid, "General Edward A. Wild and Civil War Discrimination," *Historical Journal of Massachusetts*, Vol. 13 (1), (January 1985), p. 24.
6. Edward Longacre, "Brave Radical Wild: The Contentious Career of Brigadier Edward A. Wild," *Civil War Times Illustrated* (June 1980), 19.
7. Horace N. Stevens and Gershom Bradford, "The True Man of Action." Typescript, no date, p. 4.
8. Letter from Mary Vic Stevens Griswold to Gershom Bradford, July 5, 1973. Mary Vic was a great-great niece of General Wild, daughter of Horace N. Stevens. Courtesy of Mrs. Helen Stevens Whitlock.
9. Stevens and Bradford, "The True Man of Action." Typescript, no date, p. 4.
10. Personal communication from Mrs. Helen S. Whitlock, Eastham, Mass., October 8, 2001.
11. Stevens and Bradford, "The True Man of Action," pp. 77–78

Chapter I

1. Pemberton Dudley, ed. *Transactions of the American Institute of Homeopathy: Forty-eighth Anniversary, Held at Washington, D. C., June 13 to 17, 1892* (Philadelphia: Sherman & Co., 1892), p. 227.
2. Dudley, p. 227.
3. Bradford Kingman, "General Edward Augustus Wild," in New England Historical and Genealogical Register, 49 (October) 1895, p. 407. Hereinafter cited as Kingman, "Memoir."
4. "Remarks of Hon. John W. Candler," in *Address of Martin P. Kennard* (Brookline, Mass.: Press of C. A. W. Spencer, 1894), p. 20.
5. Dick Nolan, *Benjamin Franklin Butler: The Damnedest Yankee* (Novato, Calif.: Presidio Press, 1991), p. 242.
6. *Address of Martin P. Kennard in behalf of the subscribing citizens, on presentation to the town of a memorial portrait of the late Brig.-Genl. Edward Augustus Wild, together with the response of the chairman of the Board of Selectmen, and the impromptu remarks of other gentlemen present*, p.17. Hereafter cited as *Address of Martin P. Kennard.*
7. Edward A. Wild to Edward W. Kinsley, July 28, 1863, Edward Wilkinson Kinsley Papers, Duke University, Durham, North Carolina.
8. Hartwell, in *Address of Martin P. Kennard,* p. 27.
9. *Ibid.*
10. Edward Wild to Mrs. Wild, October 18, 1861, in *Address of Martin P. Kennard*, p.11.
11. Hartwell, in *Address of Martin P. Kennard,* p. 27.
12. John W. Candler, in *Address of Martin P. Kennard,* p. 20.
13. Edward Wild to Mrs. Wild, October 18, 1861, quoted in *Address of Martin P. Kennard*, p. 11.
14. Kingman, "Memoir," p. 407.

15. Stevens and Bradford, p. 3.
16. Dudley, p. 227.
17. Clement K. Fay, in *Address of Martin P. Kennard*, pp. 24–25.
18. Fay, pp. 23–24.
19. Stevens and Bradford, pp. 20–21.
20. Mary H. Wadsworth, "Edward Atkinson," *Proceedings of the Brookline Historical Society* (Brookline, Mass.: Brookline Historical Society, 1950), p. 24.
21. Notes by Edward Wheelwright, written on announcement of a meeting of the Colonial Society of Massachusetts, Boston, March 8, 1893, Edward A. Wild Papers, Harvard University, Cambridge, Massachusetts.
22. Will of Edward A. Wild, March 4, 1888, Volume 169, p. 897–898, Probate Records, Norfolk County, Dedham, Massachusetts.
23. Kingman, "Memoir," p. 411.
24. Stevens and Bradford, p. 3.
25. John Austin Osborne, *Ancestors of Thirty-Three Rhode Island Families*, 1889, p. 1, cited in Stevens and Bradford, p. 3.
26. John William Ifkovic and Richard W. Wilkie, "Massachusetts." *Microsoft® Encarta® 97 Online Encyclopedia*, http://encarta.msn.com, copyright 1993–1996, Microsoft Corporation.
27. Kingman, "Memoir," p. 405.
28. Stevens and Bradford, pp. 18–23.
29. Harriet P. Wood, *Historical Sketches of Brookline, Massachusetts* (Robert B. Davis & Co., 1874), pp. 164–170, cited in Stevens and Bradford, p. 21–22.
30. Mary W. Poor, "Recollections of Brookline," (Brookline, Mass.: Riverdale Press: C. A. W. Spencer, 1903), pp. 2–5.
31. Wadsworth, "Edward Atkinson," p. 21.
32. Kingman, "Memoirs," p. 405. The property has since passed to William Lincoln, Stephen D. Bennett, and Arthur H. Blake, then to Blake's heirs.
33. Wadsworth, "Edward Atkinson," pp. 24–25.
34. Stevens and Bradford, p. 27.
35. Will of Edward A. Wild, dated March 4, 1888, Norfolk County, Brookline, Massachusetts, Probate, Volume 169, p. 897.
36. Wadsworth, "Edward Atkinson," p. 25.
37. *Ibid.*, p. 28.
38. *Ibid.*, p. 29.
39. Poor, "Recollections of Brookline," p. 7.
40. Stevens and Bradford, p. 28.
41. Edward A. Wild to Ned (Edward Atkinson), New York, October 18, 1872 (?), Massachusetts Historical Society, Boston, Mass.
42. Wadsworth, "Edward Atkinson," pp. 21–22.
43. *Ibid.*, pp. 28–29.
44. Poor, p. 14; also cited in Stevens and Bradford, pp. 19–20.
45. Poor, pp. 12–13.
46. Katherine Robinson Briggs, "Brookline in the Civil War," Brookline Historical Publication Society, Publication No. 10, 1896, p. 153.
47. Stevens and Bradford, p. 29. After General Wild's death, the books were passed to his widow, who gave them to Edward's sister, Mrs. Laura W. Phipps. Mrs. Phipps gave them to her daughter, Mrs. Anna M. Stevens, wife of Horace Stevens. Their son, Horace Stevens wrote "The True Man of Action" and his granddaughter, Helen M. Whitlock, is now the owner of the Sir Walter Scott novels.
48. Ifkovic and Wilkie, "Massachusetts."
49. Bruce Catton and James M. McPherson (eds.), *The American Heritage New History of the Civil War* (New York: Viking Penguin, 1996), pp. 2–3.
50. Catton and McPherson, pp. 2–3.
51. *Ibid.*
52. *Ibid.*
53. Avery Craven, *Reconstruction: The Ending of the Civil War* (New York: Holt, Rinehart, Winston, 1968), p. 21–22.
54. Stevens and Bradford, pp. 28–29.
55. D. Hamilton Hurd, compl., *History of Norfolk County, Massachusetts, with Biographical Sketches of Many of Its Pioneers and Prominent Men* (Philadelphia: J. W. Lewis & Company, 1884), p. 876.
56. Stevens and Bradford, p. 39.
57. "Edward Augustus Wild," Harvard College Class of 1844, 50th Anniversary Report, 1894, p. 252.
58. Stevens and Bradford, p. 39.
59. Wood, *Historical Sketches of Brookline, Massachusetts*, pp. 164–170, cited in Stevens and Bradford, p. 23.
60. J. Jacobs, M. Jimenez, S. Gloyd, F. Carares, G. Paniagua, and D. Crothers. "Homeopathic treatment of acute childhood diarrhea." *British Homeopathic Journal* 82:83–86, 1993.
61. "Homeopathy," *Microsoft® Encarta® Online Encyclopedia 2000*, http://encarta.msn.com, copyright 1997–2000, Microsoft Corporation.
62. Wood, *Historical Sketches of Brookline, Massachusetts*, pp. 164–170, cited in Stevens and Bradford, p. 23.
63. Hurd, D., p. 876.
64. "Necrology: Edward Wild, M.D.," *Journal of the American Medical Association* 17 (Oct. 31, 1891), 702.
65. Dudley, p. 208.
66. Frederick B. Wagner, Jr., "Growth and Consolidation," in Frederick B. Wagner, Jr., and J. Woodrow Savacool, eds. *Thomas Jefferson University: A Chronological History and Alumni directory, Annotated and Illustrated, 1824–1900* (Philadelphia: Thomas Jefferson University, 1992), pp. 53.

67. "Hippocratic Oath," *Microsoft Encarta Online Encyclopedia 2000,* http://encarta.msn.com, © 1997–2000 Microsoft Corporation.
68. Briggs, p. 154; Stevens and Bradford, p. 41.
69. Stevens and Bradford, p. 42.
70. Kingman, "Memoir," p. 406.
71. Edward Atkinson to Edward "Ned" Phibrick, Boston, December 27, 1848, Edward Atkinson Letters, Massachusetts Historical Society, Boston, Mass.
72. Stevens and Bradford, p. 42.
73. Letter from Edward Wild to Mary Howe, original in Brookline Public Library, Brookline, Massachusetts, cited in Stevens and Bradford, p. 43.
74. Stevens and Bradford, p. 43.
75. *Ibid.,* p. 44.
76. Harvard University Archives, Class of 1844, and 1896, cited in Stevens and Bradford, p. 44.
77. Edward A. Wild, "Italian War," Wild Papers, Harvard University Archives, Pusey Library, Cambridge, Massachusetts.
78. Stevens and Bradford, p. 3.
79. *Ibid.,* p. 44.
80. *Ibid.,* pp. 45–46.
81. *Ibid.,* p. 46.
82. "Garibaldi, Giuseppe," *Encarta Encyclopedia,* online at http://encarta.msn.com.
83. Edward A. Wild, "Italian War," Wild Papers, Harvard University Archives, Pusey Library, Cambridge, Massachusetts.
84. Stevens and Bradford, p. 46.
85. Edward A. Wild, "Italian War," Wild Papers, Harvard University Archives, Pusey Library, Cambridge, Massachusetts.
86. Stevens and Bradford, p. 46.
87. *Ibid.,* p. 47.
88. T. Walter Wallbank, Alastar M. Taylor, and Nels M. Bailkey, eds. *Civilization: Past & Present,* 4th edition (Glenview, IL: Scott, Foresman and Company, 1975) p. 521.
89. Briggs, p. 154.
90. Edward A. Wild, "Italian War," Wild Papers, Harvard University Archives, Pusey Library, Cambridge, Massachusetts; Stevens and Bradford, pp. 46–47.
91. Kingman, "Memoir," p. 406.
92. *Ibid.,* p. 406.
93. Edward (Ned A.) Atkinson to Ned Philbrick, Boston, November 10, 1850, cited in Stevens and Bradford, pp. 48–49.
94. John M. Blum, Edmund S. Morgan, Willie Lee Rose, et al., eds., *The National Experience,* 3rd ed. (New York: Harcourt Brace Jovanovich, Inc., 1973), pp. 277–280.
95. Stevens and Bradford, p. 48.
96. *Ibid.,* p. 48.
97. Certified copy of marriage license furnished by Office of the Secretary of State, William Francis Galvin, Secretary, Archives Division, Commonwealth of Massachusetts, Boston, Mass. 02125, from Marriage Register for the year 1855; Vol. 89, page 121, No. 48.
98. "Edward Augustus Wild," *50th Anniversary Report, Class of 1844, Harvard University,* p. 254.
99. Boatner, p. 11.
100. *Ibid.,* pp. 241–242.
101. "Widow of Gen. Wild Dead in Brookline," Boston *Globe,* October 4, 1923, page 17, column 2.
102. "The Crimean War," *The Encyclopedia Americana,* Vol. 8, International Edition (Danbury, CT: Grolier Incorporated, 1997), p. 204; Wallbank, pp. 542–543.
103. (untitled article) *The Times,* 25 December 1854, p. 6.
104. Edward A. Wild to Ned (Edward Atkinson), Port Arthur, Canada, October 12, 1889, Massachusetts Historical Society, Boston, Mass.
105. Kingman, "Memoir," p. 406.
106. John Harris, *The Gallant Six Hundred* (New York: Mason & Lipscomb Publishers, 1973), pp. 2–3.
107. E. T. Cook, *Life of Florence Nightingale* (London: Macmillan, 1913). Bay M. Notably, *Florence Nightingale and the Nursing Legacy,* 2nd ed. (London: Whurr, 1997).
108. Harris, *The Gallant Six Hundred.*
109. Edward A. Wild, "Crimean War," in Wild Papers, Harvard University Archives, Pusey Library, Cambridge, Massachusetts. Hereafter cited as Wild, "Crimean War."
110. Albert Parry, "American Doctors in the Crimean War," *The South Atlantic Quarterly,* Vol. 54 (No. 4) (October 1955), pp. 478–479.
111. Stevens and Bradford, p. 50.
112. C. B., "The Commissariat of the Crimean," *The Times* 24 January 1855, p. 10.
113. Stevens and Bradford, p. 52.
114. *Ibid.,* p. 51–52.
115. (untitled leading articles, 2nd leader) *The Times* 5 May 1855, p. 9.
116. Wallbank, pp. 542–543.
117. Parry, "American Doctors in the Crimean War," pp. 478–479.
118. *Ibid.,* pp. 482–487.
119. *Ibid.,* p. 486.
120. Wild, "Crimean War."
121. *Ibid.*
122. Stevens and Bradford, pp. 52–53; Wild, "Crimean War."
123. Wild, "Crimean War."
124. "General Wild's Turkish Medals," *The Boston Herald,* May 19, 1897, diploma translated by John P. Brown, dragoman of the American legation, cited in Stevens and Bradford, p. 53.

125. "General Wild's Turkish Medals," *The Boston Herald*, May 19, 1897.
126. Stevens and Bradford, pp. 53–4.
127. *Ibid.*, p. 54.
128. Briggs, p. 154.
129. Wild, "Crimean War."
130. Stevens and Bradford, pp. 54–55.
131. Wild, "Crimean War."
132. Letter in Brookline, Massachusetts, Public Library, cited in Stevens and Bradford, p. 55.
133. Stevens and Bradford, p. 55.
134. Wallbank, p. 544.
135. *Ibid.*, p. 543.
136. *Ibid.*, pp. 544–545.
137. "Yugoslavia's Birth to its Breakup," http://www.xs4all.nl/~frankti/Warhistory/war_hist.html.
138. *Ibid.*
139. "Edward Augustus Wild," *50th Anniversary Report, Class of 1844*, Harvard University, Cambridge, Massachusetts, p. 255.

Chapter II

1. Boatner, p. 729.
2. J. R. May and J. R. Faunt, *South Carolina Secedes* (Greenville, S.C.: University of South Carolina Press, 1960), pp. 76–81. See also web page at: http://americancivilwar.com/documents/causes_south_carolina.html.
3. Abraham Lincoln, "First Inaugural Address, Monday, March 4, 1861," http://americancivilwar.com/documents/lincoln_inaugural_1.html.
4. Boatner, pp. 15–16. See also "The Political Graveyard: Index to Politicians," online at http://politicalgraveyard.com/bio/andochick-andrew.html.
5. Boatner, p. 16.
6. John A. Andrew, Governor, to Simon Cameron, Secretary of War, April 22, 1861, *O.R.*, Ser. III, Vol. I, pp. 99–100.
7. John A. Andrew, Governor, to Simon Cameron, Secretary of War, April 25, 1861, *O.R.*, Ser. III, Vol. I, pp. 111–112.
8. William Schouler, *A History of Massachusetts*, Vol. 1 (Boston: E. P. Dutton and Company, 1868), pp. 58, and P. C. Headley, *Massachusetts in the Rebellion: A Record of the Historical Position of the Commonwealth* (Boston: Walker, Fuller and Company, 1866), pp. 485–486, cited in Stevens and Bradford, p. 60.
9. Richard Reid, "General Edward A. Wild and Civil War Discrimination," *Historical Journal of Massachusetts*, 13 (January 1985): 14.
10. Briggs, p. 143.
11. Briggs, p. 144; and Stevens and Bradford, pp. 60–62.
12. Stevens and Bradford, p. 62.
13. Simon Cameron, Secretary of War, to Wilder Dwight and George L. Andrews, Washington, D.C., April 28, 1862, cited in Briggs, p. 149.
14. Briggs, p. 153.
15. *Ibid.*, p. 145.
16. *Ibid.*, p. 145.
17. Reid, "General Edward A. Wild and Civil War Discrimination," 14.
18. *Annual Report of the Adjutant-General of the Commonwealth of Massachusetts with the Reports from the Quartermaster-General, Surgeon-General, and Master of Ordnance for the Year Ending December 31, 1864* (Boston: Wright & Potter, State Printers, 1865), pp. 224–225. Hereafter cited as *Annual Report of Adjutant-General of Commonwealth*.
19. Stevens and Bradford, pp. 64–65.
20. Official documents of Governor Andrew of Massachusetts, "Letters Sent," Volume 1, April–July 1861, 283.
21. Edward A. Wild, "Military Life of Edward A. Wild, Brig. Genl. Vol.," copy courtesy of Massachusetts Historical Society, Boston, Massachusetts, hereafter cited as Wild, "Military Life."
22. Briggs, *Brookline in the Civil War* (Brookline Historical Publication Society, 1896, number 10), 154, cited in Stevens and Bradford, p. 63.
23. Boatner, p. 919. See also "Obituary: Brig.-Gen. Edward A. Wild," *Boston Post*, September 5, 1891.
24. Massachusetts Adjutant General. *Massachusetts Soldiers, Sailors and Marines in the Great Civil War.* Vol. 1 (Norwood: Norwood Press, 1931), p. 10.
25. Alfred S. Roe, *The Fifth Regiment Massachusetts Volunteer Infantry in Its Three Tours of Duty, 1861, 1862–'63, 1864* (Boston: Fifth Regiment Veterans Association, 1911), p. 244, cited in Reid, "Raising the African Brigade," *The North Carolina Historical Review*, 70 (3), July, 1993, p. 281.
26. Briggs, p. 145.
27. *Ibid.*, p. 145.
28. *Annual Report of the Adjutant-General of the Commonwealth*, p. 79.
29. *Ibid.*, p. 75
30. *Ibid.*, p. 76.
31. Edward Wild, Capt. Co. A, 1st Regt. Mass. Foot Volunteers, to Governor John A. Andrew, Philadelphia, June 17, 1861, Massachusetts Historical Society, Boston, Massachusetts.
32. Wild, "Military Life."
33. *Annual Report of the Adjutant-General of the Commonwealth*, pp. 76–77.
34. *Ibid.*, p.77.
35. *Ibid.*, p.79.

36. Headley, *Massachusetts in the Rebellion*, p. 147, cited in Stevens and Bradford, p. 70.
37. *Annual Report of the Adjutant-General of the Commonwealth*, p. 77.
38. Boatner, p. 531.
39. Stevens and Bradford, p. 71.
40. Boatner, p. 697.
41. *Annual Report of the Adjutant-General of the Commonwealth*, p.77.
42. "Report of Col. Israel B. Richardson, Second Michigan Infantry, of action at Blackburn's Ford," July 19, 1861. O.R., Ser. I, Vol. 2, pp. 312–314.
43. *Annual Report of the Adjutant-General of the Commonwealth*, p.77.
44. William C. Davis, *Rebels & Yankees: The Battles of the Civil War* (London: Salamander Books Limited, 2001), pp. 13–15.
45. Brigadier General Irvin McDowell to Brigadier General [Daniel] Tyler, 8:15 A.M., July 18, 1861, O.R., Ser. I, Vol. 2, p. 312.
46. R. M. Johnston, *Bull Run, Its Strategy and Tactics*, 1913, pp. 91, 93, 130–131, cited in Stevens and Bradford, p. 71.
47. "Report of Col. Israel B. Richardson, Second Michigan Infantry, of action at Blackburn's Ford," July 19, 1861. O.R., Ser. I, Vol. 2, p. 313.
48. *Ibid.*, pp.312–314.
49. Stevens and Bradford, p. 73.
50. *History of the First Massachusetts*, Vol. II, cited in Stevens and Bradford, p. 73.
51. Wild, "Military Life."
52. *Ibid.*, p. 205.
53. Boatner, p. 99.
54. "Casualties at Blackburn's Ford," enclosed in "Report of Col. Israel B. Richardson, Second Michigan Infantry, of action at Blackburn's Ford," July 19, 1861. O.R., Ser. I, Vol. 2, p. 314.
55. Col. T. W. Higginson and Florence Wyman Jaques, "List of Battles and Casualties of Massachusetts Regiments During the War of the Rebellion," *New England Historical and Genealogic Register*, Vol. 46 (January 1892), p. 32.
56. *Annual Report of the Adjutant-General of the Commonwealth*, p. 79.
57. Ezra J. Warner, *Generals in Blue: Lives of the Union Commanders* (Baton Rouge, La.: Louisiana State University Press, 1972), p. 558.
58. Brigadier General Irvin McDowell to Brigadier General Tyler, Between Germantown and Centreville, July 18, 1861, O.R., Ser. I, Vol. 2, p. 312.
59. William C. Davis, *Rebels & Yankees: The Battles of the Civil War* (London: Salamander Books Limited, 2001), p. 16.
60. Stevens and Bradford, p. 74.
61. *Ibid.*, p. 74.
62. *Annual Report of the Adjutant-General of the Commonwealth*, p.77.
63. *Ibid.*, p. 80.
64. *Ibid.*, pp. 77–78.
65. Wild, "Military Life."
66. Col. T. W. Higginson and Florence Wyman Jaques, "List of Battles and Casualties of Massachusetts Regiments During the War of the Rebellion," *New England Historical and Genealogic Register*, Vol. 46 (January 1892), p. 32.
67. *Annual Report of the Adjutant-General of the Commonwealth*, p. 80.
68. *Ibid.*, p. 80–81.
69. Capt. Edward A. Wild to Col. Robert Cowdin, Fort Albany, Va., July 28, 1861, in Court Martial files, National Archives, Washington, D.C.
70. Capt. Edward A. Wild to Acting Brig. Gen. Richardson, Fort Albany, Va., August 5, 1861, Record Group 94, National Archives, Washington, D.C.
71. Col. Richardson to Col. Robert Cowdin, Fort Albany, Va., no date, but probably August 5, 1861. Record Group 94, National Archives, Washington, D.C. This was received by Capt. Wild and forwarded to Col. Cowdin in a note dated August 5, 1861.
72. Wild, "Military Life."
73. *Annual Report of the Adjutant-General of the Commonwealth*, p. 78.
74. John A. Andrew, Governor, to President Lincoln and Secretary of War, September 11, 1861, O.R., Ser. III, Vol. I, p. 499.
75. Edward G. Longacre, *Army of Amateurs* (Mechanicsville, Pa.: Stackpole Books, 1997), p. 5.
76. *Ibid.*, pp. 3–5.
77. Howard P. Nash, Jr., *Stormy Petrel: The Life and Times of General Benjamin F. Butler, 1818–1893* (Cranbury, N.J.: Associated University Presses, Inc., 1969), p. 13.
78. *Annual Report of the Adjutant-General of the Commonwealth*, p. 81.
79. *Ibid.*, p. 78; Wild, "Military Life."
80. *Annual Report of the Adjutant-General of the Commonwealth*, p. 78.
81. William Latham Candler to Brother, November 2, 1861, William Latham Candler Papers, 1861–1863, Special Collections Department, University Libraries, Virginia Polytechnic Institute and State University, Blacksburg, Virginia. See http://spec.lib.vt.edu/mss/candler/Candler5.htm.
82. Edward A. Wild to Brookline War Committee, Brookline Historical Publication Society, Publication No. 7, May, 1896, p. 68.
83. Wild, "Military Life."
84. Edward A. Wild to Brookline War Committee, Brookline Historical Publication Society, Publication No. 7, May, 1896, p. 66–67; "Report of Lieut. Col. George D. Wells, First Mass-

achusetts Infantry," Camp Hooker, Md., November 14, 1861, O.R., Ser. I, Vol. 5, p. 422.

85. Wild, "Military Life."
86. Edward A. Wild to Brookline War Committee, Brookline Historical Publication Society, Publication No. 7, May, 1896, p. 66–67; "Report of Lieut. Col. George D. Wells, First Massachusetts Infantry," Camp Hooker, Md., November 14, 1861, O.R., Ser. I, Vol. 5, p. 422.
87. Wild, "Military Life."
88. Stevens and Bradford, footnote 7, p. 30.
89. Wild, "Military Life."
90. Briggs, p. 154

Chapter III

1. Wild, "Military Life."
2. Calvin D. Cowles, compl., "Plate VIII, Survey for Military Defenses: Map of Northeastern Virginia and the Vicinity of Washington," *Atlas to Accompany the Official Records of the Union and Confederate Armies* (Washington, D.C.: Gov. Printing Office, 1891–1895, rpt. New York: The Fairfax Press, 1983).
3. "Public Document No. 7," *Annual Report of the Adjutant-General of the Commonwealth of Massachusetts with the Reports from the Quartermaster-General, Surgeon-General, and Master of Ordnance for the Year Ending December 31, 1864*, p. 81. Hereafter cited as "Public Document No. 7."
4. "Public Document No. 7," p. 82.
5. Wild, "Military Life."
6. "Public Document No. 7," p. 82; Wild, "Military Life."
7. Boatner, p. 524.
8. *Ibid.*, p. 633.
9. "Public Document No. 7," p. 82.
10. Boatner, p. 633.
11. Wild, "Military Life."
12. "Public Document No. 7," p. 82–83.
13. Colonel Robert Cowdin, reissued Brig. Gen. Naglee's Special Order No. 59, Camp Winfield Scott near Yorktown, April 14, 1862, Edward A. Wild Papers, Military History Institute, Carlisle, PA. Hereinafter cited as MHI.
14. Copy from recollection of Brig. Gen. Henry M. Naglee to Col. Robert Cowdin, Camp Winfield Scott, April 17, 1862, Edward A. Wild Papers, MHI.
15. Colonel Robert Cowdin, Special Order No. 64, Edward A. Wild Papers, MHI.
16. Capt. Edward A. Wild, reply on bottom of Colonel Robert Cowdin's Special Orders No. 64, Edward A. Wild Papers, MHI.
17. Captain Edward A. Wild to Lieutenant Joseph Hibbert, April 19, 1862, Edward A. Wild Papers, MHI.

18. *Ibid.*
19. William Latham Candler to My Dear Brother, Headquarters, Hooker's Division, Camp Near Fair Oaks, Virginia, June 24, 1862, William Latham Candler Papers, 1861–63, Virginia Polytechnic Institute and State University, Special Collections Department, Blacksburg, Virginia. Online at spec.lib.vt.edu/mss/candler/Candler 8.htm.
20. Boatner, p. 501.
21. Wild, "Military Life."
22. "Public Document No. 7," pp. 82–83.
23. Wild, "Military Life."
24. Boatner, p. 363.
25. "Public Document No. 7," pp. 82–83.
26. Wild, "Military Life."
27. *Ibid.*
28. Boatner, p. 953.
29. "Public Document No. 7," p.83.
30. Higginson and Jaques, "List of Battles and Casualties of Massachusetts Regiments During the War of the Rebellion," p. 32.
31. Boatner, 928–929.
32. Copy of letter from Edward A. Wild to Dr. Francis H. Brown, Boston, July 7, 1878, Wild Papers, Harvard University Archives, Cambridge, Massachusetts.
33. Wild, "Military Life."
34. Livermore, cited in Boatner, 929.
35. Higginson and Jaques, "List of Battles and Casualties of Massachusetts Regiments During the War of the Rebellion," p. 32.
36. *Ibid.*
37. Wild, "Military Life."
38. Boatner, p. 603–604.
39. *Ibid.*
40. Higginson and Jaques, "List of Battles and Casualties of Massachusetts Regiments During the War of the Rebellion," p. 32. The number who were wounded were not listed in the figures compiled by Lt. Col. William F. Fox, cited in Higginson and Jaques.
41. Wild, "Military Life."
42. *Ibid.*
43. Richard Henry Salter, M.D., Late Surgeon First Regiment Mass. Vols., to Whomsoever this concerns, March 25, 1878, Edward A. Wild Pension papers, Record Group 94, NA.
44. Deposition of Mrs. Susan S. Wood, February 8, 1898; Affidavit of George Augustus Wood, March 1875, Edward A. Wild Pension Papers, and Pension Application File of Mrs. Frances E. Wild, Record Group 94, NA.
45. Frances E. Wild, Deposition A, Case No. 583,593, Frances E. Wild Pension Application Papers, Record Group 94, NA.
46. "Claim for Pension Increase," Edward A. Wild, January 28, 1878, in Pension Application file of Mrs. Frances E. Wild, Record Group 94, NA.

47. Copy of letter from Edward A. Wild to Dr. Francis H. Brown, Boston, July 7, 1878.
48. Affidavit of George Augustus Wood, Philadelphia, PA, April 6, 1878, Pension Files of Mrs. Frances Wild, Record Group 94, NA.
49. William Latham Candler to Brother, Harrison's Landing, Virginia, July 15, 1862, William Latham Candler Papers, 1861–1863, Special Collections Department, University Libraries, Virginia Polytechnic Institute and State University, Blacksburg, Virginia. Online at http://spec.lib.vt.edu/mss/candler/Candler10.htm.
50. *Ibid.*
51. Wild, "Military Life."
52. *Ibid.*
53. Stevens and Bradford, p. 85.
54. B. F. Baker, Town Clerk, Brookline, Massachusetts, Special meeting, August 19, 1862, Brookline Town Records, Volume 3, p. 165; also cited in Briggs, p. 148.
55. "Thirty-Fifth Regiment—Narrative," in "Public Document No. 7," p. 474.
56. Committee of the Regimental Association, *History of the 35th Regiment, Massachusetts Volunteers, 1862–1865 with a Roster* (Boston: Mills, Knight & Co., 1884), pp. 1–19.
57. Copy of Letter from Edward A. Wild to Dr. Francis H. Brown, Boston, July 7, 1878.
58. Edward A. Wild, "History of the 35th Mass. up to January 1, 1863," Edward A Wild Papers, MHI.
59. "Public Document No. 7," p. 474.
60. Edwin M. Stanton to Governor Andrew, August 2, 1862, cited in Stevens and Bradford, p. 87.
61. Edwin M. Stanton to Governor Andrew, August 12, 1862, *O.R.*, Ser. II, Vol. 2, p. 363.
62. Boatner, p. 42.
63. Wild, "Military Life."
64. *Ibid.*
65. *The National Cyclopaedia of American Biography*, Vol. 5 (New York: James T. White & Company, 1907), p. 511.
66. "Report No. 3627," House of Representatives, 57th Congress, 2nd Session, Record Group 94, Pension Application File of Frances Ellen Wild, NA, Washington, D.C. Hereinafter cited as Frances E. Wild Pension Application papers.
67. Massachusetts Adjutant General. *Massachusetts Soldiers, Sailors and Marines in the Great Civil War.* Vol. 1 (Norwood: Norwood Press, 1931), p. 10, 647. See also "Public Document No. 7," p. 468
68. Ezra J. Warner, *Generals in Blue: Lives of the Union Commanders* (Baton Rouge: Louisiana State University Press, 1972), p. 557–558.
69. Stewart Sifakis, *Who Was Who in the Civil War* (New York: Facts on File Publications, 1988), p. 713.
70. Warner, *Generals in Blue*, p. 558.
71. Typed copy of William Schenler, Adjt. Genl. "Special Order No. 557," Headquarters, Boston, July 24, 1862, Massachusetts Adjutant Commanders Office, Term of Gov. Andrew, p. 307, in Volume 1, Notes on General Wild, notebook compiled by Horace N. Stevens, courtesy of Mrs. Helen Stevens Whitlock.
72. Frances E. Wild, Claimant's Affidavit, December 22, 1893, Frances E. Wild Pension Application Papers.
73. Typed copy of William Schenler, Adjt. Genl. "Special Order No. 562," Headquarters, Boston, July 24, 1862, Massachusetts Adjutant General's Office, Term of Gov. Andrew, p. 310, in Volume 1, Notes on General Wild, notebook compiled by Horace N. Stevens, courtesy of Mrs. Helen Stevens Whitlock.
74. Capt. Edward A. Wild to wife, Camp Union, Bladensburg, Maryland, October 18, 1861, cited in Stevens and Bradford, pp. 77–78.
75. Wild, "Military Life."
76. Wild, "History of the 35th Mass. up to January 1, 1863," Edward A. Wild Papers, MHI.
77. Committee of the Regimental Association, *History of the 35th Regiment, Massachusetts Volunteers, 1862–1865 with a Roster*, p. 17
78. Lieut.-Col. A. G. Browne, Jr., to Col. E. A. Wild, Executive Dept., Boston, August 9, 1862, "Letters Sent" August-September 1862, Volume 8, p. 182, Correspondence of Gov. Andrew, typed copy in Volume 1, Notes on General Wild, notebook compiled by Horace N. Stevens, courtesy of Mrs. Helen Stevens Whitlock.
79. John A. Andrew to Hon. E. M. Stanton, Boston, August 22, 1862, *O.R.*, Ser. III, Vol. 2, p. 438.
80. Boatner, p. 612.
81. Stevens and Bradford, p. 88.
82. *Ibid.*
83. John A. Andrew, Governor of Massachusetts to Col. Edward A. Wild, 35th Mass. Vols., Executive Dept., Boston, August 23, 1862, "Letters Sent," August-September 1862, Vol, 8, pp. 261–261, Papers of Governor John A. Andrew, typed copy in Volume 1, Notes on General Wild, notebook compiled by Horace N. Stevens, courtesy of Mrs. Helen Stevens Whitlock.
84. Stevens and Bradford, p. 88–89.
85. Kingman, "Memoir," p. 409.
86. *Ibid.*
87. Wild, "History of the 35th Mass. up to January 1, 1863," Edward A. Wild Papers, MHI.
88. Boatner, p. 131.
89. Wild, "History of the 35th Mass. up to January 1, 1863," Edward A. Wild Papers, MHI.
90. Boatner, p. 912.
91. "Troops in the Defenses of Washington, August 31, 1862," *O.R.*, Ser. I, Vol. 12, Pt. III, p. 782.

92. Wild, "History of the 35th Mass. up to January 1, 1863," Edward A. Wild Papers, MHI.
93. Stevens and Bradford, p. 90.
94. Colgrove, p. 603.
95. Hill, "The Battle of South Mountain, or Boonsboro," p. 569–570.
96. Silas Colgrove, "The Finding of Lee's Lost Order," Robert U. Johnson, and Clarence C. Buel, *Battles and Leaders of the Civil War*, Vol. II, p. 603. The lost order was found on September 13, 1862, at Frederick, Maryland, by Private B. W. Mitchell of company F, 27th Indiana Volunteers. The order was signed by Colonel Chilton, Lee's adjutant general.
97. Clint Johnson, *Civil War Blunders* (Winston-Salem, NC: John F. Blair, Publisher, 1997), p. 94–95.
98. Daniel H. Hill, "The Battle of South Mountain, or Boonsboro," Robert U. Johnson, and Clarence C. Buel, *Battles and Leaders of the Civil War*, Vol. II (1887; rpt. Secaucus, NJ: Castle, 1982), pp. 559–560.
99. "Antietam Campaign: South Mountain," Boatner, p. 20.
100. "Organization of the Army of the Potomac, Maj. Gen. George B. McClellan, U. S. Army, commanding, September 14–17, 1862," *O.R.*, Ser. I, Vol. 19, Pt. I, pp. 169–177.
101. Boatner, p. 277.
102. "Report of Brig. Gen. Edward Ferrero, U. S. Army, commanding Second Brigade, of the battles of South Mountain and Antietam," September 19, 1863, *O.R.*, Vol. 19, Pt. 1, p. 447–449.
103. "History of the 35th Regiment," Chapter 2, *Massachusetts Volunteers*, cited in Stevens and Bradford, p. 95.
104. *Ibid.*, p. 96.
105. Wild, "Military Life."
106. Stevens and Bradford, p. 96.
107. "Address of Martin P. Kennard," p. 12, cited by Stevens and Bradford, p. 87.
108. "Report of Brig. Gen. Edward Ferrero, U. S. Army, commanding Second Brigade, of the battles of South Mountain and Antietam," September 19, 1863, *O.R.*, Vol. 19, Pt. 1, p. 448.
109. "Antietam Campaign: South Mountain," Boatner, p. 20.
110. Boatner, p. 389.
111. "McKinley, William," *World Book Encyclopedia*, Vol. 12 (Chicago: Field Enterprises Educational Corporation, 1963), pp. 272–276.
112. Wild, "History of the 35th Mass. up to January 1, 1863," Edward A. Wild Papers, MHI.
113. Hill, "The Battle of South Mountain, or Boonsboro," p. 569–570.
114. Major General George B. McClellan, "Army of the Potomac," Robert U. Johnson, and Clarence C. Buel, *Battles and Leaders of the Civil War*, Vol. II, p. 600.
115. Livermore, cited in Boatner, p. 20.
116. Higginson and Jaques, "List of Battles and Casualties of Massachusetts Regiments During the War of the Rebellion," p. 34.
117. George A. Otis, *The Medical and Surgical History of the War of the Rebellion*, vol. II, part II. (Washington: Government Printing Office, 1876), p. 629..
118. Wild, "Military Life."
119. Kingman, "Memoirs" cited in Stevens and Bradford, p. 98.
120. George A. Wood, Deposition C, February 8, 1898, Case of Frances E. Wild, No. 583593, Frances E. Wild Pension Application papers.
121. John MacDonald, *Great Battles of the Civil War* (New York: Macmillan Publishing Company, 1988), pp. 62–63.
122. "Report of Brig. Gen. Edward Ferrero, U. S. Army, commanding Second Brigade, of the battles of South Mountain and Antietam," September 19, 1863, *O.R.*, Vol. 19, Pt. 1, p. 449.
123. Wild, "History of 35th Mass," Edward A. Wild Papers, MHI.
124. *Ibid.*
125. Fox, *Regimental Losses in the Civil War*, p. 172.
126. McClellan, "Army of the Potomac," *Battles and Leaders of the Civil War*, Vol. II, p. 600.
127. General Robert E. Lee, "The Confederate Army," Robert U. Johnson, and Clarence C. Buel, *Battles and Leaders of the Civil War*, Vol. II, p. 603.
128. Fox, *Regimental Losses in the American Civil War*, pp. 543, 550
129. Boatner, p. 524.
130. Wild, "Military Life."
131. O. W. Holmes, "My Hunt After 'The Captain,'" *Atlantic Monthly* Vol. 10, No. 62 (December 1862), pp.738–764.
132. Holmes, p. 740.
133. Copy of letter from Edward A. Wild to Dr. F. H. Brown, Boston, July 7, 1878, in Wild Papers, Harvard University Archives, Pusey Library, Cambridge, Massachusetts.
134. Holmes, pp.738–764.
135. Wild, "Military Life."
136. Stevens and Bradford, p. 98.
137. "Public Document No. 7," pp. 474–489.
138. Wild, "Military Life."
139. Warren H. Cudsworth, *History of the First Regiment (Massachusetts Infantry) From the 25th of May 1861, to the 25th of May 1864, including brief references to the Operations of the Army of the Potomac* (Boston: Walker, Fuller & Co., 1866), p. 96.

Chapter IV

1. P. C. Headley, *Massachusetts in the Rebellion* (Boston: Walker, Fuller & Co., 1866), p. 449.

2. Clinton Cox, *Undying Glory: The Story of the Massachusetts 54th Regiment* (New York: Scholastic Inc., 1991), pp. 8–10; Boatner, p. 265.

3. Henry Steele Commander, "The Emancipation Proclamation," *Documents of American History*, 9th ed. (Englewood Cliffs, N.J.: Prentice-Hall, Inc., 1973), pp. 420–421. The Emancipation Proclamation was enacted and made part of the United States Statues at Large, vol. XII, pp. 1268–1269.

4. "A Proclamation," Carl Sandburg, *Abraham Lincoln: The War Years*, II (New York: Harcourt, Brace & Company, 1939), pp. 17–18.

5. Abraham Lincoln to Horace Greely, August 22, 1862, Carl Sandburg, *Abraham Lincoln: The War Years*, Vol. I, p. 567.

6. Carl Sandburg, *Abraham Lincoln: The War Years*, Vol. II, p. 567.

7. "Draft Riots," Boatner, p. 245.

8. *Ibid.*, pp. 245–246.

9. "The Ferocity of the New York Rioters—Brutality of the Military," Raleigh, N.C., *The Semi-Weekly Standard* (24 July 1863).

10. "Draft Riots," Boatner, pp. 245–246.

11. Glatthaar, *Forged in Battle*, pp. 61–66, 76.

12. *Journal of the Congress of the Confederate States of America, 1861–1865*, Ninetieth Day, Friday, May 1, 1863, Closed Session, pp. 486–488, online version at: http://memory.loc.

13. *Ibid.*

14. Wilmington (North Carolina) *Journal*, May 23, 1863.

15. Dudley T. Cornish, *The Sable Arm: Negro Troops in the Union Army, 1861–1865* (New York: Longmans, Green and Co., 1956), p. 168, cited in Reid, "Raising the African Brigade," p. 279; Roy P. Basler, ed., *The Collected Works of Abraham Lincoln*, Vol. 6 (New Brunswick, N.J.), p. 195.

16. Basler, *The Collected Works of Abraham Lincoln*, Vol. 6, p. 195.

17. Warner, *Generals in Blue*, pp. 60–61.

18. Boatner, p. 172.

19. Jefferson Davis, "General Orders, No. 111," *O.R.* Ser II, Vol. 5, pp. 795–797.

20. Victor Brooks, *African Americans in the Civil War* (Philadelphia, Pa.: Chelsea House Publishers, 2000), pp. 11–15.

21. Ezra J. Warner, *Generals in Blue*, p. 61.

22. William Dana Orcutt, "Ben Butler and the 'Stolen spoons,'" *North American Review*, 207 (January 1918): 66–80, cited in Longacre, *Army of Amateurs*, pp. 5–6.

23. Boatner, p. 944.

24. *Ibid.*, p. 109.

25. Benjamin F. Butler, *Butler's Book* (Boston: A. M. Thayer & Company, 1892), pp. 437–447.

26. Richard Hofstadter, *America at 1750: A Social Portrait* (New York: Vintage Books, 1973), pp. 124–126.

27. John M. Blum, Edmund S. Morgan, Willie Lee Rose, Arthur M. Schlesinger, Jr., Kenneth M. Stampp, C. Vann Woodward, *The National Experience*, 3rd ed. (New York: Harcourt Brace Jovanovich, Inc., 1973), p. 202.

28. Hofstadter, pp. 127–128.

29. *Ibid.*, p. 129.

30. Neal R. Peirce and Jerry Hagstrom, *The Book of America: Inside the Fifty States Today* (New York: W. W. Norton & Company, 1983), p. 426.

31. Blum, Morgan, Rose, Schlesinger, Stampp, Woodward, *The National Experience*, p. 199.

32. Nat Turner, *The Confessions of Nat Turner (1800–1831)*, http://odur.let.rug.nl/~usa/D/1826-1850/slavery/confesxxhtm. This is a project for the American Revolution, under copyright of the Department of Humanities Computing.

33. William Styron, *The Confessions of Nat Turner*, Rev. Ed. (New York: Modern Library), 1994.

34. Robert Dale Owen, James McKay, Samuel G. Howe, Commissioners of the American Freedmen's Inquiry Commission, to Edward M. Stanton, Secretary of War, June 30, 1863, *O.R.*, Ser. III, Vol. 3, p. 435.

35. *Ibid.*

36. Noah Andre Trudeau, *Like Men of War: Black Troops in the Civil War, 1862–1865* (Boston: Little, Brown and Company, 1998), p. 112.

37. Cornish, *1861–1865*, pp. 126–129.

38. Assistant Adjutant General E. D. Townsend, General Order No. 143, Washington, D.C., May 22, 1863, O.R. Ser. III, Vol. 3, pp. 215–216.

39. Cornish, pp. 130–131.

40. Robert Dale Owen, James McKay, Saml. G. Howe, Commissioners, to Edward M. Stanton, Secretary of War, June 30, 1863, *O.R.*, Ser. III, Vol. 3, p. 438.

41. *Ibid.*, p. 439.

42. Trudeau, *Like Men of War*, p. 71.

43. Cornish, p. 106.

44. Russell Duncan, ed., *Blue-eyed Child of Fortune* (Athens: University of Georgia Press, 1992), pp. xv, 99.

45. Joseph T. Glatthaar, *Forged in Battle: The Civil War Alliance of Black Soldiers and White Officers* (Baton Rouge: Louisiana State University Press, 2000), pp. 13–14.

46. Cox, p. 11.

47. Duncan, pp. 24–25.
48. Oration by William James in "The Monument to Robert Gould Shaw: Its Inception, Completion, and Unveiling, 1865–1897" (Boston: Houghton Mifflin, 1897), pp. 77–85, cited in Duncan, p. 25.
49. Duncan, p. 321.
50. *Ibid.*, pp. 331–342.
51. Robert Shaw to Mother, Readville, Massachusetts, March 17, 1863, Duncan, p. 288.
52. Robert G. Shaw to Charles Russell Lowell, St. Simon's Island, Georgia, June 20, 1863, Duncan, pp. 355–356; cited in Trudeau, *Like Men of War*, p. 73.
53. Duncan, pp. 331–342.
54. Trudeau, *Like Men of War*, p. 73.
55. Brooks, pp. 33–37; Fox, p. 441.
56. Fox, p. 54.
57. Stevens and Bradford, p. 100.
58. Wild, "Military Career."
59. Trudeau, *Like Men of War*, p. 112.
60. John A. Andrew to Edwin M. Stanton, April 6, 1863, O.R. Ser. III, Vol. 3, pp. 117–118.
61. *Life of John A. Andrew* (Boston: Houghton Mifflin, 1897), p. 96, cited in Stevens and Bradford, p. 100.
62. O.R., Ser. III, Vol. 3, Pt. 3, p. 110, cited in Reid, "Raising the African Brigade," p. 274.
63. Governor John A. Andrew to Secretary of State E. M. Stanton, June 29, 1863, O.R. Ser. III, Vol. 3, pp. 423–424.
64. Robert Shaw to Mother, Readville, Massachusetts, March 17, 1863, Duncan, p. 288.
65. Boatner, p. 44.
66. Stevens and Bradford, p. 100.
67. Robert Shaw to Mother, Readville, Massachusetts, April 7, 1863, Duncan, *p.* 321.
68. Duncan, p. 323.
69. Robert G. Shaw to Lieut. Walter H. Wild, St. Helena Island, S. C., July 7, 1863, original letter, used through courtesy of Helen Stevens Whitlock; also cited in Stevens and Bradford, p. 102.
70. Special Order No. 194, Paymaster General's Office, Washington, D.C., April 29, 1863, original in Brookline Public Library, Brookline, Mass.
71. Kingman, "Memoir," pp. 405–408; *Address of Martin P. Kennard* ([Brookline, Mass]: printed for the town, 1894), 7–8, 13; "The Military Life of Edward A. Wild," Massachusetts MOLLUS Collection; Papers in Regards to Brookline in the Civil War, 1861–1865, Brookline Cadet Records, General E. A. Wild Civil War Papers, Public Library, Brookline, Mass.; Assistant Adjutant General to the War Department, July 76, 1878, Letters Received by the Commission Branch, Records of the Adjutant General's Office, Record Group 94, National Archives, Washington, D.C.; Official Records, Ser. III, Vol. 3, pp. 363, 438; cited in Reid, "Raising the African Brigade," p. 275.
72. Trudeau, *Like Men of War*, p. 113.
73. *Ibid.*
74. E. A. Wild to Calvin Cutter, March 13, 1863, Wild Correspondence, Massachusetts MOLLUS Collection, cited in Reid, "Raising the African Brigade," p. 275.
75. Reid, "Raising the African Brigade, p. 275.
76. Thomas M. Vincent, Assistant Adjutant-General to Col. Edward A. Wild, April 13, 1863, *O.R.*, Ser. III, Vol. 3, p. 122.
77. Wild, "Military Career."
78. Thomas M. Vincent, Assistant Adjutant General, War Department, to Col. Edward A. Wild, April 25, 1863, O.R., Ser III, Vol. 3, p. 167.
79. Reid, "Raising the African Brigade," p. 275.
80. Trudeau, *Like Men of War*, p. 113.
81. Maj. Gen. J. G. Foster, "General Order No. 79," New Bern, May 19, 1863, O.R., Ser. I, Vol. 18, p. 723, cited in Trudeau, *Like Men of War*, p. 113.
82. Briggs, 155.
83. *Ibid.*
84. *Ibid.*
85. Reid, "Raising the African Brigade," p. 25.
86. Ronald Melzack, "Phantom Limbs," *Scientific American* (April 1991); online at www.sciam.com/explorations/0492melzak.html; and also S. Weir Mitchell, "The Case of George Dedlow," *Atlantic Monthly*, 18 (July 1866), pp. 1–11.
87. Ira Berlin, Joseph P. Reidy, and Leslie S. Rowland, eds., *Black Military Experience*, Series 2, of *Freedom: A Documentary History of Emancipation, 1861–1867* (New York: Cambridge University Press, 1982), pp. 9, 75.
88. Trudeau, *Voices of the 55th*, p. 14.
89. Headley, p. 455.
90. *Ibid.*
91. "Troops in the Department of Virginia and North Carolina, Maj. Gen. Benjamin F. Butler, U.S. Army, commanding, April 30, 1864," O.R. Ser. I, Vol. 33, p. 1055.
92. "Organization of the Forces Operating Against Richmond Under Lieut. Gen. Ulysses S. Grant, U.S. Army, on the Morning of May 5, 1864," O.R., Ser. I, Vol. 36, Pt. I, pp. 106–118.
93. William P. Derby, *Bearing Arms in the Twenty-seventh Massachusetts Regiment of Volunteer Infantry during the Civil War, 1861–1865* (Boston: Wright and Potter Printing Co., 1883), p. 168–169, cited in Reid, "Raising the African Brigade," p. 273.
94. Governor Andrew to Major General Foster, May 14, 1863, copy in Edward Wild Papers, Military History Institute, Carlisle, Pa.; also

cited in Reid, "General Edward A Wild and Civil War Discrimination," pp.15–16.

95. "Appointment of Col. Edward A. Wild," Personnel File, Record Group 94, National Archives, Washington, D.C., and "Roster, First North Carolina African Volunteers," Massachusetts MOLLUS Collection, both cited in Reid, "Raising the African Brigade," p. 276.

96. Colonel Charles E. Griswold to General E. A. Wild, Boston, May 13, 1863, Edward A. Wild Papers, MHI.

97. G. M. Lincoln to General [Wild], Boston, May 27, 1863, Edward A. Wild Papers, MHI.

98. Stevens and Bradford, p. 102.

99. Glatthaar, *Forged in Battle*, pp. 240–241; George W. Williams, *A History of the Negro Troops in the War of the Rebellion: 1861–1865* (New York: Harper and Brothers, 1888), pp. 207–208, cited in Reid, "Raising the African Brigade," p. 277.

100. Rochester, New York *North Star,* June 8, 1849; and *Frederick Douglass' Papers* (Rochester, N.Y.), September 22, 1854, cited in Reid, "Raising the African Brigade," pp. 277–278.

101. Assistant Surgeon John De Grasse, Proceedings of General Court-Martial, Records of the Judge Advocate General's Office, Record Group 153, National Archives, Washington, D.C.; Reid, "Raising the African Brigade," p. 278.

102. John N. Mars, Compiled Military Service Records, Record Group 94, National Archives, Washington, D.C., cited in Reid, "Raising the African Brigade," p. 278.

103. Reid, "Raising the African Brigade," p. 278.

104. Derby, *Bearing Arms in the Twenty-seventh Massachusetts,*" p. 192, cited in Reid, "Raising the African Brigade," p. 266.

105. Henry A. Clapp to "Dear Willie," February 27, 1863; Henry A. Clapp to "Dear Father," March 1, 1863; Henry A. Clapp to "Dear Mother," March 14, 1863; Henry A. Clapp to Helen Clapp, March 20, 1863, and Henry A. Clapp to Louise Clapp, March 26, 1863, in Henry A. Clapp Letter Book, Collections Branch, Tryon Palace Historical Sites and Gardens, New Bern, cited in Reid, "Raising the African Brigade," p. 269.

106. Philadelphia, Pa., *Christian Recorder,* May 19, 1863, cited in Trudeau, p. 114.

107. Wild, "Military Career."

108. *Ibid.*

109. Edward W. Kinsley was "well connected in Boston, especially with those who shared his humanitarian interests." He was concerned about the "plight of the free Negro in the South during both the Civil War and Reconstruction." He solicited funds for societies aiding the freed Negroes, lobbying for Congressional legislation for equal pay for Negro soldiers. He and Governor John Andrew worked to get equal and retroactive pay for the Negro volunteers in the U.S. Army. Kinsley was involved in various projects for Negroes in New Bern, N.C.

110. Edward A. Wild to Edward Kinsley, November 30, 1863, Edward Wilkinson Kinsley Papers, Duke University, Durham, North Carolina.

111. John E. Williams, "Letter 33," June 22, 1863, published in the *Christian Recorder,* July 4, 1863, reproduced in Edwin S. Redkey, ed., *A Grand Army of Black Men: Letters from African-American Soldiers in the Union Army, 1861–1865* (New York: Cambridge University Press, 1992, rpt. 1993), p. 91.

112. Wild, "Military Career."

113. "Abstract from return of the Department of North Carolina (or Eighteenth Army Corps), Maj. Gen. John G. Foster, U.S. Army, commanding, for July 10, 1863: headquarters, New Bern, N.C.," *O.R.*, Ser. I, Vol. 27, Pt. III, p. 645.

114. Edward A. Wild to Capt. Josiah C. White, 1st Reg., N.C. Col. Vols., New Bern, June 17, 1863, Edward A. Wild Papers, MHI.

115. Edward A. Wild to Edward W. Kinsley, July 28, 1863, Kinsley Papers, Duke Manuscript Collection, Duke University, Durham, N.C.; also cited in Richard Reid, "General Edward A. Wild and Civil War Discrimination," *Historical Journal of Massachusetts* 13 (January 1985): 16.

116. Edward A. Wild to Edward W. Kinsley, July 28, 1863, Kinsley Papers, Duke Manuscript Collection, Duke University, Durham, N.C.

117. F. E. Wild to Mr. Kinsley, November 3, 1863, Edward W. Kinsley Papers, Duke University, Durham, North Carolina.

118. Major George I. Stearns to Edwin M. Stanton, August 17, 1863, *O.R.*, Ser. III, Vol. 3, p. 684.

119. Horace James, *Annual Report of the Superintendent of Negro Affairs in North Carolina 1864*, pp. 21–34, cited in W. Buck Yearns and John G. Barrett, *North Carolina Civil War Documentary* (Chapel Hill: University of North Carolina Press, 1980), pp. 50–51.

120. *Ibid.*

121. D. R. Grigs, et al., "Circular" 1864, original in Brookline Public Library, Brookline, Massachusetts.

Chapter V

1. Freddie Fields, producer, Tri-Star Pictures, *Glory*, Burbank, Calif.: RCA/Columbia

Pictures Home Video, 1990. The video, seen nationwide on television, starred Matthew Broderick, Denzel Washington, Cary Elwes, and Morgan Freeman.

2. Robert N. Rosen, *A Short History of Charleston*, 2nd ed. (Columbia: University of South Carolina Press, 1992), p. 9.

3. Boatner, p. 70.

4. Arthur M. Wilcox, "Blockade Strangled the South," Arthur M. Wilcox and Warren Ripley, *The Civil War at Charleston*, 21st edition, (Charleston, S.C.: The Post and Courier, 2000), pp. 28–29.

5. Boatner, p. 55.

6. Robert E. Lee to Jefferson Davis, in A. L. Long, *Memoirs of Robert E. Lee: His Military and Personal History Embracing a Large Amount of Information Hitherto Unpublished* (New York: J. M. Stoddart & Co., 1886), p. 570.

7. Trudeau, *Like Men of War*, footnote, p. 71. A fort is defended on all sides, and Battery Wagner had only a "low-lying breastwork" for a rear wall.

8. Quincy A. Gillmore, "The Army Before Charleston in 1865," *Battles and Leaders of the Civil War*, Vol. IV, Robert U. Johnson and Clarence C. Buel, eds. (1887, rpt. Secacus, N.J.: Castle, 1982) p. 55.

9. Steven D. Smith, *Whom We Would Never More See: History and Archaeology Recover the Lives and Deaths of African American Civil War Soldiers on Folly Island, South Carolina* (Columbia: South Carolina Department of Archives and History, 1993), pp. 2–5.

10. Ellison Capers, "South Carolina," Vol. V in Clement Evans, *Confederate Military History* (Atlanta: Confederate Publishing Co., 1899), pp. 194–195, 223.

11. Capers, p. 224.

12. *Ibid.*, p. 226.

13. *Ibid.*, pp. 226–227.

14. Arthur P. Ford and Marion Johnstone Ford, *Life in the Confederate Army and Some Experiences and Sketches* (New York: Neale Publishing Company, 1905), p. 18.

15. Major General J. G. Foster to Brig.-Gen. Q. A. Gillmore, July 29, 1863, *O.R.*, Ser. I, Vol. 28, Pt. II, p. 30.

16. Frances H. Casstevens, *Clingman's Brigade in the Confederacy, 1862–1865* (Jefferson, N.C.: McFarland, 2002), pp. 35–45; Trudeau, *Like Men of War*, p. 83.

17. Trudeau, *Like Men of War*, p. 80.

18. *Ibid.*, pp. 82–83.

19. Fox, *Regimental Losses in the Civil War*, p. 23.

20. *Ibid.*, p. 54.

21. Colonel E. N. Hallowell, to Lt. Col. E. W. Smith, December 13, 1863. *O.R.*, Ser. II, Vol. 6, p. 775.

22. Trudeau, *Like Men of War*, p. 85–87.

23. Charles Bowditch, "War Letters of Charles P. Bowditch, Capt. 55th Mass. Volunteers, 1686–1864," *Massachusetts Historical Society Proceedings*, Vol. 57, 1923/24, p. 424.

24. Charles Bowditch, Letter to Dear Mother, August 10, 1863, in "War Letters of Charles P. Bowditch, Capt. 55th Mass. Volunteers, 1686–1864," pp. 423–424.

25. Charles Barnard Fox, *Record of the Service of the Fifty-Fifth Regiment of Massachusetts Volunteer Infantry* (Cambridge: Press of John Wilson and Son, 1868), p. 9.

26. *Ibid.*, pp. 9–10.

27. Fox, *Record of the Service of the Fifty-Fifth Regiment of Massachusetts Volunteer Infantry*, pp. 10–11.

28. Wild, "Military Career;" "Troops in the Department of the South, Brig. Gen. Quincy A. Gillmore, U.S. Army, commanding, August 31, 1863: Morris Island," *O.R.*, Ser. I, Vol. 28, Pt. II, pp. 74–75.

29. Cornish, *The Sable Arm: Black Troops in the Union Army, 1861–1865*, p. 244; Stevens and Bradford, p. 104.

30. Fox, *Record of the Service of the 55th Regiment of Massachusetts Volunteer Infantry*, p. 6, cited in Smith, *Whom We Would Never More See*, p. 8.

31. *Ibid.*, p. 7.

32. *Ibid.*, p. 9.

33. Charles Bowditch, Letter to My Dear Father, Camp Near New Bern, N.C., July 29, 1863, in "War Letters of Charles P. Bowditch, Capt. 55th Mass. Volunteers, 1686–1864," Massachusetts *Historical Society Proceedings*, Vol. 57, 1923/24, pp. 423–424.

34. Smith, *Whom We Would Never More See*, p. 8.

35. Frederick H. Dyer, *A Compendium of the War of the Rebellion*, Vol. 1 (New York: Thomas Yoseloff, 1959), pp. 199–200.

36. Smith, *Whom We Would Never More See*, p. 9.

37. Glatthaar, *Forged in Battle*, p. 13.

38. The History of a Gallant Regiment," Hartford *Evening Press*, March 5, 1864, reprinted in *New England Loyal Publication Society*, No. 175, March 10, 1864.

39. Horace James, *Annual Report of the Superintendent of Negro Affairs in North Carolina, 1864*, pp. 21–34, cited in W. Buck Yearns and John G. Barrett, *North Carolina Civil War Documentary*, pp. 50–51.

40. Frederick H. Dyer, *A Compendium of the War of the Rebellion*, Vol. 1 (New York: Thomas Yoseloff, 1959), pp. 199–200.

41. Dyer, *A Compendium of the War of the Rebellion*, Vol. 1, pp. 199–200.

42. Headley, "Fifty-Fifth Regiment," p. 455.

43. Smith, *Whom We Would Never More See*, p. 9.
44. *Ibid.*, p. 20.
45. *Ibid.*, p. 9.
46. Headley, "Fifty-Fifth Regiment," p. 455.
47. *Ibid.*, p. 456.
48. Noah Andrew Trudeau, Voices *of the 55th: Letters from the 55th Massachusetts Volunteers, 1861–1865* (Dayton, Ohio: Morningside House, Inc., 1998), p. 15.
49. Stevens and Bradford, p. 104.
50. Edward A. Wild to Capt. S. L. McHenry, Folly Island, S.C., August 9, 1863, Record Group 94, NA.
51. "Abstract from 'Record of Events' on the several returns of the Department of the South, for August, 1863." *O.R.*, Ser. I, Vol. 28, Pt. II, p. 73.
52. Boatner, p. 880.
53. Bowditch, "War Letters of Charles P. Bowditch, Capt. 55th Mass. Volunteers, 1686–1864," *Massachusetts Historical Society Proceedings*, Vol. 57, 1923/24, p. 424.
54. Brig. Gen. I. Vogdes, "Announcement," Folly Island, August 6, 1863, Edward A. Wild Papers, MHI.
55. Capt. S. L. McHenry to Brig. Gen. Wild, Folly Island, 10:20 A.M., August 6, 1863, File 2162, Edward A. Wild Papers, MHI.
56. S. L. McHenry, Capt. and A.A.G., to Brig. Gen. Wild, Folly Island, 1:10 P.M., August 6, 1863, Edward A. Wild Papers, MHI.
57. S. L. McHenry, Capt. and A.A.G., to Brig. Gen. Wild, Folly Island, August 7, 1863, Edward A. Wild Papers, MHI.
58. Edward A. Wild to Capt. S. L. McHenry, Folly Island, S.C., August 9, 1863, Record Group 94, NA.
59. *Ibid.*
60. Brig. Gen. I. Vogdes, "Announcement," Folly Island, August 6, 1863, Edward A. Wild Papers, MHI.
61. Edward A. Wild to Capt. S. L. McHenry, Folly Island, S.C., August 9, 1863, Record Group 94, NA.
62. S. L. McHenry to Brig. Gen. Wild, Folly Island, August 9, 1863, Edward A. Wild Papers, MHI.
63. Edward A. Wild to Capt. S. L. McHenry, Folly Island, August 10, 1863, Edward A. Wild Papers, MHI.
64. *Ibid.*
65. Major General Q. A. Gillmore to Major General Peck, September 22, 1863, *O.R.*, Ser. I, Vol. 28, Pt. II, p. 96.
66. Bowditch to Dear Father, Folly Island, S. C., Sept. 23, 1863, "War Letters of Charles P. Bowditch, Capt. 55th Mass. Volunteers, 1686–1864," *Massachusetts Historical Society Proceedings*, Vol. 57, 1923/24, p. 447.
67. Major General Q. A. Gillmore to Major General Peck, September 22, 1863, *O.R.*, Ser. I, Vol. 28, Pt. II, p. 96.
68. Lt. Col. Alfred S. Hartwell to Brig. Gen. E. A. Wild, Headquarters 55th Regt. Mass. Infantry, October 1863, Edward A. Wild Papers, MHI.
69. Edward A. Wild to Lt. Col. Hartwell, October 4, 1863, File 2166, Edward A. Wild Papers, MHI.
70. Smith, *Whom We Would Never More See*, p. 10.
71. Letter from Capt. Walter H. Wild to sister, Laura Phipps, August 21, 1863, in Stevens and Bradford, pp. 104–106.
72. Stevens and Bradford, p. 105.
73. Ira Berlin, ed., *Freedom: A Documentary History of Emancipation 1861–1867*, Series II, *The Black Military Experience* (Cambridge: Cambridge University Press, 1982), p. 633, cited in Smith, *Whom We Would Never More See*, p. 37.
74. Letter of Lt. Frank Heimer, in James H. McKee, *Back "In War Times," A History of the 144th Regiment, New York Volunteers* (New York: H. E. Bailey, 1903), pp. 132–134, cited in Smith, *Whom We Would Never More See*, p. 38–39.
75. Smith, *Whom We Would No More See*, p. 30, cited in Trudeau, *Voices of the 55th*, p. 17.
76. Trudeau, *Voices of the 55th*, p. 16.
77. Brian Pohanka, "Morris Island Housing Development Project Proposal: December 1999 message from historian Brian Pohanka." http://www.geocities.com/Athens/Aegean/6732/Archives/morris.html.
78. Burt Green Wilder, Diary. Typed Manuscript, Wilder Collection, Division of Rare & Manuscript Collections, Carl A. Krock Library, Cornell University Library, Ithaca, New York, p. 25, cited in Smith, *Whom We Would Never More See*, p. 28.
79. Smith, *Whom We Would Never More See*, p. 29.
80. A. R. Barlow, *Company G: A Record of Services of One Company of the 157th N. Y. Volunteers in the War of the Rebellion* (Syracuse, N.Y.: A. W. Hall, 1899), p. 158, cited in Smith, *Whom We Would Never More See*, pp. 30–31.
81. See picture in Smith, *Whom We Would Never More See*, p. 31.
82. Smith, pp. 31–32.
83. Fox, *Record of the 55th Regiment of Massachusetts Volunteer Infantry*, p. 11, cited in Smith, *Whom We Would Never More See*, p. 29.
84. Trudeau, *Voices of the 55th*, p. 16.
85. Trudeau, *Like Men of War*, p. 114.
86. Bowditch, Folly Island, S.C., Sept. 15, 1863, "War Letters of Charles P. Bowditch, Capt. 55th Mass. Volunteers, 1686–1864," *Massachusetts Historical Society Proceedings*, Vol. 57, 1923/24, pp. 444–445.
87. Bowditch to Dear Mother, Folly Island,

S.C., Sept. 19, 1863, "War Letters of Charles P. Bowditch, Capt. 55th Mass. Volunteers, 1686–1864," *Massachusetts Historical Society Proceedings*, Vol. 57, 1923/24, p. 446.

88. "Major Brooks' Journal of Engineer Operations Executed Under His Direction on Morris Island, Between July 12, and September 7, 1863, Major T. S. Brooks to Major General Q. A. Gillmore," September 27, 1863, O.R., Ser. I, Vol. 28, Pt. I, p. 288.

89. *Ibid.*, p. 290.

90. Boatner, p. 320.

91. "Major Brooks' Journal of Engineer Operations Executed Under His Direction on Morris Island, Between July 12, and September 7, 1863, Major T. S. Brooks to Major General Q. A. Gillmore," September 27, 1863, O.R., Ser. I, Vol. 28, Pt. I, p. 298.

92. Samuel A. Valentine, 54th Massachusetts, Published Letter (*Christian Recorder*, August 27, 1864), cited in Smith, *Whom We Would Never More See*, p. 37.

93. "Major Brooks' Journal of Engineer Operations Executed Under His Direction on Morris Island, Between July 12, and September 7, 1863, Major T. S. Brooks to Major General Q. A. Gillmore, September 27, 1863," O.R., Ser. I, Vol. 28, Pt. I, p. 328.

94. Fox, *Record of the 55th Regiment of Massachusetts Volunteer Infantry*, p. 12, cited in Smith, *Whom We Would Never More See*, p. 30.

95. Smith, *Whom We Would No More See*, p. 30, cited in Trudeau, *Voices from the 55th*, p. 17.

96. Smith, p. 10.

97. Fox, *Record of the 55th Regiment of Massachusetts Volunteer Infantry*, p. 12, cited in Smith, *Whom We Would Never More See*, p. 30.

98. "The History of a Gallant Regiment," Hartford *Evening Press*, March 5, 1864, reprinted in *New England Loyal Publication Society*, No. 175, March 10, 1864.

99. "The History of a Gallant Regiment," Hartford *Evening Press*, March 5, 1864, reprinted in *New England Loyal Publication Society*, No. 175, March 10, 1864.

100. "Major Brooks' Journal of Engineer Operations Executed Under His Direction on Morris Island, Between July 12, and September 7, 1863, Major T. S. Brooks to Major General Q. A. Gillmore," September 27, 1863, O.R., Ser. I, Vol. 28, Pt. I, p. 296.

101. *Ibid.*, p. 297.

102. Henry F. Jackson and Thomas F. O'Donnell, eds. *Back Home in Oneida: Hermon Clarke and His Letters* (Syracuse, N.Y.: Syracuse University Press, 1965), p. 102, cited in Smith, *Whom We Would Never More See*, p. 28.

103. Fitzgerald Ross, *Cities and Camps of Confederate States*, Richard B. Harwell, ed. (1865; rpt. Urbane, Illinois: University of Illinois Press, 1958), p. 99.

104. Jackson and O'Donnell, *Back Home in Oneida*, p. 115, cited in Smith, *Whom We Would Never More See*, p. 30.

105. Bowditch, "War Letters of Charles P. Bowditch, Capt. 55th Mass. Volunteers, 1686–1864," *Massachusetts Historical Society Proceedings*, Vol. 57, 1923/24, p. 439.

106. Smith, *Whom We Would Never More See*, p. 30.

107. Capt. Walter H. Wild to Laura Phipps, Folly Island, August 21, 1863, Stevens and Bradford, p. 106.

108. Stevens and Bradford, p. 106.

109. Wild, "Military Career."

110. Glatthaar *Forged in Battle*, p. 185.

111. "The History of a Gallant Regiment," Hartford *Evening Press*, March 5, 1864, reprinted in *New England Loyal Publication Society*, No. 175, March 10, 1864.

112. Major Stearns to Edwin Stanton, August 17, 1863, *O.R.*, Ser. III, Vol. III, p. 684.

113. Ira Berlin, ed., Freedom: *A Documentary History of Emancipation 1861–1867*, Series II, *The Black Military Experience*, pp. 401–402, cited in Smith, *Whom We Would Never More See*, p. 36.

114. Smith, *Whom We Would Never More See*, p. 36. For more information on the pay dispute, see Berlin, pp. 362–368.

115. Major T. S. Brooks to Major General Q. A. Gillmore, September 27, 1863, September 27, 1863, *O.R.*, Ser. I, Vol. 28, Pt. I, pp. 268–269.

116. "Major Brooks' Journal of Engineer Operations Executed Under His Direction on Morris Island, Between July 12, and September 7, 1863, Major T. S. Brooks to Major General Q. A. Gillmore, September 27, 1863," O.R., Ser. I, Vol. 28, Pt. I, p. 285.

117. Note No. 19, "Colored Troops for Work," Major T. B. Brooks, *O.R.*, Ser. I, Vol. 28, Pt. I, p. 328.

118. Cornish, p. 246.

119. *Ibid.*

120. "Major Brooks' Journal of Engineer Operations Executed Under His Direction on Morris Island, Between July 12, and September 7, 1863, Major T. S. Brooks to Major General Q. A. Gillmore, September 27, 1863," O.R., Ser. I, Vol. 28, Pt. I, p. 281.

121. C. W. Foster, Assistant Adjutant General of Volunteers, to E. M. Stanton, Secretary of War, October 31, 1863, *O.R.*, Ser. III, Vol. 3, p. 1111–1114.

122. Robert Dale Owen, James McKay, Saml. G. Howe, Commissioners, to Edward M. Stanton, Secretary of War, June 30, 1863, *O.R.*, Ser. III, Vol. 3, p. 438.

123. Edward A. Wild to Adjutant General, War Department, from Headquarters, African

Brigade, Folly Island, S.C., September 1, 1863, War Department papers, NA.

124. Edward A. Wild, Brig. Gen. Vols. To Sergt. George H. Willis, Folly Island, S.C., October 1st, 1863, in George Willis Papers, Boston University, Special Collections, Boston, Massachusetts.

125. Assistant Adjutant-General Benj. B. Foster, General Orders, No. 12, September 10, 1863, *O.R.*, Ser. I, Vol. 29, Pt. II, p. 166.

126. Edward A. Wild to Maj. Gen. J. G. Foster, Commanding Department of N.C. and Virginia, Folly Island, S.C., September 22, 1863, Record Group 94, NA.

127. Trudeau, *Voices of the 55th*, p. 17. See also National Archives, Washington, D.C.: Compiled Service Records, 55th Massachusetts, Field and Staff Record of Events.

128. Captain and Assistant Adjutant General S. L. McHenry to Col. S. M. Alford, October 12, 1863, *O.R.*, Ser. I, Vol. 28, Pt. II, p. 106.

129. Q. A. Gillmore to General G. T. Beauregard, Morris Island, August 21, 1863, *O.R.*, Ser. I, Vol. 28, Pt. II, p. 57.

130. Wild, "Military Career."
131. *Ibid.*
132. *Ibid.*

Chapter VI

1. Wild, "Military Career."
2. Boatner, p. 45.
3. Special Order No. 105, Southard Hoffman, Assistant Adjutant General, November 2, 1863, *O. R.*, Ser. I, Vol. 29, Pt. II, p. 412.
4. Wild, "Military Career."
5. "Statement of colored troops in the service of the United States October 31, 1863, compiled from the latest official reports," *O.R.*, Ser. III, Vol. 3, p. 115.
6. Philadelphia, Pa., *Christian Recorder*, May 19, 1863, cited in Trudeau, *Like Men of War*, p. 114.
7. Ervin L. Jordan, Jr., *Black Confederates and Afro-Yankees in Civil War Virginia* (Charlottesville: University Press of Virginia, 1995), pp. 82–83.
8. Wild, "Military Career."
9. *Ibid.*
10. W. Buck Yearns and John G. Barrett, eds., *North Carolina Civil War Documentary* (Chapel Hill: University of North Carolina Press, 1980), pp. 43–44.
11. Stevens and Bradford, p. 113.
12. "Reports of Brig. Edward A. Wild, U.S. Army, commanding the expedition," December 21, 1863, Enclosure, A, and Enclosure B, *O.R.*, Series I, Vol. 29, Pt. I, p. 917.
13. *Ibid.*
14. E. D. Townsend, Assistant Adjutant General, "Special Orders No. 399," Washington, D.C., December 17, 1862, *O.R.*, Ser. III, Vol. 2, p. 951.
15. "Reports of Brig. Gen. Edward A. Wild, U.S. Army, commanding expedition," December 28, 1863, *O.R.*, Ser. I, Vol. 29, Pt. I, pp. 911–917.
16. *Ibid.*, p. 917.
17. *Ibid.*
18. James M. Matthews, ed. "An act to organize bands of Partisan Rangers," Chapter 63, *Public Laws of the Confederate States of America, Passed at the First Session of the First Congress; 1862, Carefully collated with the Original at Richmond* (Richmond: R. M. Smith, Printer to Congress, 1862), p. 48.
19. Bertil Haggman, "Confederate Irregular Warfare, 1861–1865: Partisan Rangers Units and Guerrilla commands," online site at http://hem.passagen.se/csa01/? noframe.
20. George M. Rose, "Sixty-Sixth Regiment," in Walter Clark, ed., *Histories of the Several Regiments and Battalions from North Carolina in the Great War 1861–'65*, Vol. III (Goldsboro, N.C.: Nash Brothers, 1901), pp. 685–686. Hereinafter cited as *Histories of the Several Regiments*.
21. J. W. Evans, "Sixty-Eighth Regiment," in Walter Clark, ed. *Histories of the Several Regiments*, Vol. III, pp. 713–714.
22. Louis Manarin, ed., *North Carolina Troops, 1861–1865: A Roster*, Vol. IV (Raleigh, N.C.: Department of Archives and History, 1973), p. 521.
23. "Reports of Brig. Gen. Edward A. Wild, U.S. Army, commanding expedition," December 28, 1863, *O.R.*, Ser. I, Vol. 29, Pt. I, pp. 911–917.
24. Col. Charles C. Dodge, First New York Mounted Rifles, to Brig. Gen. E. L. Viele, Military Governor of Norfolk, May 31, 1862, *O.R.*, Ser. I, Vol. LI, Pt. 1, pp. 96–98.
25. *Ibid.*
26. *Ibid.*
27. Susan B. Felker, "The Great Dismal Swamp." Online edition at http://www.vmnh.org/swmpsusn.htm.
28. The Federal Writers' Project of the Federal Works Agency, Work Projects Administration for the State of North Carolina, *North Carolina: The WPA Guide to the Old North State* (Chapel Hill: University of North Carolina Press, 1938, rpt. 1988, Columbia: University of South Carolina Press), pp. 276.
29. Porte Crayon [David Hunter Strother], "Dismal Swamp," *Harper's New Monthly Magazine* 13 (September 1856), pp. 441–455. Also cited in Jesse F. Pugh and Frank T. Williams, *The Hotel*

in the Great Dismal Swamp (Richmond, Virginia: Garrett & Massie, Inc., 1964), p. 10.

30. The Federal Writers' Project of the Federal Works Agency, Work Projects Administration for the State of North Carolina, *North Carolina: The WPA Guide to the Old North State*, p. 276.

31. Calvin D. Cowles, compl. *The Official Military Atlas of the Civil War*, plates CXXXVIII and XXVI.

32. Nathaniel H. Bishop, *"From Norfolk to Cape Hatteras," Voyage of the Paper Canoe: A Geographical Journal of 2500 miles from Quebec to the Gulf of Mexico, During the Years 1874–5* (Boston: Lee and Shepard, Publishers, 1878). Online version at: http://eldred.ne.mediaone.net/nhb/paperc/c09.html.

33. Bill Sharp, "Currituck," *A New Geography of North Carolina*, Vol. III (Raleigh: Edwards & Broughton Co., 1961), p. 11.

34. "Report of Maj. Gen. Ambrose E. Burnside, U.S. Army, New Bern, N.C., April 17, 1862, *O.R.*, Ser. I, Vol. 9, p. 271. Also cited in Barrett, *The Civil War in North Carolina*, p. 110–111.

35. Sandburg, *Abraham Lincoln: The War Years*, III, p. 65.

36. Witt, *Wild in North Carolina*, p. 4.

37. Benjamin F. Butler, *Butler's Book* (Boston: A. M. Thayer & Co., Book Publishers, 1892), pp. 617–618.

38. Wild's A.A.G., Hiram W. Allen, to Col. Alonzo Draper, November 17, 1863, NA, Record Group 393, cited in Witt, *Wild in North Carolina*, p. 49.

39. Tewksbury, "Gen. Butler's Department: Invasion of North Carolina by Gen. Wild's Colored Battalions," *New York Times*, Saturday, 9 January 1864.

40. *Ibid.*

41. Barrett, p. 177. See also *Rebellion Record*, VIII, 299–300.

42. William R. Trotter, *Ironclads and Columbiads* (Winston-Salem, N.C.: John F. Blair, Publisher, 1898), pp. 219–220.

43. Dick Nolan, *Benjamin Franklin Butler: The Damnedest Yankee* (Novato, Calif.: Presidio Press, 1991), pp. 242–242.

44. United States War Department, *Official Army Register of the Volunteer Force of the United States Army* (Washington, D.C.: The Adjutant General, 1867), Vol. 8, cited in J. V. Witt, *Wild in North Carolina* (Springfield, Virginia: privately published, 1993), p. 6, footnote 6; Trudeau, *Like Men of War*, p. 115.

45. Trudeau, *Voices of the 55th: Letters from the 55th Massachusetts Volunteers, 1861–1865*, p. 17; Bennie J. McRae, Jr., "Fifty-Fifth Massachusetts Infantry Regiment (African Descent), online at www.cozx.net/people/lwf/55mass.htm; "Union Regimental Histories: Massachusetts," The Civil War Archive, online at www.civilwararchive.com/Unreghst/unmainf5.htm, compiled from Frederick H. Dyer, *A Compendium of the War of the Rebellion,"* Part 3.

46. Edward A. Wild to Capt. George H. Johnston, Norfolk, Va., November 23, 1863, War Department files, NA.

47. Edwin S. Redkey, ed., *A Grand Army of Black Men: Letters from African American Soldiers in the Union Army, 1861–1865* (New York: Cambridge University Press), 1992, p. 84.

48. Butler, p. 618.

49. Tewksbury, "Gen. Butler's Department: Invasion of North Carolina by Gen. Wild's Colored Battalions," *New York Times*, Saturday, 9 January 1864.

50. Trotter, p. 220.

51. Bill Sharp, "Pasquotank," *A New Geography of North Carolina*, Vol. I (Raleigh, North Carolina: Edwards & Broughton Co., 1954), p. 362.

52. Bill Sharp, "Camden," *A New Geography of North Carolina*, Vol. IV (Raleigh, North Carolina: Edwards & Broughton Co., 1965), p. 1744.

53. Tewksbury, "Gen. Butler's Department: Invasion of North Carolina by Gen. Wild's Colored Battalions," *New York Times*, Saturday, 9 January 1864.

54. "Reports of Brig. Gen. Edward A. Wild, U.S. Army, commanding expedition," December 28, 1863, *O.R.*, Ser. I, Vol. 29, Pt. I, pp. 911–917.

55. Trotter, p. 220.

56. "Reports of Brig. Gen. Edward A. Wild, U.S. Army, commanding expedition," December 28, 1863, *O.R.*, Ser. I, Vol. 29, Pt. I, pp. 911–917.

57. Brig. Gen. Edward A. Wild to Brig. Gen. James Barnes, Elizabeth City, North Carolina, December 12, 1863, *O.R.*, Ser. I, Vol. 29, Pt. II, p. 562, cited in Richard Reid, "General Edward A. Wild and Civil War Discrimination," *Historical Journal of Massachusetts* 13 (January, 1985): 14.

58. Reid, "General Edward A. Wild and Civil War Discrimination," *Historical Journal of Massachusetts* 13 (January, 1985): 14.

59. Tewksbury, "Gen. Butler's Department: Invasion of North Carolina by Gen. Wild's Colored Battalions," *New York Times*, Saturday, 9 January 1864.

60. Boatner, p. 330.

61. Brigadier General Edward Wild to Brigadier General Getty, Norfolk, Va., December 4, 1863, *O.R.*, Ser. I, Vol. 29, Pt. II, p. 542.

62. Major R. S. Davis to Brig. Gen. E. A. Wild, Fortress Monroe, Va., December 12, 1863, Edward A. Wild Papers, MHI.

63. Brigadier General Edward A. Wild to Brigadier General Barnes, December 12, 1863, *O.R.*, Ser I., Vol. 29, Pt. II, p. 562.

64. Brigadier General George W. Getty to Brigadier General Wild, December 6, 1863, *O.R.*, Ser. I, Vol. 29, Pt. II, p. 543.
65. Benjamin F. Butler, "General Order No. 46," December 5, 1863, *O.R.*, Ser. III, Vol. 3, p. 1139.
66. *Ibid.*
67. Benjamin F. Butler, "General Order No. 46," December 5, 1863, *O.R.*, Ser. III, Vol. 3, p. 1144.
68. Tewksbury, "Gen. Butler's Department: Invasion of North Carolina by Gen. Wild's Colored Battalions," *New York Times*, Saturday, 9 January 1864.
69. Brigadier General Edward A. Wild to Brigadier General Barnes, Elizabeth City, Sunday, December 13, 1864, cited by Brigadier General James Barnes to Colonel J. W. Shaffer, on December 16, 1863, *O.R.*, Ser. I, Vol. 29, Pt. II, p. 564.
70. *Ibid.*
71. Tewksbury, "Gen. Butler's Department: Invasion of North Carolina by Gen. Wild's Colored Battalions," *New York Times*, 9 January 1864.
72. Trotter, p. 220.
73. Bill Sharp, "Pasquotank," *A New Geography of North Carolina*, Vol. I (Raleigh, North Carolina: Edwards & Broughton Co., 1954), p. 362.
74. Tewksbury, "Gen. Butler's Department: Invasion of North Carolina by Gen. Wild's Colored Battalions," *New York Times*, Saturday, 9 January 1864.
75. Selby Daniels and T. H. Pearce, eds., *The Diary of Captain Henry A. Chambers* (Wendell, N.C.: Broadfoot's Bookmark, 1983), pp. 182–183, cited in Trotter, p. 221.
76. *Ibid.*
77. "Reports of Brig. Gen. Edward A. Wild, U.S. Army, commanding expedition," December 28, 1863, *O.R.*, Ser. I, Vol. 29, Pt. I, pp. 911–917.
78. J. W. Evans, "Sixty-Eighth Regiment," Walter Clark, ed. *Histories of the Several Regiments*, Vol. III, p. 713.
79. Tewksbury, *New York Times*, 9 January 1864, cited in Witt, p. 12.
80. Bill Sharpe, "Camden," *A New Geography of North Carolina*, Vol. IV, p. 1742.
81. Beth Gilbert Crabtree and James W. Patton, eds. *Journal of a Secesh Lady: The Diary of Catherine Ann Devereux Edmondston, 1860–1866* (Raleigh: Department of Archives and History, 1979), pp. 509–510. Hereinafter cited as *Edmondston diary.*
82. Crabtree, *Edmondston diary*, p. 10; J. W. Evans, "Sixty-Eighth Regiment," Walter Clark, ed., *Histories of the Several Regiments*, Vol. III, p. 713.
83. Affidavit of W. J. Munden, cited in W. N. H. Smith, "Report of the special committee to inquire into certain outrages of the enemy," *O.R.*, Ser. II, Vol. 6, p. 1129.
84. *Ibid.*
85. W. N. H. Smith, "Report of the special committee to inquire into certain outrages of the enemy," *O.R.*, Ser. II, Vol. 6, p. 1128.
86. An e-mail from North Carolina State Archivist Jason Tomberlin stated: "According to the Official Records, Daniel Bright was actually in the 62nd Georgia, Company L, although he is not listed in the compiled records of that unit, in Col. Joel Griffin's command."
87. W. N. H. Smith, "Report of the special committee to inquire into certain outrages of the enemy," *O.R.*, Ser. II, Vol. 6, p. 1128.
88. Crabtree, *Edmondston diary*, p. 510.
89. Colonel Joel R. Griffin, White Mills, on Dismal Swamp, December 19, 1863, to Major General Pickett, *O.R.*, Ser. I, Vol. 29, Pt. II, p. 883.
90. Affidavit of William J. Munden, *O.R.*, Ser. II, Vol. 6, pp. 1128–1129.
91. Sharpe, "Camden," *A New Geography of North Carolina*, Vol. IV, p. 1742.
92. Affidavit of William J. Munden, February 10, 1864, *O.R.*, Ser. II, Vol. 6, pp. 1129–30.
93. Tewksbury, *New York Times*, 9 Jan. 1864; cited in Witt, pp. 16–17.
94. *Ibid.*
95. Original document from Edward A. Wild to John T. Elliott, Captain of Guerrillas, Elizabeth City, December 17, 1863, in Wild Papers, Southern Historical Collection, UNC-CH; cited in W. N. H. Smith, "Report of the special committee to inquire into certain outrages of the enemy," *O.R.*, Ser. II, Vol. 6, p. 1128.
96. Lieutenant Colonel Giles W. Shurtleff, second in command of the 5th USCT, was captured in 1861, and held prisoner at Charleston, Salisbury, and Richmond before being exchanged a year later. He was assigned to Major General Orlando Wilcox's staff, and fought at Fredericksburg, Va. *The Oberlin Review*, May 19, 1904, p. 665, and Giles W. Shurtleff, "Reminiscence of Army Life," unpublished manuscript, cited in Witt, pp. 17–19.
97. Tewksbury, *New York Times*, 9 January 1864; in Witt, pp. 17–18.
98. *Ibid.*
99. W. N. H. Smith, Chairman, "Report of the special committee to inquire into certain outrages of the enemy," *O.R.*, Ser. II, Vol. 6, p. 1127.
100. *Ibid.*, p. 1128.
101. Captain George B. Cock to Brigadier General L. Thomas, Camp near Norfolk, Va., December 29, 1863, *O.R.*, Ser. I, Vol. 51, Pt. I, p. 210.
102. Tewksbury, *New York Times*, January 9, 1864, cited in Witt, pp. 21–22.
103. "Reports of Brig. Gen. Edward A.

Wild, U.S. Army commanding expedition," December 28, 1863, *O.R.*, Ser. I, Vol. 290, Pt. I, p. 913.

104. Affidavit of William J. Munden, February 10, 1864, *O.R.*, Ser. II, Vol. 6, pp. 1129–30.

105. Edward A. Wild to Capt. Sanderlin, December 22, 1863, *O.R.*, Ser. II, Vol. 6, pp. 1128, 1130. See also footnote 52, in Witt, p. 41.

106. [Raleigh] *The North Carolina Standard*, Friday, 22 January 1864.

107. J. W. Evans, "Sixty-Eighth Regiment," Walter Clark, ed. *Histories of the Several Regiments*, Vol. III, p. 713.

108. Edward A. Wild to Willis Sanderlin, Northwest Landing, Va., December 22, 1863, in Edward A. Wild Papers, Southern Historical Collection, University of North Carolina at Chapel Hill. See also *O.R.*, Ser. II, Vol. 6, p. 1182.

109. W. N. H. Smith, "Report of the special committee to inquire into certain outrages of the enemy," *O.R.*, Ser. II, Vol. 6, p. 1129.

110. Jordan to Butler, December 31, 1863, Wild Papers, MHI; "Report of the special Committee to Inquire into Certain Outrages of the enemy," Confederate States House of Representatives February 10–17, 1864, *O.R.*, Ser. II, Vol. 6, pp. 1127–1129, cited in Witt, pp. 41–42.

111. Jeffery S. Hampton, "Rebels' descendants moved by 1863 battle," *The Virginia Pilot*, December 16, 2001, pp. Y1, Y5.

112. "Reports of Brig. Gen. Edward A. Wild, U.S. Army commanding expedition," December 28, 1863, *O.R.*, Ser. I, Vol. 29, Pt. I, p. 913.

113. Brigadier General Geo. W. Getty to Col. J. W. Shaffer, December 21, 1863, *O.R.*, Ser. I, Vol. 29, Pt. II, p. 572.

114. *Ibid.*

115. Brigadier General Geo. W. Getty to General Graham, December 21, 1863, *O.R.*, Ser. I, Vol. 29, Pt. II, p. 572–753.

116. *Ibid.*, p. 576.

117. *Ibid.*

118. "December 5–24, 1863—Expedition from Norfolk, Va., to South Mills, Camden Court House, etc., N.C.: Reports of Brig. Gen. Edward A. Wild, U.S. Army, commanding expedition," *O.R.*, Ser. I, Vol. 29, Pt. I, pp. 910–911.

119. *Ibid.*

120. Milton M. Holland, "Letter 35," Edwin S. Redkey, ed., *A Grand Army of Black Men: Letters from African-American Soldiers in the Union Army, 1861–1865*, pp. 93–94.

121. Selby Daniels and T. H. Pearce, eds., *The Diary of Captain Henry A. Chambers*, pp. 182–183, cited in Trotter, pp. 221–222.

122. *Ibid.*

123. H. Sutcliffe, Provost Sergeant to Captain J. N. Croft, Special Provost Marshal, Norfolk, Virginia, December 24, 1863, Edward A. Wild Papers, MHI.

124. "Recent Expedition to Elizabeth City," Milledgeville, Ga., *Southern Recorder*, Jan. 19, 1864, cited in Barrett, p. 180.

125. Tewksbury, "Gen. Butler's Department: Invasion of North Carolina by Gen. Wild's Colored Battalions," *New York Times*, Saturday, January 9, 1864.

126. "Reports of Brig. Edward A. Wild, U.S. Army, commanding the expedition," December 21, 1863, *O.R.*, Series I, Vol. 29, Pt. I, p. 914.

127. Holland, "Letter 35," Redkey, *A Grand Army of Black Men*, p. 94.

128. Hanibal, 5th U.S.C.T., "Letter 128," Redkey, *A Grand Army of Black Men*, pp. 289–290.

129. Tewksbury, "General Wild's Expedition, A National Account," Frank Moore, ed., *The Rebellion Record*, 8:297–304, cited in Yearns and Barrett, p. 55.

130. New York *Daily News*, cited in W. N. H. Smith, "Report of the special committee to inquire into certain outrages of the enemy," *O.R.*, Ser. II, Vol. 6, p. 1129.

131. [Raleigh] *The North Carolina Standard*, 22 January 1864.

132. *Ibid.*

133. Tewksbury, "General Wild's Expedition, A National Account," Frank Moore, ed. *The Rebellion Record*, 8:297–304, cited in Yearns and Barrett, p. 55.

134. *Ibid.*

135. D. H. Hill, Jr., *North Carolina*, Vol IV, Clement A. Evans, ed., *Confederate Military History* (Atlanta: Confederate Publishing Co., 1899; rpt. Wilmington, NC: Broadfoot Publishing Co., 1987, p. 218.

136. Tewksbury, "General Wild's Expedition, A National Account," Moore, Frank, ed. *The Rebellion Record*, 8:297–304, cited in Yearns and Barrett, pp. 54–55.

137. Holland, "Letter 35," Redkey, *A Grand Army of Black Men*, p. 94.

138. Crabtree, *Edmondston diary*, p. 517.

139. [Raleigh] *The North Carolina Standard*, 1 January 1864.

140. Crabtree, *Edmondston diary*, pp. 510.

141. Brigadier General James Barnes to Major General Butler, December 23, 1863, *O.R.*, Ser. I, Vol. 29, Pt. II, p. 581–582.

142. "Reports of Brig. Edward A. Wild, U.S. Army, commanding the expedition," December 21, 1863, *O.R.*, Series I, Vol. 29, Pt. I, p. 914.

143. *Ibid.*, p. 913.

144. Tewksbury, "General Wild's Expedition, A National Account," Frank Moore, ed. *The Rebellion Record*, 8:297–304, cited in Yearns and Barrett, p. 55.

145. Wild, "Military Career."

146. Selby Daniels and T. H. Pearce, eds., *The Diary of Captain Henry A. Chambers*, pp. 182–183, cited in Trotter, p. 221.

147. "Reports of Brig. Gen. Edward A. Wild, U.S. Army, commanding expedition," December 28, 1863, *O.R.*, Ser. I, Vol. 29, Pt. I, pp. 911–917.

148. [Raleigh] *The North Carolina Standard*, Friday, 22 January 1864.

149. *Ibid.*

150. Col. J. W. Shaffer to General Butler, January 19, 1864, Butler Papers, Library of Congress, cited in Witt, pp. 51–52.

151. Holland, "Letter 35," Redkey, *A Grand Army of Black Men*, p. 94.

Chapter VII

1. E. A. Hitchcock, "Letter to the Editor of the *New York Times*," November 28, 1863, *O.R.*, Ser. II, Vol. 6, pp. 595–596.

2. "Recent Expedition to Elizabeth City," Milledgeville, Ga., *Southern Recorder*, Jan. 19, 1864, cited in Barrett, p. 178–179; see also Moore, *The Rebellion Record*, 8:304–305, and cited in Yearns and Barrett, pp. 55–56.

3. "Recent Expedition to Elizabeth City," Milledgeville, Ga., *Southern Recorder*, Jan. 19, 1864, cited in Barrett, pp. 178–179.

4. Colonel Joel R. Griffin, White Mills, on Dismal Swamp, December 19, 1863, to Major General Pickett, *O.R.*, Ser. I, Vol. 29, Pt. II, p. 883.

5. Edward A. Wild to John T. Elliott, Elizabeth City, N.C., December 17, 1863, in Edward A. Wild Papers, Southern Historical Collection, University of North Carolina at Chapel Hill, Chapel Hill, North Carolina; see also "Report of the special committee to inquire into certain outrages of the enemy," *O.R.*, Ser II. Vol. 6, p. 1128.

6. Colonel Joel R. Griffin, White Mills, on Dismal Swamp, December 19, 1863, to Major General Pickett, *O.R.*, Ser. I, Vol. 29, Pt. II, p. 883.

7. Stewart Sifakis, *Compendium of the Confederate Armies: South Carolina and Georgia* (New York: Facts On File, Inc., 1995), pp. 151, 164–165.

8. Affidavit of W. J. Munden, cited in W. N. H. Smith, "Report of the special committee to inquire into certain outrages of the enemy," *O.R.*, Ser. II, Vol. 6, p. 1129.

9. J. D. Stokely and others to Gen. Getty, January 13, 1864, in Edward A. Wild Papers, Southern Historical Collection, University of North Carolina at Chapel Hill, Chapel Hill, North Carolina; *O.R.*, Ser. II, Vol. 6, p. 846, Appendix A, January 12, 1864.

10. Major General Benj. F. Butler to Maj. Gen. H. W. Halleck, January 17, 1864, *O.R.*, Ser. II, Vol. 6, p. 845.

11. Colonel Samuel P. Spear to Maj. Gen. B. F. Butler, January 16, 1864, *O.R.*, Ser. II, Vol. 6, pp. 845–846.

12. Kenneth W. Rendell, Inc. "Autographs and Manuscripts: The American Civil War, Catalogue No. 46" (Somerville, Mass.: Kingston Galleries, Inc., n.d.), pp. 50–51.

13. Colonel M. B. Smith to Colonel S. P. Spear, January 16, 1864, *O.R.*, Ser. II, Vol. 6, pp. 846–847. Original letter in Edward A. Wild Papers, Southern Historical Collection, University of North Carolina at Chapel Hill, Chapel Hill, North Carolina.

14. Major General Benj. F. Butler to Maj. Gen. H. W. Halleck, January 20, 1864. *O.R.*, Ser. II, Vol. 6, p. 858.

15. Milton M. Holland, "Letter 35," Redkey, *A Grand Army of Black Men*, p. 94.

16. General Order, No. 100, "Instructions for the Government of Armies of the United States in the field," *O.R.*, Ser. III, Vol. 3, pp.151, 157.

17. [name unreadable] Capt. Col. E, 66th N.C. Troops to Col., Dec. 14, 1863, in Edward A. Wild Papers, Southern Historical Collection, University of North Carolina at Chapel Hill, Chapel Hill, North Carolina.

18. Colonel James W. Hinton to Maj. Gen. Benjamin F. Butler, January 15, 1864, *O.R.*, Ser. II, Vol. 6, p. 847.

19. W. N. H. Smith, "Report of the special committee to inquire into certain outrages of the enemy," *O.R.*, Ser. II, Vol. 6, p. 1128.

20. [Raleigh] *The North Carolina Standard*, Friday, 22 January 1864.

21. "December 5–24, 1863—Expedition from Norfolk, Va., to South Mills, Camden CourtHouse, etc., N.C.: Reports of Brig. Gen. Edward A. Wild, U.S. Army, commanding expedition," *O.R.*, Ser. I, Vol. 29, Pt. I, pp. 910–911.

22. Major General Benjamin F. Butler to President Abraham Lincoln, Fort Monroe, January 26, 1864, *O.R.*, Ser. II, Vol. 6, p. 877.

23. Major General Benjamin F. Butler to Lieut. W. J. Munden and Mr. Pender Weeks, January 26, 1864, *O.R.*, Ser. II, Vol. 6, pp. 877–878; Edward Wild Papers, File 8, Box 2160, MHI.

24. *Ibid.*

25. *Ibid.*

26. B. F. Butler to Col. James W. Hinton, Fort Monroe, Va., January 27, 1864, *O.R.*, Ser. II, Vol. 6, pp. 883–884.

27. Nolan, *Benjamin Franklin Butler: The Damnedest Yankee*, p. 244.

28. [Raleigh] *The North Carolina Standard*, 22 January 1864.

29. Benjamin F. Butler to E. M. Stanton,

Secretary of War, Fortress Monroe, Va., December 31, 1863, *O.R.*, Ser. I, Vol. 29, Pt. II, p. 596.

30. *Ibid.*

31. "Reports of Brig. Edward A. Wild, U.S. Army, commanding the expedition," December 21, 1863, Enclosure, A, and Enclosure B, *O.R.*, Series I, Vol. 39, Pt. I, p. 917.

32. Benjamin F. Butler to E. M. Stanton, Secretary of War, Fortress Monroe, Va., December 31, 1863, *O.R.*, Ser. I, Vol. 29, Pt. II, p. 596.

33. Witt, pp. 49–51.

34. Benjamin F. Butler to E. M. Stanton, Secretary of War, Fortress Monroe, Va., December 31, 1863, *O.R.*, Ser. I, Vol. 29, Pt. II, p. 596.

35. *Ibid.*

36. [Raleigh] *The North Carolina Standard*, Friday, 22 January 1864.

37. J. Parker Jordan to General [Butler], Norfolk, Va., December 31, 1863, Edward A. Wild Papers, MHI.

38. Colonel James W. Hinton to Maj. Gen. Benjamin F. Butler, January 15, 1864, *O.R.*, Ser. II, Vol. 6, p. 847.

39. Governor Z. B. Vance to Judge Ould, Raleigh, North Carolina, December 29, 1863, in Joe A. Mobley, ed., *The Papers of Zebulon Baird Vance*, Vol. 2 (Raleigh, North Carolina: North Carolina Department of Cultural Resources, 1995), p. 357.

40. *Ibid.*

41. *Ibid.*

42. "Recent Expedition to Elizabeth City," Milledgeville, Ga., *Southern Recorder*, Jan. 19, 1864, cited in Barrett, pp. 178–179; see also Moore, *The Rebellion Record*, 8:304–305, and cited in Yearns and Barrett, pp. 55–56.

43. "Recent Expedition to Elizabeth City," Milledgeville, Ga., *Southern Recorder*, Jan. 19, 1864, cited in Barrett, pp. 178–179.

44. [Raleigh] *The North Carolina Standard*, 1 January 1864.

45. Affidavit of W. J. Munden, cited in W. N. H. Smith, "Report of the special committee to inquire into certain outrages of the enemy," *O.R.*, Ser. II, Vol. 6, p. 1129.

46. Handwritten copy of article, "A Wild General," New York *World*, March 5, 1864, Edward A. Wild Papers, University of North Carolina, Southern Historical Collection, Chapel Hill, North Carolina.

47. Andy Phrydas, Military Records Archivist, Department of Archives and History, 300 Capitol Ave., S.E., Atlanta, Georgia 30334, to Frances H. Casstevens, May 1, 2002.

48. Stevens and Bradford, p. 118.

49. *Ibid.*

50. Notation on announcement dated Boston, March 8, 1893, by E. W. (Edward Wheelwright, Class of 1844), Edward A. Wild Papers, Harvard University Archives, Cambridge, Mass.

Chapter VIII

1. Bill Sharp, "Currituck," *A New Geography of North Carolina*, Vol. IV, p. 1299.

2. Extracts from the diary of William Byrd II, 1728, cited in Bill Sharp, "Currituck," pp. 1292–1293.

3. Melinda J. Lukei, compl. "White Family History," typescript, p. 1, courtesy of Dale H. Beasley, Virginia Beach, Va.

4. *Cavaliers and Pioneers*, p. 272, and *Virginia Colonial Abstracts*, Vol. 31, p. 70, cited in Melinda J. Lukei, compl. "White Family History," typescript, p. 1.

5. Bill Sharp, "Currituck," *A New Geography of North Carolina*, Vol. IV, p. 1299.

6. Pauline W. Munden, "Knott's Island Then and Now," in Jo Anna Heath Bates, ed., *The Heritage of Currituck County, North Carolina, 1985* (Winston-Salem, N.C.: Hunter Publishing Company, 1985), pp. 1–2.

7. W. B. Browne, "Stranger Than Fiction," *Southern Historical Society Papers*, Vol. 29, 1914, pp. 181–185.

8. H. W. Halleck, General-in-Chief, to General John Schofield, May 25, 1863, *O.R.* Ser. II, Vol. 5, p. 696.

9. Major General N. P. Banks to Adjutant General U.S. Army, New Orleans, June [July 2], 1863, *O.R.*, Ser. II, Vol. 7, pp. 185–186.

10. W. B. Browne, "Stranger Than Fiction," *Southern Historical Society Papers* 29, pp. 181–185.

11. Browne, "Stranger Than Fiction," p. 183. See also, *O.R.*, 27, Ser. I, Pt. 2, p. 786.

12. W. Hoffman, Colonel Third Infantry and Commissary General of Prisoners to Major General N. P. Banks, Washington, D.C., July 2, 1864, *O.R.*, Ser. II, Vol. 7, p. 436.

13. Browne, "Stranger Than Fiction," pp. 181–185.

14. Boatner, p. 242.

15. Major General John A. Dix, "June 10, 1863.—Capture of the steamer Maple Leaf, off Cape Henry, Va.," *O.R.*, Ser. I, Vol. 27, Pt. II, p. 786.

16. Boatner, p. 11.

17. Lieutenant Colonel William H. Ludlow to Colonel J. C. Kelton, July 7, 1863, *O.R.*, Ser. II, Vol. 6, pp. 89–90.

18. Browne, "Stranger Than Fiction," p. 184.

19. *Ibid.*

20. Ed McHorney, "The *Maple Leaf*: How the Officers Escaped," *The Economist*, September 8, 1899, typed from microfilm by Joan H. Dunton, copy courtesy of Currituck County Public Library, Barco, North Carolina.

21. J. A. Seddon, Secretary of War to General D. H. Hill, Richmond, Va., June 17, 1863, *O.R.*, Ser. I, Vol. 27, Pt. III, p. 901.

22. Bill Sharp, "Currituck." *A New Geography of North Carolina*, Vol. IV, p. 1297.

23. Browne, "Stranger Than Fiction," p. 184.

24. Robert Ould, Agent of Exchange, Richmond, Va., to Lieutenant Colonel William H. Ludlow, July 7, 1863, *O.R.* Ser. II, Vol. 6, pp. 70–71.

25. Major General John Dix, report, 1863, *O.R.*, XXVII, Ser. I, Pt. 2, p. 786, June 11, 1863, cited in Barbara Snowden, "Civil War in Currituck," in *Heritage of Currituck County, North Carolina, 1985*, p. 17; Ed McHorney, "The *Maple Leaf*: How the Officers Escaped."

26. Thomas Waln-Morgan Draper, "General Alonzo Granville Draper," *The Drapers in America, Being a History and Genealogy of Those of that Name and Connection* (New York: J. Polhemus Printing Company, 1892), pp. 208–214. Hereinafter cited as Draper, "General Alonzo Granville Draper." See "The Draper Page," online at http://freepages.genealogy.rootsweb.com/~kenwark/samuel/samuel.htm.

27. Draper, "General Alonzo Granville Draper," p. 208.

28. *Ibid.*

29. *Ibid.*

30. *Ibid.*

31. *Ibid.*, pp. 208, 214.

32. *Ibid.*, pp. 209–210.

33. "December 5–24, 1863—Expedition from Norfolk, Va., to South Mills, Camden Court House, etc., N.C.: Reports of Brig. Gen. Edward A. Wild, U.S. Army, commanding expedition," *O.R.*, Ser. I, Vol. 29, Pt. I, p. 910–911.

34. Report of Colonel Alonzo G. Draper, December 24, 1963, Edward A. Wild Papers, Southern Historical Collection, University of North Carolina, Chapel Hill, North Carolina. See also Witt, *Wild in North Carolina*, Appendix C, pp. 69–72.

35. "General Alonzo Granville Draper," from *Drapers in America*.

36. General Wild to General Barnes, January 10, 1864, Edward Wild Papers, Southern Historical Collection, University of North Carolina at Chapel Hill, Chapel Hill, North Carolina. See also Witt, *Wild in North Carolina*, Appendix E, p. 79.

37. Lukei, "The White Family," pp. 3–4.

38. 1850 Federal Census, Currituck County, North Carolina, Knott's Island District, p. 178, lists the family of Henry White, age 32, wife Susan, age 27, daughter Nancy, age 10, son William age 4, and another son named William, age 1. Thus, Nancy White would have been 23 years old when she was taken captive in December of 1863. Image of original census page can be seen at Family Tree Maker Online, http://familytreemaker.genealogy.com.

39. Witt, *Wild in North Carolina*, pp. 32–33.

40. Draper, "General Alonzo Granville Draper," pp. 209–210.

41. Brigadier General George W. Getty to General Graham, Commanding a Naval Brigade, Norfolk, Va., December 21, 1863, *O.R.*, Ser I., Vol. 29, Pt. II, pp. 572–573.

42. Brig. Gen. James H. Ledlie to Horatio Seymour, Gov. Of New York, Norfolk, Va., Dec. 28, 1863, in Correspondence of Colonel Frederick F. Wead, New York State Library, Albany, New N.Y., hereafter cited NYSL.

43. Wead's picture can be seen at web site for "98th NY Volunteers," web page online at http://www.magpage.com/~33dny/98thnew.htm. Wead was born January 26, 1835, the son of Samuel Clark Wead and Emelina Kasson.

44. Lieut. Col. F. F. Wead to Captain A. H. Davis, Asst. Adjt. Genl., December 22, 1863, in Correspondence of Colonel Frederick F. Wead, NYSL.

45. *Ibid.*

46. *Ibid.*

47. Witt, *Wild in North Carolina*, pp. 32–33.

48. "Reports of Brig. Gen. Edward A. Wild, U.S. Army, commanding expedition," *O.R.*, Ser. I, Vol. 29, Pt. I, pp. 911–917.

49. Witt, p. 46.

50. Milton M. Holland, Letter 35, Redkey, *A Grand Army of Black Men*, p. 94.

51. Witt, p. 77.

52. Witt, pp. 45–46.

53. General Wild's Report to General Barnes Regarding Nancy White, Jan. 10, 1864, in Edward A. Wild Papers, Southern Historical Collection, University of North Carolina at Chapel Hill, Chapel Hill, North Carolina; also cited in Witt, *Wild in North Carolina*, Appendix E, pp. 77–80.

54. *Ibid.*

55. *Ibid.*

56. *Ibid.*

57. "Col. Draper, 2nd N.C. Colored Vols., Charges and Specifications against, preferred by F. F. Wead, Lt. Col. 98th N. Y. V.," December 22, 1863, in Correspondence of Colonel Frederick F. Wead, NYSL.

58. Witt, *Wild in North Carolina*, pp. 73–75.

59. Frederick F. Wead Papers, MSC Call Number SC21160, NYSL.

60. Lieut. Col. F. F. Wead to Captain A. H. Davis, Pungo, Va., December 22, 1863, in Correspondence of Colonel Frederick F. Wead, NYSL.

61. Maj. Gen. Benjamin F. Butler to Brigadier General George W. Getty, December 25, 1863, Benjamin F. Butler Papers, Library of Congress, cited in Witt, p. 45, footnote 59.

62. Brig. Gen. James H. Ledlie to Horatio

Seymour, Gov. of New York, Norfolk, Va., Dec. 28, 1863, in Correspondence of Colonel Frederick F. Wead, NYSL.

63. Witt, *Wild in North Carolina*, p. 45.

64. Special Order No. 7, Brig. Gen. James H. Ledlie, January 13, 1864, in Correspondence of Colonel Frederick F. Wead, NYSL.

65. General Order No. 8, issued by Maj. Gen. Butler, Department of Virginia, North Carolina, Fortress Monroe, January 15, 1864, in Correspondence of Colonel Frederick F. Wead, NYSL.

66. General Wild's Report to General Barnes Regarding Nancy White, Jan. 10, 1864, in Edward A. Wild Papers, Southern Historical Collection, University of North Carolina at Chapel Hill, Chapel Hill, North Carolina; also cited in Witt, *Wild in North Carolina*, Appendix E, pp. 77–80.

67. Galen D. Harrison, Prisoners' *Mail from the American Civil War* (Dexter, Mich.: Thompson-Shore, Inc., 1997), p. 215.

68. Letter from Nancy White to Brig. Gen. Wild, Norfolk, Va., January 14, 1864, from private collection of Galen Harrison, Kernersville, N.C.

69. Harrison, *Prisoners' Mail from the American Civil War*, p. 215.

70. Edw. A. Wild to Lieut. G. H. Willis, Norfolk, Va., January 14, 1864, in George Willis Papers, Boston University, Special Collections, Boston, Massachusetts.

71. Brig. Gen. Edward A. Wild to Lt. Col. F. F. Wead, Norfolk, Va., January 15, 1864, in Correspondence of Colonel Frederick F. Wead, NYSL.

72. Lt. Col. F. F. Wead to Brig. Gen. E. A. Wild, Post Headquarters, Pungo Bridge, Va., January 16, 1864, in Correspondence of Colonel Frederick F. Wead, NYSL.

73. Major General Benjamin F. Butler to President Abraham Lincoln, Fort Monroe, January 26, 1864, *O.R.*, Ser. II, Vol. 6, p. 877.

74. Benjamin F. Butler to Lieut. W. J. Munder and Mr. Pender Weeks, Fort Monroe, January 26, 1864, *O.R.* Ser. II, Vol. 6, pp. 877–878; Edward A. Wild Papers, File 8, Box 2160, MHI.

75. Nolan, *Benjamin Franklin Butler: The Damnedest Yankee*, p. 244.

76. Benjamin F. Butler to Lieut. W. J. Munder and Mr. Pender Weeks, Fort Monroe, January 26, 1864, *O.R.* Ser. II, Vol. 6, p. 877–878.

77. *Journal of the Confederate Congress,* Vol. 6, p. 600, http://memory.loc.gov/cgi-bin/ampage.

78. *Journal of the Confederate Congress,* Vol. 7, p. 107, http://memory.loc.gov/cgi-bin/ampage.

79. Longacre, "Brave Radical Wild," p. 12.

80. "Organization of troops in the Department of Virginia and North Carolina, Maj. Gen. Benjamin F. Butler, U.S. Army, commanding, January 31, 1864," *O.R.*, Ser. I, Vol. 33, p. 482.

81. Handwritten copy of "A Wild General," New York *World,* March 5, 1864, Edward A. Wild Papers, University of North Carolina at Chapel Hill.

82. "Troops in the Department of Virginia and North Carolina, Maj. Gen. Benjamin F. Butler, U.S. Army, commanding, April 30, 1864," *O.R.* Ser. I, Vol. 33, p. 1055.

83. D. Hunter to Col. James Montgomery, Hilton Head, Port Royal, S.C., June 10, 1863, *O.R.* Ser. II, Vol. 5, p. 770.

84. Edwin M. Stanton to Major General Schenck, July 1, 1863, *O.R.* Ser. II, Vol. 6, p. 69.

85. W. Hoffman, Colonel Third Infantry and Commissary General of Prisoners to Capt. E. M. Camp, Washington, D.C. July 7, 1863, *O.R.*, Ser. II, Vol. 6, p. 89.

86. William H. Ludlow to Robert Ould, July 16, 1863, *O.R.*, Ser. II, Vol. 6, p. 1127.

87. General Order No. 100, "Instructions for the Government of Armies of the United States in the Field," April 24, 1863, *O.R.*, Ser. III, Vol. 3, pp. 148–164.

88. Edward A. Wild, "Report of Brig. Gen. Edward A. Wild, U.S. Army, commanding expedition, December 31, 1863," *O.R.*, Ser. I, Vol. XXIX, Pt. 1, pp. 910–917.

89. Melinda J. Lukei, "The White Family," pp. 3–4.

90. Private correspondence from Dale Beasley to Frances H. Casstevens, December 8, 2001.

91. Alyda White Beasley, "William Henry & Susan," 1-page handwritten account, dated June 10, 1983, Currituck County Public Library, Barco, North Carolina.

92. Lukei, "The White Family."

93. Report of Gen. Gilman Marston, June 10, 1864, *O.R.*, Ser. I, Vol. 26, Pt. I, pp. 1005–1006, cited in Witt, *Wild in North Carolina*, p. 56.

94. General Order No. 80, Headquarters, Department of Virginia and North Carolina, July 15, 1864, *O.R.*, Ser. I, Vol. 40, Pt. III, p. 270, cited in Witt, *Wild in North Carolina*, p. 56.

95. Special Order No. 110, Headquarters, Department of Virginia and North Carolina, April 20, 1864, *O.R.*, Series I, Vol. 33, pp. 930–931, cited in Witt, *Wild in North Carolina*, p. 56.

96. Service and Pension Records of Alonzo G. Draper, National Archives, cited in Witt, *Wild in North Carolina*, p. 56; Draper, "General Alonzo Granville Draper," pp. 212–213.

97. Draper, "General Alonzo Granville Draper," pp. 212–214; See also online "The Draper Page," http://freepages.genealogy.rootsweb.com/~kenwark/samuel/d1154.htm

Chapter IX

1. Capt. Henry F. H. Miller, 2nd NCCV, to General Wild, Portsmouth, Va., February 3, 1864, Edward A. Wild Papers, MHI.
2. R. C. Perkins, M.D., note testifying to health of Edwin Ferebee, Camden County, N.C., February 12, 1864, Edward A. Wild Papers, MHI.
3. R. R. Overby, Pastor, note testifying that Edwin Ferebee would come to Norfolk, Camden County, N.C., February 12, 1864, Edward A. Wild Papers, MHI.
4. Capt. Henry F. H. Miller, 2nd NCCV, to General Wild, Portsmouth, Va., February 3, 1864, Edward A. Wild Papers, MHI.
5. *Ibid.*
6. Stevens and Bradford, p. 119.
7. Lawyer Charles W. Butt's letter to Edward Bates, Attorney General, in Washington, dated March 30, 1864, cited in Stevens and Bradford, p. 119.
8. Major General Benjamin F. Butler to Hon. E. M. Stanton, Secretary of War, April 6, 1864, cited in Stevens and Bradford, p. 119.
9. Major General Benjamin F. Butler, letter dated February 1, 1864, in *Benjamin F. Butler Letters*, Volume 3, p. 355–356, cited in Stevens and Bradford, p. 120.
10. *Ibid.*
11. "Special Order No. 2," *Wilmington Journal*, March 3, 1864.
12. Special Order 14, February 25, 1864, cited in Witt, p. 52. See also Moore's *Rebellion Record*, Vol. 8, p. 46, and Butler to Wild, March 11, 1864, in Marshall, *Butler Letters*, Vol. 11, p. 510.
13. Moore, *The Rebellion Record*, Vol. 8, p. 46.
14. Handwritten copy of "A Wild General," New York *World*, March 5, 1864, Edward A. Wild Papers, University of North Carolina at Chapel Hill, Southern Historical Collection, Chapel Hill, North Carolina.
15. Special Order 14, February 25, 1864, cited in Witt, p. 52. See also Moore's *Rebellion Record*, Vol. 8, p. 46, and Butler to Wild, March 11, 1864, in Marshall, *Butler Letters*, Vol. 11, p. 510.
16. Robert Seager II, *And Tyler Too: A Biography of John & Julia Gardiner Tyler* (New York: McGraw-Hill Book Company, Inc., 1963), p. 489.
17. John C. Tyler to My Dear Madam [Mrs. Julia Tyler?], Fort Hamilton near Fortress Monroe, Virginia, May 20, 1864, Tyler Family Papers, William & Mary College, Earl Gregg Swem Library, Williamsburg, Virginia. Hereafter cited as Tyler Family Papers, EGSL.
18. Seager, p. 490.
19. *Ibid.*, pp. 492–493.
20. Edward A. Wild to Mrs. Julia Gardiner Tyler, Wilson's Wharf, June 6, 1864, Tyler Family Papers, William & Mary College, EGSL.
21. Seager, pp. 492–493.
22. *Ibid.*, p. 493.
23. *Ibid.*, pp. 491–493.
24. *Ibid.*, pp. 493–494.
25. Edward Wild's Reply about Challiner prisoner at Wilson's Wharf, near Petersburg, June 30, 1864. Edward A. Wild Papers, MHI.
26. Edward A. Wild to General Robert S. Davis, Headquarters, 1st Brigade, 3rd Division, 18th A. C., Wilson's Wharf, James River, May 12, 1864, Edward A. Wild Papers, MHI.
27. Edward A. Wild, "List of wounded prisoners captured at Sandy Point Signal Station, May 6, 1864, and sent to Ft. Monroe May 8, 1864," Edward A. Wild Papers, MHI.
28. Edward A. Wild to Provost Marshal at Fort Monroe, Headquarters, 1st Brigade, 3rd Div., 18th, Corps., Wilson's Wharf, Va., May 17, 1864, Edward A. Wild Papers, MHI.
29. Seager, p. 489.
30. Charles J. Major, "Concerning George Walker of Charles City County, Va., Wilson's Wharf, May 16, 1864, Edward A. Wild Papers, MHI.
31. Joseph Bryant, "Statement Concerning George Walker of Charles City County, Va.," Edward A. Wild Papers, MHI, n.d., presumably in May of 1864.
32. Charles Kruger, Company D, 10th Virginia Cavalry, statement concerning George Walker, Wilson's Wharf, May 16, 1864, Edward A. Wild Papers, MHI.
33. Edward A. Wild, "List of prisoners sent down to Ft. Monroe, May 8th 1864 by Brig. Gen. Wild," File 7, #2158, Edward A. Wild Papers, MHI.
34. Seager, p. 490.
35. Edward Wild's Reply about Challiner prisoner at Wilson's Wharf, near Petersburg, June 30, 1864. Edward A. Wild Papers, MHI.
36. Suellen Clopton Blanton, "A Beast Comes Calling: Regarding William Henry Clopton, Sr., & the Widow of President John Tyler, Julia Gardiner Tyler," The Clopton Chronicles, online at: http://homepages.rootsweb.com/~clopton/beast.htm; Seager, *And Tyler Too*, p. 489.
37. William H. Clopton to Mrs. Julia Gardiner Tyler, Roselawn (?) Virginia, June 8, 1864, Tyler Family Papers, William & Mary College, EGSL.
38. Edward A. Wild, Report on Prisoner of War Holt, near Petersburg, Va., June 28, 1864, Edward A. Wild Papers, File No. 2156, MHI.
39. *Ibid.*
40. *Ibid.*
41. *Ibid.*
42. Edward A. Wild, page attached to "List of prisoners sent down to Ft. Monroe, May 8,

1864," Edward A. Wild Papers, File 7, #2158, MHI. Stephen V. Ash, "White Virginians Under Occupation," in *Virginia Magazine of History and Biography*, April 1990, cited in *Clopton Family Newsletter*, April 1991, p. 7.
43. William H. Clopton to Mrs. Julia Tyler, Bermuda Hundred, May 17, 1864, *Butler Letters*, Vol. 4, p. 244.
44. Ash, "White Virginians Under Occupation," *Virginia Magazine of History and Biography*, April 1990, cited in *Clopton Family Newsletter*, April 1991, p. 7. (See also Berlin's *A Documentary History of Emancipation*, 'The Black Military Experience," Series II. Also, Ransom Badger True, *Plantation of the James*, privately published, 1977.)
45. Richmond *Examiner*, 30 June 1864; *Daily Richmond Enquirer*, 1 July 1864, cited in Ervin L. Jordan, Jr., *Black Confederates and Afro-Yankees in Civil War Virginia* (Charlottesville: University Press of Virginia, 1995), p. 163, footnote 26, p. 359. See also: 8th U.S. Census, 1860, Slave Schedules, Charles City County, Virginia, June 25, 1860, p. 151, and 8th U.S. Census, Charles City County, Virginia, Dwelling No. 198, Family No. 148, p. 140; both cited in Jordan, Note. 26, p. 358. Jordan reported that both newspapers listed Clopton's name as "Clayton." In the 1860 census, William Clopton is shown as having real estate and personal property valued at $22,873. This included 25 slaves, aged 2 to 70. See also Glatthaar, *Forged in Battle*, p. 200.
46. Edward A. Wild to Captain John Cassells, Wilson's Creek, Va., May 11, 1864, Edward A. Wild Papers, MHI.
47. Henry Johnson, to Major R. S. Davis, Fortress Monroe, May 13, 1864, Court Martial files, NA, Washington, D.C.
48. William H. Clopton to Mrs. Julia Tyler, Bermuda Hundred, May 17, 1864, *Butler Letters*, Vol. 4, p. 244.
49. *Ibid.*
50. William H. Clopton to Mrs. Julia Gardiner Tyler, Roselawn (?), Virginia, May 31, 1864, Tyler Family Papers, William & Mary College, EGSL.
51. William H. Clopton to Mrs. Julia Gardiner Tyler, Roselawn (?) Virginia, June 8, 1864, Tyler Family Papers, William & Mary College, EGSL.
52. *Ibid.*
53. John C. Tyler to My Dear Madam [Mrs. Julia Tyler?], Fort Hamilton near Fortress Monroe, Virginia, May 20, 1864, Tyler Family Papers, William & Mary College, EGSL.
54. Seager, p. 490.
55. Mrs. Julia Tyler, "Letter to the Editor: Mrs. Tyler's Property," *Evening Post & Evening Express*, ca. June 27, 1864, clipping in Tyler Family Papers, William & Mary College, EGSL.

56. "Letters Found in John Tyler's House," from the Cincinnati *Commercial*, reprinted in the Evening *Post* 25 June 1864.
57. Mrs. Julia Tyler, "Letter to the Editor: Mrs. Tyler's Property," *Evening Post & Evening Express*, ca. June 27, 1864, clipping in Tyler Family Papers, William & Mary College, EGSL.
58. Seager, p. 490.
59. Frances E. Wild to Mr. Edward Kinsley, June 22, 1864, Edward Wilkinson Kinsley Collection, Duke University, Durham, North Carolina.
60. Edward A. Hinks to Brig. Gen. E. A. Wild, Head Quarters, 3rd Division, 18th Army Corps, City Point, Va., May 11, 1864, copy in File No. 2153, Edward A. Wild Papers, MHI.
61. Edward A. Wild to General Robert S. Davis, Headquarters, 1st Brigade, 3rd Division, 18th A. C., Wilson's Wharf, James River, May 12, 1864, Edward A. Wild Papers, MHI.
62. *Ibid.*
63. *Ibid.*
64. Edward A. Wild to Captain John Cassells, Wilson's Creek, Va., May 11, 1864, Edward A. Wild Papers, MHI.
65. Edward A. Wild to General Robert S. Davis, Headquarters, 1st Brigade, 3rd Division, 18th A. C., Wilson's Wharf, James River, May 12, 1864, Edward A. Wild Papers, MHI.
66. General Hinks' endorsement, Colonel Holman's copy, City Point, Va., May 13, 1864, in Edward A. Wild Papers, MHI.
67. *Ibid.*
68. Seager, pp. 489–490.
69. Sandburg, *Abraham Lincoln: The War Years*, III, p. 67

Chapter X

1. Bradford Kingman, "General Edward Augustus Wild," *New England Historical and Genealogical Register*, Vol. 29 (October 1895), p. 411.
2. Special Order No. 62, paragraphs 47 and 48, of February 8, 1864; Wild, "Military Career."
3. Major General Benj. F. Butler to Brig. Gen. E. A. Wild, Fort Monroe, January 12, 1864, O.R. Ser. I, Vol. 33, pp. 374–375.
4. Wild, "Military Career."
5. Lt. Henry T. Schroeder, "Special Order, No. 12," January 12, 1864, *O.R.*, Ser. I, Vol. 51, Pt. I, p. 1139.
6. Boatner, p. 45.
7. Wild, "Military Career."
8. Excerpt from "Journal of Laurence Bradford," typed notes by Horace Bradford, used by courtesy of Mrs. Helen Stevens Whitlock.
9. *Ibid.*
10. Jeffrey S. Mosser, "Sutler's Stores," *Camp*

Chase Gazette, XX (2) (November/December 1992), online at http://www.iprimus.ca/~nif/55virginia/article32.htm.
11. Edward A. Wild to Major Thomas M. Vincent, Asst. Adj. General, Headquarters, Colored Troops, Norfolk, Va., February 5, 1864, Edward A. Wild Papers, MHI.
12. *Ibid.*
13. Wild, "Military Career."
14. Boatner, pp. 352–353.
15. Stevens and Bradford, p. 121; Bruce Catton, *Grant Takes Command* (Boston: Little, Brown & Company), pp. 146–148.
16. Brigadier General C. A. Heckman to Brigadier General Wild, January 26, 1864, *O.R.*, Ser. I, Vol. 33, p. 645.
17. Major General B. F. Butler to Major General John J. Peck, Commanding, New Bern, N.C., March 5, 1864, *O.R.*, Ser. I, Vol. 33, p. 645.
18. Brigadier General C. A. Heckman to Brigadier General Wild, March 5, 1864, *O.R.*, Ser. I, Vol. 33, p. 645.
19. Major General B. F. Butler to Major General John J. Peck, Commanding, New Bern, N.C., March 5, 1864, *O.R.*, Ser. I, Vol. 33, p. 645.
20. Glatthaar, *Forged in Battle: The Civil War Alliance of Black Soldiers and White Officers*, p. 149.
21. Eddy W. Davison and Daniel Foxx, "A Journey to the Most Controversial Battlefield in America," Confederate *Veteran* 6:19, 2001.
22. Boatner, p. 296. See also "The Fort Pillow Massacre: A Fresh Examination of the Evidence," by Albert Castel, in *Civil War History*, Vol. 4, No. 1 (March 1958).
23. *O.R.*, Ser. I, Vol. 32, Pt. 1, pp. 534–539.
24. George Huston, report of, April 30, 1864, *O.R.*, Ser. I, Vol. 32, Pt. I, pp. 536–537.
25. James Lewis, report of, April 30, 1864, *O.R.*, Ser. I, Vol. 32, Pt. I, p. 537.
26. Davison and Foxx, "A Journey to the Most Controversial Battlefield in America," Confederate *Veteran* 6:27–32, 2001.
27. Glatthaar, *Forged in Battle*, pp. 158–159.
28. Stevens and Bradford, pp. 121–122, citing Catton, *Grant Takes Command*.
29. Stevens and Bradford, p. 122.
30. R. S. Davis, Special Order No. 110, April 20, 1864, *O.R.*, Ser. I, Vol. 33, pp. 930–931.
31. Colonel J. W. Shaffer, Chief of Staff, to Brigadier General Heckman, April 24, 1864, *O.R.*, Ser. I, Vol. 33, p. 967.
32. "Troops in the Department of Virginia and North Carolina ... April 30, 1864," *O.R.*, Ser. I, Vol. 33, p. 1055.
33. Stevens and Bradford, p. 122.
34. "Organization of the Forces Operating Against Richmond Under Lieut. Gen. Ulysses S. Grant, U.S. Army, on the Morning of May 5, 1864," *O.R.*, Ser. I, Vol. 36, Pt. I, pp. 106–118; "Organization of troops in the Department of Virginia and North Carolina, commanded by Major Gen. Benjamin F. Butler, U.S. Army, April 30, 1864," *O.R.*, Ser. I, Vol. 33, p. 1055.
35. Edward A. Wild, to Brig. Gen. Edward W. Hinks, April 28, 1864, and reply on same document from Brig. Gen. Hinks, Fort Monroe, May 1, 1864, Edward A. Wild Papers, MHI.
36. R. S. Davis, Special Order No. 110, April 20, 1864, *O.R.*, Ser. I, Vol. 33, pp. 930–931.
37. "Troops in the Department of Virginia and North Carolina, Maj. Gen. Benjamin F. Butler, U.S. Army, commanding, April 30, 1864," Ser. I, Vol. 33, p. 1055.
38. Warner, *Generals in Blue*, pp. 229–230.
39. Edward Longacre, "Brave Radical Wild: The Contentious Career of Brigadier Edward A. Wild," *Civil War Times Illustrated*, XIX (No. 3), p. 9, cited in Leonne Hudson, "Valor at Wilson's Wharf," *Civil War Times* 37 (No. 1) (March 1998), p. 46.
40. Frances Ellen Wild, wife of General Edward A. Wild, to Mr. Edward Kinsley, June 28, 1864, Edward Wilkinson Kinsley Collection, Duke University, Durham, North Carolina.
41. Stevens and Bradford, p. 128.
42. A. G. Draper to R. S. Davis, May 1, 1864, *O.R.*, Ser. I, Vol. 36, Pt. II, pp. 327–328.
43. Benjamin F. Butler to General Grant, May 2, 1864, *O.R.*, Ser. I, Vol. 36, Pt. II, p. 346.
44. Briggs, p. 155.
45. Longacre, "Brave Radical Wild," pp. 13–14.
46. Colonel J. W. Shaffer, Chief of Staff, "Circular," Headquarters, Hinks' Division, Camp Hamilton, Va., May 1, 1864, Edward A. Wild Papers, MHI.
47. "Organization of the forces operating against Richmond, under Lieut. Gen. Ulysses S. Grant, U.S. Army, on the morning of May 5, 1864," *O.R.*, Ser. I, Vol. 36, Pt. I, p. 118.
48. Longacre, "Brave Radical Wild," pp. 13–14.
49. "Sherwood Forest: Home of President John Tyler." See web page at: http://www.sherwoodforest.org/.
50. Brig. Gen. Edward A. Wild to Maj. Gen. B. F. Butler, Wilson's Wharf, May 13, 1864, Jessie Ames Marshall, ed., *Private and Official Correspondence of Gen. Benjamin F. Butler during the Period of the Civil War*, Vol. 4 (privately published, 1917), p. 203.
51. Letter from A. R. Arter to Friend, Wilson's Landing, Virginia, June 24, 1864. See Letters—Fort Pocahontas, at http://www.fortpocahontas.org/Arter.html.
52. Boatner, pp. 599–600; Fort Pocahontas: "Major General Godfrey Weitzel, United States Army," online at http://www.fortpocahontas.org/Weitzel.html.

53. Letter from A. R. Arter to Friend, Wilson's Landing, Virginia, June 24, 1864. See Letters—Fort Pocahontas, at http://www.fortpocahontas.org/Arter.html.
54. New York State Museum Collections, "The Civil War Drawings of Edward Lamson Henry." Online at http://www.Nysm.mysed.gov/history/civilwar/index.html.
55. Structures similar to those in the interior of Fort Pocahontas. Online at: http://www.fortpocahontas.org/Fortinterior.html.
56. Butler, *Butler's Book*, p. 640.
57. Lieut. Col. Wm. J. L. Nicodemus to Edwin M. Stanton, Secretary of War, October 31, 1864, "Operations of the Corps," *O.R.*, Ser. III, Vol. 4, p. 824.
58. Special Order No. 20, May 16, 1864, *O.R.*, Ser. I, Vol. 36, Pt. II, p. 838.
59. Capt. Solon A. Carter to Brig. Gen. E. A. Wild, Headquarters, 3rd Division, 18th Army Corps, City Point, Va., May 13, 1864, *O.R.*, Ser. I, Vol. 26, Pt. II, p. 744.
60. Major J. F. Milligan to Braxton Bragg, May 18, 1864, *O.R.*, Ser. I, Vol. 51, Pt. II, p. 943.
61. William Farrar Smith, Brevet Major-General, "Butler's Attack on Drewry's Bluff," in *Battles and Leaders of the Civil War*, IV (Secaucus, N.J.: Castle, 1982), pp. 206–212.
62. Edward A. Wild to Company at Wilson's Wharf, Va., May 20, 1864, in Edward A. Wild Papers, Southern Historical Collection, University of North Carolina at Chapel Hill.
63. *Ibid*.
64. Boatner, pp. 458–459.
65. Colonel J. B. Kiddoo, "Report of Col. Joseph B. Kiddoo, Twenty-Second U.S. Colored Infantry, First Brigade, of operations May 21," May 22, 1864, *O.R.*, Ser. I, Vol. 36, Pt. II, p. 168.
66. Brig. Gen. Edw. W. Hinks to Major General Butler, reporting correspondence from 1st Lieut. H. W. Allen to Capt. Solon A. Carter, May 21, 1864, *O.R.*, Ser. I, Vol. 36, Pt II, p. 167.
67. *Ibid*.
68. Stevens and Bradford, p. 124.
69. Wild, "Military Career."
70. Hudson, "Valor at Wilson's Wharf," pp. 48–49.
71. Wild, "Military Career."
72. Boatner, p. 475.
73. Louis H. Manarin, compl. *North Carolina Troops 1861–1865: A Roster*, II (Raleigh, North Carolina: State Department of Archives and History, 1968), p. 371.
74. Hudson, "Valor at Wilson's Wharf," p. 49.
75. *Ibid.*, pp. 49–50.
76. *Ibid.*, p. 50.
77. R. J. Mason to Brig. Gen. Wild, May 24, 1864, in Wild's "Military Career."
78. Briggs, p. 155; Hudson, "Valor at Wilson's Wharf," p. 50; Boatner, p. 296. See also "The Fort Pillow Massacre: A Fresh Examination of the Evidence," by Albert Castel, in *Civil War History*, Vol. 4, No. 1 (March 1958).
79. Briggs, p. 155; Kingman, "General Edward Augustus Wild," *New England Historical and Genealogical Register*, 49 (October 1895), p. 411.
80. Hudson, "Valor at Wilson's Wharf," p. 51.
81. *Ibid.*, p. 51.
82. *Ibid.*
83. Major General Benjamin F. Butler to E. M. Stanton, Secretary of War, May 25, 1864—11 A.M., *O.R.*, Ser. I, Vol. 36, Pt. II, pp. 269–270.
84. Brigadier General E. W. Hinks to Major General Butler, from City Point, Va., May 25, 1864, *O.R.*, Ser. I, Vol. 36, Pt. II, p. 270.
85. Second Lieutenant Julius M. Swaim to Captain L. B. Norton, May 25, 1864, *O.R.*, Ser. I, Vol. 36, Pt. II, p. 272.
86. Second Lieutenant Julius M. Swaim, "Report of Lieut. Julius M. Swaim, Signal Corps, U.S. Army, of operations May 1–31," May 31, 1864, *O.R.*, Ser. I, Vol. 36, Pt. II, pp. 30–31.
87. Captain L. B. Norton, to Major R. S. Davis, September 2, 1864, *O.R.*, Ser. I, Vol. 42, Pt. I, p. 651; Wm. J. L. Nicodemus to Edwin M. Stanton, October, 31, 1864, *O.R.*, Ser. I, Vol. 4, pp. 824–825.
88. Brigadier General Edward A. Wild, "Report of Brig. Gen. Edward A. Wild, U.S. Army, commanding First Brigade," Wilson's Wharf, Va., May 25, 1864, *O.R.*, Ser. I, Vol. 36, Pt. II, pp. 270–271. Also in Wild's "Military Career."
89. *Ibid.*
90. *Ibid.*
91. Trudeau, *Like Men of War*, pp. 217–218.
92. Edward A. Wild, "Report of Brig. Gen. Edward A. Wild, U.S. Army, commanding First Brigade," Wilson's Wharf, Va., May 25, 1864, *O.R.*, Ser. I, Vol. 36, Pt. II, p. 271.
93. National Park Service, "CWSAC Battle Summaries: Wilson's Wharf." http://www2.cr.nps.gov/abpp/battles/va056.htm.
94. Hudson, "Valor at Wilson's Wharf," p. 52.
95. *Ibid.*
96. Edward A. Wild, "Report of Brig. Gen. Edward A. Wild, U.S. Army, commanding First Brigade," Wilson's Wharf, Va., May 25, 1864, *O.R.*, Ser. I, Vol. 36, Pt. II, p. 271.
97. Horace N. Stevens, "A brief account of the lives of the descendants of Charles Wild of Brookline, Mass.," unpublished typescript, May 23, 1947, courtesy of Mrs. Helen Whitlock.
98. Edward A. Wild, "Report of Brig. Gen. Edward A. Wild, U.S. Army, commanding First Brigade," Wilson's Wharf, Va., May 25, 1864, *O.R.*, Ser. I, Vol. 36, Pt. II, p. 271.

99. Wild, "Military Career."
100. Brig. Gen. E. W. Hinks to Maj. Gen. Butler, 18th Army Corps Headquarters, May 18, 1864, *O.R.*, Ser. I, Vol. 26, Pt. II, pp. 270–271.
101. "Return of Casualties in the Union Forces, commanded by Maj. Gen. Benjamin F. Butler, U.S. Army (compiled from nominal lists of casualties, returns, &c.), May 5–31," *O.R.*, Ser. I, Vol. 36, Pt. II, p. 16.
102. Hudson, "Valor at Wilson's Wharf," p. 52.
103. Edward A. Wild, "Report of Brig. Gen. Edward A. Wild, U.S. Army, commanding First Brigade," Wilson's Wharf, Va., May 25, 1864, *O.R.*, Ser. I, Vol. 36, Pt. II, p. 271.
104. Hudson, "Valor at Wilson's Wharf," p. 52.
105. Acting Rear Admiral S. P. Lee to Gideon Welles, Secretary of the Navy, May 29, 1864, *O.R.*, Ser. I, Vol. 36, Pt. III, p. 321.
106. Longacre, "Brave Radical Wild," p. 15.
107. Letter from A. R. Arter to Friend, Wilson's Landing, Virginia, June 24, 1864. See Letters—Fort Pocahontas, at http://www.fortpocahontas.org/Arter.html.
108. *Ibid.*
109. Brigadier General Edward W. Hinks to Major General B. F. Butler, City Point, Va., May 28, 1864, *O.R.*, Ser. I, Vol. 36, Pt. III, pp. 287–288.
110. Wild, "Military Career."
111. "Itinerary of the First Brigade, Third Division, Eighteenth Army Corps," June, 1864, *O.R.*, Ser. I, Vol. 36, Pt. I, p. 1018.
112. Warner, *Generals in Blue*, p. 558.
113. "Itinerary of the First Brigade, Third Division, Eighteenth Army Corps," June, 1864, *O.R.*, Ser. I, Vol. 36, Pt. I, p. 1018.
114. General Hinks to General Butler, June 2, 1864, *O.R.*, Ser. I, Vol. 36, Pt. III, p. 521.
115. 115. Benj. F. Butler to Brigadier General Hinks, June 2, 1864, *O.R.*, Ser. I, Vol. 36, Pt. III, p. 523.
116. Captain Dodge, to General Hinks, June 2, 1864, *O.R.*, Ser. I, Vol. 36, Pt. III, p. 523.
117. Edward A. Wild to Henry Wilson, U.S. Senator, June 13, 1864, Edward A. Wild Papers, Southern Historical Collection, University of North Carolina at Chapel Hill, Chapel Hill, North Carolina.
118. "First Brigade, Third Division, commanded by Brig. Gen. Edward A. Wild," June 30, 1864, *O.R.*, Ser. I, Vol. 40, Pt. I, pp. 215–216.
119. B. F. Butler, "Orders," June 16, 1864, *O.R.*, Ser. I, Vol. 40, Pt. II, pp. 104–105.
120. "Fort Pocahontas," http://www.fortpocahontas.org.
121. Major R. C. Davis, Special Orders, June 16, 1864, Edward A. Wild Papers, MHI.
122. Wild, "Military Career."
123. Frances Ellen Wild, wife of General Edward A. Wild, to Mr. Edward Kinsley, June 28, 1864, Edward Wilkinson Kinsley Collection, Duke University, Durham, North Carolina.
124. General Order No.___[sic], June 19, 1864, *O.R.*, Ser. I, Vol. 40, Pt. II, pp. 224–225.
125. Frances Ellen Wild, wife of General Edward A. Wild, to Mr. Edward Kinsley, June 28, 1864, Edward Wilkinson Kinsley Collection, Duke University, Durham, North Carolina.
126. *Ibid.*
127. Ed. W. Smith, Assist. Adj. Gen., to Soldiers of the Army of the James, before Richmond, October 11, 1864, *O.R.*, Ser. I, Vol. 42, Pt. III, pp. 161–175.
128. "Return of Casualties in the Union Forces, June 15–30, 1864," *O.R.*, Ser. I, Vol. 40, Pt. I, p. 235.

Chapter XI

1. Longacre, "Brave Radical Wild: The Contentious Career of Brigadier Edward A. Wild," *Civil War Times* XIX (3) (June 1980): 10.
2. Stevens and Bradford, p. 26.
3. Copy of letter from Edwin W. Hinks to Brigadier General E. A. Wild, City Point, Va., May 11, 1864, Court-Martial files, NA.
4. Witt, p. 53. See also Longacre, "Brave Radical Wild," pp. 14–15.
5. Edward A. Wild to Major Davis, May 12, 1865, Edward A. Wild Papers, MHI.
6. Edward A. Wild to Major Davis, May 12, 1865, Edward A. Wild Papers, MHI, cited in Reid, "General Edward A. Wild and Civil War Discrimination," p. 19.
7. Edward W. Hinks, May 13, 1864, Records of Judge Advocate General's Office, Court Martial Case Files, Court-Martial of Edward A. Wild, NA. Hereinafter cited as Court-Martial files.
8. *Ibid.*
9. *Ibid.*
10. Edward W. Hinks, General Order No. 86, Hinks Papers, Boston University Library, Boston, Mass., cited in Reid, "General Edward A. Wild and Civil War Discrimination," p. 18.
11. Special Order No. 51, Paragraph III, Headquarters Third Division, XVIII Army Corps, cited in Wild, "Military Career."
12. Major General Wm. F. Smith to General John A. Rawlings, June 18 [26], 1864, *O.R.*, Ser. I, Vol. 40, Pt. II, pp. 202–203.
13. Edward W. Hinks, General Order No. 86, Hinks Papers, Boston University Library,

Boston, Mass., cited in Reid, "General Edward A. Wild and Civil War Discrimination," p. 18.

14. Captain Solon A. Carter to Edward Wild, June 22, 1864, and Edward A. Wild to Captain Solon A. Carter, June 23, 1864, Records of Judge Advocate General's Office, Court Martial Case Files, Court Martial of Edward A. Wild, National Archives, cited in Richard Reid, "General Edward A. Wild and Civil War Discrimination," p. 19.

15. Sifakis, *Who Was Who in the Civil War*, p. 713.

16. Longacre, "Brave Radical Wild," p. 15.

17. Edward A. Hinks, "Special Orders No. 52," Petersburg, June 23, 1864, Court Martial files, NA.

18. Captain Solon A. Carter to Edward A. Wild, June 22, 1864, and Edward A. Wild to Captain Solon A. Carter, June 23, 1864, Records of the Judge Advocate General's Office, Court Martial Files, NA, cited in Reid, "General Edward A. Wild and Civil War Discrimination," p. 19.

19. "Charges and Specifications against Brig Gen. Edward A. Wild, U.S. Volunteers," brought by Brig. Gen. Edw. W. Hinks, May 12, 1864, Court Martial files, NA.

20. *Ibid.*

21. *Ibid.* See also General Edward W. Hinks to Edward A. Wild, May 11, 1864, Edward A. Wild Papers, MHI, cited in Reid, "General Edward A. Wild and Civil War Discrimination," p. 19.

22. Edward A. Wild to Major Davis, May 12, 1864, Edward A. Wild Papers, MHI, cited in Reid, "General Edward A. Wild and Civil War Discrimination," p. 19.

23. *Ibid.*

24. *Ibid.*

25. *Ibid.*

26. *Ibid.*

27. "Supplemental Specifications to Charge 2nd of Charges and Specifications Preferred against Brig. Gen. Edw. A. Wild, U.S. Vols." June 2, 1864, Court Martial files, NA.

28. Capt. Solon A. Carter, "Charges and Specifications Against Brig. Gen. E. A. Wild, U.S. Vols., Petersburg, June 23, 1864, Court Martial files, NA.

29. Edward A. Wild to Capt. Solon A. Carter, June 23, 1864, Edward A. Wild Papers, MHI.

30. Mrs. Frances E. Wild to Mr. (Edward W.) Kinsley, Mansion House, Mt. Carbon, Pottsville, Pennsylvania, June 28, 1864, Kinsley Collection, Duke University, Durham, North Carolina.

31. Edward A. Wild, Brig. Gen. Vols., to Major Russell, 18th Army Corps, June 25, 1864, Court Martial files, NA.

32. "Organization of troops in the Department of Virginia and North Carolina commanded by Maj. Gen. Benjamin F. Butler, U.S. Army, May 31, 1864," *O.R.*, Ser. I, Vol. 36, Pt. II, p. 430; see also "Return of Casualties in the Union Forces, June 15–30," *O.R.*, Ser. I, Vol. 40, Pt. 1, pp. 218–236.

33. Edward W. Hinks, "Supplemental Specifications to Charge 2nd of Charges and Specifications preferred against Brig. Gen. Edward A. Wild," City Point, Va., June 27, 1864, Court Martial files, NA.

34. Longacre, "Brave Radical Wild," pp. 15–16.

35. "General Orders No. 74," Head Qrs. 18th Army Corps, near Petersburg, Va., June 28, 1864, Court Martial files, NA.

36. Edward A. Wild to Major Robert S. Davis, A. A. G., near Petersburg, Va., June 29, 1864, Wild, "Military Career," Harvard University Archives, Cambridge, Massachusetts.

37. Wild, "Military Career."

38. Edward A. Wild to Major Robert S. Davis, June 29, 1864, Edward Wild Papers, MHI, cited in Reid, "General Edward A. Wild and Civil War Discrimination," p. 19.

39. Records of Edward A. Wild's Court-Martial, Court Martial files, NA, cited in Reid, "General Edward A. Wild and Civil War Discrimination," pp. 19–20.

40. Edward A. Wild to Major Robert S. Davis, near Petersburg, June 29, 1864, Adjutant General's Papers, Court Martial files, NA.

41. *Ibid.*

42. Edward A. Wild to Major Robert S. Davis, near Petersburg, June 29, 1864, Adjutant General's Papers, Court Martial files, NA.

43. Endorsement of Maj. Gen. Comdg. William F. Smith, on back of Edward A. Wild's "Appeal to the Maj. Gen. Comdg. The Department for protection against the oppression and injustice of his superior officer states his reasons," near Petersburg, June 29, 1864, Court Martial files, NA.

44. Wild, "Military Career."

45. General Orders, No. 46, December 5, 1863, *O.R.*, Ser. III, Vol. 3, p. 1144.

46. Wild, "Military Career."

47. General Order No. 86, Hinks Papers, Boston University Library, Boston, Mass., cited in Reid, "General Edward A. Wild and Civil War Discrimination," p. 20.

48. Longacre, "Brave Radical Wild," p. 16.

49. "Report of the Military Services of Edward A. Wild," Edward A. Wild Papers, MHI, cited in Reid, "General Edward A. Wild and Civil War Discrimination," p. 20.

50. Longacre, "Brave Radical Wild," p. 16.

51. *O.R.*, Ser. I, Vol. 40, Pt. III, p. 435; New York *Times*, August ___, 1864; General Order No.

86, Hinks Papers, Boston University Library, Boston, Mass., cited in Reid, "General Edward A. Wild and Civil War Discrimination," p. 20.

52. General Orders, No. 86, issued by Major General Butler, copied into Wild, "Military Career."

53. *Ibid.*

54. Major General Benj. F. Butler to Lieutenant General Grant, July 19, 1864, *O.R.*, Ser. I, Vol. 40, Pt. III.

55. Lieutenant General U.S. Grant to Major General Butler, July 19, 1864, *O.R.*, Ser. I, Vol. 40, Pt. III, pp. 339–340.

56. Major General Benjamin F. Butler, "Orders," July 24, 1864, *O.R.*, Ser. I, Vol. 40, Pt. III, p. 435.

57. B. F. Butler to Maj. Gen. Ord, Telegram, Butler's Hd. Qrs., July 24, 1864, Edward A. Wild Papers, MHI.

58. Lieutenant General U.S. Grant to Major General Halleck, July 24, 1864, 5 P.M., *O.R.*, Ser. I, Vol. 40, Pt. III, p. 422.

59. Wild, "Military Career."

60. Sifakis, *Who Was Who in the Civil War*, p. 713.

Chapter XII

1. U.S. Grant to Maj. Gen. H. W. Halleck, City Point, Virginia, July 19, 1864, *O.R.*, Ser. I, Vol. 40, Pt. III, p. 334.

2. W. A. Nichols, A.A.G., Special Order No. 249, by order of the Secretary of War, War Department, Washington, D.C., July 26, 1864, *O.R.*, Ser. I, Vol. 40, p. 500.

3. R. S. Davis, A. A. G., to Lieut. H. T. Schroeder, Headquarters, Dept. Of Va. And N.C., July 29, 1864., *O.R.*, Ser. I, Vol. 40, p. 636.

4. Edward A. Wild to Capt. C. E. Wallbridge, in the field before Petersburg, Va., July 4, 1864, Edward A. Wild Papers, MHI.

5. General Edward A. Wild to Brig. Gen. G. F. Shepley, September 1, 1864, *O.R.*, Ser. I, Vol. 24, Pt. II, p. 653.

6. Wild, "Military Career."

7. Assistant Adjutant General R. S. Davis, "Special Order No. 212," August 4, 1864, *O.R.*, Ser. I, Vol. 42, Pt. II, p. 50.

8. "Organization of troops in the Department of Virginia and North Carolina, commanded by Maj. Gen. Benjamin F. Butler, U.S. Army, August 31, 1864," *O.R.*, Ser. I, Vol. 42, Pt. II, p. 623.

9. "Return of Casualties in the Union Forces: Chaffin's Farm, Va., September 29–30, 1864," *O.R.*, Ser. I, Vol. 42, Pt. I, p. 136.

10. Edwin W. Stanton to Major General Butler, October 28, 1864, *O.R.*, Ser. I, Vol. 42, Pt. III, p. 417; Wild, "Military Career." Special Order 372, October 29, 1864, War Department Files, NA.

11. Wild, "Military Career."

12. Edward A. Wild to My dear Walter [Wild], near Chaffin's Bluff, Nov. 18, 1865, original letter in possession of great-great niece, Helen Stevens Whitlock.

13. Major General Benj. F. Butler to Brigadier General I. N. Palmer, November 30, 1864, *O.R.*, Ser. I, Vol. 42, Pt. III, p. 765.

14. Benjamin F. Butler to Rear Admiral Porter, November 30, 1864, *O.R.*, Ser. I, Vol. 42, Pt. III, p. 761-762.

15. Wild, "Military Career."

16. William S. Powell, *The North Carolina Gazetteer* (Chapel Hill: University of North Carolina Press, 1968), p. 402.

17. Benj. Butler to Col. Webster, November 30, 1864, in Edward A. Wild Papers, Southern Historical Collection, University of North Carolina at Chapel Hill, Chapel Hill, North Carolina.

18. Derby, *Bearing Arms in the Twenty-seventh Massachusetts Regiment of Volunteer Infantry During the Civil War, 1861–1865*, p. 446.

19. Benjamin F. Butler, "Orders," December 2, 1864, Edward A. Wild Papers, MHI.

20. Wild, "Military Career."

21. Benjamin F. Butler, "Orders," December 2, 1864, Edward A. Wild Papers, MHI.

22. Barrett, *The Civil War in North Carolina*, p. 264.

23. Derby, p. 446.

24. Wild, "Military Career."

25. Derby, *p.* 447.

26. *Ibid.*

27. Wild, "Military Career."

28. Derby, p. 448.

29. *Ibid.*, pp. 448–449.

30. *Ibid.*, p. 450.

31. Brigadier General I. N. Palmer to Capt. A. L. Fitch, December 18, 1864, *O.R.*, Ser. I, Vol. 42, Pt. III, p. 1038.

32. Derby, pp. 450–451.

33. *Ibid.*, pp. 451–452.

34. *Ibid.*, p. 452.

35. Brigadier General I. N. Palmer to Capt. A. L. Fitch, December 18, 1864, *O.R.*, Ser. I, Vol. 42, Pt. III, p. 1038.

36. Wild, "Military Career."

37. Derby, p. 452.

38. General Orders, No. 297, War Dept., Adjutant General's Office, Washington, December 3, 1864, *O.R.*, Ser. I, Vol. 42, Pt. II, p. 791.

39. Brigadier General I. N. Palmer to Capt. A. L. Fitch, December 15, 1864, *O.R.*, Ser. I, Vol. 42, Pt. III, p. 1014.

40. Edward A. Wild to Lieutenant-Colonel Smith, Norfolk, December 20, 1864, *O.R.*, Ser. I, Vol. 42, Pt. III, p. 1050.

41. Wild, "Military Career."
42. John G. Barrett, *North Carolina as a Civil War Battleground, 1861–1865* (Raleigh, North Carolina: North Carolina Department of Cultural Resources, 1980), pp. 78–86.
43. *Ibid.*
44. Wild, "Military Career."
45. Longacre, "Brave Radical Wild," p. 16.
46. Special Order 25, Headquarters 25th A.C., December 30, 1864, Edward A. Wild Papers, Military History Institute; Higginson, *Massachusetts in the Army and Navy during the War of 1861–65,*" Vol. 1, p. 202; also cited in Wild, "Military Career."
47. Derby, *p.* 455.
48. Brigadier General C. A. Heckman to Major General Gibbon, January 24, 1865, *O.R.*, Ser. I, Vol. 46, Pt. II, p. 245.
49. Brigadier General C. A. Heckman to Brigadier General Turner, January 25, 1865, *O.R.*, Ser. I, Vol. 46, Pt. II, p. 260.
50. Brigadier General Edward A. Wild to Brigadier General Turner, January 26, 1865, *O.R.*, Ser. I, Vol. 46, Pt. II, p. 269.
51. Memorandum from General E. O. C. Ord to General Turner, January 26, 1865, *O.R.*, Ser. I, Vol. 46, Pt. II, p. 270.
52. Brigadier General John W. Turner to Brigadier General Heckman, January 31, 1865, *O.R.*, Ser. I, Vol. 46, Pt. II, p. 320.
53. Major General E. O. C. Ord, to General Heckman, February 6, 1865, *O.R.*, Ser. I, Vol. 46, Pt. II, p. 440.
54. A. G. Draper, Bvt. Brig. Gen., In the Field, Va., February 15, 1865, to Captain D. D. Wheeler, Court Martial files, NA.
55. "Charges and Specifications preferred against Brigadier General Edward A. Wild, U.S. Vols.," Court Martial files, NA.
56. Edward A. Wild to Lieut. Col. Edward A. Smith, A. A. G., Department of Virginia, February 19, 1865, Court Martial files, NA.
57. *Ibid.*
58. *Ibid.*
59. *Ibid.*
60. *Ibid.*
61. *Ibid.*
62. Major General Godfrey Weitzel to Lieutenant Col. E. W. Smith, Headquarters, Twenty-Fifth Army Corps, Army of the James, February 18, 1865, Court Martial files, NA.
63. Major General Ord, Special Orders, No. 48, February 14, 1865, War Department Files, NA.
64. Special Order No. 48, Ext. 9, Headquarters Dept. Of Va. Army of the James, cited in Wild, "Military Career."
65. Edward A. Wild to Capt. D. D. Wheeler, A.A.G., 25th Army Corps, February 25, 1865, War Department Files, NA.
66. E. O. C. Ord to Brig. Gen. Rawlins, Headquarters, Army of the James, February 24, 1865, *O.R.*, Ser. I, Vol. 46, Pt. II, p. 679.
67. "Special Orders, No. 85." March 27, 1865, Handwritten original copy, Edward A. Wild Papers, File 2157, MHI; also see "Special Orders, No. 85," O.R., Ser. I, Vol. 46, Pt. III, pp. 212–213.
68. Special Order No. 74, and Special Order. No. 85, Extr. 3, and General Order No. 25, cited in Wild, "Military Career."
69. Longacre, "Brave Radical Wild," p. 16.
70. "Report of Capt. George A. Bruce, Thirteenth New Hampshire Infantry, Officer of the Pickets," April 4, 1865, *O.R.*, Ser. I, Vol. 46, Pt. I, pp. 1212–1213.
71. Warner, *Generals in Blue*, p. 558.
72. Hurd, *History of Norfolk County, Massachusetts, with Biographical Sketches of Many of its Pioneers and Prominent Men*, p. 877.
73. Kingman, "General Edward Augustus Wild," *New England Historical and Genealogical Register*, 49 (October) 1895, p. 410.
74. Longacre, "Brave Radical Wild," p. 16.
75. Wild, "Military Career."
76. Fort Pocahontas: "Major General Godfrey Weitzel, United States Army," online at http://www.fortpocahontas.org/Weitzel.html.
77. "Return of casualties in the Union Forces commanded by Lieut. Gen. Ulysses S. Grant, March 29–April 9, 1865," *O.R.*, Ser. I, Vol. 46, Pt. I, pp. 581–597.
78. Special Order No. 101, Ext. 2, from Major General Ord, dated April 13, 1865, cited in Wild, "Military Career."
79. Fort Pocahontas: "Major General Godfrey Weitzel, United States Army," online at http://www.fortpocahontas.org/Weitzel.html.
80. Edward Steers, Jr. *Blood on the Moon: The Assassination of Abraham Lincoln* (Lexington, Ky.: The University Press of Kentucky, 2001), pp. 116–118.
81. Walter H. Wild, Deposition B, Case of Frances E. Wild, No. 583593, Frances E. Wild Pension Application File. National Archives, Washington, D.C.
82. Steers, pp. 272–277; Carl Sandburg, *Abraham Lincoln: The War Years*, Vol. IV, pp. 389–413.
83. Lieutenant General Grant, "Special Order No. 78," Washington, D.C., April 20, 1865, Edward A. Wild Papers, MHI.
84. Wild, "Military Career."
85. *Ibid.*
86. Reid, "General Edward A. Wild and Civil War Discrimination," p. 21.
87. Edward A. Wild to Major General Godfrey Weitzel, May 8, 1865; Wild to Wilson, May 10, 1865; Wild to Edward W. Kinsley, July 28, 1863, Edward Wild Papers, MHI and also Mrs. Wild to Edward W. Kinsley, June 28, 1864,

Kinsley Papers, Duke University, Durham, N.C., cited in Edward A. Wild Papers, MHI; cited in Reid, "General Edward A. Wild and Civil War Discrimination," p. 21.

88. Major General Godfrey Weitzel to Lieutenant Col. E. W. Smith, Headquarters, Twenty-Fifth Army Corps, Army of the James, February 18, 1865, Court Martial files, NA.

89. Longacre, "Brave Radical Wild," p. 16.

90. Major General Godfrey Weitzel to Brigadier General Edward A. Wild, May 13, 1865, cited in Reid, "General Edward A. Wild and Civil War Discrimination," p. 22.

91. *Ibid.*

92. Longacre, "Brave Radical Wild," p. 18.

93. Boatner, p. 65.

94. Correspondence of Major General Benjamin F. Butler, p. 600, cited in Reid, "General Edward A. Wild and Civil War Discrimination," p. 22.

95. *Ibid.*

96. General William Birney to General Butler, Pittsburg, Pa., April 23, 1865, *Butler Letters*, Vol. 5, pp. 600-601.

97. Boatner, p. 351.

98. Edw. A. Wild to Geo. Griggs, Brookline, May 26, 1865, original in Brookline Public Library, Brookline, Massachusetts, typed copy in files of Horace Stevens, courtesy of Mrs. Helen S. Whitlock.

Chapter XIII

1. David Lindsey, *Americans in Conflict: The Civil War and Reconstruction* (Boston: Houghton-Mifflin Company, 1974), p. 177.

2. Thomas Lately, *The First President Johnson* (New York: William Morrow & Company, Inc., 1968), pp. 405-406.

3. Margaret Green, *Defender of the Constitution: Andrew Johnson* (New York: Julian Messner, Inc., 1962), pp. 125-126.

4. "Chap. XC—An Act to Establish a Bureau for the Relief of Freedmen and Refugees," United States, *Statutes at Large, Treaties, and Proclamations of the United States of America*, Vol. 13 (Boston, 1866), pp. 507-509.

5. Paul S. Peirce, "The Freedman's Bureau, a Chapter in Reconstruction," James Truslow Adams and R. V. Coleman, *Dictionary of American History*, Vol. 2, (New York: Scribner, 1940), pp. 335-336.

6. Stevens and Bradford, p. 132.

7. E. D. Townsend, War Department, Adjutant General's Office, Special Order No. 268, *O.R.*, Ser. I, Vol. 47, Pt. 3, p. 604; also copy in Edward A. Wild Papers, MHI.

8. Paul A. Cimbala, *Under the Guardianship of the Nation: The Freedmen's Bureau and The Reconstruction of Georgia, 1865-1870* (Athens: University of Georgia Press, 1997), p. 1.

9. Boatner, pp. 722-723.

10. Cimbala, p. 3.

11. *Ibid.*, p. 23.

12. *Ibid.*, p. 23.

13. Edward A. Wild to Brevet Major General Saxton, Boston, Massachusetts, June 5, 1865, Edward A. Wild Papers, MHI.

14. Cimbala, p. 23.

15. Brevet Major General Rufus Saxton to Brig. Gen. Wild, Beaufort, South Carolina, June 20, 1865, Edward A. Wild Papers, MHI.

16. Stevens and Bradford, p. 132.

17. *Ibid.*

18. Thompson, p. 62.

19. *Ibid.*

20. *Macon Telegraph*, May 24, and June 1, 1865, cited in Thompson, pp. 45-46.

21. Shelby Foote, *The Civil War: A Narrative*, Vol. 14, pp. 288-289.

22. Wild, "Military Career."

23. Newspaper clipping from *New South*, June 24, 1865, Edward A. Wild Papers, MHI.

24. Longacre, "Brave Radical Wild," pp. 18-19.

25. Cimbala, p. 51.

26. Cimbala, pp. 1, 23.

27. William S. McFeely, *Yankee Stepfather: General O. O. Howard and the Freedmen* (New York: Norton Library, 1970), p. 11.

28. Cimbala, p. 23.

29. Edward A. Wild to John A. Andrew, Governor of Massachusetts, Augusta, Georgia, July 3, 1865, Massachusetts Historical Society, Boston, Massachusetts.

30. Cimbala, p. 23.

31. Wild to John A. Andrew, July 3, 1865, Massachusetts Historical Society, Boston, Massachusetts.

32. *Ibid.*

33. *Ibid.*

34. *Ibid.*

35. John W. Sullivan to Edward Kinsley, containing extracts of letter from Brigadier General Edward Wild, August 2, 1865, Edward Wilkinson Kinsley Papers, Duke University, Durham, North Carolina.

36. Edward A. Wild to John A. Andrew, July 3, 1865, Massachusetts Historical Society, Boston, Mass.

37. John W. Sullivan to Edward Kinsley, containing extracts of letter from Brigadier General Edward Wild, August 2, 1865, Edward Wilkinson Kinsley Papers, Duke University, Durham, North Carolina.

38. *Ibid.*

39. *Ibid.*

40. Mansfield French was born in Man-

chester, Vermont, on February 21, 1810. He studied at Bennington Seminary, and at the Divinity School of Kenyon College in Ohio. He founded Marietta College and Granville Female Seminary, and was principal of Circleville Female College. He was president of Xenia, Ohio, Female College, and agent for Wesleyan University. He became an itinerant minister in North Ohio for the Methodist Church. He became a strong anti-slavery agitator through his newspaper, *The Beauty of Holiness*, and was one of the first to propose the education of the freed slaves. "Mansfield French," James Grant Wilson and John Fiske, eds. *Appleton's Cyclopedia of American Biography*, at Virtual American Biographies, http://famousamericans.net/mansfieldfrench/.

41. McFeely, p. 91.
42. Andrews, *War-Time Journal of a Georgia Girl*, p. 359.
43. [Clipping from unidentified newspaper and city] "Dr. French's Lecture," July 1865, Edward A. Wild Papers, MHI.
44. Andrews, *War-Time Journal of a Georgia Girl, 1864–1865*, pp. 337–339.
45. Portion of an article from unidentified newspaper, Edward Wild Papers, M.H.I.
46. Boatner, p. 842.
47. Cimbala, p. 106.
48. John W. Sullivan to Edward Kinsley, containing extracts of letter from Brigadier General Edward Wild, August 2, 1865, Edward Wilkinson Kinsley Papers, Duke University, Durham, North Carolina.
49. Edward A. Wild to Capt. A. P. Ketchum, Augusta, Georgia, July 14, 1865, Edward A. Wild Papers, MHI.
50. *Ibid.*
51. *Ibid.*
52. *Ibid.*
53. *Ibid.*
54. Cimbala, p. 24.
55. Willingham, *No Jubilee: The Story of Confederate Wilkes*, pp. 97–98.
56. Colonel Jack "Black Jack" Travis, "General Edward Porter Alexander: Soldier, Author, Scholar, and Captain of Industry," *Confederate Veteran*, 1:22–32, 2002.
57. Willingham, *No Jubilee: The Story of Confederate Wilkes*, pp. 96–97.
58. *Ibid.*, pp. 102–103.
59. J. Frank Carroll, *Confederate Treasure in Danville* (Danville, Virginia: URE Press, 1996), p. 13.
60. Medora Fields Perkerson, *White Columns in Georgia* (New York: Bonanza Books, 1956), p. 1643.
61. Carroll, pp. 12–13.
62. Strode, pp. 167–168.
63. *Ibid.*
64. Carroll, pp. 2–3.

65. Strode, pp. 180–182.
66. M. H. Clark, "The Last Days of the Confederate Treasury and What Became of the Specie," *Southern Historical Society Papers*, IX (rpt. Broadfoot Publishing Company, 1990), p. 545. According to Clark, about $40,000 in silver, generally reported at $39,000, was left at Greensboro.
67. Barrett, *The Civil War in North Carolina*, p. 378.
68. Strode, p. 185.
69. Willingham, pp. 191–192.
70. Perkerson, pp. 166–167.
71. *Ibid.*, p. 166.
72. *Ibid.*
73. Willingham, pp. 192–193.
74. Clark, pp. 542–556.
75. Basil W. Duke, "Last Days of the Confederacy," in Johnson, Robert U., and Clarence C. Buel, *Battles and Leaders of the Civil War*, Vol. IV (1887; rpt. Secaucus, N.J.: Castle, 1982), pp. 764–765.
76. Duke, pp. 764–765.
77. Perkerson, p. 164.
78. Willingham, pp. 193–194.
79. *Ibid.*, pp. 204–205.
80. Evans, *Confederate Military History*, VI, p. 384.
81. Willingham, p. 194; and Perkerson, p. 167.
82. Strode, pp. 212–213.
83. Evans, *Confederate Military History*, VI, p. 384.
84. Willingham, pp. 204–205.
85. [Mrs. Robertson], "The Money of the Richmond Banks That was in Washington at the Close of the War. Another Account of What Became of It," *Washington Gazette*, October 18, 1895, reprinted from an article in the *Savanna Press*, October 15, 1895, in Warren, *Chronicles of Wilkes County, Georgia*, p. 305.
86. Carroll, p. 13.
87. *Ibid.*, p. 196.
88. [Mrs. Robertson], "The Money of the Richmond Banks That was in Washington at the Close of the War. Another Account of What Became of It," *Washington Gazette*, October 18, 1895, reprinted from an article in the *Savanna Press*, October 15, 1895, in Warren, *Chronicles of Wilkes County, Georgia*, p. 305.
89. Willingham, *No Jubilee: The Story of Confederate Wilkes*, p. 196.
90. *Washington Chronicle*, July 31, 1889, cited in Warren, Mary Boudurant, ed. *Chronicles of Wilkes County, Georgia, from Washington's Newspaper 1889–1898* (Danielsville, Ga.: Heritage Papers, 1978), pp. 188–189.
91. Andrews, *War-Time Journal of a Georgia Girl*, p. 368.
92. "Legends of Lost Gold," online at http://www.kudcom.com/www.gold.html.

93. Perkerson, p. 167.
94. "A Romance of Robbery," *The New York World*, August 21, 1865.
95. Willingham, *No Jubilee: The Story of Confederate Wilkes*, pp. 196–197.
96. *Ibid.*, p. 197.
97. *Ibid.*
98. Andrews, *War-Time Journal of a Georgia Girl*, pp. 269.
99. "A Romance of Robbery," *The New York World*, August 21, 1865.
100. Andrews, *War-Time Journal of a Georgia Girl*, p. 289.
101. [Mrs. Robertson], "The Money of the Richmond Banks That was in Washington at the Close of the War. Another Account of What Became of It," *Washington Gazette*, October 18, 1895, reprinted from an article in the *Savanna Press*, October 15, 1895, in Warren, *Chronicles of Wilkes County, Georgia*, p. 306.
102. *Ibid.*, p. 307.
103. *Ibid.*, pp. 341–342.
104. *Ibid.*, p. 361.
105. *Ibid.*, pp. 356–357.
106. *Ibid.*, p. 352.
107. Willingham, pp. 198–199.
108. Andrew, *War-Time Journal of a Georgia Girl*, p. 352.
109. Willingham, pp. 198–199.
110. "A Romance of Robbery," *The New York World*, August 21, 1865.
111. *Ibid.*
112. Willingham, p. 199.
113. "A Romance of Robbery," *The New York World*, August 21, 1865.
114. Willingham, p. 234.
115. *Washington Chronicle*, July 31, 1889, cited in Warren, Mary Boudurant, ed. *Chronicles of Wilkes County, Georgia, from Washington's Newspaper 1889–1898* (Danielsville, Ga.: Heritage Papers, 1978), pp. 188–189.
116. "A Romance of Robbery," *The New York World*, August 21, 1865.
117. Letter from John B. Weems, Macon, Georgia, to Henry Clay Dean, Mount Pleasant, Iowa, October 7, 1867, *Southern Historical Society Papers*, Vol. I (Richmond, Va., 1876, rpt. Wilmington, N.C.: Broadfoot Publishing Co., 1990), pp. 232–234.
118. J. F. Schaffer, "Treatment of Prisoners in Castle Thunder, Richmond, Va., *O.R.* Ser. II, Vol. 5, p. 878.
119. Andrews, *War-Time Journal of a Georgia Girl*, p. 340.
120. Willingham, p. 199.
121. Weems to Dean, October 7, 1867, *Southern Historical Society Papers*, Vol. I, pp. 232–234.
122. "A Romance of Robbery," *The New York World*, August 21, 1865.
123. Weems to Dean, October 7, 1867, *Southern Historical Society Papers*, Vol. I, pp. 232–234.
124. Willingham, p. 199.
125. Andrews, *War-Time Journal of a Georgia Girl*, p. 352.
126. Edward A. Wild, "Charges vs. Chennault family" (List of charges against Mrs. Dionysius Chennault and Mrs. John N. Chennault), July 28, 1865, Edward A. Wild Papers, MHI.
127. *Ibid.*
128. *Ibid.*
129. Andrews, *War-Time Journal of a Georgia Girl*, p. 353.
130. Weems to Dean, October 7, 1867, *Southern Historical Society Papers*, Vol. I, pp. 232–234.
131. Willingham, p. 199.
132. Weems to Dean, October 7, 1867, *Southern Historical Society Papers*, Vol. I, pp. 232–234.
133. Edward A. Wild to Major General James B. Steedman, Washington, Wilkes County, Georgia, July 29, 1863, Edward A. Wild Papers, MHI.
134. *Ibid.*
135. Boatner, pp. 413–414.
136. Edward A. Wild to "The Occupants of the Premises of Robert Toombs," Washington, Wilkes Co., Ga., July 28, 1865, Edward A. Wild Papers, MHI.
137. Perkerson, p. 165.
138. Andrews, *War-Time Journal of a Georgia Girl*, pp. 355–356.
139. Washington, D.C., *Daily National Intelligencer*, August 25, 1865.
140. Andrews, *War-Time Journal of a Georgia Girl*, pp. 357–358.
141. Cimbala, p. 115.
142. Andrews, *War-Time Journal of a Georgia Girl*, p. 358.
143. *Ibid.*, p. 360.
144. *Ibid.*, p. 362.
145. *Ibid.*, pp. 363–364.
146. Boatner, p. 727; Lindsey, p. 179.
147. Carl Schurz to General Steedman (which was forwarded on to President Johnson), Augusta, Ga., August 7, 1865, "Views expressed by Major Gen. Steedman in Conversation with Carl Schurz, 1865," U.S. 39th Congress, 1st Session 1865–66, Senate Executive document No. I, p. 52, Carl Schurz report on condition in South, in that portion of the Union lately in rebellion, cited in Stevens and Bradford, pp. 133–135.
148. Lindsey, p. 179.
149. Carl Schurz to General Steedman, Augusta, Ga., August 7, 1865, cited in Stevens and Bradford, pp. 133–135.
150. *Ibid.*
151. Senate Executive Document No. 2,

39th Congress, 1st Session, p. 40, Carl Schurz's Report to the President, 1865, in Walter L. Fleming, *Documentary History of Reconstruction, Political, Military, Social, Religious, Educational and Industrial, 1865 to the Present Time*, Vol. I, (Cleveland, Ohio: Arthur H. Clark Co., 1906), p. 31.

152. Edward A. Wild to Maj. Gen. Steedman, Commanding Georgia, Atlanta, Ga., August 2, 1865, Edward A. Wild Papers, MHI.
153. *Ibid.*
154. *Ibid.*
155. *Ibid.*
156. Weems to Dean, October 7, 1867, *Southern Historical Society Papers*, Vol. I, pp. 232–234.
157. Brevet Major Gen. R. Saxton, "General Orders, No. 7," Beaufort, South Carolina, August 9, 1865, Edward A. Wild Papers, MHI. This document can also be found in the U.S. 39th Congress, 1st Session, House Executive Document, Vol. 8, No. 1256, Executive Document No. 70, Freedmen's Bureau, p. 107.
158. Cimbala, p. 25
159. Saxton to Wild, August 17, 1865, Wild Papers, MHI, cited in Reid, "General Edward A. Wild and Civil War Discrimination," *Historical Journal of Massachusetts*, 13 (1) January, 1985, p. 23.
160. Cimbala, p. 26.
161. Edward A. Wild to General Saxton, Macon, Ga., August 23, 1865, Edward A. Wild Papers, MHI.
162. *Ibid.*
163. *Ibid.*
164. *Ibid.*, p. 27.
165. *Ibid.*
166. *Ibid.*
167. McFeely, p. 104.
168. O. O. Howard, Circular No. 13, July 28, 1865, National Archives, Washington, D.C., Record Group 105, Bureau of Refugees, Freedmen, and Abandoned Lands, cited in McFeely, p. 104.
169. McFeely, p. 105.
170. *Ibid.*, p. 108–109.
171. *Ibid.*, pp. 133–134.
172. Correspondence of John Emory Bryant, "Letter Book of J. E. Bryant, Freedmen's Bureau, Augusta, Ga., 1865," pp. 210–215, in C.S.A. *Army Letter Book for Conscription, 1863–1864, 8th Congressional District of Georgia*, John Emory Bryant Papers, Duke University, Durham.
173. Cimbala, p. 133.
174. Correspondence of John Emory Bryant, "Letter Book of J. E. Bryant, Freedmen's Bureau, Augusta, Ga., 1865," pp. 210–215, in C.S.A. *Army Letter Book for Conscription, 1863–1864, 8th Congressional District of Georgia*, John Emory Bryant Papers, Duke University, Durham.
175. Wild, "Military Career."
176. Edward A. Wild to Brevet Major General Rufus Saxton, Macon, Georgia, August 26, 1865, Edward A. Wild Papers, MHI.
177. Edward A. Wild, "Roster, Sept. 1, 1865," Edward A. Wild Papers, M.H.I.
178. Telegram from Brevet Major General R. Saxton to John Bryant, Beaufort, South Carolina, September 1, 1865, Edward A. Wild Papers, MHI.
179. Cimbala, p. 75.
180. *The Commonwealth*, September 30, 1865.
181. "The Troubles in Georgia between the Citizens and Colored Troops," Savannah *Republican*, September 21, 1865, p. 1; Cimbala, p. 75.
182. "The Murder of Capt. Healy at Augusta, Ga.," New York *Tribune*, September 15, 1865.
183. "The Troubles in Georgia between the Citizens and Colored Troops," Savannah *Republican*, September 21, 1865, p. 1.
184. Edward A. Wild to Edward Atkinson, Augusta, Ga., September 16, 1865, Massachusetts Historical Society, Boston, Mass.
185. *Ibid.*
186. *Ibid.*
187. Edward A. Wild to General Saxton, Augusta, Georgia, September 13, 1865, Edward A. Wild Papers, MHI.
188. Official copy of telegram from Lt. Gen. U.S. Grant to Edwin M. Stanton, Secretary of War, Galena, Ill., September 2, 1865, Edward A. Wild Papers, MHI.
189. Official copy of telegram from Lt. Gen. U.S. Grant to Edwin M. Stanton, Secretary of War, Galena, Ill., September 2, 1865, and from J. S. Fullerton, A.A.G., to Brev. Maj. Gen. R. Saxton, Washington, D.C., September 2, 1865, Edward A. Wild Papers, MHI.
190. Saxton to Wild (no date), Wild Papers, MHI, cited in Reid, "General Edward A. Wild and Civil War Discrimination, p. 23.
191. Joseph A. Staden, secretary to General Howard, October 24, 1865, Wild Papers, M.H.I, cited in Reid, "General Edward A. Wild and Civil War Discrimination," p. 23.
192. Stuart M. Taylor to E. A. Wild, Beaufort, S.C., September 12, 1865, Edward A. Wild Papers, MHI.
193. Wild, "Military Career."
194. Stuart M. Taylor, "Special Order No. 16," Beaufort S.C., September 12, 1865, Edward A. Wild Papers, MHI; see also Wild, "Military Career."
195. Weems to Dean, October 7, 1867, *Southern Historical Society Papers*, Vol. I, pp. 232–234.
196. "A Romance of Robbery," *The New York World*, August 21, 1865.

197. "Antics of a Wild Massachusetts General," article from the New York *Times*, reprinted in an unidentified newspaper clipping, Edward A. Wild Papers, File 6, #2158, MHI.

198. *Ibid.*

199. Unidentified newspaper clipping, "Opposition to the Freedmen's Bureau," with handwritten date, "Sept. 30, 1865," in Edward A. Wild Papers, MHI.

200. E. D. Townsend, A.A.G., Special Order No. 501, Edward A. Wild Papers, M.H.I.

201. Edward A. Wild to Col. Frank E. Howe, Augusta, Ga., September 19, 1865, National Archives, Washington, D.C.

202. Reid, "General Edward A. Wild and Civil War Discrimination," p. 23.

203. *Ibid.*

204. *Ibid.*, pp. 23–24.

205. *Ibid.*, p. 24.

206. Edward A. Wild to Gov. John A. Andrew, New York, October 15, 1865, Massachusetts Historical Society, Boston, Massachusetts; also cited in Stevens and Bradford, pp. 135–136.

207. *Ibid.*

208. Lieutenant Joseph A. Staden for General Howard to John W. Sullivan, Washington, Georgia (?), October 24, 1865, copy in Edward A. Wild Papers, M.H.I.

209. Edward A. Wild to Gov. John A. Andrew, New York, October 15, 1865, Massachusetts Historical Society, Boston, Massachusetts.

210. *Ibid.*

211. *Ibid.*

212. Wild, "Military Career."

213. Special Orders, No. 652, E. D. Townsend, War Department, December 22, 1865, War Department Files, National Archives, Washington, D.C.

214. Weems to Dean, October 7, 1867, *Southern Historical Society Papers*, Vol. I, pp. 232–234.

215. *Washington Chronicle*, July 31, 1889, and August 21, 1889, cited in Warren, Mary Boudurant, ed. *Chronicles of Wilkes County, Georgia, from Washington's Newspaper 1889–1898*, pp. 188–189.

216. Willingham, p. 200.

217. James MacGregor Burns, J. W. Peltason, *Government by the People*, 8th ed. (Englewood Cliffs, New Jersey: Prentice-Hall, Inc., 1972), pp. 473–474.

218. Robert Willingham, "Wilkes County, Georgia: An Overview of Local History." Online at http://www.rootsweb.com/~gawilkes/localhst.htm.

219. *Washington Chronicle*, July 31, 1889, and August 21, 1889, cited in Warren, Mary Boudurant, ed. *Chronicles of Wilkes County, Georgia, from Washington's Newspaper 1889–1898*, pp. 188–189.

Chapter XIV

1. "Letters of the Civil War: Return of the Flags," http://www.letterscivilwar.com/returnflag.html.

2. *Ibid.*

3. Massachusetts Adjutant-General's Report, January, 1863, pp. 83–85.

4. *Ibid.*, pp. 86–88.

5. *Ibid.*

6. "[Harvard] Class of 1844, 50th Annual Report," p. 257.

7. J. Heber Smith, M.D., Deposition B, March 18, 1898, Case of Frances E. Wild, No. 583593, Frances E. Wild Pension Application papers.

8. Edward A. Wild's "Claim for Invalid Pension," County of Suffolk, State of Massachusetts, January 31, 1866, Edward A. Wild Pension Papers, NA, Record Group 94, Washington, D.C. Hereinafter cited as Edward A. Wild Pension Papers.

9. Edward A. Wild, "War of 1861. Act July 14, 1862, Claim for an Invalid Pension," Edward A. Wild Pension Papers.

10. "[Harvard] Class of 1844, 50th Annual Report," p. 257.

11. Frances E. Wild, Deposition A, Case No. 583593, June 17, 1897, Frances E. Wild Pension Application Papers.

12. Emily J. Jones, Deposition B, February 4, 1898, Case of Frances E. Wild, No. 583593, Frances E. Wild Pension Application papers.

13. Walter H. Wild, Deposition B, Case of Frances E. Wild, No. 583593, Frances E. Wild Pension Application Papers.

14. Anthony Jones, Deposition A, February 4, 1898, Case of Frances E. Wild, No. 583593, Frances E. Wild Pension Application Papers.

15. Emily J. Jones, Deposition B, February 4, 1898, Case of Frances E. Wild, No. 583593, Frances E. Wild Pension Application papers.

16. Anna F. Sullivan, affidavit, October 1896, Case of Frances E. Wild, No. 583593, Frances E. Wild Pension Application Papers.

17. Edward A. Wild, "Application for an Artificial Limb," to Surgeon General, Washington, D.C., November 19, 1875, Edward A. Wild Pension Papers.

18. William L. Candler, formerly 1st Lieutenant, Company A, First Massachusetts Infantry Volunteers, "Officer's Certificate of Disability," January 26, 1878, Edward A. Wild Pension Papers.

19. Edward A Wild, "Claim for Pension Increase," Certificate #65,294, filed by Massachusetts State Agency, Boston, Mass., Edward A. Wild Pension Papers.

20. "Increase Invalid Pension, Claimant Edward A. Wild," Edward A. Wild Pension Papers.

21. Hannibal Williams and J. H. Thompson, "Affidavit," November 13, 1878, San Francisco, California, Edward A. Wild Pension Papers.
22. Edward A. Wild to Hon. J. A. Bentley, Commissioner of Pensions, notarized on June 9, 1879, San Francisco, California, in Edward A. Wild Pension Papers.
23. Frances E. Wild, Deposition A, No. 583593, June 17, 1897, Frances E. Wild Pension Application Papers.
24. Edward A. Wild to Edward Atkinson, September 16, 1865, Atkinson Papers, Massachusetts Historical Society, cited in Stevens and Bradford, p. 138.
25. "Memorial Service" in Pemberton Dudley, ed., Transactions of the Forty-Fifth Session of the American Institute of Homeopathy, Forty-eighth Anniversary, Held at Washington, D.C., June 13 to 17, 1892, Philadelphia: Sherman & Company, 1892, p. 209.
26. Edward A. Wild to Walter Wild, Chaffin's Bluff, November 18, 1864, cited in Stevens and Bradford, pp. 138–139.
27. J. T. Talbor, "Remarks," *Transactions of the Forty-Fifth Session of the American Institute of Homeopathy*, pp. 227–228.
28. SENEX, "The Late General Wild," Letter to the Editor of the Nation. *The Nation* 83 (29 October 1891), p. 334.
29. J. T. Talbor, "Remarks," *Transactions of the Forty-Fifth Session of the American Institute of Homeopathy*, pp. 227–228.
30. Robert Wallace, ed. *The Old West: The Miners* (New York: Time-Life Books, 1976), pp. 32–35.
31. Wallace, The *Old West: The Miners*, pp. 57–59.
32. *The World Book Encyclopedia*, Vol. 16 (Chicago: Field Enterprises Educational Corporation, 1963), pp. 38–39.
33. Edward A. Atkinson to Gen. Edward A. Wild, Boston, February 8, 1866, Edward Atkinson Letters, October 17, 1865, to July 23, 1867, No. 159, Edward A. Atkinson Collection, Massachusetts Historical Society, Boston, Mass.
34. Robert Silverberg, *Ghost Towns of the American West* (New York: Thomas Y. Crowell Company, 1968), pp. 134–135.
35. *Ibid.*, p. 136.
36. *Ibid.*, pp. 141–142.
37. *Ibid.*, pp. 143–144.
38. Stevens and Bradford, p. 139.
39. "Edward Augustus Wild," [Harvard] Class of 1844, 25th Anniversary Report," May 1869, p. 189.
40. W. C. Bryant, *Silver District of Nevada*, New York, 1865, p. 24, cited in Stevens and Bradford, p. 140.
41. B. Silliman, "Reece River Consolidated Company mines located in Austin, Lander Co., Nevada. Prospectus of the Company and report by B. Silliman, M.A., M.D. of Yale College" (New York: John W. Ameriana, Printer, 1866), p. 22.
42. *Silver Mines of Nevada* (New York: W. C. Bryant & Company, 1864), p. 63.
43. B. Silliman, "Reece River Consolidated Company mines located in Austin, Lander Co., Nevada. Prospectus of the Company and report by B. Silliman, M.A., M.D. of Yale College," p. 6.
44. *Silver Mines of Nevada* (New York: W. C. Bryant & Company, 1865), p. 24.
45. Edward A. Wild to Edward Atkinson, Austin, Nevada, September 19, 1866, Edward Atkinson Papers, Massachusetts Historical Society; also cited in Stevens and Bradford, pp. 139–140.
46. Edward Atkinson to Edward Wild, cited in Stevens and Bradford, p. 140.
47. *Ibid.*
48. *Ibid.*, p. 141.
49. Edward Atkinson to General E. A. Wild, Boston, June 19, 1866, "Copy Book," Vol. 2, pp. 655–656, Edward A. Atkinson Collection, Massachusetts Historical Society, Boston, Mass.
50. Ned Atkinson to Ned Wild, Boston, May 4, 1867, Vol. 2, pp. 653–654.
51. Edward A. Wild to Ned [Atkinson], Austin, Nevada, September 27, 1866, Massachusetts Historical Society, Boston, Mass.
52. Edward Atkinson to Edward Wild, Boston, October 2, 1866, "Copy Book," Vol. 2, p. 437, Edward A. Atkinson Collection, Massachusetts Historical Society, Boston, Mass.
53. Edward Atkinson to Edward Wild, Boston, November 13, 1866, "Copy Book," Vol. 2, pp. 454–457, Edward A. Atkinson Collection, Massachusetts Historical Society, Boston, Mass.
54. Edward Atkinson to Edward Wild, cited in Stevens and Bradford, pp. 141–142.
55. Ned Atkinson to Ned Wild, Boston, December 3, 1866, "Copy Book," Vol. 2, pp. 499–501, Edward A. Atkinson Collection, Massachusetts Historical Society, Boston, Mass.
56. *Ibid.*
57. Frances E. Wild, Deposition A, Case No. 583593, June 17, 1897, Frances E. Wild Pension Application Papers.
58. Stevens and Bradford, p. 141.
59. "[Harvard] Class of 1844, 50th Annual Report," p. 256.
60. E. Wainwright to Dr. Talbot, 22 Chestnut Street, Boston, Mass., April 16, 1893, in Harvard University Archives.
61. Stevens and Bradford, p. 141.
62. Frances E. Wild to Edward Atkinson, December 1, 1881, Atkinson Papers, Massachu-

setts Historical Society, cited in Stevens and Bradford, p. 141.

63. Frances E. Wild, Deposition A, Case No. 583593, June 17, 1897, Frances E. Wild Pension Application Papers.

64. "[Harvard] Class of 1844, 50th Annual Report," p. 257.

65. Walter H. Wild, Deposition B, Case of Frances E. Wild, No. 583593, Frances E. Wild Pension Application Papers.

66. Walter H. Wild, Deposition B, Case of Frances E. Wild, No. 583593, Frances E. Wild Pension Application Papers

67. Walter H. Wild to Mesesrs. Brower & Colgate of New York, Trustees, April 22, 1875, personal correspondence, courtesy of Mrs. Helen Stevens Whitlock.

68. Ministry of Northern Development and Mines, "A proven mineral producer," online at http://www.mndm.gov.on.ca/MNDM/.

69. Stevens and Bradford, p. 141.

70. *Ibid.*, p. 142.

71. Walter H. Wild, Deposition B, Case of Frances E. Wild, No. 583593, Frances E. Wild Pension Application Papers.

72. Emily J. Jones, Deposition B, February 4, 1898, Case of Frances E. Wild, No. 583593, Frances E. Wild Pension Application papers.

73. *Ibid.*

74. Edward A. Wild to Walter Wild, September 19, 1883, Providence, Rhode Island, cited in Stevens and Bradford, p. 142.

75. Stevens and Bradford, p. 142.

76. Edward A. Wild, "Brief for Duplicate Certificate," filed at Boston, Mass., January 16, 1885, Edward A. Wild Pension Papers, National Archives, Washington, D.C.

77. *Ibid.*

78. Description of cabin from George Bullock, an engineer who visited the cabin, cited in Stevens and Bradford, p. 143.

79. Anthony Jones, Deposition A, February 4, 1898, Case of Frances E. Wild, No. 583593, Frances E. Wild Pension Application Papers.

80. Frances E. Wild, Deposition A, Case No. 583593, June 17, 1897, Frances E. Wild Pension Application Papers.

81. Stevens and Bradford, p. 143.

82. Thomas A. Gorham, Esq., to Amos G. Hull, of New York, cited in Stevens and Bradford, p. 144.

83. *Ibid.*

84. Stevens and Bradford, p. 143.

85. Thomas A. Gorham to Amos G. Hill, quoted in Stevens and Bradford, p. 144.

86. "Memorial Service" in Pemberton Dudley, ed., Transactions of the Forty-Fifth Session of the American Institute of Homeopathy, Forty-eighth Anniversary, Held at Washington, D.C., June 13 to 17, 1892, Philadelphia: Sherman & Company, 1892, p. 209.

87. *Ibid.*

88. Frances E. Wild, Deposition A, June 17, 1897, Frances E. Wild Pension Application Papers.

89. Rebecca P. Hunt, Deposition D, February 21, 1898, Case of Frances E. Wild, No. 58593, Frances E. Wild Pension Application Papers.

90. Hiram W. Allen, Deposition A, January 20, 1898, Case of Frances E. Wild, No. 583598, Frances E. Wild Pension Application papers.

91. Anthony Jones to Mrs. E. A. Wild, Colombia, South America, Sept. 3, 1891, in Class of 1844 Secretary's Papers, Harvard University Archives, Cambridge, Mass.

92. Anthony Jones, Deposition A, February 4, 1898, Case of Frances E. Wild, No. 583593, Frances E. Wild Pension Application Papers.

93. "[Harvard] Class of 1844, 50th Annual Report," pp. 257–258.

94. Anthony Jones to Mrs. E. A. Wild, Colombia, South America, Sept. 3, 1891, in Class of 1844 Secretary's Papers, Harvard University Archives, Cambridge, Mass.

95. "General Edward Augustus Wild: Enlightened Article Concerning Distinguished Son of Brookline in Civil War by Colombian Consul at Anniversary of his death," *The Chronicle* (Brookline, Mass.), 25 August, 1932.

96. "[Harvard] Class of 1844, 50th Annual Report," pp. 257–258.

97. Anthony Jones to Mrs. E. A. Wild, Colombia, South America, Sept. 3, 1891, in Class of 1844 Secretary's Papers, Harvard University Archives, Cambridge, Mass.

98. Frances E. Wild, Deposition A, Case No. 583593, June 17, 1897, Frances E. Wild Pension Application Papers.

99. Anthony Jones to Mrs. E. A. Wild, Colombia, South America, Sept. 3, 1891, in Class of 1844 Secretary's Papers, Harvard University Archives, Cambridge, Mass.

100. *Ibid.*

101. "[Harvard] Class of 1844, 50th Annual Report," pp. 257–258.

102. Anthony Jones to Mrs. E. A. Wild, Colombia, South America, Sept. 3, 1891, in Class of 1844 Secretary's Papers, Harvard University Archives, Cambridge, Mass.

103. *Ibid.*

104. Extracts from a letter of Miss Katherine Wild, dated Swamp Scott, September 4, 1891, in Class of 1844 Secretary's Papers, Harvard University Archives, Cambridge, Mass.

105. Anthony Jones to Mrs. E. A. Wild, Colombia, South America, Sept. 3, 1891, in Class

of 1844 Secretary's Papers, Harvard University Archives, Cambridge, Mass.
106. *Ibid.*; Bradford Kingman, "General Edward Augustus Wild," *New England Historical and Genealogical Register,* p. 413.
107. Anthony Jones to Mrs. E. A. Wild, Colombia, South America, Sept. 3, 1891, in Class of 1844 Secretary's Papers, Harvard University Archives, Cambridge, Mass.
108. Extracts from a letter of Miss Katherine Wild, dated Swamp Scott, September 4, 1891, in Class of 1844 Secretary's Papers, Harvard University Archives, Cambridge, Mass.
109. "Obituary: Brig.-Gen. Edward A. Wild," *Boston Post,* September 5, 1891.
110. Anthony Jones to Mrs. E. A. Wild, Colombia, South America, Sept. 3, 1891, in Class of 1844 Secretary's Papers, Harvard University Archives, Cambridge, Mass.
111. Note from Edward Wheelwright, Secretary Class of 1844, to N. B., October 13, 1891, Harvard University Archives, Cambridge, Massachusetts.
112. Anthony Jones to Mrs. E. A. Wild, Colombia, South America, Sept. 3, 1891, in Class of 1844 Secretary's Papers, Harvard University Archives, Cambridge, Mass.
113. Extracts from a letter of Miss Katherine Wild, dated Swamp Scott, September 4, 1891, in Class of 1844 Secretary's Papers, Harvard University Archives, Cambridge, Mass.
114. *JAMA* 17 (October 31): 702, 1891.
115. "Lonely Grave of Hero Is Located: G.A.R. to Bring Remains of Gen. Wild from Colombian City," *The Boston Journal,* February 2, 1910.
116. "Widow Averse to Having Gen. Wild's Body Removed. Does Not Object to Bronze Tablet to Veteran's Memory," *The Boston Journal,* February 3, 1910.
117. Edward A. Wild to wife, November 29, 1861, cited in Stevens and Bradford, p. 78.
118. Colonel Samuel M. Ray, report of securities in his possession, quoted in Stevens and Bradford, pp. 143–144.
119. Horace N. Stevens, "Supplement to the life of General Wild," typescript, pp. 1–3, courtesy of Mrs. Helen S. Whitlock.
120. Helen S. Whitlock, Eastham, Mass., May 7, 2002, personal correspondence.
121. Stevens and Bradford, "The True Man of Action."
122. Edward W. Smith to Soldiers of the Army of the James, Before Richmond, October 11, 1864, *O.R.,* Ser. I, Vol. 42, Pt. III, pp. 161–175.
123. Longacre, "Brave Radical Wild," p. 9.
124. *Ibid.*
125. "Widow Averse to Having Gen. Wild's Body Removed," *The Boston Journal,* February 3, 1910.

126. "[Harvard] Class of 1844, 50th Annual Report," p. 258.
127. Harvard University, "About Memorial Hall," online at http://www.fas.harvard.edu/~memhall/exterior.html.
128. "[Harvard] Class of 1844, 50th Annual Report," p. 258; Bradford Kingman, "General Edward Augustus Wild," p. 412.
129. "[Harvard] Class of 1844, 50th Annual Report," p. 258.
130. *Ibid.,* p. 258.
131. "Recall Career of Local War Hero with Memorial Day again at hand," *The Chronicle* (Brookline, Mass.), 27 May 1926.
132. "Address of Martin P. Kennard, In Behalf of the Subscribing Citizens, on Presentation to the Town of a Memorial Portrait of the late Brig.-Gen'l Edward Augustus Wild, together with the response of the Chairman of the Board of Selectmen, and the impromptu remarks of other gentlemen present." Brookline, Mass., 1894, privately published by the town.
133. Inscription below portrait of General Wild in the Brookline Public Library, courtesy of the Brookline Public Library, Brookline, Mass.
134. "Widow Averse to Having Gen. Wild's Body Removed," *The Boston Journal,* 3 February 1910.
135. "General Wild's Turkish Medals," Boston *Herald,* 19 May 1897.
136. *Ibid.*
137. Sifakis, *Who Was Who in the Civil War,* p. 713.
138. "Address of Martin P. Kennard, In Behalf of the Subscribing Citizens, on Presentation to the Town of a Memorial Portrait of the late Brig.-Gen'l Edward Augustus Wild, together with the response of the Chairman of the Board of Selectmen, and the impromptu remarks of other gentlemen present." Brookline, Mass., 1894, privately published by the town, p. 20.
139. Bradford Kingman, "General Edward Augustus Wild," p. 411.

Epilogue

1. Last Will and Testament of Edward A. Wild, Norfolk County Probate Court, Norfolk County Courthouse, 649 High Street, Dedham, Massachusetts 02026, Book 169, pp. 897–898.
2. *Ibid.*
3. Arthur Cushing to Pension Office, stamped October 22, 1895, National Archives, Pension Files of Brigadier General Edward A. Wild, and widow, Frances Ellen Wild Pension Application papers, Record Group 94, Washington, D.C.

4. Horace N. Stevens, "A brief account of the lives of the descendants of Dr. Charles Wild of Brookline, Mass." (Typescript, May 23, 1947), p. 1.

5. Congressional Act of June 27, 1890.

6. "Civil War Pension Acts (1865–1930)," online at: www.hartslog.com/pensions/page2.htm.

7. Frances E. Wild, Application for Accrued Pension. (Widows.) Frances Ellen Wild Pension Application papers.

8. *Ibid.*

9. Frances E. Wild, Claimant, for Widow's Pension, 583593, Frances E. Wild Pension Application papers.

10. Private Act No. 931, Department of the Interior, March 3, 1903, National Archives, Pension Files of Brigadier General Edward A. Wild, and widow, Frances Ellen Wild, Record Group 94, Washington, D.C.

11. "Civil War Pension Acts (1865–1930)," online at: www.hartslog.com/pensions/page2.htm.

12. "Drop Report-Pensioner," O J. Randall, Chief, Finance Division, October 12, 192, National Archives, Pension Files of Brigadier General Edward A. Wild, and widow, Frances Ellen Wild, Record Group 94, Washington, D.C.

13. Obituary notice of Mrs. Frances Ellen Wild, in Boston *Evening Transcript*, October 3, 1923, part 2, page 2, column 7; see also "Widow of Gen. Wild Dead in Brookline," Boston *Globe*, October 4, 1923, page 17, column 2.

14. Death certificate of Frances Ellen Wild, Brookline, Norfolk County, Massachusetts.

15. Will of Frances E. Wild, #64143, Probate Office, Norfolk County, Massachusetts.

Appendix

1. Brigadier General Edward A. Wild to General Barnes, *O.R.*, Ser. I, Vol. 29, Pt. II, p. 562; "Reports of Brig. Gen. Edward A. Wild, U.S. Army, commanding expedition," Edward A. Wild, Brigadier General of Volunteers to Capt. George H. Johnston, Assistant Adjutant General, Norfolk, Va., December 28, 1863, *O.R.*, Ser. I, Vol. 29, Pt. I, pp. 911–917; Captain George B. Cock, 5th USCT to Brigadier General Lorenzo Thomas, December 29, 1863, *O.R.*, Ser. I, Vol. 51, Pt. I, p. 20; and J. V. Witt, *Wild in North Carolina*, pp. 1–60.

2. Beth Gilbert Crabtree and James W. Patton, eds. *Journal of a Secesh Lady: The Diary of Catherine Ann Devereux Edmondston, 1860–1866.* (Raleigh, N.C.: Division of Archives and History, 1979), pp. 509–510.

3. Brigadier General Edward A. Wild to General Barnes, *O.R.*, Ser. I, Vol. 29, Pt. II, p. 562.

4. J. V. Witt, *Wild in North Carolina*, p. 18.

5. Selby Daniels and T. H. Pearce, eds., *The Diary of Captain Henry A. Chambers*, pp. 182–183.

6. "Reports of Brig. Gen. Edward A. Wild, U.S. Army, commanding expedition," Edward A. Wild, Brigadier General of Volunteers to Capt. George H. Johnston, Assistant Adjutant General, Norfolk, Va., *O.R.*, Ser. I, Vol. 29, Pt. I, pp. 911–917.

7. Report of Colonel Alonzo G. Draper, to Lieutenant Hiram W. Allen, A.A.A.G., Colored Troops, District of Norfolk and Portsmouth, Va., December 24, 1863, Portsmouth, Va., Edward A. Wild Papers, Southern Historical Collection, University of North Carolina, Chapel Hill, North Carolina. Note: This report is not to be found in the *Official Records of the War of Rebellion*, but the information is included in Brigadier General Wild's report of December 23, "Reports of Brig. Gen. Edward A. Wild, U.S. Army, commanding expedition," *O.R.*, Ser. I, Vol. 29, Pt. I, pp. 911–917.

8. "Reports of Brig. Gen. Edward A. Wild, U.S. Army, commanding expedition," Edward A. Wild, Brigadier General of Volunteers to Capt. George H. Johnston, Assistant Adjutant General, Norfolk, Va., *O.R.*, Ser. I, Vol. 29, Pt. I, pp. 911–917.

Bibliography

Manuscript Sources

Assistant Adjutant General's Office, Record Group 94, National Archives, Washington, D.C.
Atkinson, Edward, Letters. Massachusetts Historical Society, Boston, Massachusetts.
Beasley, Alyda White papers. Special collections. Currituck County Library, Barco, North Carolina.
Brookline, Massachusetts, Town Records.
Bryant, John Emory, papers. Duke University, Durham, North Carolina.
Bureau of Refugees, Freedmen, and Abandoned Lands, Record Group 105, National Archives, Washington, D.C.
Butler, Benjamin F., papers. Manuscript collection, Library of Congress, Washington, D.C.
Candler, William Latham, papers, 1861–1863, Special Collections Department, University Libraries, Virginia Polytechnic Institute, Blacksburg, Virginia.
Clapp, Henry A., Letter Book, Collections branch, Tryon Palace Historical Sites and Gardens, New Bern, North Carolina.
8th United States Census, Charles City County, Virginia.
8th United States Census, 1860, Slave Schedules, Charles City County, Virginia.
Kinsey, Edward W., Papers, Southern Historical Collection, University of North Carolina at Chapel Hill, Chapel Hill, North Carolina.
Lukei, Melinda J. "The White Family." 5 page typescript, n.d., courtesy of Dale H. Beasley, Norfolk, Virginia.
Military service and pension records of Union Soldiers in the Civil War. Record Group 94. National Archives, Washington, D.C.
Moore, Timothy. *First to Richmond*. Unpublished manuscript in files of author (Jerry V. Witt).
Probate Records, Brookline, Suffolk County, Massachusetts.
Proceedings of General Court-Martial, Records of the Judge Advocate General's Office, Record Group 153, National Archives, Washington, D.C.
Quartermaster General, Consolidated Correspondence File, Ser. 225, Record Group 92, National Archives, Washington, D.C.
Shurtlett, Giles Waldo and Mary E. Burton Shurtlett Papers, Oberlin College Archives, Oberlin, Ohio.
Stevens, Horace, Papers, Private Collection, Mrs. Helen Stevens Whitlock, Eastham, Massachusetts.

Stevens, Horace N. "A brief account of the lives of the descendants of Dr. Charles Wild of Brookline, Mass." Typescript, May 23, 1947.
____, and Bradford, Gersham. *The True Man of Action*, typescript, n.d. Brookline Public Library, Brookline, Mass.
Tyler Family Papers, Earl Gregg Swem Library, the College of William & Mary, Williamsburg, Virginia.
Wead, Frederick F., Papers, New York State Library, Albany, New York.
Wild, Edward A., Civil War Papers, Brookline Public Library, Brookline, Massachusetts.
____, papers. Massachusetts Commandery, Military Order of Loyal Legions of the United States Collection (MOLLUS), U. S. Army Military History Institute, Carlisle Barracks, Pennsylvania.
____, papers. Southern Historical Collection. Manuscript Department, University of North Carolina, Chapel Hill, North Carolina.
Willis, George H., papers. Mugar Memorial Library, Boston University, Boston, Massachusetts.

Newspapers

Boston Journal, February 2, 1910, and February 3, 1910; Boston [Mass.] *Post*, September 5, 1891; [Brookline, Mass.] *Chronicle*, May 27, 1926; *Daily Confederate* [Raleigh, North Carolina,] 1863–1865;
Daily Richmond Enquirer, July 1, 1864; [Elizabeth City, North Carolina] *Economist*, 1899–1900;
[London] *Times;* [Lorain, Ohio] *Chronicle-Telegram; Milledgeville* [Georgia] *Southern Record*, 1864; New York *Daily Tribune*, 1865;
New York *Globe*, March 4, 1864; New York *Times*, 1863, 1864;
New York *World*, 1864; *Norfolk* [Virginia] *Ledger Dispatch;* [Norfolk] *Virginia Pilot; North Carolina Standard*, [Raleigh, North Carolina], 1863–1864;
Richmond [Virginia] *Examiner*, June 30, 1864; Savannah, Georgia, Republican, September 21, 1865; *Semi-Weekly Standard*, Raleigh, North Carolina, 1863;
Virginia Pilot, December 16, 2001; [Washington, D.C.], *Daily National Intelligencer*, 1865;
Washington [Georgia] *Chronicle*, 1889–1898; *Weekly Register* [Petersburg, Virginia], 1863–1864;
Wilmington [North Carolina] *Journal*, 1863–1866.

Primary Printed Sources

Andrews, Eliza Frances. *The War-Time Journal of a Georgia Girl*. New York: D. Appleton & Co., 1908.
Annual Report of the Adjutant-General of the Commonwealth of Massachusetts with the Reports from the Quartermaster-General, Surgeon General, and Master of Ordinance for the Year Ending December 31, 1864. Boston: Wright & Potter, State Printers, 1865.
Basler, Roy P., et al., eds. *The Collected Works of Abraham Lincoln*. 9 vols. New Brunswick, New Jersey: 1953–1955.
Blackett, R. J. M., ed. *Thomas Morris Chester, Black Civil War Correspondent: His Dispatches from the Virginia Front*. Baton Rouge: Louisiana State University Press, 1989.
Calvin D. Cowles, compl., *Atlas to Accompany the Official Records of the Union and Confederate Armies*. Washington, D.C.: Government Printing Office, 1891–1895, rpt. New York: Fairfax Press, 1983.
Commander, Henry Steele. *Documents of American History*, 9th ed. Englewood Cliffs, N.J.: Prentice-Hall, Inc., 1973.
Crabtree, Beth Gilbert, and James W. Patton, eds. *Journal of a Secesh Lady: The Diary of Catherine Ann Devereux Edmondston, 1860–1866*. Raleigh, N.C.: Division of Archives and History, 1979.
Daniels, Selby, and Pearce, T. H., eds. *The Diary of Captain Henry A. Chambers*. Wendell, N.C.: Broadfoot's Bookmark, 1983.

Duncan, Russell, ed. *Blue Eyed Child of Fortune: The Civil War Letters of Robert Gould Shaw.* Athens: University of Georgia Press, 1992.
Harris, William C., ed. *"In the Country of the Enemy": The Civil War Reports of a Massachusetts Corporal.* Gainesville: University Press of Florida, 1999.
Harrison, Galen D. *Prisoners' Mail from the American Civil War.* Dexter, Mich.: Thomson-Shore, Inc., 1997.
Marshall, Jessie Ames, ed. *Private and Official Correspondence of Gen. Benjamin F. Butle.* 5 vols., Norwood, Mass., Privately published, 1917.
Massachusetts Adjutant General. *Massachusetts Soldiers, Sailors and Marines in the Great Civil War.* 8 vols. Norwood, Mass.: Norwood Press, 1931.
Matthews, James M. *Public Laws of the Confederate States of America, Passed at the First Session of the First Congress; 1862, Carefully Collated with the Original at Richmond.* Richmond: R. M. Smith, Printer to Congress, 1862.
Mobley, Joe A., ed. *The Papers of Zebulon Baird Vance.* 2 vols. Raleigh: North Carolina Department of Cultural Resources, Division of Archives and History, 1963, 1995.
Moore, Frank, ed. *The Rebellion Record: A Diary of American Events, with Documents, Narratives, Illustrative Incidents, Poetry, etc.* 8 vols. New York: Putnam, 1861–1871.
Otis, George A., *The Medical and Surgical History of the War of the Rebellion,* 6 vols. Washington, D.C.: Government Printing Office, 1876.
Pugh, Jesse F., and Frank T. Williams. *The Hotel in the Great Dismal Swamp and Contemporary Events Thereabouts.* Richmond, Va.: Garrett & Massie, Inc., 1964.
Ross, Fitzgerald. *Cities and Camps of Confederate States,* Richard B. Harwell, ed. 1865; rpt. Urbana: University of Illinois Press, 1958.
Ruffin, Edmond. *The Diary of Edmund Ruffin.* Edited by William Kauffman. Baton Rouge: Louisiana State University Press, 1989.
United States. "Chap. XC—An Act to establish a Bureau for the Relief of Freedmen and Refugees," United States, *Statutes at Large, Treaties, and Proclamations of the United States of America,* Vol. 13 Boston, 1866.
_____. War Department. *Official Army Register of the Volunteer Force of the United States Army.* Washington, D.C.: Government Printing Office, 1867, Part 8.
_____. _____. *The War of the Rebellion: A Compilation of the Official Records of the Union and Confederate Armies.* 130 vols. Washington, D.C.: Government Printing Office, 1880–1901.
Wallace, Elizabeth Curtin. *Glencoe Diary: The War-Time Journal of Elizabeth Curtis Wallace.* Edited by Eleanor P. Cross and Charles B. Cross, Jr. Norfolk: Norfolk County Historical Society of Chesapeake, Va., 1968.
Warren, Mary Boudurant, ed. *Chronicles of Wilkes County, Georgia, from Washington's Newspaper 1889–1898.* Danielsville, Ga.: Heritage Papers, 1978.
Yearns, W. Buck, and John G. Barrett, eds. *North Carolina Civil War Documentary.* Chapel Hill: University of North Carolina Press, 1980.

Other Primary Public Sources

Marriage Register, Office of the Secretary of State, William Francis Galvin, Secretary, Archives Division, Commonwealth of Massachusetts, Boston, Massachusetts.
Probate Records, Norfolk County, Massachusetts, Dedham, Massachusetts.

Memoirs

Briggs, Katherine Robinson. "Brookline in the Civil War." Brookline Historical Publication Society, Publication No. 10, December 1896.

Butler, Benjamin F. *Butler's Book: The Autobiography and Personal Reminiscences of Major-General Benj. F. Butler.* Boston: A. M. Thayer & Co., Book Publishers, 1892.

Clark, Walter, ed. *Histories of the Several Regiments and Battalions from North Carolina in the Great War, 1861–1865.* 5 vols. Goldsboro, N.C.: Nash Brothers, 1901; repr. Wendell, N.C.: Broadfoot's Bookmark, 1982.

Cowdin, Robert, compl. *First Regiment of Infantry, Massachusetts Volunteer Militia.* Boston: Wright and Potter Printing Co., 1903.

Cudworth, Warren H. *History of the First Regiment (Massachusetts Infantry) from the 25th of May, 1861, to the 25th of May, 1864: Including Brief References to the Operations of the Army of the Potomac.* Boston: Walker, Fuller, and Company, 1866.

Ford, Arthur P., and Marion Johnstone Ford, *Life in the Confederate Army and Some Experiences and Sketches.* New York: Neale Publishing Company, 1905.

Kingman, Bradford. *Memoir of Gen. Edward Augustus Wild.* Boston: Privately printed, 1895. Parker, William Harwar. *Recollections of a Naval Officer, 1841–1865.* New York: Charles Scribner's Sons, 1883, rpt. Annapolis, Md.: Naval Institute Press, 1985.

Kreutzer, William. *Notes and Observations Made During Four Years of Service with the Ninety-Eighth N.Y. Volunteers in the War of 1861.* Philadelphia: Grant, Faires & Rogers, Printers, 1878.

Long, A. L. *Memoirs of Robert E. Lee: His Military and Personal History Embracing a Large Amount of Information Hitherto Unpublished.* New York: J. M. Stoddart & Co., 1886.

Poor, Mary W. *Recollections of Brookline.* Brookline, Mass.: Riverdale Press: Reprinted from Brookline Historical Society publication of August 1903.

Woods, Harriet P. *Historical Sketches of Brookline, Massachusetts.* Boston: Robert B. Davis & Co, 1874.

Secondary Sources

Adams, James Truslow, and R. V. Coleman. *Dictionary of American History.* New York: Scribner, 1940.

Avary, Myrta Lockett. *Dixie After the War: An Exposition of Social Conditions Existing in the South, during the Twelve Years Succeeding the Fall of Richmond.* New York: Doubleday, 1906.

Barrett, John G. *The Civil War in North Carolina.* Chapel Hill: University of North Carolina Press, 1963.

_____. *North Carolina as a Civil War Battleground 1861–1865.* Raleigh: North Carolina Department of Cultural Resources, 1980.

Berlin, Ira, ed. *Freedom: A Documentary History of Emancipation, 1861–1867.* Series 1, Vol. 1, *The Destruction of Slavery*, and Series 2, *The Black Military Experience.* Cambridge: Cambridge University Press, 1982 and 1985.

Blum, John M., Edmund S. Morgan, Willie Lee Rose, Arthur M. Schlesinger, Jr., Kenneth M. Stampp, and C. Vann Woodward. *The National Experience*, 3rd ed. New York: Harcourt Brace Jovanovich, Inc., 1973.

Boatner, Mark M., III. *The Civil War Dictionary*, rev. ed. New York: Vintage Books, 1991.

Brooks, Victor. *African Americans in the Civil War.* Philadelphia, Pa.: Chelsea House Publishers, 2000.

Burns, James MacGregor, and J. W. Peltason. *Government by the People*, 8th ed. Englewood Cliffs, N.J.: Prentice-Hall, Inc., 1972.

Butchko, Thomas R. *Shores of the Pasquotank.* Elizabeth City: Museum of the Albemarle, 1989.

Capers, Ellison. *South Carolina*, Vol. V, *Confederate Military History.* Ed. Clement A. Evans. Atlanta: Confederate Publishing Co., 1899; repr. Washington, N.C.: Broadfoot Publishing Co., 1987.

Carroll, J. Frank. *Confederate Treasure.* Danville, Va.: URE Press, 1996.

Casstevens, Frances H. *Clingman's Brigade in the Confederacy, 1862–1865.* Jefferson, N.C.: McFarland, 2002.

Cimbala, Paul A. *Under the Guardianship of the Nation: The Freedmen's Bureau and the Reconstruction of Georgia 1865–1870*. Athens: University of Georgia Press, 1997.

Cook, E. T. *Life of Florence Nightingale*. 2 vols. London: Macmillan, 1913.

Cook, Gerald Wilson. *The Last Tarheel Militia 1861–1865*. Privately published, 1987.

Cornish, Dudley Taylor. *The Sable Arm: Black Troops in the Union Army, 1861–1865*. Lawrence: University of Kansas Press, 1987.

Cox, Clinton. *Undying Glory: The Story of the Massachusetts 54th Regiment*. New York: Scholastic, Inc., 1991.

Craven, Avery. *Reconstruction: The Ending of the Civil War*. New York: Holt, Rinehart, Winston, 1968.

Davis, William C. *Rebels and Yankees*. 3 vols. London: Salamander Books Limited, 1990, 1999–2001.

Derby, William P. *Bearing Arms in the Twenty-seventh Massachusetts Regiment of Volunteer Infantry during the Civil War, 1861–1865*. Boston: Wright and Potter Printing Co., 1883.

Draper, Thomas Wain-Morgan. *Drapers in America, being a history and genealogy of those with that name and connection*. New York: J. Polhemus Printing Co., 1892.

Dyer, Frederick H. *Compendium of the War of the Rebellion. Compiled and Arranged from Official Records of the Federal and Confederate Armies*. Des Moines, Iowa: Dyer Publishing Co., 1908.

The Encyclopedia Americana. International edition, 30 vols. Danbury, Conn.: Grolier Incorporated, 1997.

Evans, Bruce A. *A Primer of Civil War Medicine: Non Surgical Medical Practices during the Civil War Years*. Knoxville, Tenn.: Bohemian Brigade Bookshop Publishers, 1998.

The Federal Writers' Project of the Federal Works Agency, Work Projects Administration for the State of North Carolina. *North Carolina: The WPA Guide to the Old North State*. 1938, rpt. 1988, Columbia: University of South Carolina Press.

Fleming, Walter L. *Documentary History of Reconstruction, Political, Military, Social, Religious, Educational and Industrial, 1865 to the Present Time*, 2 vols. Cleveland, Ohio: Arthur H. Clark Co., 1906.

Foote, Shelby. *The Civil War: A Narrative*. 14 vols. Alexandria, Va.: Time-Life Books, 1998.

Fox, Charles Barnard. *Record of the Service of the Fifty-Fifth Regiment of Massachusetts Volunteer Infantry*. Cambridge: Press of John Wilson and Son, 1868.

Garrison, Webb. *The Encyclopedia of Civil War Usage*. Nashville, Tenn.: Cumberland House, 2001.

Glatthaar, Joseph T. *Forged in Battle: The Civil War Alliance of Black Soldiers and White Officers*. New York: Free Press, 1990.

Green, Margaret. *Defender of the Constitution: Andrew Johnson*. New York: Julian Messner, Inc., 1962.

Harris, John. *The Gallant Six Hundred*. New York: Mason & Lipscomb Publishers, 1973.

Headley, P. C. *Massachusetts in the Rebellion: A Record of the Historical Position of the Commonwealth*. Boston: Walker, Fuller and Co., 1866.

Higginson, Thomas Wentworth. *Massachusetts in the Army and Navy during the War of 1861–65*. 2 vols. Boston: Wright and Potter, 1895.

Hill, D. H., Jr. *North Carolina*, Vol. IV, *Confederate Military History*. Ed. Clement A. Evans. Atlanta: Confederate Publishing Co., 1899; repr. Washington, N.C.: Broadfoot Publishing Co., 1987.

Hofstadter, Richard. *America at 1750: A Social Portrait*. New York: Vintage Books, 1973.

Hunt, Robert D., and Jack R. Brown. *Brevet Brigadier Generals in Blue*. Gaithersburg, Md.: Olde Soldier Books, Inc., 1990.

Hurd, D. Hamilton, compl. *History of Norfolk County, Massachusetts, with Biographical Sketches of Many of its Pioneers and Prominent Men*. Philadelphia: J. W. Lewis & Company, 1884.

Johnson, Clint. *Civil War Blunders*. Winston-Salem, N.C.: John F. Blair, Publisher, 1997.

Johnson, Robert U., and Clarence C. Buel. *Battles and Leaders of the Civil War*, 4 vols. 1887; rpt. Secaucus, N.J.: Castle, 1982.

Jordan, Ervin L., Jr. *Black Confederates and Afro-Yankees in Civil War Virginia*. Charlottesville: University Press of Virginia, 1995.

Lewis, Emanuel Raymond. *Seacoast Fortifications of the United States.* Washington, D.C.: Smithsonian Institution Press, 1970.
Lindsey, David. *Americans in Conflict: The Civil War and Reconstruction.* Boston: Houghton-Mifflin Company, 1974.
Longacre, Edward G. *Army of Amateurs: General Benjamin F. Butler and the Army of the James, 1863–1865.* Mechanicsburg, Pa.: Stackpole Books, 1997.
MacDonald, John. *Great Battles of the Civil War.* New York: Macmillan Publishing Company, 1988.
McFeely, William S. *Yankee Stepfather: General O. O. Howard and the Freedmen.* New York: Norton Library, 1970.
Moore, John W. *Roster of North Carolina Troops in the War Between the States.* Raleigh: Ashe & Gatling, State Printers, 1882, Vol. 4.
Nash, Howard P., Jr. *Stormy Petrel: The Life and Times of General Benjamin F. Butler, 1818–1893.* Cranbury, N.J.: Associated University Presses, Inc, 1969.
The National Cyclopaedia of American Biography, 37 Volumes. New York: James T. White & Company, 1907 [Vol. 5, p. 511].
Nolan, Dick. *Benjamin Franklin Butler: The Damnest Yankee.* Novato, Calif.: Presidio Press, 1991.
Notably, Baly M. *Florence Nightingale and the Nursing Legacy*, 2nd ed. London: Whurr, 1997.
Parker, Derek, and Julia Parker. *The Complete Astrologer.* New York: McGraw-Hill Book Company, 1971.
Peirce, Neal R., and Jerry Hagstrom. *The Book of America: Inside the Fifty States Today.* New York: W. W. Norton & Company, 1983.
Peirce, Paul Skeels. *The Freedman's Bureau: A Chapter in the History of Reconstruction.* Iowa City: State University of Iowa, 1904.
Perkerson, Medora Field. *White Columns in Georgia.* New York: Bonanza Books, 1956.
Powell, William S. *The North Carolina Gazetteer: A Dictionary of Tar Heel Places.* Chapel Hill: University of North Carolina Press, 1968.
Redkey, Edwin S., editor. *A Grand Army of Black Men: Letters from African American Soldiers in the Union Army, 1861–1865.* New York: Cambridge University Press, 1992.
Roe, Alfred S. *The Fifth Regiment Massachusetts Volunteer Infantry in Its Three Tours of Duty, 1861, 1862–'63, 1864.* Boston: Fifth Regiment Veterans Association, 1911.
Rosen, Robert N. *A Short History of Charleston*, 2nd ed. Columbia: University of South Carolina Press, 1992.
Schouler, William. *A History of Massachusetts,* Vol. 1. Boston: E. P. Dutton and Company, 1868.
Seager, Robert, II. *And Tyler Too: A Biography of John & Julia Gardiner Tyler.* New York: McGraw-Hill Book Company, Inc., 1963.
Shannonhouse, Edna M., ed. and compl. *YearBook, Pasquotank Historical Society.* Baltimore: Gateway Press, Inc., 1983.
Sharp, Bill. *A New Geography of North Carolina.* 4 volumes. Raleigh, N.C.: Edwards & Broghton, Inc., 1954–1965.
Sifakis, Stewart. *Compendium of the Confederate Armies: North Carolina.* New York: Facts on File, 1992.
_____. *Compendium of the Confederate Armies: South Carolina and Georgia.* New York: Facts on File, 1995.
_____. *Who Was Who in the Civil War.* New York: Facts on File, 1988.
Silliman, B. *Reece River Consolidated Company Mines located in Austin, Lander Co., Nevada.*
Prospectus of the Company and Report by B. Silliman, M.A., M.D. of Yale College. New York: John W. Amerinan, Printer, 1866.
Silver Mines of Nevada. New York: W. C. Bryant & Co., 1864.
Silver Mines of Nevada. New York: W. C. Bryant & Co., 1865.
Silverberg, Robert. *Ghost Towns of the American West.* New York: Thomas Y. Crowell Company, 1968.
Smith, Steven D. *Whom We Would Never More See: History and Archaeology Recover the Lives and Deaths of African American Civil War Soldiers on Folly Island, South Carolina.* Columbia: South Carolina Department of Archives and History, 1993.

Steers, Edward, Jr. *Blood on the Moon: The Assassination of Abraham Lincoln.* Lexington: University Press of Kentucky, 2001.
Strode, Hudson. *Jefferson Davis: Tragic Hero.* 3 vols. New York: Harcourt, Brace & World, Inc., 1964.
Styron, William. *The Confessions of Nat Turner,* rev. ed. New York: Modern Library, 1994.
Thomas, Lately. *The First President Johnson.* New York: William Morrow & Company, Inc., 1968.
Trotter, William R. *Ironclads and Columbiads: The Civil War in North Carolina—The Coast.* Winston-Salem, N.C.: John F. Blair, Publisher, 1989.
Trudeau, Noah Andre. *Like Men of War: Black Troops in the Civil War, 1862–1865.* Boston: Little, Brown and Company, 1998.
_____. *Out of the Storm: The End of the Civil War, April–June, 1865.* Boston: Little, Brown and Company, 1994.
_____. *Voices of the 55th: Letters from the 55th Massachusetts Volunteers, 1861–1865.* Dayton, Ohio: Morningside House, Inc., 1998.
Wagner, Frederick B., Jr., and J. Woodrow Savacool, eds. *Thomas Jefferson University: A Chronological History and Alumni Directory, Annotated and Illustrated, 1824–1900.* Philadelphia: Thomas Jefferson University, 1992.
Wallace, Robert, ed. *The Old West: The Miners.* New York: Time-Life Books, 1976.
Wallbank, T. Walter, Alastar M. Taylor, and Nels M. Bailkey, eds. *Civilization: Past & Present,* 4th edition. Glenview, Ill.: Scott, Foresman and Company, 1975.
Warner, Ezra J. *Generals in Blue: Lives of the Union Commanders.* Baton Rouge: Louisiana State University Press, 1972.
West, Richard S., Jr. *Lincoln's Scapegoat General: A Life of Benjamin F. Butler, 1818–1893.* Boston: Houghton Mifflin Company, 1965.
Wilcox, Arthur M., and Warren Ripley. *The Civil War at Charleston,* 21st ed. Charleston, S.C.: The Post and Courier, 2000.
Williams, George W. *A History of the Negro Troops in the War of the Rebellion, 1861–1865.* New York: Harper and Brothers, 1888.
Willingham, Robert M., Jr. *No Jubilee: The Story of Confederate Wilkes.* Washington, Ga.: Wilkes Publishing Company, 1976.
Witt, J. V. *Wild in North Carolina.* Privately published, 1993, distributed by the Family Research Society of Northeastern North Carolina, Belvidere, N.C. 27919.

Articles and Pamphlets

Barrow, Mary Reid. "The History Beat—Farragut and the Confederate Mutiny," *Virginia Pilot,* 1982.
Browne, W. B. "Stranger than Fiction: Capture of United States Steamer Maple Leaf, Near Cape Henry, Half a Century Ago," *Southern Historical Society Papers,* 29 (April 1914): 181–185.
Clarke, M. H. "The Last Days of the Confederate Treasury and What Became of its Specie." *Southern Historical Society Papers* IX (rpt. Broadfoot Publishing co., 1990), pp. 542–556.
Crayon, Porte [David Hunter Strother]. "Dismal Swamp." *Harper's New Monthly Magazine,* 13 (September 1856): 441–455.
Creecy, Richard B. "Old Times in Betsy." *Elizabeth City Economist,* 24 August 1900.
Davison, Eddy W., and Daniel Foxx. "A Journey to the Most Controversial Battlefield in America." *Confederate Veteran,* 6:15–33, 2001.
Du Bois, W. E. Burghardt. "The Freedmen's Bureau." *Atlantic Monthly,* 87:354–365, 1901.
Duke, Basil W. "Last Days of the Confederacy." In Johnson, Robert U., and Clarence C. Buel, *Battles and Leaders of the Civil War,* Vol. IV. 1887; rpt. Secaucus, N.J.: Castle, 1982.
Forehand, Billy. "Shiloh Baptist Church," *Carolina Trees & Branches,* 1 (September 1992): 3.
Hampton, Jeffrey S. "Rebels' descendants moved by 1863 battle." *The Virginia Pilot,* Sunday (16 December 2001): Y1, Y5.

[Harvard] "Class of 1844, 25th Anniversary Report." May 1869.
[Harvard] "Class of 1844, 50th Anniversary Report." 1894.
Higginson, T. W., and Florence Wyman Jaques. "List of Battles and Casualties of the Massachusetts Regiments during the War of the Rebellion." *New England Historical and Genealogic Register Vol.* 46 (January 1892), pp. 31–45.
"The History of a Gallant Regiment." Hartford *Evening Press,* March 5, 1864, reprinted in *New England Loyal Publication Society,* No. 175, March 10, 1864.
Holmes, O. W. "My Hunt After 'The Captain.'" *Atlantic Monthly,* Vol. 10, No. 62 (December 1862), pp.738–764.
Hudson, Leonne. "Valor at Wilson's Wharf," *Civil War Times Illustrated,* 37(1): 46–52, March 1998.
Hutchens, James Albert. "Distinguished Jurist Operated Law School." In: Rutledge, William E., ed., *An Illustrated History of Yadkin County, North Carolina, 1850–1865.* Yadkinville, N.C.: Privately published, 1965.
_____. "Richmond Mumford Pearson: Founder of Richmond Hill Law School," In: Casstevens, Frances H. ed., *Heritage of Yadkin County, North Carolina.* Winston-Salem, N.C.: Hunter Publishing Co., 1981.
Kennard, Martin P. *Address in Behalf of the Subscribing Citizens on Presentation to the Town of a Memorial Portrait of the late Brig. Gen'l Edward Augustus Wild.* Brookline, Mass.: C. A. W. Spencer, 1894.
Kingman, Bradford. "General Edward Augustus Wild." *New England Historical and Genealogical Register,* 49 (October), 1895, pp. 405–413.
Kitrell, Irvin, III. "40 Acres and a Mule." *The Civil War Times Illustrated,* XLI (No. 2) (May) 2002, pp. 54–61.
Longacre, Edward. "Brave Radical Wild," *Civil War Times Illustrated,* XIX (3) (June 1980): 8–19.
Melzack, Ronald. "Phantom Limbs." *Scientific American.* April 1992. Online edition: www.sciam.com/explorations/0492melzak.html.
Mitchell, S. Weir. "The Case of George Dedlow." *Atlantic Monthly,* XVIII (July 1866), pp. 1–11.
Mosser, Jeffrey S. "Suttler's Stores." *Camp Chase Gazette* XX (2), 1992.
Munden, Pauline W. "Knott's Island Then and Now," in Jo Anna Heath Bates, ed., *The Heritage of Currituck County, North Carolina, 1985.* Winston-Salem, N.C.: Hunter Publishing Company, 1985, pp. 1–2.
"Necrology: Edward Wild, M.D." *Journal of the American Medical Association,* 17 (October 31), 1891:702.
Novak, Steve. "Glory Trail: Oberlin to Ft. Wagner." Lorain, Ohio *Chronicle-Telegram,* 26 January 1990.
Oberlin College. *The Oberlin Review.* 19 May 1904.
[Obituary] "Edward Wild, M.D." *Journal of the American Medical Association,* 17:702, 1891.
Orcutt, William Dana. "Ben Butler and the 'Stolen Spoons,'" *North American Review,* 207 (January 1918): 66–80.
Perry, Albert. "American Doctors in the Crimean War." *The South Atlantic Quarterly,* Vol. 54 (No. 4), (October, 1955), pp. 478–490.
Reid, Richard. "General Edward A. Wild and Civil War Discrimination." *Historical Journal of Massachusetts,* 13 (No. 1 (January 1985): 14–29.
_____. "Raising the African Brigade: Early Black Recruitment in Civil War North Carolina." *North Carolina Historical Review,* 70 (3) (July 1993): 266–297.
Rendell, Kenneth W., Inc. "Autographs and Manuscripts: The American Civil War, Catalogue No. 46." Somerville, Mass.: Kinston Galleries, Inc.
Squires, W. H. T. "Norfolk in By-Gone Days." *Norfolk Ledger Dispatch,* 3 October 1935.
Travis, Jack, "General Edward Porter Alexander: Soldier, Author, Scholar, and Captain of Industry." *Confederate Veteran,* 1 (January 2002): 22–32.
Wadsworth, Mary H. "Edward Atkinson." *Proceedings of the Brookline Historical Society at the Annual Meeting, January 22, 1950, Meeting, March 19, 1950, Spring Meeting, May 19, 1950.* Brookline, Massachusetts: Brookline Historical Society, 1950.

Index

Abbeville, South Carolina 220-1
African Brigade 1
Albemarle & Chesapeake Canal Co. 97
Albemarle Sound 97
Alexander, Edward Porter 219, 225
Alexander, Louisa Fredericka 219
Alford, Col. Samuel 88, 92
Allen, 1st. Lt. Hiram W. 171, 255
American Institute of Homeopathy 18
Anderson, Maj. Robert 19.73
Andrew, Gov. John A. 21, 25, 41, 56, 63, 68, 70, 210, 242, 245
Andrews, Eliza Frances 216, 223, 225, 231-2
Andrews, Judge Garnett 220, 223, 226
Andrews, Corp. Richard F. 163
Andrews, Sarah Elizabeth 132
Antietam 22
Antietam, battle of, 9/17/1862 50-52
Antietam Creek 51
Anti-slavery movement 9-10
Arlington Heights, Va. 29
Army of the Potomac 52
Arrest 29
Articles of War 30, 138
Asbury, Lt. A. E. 129
Assassination attempt on Wild 237-8
Atkinson, Edward 8, 9, 238, 247-8, 251-2, 262
Audubon, John James 8
Augusta, Georgia 216

Austin, Nevada 246, 249-50
Austria 18

Balaklava 15
Balkan states 17
Ballance, Arsenth 144
Ballance, Eugene 144
Ballance, Mary 144
Ballance, Nancy White 144
Ballance, Nannie 144
Ballance, Susan 144
Ballance, Willoughby 144
Baltimore, Maryland 25
Bank of Georgia 222
Banks, Maj. Gen. Nathaniel P. 25
Barlow, Brig. Gen. Francis C. 64-5
Barnard, Brig. Gen. John Gross 37
Barnes, Brig. Gen. James 93, 102, 114, 162
Barney, 2nd Lt. John G. 237
Barry, Brig. Gen. William F. 37
Bates, Atty. Gen. Edward 148, 160
Battery Gregg, Morris Island 86
Battery Wagner 2, 62, 73, 86
Battle at Wilson's Wharf, 5/24/1864 171-178
Battle of Antietam (Sharpsburg) 56
Battle of Williamsburg 38
Beasley, Mrs. 144
Beaufort, North Carolina 70
Beauregard, Gen. P.G.T. 27, 74, 92
Beecher, Henry Ward 79
Berkley Plantation, James River 170

Bermuda Hundred 170
Birdsall, Lt. 186
Birney, D. B. 39
Birney, William 208
Birney's Brigade 39
Black Sea 15, 18
Black troops, evolution of 55-6
Blackburn's Ford, VA, 7/18/1861 26-28
Blackwater River 124
Bladensburg, Md. 29
Blockade runner 130
The Blue Juanita 14
Booth, John Wilkes 206
Boston Independent Corps 14
Boston parade, 12/22/1865 245
Bowden, Verna Irene 144
Bowditch, Capt., 55th Mass. 81, 85, 88
Bowditch, W. I. 262
Boyden, Capt. Stephen A. 173
Bradford, Gershom 6, 126
Bradford, Laurence 162
Bradford, Maj. William B. 164
Bragg, Gen. Braxton 170, 221
Breckinridge, Maj. Cary, killed 174, 177
Breckinridge, Maj. Gen. John C. 220-1
Bright, Daniel 57, 102, 106, 114; hanging of 107-8, 117, 120-21, 125
Brookline, Massachusetts 6, 14, 72, 246
Brookline Military Committee 23
Brookline Public Library 262
Brookline War Committee 32
Brooks, Maj. T. B. 89
Brown, Dr. Francis H. 53
Brown, William H. 6
Brown, Surgeon William S. 67

Browne, W. B. 129
Bruce, Capt. George A. 204
Bryant, John Emory 215–6, 218, 236–7
Bryant, Joseph 152
Budd's Ferry 31
Buffaloes 104
Bullifant, R. W. 156
Bunt, William B. 153
Bureau for Colored Troops 61
Burnham, Brig. Gen. H. 189
Burns, Anthony 14
Burnside, Maj. Gen. Ambrose 51, 52, 97
Burroughs, Maj. 94
Butler, Maj.Gen. Benjamin F. 5, 30–1, 58–59, 93, 98.101–2, 119, 120–23, 139, 140, 142, 145, 166.193, 194, 196, 201
Butts, Atty. Charles W. 136–7, 148, 174, 189–192, 200–201
Byrd, William II 97, 128

C&A Canal 137
Calvert County, Md. 30
Cambridge, Massachusetts 24
Camden County, North Carolina 104
Camden Court House 111
Cameron, Simon (Sec. of War) 21, 23
Camp Banks 25
Camp Cameron 24
Camp Hooker, Charles Co., Md. 31
Camp Scott 29
Camp Stanton 41
Camp Union 29
Camp Winfield Scott 37
Candler, John W. 262
Candler, William Latham 22, 23, 24, 31, 36, 40, 49, 262
Capen, Charles 262
Captain of Guerrillas 123
Carr, General 208
Carrington, S. P. 153
Carter, Capt. Solon A. 170, 188
Cassells, Capt. John 155
Castle Thunder 142, 228
Casualties: Antietam/Sharpsburg 51–2; Battery Wagner, 7/18/63 63; Blackburn's Ford 28; First Bull Run 29; Fort Pillow, 1864 165; Indiantown 108; June 15–30, 1864 181–2; South Mountain 50–1; Wild's raid 115; Wilson's Wharf 174–5, 177
Caucasus Mountains 16
Centreville, Virginia 27
Chaffin's Bluff 196
Chain bridge across Potomac River 25

Challiner, James 151, 153
Chamberlain, Lt. Col. Abial G. 142, 166
Chambers, Capt. Henry A. 111
Chandler, Lt. Charles P. 22, 23, 32, 34
Charge of the Light Brigade 15
Charles Albert, King of Sardinia 13
Charles City County, Virginia 152
Charles County, Maryland 34
Charles home, Elizabeth City 103
Charleston, South Carolina, 1863 73
Charleston Battalion 76
Charleston Harbor 2, 62; sketch 75
Chase, William F. 176
Chennault, the Rev. A. Dionysius 224, 226–9
Chennault, Mrs. Dionysius 229
Chennault, Frank 227
Chennault, John N. 227–8, 243
Chennault, Mrs. John N. 229
Chennault, Mary A. 228
Chennault family 221, 230
Chennault plantation 223
Chesapeake Hospital Prison 156
Chicamoxen Creek 31
Chickahominy River 39
Choat, Capt. 159
Civilian prisoners 152–3
Clapp, Pvt. Henry A. 69
Clarke, Acting Sec. M. H. 220
Clingman's Brigade 76
Clopton, Mrs. Luella 156
Clopton, William 154–8, 159–60, 184
Cock, Capt. George B. 108
Coffee, Solomon W. 137
Coffee's Guerrilla Co. 135
Cold Harbor, Va., 5/31–6/12/1864 179
Coleman, 1st Lt. George B., Jr. 117
Colgin, G. W. 156
Colombia, South America 256–258
Colyer, Vincent 71
Commadore (gunboat) 169
Company A, First Regiment, Mass. 24, 26
Company E, 66th North Carolina 120
Compromise of 1850 14
Confederate cavalry of Fitzhugh Lee 165
Confederate Congress 141

Confederate Congress Committee 105
Confederate dog 154–5
Confederate treasure 219–222
Conine, Col. James W. 100
Constantinople 15
Contraband 58, 61, 195
Cook, Maj. 159
Cooley, Capt. 228
Corps d'Afrique 61, 117
Cotting, Dr. Benjamin Eddy 10
Coughlin, Lt. Col. J. 189
Court martial charges 185–
Court martial of Draper 137–9
Court martial of Wild 183–193
Court martial verdict 191
Cowdin, Col. Robert 2, 25–6, 29–32, 36, 41
Cox, Gen. J. D. 48
Crab Island 110
Crimean War 15
Croatia 18
Croft, Capt. James 139
Croft, Mrs. 8
Crofton, Brig. Gen. F. 237
Croper, Golmore 156
Crump, Judge W. W. 219
Cullen, Col. 135
Currituck Court House 111
Currituck Sound 103
Curtis, Col. N. M. 189

Dahlgren, Rear Adm. J. A. 75
Danburg, Georgia 225
Danville, Virginia 220
Darien, Georgia, destruction of 61
Davis, Capt. A. H. 135–6
Davis, Jefferson 31
Davis, Pres. Jefferson 58, 205, 220–1
Davis, Maj. Robert S. 101, 156, 158, 184, 187, 190
Davis, Varina Howell 222
Davison, Eddy W. 165
Dean, Henry Clay 243
Death of Wild in South America 255–259
Decker, Charles Patrick 258
Dedlow, George, case of 66
Deep Creek 100
De Grasse, Dr. John V. 69
De Hanne, J. V. 237
Delaware 32
Derby, William 67
DeRussy's battery 39
Dey, Mary Ballance 144
Diana Mine 250, 252
Dibble, George C. 221
Discrimination against black troops 88
Disloyalty and treason 149
Dismal Swamp 60

Dismal Swamp Canal 99, 109
Dix, Gen. John Adams 14, 129, 131
Dodge, Col. Charles C. 96
Dorton, Jordon 108
Douglass, Frederick 61
Douthat, Thomas 153
Draft riots 56–7
Draper, Pvt. Algernon 163
Draper, Col. Alonzo G. 79, 98, 100, 110–11, 113, 127, 131–4, 140–1, 148, 161, 163; death of 145
Draper, Capt. James S. 91
Draper files charges against Wild 202
Draper's court martial 137–30
Drayton, Capt. 8
Drayton, Col. 240
Drayton, Maj. James Spencer 246
Drewry's Bluff 170
Drum-head court 106
Duke, Gen. Basil 220–1
Duncan, Col. Samuel A. 166, 168
Dunston, Capt., Quartermaster 82
DuPoint, Rear Adm. 75

Ealey, R. H. 152
Easby, David 112
Edenton, North Carolina 96
Edmondston, Mrs. Catherine 105–6, 114
Egman, J. L. 151
Eighteenth Army Corps 67
Eleventh Pennsylvania Cavalry 162
Elizabeth City, North Carolina 100, 103, 146
Elliott, John T., Capt. 104, 106–07, 118, 121, 123
Emancipation Proclamation 56, 69
Escape from *Maple Leaf* 128–30

Fair Oaks, Virginia, 6/25/1862 38–40
Fall of Richmond 204–5
Faneuil Hall 24
Federal blockage 74
Female hostage 111
Ferebee, Edwin 146–7
Ferguson, A. H. 151
Ferrero, Gen. Edward 48, 51
Fiasco at Fort Fisher 200
Fifth New Jersey Volunteers 34
Fifth Ohio, Company B 118–9
Fifth U.S. Colored Troops, Co. D. 119
Fifty-fifth Massachusetts 67, 78
Fifty-first New York 48

Fifty-first Pennsylvania 48
Fifty-fourth Massachusetts 61, 76
First Bull Run, 7/21/1861 29
First Manassas, 7/21/1861 29
First Massachusetts Regiment 2, 22, 26, 29, 31, 34, 38
First North Carolina Colored Vol. 68, 78–79
First Regiment Colored Cavalry 195–6
Fitch, Capt. A. J. 200
Flag, 1st NCCV 70
Flinn, Capt. John M. 143
Flora Temple (gunboat) 111
Flusser, Capt. 103
Folly Island 74–92
Ford, John 112
Forrest, Gen. Nathan Bedford 164
Fort Albany 29
Fort Brady, James River 201
Fort Branch 198–200
Fort Fisher, North Carolina 196
Fort Gilmer 196
Fort Hamilton 157
Fort Harrison 196
Fort Magruder 38
Fort Monroe 35, 99, 129, 131, 153, 193
Fort Pillow massacre 164–5, 174
Fort Pocahontas 168–9
Fort Powhatan 167–9
Fort Sumter 19, 73
Fort Wagner 74
Forty-eighth New York 76
Foster, A.A.G. C. W. 90
Foster, Charles W. 61
Foster, Brig. Gen. John G. 61, 63, 70, 91, 93, 98
Foster, Brig. Gen. Richard S. 88
Fourth of July Parade, 1865 216
Fox, Maj. Charles B. 67
Fox, Daniel 165
Fox, Pvt. Richard H. 108
Fox, Lt. Col. William F. 28
Fox's Gap 48
Francis, Dr. Tappan E. 262
Francis Ferdinand (Archduke) 18
Frankle, Colonel 197–9
Franklin, Pvt. Jeremiah 108
Freedman's Court of Claims 218
Freedmen's Bureau 61, 210–214
Freeman, John H. 152
Freemasony 17
French, Dr. Mansfield 216, 226, 232, 234
Fugitive Slave Act 14

Fuller, Capt. E. C. 129
Fullerton, Col. Joseph S. 233, 235–6, 241

Galloway, Abraham H. 70
Gannett, Lt. 80
Garibaldi, Giuseppe 13
Garland, Brig. Gen. Samuel, Jr. 49
Garrison, William Lloyd 9
Gaskill, Pvt. Edward C. 163
Gaskill, 2nd Lt. Leonard T. 162–3
General Order No. 28 59
General Order No. 46 189, 191
Geneva, Switzerland 13
George Peabody (steamer) 79
Georgetown College 25
Getty, Brig. Gen. George W. 101–02, 110, 118
Gibson, Col. 189
Gilchrist, Capt., Provost Marshal 189
Gilchrist, Daniel 9
Gillmore, Brig. Gen. Quincy A. 75, 81–2, 92, 165, 234
Gilmer, Maj. Gen. Jeremy Francis 219
Gordon, Dunbar 153
Gordon, Grenbow 151
Gorham, Thomas A. 254–5
Graham, Charles K., Gen. 110, 142, 166
Grand Army of the Republic 209
Grant, Ulysses S. 5, 163, 165, 193, 194, 212, 240
Graves, Richard M. 156
Graves, W. S. 151
Great Bridge, Va. 101
Great Dismal Swamp 96–98
Great Falls 26
Greek Orthodox Church 15
Green, Col. J. J. 129, 131
Gregory, Maj., hostage 109
Griffin, Col. Joel R. 106, 108, 117–9, 124
Griggs, George 209
Grimke, Angelina 10
Grimke, Sarah 10
Griswold, Col. Charles E. 68
Griswold, Mary Vic 259
Gross, W. Y. 252
Grover, Brig. Gen. Cuvier 37
Grove's Wharf on James River 170
Grush, Job 6
Guerrillas 94, 95, 98, 106, 107, 117, 121–2, 147, 159

Hale, George Silsbee 12
Hall, James 153
Hall, Col. Robert M. 202–3

Index

Hallowell, Col. N. P. 65, 67, 92
Hallux, Gen. H. W. 92, 129, 193, 194
Hamilton, North Carolina 198
Hancock, Gen. Winfield S. 38
Harding, William 128
Harman, Lt. 80
Harris, Henry 159
Harris, William 155
Harrison, Galen 1, 140
Harrison, Pres. William H. 168
Harrison's Landing 152
Hartwell, Lt. Col. Alfred S. 67, 82, 92
Harvard College 10; Class of 1844 261; Medical School 7
Hatlinger, 1st Lt. Joseph J. 162
Hayes, Rutherford B. 49
Hayward, Lt. 162
Hayward, 2nd Lt. Waldo F. 166
Healy, Capt., killed 238
Heath, Charles 9
Heckman, Brig. Gen. C. A. 163
Heimer, Lt. Frank, 84
Heintzelman's Corps 37, 39
Henry, Edward Lamson 169
Hertford, North Carolina 96, 104
Hibbert, Lt. Joseph 36
Hill, Gen. D. H. 38, 48, 130
Hill, James 112
Hill, Brig. Gen. T. H. 189
Hindon, Col. James W. 95, 121, 123–4
Hinks, Brig. Gen. Edward W. 158, 160, 163, 166–7, 171, 178, 179–80, 184–9, 245
Hinton, Col. 198
Hinton's Crossroads 107
Hodges, Capt. Thorndike D. 91
Hoke, Brig. Gen. Robert F. 164
Holman, Col. John H. 100, 104, 142, 156, 166, 184, 196, 200
Holmes, Dr. Oliver Wendell 52
Holt, Col. Joseph 157
Holt affair 154
Homeguard 104
Homeopathy 10–11
Hooker, Gen. Joseph 30, 40
Hooker's Brigade 29
Hostages 105–6, 116, 118, 135–6, 140; male 143
Howard, Maj. Gen. Oliver Otis 214, 230, 234, 239, 241
Howe, Frank 9
Howe, Col. Frank E. 241
Howe, Mary 11, 14
Howe, Samuel G. 60, 90
Howell, Col. Joshua B. 74
Howell, Midshipman 222

Huger, Maj. Gen. Benjamin 39
Huger's Division 39
Hughes, Edward 70
Hunt, Rebecca P. 255
Hunt, Dr. William P. 50, 255
Hunter, Gen. David 142
Huston, Pvt. George 165
Hypnophonians 6

Indiantown, North Carolina 108
Indiantown Bridge 109
Italy 12
Ives, George W. 162

Jackson, Chaplain William 67
Jamaica Plain, Mass. 23
James, Lt. Garth Wilkinson 61
James, the Rev. Horace 71, 91, 262
James, William 61
James River 35
Jefferson Medical College 11
Jennings, Ed 105
Johnson, Pres. Andrew 211, 242
Johnston, Gen. Joseph E. 26, 220, 236
Jones, Anthony 253, 255–6
Jones, Emily J. 253
Jones, Pvt. Samuel 119
Jones, Capt. W. Hemphill 130
Jordan, Atty. J. Parker 123
Jordan, Pvt. Samuel 103, 106; hanging 118, 120–21, 125
Junior Reserves 199

Kautz, Brig. Gen. A. V. 165–6, 204
Kennard, M. P. 262
Kennon's Landing 149
Ketchum, Capt. A. P. 217–8
Kholoussy Bey 16
Kiddoo, Col. Joseph B. 142, 166, 169
Kilpatrick, Brig. Gen. Hugh J. 164
Kingman, Bradford 6, 263
King's School House 38
Kinsley, Edward Wilkinson 70, 181, 188
Kirk, Private 150
Knapp, Joseph P. 128
Knight, Dempsey 130
Knott's Island 111, 127–128
Kruger, Charles H. 152
Kruntzer, Capt. 135

Lafayette, Gen. 8
Lake Garda 13
Lamb, Col. William 200
Land pirates 94
Lawson, Alexander Robert 221
Lawsuits 252

Lawton, Surgeon J. W. 237
Ledlie, Brig. Gen. James H. 134, 138
Lee, Maj. Gen. Fitzhugh 150, 154, 172–176
Lee, Acting Rear Adm. S. P. 169
Lee, Brig. Gen. William Fitzhugh 143
Lieber, Professor Francis 94
Lincoln, A. L. 262
Lincoln, Pres. Abraham 19, 20, 25, 29, 56, 60–1, 121, 140, 147, 205–6; funeral 206
Lincoln, Dr. Francis M. 68
Livermore, Capt. Thos. L. 187
Longstreet, Gen. James 38
Louisiana Native Guards, 1st Reg. 58
Ludlow, Lt. Col. William H. 130, 143
Lyon, Charles 6

Mackey's Island 128
Magruder, Maj. Gen. John B. 36–7
Magruder's Army 36
Major, Charles J. 152
Major, George B. 153
Malta 17
Manassas Gap Railroad 26
Maple Leaf 79, 127–129
Marklin, Charles 156
Mars, the Rev. John N. 69
Martial law 147
Mary Benton (steamer) 80
Mason-Dixon line 61
Massachusetts Bay Colony 7
Massachusetts Medical Society 11, 69
Massachusetts Volunteer Militia 14
McClellan, Gen. George B. 29, 35, 39, 52, 152
McDowell, Brig. Gen. Irvin 26, 27
McGougal, Sen. 26
McHenry, Capt. S. L. 81–2
McHorney, Dr. Ed 130
McIntosh 108
McKay, James 90
McKinley, William 49
Medellín, Colombia 256
Mejid, Sultan Abdul 15, 16, 17
Memminger, Christopher G. 20
Middletown, Maryland 52
Milan, Italy 13
Miller, Capt. Henry F. H. 146
Milligan, Maj. J. F. 170
Milliken's Bend, La. 164
Minge, Collie 168
Mitchell, S. Weir 66
Monroe, Elsie Wild 259

Montgomery, Col. James 61, 142
Moore, Capt. 26, 82
Morris Island 62.73–7, 125
Morrisetts, Mr., Camden County 123
Morrison, Samuel 155
Moses, Maj. Raphael J. 222
Moss, Mrs. J. D. 221
Mumford, Mrs. 59–60
Mumford, William B., hanging of 59
Munden, Mrs. Phoebe 105, 118–20, 123, 141
Munden, Lt. William J. 105–6, 118, 124, 140
Murat, Mrs. 11, 12
Murdock, George 6

Naglee, Brig. Gen. H. M. 36, 122
Napia, Lord 17
Nat Turner Rebellion, 1831 60
NCCV 68
Negro Plot of 1741 60
New, Nelson R. 156
New Bern, North Carolina 68
New England Education Commission 72
New Market Heights 196
Newell, Artemus 6
Newport News, Va. 195
Newton, Mrs. Courtney 148
Nicholas (tsar) 15
Nichols, Lt. J. T. 77
Nightingale, Florence 15, 16, 18
Ninety-eighth New York Reg. 110
Ninety-eighth New York Vol. 135
Ninety-sixth New York Vol. 135
Ninth Army Corp, 2nd Div. 51
Norfolk, Va. 100
Normandy, France 12
Norris, Dr. George W. 40
North Carolina Defenders 95
North Carolina raid 113–6
North State (gunboat) 103
Northwest Landing, Va. 101, 110, 138

Oak Grove/Fair Oaks, 6/25/1862 40
Oath of allegiance 147
O'Brien, Col. H. F., killed 57
Ord, Maj. Gen. Edward O. C. 201–5, 207–8
Otis, Mr. 12
Ottoman Empire 15, 18
Ould, Judge 123
Ould, Robert 131, 143
Overby, Pastor R. R. 146

Overland campaign 163
Owen, Robert Dale 90

Paine, Charles J. 208
Palmer, Rear Adm. David 196
Palmer's brigade 39
Paris, France 12
Parker, 2nd Lt. 162
Parker, Capt. William Harwar 219
Partisan rangers 94, 126
Pasha, Omar 16
Pasquotank County, North Carolina 119
Pasquotank River 97
Pawnee Landing 83
Peck, Maj. Gen. John J. 83, 91, 164
Peninsular Campaign, 1862 35
Peninsular Campaign, 1864 149
Perkerson, Medora 220
Perkins, Dr. R. C. 146
Perquimans County, North Carolina 104
Perry's Woods 8
Petersburg, Va. 180–1
Petition from citizens 122
Phantom limb pain 66
Philbrick, Edward S. 8, 9
Philbrick, Samuel 10
Philbrook, Walter 219
Phipps, Hattie 162
Phipps, Laura W. 83
Phrydas, Andy 119
Pickett, Maj. Gen. George 118–9, 121
Pierce, John H. 6
Plymouth, North Carolina 164, 200
Point Lookout, Maryland 145
Pool, Dr. W. G. 106
Poquosen Creek 35
Port Arthur, Ontario, Canada 256
Port Crayon 97
Portsmouth, Va. 100, 149
Portuguese Man-of-War 84
Posey Plantation 31
Posey's house 34
Post-war years of Wild 245–263
Powell, Lt. Col. Edward H. 142, 166
Princess Ann County, Va. 98
Prisoners and punishment 143
Proctor, 1st. Lt. George B. 162
Pungo Bridge 134
Pungo Point 138
Putnam, Col. Haldimand S. 76

Quan, David 108
Queen Hotel fire 254

Rabbit Mountain Silver Mine 253
Radical Republicans 211
Rainbow Banks 197
Rainbow Bluff Expedition 197–200
Rainbow Bluffs 197
Randall, Richard B. 153
Randall, Samuel 153
Randall, Tabornto 153
Ransom's Brigade 111
Rawlings, Gen. John A. 185
Rawlston, Lt. Col. J. B. 189
Ray, Col. Samuel M. 259
Rebel signal station 151
Reconstruction in Georgia 243–4
Recruit (schooner) 79, 80
Reed, Col. William N. 69
Regan's 7th New York Battery 162
Reno, Gen. Jesse Lee 48, 98
Revere, Col. Joseph W. 34
Review of Army, May 1865 209
Rhodes, Mary Joanna 7, 8
Rich, Capt. Giles H. 173, 176
Richard's Brigade 26
Richardson, Act. Brig. Gen. Israel 30
Richardson, Col. Israel Bush 26
Roanoke Island, North Carolina 94
Roanoke River 198
Robertson, Dr. J. J. 222–3
Rogers, Dr. Samuel 10, 50
Roman Catholic Church 15
Rudetsky, Marshal 13
Russell, A.A.G., Jr., XVIII Army 188
Russo-Turkish War, 1877–1878 18

St. John's Lodge 17
Salter, Dr. Richard H. 40
Sandburg, Carl 160
Sanderlin, Capt. Willis, 68th NC 109
Sanderson, Serg. George O. 72
Sandy Swamp 108
Sanitary Commission Fair 168
Sargent, Binney 23
Sawtelle, Col. 149
Saxton, Maj. Gen. Rufus 212–3, 234, 236–7, 243
Sayers, Capt. H. W. 143
Schley, Col. Wm. L. 189
Schroeder, A.A.A-G. Henry T. 162
Schurz, Maj. Gen. Carl 232, 235

Scott, Gen. Winfield 35
Scutari 15
Seager, Robert, II 150
Sebastopol 16
Second Massachusetts Heavy Artillery 142
Second Massachusetts Reg. Heavy Artillery 162
Second Michigan Regiment 26
Second North Carolina Colored 79, 133
Second South Carolina Reg. 61
Second U.S. Colored Troops 70
Seddon, James A. 130
Seizure of private homes 147
Selwood Plantation 156
Semmes, Paul Jones 219
Seven Days' Battles 38–40
Seven Pines Battlefield 39
Seventh New York Battery 142
Seward, William (Sec. of State) 56
Seyden, Lt. 135
Sharpsburg, Md., 9/17/1862 50–2
Shaw, Francis George 61
Shaw, Mrs. 147
Shaw, Col. Robert Gould 61–5, 77, 126
Shaw's 54th Massachusetts 68
Shawsheen (gunboat) 169
Shepherd, Lewis 224
Shepley, Brig. Gen. George F. 196
Sherman, Brig. Gen. Thomas W. 30
Sherman, Gen. William Tecumseh 100, 196
Sherwood Forest Plantation 149, 157–8, 168
Shiloh, North Carolina 111
Shipping Point 31, 34
Shockokon (gunboat) 162
Shurtleff, Lt. Col. Giles W. 107
Sickles' Brigade 39
Sixth Connecticut 76
Sixth Massachusetts Regiment 21
Sixty-eighth North Carolina Reg. 95
Sixty-second Georgia Reg. 118
Sixty-sixth North Carolina Reg. 95, 120
Slaves: price of 114; revolts 60
Slovenia 18
Small, Judge: house in Elizabeth City 103
Smallpox 72
Smith, A.A.G. Edward A. 202
Smith, Dr. J. Heber 246
Smith, M. B. 119
Smith, Gen. W. F. 38

Smith, Maj. Gen. William F. "Baldy" 163, 165, 188–9
Smith, William G. 153
Smith's Division 38
Sons of Confederate Veterans 1
South Mills, North Carolina 97, 101, 107
South Mountain, 9/4/1862 48–50
Spear, Col. Samuel P. 119
Special Committee, CSA Congress 124
Spring Green Church 198
Stanton, Edwin (Sec. of War) 63
Star of the West 129
States' Rights 20
Steadman, Col. G. A. 189
Stearns, J. P. 262
Steedman, Maj. Gen. James B. 217, 233, 239
Stevens, Horace 6, 126
Stevens, Horace N., Jr. 259
Stevenson, Brig. Gen. Thomas G. 76
Stoneman, George, cavalry of 220
Stono Revolt, 1739 60
Stowe, Harriet Beecher 22, 61, 79, 97
Strong's Brigade 76
Strother, David Hunter 97
Styles, Wagon-Master 195
Styron, William 60
Suffolk, Va. 164
Sullivan, Anna F. 246
Sullivan, Frances Ellen 14
Sullivan, John Whiting 14, 242
Sullivan, Marian Dix 14
Sullivan's Island 77, 86
Swaim, 2nd Lt. Julius M. 175

Talbot, Dr. J. T. 5
Tannat, Col. Thomas B. 132
Tenny, Alfred, Lord 15, 18
Tenth Army Corps 75
Terracina, Italy 13
Terry, Gen. Alfred H. 75, 200
Tewksbury 105, 114
Thayer, Dr. David 246
Third Michigan Regiment 26
Third N. C. Colored Vol. 79, 140
Third New York Cavalry 135
Thirty-fifth Massachusetts Reg. 2, 34–54, 78–9
Thirty-seventh U.S. Colored Vol. 79
Thirty-sixth U. S. Colored Vol. 79
Thompson, J. H. 247
Three Brothers 111

Thunder Bay, Lake Superior 253–4, 259
Thurber, Lt. 84
Titcomb, 2nd Lt. 162
Tito, Marshal 18
Toombs, Brig. Gen. Robert 51, 217, 221
Toombs, Mrs. Robert, evicted 230–1
Toombs house 235
Treaty of Paris, 1865 17
Treaty of San Stefano, 1878 18
Troad 17
Turkey, Ottoman Empire 17
Turkish "Fez" 262
Turner, Fergus B.
Turner, Chaplin Henry M.. 176
Turner, Brig. Gen. J. W. 189
Turner's Gap 48
Twelfth New York Regiment 26
Twentieth New York Cavalry 142
Twenty-first Massachusetts Reg. 48
Twenty-seventh Massachusetts Reg. 162
Tyler, Brig. Gen. Daniel 27, 28
Tyler, David Gardiner "Gardie" 156
Tyler, John C. 150, 153, 156, 157
Tyler, Julia Gardiner 150, 154, 156–7
Tyler, Maria 150, 156
Tyler, Robert 156

Uncle Tom's Cabin 79
Union sympathizers 99
United States Hotel 142
USCT 70

Vaiden, J. M. 156
Vaiden, M. F. 156
Vaiden, R. J. 153.156
Vance, Gov. Zebulon B. 95, 96, 122–3
Vandalism at Sherwood Forest 178
Vaughan, James C. 153, 221
Vaughan's Brigade 224
Vickers, R. H. 221
Vincent, Pvt. Thos. R. 151, 153, 162
Virginia bank funds, private 219
Vogdes, Brig. Gen. Israel 75, 80, 81, 84, 86, 88

Walker, George 151
Walker, Wm. R. 156
Walker Memorial Porch 261
Wallbridge, Capt. C. E. 194
Walton, Richard T. 229

Ward, Col. John, 8th Conn. Reg. 101–02
Washington, D.C. 25
Washington, Georgia 216
Washington, North Carolina 67
Wead, Lt. Col. Frederick F. 134–139, 144–5
Weeks, Mrs. Elizabeth, hostage 106, 118, 123, 141
Weeks, Pvt. Pender 140
Weems, John G. 229, 234, 243
Weitzel, Maj. Gen. Godfrey 169, 197, 204, 207
Weldon, Lt. Col., Provost marshal 148
Weless, Gen. John F. 202
Wells, Lt. Col. George D. 24, 31, 37
Wells, Gideon (Secretary of Navy) 178
Wheelwright, Edward 6, 126
William A. Crocker (schooner) 79
Wingfield, Francis G 229
White, Alyda 144
White, Caleb 134–5
White, Charles 153
White, Elizabeth 128
White, Henry 130, 135, 137
White, James 134, 137
White, Josiah C. 70
White, Marshall 134
White, Nancy 1, 116, 127–8, 133–41; tombstone 144
White, Patrick 128
White, Solomon 128
White, Mrs. Susan 133, 136
White, William Fentress 144
White, William Henry 134, 144
White Oak Swamp Bridge 38
Whiteman, Capt. 195
Whitlock, Helen Stevens 4, 259
Wigfall, Brig. Gen. Louis T. 32
Wilcox, Lamb 153–4
Wild, Abraham 7
Wild, Dr. Charles 6, 7, 10, 11, 183
Wild, Frances (Ellen) 17, 40, 262
Wild, Mrs. 71, 126, 181, 188, 252–3, 258–9
Wild, "Ned" 4
Wild, Susanna 7, 33
Wild, Capt. Walter H. 65, 83–4, 88, 91, 100, 177, 181, 253; injured 177
Wilder, Dr. Burt G. 67, 84, 76
Wilder, Dwight 2
Wilder, Capt. John 70
Wilkes County, Georgia 218
Williams, George N. 69
Williams, Hannibal 247
Williams, John 147
Williams, the Rev. Roger 7
Williamsburg, Virginia, 5/4/1862 38
Williamston, North Carolina 198
Willis, Sgt. George H. 91, 140
Wilmington, North Carolina 196
Wilmot Proviso 20
Wilson, Dr. 152
Wilson, George W. 153
Wilson, Henry (U.S. Senator) 180, 207
Wilson, J. C. 153
Wilson, Josiah 153
Wilson, Mrs. 152
Wilson's Landing 169
Wilson's Wharf 2, 149, 151, 154; results of 176
Wingfield, the Rev. S. H. 148–9
Winship, Dr. 71
Wise, Pvt. W. D. 151, 153
Wistar, Gen. Isaac J. 112
Wood, George Augustus 33, 40, 168
Wood, Susanna S. 40
Worthington, Dennison 153
Wright, Maj. Elias 142
Wright, Mrs. 105
Wright, William T. 105

Yellowly, Lt. Col. Edward C. 95
Yorktown, Virginia 35
Yorktown, battle of, 4/5/1862 36–7
Yugoslavia 18

www.ingramcontent.com/pod-product-compliance
Lightning Source LLC
Chambersburg PA
CBHW081538300426
44116CB00015B/2674